THE HOOVER LIBRARY ON WAR, REVOLUTION, AND PEACE

—————————————————PUBLICATION No. 26—————————————————

Soviet Russia and the West
1920–1927

PUBLISHED under the authority of the Publication Committee
of the Hoover Library on War, Revolution, and Peace

SOVIET RUSSIA and the WEST

1920-1927

A Documentary Survey

by
XENIA JOUKOFF EUDIN
and
HAROLD H. FISHER
in collaboration with
ROSEMARY BROWN JONES

1957
STANFORD UNIVERSITY PRESS / STANFORD, CALIFORNIA

STANFORD UNIVERSITY PRESS, STANFORD, CALIFORNIA

London: Oxford University Press

© 1957 by the Board of Trustees of the Leland Stanford Junior University

Printed in the United States of America

Library of Congress Catalog Card Number: 57-6013

FOREWORD

This volume on *Soviet Russia and the West, 1920–1927* is one of two companion studies of Soviet foreign policy in this period. The second, published simultaneously, presents the relations of the Soviet Union with the East. Both volumes are composed principally of documents. In each, brief introductory narratives provide the historical setting for the documents.

The Hoover Institute and Library is following a long-established policy in making these documents, drawn almost entirely from its own collections, available in English. The intention is to serve scholars and a broader public by placing at their disposal source materials upon which understanding and interpretation of Soviet foreign policy in the years 1920–27 must be based. Every effort has been made by the authors and editors to present a representative and objectively chosen selection of documents. It goes without saying that the Institute and Library does not assume responsibility for the views contained in these documents.

A few words about the author-editors of these volumes are in order. Mrs. Xenia Joukoff Eudin has been associated with the Hoover Institute and Library since 1932. Earlier she was a student at the University of London, and before the revolution she attended Moscow University. She is coeditor of two other volumes in the series of Hoover Library Publications: *Features and Figures of the Past: Government and Opinion in the Reign of Nicholas II* (1939), and *The Life of a Chemist: Memoirs of V. N. Ipatieff* (1946).

Harold Henry Fisher is professor of history emeritus at Stanford University. He was associated with the Hoover Library from 1924 until his retirement in 1955. He served successively as secretary, vice-chairman, and chairman. Most of his work has been with documents in the Russian and Eastern European collections. He is the author, coauthor, or editor of eight other volumes of the Hoover Library Publications series, and the author of a study on *The Communist Revolution* published in the Hoover Institute Studies series. His books *America and the New Poland* and *America and Russia in the World Community* were published under other auspices.

Mrs. Rosemary Brown Jones, a journalist and wartime White House correspondent who has many articles to her credit, co-operated in the editorial preparation of the volume.

Much of the preliminary research for this volume was conducted under the Slavic Fellowship Program made possible by a grant from the Rockefeller Foundation in 1946. Additional research and editorial assistance, together with the costs of publication, have come from the private gift funds of the Hoover Institute and Library and from those of Stanford University. It is understood that the Rockefeller Foundation, despite its generous contribution to the preparation of this volume, bears no responsibility for its contents.

Stanford University
March 1957

C. EASTON ROTHWELL
Director, Hoover Institute
and Library

PREFACE

In 1920 the Soviet government entered a new phase in its foreign relations. Events had shown that the Communists were strong enough to defeat their domestic enemies but not to reconquer the peoples of the western borderlands who had declared their independence. Events had also shown that the communist revolution was not going to spread into Central and Western Europe and that the Western powers and Japan would not and perhaps could not continue their intervention in Russia with sufficient strength to overthrow the Soviet regime. A stalemate had been reached in the undeclared war that had begun when the Bolsheviks seized power and proclaimed their intention to promote the overthrow of the governments of other countries. The Soviet government, and similarly the governments of the western borderlands and of Western Europe, had concluded that even if friendly relations between them were not immediately possible, formal diplomatic and economic relations were preferable to war.

The materials presented in this volume relate to the eight years, 1920–27, during which the Russian Communists experimented with the dual policy of carrying on, through the Soviet government, ostensibly normal diplomatic, economic, and cultural relations with the noncommunist countries, while at the same time promoting political disagreements between, and social tensions and revolution within, those same powers through the Communist International. These were also the years when Soviet Russia's foreign and domestic policies were affected by the transition from Lenin and Leninism to Stalin and Stalinism.

Most of the documents are translations from Soviet and Comintern sources. In a very few cases we have included documents expressing the views of the Western governments in their dealings with Soviet Russia, but we have not tried to show in any detail Western opinions of Soviet policies. This would have involved the inclusion of a large number of documents available elsewhere in Western languages.

In the selection of the materials for this book we have tried to do three things: first, to recall the principal events in Soviet-Western relations during these years; second, to present communist descriptions and analyses of these events; and third, to show the communist explanations of their policy decisions. From the vast amount of available Soviet materials we have made excerpts from reports and minutes of Soviet, Communist Party, and Comintern congresses and conferences. We have also drawn upon Soviet newspapers and periodicals more heavily than upon official texts of treaties, diplomatic correspondence, and similar documents which are now easily accessible in Western-language publications. In these official diplomatic utterances the communist leaders are, so to say, speaking to the world; but in their published explanations, discussions, and comments they are talking to themselves and to those over whom they rule. These "family discussions" seemed to us essential for the understanding of how the Russian Communists interpreted world affairs and how they explained their policies to the members of the Communist Party and to the Soviet public at large.

The documents have been arranged chronologically but with subdivisions under subject headings. With each section we have given a summary of the events to which the documents relate. In some cases these narratives contain phrases or quotations from documents which lack of space did not permit us to reproduce *in extenso*.

Our principal source material is in the Hoover Library, and we wish to thank our colleagues in the reference, research, and administrative divisions of the Library for their generous and indispensable help. We are particularly grateful to Dr. Merrill Spalding, a specialist in early Soviet history, who wrote most of the Historical Introduction; to Mrs. Helen Dwight Fisher for a critical reading of the translations and for her suggestions for their improvement; and to Mrs. Marina Stragus Tinkoff for her thorough and expert help in technical matters. The index has been prepared by Mrs. Laura M. Bell.

XENIA J. EUDIN
HAROLD H. FISHER

Stanford, California
March 1957

CONTENTS

HISTORICAL INTRODUCTION   xxi

PART I   REOPENING THE WINDOW TO EUROPE, 1920–1921   3

The Strategic Retreat on the Domestic Front. Reorientation of Soviet Foreign Policy: From the World Revolution to "Peaceful Coexistence." Reorientation of Allied Policy: From *Cordon Sanitaire* to Fighting Anarchy with Abundance. The Treaty with Estonia. The Treaty with Lithuania. The Treaty with Latvia. The Treaty with Finland. The Treaty with Poland. Beginning Negotiations with the West. British Trade Negotiations. Negotiations with Italy. Resumption of Relations with Germany and Other Countries. Relations with the United States. The Famine of 1921–23. Charges and Countercharges. The Third Congress of the Comintern. Defensive Revolutionary Strategy.

DOCUMENTS (for detailed list see pp. x–xii)   37

PART II   THE BEGINNING OF "PEACEFUL COEXISTENCE," 1922–1923   97

The Genoa Conference Preliminaries. The Genoa Conference. The Hague Conference. Disarmament. The Lausanne Conference. The Rome Conference. The Congress on War Against War. The Soviet Attitude Toward the League of Nations.

DOCUMENTS (for detailed list see pp. xii–xiv)   123

PART III   DIPLOMATIC TRIUMPHS AND REVOLUTIONARY FAILURES, 1922–1924   163

Nationality Relations—The Union of Soviet Socialist Republics. The Party's Estimate of the International Situation, 1922–24. Extension of the Breathing Space: Coexistence and Revolution. German Rapprochement and the German Revolution. Soviet Relations with German Nationalists, Militarists, and Industrialists. Indecision and Failure of the German "October," 1923. Communist Reasons for the Failure of the German "October." The Anglo-Soviet Crisis, 1923. Communist Interpretation of the Anglo-Soviet Crisis. *De Jure* Recognition by the British and Other Governments. Aloofness of the United States. The Soviet Government and the League of Nations. The Communist Estimate of the Situation in 1924.

DOCUMENTS (for detailed list see pp. xiv–xvi)   197

PART IV   "SOCIALISM IN ONE COUNTRY" AND THE
              PACIFIST-REFORMIST INTERLUDE, 1924–1926   253

Stalin and the Party Machine. Lenin's Testament. Socialism in
One Country *vs.* Permanent Revolution. Anglo-Soviet Treaties of
August 8, 1924. The Soviet Government and the Dawes Plan. The
Zinoviev Letter. United Fronts. Locarno. Soviet Suspicions
About the League of Nations. Communist Theory of International
Law. Bilateral Neutrality and Nonaggression Pacts with Turkey,
Afghanistan, and Persia. The Soviet-German Neutrality and Non-
aggression Treaty of April 24, 1926. Negotiations with Poland and
the Baltic States. The Soviet-Lithuanian Neutrality and Nonag-
gression Pact. The Soviet Leaders' Estimate of the International
Position of the U.S.S.R. at the End of 1926. The Communist International Party Line in 1926.

DOCUMENTS (for detailed list see pp. xvi–xvii)   286

PART V   RENEWAL OF SUSPICION AND HOSTILITY,
          1926–1927   341

The British General Strike and the Arcos Raid. France: Tsarist
Debts and the Rakovsky Affair. Poland: The Pilsudski Coup.
World Economic Conference. The Preparatory Commission on
Disarmament. The Kellogg-Briand Pact. Disarmament and the
Territorial Militia Program. The First Five-Year Plan. The Fif-
teenth Party Congress.

DOCUMENTS (for detailed list see pp. xviii–xix)   358

CHRONOLOGY   411

BIBLIOGRAPHY   419

INDEX   443

DOCUMENTS

PART I

1. Stalin on the Three Years of the Proletarian Dictatorship [Speech
   at a Session of the Baku Soviet, November 6, 1920]   37

2. Trotsky on Postwar Imperialism, the Role of the Second International, and the Road to Victory [Excerpt from a Speech at the Final
   and Joint Session of the Second Congress of the Communist International, the All-Russian Central Executive Committee, the Moscow
   Soviet, the All-Russian Council of Trade Unions, and the Factory
   Committees, August 7, 1920]   41

3. Lenin on Foreign Trade and the Advantages Inherent in the Policy of Concessions [Report on Concessions to the Communist Party Faction at the Eighth Congress of Soviets of the R.S.F.S.R., December 1920]   44

4. Lenin on Peace with Estonia [Speech Delivered at the First Session of the All-Russian Central Executive Committee, February 2, 1920]   48

5. Ioffe Interprets the Significance of the Treaty of Peace with Latvia of August 11, 1920   48

6. Soviet Policy of "Peaceful Advance" [Ioffe's Statement in 1921 on Peace with the Baltic States]   49

7. Reply of the All-Russian Central Executive Committee to the League of Nations' Proposal to Send a Commission of Inquiry to Russia, May 14, 1920   52

8. Lenin Criticizes British Labor Leaders and Defends the Red Terror [Letter to the British Workers, May 30, 1920]   53

9. Peace Negotiations Between Soviet and Polish Delegations at Minsk [First Meeting, August 17, 1920]   54

10. New Peace Proposals by the Soviet Government [Declaration of the All-Russian Central Executive Committee, September 23, 1920, Signed by Kalinin, Its Chairman, and Chicherin, People's Commissar of Foreign Affairs]   57

11. Statements on the Conclusion of the Soviet-Polish Treaty   59

12. Lenin on War with Poland [Speech at a Congress of Leather Industry Workers, October 2, 1920]   61

13. The Failure to Establish Soviets in Poland [a, Statement by Trotsky, October 20, 1920; b, Statement by Julian Marchlewski; c, Statement by D. Z. Manuilsky]   62

14. The End of Proletarian and Imperialist Offensives [Ioffe's Statement in 1921 on the Significance of Peace with Poland]   63

15. Criticism of the British Draft of the Trade Agreement [Editorial by Iu. M. Steklov]   64

16. Shortcomings and Advantages of the Anglo-Soviet Trade Agreement [Krasin's Comments]   65

17. The Absence of Rapprochement Between Soviet Russia and the United States [a, American Policy Toward Soviet Russia Defined by Bainbridge Colby, United States Secretary of State, in a Letter to the Italian Ambassador, August 10, 1920, Usually Spoken of as "the Colby Note"; b, A Circular Letter from the People's Commissar of Foreign Affairs of the R.S.F.S.R., G. V. Chicherin, to the Russian Plenipotentiaries Abroad, September 10, 1920]   66

18. Maxim Gorky's Appeal to the American People, Moscow, July 13, 1921   73

19. Mr. Hoover's Reply to Maxim Gorky's Appeal, July 23, 1921   74

20. Official Soviet Appreciation of American Help [Resolution of the Council of People's Commissars, Moscow, July 10, 1923]   75

21. Lenin's Appeal to the International Proletariat, August 2, 1921   75

22. Soviet Suspicion of the Little Entente [Iu. M. Steklov's Comment]   76

23. The Soviet Government Charges That France Incites Poland and
    Rumania to New Anti-Soviet Activity [Declaration by the People's
    Commissariat of Foreign Affairs, Moscow, September 13, 1921]   77

24. Proposed Warning to Soviet Russia's Neighbors [Lenin to the
    Politburo, December 22, 1921]   78

25. The Soviet Government Calls for an International Conference to
    Settle Outstanding Problems Between Russia and the Allies [Offi-
    cial Note of the People's Commissar of Foreign Affairs to the Gov-
    ernments of Great Britain, France, Italy, Japan, and the United
    States, October 28, 1921]   79

26. On the Eve of the Third Congress of the Communist International
    [Editorial by Karl Radek]   80

27. Lenin's Estimate of the International Situation, July 5, 1921   82

28. The Third Congress of the Communist International on the World
    Situation [Excerpts from the Theses Adopted by the Third Con-
    gress of the Communist International, July 4, 1921]   84

29. Lenin on a Dual Policy to Take Advantage of the Weakness of Capi-
    talist States [Excerpts from the Stenographic Notes on Lenin's
    Speech at a Meeting of the All-Russian Central Council of Trade
    Unions, April 11, 1921]   90

30. Kamenev's Estimate of the World Situation and the Objectives of
    Communist Foreign Policy [Speech at the Tenth Party Congress,
    Moscow, March 15, 1921]   91

PART II

31. Lenin on Domestic and Foreign Policies of the Republic [Report
    of the All-Russian Central Executive Committee and the Council of
    People's Commissars to the Ninth All-Russian Congress of Soviets,
    December 23, 1921]   123

32. Radek on the Invitation to the Genoa Conference   124

33. Chicherin's Pre-Genoa Report on the International Situation to the
    All-Russian Central Executive Committee, January 27, 1922   126

34. A Member of the Soviet Delegation on the Genoa Conference
    [Rakovsky's Forecast]   128

35. Soviet Policies on Coexistence of Old and New Systems, Economic
    Concessions, Peace, Disarmament, Equality of All Peoples, Partici-
    pation of Workers' Organizations, Reform of the League of Nations
    [Chicherin's Speech at the Genoa Conference, April 10, 1922, De-
    livered in French]   131

36. "Finita la Commedia!" Says Steklov [Soviet Explanation of the
    Failure of the Hague Conference]   133

37. Soviet Proposals for Reducing Armies by Two-Thirds and Limiting
    Military Budgets [The First Session of the Moscow Conference on
    the Reduction of Armaments, December 2, 1922]   135

38. The Reply of the Delegations of Estonia, Latvia, Finland, and
    Poland to Soviet Proposals, Read by the Polish Delegate, Prince

Radziwill [Session of the Military and Technical Commission of the Conference, December 11, 1922] 137

39. Soviet Rejection of Counterproposals by Poland and the Baltic States [Declaration of the Russian Delegation at the Final Session of the Military and Technical Commission, December 12, 1922] 138

40. The Soviet Government's Offer to Convene a Conference on the Problems of the Near East [Telegram of the Assistant Commissar of Foreign Affairs, L. M. Karakhan, to Great Britain, France, Italy, Yugoslavia, Bulgaria, Rumania, Greece, and Egypt, September 24, 1922] 141

41. Russia's Reply to the Allied Proposal of Limited Participation at the Lausanne Conference [Chicherin to the Soviet Official Agent in London, Krasin, November 2, 1922; Copies Directly to the Foreign Ministers of France and Italy] 143

42. Lenin on the Straits [Lenin Interviewed by a British Journalist, October 27, 1922] 144

43. Soviet Interpretation of the Significance of the Turkish Nationalist Movement [Excerpts from Chicherin's Article on the Lausanne Conference and the World Situation] 145

44. Lenin Outlines the Tasks of the Soviet Delegation at The Hague, December 4, 1922 148

45. Fourteen-Point Program Proposed by the Russian Delegates and Rejected by Noncommunist Delegates [Excerpt from Rotshtein's Speech at the Sixth Session of the International Peace Congress, December 13, 1922] 149

46. Stalin on the Need of Confederation as Well as Federation of Soviet Republics [Stalin's Remarks on the Theses on the National and Colonial Questions Drafted by Lenin and Adopted by the Second Congress of the Communist International, July-August, 1920] 150

47. Lenin on the Disunity and Ineffectiveness of the League of Nations [Excerpt from Speech at a Conference of the Members of the Local Party Executive Committees of the Moscow Province, October 15, 1920] 151

48. Stalin on the Socialist and Capitalist Camps [Excerpts from Stalin's Statements in Connection with the Formation of the Union of Soviet Socialist Republics, November 18 and December 26, 1922] 152

49. Toward a World Soviet Socialist Republic [Excerpts from the Declaration Concerning the Formation of the Union of Soviet Socialist Republics, Adopted at the First Congress of Soviets of the Union, December 30, 1922] 155

50. Soviet Attitude Toward the League of Nations [Excerpt from the Note of the People's Commissariat of Foreign Affairs of the R.S.F.S.R. to the Secretary General of the League of Nations Stating Russia's Willingness to Participate in the Conference on the Limitation of Naval Armament, March 15, 1923] 155

51. Russia, the Great Powers, and the World Revolution [Radek's Report on the International Situation to the Fourth Congress of the Communist International, October 28, 1922] 156

52. The Right of Red Intervention to Extend Socialism [Bukharin's Explanation of the Russian Party's Position on This Issue at the Fourth Congress of the Comintern, 1922]   159

53. Soviet Russia's Leadership in the World Revolution and the Duty of All Workers to Support Russia [Resolution of the Fourth Congress of the Communist International on the Russian Revolution]   160

PART III

54. Chicherin on the International Situation [Speech at an Improvised Meeting at the Station of Sebezh on His Way to Moscow from the Lausanne Conference, February 1923]   197

55. The Threat of a New War [Editorial by Iu. M. Steklov in *Izvestiia*]   200

56. Moscow's Determination to Win the Masses [Excerpts from the "Theses on the Tactics of the Communist International" adopted by the Fourth Congress of the Communist International, November 5–December 5, 1922]   201

57. Soviet Denial of Secret Clauses in the Rapallo Treaty [Chicherin to M. Barthou, April 29, 1922]   202

58. Soviet Evaluation of the Rapallo Treaty a Quarter of a Century Later   203

59. Radek's Contact with the German Nationalists During His Imprisonment in Berlin in 1919–20 [Excerpt from Radek's Reminiscences]   203

60. Secret Transactions Between German and Soviet Representatives in the Early Twenties [Account Based on General von Seeckt's Personal Papers]   205

61. Seeckt on the Russian Problem [Excerpts from Letters to General von Hasse and Chancellor Wirth, 1922]   206

62. Soviet-German Co-operation in Producing Poison Gas [General V. N. Ipatieff's Recollections]   207

63. Soviet Explanation of Soviet-German Military Co-operation   208

64. Bukharin on Military Alliance with Bourgeois States [Excerpt from Speech at the Fourth Congress of the Communist International on Its New Program, November 18, 1922]   209

65. Soviet Reaction to the Occupation of the Ruhr   210

66. Bukharin on the Occupation of the Ruhr [Speech Delivered at the Fourth All-Russian Congress of Press Workers]   211

67. Communist Propaganda on the Ruhr Occupation [Appeal of the All-Russian Central Council of Trade Unions to the Workers of the Ruhr Coal Basin, the Workers of the World, and the Workers of Russia]   211

68. Stalin's Ideas on Help to the German Revolutionaries [Stalin's Letter to Zinoviev and Bukharin in the Summer of 1923]   212

69. The Time to Provoke Communist Action in Germany Is Not at Hand [Radek's Statement in the Summer of 1923]   213

70. Zinoviev on the United Front with the Saxon Government, October 1923   213

71. Zinoviev on the Problems of the German Revolution, October 1923   214

72. Poland: Bridge or Barrier? [Trotsky Speaking on the International Situation at the Moscow Province Congress of Metalworkers, October 1923]   217

73. Analysis of the Failure in Germany [Zinoviev on the Lessons of German Events and United Front Tactics]   218

74. Zinoviev Does Not Abandon Hope for the German Revolution [Description of the Hamburg Uprising]   220

75. Mistakes Made in Germany in 1923 [Resolution of the Fifth Enlarged Plenum of the Executive Committee of the Communist International, April 4, 1925]   221

76. The Petrograd Soviet on the War Danger [A Declaration of the Petrograd Soviet to the Workers of All Countries, May 1923]   222

77. The Soviet Government Replies to the British Ultimatum [Note of the Assistant People's Commissar of Foreign Affairs of the R.S.F.S.R., Litvinov, to Mr. Hodgson, May 11, 1923]   223

78. A Communist Analysis of the World Situation at the Beginning of 1924 [Excerpts from Kamenev's Speech at the Second Congress of Soviets of the U.S.S.R., January 30, 1924]   228

79. Soviet Explanation of the Significance of British Recognition [Resolution Adopted by the Second Congress of Soviets of the U.S.S.R., February 2, 1924]   233

80. A Communist Interpretation of Russia's Recognition by Italy [From an Article by Karl Radek in *Pravda*]   234

81. A Communist Interpretation of the Role of Soviet Diplomacy After Recognition [From an Article by F. A. Rotshtein in *Pravda*]   235

82. Notes Exchanged Between the French Premier and Chicherin Concerning the Recognition of the U.S.S.R. by France [a, The Telegram of the Chairman of the Council of Ministers and Foreign Minister of France, Herriot, to the Chairman of the Council of People's Commissars of the U.S.S.R., Rykov, and the People's Commissar of Foreign Affairs of the U.S.S.R., Chicherin, Paris, October 28, 1924; b, Telegram of the Chairman of the Central Executive Committee of the U.S.S.R., Kalinin; the Chairman of the Council of People's Commissars of the U.S.S.R., Rykov; and the People's Commissar of Foreign Affairs of the U.S.S.R., Chicherin, to Herriot]   236

83. A Communist Interpretation of French Recognition [Iu. M. Steklov in *Izvestiia*]   237

84. The Soviet Government's Failure to Re-establish Friendly Relations with the American Government [a, Excerpt from President Coolidge's Message to Congress, December 6, 1923; b, Chicherin, People's Commissar of Foreign Affairs, to President Coolidge; c, American Reply to Chicherin's Note: Instructions from Secretary of State Charles Evans Hughes to the American Consul at Tallinn, December 18, 1923]   239

85. A Soviet Interpretation of American Refusal to Recognize the Soviet Government [Statement by Chicherin in a Newspaper Interview]   241

86. Review of the International Situation in 1924 [Stalin's Report on the Results of the Thirteenth Congress of the Russian Communist Party to the School of Secretaries of the County Committees of the Central Committee of the Party, June 17, 1924]   243

87. Trotsky on the Chances of American Domination in Europe During the Pacifist-Reformist Era [Speech Delivered on the Tenth Anniversary of World War I at a Meeting of the Society of Friends of the Physics and Mathematics Faculty, July 28, 1924]   244

PART IV

88. Stalin on the Theory of the Proletarian Revolution, April 1924 [Excerpts from Lectures on the Foundations of Leninism at the Sverdlov University, April-May, 1924]   286

89. Stalin on the Strategy and Tactics of the Revolution [Excerpts from Lectures on the Foundations of Leninism at the Sverdlov University, April-May, 1924]   287

90. Stalin on the October Revolution as the Beginning of and the Prerequisite for World Revolution [Introduction to Stalin's Book *Na putiakh k Oktiabriu*, December 17, 1924]   289

91. Soviet Strength Lies in the Success of Soviet Economic Development [Kamenev at a Party Conference at Krasnaia Presnia, May 8, 1924]   291

92. Rakovsky Answers MacDonald at the Opening of the Conference in London, April 14, 1924   292

93. Rakovsky's Comment to the Press on the British Bankers' Memorandum, April 25, 1924   295

94. Chicherin on the Anglo-Soviet Treaty, at the Special Plenary Session of the Moscow Soviet, August 20, 1924   296

95. The Dawes Plan and the Communists [a, The Principles Outlining the Committee of Experts' Plan, known as the Dawes Plan; Letter of Charles G. Dawes, Chairman of the Committee of Experts, to the Reparations Committee, April 9, 1924, Attached to the Report of the Committee of Experts; b, The Closing Part of the Manifesto of the Fifth Congress of the Communist International to the World Proletariat, on the Occasion of the Tenth Anniversary of World War I, July 5, 1924, Signed by the Presidium of the Congress]   296

96. Stalin on the International Situation, September 1924   299

97. Zinoviev on the British Labour Government at the Fifth Congress of the Comintern, June 26, 1924   301

98. The Concrete Tasks of the British Communist Party Outlined by the Fifth Congress of the Communist International, June 17–July 8, 1924   302

99. "The Zinoviev Letter" [a, Zinoviev's Alleged Instructions to the British Communist Party; b, Zinoviev's Statement to Representatives of the Foreign Press, October 27, 1924]   303

100. The Official Soviet Position in Regard to the "Zinoviev Letter" Incident [Rakovsky's Acknowledgment of Chamberlain's Note of

November 21 and Recapitulation of the Preceding Correspondence, November 28, 1924] 306

101. Excerpts from the Theses on Tactics Adopted at the Fifth Congress of the Communist International, June 17–July 8, 1924 308

102. The Workers' United Front [Joint Declaration of International Unity by the Anglo-Russian Conference of Trade Unions in London, Which Met on April 6, 7, and 8, 1925] 309

103. Chicherin's Report to the Third Congress of Soviets on the Relation of Propaganda to Relations with Capitalist Governments in General and Soviet-British Relations in Particular, May 14, 1925 309

104. The International Situation and the Military Tasks of the Soviet Union [Speech by M. V. Frunze at a Meeting of Cadets, Commanding Officers, and Political Workers of the Moscow Garrison, February 16, 1925] 311

105. The Extension of the Breathing Space for Soviet Russian Foreign Policy [Directives to the Central Committee by the Fourteenth Congress of the Russian Communist Party, December 18–31, 1925] 314

106. Karl Radek on Locarno 316

107. The Meaning of Locarno for the U.S.S.R. [Statement by Rakovsky] 317

108. Rykov on the League of Nations [Excerpt from the Report to the Fourteenth Moscow Province Party Conference, December 5, 1925] 320

109. On the Impossibility of Solving Disputes by Arbitration 322

110. First Soviet Nonaggression Treaty [Litvinov on the Soviet-Turkish Treaty of Friendship and Neutrality, December 17, 1925] 323

111. Litvinov on the Signing of the Soviet-German Treaty and Russia's Desire for Peace [Excerpt from a Speech to the All-Russian Central Executive Committee, April 24, 1926] 324

112. The Fourth Nonaggression Treaty [The Treaty of Neutrality and Nonaggression Between Lithuania and Soviet Russia, Known as the Treaty of Moscow, September 28, 1926] 326

113. The Nonaggression Treaties and the System of Coexistence [An Editorial in *Izvestiia*] 326

114. Zinoviev on the Theory of Socialism in One Country [Excerpt from a Speech at the Fourteenth Party Conference, April 29, 1925] 327

115. The Temporary Nature of Capitalist Stabilization and the Tasks of the Comintern [Resolution on the Immediate Problems of the International Communist Movement, Adopted at the Sixth Enlarged Plenum of the ECCI, February 17–March 15, 1926] 330

116. "Socialism in One Country" and the World Policies of Soviet Russia and the Communist Party [Excerpts from Stalin's Speech at the Fifteenth Party Conference, November 1, 1926] 333

117. The Main Tendencies of Capitalism and the Aims and Effects of Socialist Policies [Excerpts from Bukharin's Report Prepared for the Seventh Enlarged Plenum of the ECCI, November 22–December 16, 1926] 336

PART V

118. Stalin on the International Significance of Building Socialism in One Country [Report to the Seventh Enlarged Plenum of the ECCI, December 7, 1926]   358

119. Bukharin on the International Revolution [Excerpt from His Report on the International and Domestic Situation at the Fifteenth Moscow Province Party Conference, January 1927]   359

120. The Fundamental Principles of the Foreign Policy of the U.S.S.R. [Outlined by A. I. Rykov, Chairman of the Council of People's Commissars, at the Fourth Congress of Soviets of the U.S.S.R., April 19, 1927]   364

121. Lessons of the British Strike [Excerpt from Stalin's Speech Delivered at a Meeting of the Railway Shop Workers in Tiflis, June 8, 1926]   368

122. Analysis of the Soviet Reply to the British Warning Concerning Diplomatic Relations, February 1927   370

123. Rykov on Relations with Britain [Speech at the Fourth Congress of Soviets of the U.S.S.R., April 19, 1927]   371

124. The Soviet Government Protests the Raid on Arcos [Litvinov to William Peters, British Representative in Moscow, May 17, 1927]   375

125. Litvinov's Statement on Soviet-British Relations [An Interview with Representatives of the Soviet Press, May 1927]   377

126. The British Break Interpreted as New Evidence of Class Hatred [Resolution of the Plenum of the Moscow Soviet on the Report of A. I. Rykov, June 1, 1927]   379

127. Soviet-French Relations [Declaration of the Assistant Commissar of Foreign Affairs, Litvinov, to Representatives of the Press, Moscow, September 16, 1927]   381

128. Soviet Estimate of the World Economic Situation [Speech by the Soviet Delegate, Obolenski-Ossinski, at the World Economic Conference, Geneva, May 7, 1927]   382

129. Obolenski-Ossinski Sums up the Results of the Conference at the Session of May 23, 1927   386

130. Zinoviev on How to Prevent War   388

131. The U.S.S.R., the League of Nations, and Disarmament [Excerpt from Rykov's Report to the Fourth Congress of Soviets of the U.S.S.R., April 19, 1927]   388

132. Total Disarmament Proposed by Litvinov at the Preparatory Commission on Disarmament, November 30, 1927   390

133. Litvinov's Comments on the Preparatory Commission for the Disarmament Conference [Report to the Fifteenth Party Congress, December 14, 1927]   393

134. Stalin on Capitalist Disarmament [Excerpt from the Political Report of the Central Committee of the VKP to the Fifteenth Congress of the Party, Delivered by Stalin, December 3, 1927]   397

135. M. V. Frunze on Soviet Military Organization, 1922 [Excerpts from an Article Entitled "Regular Army and Militia," March 1922]   399

136. Soviet Armed Strength Based on the Principle of the Territorial Militia System [Frunze's Report to the Secretaries of Party Cells, February 27, 1925]   399

137. The Militarization of the Entire Population [I. S. Unschlicht, Acting People's Commissar for Military and Naval Affairs, on the Ninth Anniversary of the Red Army]   401

138. K. E. Voroshilov, People's Commissar for Military and Naval Affairs, on the Five-Year Plan for the Army [Speech at the Fifteenth Party Congress, December 1927]   402

139. Stalin on the Need for a Strong Red Army [Excerpt from a Speech at a Plenary Session of the Central Committee of the Party, January 19, 1925]   403

140. Stalin on the World Significance of the October Revolution [On the Occasion of the Tenth Anniversary of the October Revolution]   403

141. The Future Is on the Side of the Comintern [Bukharin's Final Remarks in His Speech at the Fifteenth Party Congress, December 10, 1927]   405

142. Establishing Socialism in the U.S.S.R. Essential to the World Communist Movement [Stalin at the Plenum of the Central Committee and Central Control Commission of the Party, October 23, 1927]   406

143. Stalin on the Capitalist World and the U.S.S.R. [Excerpt from His Report to the Fifteenth Party Congress, December 3, 1927]   407

HISTORICAL INTRODUCTION

The Soviet communist regime, like other revolutionary regimes, inherited both the assets and the liabilities of its predecessors. As a geographical legacy it received vast territories embracing the heartland of the Eurasian continent. It also took over from Imperial Russia and the short-lived Provisional Government a large, rapidly growing, polyglot population, as well as an underdeveloped economic and technological system. Perhaps most significant of all, it was heir to historic traditions imbued with the spirit of political autocracy, religious orthodoxy, and a strong Russian nationalism. Such traditions had fostered a policy of territorial aggrandizement, which was based on the conviction that Russia, in order to fulfill its destiny, should dominate certain non-Russian lands, and that it must have access to the outside world both by land and through warm-water ports.

Russian expansionism, at least in its earlier stages, had grown out of the experience and the continuing fear of foreign inroads upon territory once ruled by the Kievan state. The Russians had long been the objects of aggression from the east and south by Tatars, Turks, and other Asian peoples, and from the west by Germans, Swedes, Lithuanians, and Poles. In the face of such attacks they had developed their own military power under their Muscovite tsars, and in time had succeeded in pushing the boundaries of their nation eastward into Asia, southward toward the Black Sea, and westward into regions formerly annexed by Poland and Lithuania. In this fashion they were able to make good their claims to many territories of the former Kievan state and to control certain areas which had been, or which might have become, staging grounds for foreign aggression. Eventually, under Peter the Great and his eighteenth- and early-nineteenth-century successors, the Russians occupied ports on the Baltic, Black, and Caspian seas and brought many non-Russian peoples under tsarist rule.

The territorial gains of the eighteenth and early nineteenth centuries failed, however, to provide Russia with adequate outlets to the open sea. In the west, German and Scandinavian states controlled the waterways leading to the North Sea and the Atlantic Ocean. In the Middle East, the Persian monarchy—with growing English assistance—blocked any Russian advance to the Persian Gulf. In the Far East, an independent Korea and a Chinese-ruled Manchuria served as barriers to Russian expansion. Finally, in the south, the route to the Mediterranean by way of Constantinople and the Straits remained in Turkish hands. Russia still had few warm-water ports. Yet several of the most coveted naval or commercial bases had been brought within striking distance, and the growing weakness of some of Russia's neighbors—particularly the Ottoman Empire—seemed to invite further aggression.

While this military and political advance was in progress, Russia became increasingly conscious of what many of its leaders regarded as its world mission. The concept of Russia's historic role as a great civilizing force had originally sprung from close association with the Byzantine Empire, whose collapse in 1453, followed by the marriage of Ivan III to a niece of the last Byzantine emperor, fostered the belief that autocratic Russia was the third—and final—Rome. This belief was accompanied by a Byzantine-inspired conviction that the West, through heresy and wrongheadedness, had failed humanity and that mankind could be saved only by apostles of the true (Eastern Orthodox) faith, which had gained new strength and vitality in its predominantly Slavic environment. To the leaders of Holy Russia the West appeared corrupt and decadent; it could best be revitalized by an infusion of Russian culture and by accepting a social and religious outlook to which Eastern mysticism had generously contributed and in which the Slav feeling of world brotherhood played a conspicuous role.

The Russians are, of course, not the only people to have grandiose ideas about their destiny, but no other nation has had any more exalted ones. Two great writers are often quoted in this connection. In *Dead Souls*, Gogol apostrophizes his native land: "And you, Russia—are you not speeding like a *troika* which nought can overtake? . . . while the other states and nations, with looks askance, make way for you and draw aside."[1] And Dostoevsky, in his famous address on Pushkin delivered June 8, 1880, gives this eloquent description of the nature and mission of the Russian soul: "We, well, not we, but the future Russians, to the last man will comprehend that to become a genuine Russian means to seek finally to reconcile all European controversies, to show the solution of European anguish in our all-humanitarian and all-unifying Russian soul, to embrace in it with brotherly love all our brethren, and finally, perhaps, to utter the ultimate word of great universal harmony, of the brotherly accord of all nations abiding by the law of Christ's Gospel."[2]

This sense of mission, together with the other factors just discussed, was the chief motivating force in the tsarist empire's expansionist policy up to 1917. Backed by a huge population and by an abundance of natural resources, Russia's advance seemed difficult to contain, not only in backward Asia but in Europe itself. Yet there were certain obstacles—social and psychological, as well as political and military—which eventually caused the advance to lose momentum. By the early twentieth century these obstacles had become so formidable that Russia, under its Provisional Government of 1917, appeared ready to abandon its territorial ambitions, reject the concept of a decadent West, and join Western nations in realizing commonly shared ideals of political and social democracy and of international co-operation.

One of the most effective brakes upon Russian expansionism was the growing belief of progressively inclined groups that further territorial acquisitions were unnecessary, and that the tsarist government should concentrate on urgent problems of economic development and social reform. This pressure first manifested itself under Catherine II and Alexander I; it acquired almost explosive

[1] N. V. Gogol, *Polnoe sobranie khudozhestvennykh proizvedenii*, p. 738.

[2] F. M. Dostoevsky, *The Diary of a Writer* (translated and annotated by Boris Brasol), II, 980.

force during the second half of the nineteenth century; and early in the twentieth century it generated a movement for constitutional government and social
reorganization which deeply impressed foreign observers. The movement,
moreover, was truly national in scope, embracing trusted government officials
as well as "bourgeois" liberals, unruly urban workers, the dissatisfied peasantry,
and the more clamorous national minorities. Although Nicholas II was reluctant to face the full implications of the new reform program, his two ablest
ministers, Witte and Stolypin, devoted their major efforts to modernizing the
nation's economy; and one of his most experienced diplomats, Baron Rosen,
asserted that Russia had reached the limit of its westward advance, that the
genius of the Russian people was averse to armed aggression, and that the empire's real mission lay in raising the cultural level of its own peoples, particularly
in Asia, rather than in attempting to influence the more highly developed civilization of the West.

A second brake upon the tsarist expansionist movement was the growing
uncertainty about what type of culture Russia was supposed to spread to foreign peoples. The traditional "Third Rome" view stressed the three "pillars"
of autocracy, orthodoxy, and nationalism. In the course of the nineteenth
century, however, these three pillars began to be undermined. Gogol and
Dostoevsky, to be sure, were basically conservative in their views, although
they sometimes criticized the repressive features and bureaucratic incompetence
of the Russian government. On the other hand, the early Slavophils—Khomiakov, Samarin, Ivan Kireevsky, and Konstantin Aksakov—paid such glowing
tribute to an idealized Orthodox Church and an equally idealized and democratic peasant commune that their writings became a rather disruptive critique
of the existing tsarist regime even while proclaiming loyalty to the tsar. It is
quite true that the later Pan-Slavists, for the most part Russian chauvinists
wedded to autocratic principles, succeeded in forcing Slavophil nonconformity
into the background of Russian political life. But the seeds of discord had been
planted: Russia was now confronted with the dilemma of reconciling two apparently irreconcilable ideals—that of the absolutist and increasingly nationalistic
"Third Rome" and that of the more freedom-conscious "Russian soul."

A third brake upon the tsarist expansionist movement was the conflict between its long-range messianic aims and its tendency to follow a more selfishly
acquisitive policy. In theory, Russian territorial ambitions were supposed to
benefit both Russia and the newly annexed or protected peoples; in practice, the
Russian government often waged its wars or conducted its diplomacy merely
to serve its own political or economic interests. This opportunist policy was at
times pushed so far that nations with which Russia had strong racial or religious ties found their territorial integrity and their legitimate political aspirations jeopardized by a self-seeking type of imperialism.

Russian activity in the Balkans offered a striking example of such *realpolitik*.
Since the early nineteenth century the tsarist government had displayed a growing readiness to help the Greeks, Rumanians, Bulgars, and Serbs emancipate
themselves from Ottoman rule. Russia had contributed to the winning of Greek
independence in 1829 and of Rumanian and Serbian independence after the
war of 1877–78. It had also helped Bulgaria secure a broad degree of autonomy
and a widely acclaimed constitution. However, it sharply deviated from this
co-operative and liberating policy by demanding part of Bessarabia from Ru-

mania, its wartime ally, and by imposing upon Bulgaria military and political controls that were deeply resented and eventually rejected by the Bulgarian people. Even Serbia, the most pro-Russian of all the larger Balkan states in the early twentieth century, saw its hopes of territorial expansion partially blocked by an Austro-Russian agreement in 1908, which permitted the Hapsburg empire to annex Bosnia and Herzegovina in exchange for contemplated Russian transit privileges from the Black Sea to the Mediterranean.

The most glaring departure from Russia's professed ideals was its treatment of the Poles. United since 1386 with a militant Lithuania, Poland had become in the sixteenth century a most formidable enemy of the Muscovite state. Early in the seventeenth century Polish armies had occupied Moscow, and a Polish prince had succeeded in ascending the Muscovite throne. Russian enmity toward Poland at that time was, therefore, understandable. But the subsequent military weakness of Poland removed any threat to the Russian nation, and there was little justification for Russia's Polish policy of the late eighteenth and nineteenth centuries. Catherine II took a leading part in the partitions of Poland and virtually destroyed a reformed Polish state in 1793. The autonomy Alexander I conferred upon the Poles under Russian rule was too fragile to withstand the combined impact of Polish revolts and Russian political reprisals. And even the last remnant of Polish sovereignty—the independent Republic of Cracow—was condemned to extinction by another Russian emperor, Nicholas I, who encouraged Austria to annex this tiny state in 1846.

The fourth and perhaps most effective brake upon the tsarist expansionist movement was the resistance it met from the other nations of Europe. This resistance, which stiffened or relaxed in accordance with the changing alignments of international politics, was caused basically by fear of Russian political and territorial aggression, a fear that had been aggravated in Western Europe by Russia's treatment of the Poles.

The partitions did not arouse hostility toward Russia in Austria and Prussia, the two other powers that had shared in the dismemberment of Poland. This new community of interest was, of course, strengthened by the attempt of the three conservative monarchies to combat French revolutionary ideas in their wars against Napoleon, and it assumed even more definite form in the policing of Europe after Napoleon's defeat. The close association of the three monarchies came to an end only after the middle of the nineteenth century, partly because of Austria's growing Balkan ambitions, and partly because the Hapsburg empire refused to help Russia in the Crimean War after Russian troops, in 1849, had suppressed a serious Hungarian rebellion led by Louis Kossuth.

Despite Austria's antagonistic policies, the tsarist government did not wish to abandon its pro-German orientation. Close dynastic ties with a number of German states remained, and there was still a strong aversion, shared by Austria and Prussia, to the liberal and republican doctrines of the West. Moreover, the new German empire under Bismarck's leadership was determined to maintain friendly relations with its Russian neighbor. Thanks to Bismarck's vigorous support, the tsarist government found it comparatively easy to terminate the neutralization of the Black Sea, which had been forced upon Russia after the Crimean War. And it was largely owing to Bismarck's diplomatic skill that Russia and Germany signed the famous Reinsurance Treaty, which remained in force as long as Bismarck remained Chancellor.

The tsarist government was deeply impressed by this display of German friendship. Although the German emperor, William II, allowed the Reinsurance Treaty to lapse—thereby driving Russia into an alliance with republican France—a more limited kind of Russo-German co-operation continued almost up to World War I. It was the folly of German statesmen in underwriting Austria's Balkan policy, rather than any deep-seated Russo-German antagonism, that ultimately led to war between Germany and Russia in 1914.

One final reason for the close ties between Russia and Germany should be noted, namely, the impact on the tsarist empire of German industrialization and of the unrest it provoked. German businessmen were eager to increase their trade with Russia during the late nineteenth and early twentieth centuries, as well as to invest some of their capital in Russia's rapidly growing industry. Meanwhile, German socialists provided a new revolutionary gospel to those Russians who sought to free themselves from capitalistic controls. It is true that a large percentage of Russian socialists, notably the Socialist Revolutionaries, remained loyal to a distinctly Russian type of socialism aimed primarily at land distribution among the peasants. However, the Russian Social Democrats, among whom Lenin was soon to play a dominant role, derived their chief inspiration from the doctrines of Karl Marx, and at first looked upon the highly industrialized German nation as the leader of the anticipated social revolution.

The more democratically inclined nations of the West—particularly England, France, and the United States—were at one time or another prepared to resist Russia's expansionist policy, even though they were seldom in danger of Russian encroachment. To be sure, Russia entered the final coalition against the Napoleonic empire, and later pushed southward into California; but those crises were quickly ended, the first by the victory over Napoleon, the second by Russia's peaceful withdrawal following the promulgation of the Monroe Doctrine. More serious matters were the aversion felt by Western liberals to the dictatorial methods of the tsarist system at home and abroad, and the growing clash of economic interests in Asia between Russia and the Western nations.

Largely because of its geographical remoteness, the United States was slower than the other two nations to distrust Russia. Anti-Russian sentiment at the time of Kossuth's visit to America was soon replaced by a strong feeling of friendship for Alexander II, whose territorial ambitions in no way clashed with those of the United States and whose actions—notably liberating the serfs and sending Russian fleets to New York and San Francisco during the Civil War—were widely acclaimed, though partially misunderstood. Under Alexander III and Nicholas II, however, tsarist political repression, particularly against Russian Jews, and the tsarist government's refusal to recognize the full American citizenship of some of its former subjects, led to much angry newspaper comment, dramatic mass meetings, and sharp diplomatic notes. Finally, in 1911, the Russo-American commercial treaty of 1832 was abrogated as a protest against tsarist political and legal concepts. Meanwhile, the growing interest of American businessmen in Manchuria, and the clash of America's "Open Door" doctrine with Russia's aggressive policies in that area, strengthened the anti-Russian feeling of the American government to such a point that it encouraged Japan to attack Russia in the Far East and gave Japan considerable diplomatic and financial aid in the ensuing struggle.

The French and British governments were more consistent in their anti-Russian orientation, particularly during the reigns of Nicholas I and Alexander II. Up to the end of the eighteenth century these two countries had not been traditional enemies of the tsarist empire. England had old commercial ties with Russia, and the desire of British merchants to maintain this profitable relationship was so strong in 1791 that they were able to circumvent the efforts of Pitt to check tsarist aggression in Poland and along the northern coast of the Black Sea. France, meanwhile, had intermittently regarded Russia as a useful ally against its Hapsburg and Hohenzollern enemies of the era preceding the partitions of Poland. It had likewise extended its cultural influence into Russian governmental circles during the reigns of Elizabeth and Catherine II.

The outbreak of the French Revolution, together with Napoleon's policy of aggressive war and of continental blockade, undermined these friendly relationships. Shortly afterward, nineteenth-century liberalism and the spreading Industrial Revolution brought them to an end. Both the "liberal" French monarch, Louis Philippe, and the liberally inclined French emperor, Napoleon III, were snubbed by Nicholas I, and they reciprocated his unfriendly feelings. The more republican-minded Frenchmen, as well as Englishmen of both major political parties, became equally antagonistic to Nicholas I, seeing in his policy of supporting "legitimate" governments throughout Europe an illegal and anachronistic extension of discredited political controls. The suppression of the Polish rebellion of 1863 led to further dislike of the tsarist regime, despite its reformist legislation under Alexander II. However, French anti-Russian feeling abated to a considerable extent late in the nineteenth century as a result of common military interests, which culminated in the Franco-Russian alliance, and also because of the two countries' growing financial interdependence, which expressed itself in widely subscribed French loans to the tsarist government. England, on the other hand, became increasingly fearful of Russian colonial ambitions in Asia, and its concern for India and British economic interests overseas led to a series of war scares that lasted until early in the twentieth century. By that time British government leaders, following the French example, had decided that Germany was a more dangerous rival than the Russian empire. They also realized that Russia's national economy, under the prodding of men like Witte, offered an inviting field for British capital investment and British trade. The two countries accordingly reached mutually satisfactory agreements on Asian spheres of influence in 1907.

The most persistent and troublesome of all the issues between the Anglo-French and tsarist governments was the question of Constantinople and the Straits. This strategically important area had been a major concern of tsarist foreign policy ever since the reign of Catherine II, who won from the Turks the right of free transit for Russian merchant ships. Early in the nineteenth century, Nicholas I managed to obtain certain exclusive rights to send Russian warships through the Straits, but the combined diplomatic pressure of other European powers forced Nicholas to substitute an agreement, signed in 1841, that barred the Straits to all foreign warships in time of peace. This Convention of 1841 remained unchanged in its essential provisions until World War I. It led, however, to restrictions which Russia found increasingly irksome and which the tsarist government repeatedly sought to remove in favor of exclusive rights of passage for Russian naval vessels.

The French and British governments were by no means disposed to comply with Russian proposals to this end. France had long enjoyed certain treaty rights as an ally of Turkey, rights which Napoleon III considered important enough to justify his anti-Russian policy leading to the Crimean War. Even the conclusion of the Franco-Russian alliance late in the nineteenth century and the close financial ties between Russia and France at that time failed to erase this old antagonism. Up to the very outbreak of World War I, France would not give its official blessing to Russia's demand for exclusive rights of passage for Russian warships from the Black Sea to the Mediterranean.

British opposition to Russian naval privileges in the Straits was linked to long-standing British fears of a Russian advance on India and of Russian aggression in the Near East. It is true that after the Anglo-Russian agreements of 1907, Sir Edward Grey began to view Russian claims in the Straits area with some degree of sympathy. But prior to World War I, Grey and his colleagues never felt free to grant Russian warships the exclusive right to pass through the Straits. They claimed that English public opinion would not tolerate such a one-sided arrangement; if the Straits were opened to warships in time of peace, all nations should share the privilege.

The outbreak of World War I compelled both the French and the British to reconsider their Turkish policy. In 1915 Russia demanded not only special rights for its warships but also possession of the city of Constantinople and of strategically situated territory on both sides of the Straits. Under the pressure of wartime expediency England and France accepted the Russian proposals. The British and French governments insisted, however, on adequate "compensation," particularly in Asiatic Turkey and in Persia, thus effectively blocking any serious Russian threat to Anglo-French interests in the Near East.

Such were the major obstacles to tsarist expansionist policy. The first three—pressures for internal reforms, skepticism at home concerning the nature of Russia's civilizing mission, and the betrayal in practice of long-range messianic aims—were so varied in nature that it is difficult to estimate their combined effect. The fourth—specific acts of resistance by foreign nations—operated only sporadically. Nevertheless, by March 1917, when the tsarist regime was overthrown, these four obstacles had definitely proved their strength. The tsarist government itself had not abandoned the idea of future territorial acquisitions, which had been sanctioned by Russia's secret treaties with its wartime allies. However, the overwhelming mass of the Russian people, sick of war, eager to control their own national destiny, and increasingly receptive to Western constitutional and socialistic ideas, supported a peace program that rejected all annexations and indemnities and called for a concentration of the nation's energies on problems of political reconstruction and social reform.

A striking example of this new Russian orientation was the Provisional Government's renunciation of Russia's claims to Constantinople and to territory adjoining the Straits. Another example was the new government's relatively generous treatment of Russia's national minorities, which, despite growing disorder and Left-wing separatist agitation, seemed willing—except in officially liberated Poland—to accept an autonomous existence within a new federal and democratic Russian state. Perhaps the most interesting example of all was the readiness with which Russia turned to the West to rehabilitate its sagging economy and to work out a pattern of close political co-operation. Western transportation experts were invited to Russia to help increase the efficiency of the nation's overburdened railways. Western diplomats, expressing the new feeling of solidarity between their governments and democratic Russia, encountered a friendliness and appreciation which their demands for an all-out Russian war effort could not completely destroy. The assistance of Western socialist leaders was also sought, sometimes without success, in an attempt to strengthen Russia's own movement for an early negotiated peace. And had it not been for the disorderly state of Russian industry and the unruly behavior of many Russian workmen, real progress might have been made in enlisting the aid of Western businessmen and engineers, whose activity in raising the level of Russian industrial production had become more and more conspicuous during the last years of the tsarist regime.

One final point should be noted with respect to Western aid to the Russian nation in 1917. During the reigns of Alexander III and Nicholas II the more severe Russian famines had not been ignored by the peoples of Western Europe and America. The Americans, in particular, had generously contributed to Russian famine relief in 1891–92, despite the strained diplomatic relations between the two countries. Although there was no famine in 1917, the scarcity of food was a serious problem in Russia's urban centers, and bread, meat, milk, and sugar lines sometimes lasted all day and far into the night. In an effort to meet this problem the American Red Cross played a most active and beneficial role, especially during the last months of the Provisional Government.

Russia's rapprochement with the West in 1917 was thus a widely attested fact. Whether this new trend would have persisted if the Provisional Government had remained in power long enough to encounter the manifold problems of postwar readjustment is, of course, another matter. Heavy financial indebtedness to the Western nations and a demand for the scaling down of interest payments could have led to acrimonious disputes. Urgent economic needs were likely to revive the traditional pressure for better trade outlets and easier access to the open sea. And the great popularity of the Socialist Revolutionary Party, with its emphasis upon an agrarian type of socialism, might have weakened Russia's ties with the Western labor and socialist movements enough to give the old belief in Russia's special civilizing mission a new lease on life. Russia, even after the kaleidoscopic changes of 1917, was still a product of past experiences. Habits that had developed over centuries could not be broken in a few months by revolutionary slogans or the ideas of the democratic West.

Once the Bolsheviks were entrenched in power, the readiness of a revolutionary-minded Russia to return to certain practices and traditions of the tsarist period was made abundantly clear. To be sure, Lenin and his associates spared no effort in "exposing" and vilifying the tsarist regime. They rejected the principle of political autocracy, denounced bureaucratic methods, sought to destroy the Orthodox Church, and redefined the doctrine of Russian nationalism so as to strip it of all vestiges of "oppressive" Russification and "predatory" imperialism. Yet within a short period of time they found themselves yielding to the pressure of historical forces which no revolutionary fanaticism could conjure away. Defense of Russian national interests, enlargement of the Russian sphere of political influence, ready access to the outside world through warm-water ports, extension of Russian-inspired reforms to "misguided" foreign nations—to all these elements of traditional Russian expansionism the Bolsheviks brought their own form of the old crusading zeal. The language of this policy was new, its aims revolutionary, its methods highly unconventional. But by reasserting Russia's long-felt political and economic needs, and by reformulating Russia's long-cherished ideal of world brotherhood, the Soviet regime brought itself into imperfect but still logical alignment with the general course of Russian history.

Needless to say, the Bolsheviks' attempt to defend Russia's national interests and to enlarge Russia's sphere of political influence was part of a much larger and far more ambitious revolutionary program. Their strategy was world-wide in scope: it called for an international communist revolution growing out of international class war that would "inevitably" result from the international rivalries and armed conflicts of capitalist groups. To reach such a goal, according to the Bolsheviks, Soviet Russia would have to protect itself against capitalist attacks and eventually join forces with other sovietized nations in an expanding communist movement. Once the movement reached its presumably final stage of a complete victory over capitalism, all national frontiers, like the political state with its coercive power, would begin to "wither away." Meanwhile, political boundaries would continue to exist, although they would be drawn in rigid compliance with the Bolsheviks' own formula of national self-determination.

This formula reflected a characteristically communist point of view. Lenin and his followers believed that any attempt at national self-determination should not involve the participation of all the inhabitants of a given country. They insisted that "bourgeois" and "reactionary" groups, with their financial power, their systems of police "intimidation," and their "corrupting" press, should be denied voting privileges. For, to the Bolsheviks' way of thinking, any election, in order to be truly free, would have to be based on the will of the workers and poorer peasants, who represented an actual or potential majority of the population, and whose temporary "dictatorship" was essential to the success of the revolutionary movement. The workers and poorer peasants were, in turn, to be led by dedicated and well-disciplined Bolshevik—or Communist—parties having close organizational and ideological ties with similar parties in other nations. Since Lenin and his followers had taken the initiative in translating communist doctrines into revolutionary action, it was obvious that Russia, as the leader of the entire communist movement, would be able to exert great, perhaps decisive, pressure upon the policies of other sovietized and Bolshevized states.

The Bolshevik formula of national freedom and legitimate national defense likewise promised to satisfy Russia's "urge to the sea." Soviet leaders were well aware of the importance of warm-water ports; in fact, Trotsky, in his early negotiations with the Central Powers, showed himself at least temporarily willing to violate every principle of national self-determination in order to maintain Russian control over the port of Riga, with its many German- and Lettish-speaking inhabitants. In their official statements of policy, however, the Bolsheviks invariably stressed the "inquity" of such imposed controls over foreign peoples, and they spared no effort in denouncing the "predatory" imperialism of the tsarist government in Persia, Manchuria, and Korea, as well as with respect to Constantinople and the Straits. All such territory, they insisted, should be governed by its own working-class population, who, thanks to the Bolshevik triumph in 1917, would henceforth be free from any fear of Russian aggression. In making these ringing pronouncements, the Bolsheviks refrained from adding that the workers and peasants of Persia, Manchuria, Korea, and Turkey were expected, once they had overthrown their capitalist governments, to join a federation of soviet republics under vigorous Russian leadership and thus provide the Russian soviet state with easy access to the Persian Gulf, the Pacific Ocean, and the Mediterranean.

A much more obvious example of Bolshevik indebtedness to old tsarist traditions was the revived consciousness of Russia's duty to reform the world. The new and revolutionary form of this crusade was Western in origin, drawing its basic doctrines from such German thinkers as Hegel, Feuerbach, Engels, and Marx. Lenin was an orthodox and loyal Marxist in the sense that he subscribed to Marxist economic principles and "laws" of history. But, like other Marxist leaders of the late nineteenth and early twentieth centuries, he realized that Marx and Engels had been too confident in predicting the almost automatic collapse of capitalism as a result of progressively severe business crises, increasing misery, and the relentless growth of a revolutionary-minded proletariat which would seize power first in the more highly industrialized nations of the West. Obviously, it had become essential to revise Marx, and the task was resolutely undertaken by Western socialists, some of whom stressed the need of revolutionary violence while others advocated a more cautious and flexible strategy based on parliamentary action and a strong and flourishing labor movement. Lenin bitterly opposed the latter—or "gradualist"—viewpoint. In close touch with Russian and Asian as well as Western political and social developments, he had been deeply impressed by the immense, spontaneous character of Russian peasant uprisings and by the revolutionary potential of "exploited" colonial areas. He had likewise paid considerable attention to the more nihilistically inclined Russian socialists of the nineteenth century—particularly the champions of revolutionary violence, Bakunin, Nechaiev, and Tkachev.

Such Russian and Asian influences, supplemented by a painstaking study of the development of finance capitalism in the West, led to the formulation of Lenin's doctrine of imperialism, a restatement of Marxist theory in relatively uncompromising and militant terms. According to this doctrine capitalism had survived its periodical crises largely by exploiting colonial and semicolonial areas. It had thus been able to augment its profits and to create an artificial prosperity, in which corruptible labor leaders and their deluded followers might participate to a very limited extent. But, as Lenin was quick to point out, such prosperity was ephemeral. There were only so many colonial or semicolonial areas for Western finance capitalism to exploit, and the growing competition for these areas was bound to lead to a series of armed conflicts among the capitalist nations. Under such conditions a real and lasting peace could only be obtained by converting the "imperialistic" World War into an international civil conflict which would bring about the destruction of the capitalist system. Hence the need for violence, for the forced development of the class struggle to its most explosive point; and violent action, to be fully effective, had to be taken not only by the more class-conscious industrial workers, but by the less articulate peasantry and by the oppressed and hitherto leaderless masses of the colonial areas.

Moreover, the political and social immaturity of the peasantry and the colonial masses, as well as the unreliability of certain urban workers themselves, called for a kind of professional leadership. Such leadership, in Lenin's opinion, was to be exercised by rigorously disciplined and thoroughly indoctrinated party organizations acting as the vanguard of the new revolutionary offensive.

Lenin's radical program was elaborated still further after the overthrow of the tsarist government in March 1917. Russia then began to play a leading and decisive role in Lenin's revolutionary strategy. The comparatively rapid industrialization of the tsarist empire in the early twentieth century, its increasingly rebellious peasantry, its growing contacts with "exploited" colonial areas in Asia, and its critical wartime situation, loaded with revolutionary possibilities, all lent encouragement to Lenin's belief that his own country could become the temporary headquarters of the anticipated drive toward international communism. Russia was being offered an unexpected, almost unique opportunity. It could launch a crusade as world-wide in scope as that contemplated by the most enthusiastic and visionary sponsors of the "Third Rome." Lenin himself would have resented such an analogy, and he would have gone to great lengths to discount the indebtedness of his Marxist messianism to the messianism of tsarist Russia. But historical tradition cannot be discounted. Even the Communist Party, in formulating its theses on the role it should play, re-expressed some of the aspirations of Holy Russia, of Dostoevsky, and of the Slavophils when it announced: "Strong in its close association with worker and peasant masses, in its good organization, discipline, self-control, and unshakable faith in the victory of the working class, and acting in solidarity with the communist proletariat of the world, the Russian Communist Party will fulfill its historic mission by reaching its final goal of rejuvenating human society."[3]

Lenin's revolutionary program naturally affected Bolshevik views of foreign relations. Since, as he believed, the capitalists dominated most of the states of the world, any state ruled by or in the name of the proletariat would be regarded by the capitalists as an enemy and a threat, and hence, if possible, destroyed. The new Bolshevik government of Russia could therefore expect direct or indirect aggression from other states. In communist terms, there could be no such thing as "permanent peace" between the workers' and peasants' government and capitalist governments. The best that the Bolsheviks could hope for would be a kind of truce, which, according to the official viewpoint of 1917–18, would be of short duration.

Such beliefs decisively influenced the Bolshevik attitude toward international law. To the Bolshevik way of thinking, international law was a set of rules drawn up and enforced to serve the needs and interests of the ruling classes. Since the ruling classes outside Soviet Russia were regarded as capitalist imperialists, the Bolsheviks could not willingly acknowledge the validity of existing international law or agree to such international practices as arbitration. Furthermore, the Bolsheviks maintained that the government and diplomats of a bourgeois state could not speak for the people as a whole but only for the ruling class. Who then did speak for the majority of the people, for "the toiling and exploited masses"? The Bolsheviks had the answer to this in what A. V. Sabanin called the basic principle of the proletarian revolution, namely, "the solidarity of the toiling masses of the world,"[4] or what Trotsky referred to as the "one unwritten but sacred treaty, the treaty of the international solidarity of the proletariat."[5]

[3] *Izvestiia*, No. 206, September 17, 1920, p. 2.

[4] "Sovetskaia vlast i mezhdunarodnoe pravo," *Mezhdunarodnaia Zhizn*, No. 15 (133), Nov. 7, 1922, p. 11.

[5] *Protokoly zasedanii VTSIK* [Vserossiiskogo Tsentralnogo Ispolnitelnogo Komiteta] *2 sozyva* (1918), p. 154.

This viewpoint produced certain practical results. The Soviet government claimed to speak for the toiling and exploited masses not only of Russia but of all countries, and it appealed to the workers of the world to unite against their own rulers and in support of the "real" representatives of their interests, the Russian Bolsheviks.

On the basis of this principle of proletarian solidarity or proletarian internationalism, Soviet leaders repudiated the traditional concept of "foreigner" and the legal concept of "citizenship" and recognized as citizens of the Soviet republic prisoners of war or other "nationals" of foreign countries who accepted Bolshevism, or as Sabanin put it, were "ideologically close to the Soviet regime." From this principle the Soviet government also assumed the right to intervene on behalf of its supporters in other countries who were being "persecuted" under the laws of bourgeois states.

The Soviet peace program thus had no roots in traditional concepts of international law. The Bolsheviks' immediate aim in the months following the October Revolution was to withdraw from the war and to have the Soviet government recognized as the successor of the Imperial and the Provisional governments; but their major objective was "the transformation of the imperialist war into a world-wide struggle against capitalism." This meant that the Bolsheviks' foreign policy was two-edged. Even while endeavoring to establish temporary relations with capitalist governments, they sought to undermine and if possible overthrow them by anticapitalist insurrections.

The Bolsheviks' initial attitude toward diplomatic procedure was in line with their revolutionary doctrines. When Trotsky, somewhat against his will, took over the People's Commissariat of Foreign Affairs on November 8, 1917, he apparently did so in the belief that his task was not to reform the organization and personnel of the foreign service but to liquidate the entire apparatus of diplomacy along with the other government departments that had no function in a revolutionary regime. In his memoirs, Trotsky quotes Lenin's astonished comment: "What foreign affairs will we have now?"[6] He recalls his own remark that he would issue some revolutionary proclamations "and then shut up shop" as indicating his opinion that other things were more important than diplomacy.

These observations, whether serious or not, were in harmony with the views of Bolshevik leaders late in 1917. Soviet Russia, they believed, was at war with international capitalism; and unless the capitalists were speedily replaced by friendly revolutionary governments, the Soviet republic would be overthrown. In either case there would be no job for the old-style foreign office or the old-style diplomat.

Trotsky's career as head of the People's Commissariat of Foreign Affairs ended in March 1918, when he resigned to become Commissar of War. He did not succeed in liquidating diplomacy, but thanks to some of his innovations it has never been the same since his time. His successor was G. V. Chicherin, a Russian *gentilhomme,* who had joined the Imperial Ministry of Foreign Affairs as an archivist and research worker, and had left the Ministry to study abroad, where he became a Marxist and an official of the Russian Social Democratic Labor Party's Foreign Bureau. On his return to Russia in January 1918, Lenin

---

[6] L. D. Trotsky, *My Life; An Attempt at an Autobiography,* p. 341.

assigned him to the People's Commissariat of Foreign Affairs. Within a short time he brought Soviet diplomatic procedure into somewhat closer alignment with that of foreign nations.[7]

Thus, while Soviet foreign policy set an absolutely new course, in the sense that it repudiated both conventional doctrines of international law and conventional codes of ethics, it could not break wholly with the past. Certain of its motivations were as old as history, and were as relevant to Soviet needs as they had been to those of the tsars.

The continuing influence of historical forces was also revealed in the obstacles which the Bolshevik expansionist movement encountered. As under the tsars, the demands of an aggressive foreign policy clashed sharply with those of a constructive program of internal reform. As in prerevolutionary Russia, there were ideological disagreements, which now centered on the methods rather than the principles of political control. There was also the rude intrusion of a self-seeking *realpolitik* upon the idealism underlying Russia's historic mission. Finally—and inevitably—there was the resistance of foreign peoples and foreign governments opposed to any further extension of Russian power.

The first obstacle to Soviet expansion—the clash between an aggressive foreign policy and the requirements of internal reorganization—became painfully evident during the early months of 1918. The Bolsheviks had expected a series of proletarian uprisings in foreign countries as soon as Russia gave the necessary signal. They had likewise felt great confidence in the ability of the Russian working class to invigorate the Russian administrative system and infuse Russian industry with new productive power. In both respects, they were grievously disappointed. The inertia and innate conservatism of most foreign workers, together with their war-inflamed patriotism and their subjection to wartime controls, blocked any immediate extension of the Soviet system. Meanwhile the inexperience, selfishness, and lack of discipline displayed by the Russian masses made a shambles of Lenin's initial plan for a well-integrated and efficient system of "workers' control" within the new Soviet state. The Bolsheviks were therefore compelled to reconsider their revolutionary strategy. Just as Witte and Stolypin had stressed the paramount need of far-reaching internal reforms at the expense of new foreign adventures, so Lenin and his more loyal followers began to direct their attention toward giving Russia a "breathing spell," in which earlier communist mismanagement could be corrected and the pressure toward extending the communist movement relaxed. Lenin's sober reasoning was bitterly assailed by many party members, who called themselves Left communists, as well as by other Left-wing groups who still wished to carry on their revolutionary crusade at almost any price. But Lenin eventually had his way. He thus set a precedent of interrupting the forward drive of communism which was to be carefully followed in subsequent years, particularly during the early 1920's, when the N.E.P. was introduced, and a few years later, when Stalin's "socialism in one country" triumphed over Trotsky's doctrine of "permanent revolution."

The second obstacle to Soviet expansion—disagreements over the methods of applying Soviet political controls—was equally disturbing. Russia's chaotic

[7] T. H. von Laue, "Soviet Diplomacy: G. V. Chicherin, Peoples Commissar for Foreign Affairs, 1918–1930," Chapter 8 in Gordon A. Craig and Felix Gilbert (eds.), *The Diplomats 1919–1939*, pp. 234–46.

situation early in 1918 called not only for a "breathing spell" but for a distasteful kind of administrative centralization to make the "breathing spell" effective. Before the October Revolution the Bolshevik program had stressed certain democratic or quasi-democratic practices, notably the election by the working classes of all government officials and of all officers in the armed forces. Shortly after the October Revolution, however, the more realistic Bolshevik leaders saw that they must return, temporarily, to the old-fashioned methods of administering the country and of organizing the army, even though this meant employing the services of many former tsarist officials and tsarist officers. Such a justification of "bureaucratic" methods at the expense of "democratic principles" was the exact opposite of the Slavophil critique of tsarist policy, but it was equally embarrassing and even more serious in its effects. To be sure, opposition to the new centralized controls by nonparty groups could be faced and eventually brushed aside, as Slavophil dissatisfaction with the tsarist regime had been. But when sharp objections were raised within the party, by the Left communists, the problem became quite complicated. Moreover, the application of the new system of centralized controls—by a rapidly expanding bureaucracy and an almost irresponsible political police—was bound to confuse and even alienate foreign sympathizers. It is hard to say how much this shift in tactics impeded the progress of the communist movement. There can be no doubt, however, that Soviet Russia's "world mission" lost both its logical justification and much of its emotional appeal soon after the revolution. This happened because of the swing toward totalitarian methods which began in 1918, developed into the bureaucratized "War Communism" of 1920, and culminated in the final years of Stalin's dictatorship.

A third obstacle to Soviet expansionism, as it had been to tsarist expansionism, was the apparent perversion of Russia's "civilizing mission" by considerations of immediate political or economic advantage. The tsarist government had made a mockery of Pan-Slavic doctrines, and in some of its dealings with Rumania, Bulgaria, and Serbia it had shown little concern for the "brotherly accord of all nations." The Soviet government was even more vulnerable to charges of inconsistency in its foreign policies. The Bolsheviks' emphasis upon the principle of working class self-determination called for a truly representative expression of working class opinion in every country whose territory they wished to control and whose support they definitely claimed. Yet this kind of national plebiscite was avoided whenever they felt they must possess certain territory without delay. The Ukraine, for example, which in early 1918 seemed of vital importance to the survival of the Soviet system, was quickly overrun by Soviet military forces, despite a declaration of independence by its own national *Rada* and earlier support of the *Rada*'s policies by an All-Ukrainian Congress of Soviets. Subsequent developments led to similar moves—the invasion of Poland in 1920, the annexation of Georgia in 1921, the occupation of numerous Eastern European countries during and immediately after World War II.

The fourth and most important obstacle to Bolshevik expansion was the resistence of foreign powers, which flared up immediately after the October Revolution and has persisted to the present day.

Germany was both the chief enemy of the Soviet republic and the chief target of Soviet propaganda in 1918. After the Entente's refusal to consider Bolshevik proposals for ending the "imperialistic" war, Lenin and his associates had been compelled to negotiate a separate peace with the Central Powers, who took full advantage of their new opportunity to dominate Eastern Europe. The treaty of peace, signed at Brest-Litovsk on March 3, 1918, was a Russian disaster. The Soviet government lost control over Finland, the Ukraine, Transcaucasia, and most of Russia's western borderlands; it had to accept unfavorable commercial arrangements and, later, the demand for a large indemnity; and, in theory at least, it was obliged to disband its armed forces. The Bolsheviks signed the peace treaty under protest, having every intention of sabotaging it whenever possible and of repudiating it as soon as the war situation changed to Germany's disadvantage. Their military weakness, however, forced them to adopt a relatively cautious policy: "correct" diplomatic relations with the German empire, partial disarmament at sea but not on land, protests against any German violations of the Brest-Litovsk treaty, and unremitting efforts to weaken Germany and its allies by subversive activity and revolutionary propaganda. On the whole, this defensive strategy proved successful. The most dangerous military threats—by German sponsored counterrevolutionary groups—were parried, and Soviet Russia emerged from the World War with its revolutionary system still functioning and the most vital areas of central Russia still under its control. For such a favorable turn of events Entente military victories were, of course, largely responsible. Yet the Bolsheviks helped their own cause to a very appreciable extent by their skill in delaying and eventually containing Entente efforts to reactivate the eastern front against Germany and by their shrewdness in exploiting the disagreements between German militarists, who wanted to destroy the Soviet regime, and German civilian leaders, who feared the effect of further German aggression upon public opinion both at home and abroad.

The Armistice of November 11, 1918, and the outbreak of revolutionary movements in Central Europe seemed to offer the Bolsheviks a long-sought opportunity to spread communism to foreign countries. The Brest-Litovsk treaty was promptly denounced; but the conservative instincts of the peoples of Germany and the former Austro-Hungarian empire prevented any immediate or widespread acceptance of Bolshevik doctrines. The first great test of the strength of the communist movement came in January 1919, when the Spartakus rising in Berlin was suppressed and its leaders, Karl Liebknecht and Rosa Luxemburg, were killed. There were later, and temporarily more successful, insurrections during the spring of 1919, particularly in Hungary. But the vast majority of the people of Central Europe stood firm against the Bolshevik revolutionary offensive.

Since Soviet Russia seemed unable to realize its expansionist program by force of example and subversive activity, it fell back upon the more direct method of force of arms. Early in 1919 it attempted to regain control over Russian territory formerly occupied by Austro-German troops and to use this territory as a staging ground for a political and military advance toward Central Europe.[8] Needless to say, the Bolshevik formula of national self-determination was used to justify the new communist offensive. Yet most of the peoples inhabiting Russia's western borderlands were inclined toward more conservative political

[8] A detailed survey of Soviet foreign policy during the years 1918–20 will be contained in two forthcoming volumes by Merrill Spalding and Xenia J. Eudin. This survey will provide extensive documentation on Soviet Russia's armed offensive of 1919, as well as on other related topics.

and social ideals, and they stubbornly resisted the encroachment of both Russian communist troops and the troops recruited by their own communist minorities. Finland, which had overthrown its Left-wing socialist government early in 1918, would not surrender an inch of its territory. Estonia, after temporarily yielding to Soviet pressure along its eastern frontier, soon drove the Bolsheviks out. Latvia experienced a somewhat longer period of Bolshevik domination, but eventually rallied, together with neighboring Lithuania and Belorussia, to free itself from Soviet control. Poland was strongly anti-Bolshevik from the very beginning of its new national existence, and it not only succeeded in defending its own territory but materially aided Lithuania and Belorussia in their efforts to check revolutionary communism. Finally, the Ukraine, after accepting a communist regime early in 1919, remained in a state of political turmoil; its new soviet government had to face the combined opposition of Ukrainian nationalists, peasant insurgents, and newly arrived Entente troops.

Thus the attempt to spread communism by force of arms quickly lost its momentum. Nothing came of plans that were drawn up during the late spring of 1919 to send troops, by way of Rumania, to aid the communist uprising in Hungary. Soviet troops were needed elsewhere—to suppress the insurrections of Ukrainian peasant guerrillas, and, more important, to check the growing pressure of Russian counterrevolutionary forces supported by the Entente.

Entente intervention in Soviet affairs had actually commenced in the summer of 1918, when troops were sent to North Russia and Siberia to guard war supplies and, if possible, reactivate the eastern front against Germany. With the Armistice of November 11, 1918, such intervention automatically came to an end. Nevertheless, Entente troops still occupied Russian territory and Entente pressure against revolutionary Bolshevism continued. There was a widely expressed desire to encourage the Russians to set up a new, popularly elected government which would eradicate the "disease" of Bolshevism, compensate Western businessmen for their property losses, acknowledge Russia's debts, and restore the friendly relations which had existed under the Provisional Government. There may also have been a desire to convert the struggle against Bolshevism into an attempt to weaken the Russian empire, by getting the new government to grant economic concessions or acknowledge the independence of many of Russia's former national minorities. Last, but by no means least, there was the feeling that the Russian counterrevolutionary—or White—movement, which had largely supported Entente efforts to restore an anti-German front in Russia, should in turn receive some effective support against its Bolshevik opponents.

During the Paris Peace Conference these various policies came into sharp collision. In January, and again during the spring months of 1919, an attempt was made to compromise existing differences of opinion by arranging an armistice between the warring political groups in Russia and by providing the long-suffering Russian people with necessary food supplies. The attempt failed, partly because of indecision and continuing disagreement at Paris, and partly because of the stepping up of the Bolshevik military and propaganda offensive in the West. Propaganda assumed more formidable proportions in March 1919, when a Third—or Communist—International was organized in Moscow to direct and implement the Bolshevik drive to overthrow existing capitalist governments.

In the late spring of 1919 Entente leaders broke off all relations with the Bolsheviks, intensified their blockade of Soviet territory, and announced their readiness to support the Russian counterrevolutionary movement. Official recognition was promised its leader, Admiral Kolchak, if he could give assurance that the new Russian state he hoped to found would rest on a basis of full popular approval. Meanwhile, the flow of military supplies was increased to the various anti-Bolshevik fronts, especially Siberia, southeastern Russia, and the area near Petrograd. However, this second attempt to solve the Russian problem proved unsuccessful. Entente aid to the White forces soon began to dwindle because of the pressure of Left-wing groups in the West against further intervention in Russia; and the White leaders were, on the whole, so conservative in their aims that they lost the support of the Russian masses and antagonized former national minorities, like the Finns and Estonians, who were more disposed to negotiate with an officially anti-imperialist Soviet state than to back Russian counterrevolutionaries who proclaimed the old doctrine of "Russia one and indivisible." Kolchak's forces were routed; the White advance from southeastern Russia was checked and then driven back; and the threat to Petrograd, based largely on Finnish and Estonian co-operation, came to an end.

In the first weeks of 1920 it was becoming clear that a kind of military stalemate had been reached. The Bolsheviks had gained the upper hand in Russia's civil war, but in so doing, they had seen their armed offensive against the West lose its momentum. Moreover, their economic situation, already critical in 1918, had become almost catastrophic. Mobilization of available Soviet resources on the "labor front" was now the Bolsheviks' immediate aim. They desperately needed another "breathing spell"; and the inability of Western nations to pursue their interventionist campaign, the evidence of mutiny among Western troops sent to Russia, the obvious unwillingness of Russia's western borderlands to support the White armies, and the West's own growing interest in more normal economic relationships with Eastern Europe all led Lenin and his associates to believe that this new "breathing spell" would be longer than the one in 1918.

It was to be a temporary respite, however, and nothing more. No real rapprochement with the West was conceivable, in view of the Bolsheviks' rigid adherence to their basic program of world revolution. They had no intention of seeking a permanent peace with the West. They wished merely to play off one capitalist nation against another; to combine, if possible, with a once friendly Germany against a traditionally hostile Poland; to seek the support of a trade-conscious England against a France embittered by unpaid debts; to join the new nationalist Turkey in common opposition to the 1919–20 peace settlement; to use this pro-Turkish orientation as a means of solving the troublesome Straits problem; and to overcome the growing aloofness and vehement anti-Bolshevism of the United States. In short, the Bolsheviks, having abandoned their initial overconfidence and their almost utopian crusading zeal, seemed ready to adopt a new type of revolutionary strategy. They would cease their frontal attack upon Western capitalism and try, for some time at least, to coexist "peacefully" with Western nations.

The beginnings of this policy of "peaceful coexistence," its early development, its temporary setbacks, and its general acceptance as a major instrument of Soviet revolutionary strategy are the topics with which the present volume is concerned.

PART I

Reopening the Window to Europe
1920–1921

PART I

"The international position of the Soviet republic has never been as favorable and triumphant as it is at present."

Lenin said this on March 1, 1920.[1] In part, no doubt, he hoped to raise the spirits of his party comrades and those workers and peasants who had been supporting the Communists in the civil war, men who were still mired so deep in so many difficulties that their situation could scarcely seem either favorable or triumphant. But in view of the situation a year before, Lenin's optimism was justified. The Red armies had beaten their most dangerous enemies. The foreign governments, except the Japanese, had given up their half-hearted intervention. Kolchak had been defeated in Siberia, Denikin's southern armies had disintegrated and were in full retreat, Yudenich had fallen back into Estonia. Foreign troops had been evacuated from Siberia, Arkhangelsk, the Crimea, and the Caucasus. Japanese troops remained in the Russian Far East, problems remained to be settled with Poland, the Western powers continued to treat the Soviet government as an outlaw in the society of nations, but the tide had turned. The Allies had just lifted their blockade against Russia. Fewer foreigners believed that the Soviet government was on the verge of collapse, and more were coming to view the Communists as an evil that must be endured until they either came to grief through their own errors or recognized their folly and mended their ways.

Yet, in spite of military and political success, the whole economic structure of the new state was near collapse. Poverty, disease, and famine had come on the heels of victory.

The Strategic Retreat on the Domestic Front

In 1921 mass discontent reached such proportions, even in the face of harsh repression, that the Soviet government abandoned War Communism and relaxed or removed some of its severest measures of regimentation. Several factors forced the change. In March 1921, the sailors of Kronstadt staged an armed revolt under the slogans "All power to the soviets" and "Down with the Communists' dictatorship." Besides this revolt of forces previously loyal to the Bolsheviks, there were widespread uprisings among the peasants of Tambov Province protesting the government's policy in the countryside. Communist leaders, Lenin in particular, realized that they had either to crush the opposition in a new and bloody civil war or to appease the opposition by a retreat from War Communism. They decided to retreat.

Accordingly, on March 15, 1921, the Tenth Congress of the Communist Party inaugurated the New Economic Policy by decreeing the replacement of grain requisitioning by a tax in kind. Other steps followed; money came back into use and market conditions were restored. By decrees of October 4 and

[1] V. I. Lenin, *Sochineniia*, XXV, 47.

October 27, 1921, the peasants were permitted, after paying their taxes, to sell their surplus agricultural products in the free market. A decree of May 22, 1922, legalized private ownership of new property acquired under the new regime. In a way, the New Economic Policy tried to reconcile two contradictory principles, socialism and capitalism, but it proved to be a relatively minor and temporary concession to capitalism. The government held the so-called "commanding heights"—control of foreign trade, large-scale enterprises, transportation, etc. In his closing speech at the Eleventh Party Congress, April 2, 1922, Lenin said of the new policies:

When, during the spring of 1921, the vanguard of the revolution was in danger of becoming isolated from the masses of the people, from the masses of the peasants, whom it must skillfully lead forward, we unanimously and firmly decided to retreat. And on the whole, during the past year, we retreated in good revolutionary order.[2]

While War Communism was in effect, the Communists claimed or implied that they were achieving communism. When War Communism had to be abandoned, the Communists naturally had no intention of admitting that communism had failed and that Soviet Russia had been forced to go back to capitalism. Some said that War Communism was not an attempt to introduce communism but a policy forced on the country by intervention and civil war.[3] But Lenin stressed the idea of a temporary strategic retreat. At the plenum of the Moscow soviet, November 20, 1922, he said: "We are now retreating, going back, as it were; but we are doing this in order to get a better run for our longer leap forward." And he promised that "not in our day but in the course of several years . . . N.E.P. Russia will be transformed into Socialist Russia."[4]

A later authorized explanation is this:

War Communism had been an attempt to take the fortress of the capitalist elements in town and countryside by assault, by a frontal attack. In this offensive the party had gone too far ahead, and ran the risk of being cut off from its base. Now Lenin proposed to retire a little, to retreat for a while nearer to the base, to change from assault to the slower method of siege, so as to gather strength and resume the offensive.[5]

Reorientation of Soviet Foreign Policy: From World Revolution to "Peaceful Coexistence"

During 1920–21 the Communists also changed the orientation of Soviet foreign policy. In preceding years communist leaders had exultantly awaited the coming world revolution, but by 1920 enthusiastic hopes were giving way

[2] Lenin, Sochineniia, XXVII, 271.

[3] L. D. Trotsky, Sochineniia, XII, 306–12; also A. Iu. Aikhenvald, Sovetskaia ekonomika. Ekonomika i ekonomicheskaia politika SSSR, p. 27.

[4] Lenin, Sochineniia, XXVII, 361–62, 366.

[5] Istoriia Vsesoiuznoi Kommunisticheskoi Partii (Bolshevikov). Kratkii kurs, p. 245. The first edition of this volume, edited and authorized by the Central Committee of the party, appeared in 1938; its authorship has often been ascribed to Stalin, and as long as Stalin lived it was quoted by Soviet writers as an infallible source of information. An English translation appeared in 1939 under the title History of the Communist Party of the Soviet Union (B).

to realistic appraisal and the reluctant recognition that revolution was to be, at the very least, slower in coming about than had been anticipated.

Spartakus week, ten days of revolutionary uprising in Berlin (January 6–15, 1919) staged by the Spartakusbund,[6] not only failed to touch off an "October" revolution in Germany but ended in the defeat of the Spartakists and the killing of Karl Liebknecht and Rosa Luxemburg, the two outstanding leaders of German communism. The Munich soviet with its odd assortment of revolutionary characters collapsed after a few weeks, and the Hungarian soviets, led by the Russian-trained Bela Kun, disintegrated in August 1919 under pressure from within and without. In the summer of 1920, when Red Army forces were standing at the gates of Warsaw, renewed hope flickered briefly, but the defeat before Warsaw, the failure of the Left parties in the West to follow the Russian example, and Russia's own desperate economic plight all pointed to the likelihood of a long period of coexistence with capitalist states.

The problem of survival within capitalist encirclement thus became the chief concern of the Communists. Although Soviet Russia's position had improved, it was by no means secure; all around were enemies who might attack as soon as they had recovered sufficiently from the war. The situation might be summed up in this fashion:

1. The Soviet republic is weak. To overcome famine and internal confusion and to build up its defenses, it needs both an extension of the breathing space granted by the Brest-Litovsk treaty and economic aid from its capitalist enemies. Therefore the Soviet government must advocate international peace and try to establish relations with the capitalist states.

2. In order to get the best terms and to minimize the danger of capitalist attack, Soviet diplomats must make use of the capitalists' greed for profits and at the same time do everything possible to keep alive the rivalries between capitalist groups and states.

3. Since security for Soviet Russia and permanent peace can be won only by the defeat of capitalism, the Soviet government has the duty, both as the leader of the world revolution and in the interest of its own security, to inspire and support revolutionary movements everywhere. (It was particularly important, in Lenin's view, to encourage revolution in colonial and semicolonial countries, because the great imperialist powers were dependent on the exploitation of these regions for the survival of their system.)

In short, the Communists hoped for a long period of peaceful coexistence during which they could co-operate or struggle with their enemies as the situation dictated. The People's Commissariat of Foreign Affairs had the job of developing co-operation with and encouraging antagonisms between the capi-

[6] The Spartakusbund, a revolutionary Left-wing group, was founded in Germany during World War I by radical opposition within the German Social Democratic Party. Leaders of the group were Rosa Luxemburg, Karl Liebknecht, Klara Zetkin, and Franz Mehring. This group supported the Zimmerwald movement, which was inaugurated at a conference held September 5–8, 1915, in the little village of Zimmerwald near Berne (see Olga Hess Gankin and H. H. Fisher, *The Bolsheviks and the World War: The Origin of the Third International,* pp. 309 ff.). The group played an active and explosive role in the German revolutionary movement, and at a conference held on December 29, 1918, voted to form a German communist party.

talist countries. The Communist International (Comintern) had the duty of
leading the world revolutionary struggle.

Lenin never forgot that Soviet success during the civil war and intervention
had been due in large measure to irreconcilable differences among the anti-
Bolshevik forces. He believed that the Soviet government would have to take full
advantage of the antagonisms among its enemies. These antagonisms, the Communists believed, were centered around a race for world hegemony between
the United States and Great Britain; unless a proletarian revolution intervened,
war between these two powers for control of the Pacific was inevitable. The
Soviet government also hoped to exploit conflicts of interest between Britain
and France, between the United States and Japan, between the Entente and
Germany, and between the imperialist powers and their colonies. Even the
policy of giving concessions to foreigners in order to attract capital investment
was to be used to cultivate antagonisms. Thus Lenin defined the policy of concessions, introduced by the decree of the Council of People's Commissars on
November 23, 1920, as being

also the policy of the continuation of the war . . . Our task is to maintain the existence of our isolated socialist republic . . . which is so much weaker than the capitalist enemies who surround it; to remove the opportunity for the enemies to create
an alliance among themselves for a struggle against us; to keep on interfering with
their policies; to prevent them from winning.[7]

In this same speech, Lenin declared that it was essential to re-establish trade
relations, but added: "We do not for a moment believe in lasting trade relations
with the imperialist powers; what we shall obtain will be simply a breathing
space [peredyshka]."[8]

The breathing space, like the New Economic Policy, was a kind of strategic
retreat. The communist leaders renounced neither the idea of spreading the
world revolution nor the idea of socializing the means of production and distribution in Russia. They simply fell back, in the face of unexpected resistance
to revolution abroad, from the revolutionary diplomacy of the first two years
to the conventional diplomacy of the balance-of-power system. As the N.E.P.
became gradually transformed into the idea of "socialism in one country," so
in the course of time the doctrine of the breathing space was merged into the
doctrine of peaceful coexistence and competition between different social and
political systems.

Reorientation of Allied Policy: From *Cordon Sanitaire* to Fighting Anarchy with Abundance

Meanwhile the Western powers were revising their ideas of how the Russian situation could best be dealt with. By November 1919, it was apparent
to all except the most embittered anti-Bolsheviks that in spite of the devastation
and exhaustion of the country, the Soviet government was not likely to be overthrown by any of the White forces or to collapse from internal weakness or
mismanagement. At the same time the Entente powers were experiencing the

[7] Lenin, *Sochineniia,* XXVI, 23; see Document 3.
[8] *Ibid.,* p. 12.

economic and moral after-effects of a long and exhausting war. War-weary peoples began to question more and more the wisdom of pursuing an undeclared war against Russia—a war that was costly, indecisive, and interminable. The "Hands off Russia" movement in Britain expressed the mood of an increasing number of people. Hunger, discontent, and confusion harassed most of Europe. Britain and France were having trouble with their colonies, and a darkening economic horizon strengthened the arguments of those who claimed that there were other and better methods of curing Bolshevism than by force.

Prime Minister David Lloyd George, with his characteristic agility, proposed a new treatment in a speech in the House of Commons on February 10, 1920. He called it fighting anarchy with abundance. He put it this way: Russia is necessary for the recovery of Europe. Russia cannot be restored to sanity by force, as events have proved. Commerce has sobering as well as beneficial effects. The way to help Russia and Europe and Britain is by trade—that is, to fight anarchy, wherever it appears, with abundance.[9]

A little earlier the Allied Supreme Council had taken steps to clear the way for such a program. On January 16, 1920, the Council lifted the blockade of Russia, without any recognition of the Soviet government. On February 24, 1920, the Council suggested to the Russian border states that they end hostilities and begin trade with Russia. The Council did not put it so bluntly, of course; it simply said it could not take the responsibility for advising that war be continued and added that trade between Russia and Europe would be good for everybody.[10]

Thus encouraged, the Baltic states entered into negotiations with the Soviet government, and during 1920 peace treaties were signed and diplomatic and trade agreements worked out. Actually the Estonian government had not waited for the Allied Supreme Council's action. As early as August 13, 1919, it had accepted a Soviet invitation for peace negotiations, which had been initiated within a month. Discussions were soon interrupted, however, by the advance on Petrograd from Estonia by the anti-Bolshevik forces of General Yudenich. With the defeat of Yudenich in October, the discussions were resumed, and delegations representing the two countries met at Tartu (in German, Dorpat; in Russian, Iuriev), December 5, 1919. After some two months of negotiations the Treaty of Tartu was signed on February 2, 1920.

The Soviet government was willing to fight anarchy with abundance, too, but it also had other aims in these negotiations with the Russian succession states in the West. One aim was to reopen, at least part way, the window on the Baltic that Peter the Great had forced open two hundred years before. Another aim was to prevent, as far as possible, the use of the Baltic states as staging areas for attacks against Soviet Russia such as that led by Yudenich. To realize these aims the Communists were willing to recognize the anticommunist governments of countries in which they had recently helped to install communist governments. This, as elsewhere, was a strategic retreat.

Chicherin, the Commissar of Foreign Affairs, explained that the Estonian treaty was a dress rehearsal for an understanding with the Entente, a first at-

[9] *Debates 1920* (Great Britain, House of Commons, Fifth Series, Vol. 125), pp. 40–46.
[10] *Papers Relating to the Foreign Relations of the United States, 1919. The Paris Peace Conference*, IX, 886–87. See also *Debates 1920* (Great Britain, House of Commons, Fifth Series, Vol. 125), pp. 1501–2.

tempt to break through the blockade, and the first "experiment in peaceful coexistence between the Soviet republic and bourgeois states."[11]

The Treaty with Estonia

The treaty with Estonia, the first of the Baltic treaties, declared the war between the two countries at an end, delimited boundaries, introduced the principle of the neutralization of the Gulf of Finland, and provided for the right of citizens to choose the country to which they owed allegiance and for their exchange, as well as for the repatriation of war prisoners. The treaty set forth the principle of a broad amnesty for all offenses committed during the war, declared mutual annulment of claims for war damages, and provided for the establishment of diplomatic and commercial relations.

In line with the desire of the Soviet government to secure its borders, the treaty obligated the contracting parties

to refuse to countries which are *de facto* in a state of war with either of the Contracting Parties, and to organizations or groups whose object is armed warfare against either of the Contracting Parties, the passage through their ports and their territory of anything which might be used in attacking the other Contracting Party . . . [and] to forbid the formation and the presence on their territory, of any organizations or groups whatsoever claiming to govern all or part of the territory of the other Contracting Party, and the presence of representatives or officials of organizations or groups whose object is to overthrow the Government of the other Party of the Treaty.[12]

The disarmament of alien military forces was also required, a provision clearly directed toward the men under the command of General Yudenich, for by the time the treaty was signed Yudenich and his troops had retreated into Estonia. These provisions are particularly interesting in the light of the Communist policy in later years of supporting guerrillas and rebels in civil wars "of liberation."

As to Estonian independence, the treaty stated:

On the basis of the right of all peoples freely to decide their own destinies, and even to separate themselves completely from the state of which they form part, a right proclaimed by the Federal [Federated] Socialist Republic of Soviet Russia, Russia unreservedly recognizes the independence and autonomy of the State of Estonia, and renounces voluntarily and forever all rights of sovereignty formerly held by Russia over the Estonian people and territory by virtue of the former legal situation, and by virtue of international treaties, which, in respect of such rights, shall henceforth lose their force. No obligation towards Russia devolves upon the Estonian people and territory from the fact that Estonia was formerly part of Russia.[13]

The economic provisions of the treaty with Estonia included a mutual waiver of claims arising from Estonia's previous inclusion within the Russian Empire; a financial settlement with Russia granting Estonia fifteen million gold rubles; a specific statement that Estonia "shall bear no responsibility for any debts or other obligations of Russia"; and concessions from Russia to Estonia for the construction and working of a railway line between Moscow and some point on

---

[11] *Izvestiia,* No. 25, February 5, 1920, p. 1.
[12] L. Shapiro (comp. and ed.), *Soviet Treaty Series,* I, 35 (cited hereafter as Shapiro).
[13] Shapiro, I, 34.

the Russo-Estonian frontier, and (because of Estonia's shortage of forest land) for exploiting one million desiatinas of Russian forest land.[14]

The Treaty with Lithuania

The next of the Baltic states to enter into negotiations with the Soviets was Lithuania. Late in February, 1920, the Lithuanian government agreed to negotiations; a conference met in Moscow May 9, the outcome of which was the signing, on July 12, of the Treaty of Moscow. Since the two countries had not been at war, there was no necessity in this case for a declaration of peace. But the Treaty of Moscow, like the Treaty of Tartu, included clauses prohibiting, on the territory of either party, activity by or recruitment of forces hostile to the other party, and recognition by Russia of the independence of Lithuania. The treaty further provided for the right of choice of citizenship and exchange of citizens, the return of refugees, a general amnesty, and the establishment of diplomatic and commercial relations. The Soviet government, moreover, agreed to a financial settlement with the Lithuanian government and agreed to grant Lithuania timber concessions. Lastly, by the terms of the treaty, the city of Vilna (in Lithuanian, Vilnius; in Polish, Wilno) and the greater part of the province of Vilna, temporarily occupied by Red troops, were ceded by Russia to Lithuania.

Vilna was the ancient capital of the independent Grand Duchy of Lithuania. After the union of Poland and Lithuania in 1569, it became a center of Polish culture with a mixed population of Lithuanians, Poles, Belorussians, and Jews. But in 1795, as a result of the third partition of Poland, the greater part of Lithuania, including Vilna, passed to Russia, under whose jurisdiction it remained until World War I. In 1915 German forces occupied the city; when forced to retreat in November 1918, these forces turned it over to the Lithuanians. It did not long remain in their hands, however, for in January 1919 it fell to the Bolsheviks; in April it was taken by the Poles; and finally in 1920, in the course of the Soviet-Polish war, it was recaptured by the Russians. Although the Soviet government shortly thereafter ceded Vilna to the Lithuanians, as mentioned above, a Polish advance in August 1920 forced the Red troops that had been occupying the city to abandon it, leaving the Lithuanians to defend it against the invading Poles. The Lithuanian government immediately appealed to the League of Nations for aid. The League effected an armistice, signed at Suwalki, October 7, 1920, by the terms of which the city was to remain under Lithuanian jurisdiction. This agreement was to have come into force October 10, but the day before, October 9, troops of General Zeligowski, a Polish officer, drove the Lithuanians from the city. Thereafter, the Poles refused to be moved by either Lithuanian protests or League efforts.

In their subsequent claims to Vilna the Poles said that Lithuania had violated its neutrality in the Soviet-Polish war of 1920 and signed a secret military agreement with the Soviet government. Although the note addressed to the Polish government by the Lithuanian government, August 28, 1920, reaffirmed Lithuanian neutrality, Polish suspicions persisted. These suspicions were substantiated by the fact that on July 14, 1920, two days after the signing of the Soviet-Lithuanian treaty, the Soviet and Lithuanian governments had ex-

[14] *Ibid.*, pp. 37, 38; full text, pp. 34–38. One desiatina is equivalent to 2.7 acres.

changed secret notes arranging for "the crossing of the Lithuanian frontier by Russian troops and the occupation by them of a part of [Lithuanian] territories."[15] The Poles further claimed that the Lithuanians actively participated in the military operations of the Red Army. This fact is also substantiated in the statements of Soviet military writers on the Soviet-Polish war.[16]

Finally, the Conference of Allied Ambassadors, acting under the authority of Article 87 of the Treaty of Versailles, took up the whole matter of Polish-Lithuanian frontiers, and on March 15, 1923, a new frontier was delimited by which Vilna was awarded to the Poles. The Lithuanian government, however, refused to accept this decision. Diplomatic relations between the two countries were broken off, not to be resumed until March 1938.

The Treaty with Latvia

On April 16, 1920, the Soviet government and the Latvian government began negotiations. The conference settled territorial questions without great difficulty, but economic problems took longer. A compromise was eventually reached, however, and on August 11 a treaty was signed in Riga.

Its provisions were in general similar to those of the treaties with Estonia and Lithuania. Peace was declared; Russian recognition of Latvian independence was proclaimed; the Soviet-Latvian frontier was delimited, with Latvia getting southern Livonia, Kurland, and Latgalia; and a clause was included concerning suppression of hostile organizations. Again there appeared provisions regarding the restoration of property, the renunciation of compensation for war damages, the repatriation of prisoners, the right of choice of citizenship, the establishment of diplomatic and commercial relations, etc. The treaty also provided for a financial settlement, for the return to Latvia of railway equipment that had been removed into the interior of Russia during the war, and for Soviet assistance in the restoration of Latvian telegraph lines and lighthouses. Like Estonia and Lithuania, Latvia was exempted from responsibility for Russian debts and

---

[15] The text of these notes appeared in *The Times* (London), August 5, 1920, p. 9, but no Russian text is available. However, the chronological table in the first edition of Lenin's *Sochineniia*, XVII, 473, reads as follows: "July 14, 1920. Agreement with Lithuania regarding the passage of the Red Army through its territory." The Lithuanian confirmation of this agreement is found in a statement by Professor Voldemaras, who represented Lithuania at the Ninth Session of the Council of the League of Nations: "By the declaration annexed to the Treaty Lithuania had authorized the Soviet troops to use her territory." *Procès verbal . . . Minutes of the Ninth Session of the Council of the League of Nations Held in Paris from 16th to 20th September, 1920*, p. 13.)

[16] M. Tuchaczewski [Tukhachevskii], "Pochód za Wisłe," in Józef Pilsudski, *Rok 1920*, p. 256 (French translation: J. Pilsudski, *L'Année 1920*, p. 226); also in N. E. Kakurin and V. A. Melikov, *Voina s belopoliakami, 1920 g.*, p. 204. For further details on the Vilna problem see J. Makowski, "La question lithuanienne," *Revue Générale de Droit International Public*, XXXVII, January–April, 1930 (Paris), 43–61, and S. Kutrzeba, "La question de Wilno," *ibid.*, XXXV, 1928, 626–44. For official interpretation of the problem see *The Lithuanian-Polish Dispute*, an official publication of the Lithuanian Information Bureau, 3 vols. (London, 1921–23), and *Documents diplomatiques concernant les relations polono-lithuaniennes*, an official publication of the Polish Ministry of Foreign Affairs, 2 vols. (Warsaw, 1920–21).

obligations, the treaty stating that "all claims of this nature lodged by creditors of Russia must be exclusively addressed to Russia."[17]

One new element appeared in the Latvian treaty, a plan for the promotion of general recovery from the war. In this regard the treaty stated:

In view of the fact that it is necessary to apportion in an equitable manner among the states of the world, the obligation to make good the damages caused by the World War of 1914–1917 to states that have been ruined, or to portions of states on whose territory military operations have taken place, the two Contracting Parties undertake to do all in their power to secure an agreement among all states in order to establish an international fund, which would be used to cover the sums intended for the reparation of damages due to the war. Independently of the creation of this international fund, the Contracting Parties consider it necessary that Russia and all new states constituting independent republics in what was formerly Russian territory, should render each other, as far as possible, mutual support to make good from their own resources the damage caused by the World War, and undertake to do all in their power to secure this agreement between the above-mentioned republics.[18]

The Treaty with Finland

Peace with Finland proved more difficult to negotiate. The Soviet government made overtures to the Finnish government in the fall of 1919, but the Finnish government did not respond until June 1920. In that month a conference was convened, but it took four months for the negotiators to complete the agreement. The head of the Soviet delegation, J. A. Berzin, in his last speech to the conference gave the following Soviet interpretation of the treaty:

By this Treaty not only does the abnormal condition come to an end which has prevailed during the last period of nearly three years, but also the whole of that past which rose out of the oppression of the Finnish people by Russian tsarism. Soviet Russia is proud of being the first Power to grant to small nations, which the ruling classes formerly oppressed, the possibility of self-determination, the possibility to organize their life freely.[19]

The treaty with Finland, like the Estonian treaty titled the Treaty of Tartu (Dorpat) after the city in which it was negotiated, was signed October 14, 1920. Although in many ways similar to the treaties with Estonia, Lithuania, and Latvia, it differed from them to the extent that military and defense questions received considerably greater attention.

Territorial problems were resolved as follows: Russia ceded to Finland Pechenga (Petsamo) and a strip of land leading to that Arctic port, but at the same time retained the right of passage to Norway; the Finns secured a good boundary on the Karelian Isthmus, but surrendered to Russia the communes of Repola and Porajärvi, which were to be attached to the autonomous territory of East Karelia. East Karelia was to be formed of the Karelian population inhabiting the R.S.F.S.R.'s Arkhangelsk and Olonetsk provinces; Russia was obligated to maintain its political, economic, and cultural autonomy.

Military stipulations included limitations on fortifications, military ports, naval bases, and military personnel in the border areas; the neutralization of

[17] Shapiro, I, 57–58.
[18] *Ibid.*, p. 55; full text, pp. 54–58.
[19] *The Treaty of Peace Between Finland and the Russian Soviet Republic*, p. 32.

various islands in the Gulf of Finland; the demilitarization of Lake Ladoga; and destruction by Finland of the fortifications of Ino and Puumala, which were within firing range of the Soviet base of Kronstadt.

Although the Finnish government had originally demanded compensation to Finnish citizens for their losses in the Russian revolution and the civil war in Finland, this demand was dropped, and the treaty provided for mutual renunciation of claims for damages. However, ships seized by the two governments during the course of hostilities were to be returned.

The treaty also stated that "Finland will take no share in the expenses incurred by Russia in the World War of 1914–1918."[20] Finland further agreed to give Russia full rights to use the direct telegraphic lines across Finland that connected Petrograd with Stockholm, while other clauses of the treaty paved the way for the resumption of diplomatic and commercial relations. A special commission of representatives of the two contracting parties was to meet immediately after the signing of the treaty[21] to draft a commercial treaty between the two countries.

On December 1, 1920, the Finnish Diet ratified the treaty, and the Soviet government soon followed, but Soviet-Finnish differences remained. A Soviet trade delegation was unable to go to Helsinki until May 1921; hence trade was not resumed until that month. One of the disputes that disturbed relations between the two countries, the flotage of lumber through Karelia and on Lake Ladoga, required special agreements that were not concluded until October 28, 1922.[22] But the most serious difficulties concerned the status of East Karelia, a region inhabited largely by Finnish-speaking people but lying on the Russian side of the historic boundary between Russia and Finland. After the October Revolution and during the civil war, East Karelians strongly resisted communist rule. The Soviet government maintained that the discontented Karelians received encouragement and help from Finland. On the eve of the Finnish-Soviet peace conference the Soviet government issued a decree (June 8, 1920) which apparently gave East Karelia a special status as the Karelian Labor Commune within the R.S.F.S.R.[23] This action was taken in deference to the national sentiment of the East Karelians and in anticipation of a demand from the Finnish government that the Soviet government apply its vaunted principle of national self-determination.

After heated discussions during the peace negotiations, it was agreed and the Treaty of Tartu provided, as stated above, that East Karelia would remain an autonomous region within the R.S.F.S.R. But this did not dispose of the East Karelian issue. In the summer of 1921, the Finnish government sent several notes to Moscow charging the Soviets with failure to carry out their treaty obligations regarding autonomy. The Soviet government countercharged that Finland was promoting a plan for a Greater Finland that would include

---

[20] Shapiro, I, 72.

[21] Full text, *ibid.*, pp. 69–75.

[22] These agreements were: *Convention Regarding the Floating of Timber in the Watercourses Between Finland and Russia,* Helsinki, October 22, 1922, and *Convention Regarding the Maintenance of River Channels and the Regulation of Fishing on Watercourses Forming Part of the Finnish-Russian Frontier,* Helsinki, October 28, 1922 (texts appear in Shapiro, I, 193–96 and 197–98 respectively).

[23] This decree appears in *Sobranie Uzakonenii i Rasporiazhenii . . . ,* No. 53, June 14, 1920, p. 234.

all Karelia, the Petrograd region and the city of Petrograd, the Kola Peninsula and the port of Murmansk, and all the territory of northeast Russia to the Urals.

Meanwhile, in East Karelia rebellion against the Soviet government broke out. The Finnish people gave moral and material support to the rebels, and volunteers from Finland joined in the fighting. The Russians alleged that the revolt had been instigated by Finland. This the Finnish government denied, declaring that it was an uprising of the Karelians themselves against Soviet rule, and proposing that the whole Karelian question be discussed by a mixed Soviet-Finnish commission. The Soviet government refused and Finland, supported by Estonia, appealed to the League of Nations for a settlement. The Soviet government responded by demanding, December 5, 1921, that the Finnish government cease interfering in East Karelian affairs. An exchange of notes followed,[24] but meanwhile Soviet troops had moved into the area and crushed the revolt (January-March, 1922).

The Aaland Islands in the Baltic Sea were another cause of dispute. These strategic islands, controlling the entrance to the Gulf of Finland and the Gulf of Bothnia, have been inhabited since the Middle Ages by Swedish-speaking people. Nonetheless, and although the largest island is nearer Sweden than Finland, the archipelago as a whole has always been considered part of Finland. When Sweden ceded Finland to Russia in 1809, the Aaland Islands were included, and from then on they were treated by Russia in all administrative matters as an integral part of Finland. In 1835 Russia erected a fortress on the Islands, but during the Crimean War the fortress was destroyed by the British fleet. The Treaty of Paris of 1856, after the Crimean War, forbade fortification of the Islands, but in 1915, after the outbreak of World War I, Russia again fortified them (with British and French consent). In 1917, when Finland declared herself independent of Russia, the Aaland Islanders used the occasion to claim the right of self-determination in favor of union with Sweden. The Soviet-Finnish Treaty of Tartu did not specifically mention the Islands, but the frontiers drawn in that agreement included them as part of Finland.

Since Sweden supported and Finland opposed the claims of the Islanders, the Council of the League of Nations took up the controversy. A committee of three international jurists appointed by the Council decided against Finland, but a second League committee decided for Finland. In June 1921, the League recognized Finnish sovereignty. The Finnish Diet in 1922 passed a law giving a large measure of self-government and a guarantee of cultural autonomy to the Islanders. The governments of Denmark, Estonia, Finland, France, Germany, Great Britain, Italy, Latvia, Poland, and Sweden were invited by the League of Nations to a special conference in October 1921, which agreed on the non-fortification of the Islands in time of peace and their neutrality in time of war. Of Finland's neighbors only Russia and Norway were not parties to this agreement. On November 13, 1921, the Soviet government warned each government

---

[24] Texts of the Soviet demand, the Finnish reply, and Chicherin's retort appear in Iu. V. Kliuchnikov and A. Sabanin, *Mezhdunarodnaia politika noveishego vremeni v dogovorakh, notakh i deklaratsiiakh . . . ,* III, 149–54 (cited hereafter as Kliuchnikov and Sabanin). English text of Chicherin's note of December 5, 1921, appears in Jane Degras (comp. and ed.), *Soviet Documents on Foreign Policy,* I, 280–82 (cited hereafter as Degras). For official Karelian and Russian documents concerning the Karelian question, see *Livre vert; Actes et documents concernant la question carélienne (1922),* published by the Finnish Ministry of Foreign Affairs.

that had participated in the special conference that Soviet Russia would not abide by a decision taken without her participation on a question of vital interest to her.[25]

Thus in the first two years after the negotiation of the Treaty of Tartu, relations between Soviet Russia and Finland were anything but cordial. On June 1, 1922, however, the two governments concluded a new agreement designed to assure the safety of their respective frontiers. Article VI of this agreement significantly stated that:

The two Contracting Parties bind themselves to take active measures forthwith to prohibit the organization within their territory of detachments or groups formed for the purpose of making attacks upon or of invading the territory of the other Party, and also to prevent their crossing into the said territory. Likewise, the two contracting countries undertake, in the event of armed risings occurring in the territory of the other state, to observe the precepts laid down by international law.[26]

In addition to these treaties with the Baltic republics and Finland, Soviet Russia also recognized the independence of yet another state within the borders of the former tsarist empire—the republic of Georgia. The treaty with Georgia, which remained in force for only one year, was signed May 7, 1920.[27] On February 25, 1921, the Menshevik government in Tiflis was overthrown by a communist-led revolt encouraged by the Soviet ambassador, S. M. Kirov, and aided by the Eleventh Red Army.

The Treaty with Poland

Relations with Poland during 1920 presented quite another picture, for in that year the state of war that had existed ever since German troops evacuated Poland in 1918 flared up with great intensity.

The separation of Poland from Russia had first been formally recognized by the Soviet government in the Treaty of Brest-Litovsk, March 3, 1918. During the Brest negotiations Trotsky had declared that Soviet Russia "recognized fully and without any reservations the independence of the Polish people and the Polish state."[28] Moreover, a few weeks after the collapse of the Central Powers, the Soviet government issued a decree abrogating all treaties and acts between the former Russian Empire and the Kingdom of Prussia and the Austro-Hungarian Empire relating to the partition of Poland, and declaring the partition to have been "contrary to the principle of self-determination of nations and contrary to the revolutionary interpretation of law by the Russian people, who have recognized the inalienable right of the Polish people to independence and unity."[29]

But although the Soviet government thus appeared from the first to have

[25] Text of this note is found in Kliuchnikov and Sabanin, III, 146–47. English text appears in Degras, I, 276–77.

[26] Text of this agreement appears in Shapiro, I, 171–73.

[27] For the text of this treaty, see *ibid.,* pp. 44–46.

[28] Trotsky, *Sochineniia,* XVII, Part I, p. 86.

[29] Article Three of the Decree of the Council of People's Commissars, August 29, 1918; appears in *Sobranie Uzakonenii i Rasporiazhenii,* No. 64, September 9, 1918, p. 776.

taken the independence of Poland for granted, it had its own ideas about the composition of the Polish government and the territorial boundaries of the Polish state. In point of fact, the Communists disapproved of the new Polish government, claiming that it had been set up during the German occupation against the will of the people. In practice, moreover, Soviet recognition of the right of peoples to self-determination applied only to the "toiling masses," and only the Communists could speak for the "toiling masses."

After the defeat of Germany and the beginning of the withdrawal of German forces from the territories of the former Russian Empire, the frontier line between Soviet Russia and Poland, whose independence the Soviet government had officially recognized, remained temporarily undetermined.[30] Moscow's efforts to set up Soviet regimes in the newly formed border states caused alarm in Poland. The Polish National Committee, through its representative in Paris, Roman Dmowski, asked for and secured permission from the Allied authorities for German troops to remain in the Ober-Ost as protection against the Communists until such time as Poland might be able to handle the situation without aid. But German troops in Poland and Lithuania took matters into their own hands and started home. As they left, Red Army detachments moved in. A prominent Polish-born Communist explained this action by saying that since the local population could not drive off the marauding Germans, "the Red Army came in to chase off the armies of occupation."[31]

The Poles were soon able to advance into these eastern borderlands, for in the early months of 1919 the Soviet government had its hands full with the anti-Bolshevik armies of Kolchak, Krasnov, Denikin, Yudenich, and Miller, which began to press in upon Soviet territory from the east, the south, the west, and the north. The Poles were not strong enough to push ahead very far, and Józef Pilsudski, the commander of the Polish army, was apparently not anxious to contribute to a victory by Kolchak, Denikin, or any other believer in the doctrine of "Russia, one and indivisible" who might be less ready than Lenin to recognize Poland's independence and unity.

In 1920, the desultory fighting between the two countries flared into a full-fledged war when Polish forces, together with those of the Ukrainian anti-Bolshevik leader S. V. Petliura, sought to move the Polish borders eastward and to transform the Communist-enforced Ukrainian union with Russia into a Polish-

---

[30] The question of Poland's eastern frontier was taken up by the Peace Conference in 1919. Two things had to be settled. First, there was the question of Eastern Galicia, once the territory of the Great Kingdom of Poland, and later that of Austria-Hungary, inhabited by the Ukrainians who desired independence from the Poles and leaned toward the Ukrainians of the former Russian Empire. Second, there was the question of the frontier line between Poland and Russia. Eastern Galicia was temporarily ignored, and the question of the Russian-Polish frontier was studied by a special committee of the Supreme Council. The outcome of this study was an official declaration by the Supreme Council on December 8, 1919, tracing the eastern frontier of Poland along a line that later became known as the Curzon line. This line passed much further to the west than the old Polish frontier of 1772. The Supreme Council's declaration did not pertain to Eastern Galicia and that problem remained in abeyance until March 16, 1923, when Polish sovereignty over the region was recognized. See Witold Sworakowski, "An Error Regarding Eastern Galicia in Curzon's Note to the Soviet Government of July 11, 1920," *Journal of Central European Affairs,* Vol. IV, No. 1, April 1944.

[31] Julian Marchlewski, *Voina i mir mezhdu burzhuaznoi Polshei i proletarskoi Rossiei,* p. 7.

enforced Ukrainian union with Poland.[32] Soviet historians have since claimed
that this was an unprovoked war started by the Poles for the purpose of establishing the old Great Poland stretching from the Baltic to the Black Sea. Polish
sources, however, claim that Russia was preparing to launch an attack on Poland
as soon as her forces could safely leave the various civil war fronts. The details
of the Soviet-Polish war—during the course of which Polish forces captured
Kiev, were then thrown back by a Soviet counterattack that penetrated to the
gates of Warsaw, and finally rallied to hurl back the Red forces and drive them
out of Poland—are beyond the scope of this volume.[33]

There is no doubt about the Communists' plans for Poland. At the height
of the Red Army's advance, Felix Dzierzynski and other Polish Communists
in the Soviet government set up a Provisional Revolutionary Committee of
Poland. This committee, created July 31, 1920, immediately issued a manifesto,
which declared that

a lasting peace is possible only between socialist Russia and a socialist Poland of
workers' soviets . . . Factories and mines must be torn from the capitalists and
speculators and turned over to the people, represented by workers' committees.
Lands and forests must be owned and managed by the people. Landowners must be
driven away; poor peasants' committees will take charge of the land. The land of
the toiling peasants will remain untouched. In towns the authority will pass to the
workers' deputies, and in the villages provisional soviets will be formed. When
throughout Poland the representatives of the bloody government that plunged the
country into war have been overthrown, the soviets of workers' deputies in the
towns and villages will establish a Soviet Socialist Republic of Poland.[34]

Equally significant were the pronouncements of the Communist International
at its Second Congress, July 19–August 7, 1920. One of the first moves of the
Congress was to address a proclamation to the Red soldiers at the front:

You are fighting not only for the interests of Soviet Russia, but for the interests of
all toiling mankind, for the Communist International . . . The toiling masses can-
not break the yoke of the rich and destroy wage slavery except by force of arms. . . .
The Red Army is now one of the chief forces of world history. You are not alone.
The toilers of the world are all on your side. The time is near when an International
Red Army will be organized.[35]

The Second Congress also addressed a proclamation to the workers of the
world, claiming that the British had armed the Poles for the attack on Russia,
that Britain and her allies had refused to hold back the Poles when the Russians
had been ready to negotiate, and that they were now threatening to attack Soviet
Russia unless the Soviets would sign an armistice. The Comintern claimed that

[32] Texts of the secret political and military agreements between the Polish government
and Petliura, April 21 and April 24 respectively, appear in N. Filippov, *Ukrainskaia kontr-
revoliutsiia na sluzhbe u Anglii, Frantsii i Polshi,* pp. 71–78.

[33] This phase of Soviet history will be dealt with in a forthcoming Hoover Library study,
now in preparation and tentatively titled "The Foundations of Soviet Foreign Policy."

[34] The following give the Soviet and Polish versions of the war of 1920 and the events
leading up to it: "Krasnaia Kniga," *Sbornik diplomaticheskikh dokumentov o russko-polskikh otnosheniiakh, 1918–1920 gg.;* P. V. Suslov, *Politicheskoe obespechenie sovetsko-
polskoi kampanii, 1920 goda;* Jósef Pilsudski, *Rok 1920* (also in French, *L'Année 1920*);
Adam Przybylski, *Wojna Polska, 1918–1921.*

[35] *Vtoroi Kongress Kominterna, iiul–avgust, 1920 g.,* pp. 31–32.

Britain and France were not really interested in the independence of Poland because in 1917 they had been willing to sacrifice Polish independence in return for tsarist support of British and French interests in Western Europe.[36]

In the first weeks of August, 1920, while Red forces were pressing upon Warsaw, a Polish delegation left Warsaw for Minsk, empowered to open peace negotiations with the Russians. Upon their arrival in Minsk, the negotiators were cut off from news of the front, and accordingly from news of the radical shift in fortunes which started August 16 with a Polish counterattack and the beginning of a general retreat by the Red Army.

In Minsk the Soviet delegation — which also represented the Soviet Ukraine—outlined drastic demands, among them the demobilization of the Polish army within a month; the reduction of Polish armed forces to 50,000 men, and the substitution for the Polish army of a militia made up of workers; the delivery of all ammunition exceeding the amount needed for these forces to Russian and Ukrainian authorities, who in turn would have charge of supplying the civil militia; the end of ammunition production within Poland and the demobilization of war industries; and recognition of Polish independence up to the frontier running approximately along the Curzon line.[37]

The Polish reply, delivered on August 23, stated among other things that the government of the R.S.F.S.R. was attempting to force upon Poland a peace that violated Poland's independence and sovereignty. Referring to the proposed frontier line between the two countries, the Polish delegates claimed that "the so-called Curzon line proposed by the Soviet government is almost identical with the line of the third partition of Poland as far as Russia is concerned. In that way, it appears that the Soviet government wishes to keep for Russia most of the territories that were conquered by tsarist Russia from Poland." As for the reduction of armaments, which according to the Russian proposal was to be applied to Poland alone and not to the other parties (the R.S.F.S.R. and the Ukraine), the delegates stated: "We reject it most categorically as damaging the dignity of the Polish people. We find to our great amazement that the government of the Soviet republic is consciously or unconsciously following the policy of Peter the Great and Catherine the Second."[38]

A change soon became apparent in the attitude of the Soviet delegates, as news arrived of the Red Army's retreat. After the Warsaw defeat, the Soviet government appeared very anxious to speed up the negotiations. In September the conference was transferred from Minsk to Riga, where it resumed on September 21 with a statement by A. A. Ioffe, head of the Soviet delegation, that the Soviet government wished a just and democratic peace without victors and vanquished, a peace of understanding and not a peace of force. During its second session, September 24, the conference heard a declaration of the views of the All-Russian Central Executive Committee, signed by Kalinin, its chairman, and Chicherin, People's Commissar of Foreign Affairs.[39]

The attempt to dictate the size and composition of Polish armed forces was dropped, and Poland was offered a far more favorable frontier. On October 5,

[36] *Ibid.*, pp. 37–41.

[37] *Izvestiia,* No. 184, August 21, 1920, p. 1; also Jan Dąbski, *Pokój Ryski,* pp. 48–51. See Document 9.

[38] *Izvestiia,* No. 190, August 28, 1920, p. 2; and Dąbski, *Pokój Ryski,* p. 62.

[39] *Izvestiia,* No. 213, September 25, 1920, p. 1; see Document 10.

to the surprise of Western Europe, an agreement concerning an armistice was announced. On October 12 a *Preliminary Treaty of Peace with Armistice Conditions*[40] was signed, and within two weeks both governments ratified the agreement. Military operations were suspended on October 18, and a month later, November 18, the conference set to work to draw up a permanent peace settlement. After prolonged argument, particularly over Polish financial claims, terms were agreed upon, and on March 18, 1921, the Treaty of Riga between Poland and Russia was signed. Communist leaders immediately hailed the event as marking the end of open armed intervention against the Soviet republic by the agents of world imperialism.[41]

The treaty with Poland declared the war at an end, included a mutual guarantee concerning political sovereignty, and provided that each signatory would refrain from interference in the internal affairs of the other and would suppress on its territory the organization of armed groups hostile to the other party. Poland obtained a frontier considerably to the east of the Curzon line, running instead along the line of the German front at the outbreak of the Bolshevik revolution. Each party agreed to protect the rights of the national minorities of the other within its territory, including the right to free intellectual development, the use of their own language, and the practice of the religion of their choice. Diplomatic and trade relations were arranged, provisions were made for the transit of goods, a mutual amnesty was declared, and a financial settlement was detailed.[42]

Upon the conclusion of the treaty both delegations hailed the terms of the settlement as introducing a new era of understanding between the Polish and the Russian states, based on independence, self-determination, and noninterference in each other's domestic affairs. Dąbski, the head of the Polish delegation, said that Poland desired to be a bridge and not a barrier in the development of economic relations between East and West, and that the mutual economic interests of the parties concerned would be the surest foundation of peace.

Ioffe, speaking for the Soviet delegation, said: "We have signed a peace treaty that gives satisfaction to the vital, legitimate, and essential interests of the Polish nation." Referring to Russia's recent peace treaties, including the one just signed, Ioffe observed:

None of the peace treaties concluded by Russia and the Ukraine permits preparations for a new war, because none of these treaties leaves any problems unsolved, nor are any solved simply on the basis of a relationship of forces [of the contracting parties], as was formerly done at the expense of some other nations concluding such treaties. Nations which receive all that is essential to them will themselves take care to see that such a peace is permanent.

By the conclusion of the peace treaty with Poland a series of arrangements has been set for peaceful relations between all the states that belonged to the former Russian Empire, and the tsarist regime of violence has been ended; the nations that have separated without hate or ill-feeling, and are animated by sincere friendship, can and should now develop on the basis of good neighborly relations those bonds of economic rapprochement and community which exist among them as the result of belonging for some centuries to the same state.

[40] Text in Shapiro, I, 67–69.

[41] A. A. Ioffe, *Mirnoe nastuplenie*, pp. 3–4; see Document 14.

[42] For text of the treaty and its five annexes see Shapiro, I, 105–16.

. . . The establishing of close economic relations with a free Poland, with an independent policy of her own, is the aim the governments of Russia, the Ukraine, and Belorussia have in view.[43]

The aims of the Soviet government with respect to Poland underwent a considerable change in the course of time, and so did the communist estimate of this treaty that the Soviet delegate praised so highly. After Russia had taken part, with Nazi Germany, in a fourth partition of Poland, a Soviet historian wrote in 1939:

By the Versailles treaty, the Entente imperialists artificially created a motley Poland made up of many nationalities. So that this state could be used as a battering-ram against Germany, and a starting point in the attack on the U.S.S.R., Western Ukraine and Western Belorussia were forcibly joined to Poland . . . The new Polish state included no fewer than eight million Ukrainians and three million Belorussians. The years that followed were years of the most cruel exploitation of these peoples. . . . The Soviet Union has now brought release to the population of Western Ukraine and Western Belorussia . . .[44]

On October 31, 1939, V. M. Molotov had this to say about the new Soviet policy toward Poland: "There can be no question, of course, of the re-establishment of old Poland. Therefore it appears senseless to maintain in the present war the slogan of the re-establishment of old Poland . . ."[45]

Beginning Negotiations with the West

While the Soviet-Polish hostilities were still in progress, Soviet Russia had received certain overtures from Western Europe. The first of these was a proposal that the League of Nations send a commission of inquiry to Russia to gather information about actual conditions there. This proposal the Soviet government declined, on the grounds that Poland, a member of the League, was at war with Russia, and that other members of the League were supporting the Poles.[46] But when British labor leaders asked that they be permitted to send a delegation to Russia, the Soviet government quickly agreed, seeing in the proposed visit an excellent opportunity to "gain the friendship of hundreds of thousands of workers."[47] A delegation of twelve representatives of the British Trades Union Congress and the British Labour Party accordingly visited Russia in May 1920.[48]

In order to take advantage of the new trend in the policies of the Allies, Lenin sent Maxim Litvinov, the Assistant People's Commissar of Foreign Affairs, to Copenhagen to open negotiations on a number of matters that had to be cleared up if normal relations were to be established. Litvinov had lived many

[43] Dąbski, *Pokój Ryski*, pp. 190–92; English text of this speech appears in Degras, I, 242–44.

[44] P. Rubinshtein, "Zapadnaia Ukraina i Zapadnaia Belorussiia," *Istoricheskii Zhurnal*, No. 10, 1939, p. 15.

[45] *Istoricheskii Zhurnal*, No. 11, 1939, p. 3.

[46] Text of the Soviet government's reply appears in Kliuchnikov and Sabanin, III, 23–24. For English text see Degras, I, 186–87.

[47] *Izvestiia*, No. 106, May 18, 1920, p. 1.

[48] An account of this visit was published in 1920 by the British Labour Party under the title *British Labour Delegation to Russia, 1920. Report.*

years in England and his wife was English. He and L. B. Krasin, who also had many Western connections, were admirably suited to personify the spirit of peaceful coexistence. Their appearance on the diplomatic scene was calculated to show the West that not all Bolsheviks were such wild men as Lenin and Trotsky were believed to be; that Bolshevism had its peaceful side, represented by men with civilized manners who could speak and understand the language of commerce and diplomacy.

Litvinov's first negotiations concerned the exchange of civil and military prisoners. On February 12, 1920, Litvinov and James O'Grady, a British Labour Party M.P., signed an agreement according to which the British would supply ships for the repatriation of British, Allied, and neutral prisoners in Russia.[49] Litvinov signed similar agreements with Austria, Belgium, France, Hungary, and Italy.[50]

The French agreement (April 20, 1920) had a political clause binding France not to intervene or to co-operate in aggressive measures against the Soviet republic. In late August, the Soviet government protested that France had violated this agreement (presumably by rendering material and moral support to the anti-Soviet armed forces in southern Russia) and thereby rendered it invalid. Chicherin's note to the French government was firm: "Owing to the fact that this promise has not been kept, and that the whole policy of France with regard to Russia has been a direct violation of the obligations accepted at Copenhagen, the treaty which was based on this condition becomes invalid, as our representative Litvinov stated at the proper time to the French representative in Copenhagen."[51]

British Trade Negotiations

The greatest single triumph of the new Soviet diplomatic policy in the period 1920–21 was the successful negotiation of a trade agreement with Great Britain, signed March 16, 1921. Although Soviet leaders had attempted to gain full *de jure* recognition of the Soviet republic, the *de facto* recognition implicit in the agreement represented a major victory. Moreover, it paved the way for the establishment of economic relations with other Western Europe states. Soviet leaders looked upon the agreement as an armistice between Russia and Britain in preparation for the conclusion of a definite peace, a view not entirely without foundation.

The shattered Soviet economy needed finished goods of all sorts; British business needed raw materials and markets. These needs overcame the barriers of fear and enmity, although it was only after more than a year of spasmodic negotiation that the trade agreement was finally signed. Immediately after the January 16, 1920, decision of the Allied Supreme Council to lift the blockade of Russia and to negotiate with Russian co-operative organizations, the Russian Tsentrosoiuz[52] appointed a delegation headed by Krasin, the Soviet Commissar of Communications and Foreign Trade, and Litvinov, the Assistant People's Commissar of Foreign Affairs, to confer with Allied representatives. The Com-

---

[49] Text in Shapiro, I, 38–39.
[50] Text of these agreements in *ibid.*, pp. 49–50, 42, 41–42, 47, 43, respectively.
[51] *Soviet Russia,* No. 17, October 23, 1920, p. 413.
[52] An abbreviation of *Vserossiiskii Tsentralnyi Soiuz Potrebitelskoi Kooperatsii,* the All-Russian Central Union of Consumers' Cooperatives.

munists encouraged and the West accepted the fiction that despite the Soviet monopoly of foreign trade, the Soviet economic branches of the government were less official than the political. The delegation met Allied representatives in Copenhagen, where the French proved to be interested primarily in what the Soviet government would do about recognizing tsarist debts. The British agreed to open trade talks, but asked that the negotiations be transferred to London. Although the Soviet delegation was perfectly willing to go to London, the British government at first refused to grant a visa to Litvinov and the Russian delegation refused to proceed without him.

Meanwhile, political questions were also coming to the fore. On February 21, 1920, Lord Curzon forwarded to the Soviet government a request on behalf of General Miller, commander of the defeated anti-Bolshevik forces in Arkhangelsk, that no mass reprisals be undertaken by the triumphant Red troops.[53] On April 14, Curzon proposed that the fighting cease in the Crimea between Red forces and Whites under General Wrangel, upon condition of a guarantee of amnesty for Wrangel. Curzon added that the opening of trade negotiations with the Russian co-operative organizations would hinge on the Soviet reply.

In his reply Chicherin proposed that in return for amnesty for Wrangel, the members of the Hungarian soviet government (April–August, 1919), who had escaped to Austria, be allowed to go to Russia.[54] In his note of April 25, Chicherin offered to guarantee to Wrangel, as he had guaranteed to Miller, life and safe departure from Russia if he capitulated. Lord Curzon replied that the point in question was not capitulation by Wrangel but an armistice, and offered to act as mediator in the negotiations between the two parties.[55] Further notes followed, after which the negotiations bogged down.

Toward the end of May the Soviet trade delegation, headed by Krasin, finally arrived in London, and on May 31 it held its first meeting with the British. Krasin outlined the following Soviet proposals: completion of the lifting of the blockade; mutual trade representation; inviolability of Soviet funds and property in Britain; elimination of mines in the Baltic; and an end to British support of Poland in the Soviet-Polish war. Lord Curzon insisted that as a preliminary to a trade agreement, the Soviets should guarantee to end anti-British propaganda in the Near East, Persia, Afghanistan, and India and also give a guarantee against Soviet attack upon the Baltic states and upon Wrangel from the Black Sea. Shortly thereafter Lloyd George made a further condition that the Soviet government recognize the tsarist government's debts.

Krasin replied on June 9 that the Soviet government was willing to revise its foreign policy and cease all propaganda and other activity hostile to Britain, and also to re-examine British financial claims and the question of Russian liability for property expropriated and debts repudiated, but only on the basis of reciprocity and on condition that a definite formal peace be established between the two governments. This meant counterclaims for damage caused by British

[53] Texts of Curzon's note and Chicherin's reply appear in *Izvestiia*, No. 41, February 24, 1920, p. 2.

[54] For Curzon's note and Chicherin's reply, see *Izvestiia*, No. 80, April 16, 1920, p. 1. English text of Chicherin's reply appears in Degras, I, 184–85.

[55] *Izvestiia*, No. 92, April 30, 1920, p. 1. Wrangel and his forces were finally defeated by the Reds in November 1920. The Hungarian Communists soon succeeded in reaching Soviet Russia.

intervention and for *de jure* recognition. Nothing, however, was said about the activities of the Communist International, which, since its founding in 1919, had been nominally carrying on the activities of which the British complained and for which the Soviet government consistently refused to take any responsibility.[56]

For several months trade negotiations were stalled in recriminations over the Soviet-Polish war, the revolutionary tone of the Second Congress of the Comintern (July 1920) and the Baku Congress of the Peoples of the East (September 1920),[57] and the failure of the agreement on repatriation of nationals.

On November 29, 1920, the British submitted a draft trade agreement; the Soviet government responded with a counterdraft, and after further negotiation and compromise an agreement was finally signed, as previously noted, March 16, 1921.[58] Krasin later surmised that a Soviet contract for 600 German-made locomotives was what induced the British to sign the agreement.[59]

One of the most difficult problems was how to word the preamble with regard to propaganda and other hostile activities. The British draft had originally included among the countries in which Russia was to agree to refrain from anti-British activity the Caucasus, Persia, and Asia Minor, as well as India and Afghanistan. The Soviet government objected especially to the inclusion of the Caucasus, and pointed out that this British draft differed from the preliminary British proposals of June 30. Eventually the British accepted the exclusion of the Caucasus, Persia, and Asia Minor, and moreover agreed to refrain from anti-Soviet activities in those former areas of the tsarist empire which were now independent.

The negotiators also had trouble over the question of the immunity from seizure or attachment for past Russian debts of such Russian funds and property as might be sent to Britain.

In its final form the trade agreement with Britain consisted of a preamble, fourteen articles, and an annex entitled *The Declaration of Recognition of Claims*. The preamble, which described the document as a preliminary agreement pending the conclusion of a formal general peace treaty, stipulated that neither country would engage in hostile action or propaganda, direct or indirect, against the other country or its institutions. The body of the agreement forbade either country to blockade the other; provided for removing obstacles to the resumption of trade; guaranteed the rights and immunities of official representatives of each country while in the territory of the other for the purpose of carrying on trade, including "immunity from arrest and search, provided that either

[56] For the official Soviet analysis of the British and Soviet notes of May 31 and June 9, see *Izvestiia*, No. 149, July 9, 1920, p. 1.

[57] The Baku Congress of the Peoples of the East met in Baku in September 1920; 1,891 persons attended it, representing various nationalities inhabiting the former Russian Empire as well as independent Near Eastern states. The chief speakers representing the Russian Communist Party were Karl Radek, G. E. Zinoviev, and M. L. Pavlovich (M. Veltman). Delegates to the congress were exhorted to declare a holy war against British and French capitalists and to join with Soviet Russia in a common struggle. (For more on this congress, see the companion volume, *Soviet Russia and the East, 1920–1927*.)

[58] For the British draft of November 29, 1920, and the Russian counterdraft of December 13, 1920, see *Izvestiia*, No. 295, December 30, 1920, pp. 1–2; and *Soviet Russia*, No. 4, January 22, 1921, pp. 99–102. For Chicherin's final amendments to the British draft, February 4, 1921, see *Izvestiia*, No. 27, February 8, 1921, pp. 1–2, and *Soviet Russia*, No. 11, March 12, 1921, pp. 268–70.

[59] L. B. Krasin, *Vneshtorg i vneshniia ekonomicheskaia politika sovetskogo pravitelstva*, p. 11; see Document 16.

Party may refuse to admit any individual as an official agent who is *persona non grata* to itself or may require the other Party to withdraw him should it find it necessary to do so on grounds of public interest or security";[60] guaranteed that the British government would not initiate steps to seize Soviet funds or commodities in Britain; and provided for the termination of the agreement by either party on six months' notice under certain agreed-upon conditions, among them violation of the preamble's strictures on propaganda and other hostile activities.

The annex dealt primarily, as indicated by the title, with the question of claims arising out of previous relations. In this regard it stated:

At the moment of signature of the preceding Trade Agreement both parties declare that all claims of either Party or of its nationals against the other Party in respect of property or rights or in respect of obligations incurred by the existing or former Governments of either country shall be equitably dealt with in the formal general peace treaty referred to in the Preamble.

In the meantime and without prejudice to the generality of the above stipulation the Russian Soviet Government declares that it recognizes in principle that it is liable to pay compensation to private persons who have supplied goods or services to Russia for which they have not been paid. The detailed mode of discharging this liability shall be regulated by the treaty referred to in the Preamble.

The British Government hereby makes a corresponding declaration.[61]

The signing of the Anglo-Soviet trade agreement was a formal but indirect acknowledgment that an undeclared war had existed between the Entente and Soviet Russia. The war-weary victors of World War I had not shown the will or the strength to make their intervention in the Russian civil war decisive. The Communists had not had the strength to maintain Red regimes in Finland, Poland, and the Baltic states, or in Hungary and Germany. Their revolutionary propaganda had failed to set off the sparks of revolt in the great citadels of capitalism. Western Europe wanted to trade with Russia; having failed to destroy the Communists by force, the Western leaders decided to cure them with kindness.

The Communists, victorious in the civil war but faced with spreading peasant revolt and the grim menace of famine, desperately needed goods that only the West could provide. On the home front, Lenin carried through the strategic retreat of the New Economic Policy without surrendering the "commanding heights" of nationalized industry, communications, and foreign trade, and without repudiating the objective of achieving socialism and ultimately communism. On the international front, the Communists made a comparable strategic retreat without surrendering the weapon of organized revolutionary propaganda represented in the Comintern, and without abandoning the objective of spreading the communist revolution until ultimately it embraced the whole world.

Negotiations with Italy

The Anglo-Soviet agreement ended the diplomatic ostracism of the Soviet government, and other states quickly followed the British in order to have their share in whatever advantages were to be had from this new trade.

The first country to do so was Italy. As early as March 19, 1919, the Italian premier, Sforza, had proposed to his parliament that Italy negotiate a trade agreement to secure coal concessions in southern Russia. The following Decem-

[60] Article V.
[61] Shapiro, I, 104; for full text of the trade agreement see *ibid.*, pp. 102–4.

ber Premier Nitti had urged the lifting of the Russian blockade. Shortly thereafter Italy had opened negotiations with Litvinov in Copenhagen. Meanwhile, at the nongovernmental level Russian and Italian co-operatives had reached an agreement that Russian wheat would be shipped to Italy during the summer of 1920. The Copenhagen negotiations bogged down, however, and agreement on sending a Soviet trade mission to Italy was not reached until October. A mission headed by V. V. Vorovsky arrived in Italy the same month. The following May (1921) Vorovsky and Italian representatives opened trade discussions, and on December 26, 1921, a *Preliminary Economic and Political Agreement* was signed in Rome between the two countries.[62]

Resumption of Relations with Germany and Other Countries

The resumption of relations with Germany proved less difficult, for the two outcasts from the community of nations were naturally drawn toward one another in their isolation. At the Eighth Congress of Soviets of the R.S.F.S.R. on December 21, 1920, Lenin had explained why Russia was important to Germany and Germany to Russia in communist diplomatic strategy.

[Industrially] Germany is the most advanced country, with the exception of America . . . Yet this country, tied hand and foot by the Versailles treaty, finds itself facing conditions that make its very existence impossible. Under such circumstances, Germany naturally is inclined toward an alliance with Russia. When the Russian troops were approaching Warsaw, the whole of Germany was seething. [The desire] of Germany, which is strangled, but which has a chance to start up some of her gigantic productive forces, for a union with Russia has produced something of a political mix-up in Germany. The German Black Hundreds[63] are inclined to be sympathetic with the Bolsheviks and Spartakists. This can be easily understood, for it grows out of economic conditions, and it also creates for us the basis of our entire economic position and of our foreign policy.

Our foreign policy, while we are alone and the capitalist world is strong, consists of making use of existing antagonisms (to win over the imperialist powers would be still better, of course, but we shall not be able to do that for quite a while). Our existence depends on two facts: (1) that there exist basic differences among the imperialist powers, and (2) that the victory of the Entente and the Versailles treaty have thrown back the great majority of the German people into a situation in which they cannot survive. Because of the Versailles peace, Germany cannot even dream of a time when she will no longer be plundered of the very means of her existence, when her population will not be condemned to starvation and death. Germany cannot dream of this, and therefore, naturally, her only means of saving herself is an alliance with Soviet Russia, toward whom she turns her gaze.[64]

Shortly after the German collapse in 1918, the German socialist government expelled the Soviet representative, Ioffe, and broke off relations with Moscow,

---

[62] Shapiro, I, 158-59. An identical treaty was signed on the same day between Italy and the Ukrainian S.S.R.

[63] The term "Black Hundred" was applied to the extreme conservative and monarchist groups at the time of the first Russian revolution in 1905. Originally the term was used in Muscovite Russia for special armed bands enlisted from the lowest elements of the population to suppress opposition to the regime in power.

[64] Lenin, *Sochineniia*, XXVI, 14-15; see Document 3.

charging the Bolsheviks with revolutionary propaganda and intervention. But on February 20, 1920, official diplomatic relations between the two governments were restored, and V. L. Kopp was recognized as the official Soviet representative in Germany. In the meantime, at the unofficial level, Karl Radek had gone to Germany incognito and had taken over the leadership of revolutionary activities there. In January 1919 he was locked up in Moabit prison, but during his imprisonment he managed to continue to give directives to the German Communist Party.[65]

In spite of continued conflict between the German Communists and the Social Democrats who controlled the government, relations between Germany and Soviet Russia gradually improved and measures were taken regarding the repatriation of prisoners of war of the two countries.[66] In the early months of 1921 German business and political circles declared their willingness to enter into a trade agreement with Russia, and on May 6, 1921, a *Provisional Agreement Regarding the Extension of the Sphere of Activity of Their Mutual Delegations Engaged in the Assistance of Prisoners of War*[67] was signed in Berlin. In the autumn trade representatives were exchanged. During the winter of 1921–22 Russo-German trade operations considerably increased, and certain German firms began negotiating for concessions in Russia.

Austria soon followed the German example, and on December 7, 1921, signed a *Provisional Agreement Regarding Future Relations* with both the R.S.F.S.R. and the Ukrainian S.S.R.[68]

Czechoslovakia was badly in need of foreign markets, but bitter memories of conflict between the Czechoslovak Legion and the Soviet forces during the Russian civil war led the Czech government to ignore the first Soviet offer of commercial relations between the two countries, made on February 25, 1920.[69] Ultimately, however, on June 5, 1922, a *Provisional Treaty of Friendship and Commerce* was signed between Czechoslovakia and the R.S.F.S.R., followed on June 6 by an identical treaty between Czechoslovakia and the Ukrainian S.S.R.[70]

Norway, Sweden, and Denmark also showed interest in resuming diplomatic relations with Russia. On September 1, 1921, the Norwegian and Russian governments signed a *Preliminary Agreement Regarding Political and Economic Relations,* similar in general to the Anglo-Soviet agreement, but in addition stating (Article III) that "The heads of the delegations of both countries will have quality and full power to act in the name of their Governments."[71]

Negotiations with Sweden and Denmark went more slowly. A trade agreement was eventually signed with Sweden on March 1, 1922, but was not ratified by the Swedish parliament. Negotiations with Denmark did not produce results

[65] See his own account in *Krasnaia Nov,* No. 10, 1926, pp. 155–72; for excerpts, see Document 59.

[66] There are evidences that the two countries signed a secret agreement in the summer of 1920, defining their political, economic, and military relations with each other. The authenticity of this document has not been definitely established. For full text see Shapiro, I, 381–82.

[67] *Ibid.,* pp. 119–20.

[68] *Ibid.,* pp. 147–48.

[69] For Chicherin's message to Dr. Beneš, the foreign minister of Czechoslovakia, see *Soviet Russia,* No. 25, June 19, 1920, p. 615.

[70] Shapiro, I, 173–74, 175.

[71] Full text, *ibid.,* p. 131.

until April 23, 1923, when a *Preliminary Agreement Regarding Economic Relations* was signed.[72]

During this same period Soviet Russia signed treaties of friendship with Persia, February 26, with Afghanistan, February 28, and with Turkey, March 16, 1921.[73]

During the period under consideration France declined to join the other European states in establishing trade relations. For one thing, the Soviet government claimed to have discovered a secret agreement of March 12, 1921, between France and Japan, providing for the transfer of General Wrangel's remaining forces from Constantinople to Vladivostok and recognizing the Japanese government's right to establish itself in Siberia and to place under Japanese control all White governments that might be created in the Far East.[74] The Soviet repudiation of foreign loans contracted by the tsarist government, in which the French had invested heavily, and France's support of Poland and Wrangel were even more formidable barriers to any improvement in Franco-Soviet relations.

Relations with the United States

The United States also took a firm stand against any kind of recognition of the Soviet government. Soviet leaders, however, were anxious to establish contact with the United States for several reasons. They hoped to derive both economic and diplomatic benefits from British and American competition for commercial advantages; and they looked upon the United States as less of a menace to Soviet Russia's security than Britain, France, or Japan. On January 2, 1919, Ludwig C. A. K. Martens (a Soviet citizen, then living in the United States), was appointed by the Soviet government to represent the People's Commissariat of Foreign Affairs in the United States. On March 18 he sent his credentials to the State Department, along with a memorandum proposing the opening of commercial relations. The memorandum stated, among other things:

Fully realizing that the economic prosperity of the world at large, including Soviet Russia, depends on uninterrupted interchange of products between various countries, the Soviet Government of Russia desires to establish commercial relations with other countries, and especially with the United States. . . . The Soviet Government of Russia is willing to open its doors to citizens of other countries for peaceful pursuit of opportunity, and it invites any scrutiny and investigation of its conditions which I feel sure will prove that peace and prosperity in Russia—and elsewhere, in as far as the prosperity of Russia affects other countries—may be attained by the cessation of the present policy of non-intercourse with Soviet Russia, and by the establishment of material and intellectual intercourse.

[72] For text of the agreement with Denmark, see *ibid.,* pp. 205–6.

[73] Texts of these treaties appear in Shapiro, I, 92–94, 96–97, 100–102, respectively. See also the companion volume, *Soviet Russia and the East, 1920–1927.*

[74] See N. L. Rubinshtein, *Sovetskaia Rossiia i kapitalisticheskie gosudarstva v gody perekhoda ot voiny k miru (1921–1922 gg.),* pp. 43–44; also Chicherin's protest to the foreign ministers of France, Great Britain, and Italy on June 1, 1921 (*Izvestiia,* No. 120, June 3, 1921, p. 1). The Russian charge was denied in an official communiqué of the American High Commissioner in Constantinople to the U.S. Secretary of State, June 9, 1921 (*Papers Relating to the Foreign Relations of the United States, 1921,* II, 726; cited hereafter as *Foreign Relations of the United States*).

Also included was a list of the amount and types of commodities the Soviet government desired to purchase in the American market.[75]

The State Department ignored both Martens' credentials and the memorandum. Martens himself was arrested later for subversive activity and ordered deported. He was eventually permitted, however, to leave the country of his own accord, which he did January 21, 1921.[76]

The United States government had stated its general attitude toward the situation in Russia on August 10, 1920, in Secretary of State Bainbridge Colby's reply to an Italian request for information concerning American policy toward Russia. The Colby note stated that the United States opposed both recognition of the Soviet government and dismemberment of the Russian state, and that accordingly the United States recognized neither the Baltic states nor the republics of Georgia and Azerbaijan, though on historical grounds it made exceptions of Poland, Finland, and Armenia. This attitude, so the note explained, was based on the belief that "the present rulers of Russia do not rule by the will or the consent of any considerable proportion of the Russian people." Moreover, said Colby, nonrecognition had

nothing to do with any particular political or social structure which the Russian people themselves may see fit to embrace. It rests upon a wholly different set of facts. These facts, which none dispute, have convinced the Government of the United States, against its will, that the existing regime in Russia is based upon the negation of every principle of honor and good faith, and every usage and convention, underlying the whole structure of international law; the negation, in short, of every principle upon which it is possible to base harmonious and trustful relations, whether of nations or of individuals.

Colby also emphasized a lack of faith in the intention of Russian leaders to carry out any undertakings or agreements into which they might enter.[77]

In its reply the Soviet government denied that it had violated its agreements and accused the American government of unwillingness to recognize any Russian government that was not subservient to financial groups in the United States. With an eye to sharpening Anglo-American rivalry, the Soviet government further charged that the American government was unwilling to recognize the new states along Russia's borders because British financial groups had already gained predominance there, and that rather than see such a situation continue, the United States would prefer that the independence of the states be abrogated.[78]

On March 20, 1921, shortly after the inauguration of President Harding, Litvinov, then in Estonia, forwarded an official note from the All-Russian Central Executive Committee to the Congress of the United States and the new President proposing the opening of trade relations between the two countries. Although he appealed primarily to the capitalistic acquisitiveness which the Communists assumed dominated American policy, Litvinov was careful to emphasize Soviet Russia's great need of internal reconstruction, and the fact that his government had "no intention of intervening in the internal affairs of America."

[75] *Foreign Relations of the United States, 1918[-1919], Russia*, IV, 140.

[76] For further details see *Russian Propaganda. Hearing Before a Sub-Committee of the Committee on Foreign Relations. United States Senate, 66th Congress, 1920.*

[77] *Foreign Relations of the United States, 1920*, III, 466; see Document 17a.

[78] Kliuchnikov and Sabanin, III, 56-60; see Document 17b.

Charles Evans Hughes, the new Secretary of State, replied on March 25, 1921, that no resumption of trade relations was possible as long as Russia did not recognize "the sanctity of private property, the sanctity of contract, and the rights of free labor."[79]

The Famine of 1921–23

Meanwhile, although the lifting of the blockade, the peace treaties with the Baltic states, the trade agreement with Britain, and similar agreements with other countries were increasing the international status of the Soviet republic, the domestic economic situation was deteriorating rapidly. Finally, in the summer and fall of 1921, disaster struck. To the chaos of war, revolution, and civil war was added the horror of famine. In March, 1921, as previously noted, communist leaders had introduced the New Economic Policy in a desperate attempt to bolster sagging industrial and agricultural production, but by then the food shortage throughout Russia was already acute. The following spring and summer in the great grain-producing areas of southern and eastern European Russia no rain fell. With drought came crop failure. Grain reserves had long since been requisitioned or consumed, and soon vast numbers of Russians were without food. On June 26, 1921, *Pravda* admitted that twenty-five million people in Russia were starving.

The situation was so desperate that Soviet leaders decided to ask for outside aid. On July 13, Maxim Gorky, the most widely known Russian writer then living, addressed an appeal to the peoples of the world.[80] On August 2, Lenin called upon the international proletariat for help, and on the same day Chicherin, People's Commissar of Foreign Affairs, sent a circular note to the governments of Europe and the United States, informing them of the extent of the catastrophe, and urging them not to interfere with the rendering of assistance. Chicherin's note stated in part:

Information received daily of numerous organizations in all countries willing to help famine stricken population in Russia meets with wishes of Russian people and government and with urgent need of famine stricken provinces for foreign aid. Addressing itself to all governments upon this subject the Russian government permits itself to express the hope that latter will present no obstacles to public bodies and individual citizens of their countries desirous to help famine stricken Russian citizens. Russian government will accept for this purpose any aid from whatever source it may come disregarding entirely existing political co-relations. Expressing on behalf of Russian people warmest gratitude to foreign organizations and individuals manifesting such ardent desire to help famine stricken Russian citizens the Russian government thinks itself entitled to hope that the governments of other countries will present no obstacles nor barriers to these desires of their citizens.[81]

Meanwhile, on July 23, Herbert Hoover, as chairman of the American Relief Administration, a nongovernmental organization, replied to Gorky's appeal by offering assistance to the starving. The only stipulations were that the Soviet government would immediately release Americans held prisoner in Russia and

[79] *Foreign Relations of the United States, 1921,* II, 763–64, 768.
[80] *American Relief Administration Bulletin,* Second Series, No. 16, September 1, 1921, p. 2; see Document 18.
[81] *Foreign Relations of the United States, 1921,* II, 811–12.

that it would provide adequate means for relief administration, including liberty for personnel to move about freely in Russia, permission to organize local distribution committees free from governmental interference, and operating conditions similar to those which had been established in the twenty-three other countries in which the A.R.A. had operated.[82] Two days later, Gorky responded that the Soviet government accepted the offer, and on July 31 the Soviet government made the acceptance official. In August, Walter Lyman Brown, European Director of the A.R.A., and Maxim Litvinov, representing Soviet Russia, worked out an agreement concerning the terms and details of the aid to be rendered.

During the course of the negotiations, Litvinov had argued that since, in his words, "food is a weapon," the Soviet government should have control of the local distributing committees that were to be set up, the right to decide which areas were to receive American relief, and the right to demand the withdrawal of any American personnel accused of political activity. In general, however, the agreement met Hoover's original stipulations.

The terms of the agreement between the A.R.A. and the Soviet government, signed August 20, provided that the A.R.A. would extend what assistance it could to the Russian people on the following conditions: Soviet authorities were to grant full diplomatic immunity to all personnel brought into Russia by the A.R.A.; such personnel were to be free to move about Russia on official business; the A.R.A. was to have complete freedom in selecting what Russian personnel it needed; A.R.A. supplies were to remain the property of the A.R.A. until distributed to the actual recipients; the A.R.A. was to be allowed to set up organizations necessary for carrying out its work without governmental interference; and the Soviet government was to provide the necessary kitchens, dispensaries, hospitals, fuel, transportation, etc., when available. The A.R.A. on its part agreed to provide food, clothing, and medical relief without regard to race, religion, or social or political status, and agreed that its personnel in Russia would confine themselves to the ministration of relief. Personnel who violated this agreement by engaging in political or commercial activities would be withdrawn upon the request of the central Soviet authorities. Lastly, the agreement stated:

The Soviet Authorities having previously agreed as the absolute *sine qua non* of any assistance on the part of the American people to release all Americans detained in Russia and to facilitate the departure from Russia of all Americans so desiring, the A.R.A. reserves to itself the right to suspend temporarily or terminate all of its relief work in Russia in case of failure on the part of the Soviet Authorities to fully comply with this primary condition or with any condition set forth in the above agreement. The Soviet Authorities equally reserve the right of cancelling this Agreement in case of non-fulfillment of any of the above clauses on the part of the A.R.A.[83]

As soon as the agreement was signed, the A.R.A. proceeded with the delivery of food and medical supplies. Despite broken-down and disorganized transportation, the A.R.A. was able at the height of its operations to feed eleven million people and provide medical and clothing supplies to other millions. In July 1923, the Council of People's Commissars paid tribute to this vast enterprise:

[82] *American Relief Administration Bulletin,* Second Series, No. 16, September 1, 1921, pp. 3–4; see Document 19.

[83] Text in H. H. Fisher, *The Famine in Soviet Russia, 1919–1923,* pp. 507–10.

Thanks to the enormous and entirely disinterested efforts of the A.R.A., millions of people of all ages were saved from death, and entire districts and even cities were saved from the horrible catastrophe which threatened them. . . . The people inhabiting the Union of Soviet Socialist Republics will never forget the help given them by the American people, through the A.R.A., seeing in it a pledge of the future friendship of the two nations.[84]

While the negotiations between Brown and Litvinov were in progress, other efforts were also being made outside Russia to alleviate the famine. On August 15, a joint committee representing the International Red Cross and the League of Red Cross Societies met in Geneva and set up an International Committee for Russian Relief. Dr. Fridtjof Nansen and Hoover were asked to serve as its High Commissioners. Hoover was obliged to decline because of his official duties, but Nansen accepted and soon left for Moscow, where, on August 27, he signed an agreement with the Soviets on behalf of his organization.

Although the Nansen Agreement provided that the earlier agreement with the A.R.A. should be used as a basis for the general techniques of supply distribution, it differed significantly from the Brown-Litvinov pact in two respects: (1) I.C.R.R. operations in Russia were to be directed by a committee of two, a representative of Nansen and the International Committee in Geneva, and a representative of the Soviet government; (2) Nansen, as High Commissioner, was to act as intermediary between Russia and the Western European nations in negotiating the credits by which the relief supplies were to be purchased. That is, foreign governments were expected to underwrite the cost of the operations, while the Soviet government would have a hand in controlling the distribution of the supplies.[85]

---

[84] A photograph of the original resolution is given in Fisher, *op. cit.,* opposite p. 398. That memories are sometimes short, however, was demonstrated by the following evaluation made several years later by a Soviet historian: "Thanks to the light hand of Hoover and his officials, first of all Brown, and then the Chief of the History Department of the A.R.A., Fisher, information has been circulated in literature that the A.R.A. allegedly played an almost decisive role in overcoming the famine in Soviet Russia. However, the facts tell a different story, indicating that such statements were only political propaganda unconfirmed by actuality. The A.R.A. brought to Russia in 1921 all in all 25,000 tons of foodstuffs, i.e., a very small amount of what was required." (Rubinshtein, *Sovetskaia Rossiia i kapitalisticheskie gosudarstva v gody perekhoda ot voiny k miru (1921–1922 gg.),* p. 140.) The accountant's final figures show that the A.R.A. actually brought to Russia, from the beginning of the relief operations in August 1921 to their close in 1923, a total of 741,572.7 metric tons of relief supplies, with a total value, including the contribution of facilities by other European governments, of $63,174,848.78. These supplies included 1,447.8 tons of clothing worth $1,700,795.00 and 8,281.9 tons of medical supplies worth $8,072,256.03. Of the total amount spent on the operation, the United States Congress appropriated $20,000,000, the Russian and Ukrainian soviet governments contributed $12,000,000, and other governments supplied $115,360. The rest came from gifts of American individuals and organizations. (Frank M. Surface and Raymond L. Bland, *American Food in the World War and Reconstruction Period,* pp. 246–48.) As the resolution of the Council of People's Commissars (Document 20) shows, the Soviet government expressed full satisfaction over the way the A.R.A. conducted its operations, including the expenditure of Soviet funds.

[85] As head of the International Committee for Russian Relief, Nansen was able to supply to Russia, from September 1921 to September 1922, over 90,700 tons of foodstuffs. The Committee was dissolved on September 19, 1922, having by that time appropriated over 42,000,000 Swiss francs. For particulars concerning the organization and work of the Committee, see Georges Vaucher, "Le Comité international de secours à la Russie et son haut commissariat," *Revue Internationale de la Croix Rouge,* No. 37, January 15, 1922, pp. 1–13;

When the Assembly of the League of Nations next met in Geneva in September 1921, Nansen attempted to persuade the League to take the lead in Russian relief and to raise an international governmental loan for this purpose. Commenting later on this effort, Nansen wrote:

There was superabundance of food, transport, and workmen in the world. The maize was used as fuel in the locomotives of Argentina, the ships lay idle in many countries, and thousands of men were unemployed. Some of the idle ships, with a small part of the unemployed men, could easily carry sufficient superfluous American corn to save the starving and dying millions.[86]

The League did not agree to Nansen's plea. Few delegates respected Russia's ability to make good on the bonds that were to be floated to back the credits; some even believed that to help the starving would be tantamount to supporting the communist government. Nansen sadly observed that "the hearts of politicians are often hard and inhuman."[87]

Lenin's appeal to the international proletariat also had some success. Workers' organizations throughout the world sent considerable amounts of food and money to Russia.[88] Among these was Mezhrabpom (Mezhdunarodnaia Rabochaia Pomoshch), the International Workers' Aid, founded in Berlin in September 1921 and one of the earliest nongovernmental organizations to be made use of by the Russian Communists in their foreign relations.

The International Workers' Aid, or I.W.A., continued to function under communist guidance long after the famine emergency had abated. A German communist member of the Reichstag, Willi Münzenberg, was appointed secretary of the organization, and at the Fourth Congress of the Comintern in 1922 reported on its activities. Officially it was a relief organization to render aid to needy workers and their families, but in 1926 Münzenberg revealed that it also served another purpose: "The I.W.A. is an indispensable organization; its national organizations are indissolubly associated with the revolutionary workers' movements of their respective countries." Although its beginnings in 1921 had been modest, said Münzenberg, by 1926 it had branches in most countries and a membership of more than fifteen million workers. He further stated that members of the organization had raised the sum of £1,250,000 within five years.[89]

The International Workers' Aid should not be confused with another Moscow-sponsored international organization for foreign aid which was similar in name but different in purpose. This was the International Organization to Aid the Revolutionary Fighters (Mezhdunarodnaia Organizatsiia Pomoshchi Bort-

---

and "Work Accomplished by the International Committee of the Russian Relief Fund Under the Superintendence of Dr. Nansen from September 1921 to September 1922," *Report on Economic Conditions in Russia with Special Reference to Famine of 1921–1922 and the State of Agriculture,* Annex IV, pp. 103–6. (This report was issued by the League of Nations Secretariat.)

[86] Fridtjof Nansen, *Russia and Peace,* p. 37.

[87] *Ibid.,* p. 39. See also Nansen's plea for the starving people of Russia at the Assembly of the League of Nations, September 9, 1921, in *Records of the Second Assembly. Plenary Meetings. Text of the Debates,* pp. 171–78.

[88] Lenin's letter to Sidney Hillman, president of the Amalgamated Union of Clothing Workers of America, appears in Lenin, *Sochineniia,* XXVII, 23–24.

[89] Willi Münzenberg, "Five Years of Workers International Relief," *International Press Correspondence,* No. 61, September 9, 1926, p. 1045.

sam Revoliutsii, or M.O.P.R.), initiated on September 22, 1922, by the Association of Old Bolsheviks for the purpose of helping political prisoners abroad and political exiles living in Russia. The Fourth Congress of the Comintern in November 1922 endorsed the idea, calling upon all communist parties "to assist with the establishment of an organization aimed at rendering material and moral aid to the prisoners of capital."[90]

The first World Conference of the M.O.P.R. met in Moscow in the summer of 1924, attended by representatives from Soviet Russia, Germany, Poland, Czechoslovakia, Bulgaria, Hungary, Rumania, Yugoslavia, Lithuania, Estonia, Italy, France, Spain, Turkey, Argentina, and Brazil. The conference called upon all its national sections to organize a united front with all proletarian political parties, trade unions, co-operative organizations, youth and women's organizations, etc. Meanwhile, the Fifth Congress of the Comintern, which met in June and July of 1924, had adopted a special resolution calling upon all communist parties to support the M.O.P.R., to promote the establishment of its sections and branches in their respective countries, and to urge their members to take an active part in these branches and sections and pay their dues. This resolution also called upon the party press to devote "due attention to agitation and propaganda for aid to revolutionary fighters."[91]

In the years that followed, the M.O.P.R. continued to expand, and by January 1929 it listed 7,831,712 members, individual and collective, in forty-eight countries. It published a considerable amount of literature and two periodicals: Put MOPR ("The Path of the M.O.P.R.") and Biulleten TS.K. MOPR ("Bulletin of the Central Committee of the M.O.P.R."). The M.O.P.R. worked to improve conditions in some 226 prisons in twenty-five European countries and made propaganda in the Sacco-Vanzetti case in the United States. It also campaigned extensively against fascism in Italy, the Balkans, Rumania, Poland, and China.[92]

The Allied Supreme Council also made a gesture in the direction of aiding the stricken by creating an International Commission for Russian Relief (not to be confused with Nansen's organization). Joseph Noulens, the former French ambassador to Russia, was appointed chairman, not a very happy selection, since he had been identified with anti-Bolshevik activities. Immediately it became apparent that political considerations were to outweigh charitable motives. It was decided that the situation should first be thoroughly investigated, that credits should be granted Russia only if the Soviet government recognized its responsibility for the discharge of existing debts and other obligations and liabilities, and that adequate security should be given for the future. It was further suggested that relief be conditional upon Allied control of the Russian transportation system, but this suggestion was not adopted. Finally a note was drafted indicating that aid would be forthcoming only if a commission of foreign experts were allowed to investigate actual conditions in Russia. Similar attitudes and resolutions reappeared at a later conference attended by representatives of twelve governments in Brussels in September and October.[93]

[90] Malaia Sovetskaia Entsiklopediia, V, 362–63.
[91] Piatyi Vsemirnyi Kongress Kommunisticheskogo Internatsionala, II, 78. (Hereafter cited as Piatyi Vsemirnyi Kongress K.I.)
[92] Malaia Sovetskaia Entsiklopediia, V, 363.
[93] Commission Internationale de Secours à la Russie. Procès verbaux . . . Séances tenues à Paris, les 30, 31 août et les 1, 15, et 16 septembre; à Bruxelles les 6, 7, et 8 octobre, 1921.

The Soviet government sent an angry reply, protesting the appointment of Noulens, branding the proposal for an investigation a "mockery of the dying millions," and writing off the whole scheme as a French plot to gain entry into Russia for espionage purposes.[94]

The Soviet reply also questioned the intentions of the commission, charging that at the same time that the commission was proposing an investigation, a member government, the French government, was supplying tremendous quantities of war material to Poland and Rumania and hence indirectly to the White bands operating along Russian borders.

Charges and Countercharges

Soviet leaders believed, in addition, that the French government intended to use the famine to cover a new attempt to overthrow the Soviet government, and that to this end the French planned to use the border states as staging areas for an attack. The Communists viewed both the creation of the Little Entente and the organization of cultural and economic conferences of the Baltic states as hostile moves. The chief regions of concern, however, were Poland and Rumania.[95] For one thing, anticommunist Russian and Ukrainian forces of Savinkov, Bulakh-Balakhovich,[96] and Petliura had retreated into these countries and were using them, particularly Poland, as bases for forays into adjacent Soviet territories. For another, on March 4, 1921, Rumania and Poland signed a military convention guaranteeing each other mutual assistance in the event of an attack on the eastern frontier of either.

Finally, on September 13, 1921, the People's Commissariat of Foreign Affairs claimed to have come into possession of reliable information that France was attempting to force Poland and Rumania to make maximum demands on the Soviet government, with a threat of military action if the demands were not complied with. According to this Soviet charge, the French government then intended to demand that all communist-held hostages and civil war prisoners in

[94] See full text of the Soviet reply in Kliuchnikov and Sabanin, III, 115–18.

[95] Tension between Soviet Russia and Rumania during this period derived primarily from disputes concerning jurisdiction over the region of Bessarabia, between the Pruth, the Dniester, and the Black Sea. Bessarabia had been incorporated within the Russian Empire in 1812, when it was ceded to Russia by the terms of the Treaty of Bucharest with the Ottoman Empire. In May 1917, during the period when other Russian borderlands were beginning to claim independence, a Bessarabian council (Sfatul Tärei) claimed autonomy for the region. On January 24, 1918, an "Independent Moldavian Republic" was proclaimed. Shortly thereafter Rumanian troops were invited into the region, with the approval of the Allied powers, to preserve order. The Soviet government opposed the move, and fighting resulted. On March 9, 1918, at Odessa, the R.S.F.S.R. and Rumania signed an *Agreement Regarding Military and Political Matters* by which Rumanian troops were to evacuate Bessarabia (text in Shapiro, I, 22). But the troops were not withdrawn; instead, on April 8, 1918, the Bessarabian National Council voted for political union with Rumania, a decision the Soviet government refused to recognize. On October 28, 1920, the principal Allied powers signed a treaty with Rumania recognizing Rumanian sovereignty in Bessarabia and stating that "the High Contracting Powers will invite Russia to adhere to the present Treaty as soon as a Russian Government recognised by them shall be in existence." (A. J. Toynbee, *A Survey of International Affairs, 1920–1923,* p. 503. For Soviet account see Kh. G. Rakovsky, *Roumania and Bessarabia,* p. 22 ff.)

[96] B. V. Savinkov, an old Russian revolutionist, was active in the anti-Bolshevik movements in Russia and Poland. Major Bulakh-Balakhovich, an adventurous figure at the northwestern front of civil war in 1919, continued his anti-Soviet guerrilla activities in 1920.

Russia be liberated and that all organizations in France engaged in communist propaganda be liquidated.[97]

On September 14 the Polish government did, in fact, send a note to the Soviet government insisting that the provisions of the Riga treaty be carried out, and on September 18 this note was followed by another in which the Polish government threatened to recall its representatives in Moscow if its demands were not carried out before October 1.[98]

Moscow replied that the Polish government had failed to carry out its obligation to end the activity of anti-Soviet organizations in its territory. If one side lived up to the agreements, said the Russians, so should the other.[99] On December 28, 1921, on Lenin's personal recommendation,[100] the Ninth Congress of Soviets of the R.S.F.S.R. declared that unless the border raids from Poland were terminated, the Soviet peoples would rise in a patriotic war.[101] Whereupon Savinkov and other anti-Communist Russian leaders were required by the Warsaw government to leave Poland, and thereafter relations between Russia and Poland improved slightly.

About this time Anglo-Soviet relations also deteriorated, as a result of British charges that the Soviet government was violating the trade agreement by continuing to conduct anti-British propaganda in Asia.[102]

Along with this hostility toward and suspicion of the border states and the Great Powers, Soviet diplomacy continued its pursuit of greater security for its frontiers and increased trade with the West. On October 28, 1921, the People's Commissariat of Foreign Affairs sent a note to the governments of Great Britain, France, Italy, Japan, and the United States, offering to make certain concessions with regard to tsarist debts in return for a definite peace and recognition for the Soviet government.[103]

On November 1, Lord Curzon replied: "His Majesty's Government feel that in making this announcement the Soviet Government have set their feet upon the only path by which they can hope to attain the goal they here profess to desire, namely, economic co-operation with other nations." But he pointed out that a number of points raised in the Soviet note would require further explanation, as for example, "whether recognition of other classes of obligations, e.g., loans to the Czarist Government since 1914, municipal and railway loans and claims by foreign owners of property in Russia confiscated or destroyed by the Soviet Government, also corresponds with the intention of the Soviet Government at the moment; and they invite that government explicitly to define their attitude in regard to all such other classes of claims."[104]

[97] *Sovetskaia Rossiia i Polsha*, pp. 49–50; see Document 23.

[98] The notes of September 14 and 18 appear in *ibid.*, pp. 50–51 and 60–62 respectively.

[99] *Ibid.*, pp. 62–64. English text appears in Degras, I, 254–57.

[100] *Leninskii Sbornik*, XXXV, 304; see Document 24.

[101] This declaration appeared in *Izvestiia*, No. 1, January 1, 1922, p. 1.

[102] For the text of the British protest to the Soviet government, see *A Selection of Papers Dealing with the Relations between His Majesty's Government and the Soviet Government, 1921–1927* (Cmd. 2895), pp. 4–12. (Cited hereafter as *A Selection of Papers, 1921–1927*.)

[103] *Izvestiia*, No. 243, October 29, 1921, p. 1; also Kliuchnikov and Sabanin, III, 140–42. See Document 25.

[104] *Correspondence with M. Krassin respecting Russia's Foreign Indebtedness* (Cmd. 1546), pp. 5, 6.

The Third Congress of the Comintern

The Soviet diplomatic pursuit of reconciliation with the West during the years 1920–21 in no way implied the abandonment of communist revolutionary goals. This was made abundantly clear at the Third Congress of the Communist International, which met in the summer of 1921. The theses of that Congress, drafted by Lenin, took note of the temporary stabilization of capitalism and the consequent slackening of the pace of the revolution. The Comintern, it was pointed out, had never guaranteed it would bring about the proletarian revolution at a given date; nonetheless the curve of capitalist development was proceeding, despite temporary rises, constantly downward, while the curve of the revolution was proceeding, despite certain ebbs, constantly upward. The Comintern foresaw the aggravation of social antagonisms and social struggles and the transition to open civil war in capitalist countries. Every communist party was ordered to take advantage of every lull in order to "deepen and widen the class conflicts, to combine them nationally and internationally by unity of goal and practical activity, and in this way, at the head of the proletariat, to shatter all resistance on the road to its dictatorship and the socialist revolution." The Cominern's most important task was to rally behind it the majority of the working class. To this end the communist parties were again called upon, as they had been at the two earlier congresses, to support each other in the struggle; to use as weapons of agitation such bourgeois institutions as freedom of the press and freedom of assembly; to support Soviet Russia unconditionally; to work for those ends which would help the Soviet government build a strong economy; and, primarily, to carry on constant revolutionary propaganda and agitation. Finally, the theses declared: "It is only by leading the working masses in the daily warfare against the onslaughts of capitalism that the communist party will become the vanguard of the working class, will acquire the capacity for systematic leadership of the proletariat, and will be fully prepared [for the struggle] for the complete elimination of the bourgeoisie. . . ."[105]

These admonitions and directives chiefly concerned communist activity in the West, but the Comintern did not overlook the significance of the revolutionary move in the East. In a speech to the Congress, Lenin declared that Eastern national-revolutionary movements "will perhaps play a much greater revolutionary role than we expect."[106]

Defensive Revolutionary Strategy

As 1921 drew to a close, communist leaders had put in cold storage their earlier dreams of immediate revolution in other countries, and were directing their diplomacy toward strengthening Russia's economy and protecting her frontiers. Their goal was to preserve the isolated Soviet republic within what they liked to speak of as the "capitalist encirclement," a phrase suggesting a state of siege in which major offensive operations were suspended but minor hostilities continued. So preserved and strengthened, the Communists' argument ran, Soviet Russia would be prepared to take full advantage of the coming capitalist

105 *Kommunisticheskii Internatsional v dokumentakh,* pp. 180, 208; see Document 28.
106 Lenin, *Sochineniia,* XXVI, 453; see Document 27. See also the companion volume, *Soviet Russia and the East, 1920–1927.*

crisis. Thus, if the Russian Communist leaders were working to make treaties and establish normal diplomatic relations in place of armed encounters, they were far from expecting these new agreements to lead to permanent peace between the Soviet republic and the non-Soviet world. On the contrary, as L. B. Kamenev put it, "our agreements represent only a new form of struggle, the struggle to establish communism in one isolated country."[107]

As for trade relations, the Communists believed that such benefits as the capitalists received would eventually do capitalism more harm than good. According to Kamenev:

The disintegration of the capitalist economy in Western Europe is so advanced that our raw materials, which will bring us into the world economy, cannot delay the revolutionary process there even for a day, not for an hour. Moreover, the development of the productive forces of the world economy does not contradict the proletarian revolution, but, on the contrary, only stimulates its development, because it intensifies [class] differences.[108]

By the end of 1921, communist leaders had worked out a strategy of foreign relations that seemed to serve Russia's need for a breathing space and for economic and technical aid from the capitalist powers, without sacrificing either the gains of the October Revolution or the communist aim of achieving permanent peace and social justice by world revolution.

The Soviet government professed a desire to live in peace and harmony with the other nations of the world, and negotiated with them for the resumption of normal diplomatic and trade relations. The Comintern at the same time did its utmost to foment revolution in the same countries, by furnishing likely revolutionary groups with leadership, an ideology, and moral and material support. The People's Commissariat of Foreign Affairs, upon which in the normal diplomatic course of things fell the brunt of foreign complaints about the Comintern's activities, stoutly upheld the fiction that the Comintern was an international body for whose actions the Soviet government had no responsibility.

When the situation seemed to require the Soviet government to abandon revolutionary diplomacy, confiding that function to the Comintern, and to take up the traditional balance-of-power diplomacy, the Communists adopted the form rather than the substance of twentieth-century diplomatic relations. The Communists wanted time and used diplomacy to gain it, but their diplomacy was not ultimately aimed at strengthening world capitalism by diminishing world tensions. Soviet diplomacy, as Kamenev said, was a means of struggle. While championing the cause of peace, the Communists scorned the new League of Nations as a means of lessening the danger of war.

The Great Powers were well aware of the objectives of Soviet diplomacy, which the Communists did not try to conceal. But gradually their governments, except those of the United States and France, came to the conclusion that it was safe and to their advantage to accept the formula that the Soviets offered.

[107] *Desiatyi sezd R.K.P. (B). Mart, 1921*, p. 458 (cited hereafter as *Desiatyi sezd R.K.P.*) ; see Document 30.
[108] *Desiatyi sezd R.K.P.*, p. 464.

DOCUMENTS

SOVIET RUSSIA'S INTERNATIONAL POSITION IN 1920

1

Stalin on the Three Years of the Proletarian Dictatorship

[Speech at a Session of the Baku Soviet, November 6, 1920][1]

. . .

There is no doubt that the international position of Soviet Russia has been the basic problem in the life of our country during the last three years. There was a time when Soviet Russia was not noticed, was ignored, was not recognized. This was the first period, beginning with the establishment of the Soviet government in Russia and until the defeat of German imperialism. At that time the imperialists of both the Western coalitions, i.e., the British and the German, were battling with each other, and they simply did not notice Russia, that is, were too busy, so to speak, to notice Russia.

The second period covers the time from the defeat of German imperialism and the beginning of the German revolution to the time of the all-out advance by Denikin on Russia, when he approached the gates of Tula. This period differs from the first in so far as the international position of Russia was concerned: having defeated Germany, the Entente, i.e., the Anglo-French-American coalition, now directed all its free forces against Soviet Russia. This was the period when we were threatened by an alliance of fourteen states, an alliance that later proved to be a myth.[2]

First Period

Three years ago, on October 25 (November 7, N.S.), 1917, a small group of Bolsheviks, the active members of the Petrograd soviet, met together and decided to surround Kerensky's palace, take control over the already disintegrated troops, and pass on the authority to the Second Congress of Soviets of Workers', Peasants', and Soldiers' Deputies, which had just begun its sitting.

At that time many people considered us odd fellows at best, and, at worst, agents of German imperialism.

From the viewpoint of [our] international position, this period can be called the period of complete isolation of Soviet Russia. Not only were the bourgeois countries that surround us hostile to Russia, but even our socialist comrades in the West looked upon us with suspicion.

Nevertheless, Soviet Russia was able to survive as a state, chiefly because the imperialists of the West were engaged in a serious struggle among themselves. In

---

[1] Stalin, *Sochineniia,* IV, 382–93. Appeared originally in *Baku Kommunist,* Nos. 157 and 160, November 7 and 11, 1920.

[2] This refers to an alleged statement by Winston Churchill to the effect that the Entente was preparing a coalition of fourteen states against Soviet Russia. The report appeared in the Swedish newspaper *Folkets Dagblad Politiken,* No. 195, August 25, 1919. The authenticity of this document has never been verified.

addition, they treated the Bolshevik experiment in Russia with irony and believed that the Bolsheviks would die their own death [as a political force].

From the viewpoint of the internal situation, this period saw the destruction of the old world in Russia, and of the entire machinery of the old bourgeois authority.

We knew that the proletariat could not simply take over the old state machinery and make it work. The theoretical thesis given by Marx was fully confirmed [at that time] by facts; we met with numerous instances of sabotage by tsarist officials, employees, and certain sections of the higher strata of the proletariat. This was the period of complete disorganization of the state machinery.

A very important apparatus of the bourgeois state, the old army and its generals, we simply pushed aside and demolished. This was an expensive undertaking. It left us without any army for a while and obliged us to sign the Brest-Litovsk treaty. But there was no other choice; history gave us no other way to liberate the proletariat.

Later, an equally important piece of bourgeois machinery was done away with, the machinery of officialdom, the machinery of the bourgeois administration.

As for [our third target,] the administration of the national economy, our most characteristic act of that time was to deprive the bourgeoisie of the backbone of its economy, namely the banks. Without its banks, the bourgeoisie was left, so to speak, without a soul. Next, steps were taken to demolish the old machinery of the country's economy and to expropriate the bourgeoisie, whose factories and mills were handed over to the working class. Finally, the old machinery of food supply was demolished, and an attempt was made to organize new machinery capable of collecting grain and distributing it among the population. Then the Constituent Assembly was liquidated. These were approximately the measures Soviet Russia was obliged to take in this period in order to destroy the bourgeois state machinery.

Second Period

The second period dates from the defeat of German imperialism by the Anglo-French-American coalition, and the launching of the latter's campaign to defeat Soviet Russia.

From the standpoint of international relations, this period saw open warfare between the Entente's forces and those of Soviet Russia. In contrast to the first period, when we were either not noticed or laughed at and mocked, the second period saw the dark forces become anxious to put an end to the so-called "anarchy" in Russia, which threatened to disintegrate the entire capitalist world.

Internally, this was a constructive period. The destruction of the old machinery of the bourgeois state had on the whole been completed, and a new period of construction was under way. The expropriated factories and mills were organized, true workers' control of them was worked out, and the proletariat passed from controlling them to managing them directly. A new food supply apparatus replaced the destroyed one, and new organizations for managing the railways were set up both at the center and locally. To replace the old army, a new army was formed.

We must admit, however, that the constructive work of that period was rather weak, since the basic constructive energy, i.e., nine-tenths of it, was directed to building up the Red Army. This was necessary because of the death struggle against the Entente, because the very existence of Soviet Russia was at stake, and because Russia could be defended only by a powerful Red Army. We must say that our efforts were not in vain; the Red Army defeated Yudenich and Kolchak and even in that period revealed its full power.

From the standpoint of Russia's internal position, this period saw a gradual abandonment of Russia's isolation. Russia soon acquired allies. The German revolution produced closely-welded cadres of workers, the communist cadres, and, in the Liebknecht group, laid the foundation for a new communist party.

In France a small group which was not noticed before, the group led by [Fernand]

Loriot, became important in the communist movement. In Italy the communist movement, weak at first, soon drew to itself most of the members of the Italian Socialist Party.

In the East, the Red Army's success caused unrest: Witness the example of Turkey, where actual war against the Entente and its allies broke out.

The bourgeois states themselves were no longer united in their hostility to Russia, as they had been in the first period. Increasing differences were revealed within the Entente on the question of recognizing Soviet Russia. Some voices now favored negotiations with Russia, an agreement with her. Such were the voices of Estonia, Latvia, and Finland.

Finally, the growing popularity among the British and French workers of the slogan "Hands off Russia" made direct armed intervention by the Entente in Russia no longer possible. Unable to send Anglo-French soldiers against Russia, the Entente continued to support such foreign armies as it expected to be obedient to its wishes.

Third Period

This is the period through which we are now passing. It can be called a period of transition. In its first stage, Russia, having defeated its chief enemy, Denikin, and anticipating the end of the war, set about converting the state machinery from war purposes to economic reconstruction. The earlier slogans were "Everything for the war," "Everything for the Red Army," "Everything for victory over the foreign foe." Now a new slogan was advanced: "Everything for the consolidation of the economic life of the country." The third period, however, which began with the defeat of Denikin and his expulsion from the Ukraine, was soon interrupted by the attack launched by Poland on Russia. The Entente had incited Poland against Russia to prevent Russia from becoming economically strong and thus becoming one of the most powerful states in the world.

It became necessary once more to reorganize the state machinery, which had already been converted to economic reconstruction. The labor armies of the Ukraine, the Ural region, and the Don had to be put once more on a war footing, as a cadre for new fighting units to be sent against Poland. This period has seen the neutralization of Poland, and no new foreign enemies seem to be in sight. The only enemy that is still left is the remnant of Denikin's army headed by Wrangel, whom our Comrade Budenny is defeating right now.

There is reason to suppose that at least for a time Soviet Russia will be given a considerable breathing space and will be able to turn the energy of its indefatigable workers, who organized the Red Army almost in one day, to the tasks of economic reconstruction—to making the factories, the farms, and the food supply machinery work to their full capacity.

From the viewpoint of foreign relations, in the third period the Entente not only noticed and opposed Russia in an armed struggle with all the strength it could muster (that is, with the fourteen states, as Churchill had once threatened Russia), but, having been beaten several times, grew apprehensive of Russia. They [Russia's enemies] came to realize that a great people's socialist state was emerging and that this state would not allow anyone to mistreat it.

.   .   .

Prospects for the Future

Our constructive work during the past three years has been less successful than we might have wished, but it should be remembered how difficult and almost impossible were the conditions of work during that time and that such conditions were inevitable. We cannot quarrel about such a situation; we must overcome it.

We were obliged to carry on constructive work under fire. Imagine a mason who builds with one hand and defends his home with the other.

We were not organizing a bourgeois economy in which everyone pursues his own private interests and is not concerned with the state as a whole . . . No, we were organizing a socialist society. This meant that the requirements of the society as a whole had to be taken into account, that the national economy had to be organized systematically, class-consciously, and on an all-Russian scale. Such a task is clearly much more complicated and much more difficult. That is why our constructive work could not be highly successful [at first].

Our future prospects are clear: We stand on the threshold of liquidating our foreign enemies and of converting our state machinery to economic reconstruction. We are for peace in our foreign policy; we do not favor war. But if a war is forced upon us (and there are some indications that the Entente is trying to launch military actions in the South, i.e., in Transcaucasia), if the Entente, which has been beaten by us several times, again forces a war upon us, it goes without saying that we shall not let the arms out of our hands, and shall not disband our troops. As before, we shall see to it that the Red Army prospers, so that it is in battle readiness to defend Soviet Russia from her enemies as valiantly and courageously as it has done in the past.

In reviewing the past work of the Soviet government, one involuntarily recalls the evening of October 25, 1917, three years ago, when a small group of Bolsheviks, headed by Comrade Lenin and in control of the Petrograd soviet (it was a pro-Bolshevik soviet) and a small Red Guard, having at our disposal a small and not as yet fully organized Communist Party of between 200,000 and 250,000 members, removed from power the representatives of the bourgeoisie and transferred authority to the Second Congress of Soviets of Workers', Peasants', and Soldiers' Deputies.

Three years have gone by. During these three years Russia has gone through water and fire, and has molded a great socialist world power. Three years ago we had control of only the Petrograd soviet; now we have around us the closed ranks of the soviets of all Russia. Instead of the Constituent Assembly for which our enemies were preparing themselves, we now have the All-Russian Central Executive Committee of Soviets, which grew out of the Petrograd soviet. Three years ago we had a small guard made up of the Petrograd workers, who were able to suppress the mutinous Cadets in Petrograd but were not yet capable of opposing the foreign foe. Now we have a glorious Red Army, millions strong, which fought the enemies of Soviet Russia, defeated Kolchak and Denikin, and now, led by the experienced commander of our cavalry, Comrade Budenny, storms the remnants of Wrangel's army.

Three years ago we had a small and not fully organized Communist Party, with some 200,000–250,000 members. Now . . . the party has 700,000 members, and is a party closely welded and steeled, a party whose members can be mobilized and concentrated at a moment's notice on any party work, a party that fears no confusion and is able with its Central Committee to re-form its ranks and advance against the enemy.

Three years ago we had only small groups of sympathizers in the West, such as Loriot's group, McLean's in Britain, and Liebknecht's in Germany. Now we have a great organization for the international revolutionary movement, the Third International, which has won over the most important parties in Europe: the German, the French, and the Italian. We have now the basic center of the international socialist movement represented by the Communist International, which has defeated the Second International. . . .

And finally, three years ago, we found in the oppressed countries of the East only indifference toward the revolution. Now the East has come into motion, and a number of movements of liberation directed against the Entente, against imperialism, exist there. There is now a revolutionary center [in the East] which attracts all colonial and semicolonial countries, namely the government of Kemal, who, although a bourgeois revolutionary, nevertheless carries on an armed struggle against the Entente.

Three years ago we could not even dream that the East would arise. Now we have not only a revolutionary center in the East, represented by the bourgeois revolution in Turkey, but also a socialist organization for the East, namely, the Committee for Action and Propaganda.[3]

. . . All the above facts make it possible for us to affirm that Soviet Russia will live, develop, and defeat all its enemies.

Our path will not be an easy one, but no difficulties will frighten us. To paraphrase the well-known words of Luther, Russia can now say:

"Here I stand, on the borderline between the old capitalist world and the new socialist world. Here, on this borderline, I unite the efforts of the proletarians of the West and of the peasants of the East in order to smash the old world. The God of history grant me help."

2

Trotsky on Postwar Imperialism, the Role of the Second International, and the Road to Victory

[Excerpt from a Speech at the Final and Joint Session of the Second Congress of the Communist International, the All-Russian Central Executive Committee, the Moscow Soviet, the All-Russian Council of Trade Unions, and the Factory Committees, August 7, 1920][4]

. . .

Now, what is the state of Europe and of the whole world after it has emerged from the world butchery and from the workshop of the Versailles Peace? There is not a single point of support for the bourgeois order anywhere. All things are in a state of flux. All the mainstays have been shaken, all the State programs of the bourgeoisie have been annulled, all international ties have been broken, and the bourgeoisie, in fear and trembling for the morrow, is looking for a way out of the position created by centuries of robbery and violence, but cannot find one.

England, France and the United States have promised their peoples a world union, the League of Nations, which was to put an end to imperialist conflicts, to international wars. Now the League of Nations is in being, but hardly had it come out of the Chancelleries of diplomacy than its father, President Wilson, turned his face away from it. . . .

. . . Wilson, the American provincial, carrying the highly rated dollar not only in his pocket but also on his forehead, had made up his mind that his fourteen points

---

[3] The Committee for Action and Propaganda (formally, the Council for Propaganda and Action of the Peoples of the East), was created by the Baku Congress of the Peoples of the East in September 1920. It was to serve as a sort of central clearinghouse for propaganda and revolutionary strategy for all the national-liberation movements in the East. Although this particular committee lasted only a year (a second Baku congress that was to review its work and reorganize it as necessary was never held), similar organizations were soon created within the Comintern. See the companion volume, *Soviet Russia and the East, 1920–1927.*

[4] *The Second Congress of the Communist International. Proceedings of Petrograd Session of July 17th, and of Moscow Sessions of July 19th–August 7th, 1920,* pp. 430–37. The English and German editions of the proceedings of the Second Congress were published in Moscow in 1920; the Russian edition appeared in 1921, and the second revised Russian edition in 1934. Only the early English edition includes the proceedings of the last, joint session in which the All-Russian Central Executive Committee and the All-Russian Council of Trade Unions participated. The German edition gives only a summary of this session; the Russian editions give nothing at all.

should become the new Gospel of the world. He had, however, come up against the English fleet and against something more formidable, viz., Soviet Russia and Communism, and the vexed American apostle went back to the White House at Washington, to his Mount Sinai. Do not, however, imagine, comrades, that this means renunciation of the policy of world domination on the part of American Capital. It cannot do that . . . The American Admiralty is drawing up a new naval program to be completed before 1925, so as to make the American fleet by that time—some say it will be even earlier: by 1923—incomparably stronger than the fleet of England. Now, what does this mean? The strength of England is based on the fleet, which holds all the maritime routes, giving her the power for her world robbery. . . . Now, America, with its shining dollar, the rate of which is sky high on the Stock Exchange, says: "My fleet will in three years time be stronger than the fleet of England." That means that the question of "to be or not to be" is now confronting British imperialism. That means that England and the United States are rushing headlong towards a new sanguinary world conflict, because in the world of imperialist states there can be no dual authority, and the crown of world domination must in the long run belong either to England or America, provided it is not wrested from them by the world proletariat. And now after four years of the bitterest world war which has crushed the mighty powers of Central Europe, has laid Europe waste, and ruined the whole world, a new, even more gigantic war is being prepared over the bones of the fallen.

France, the arch enemy of Soviet Russia, the bitterest opponent of the world proletariat, thinks itself victor; or, more correctly, the simpletons, the petty bourgeoisie, the middle class, the social patriots, a part of the deceived workers, think that France has come out victorious. This is a mistake, a bitter mistake. . . . And now France is of all the independent countries of the world the most exhausted, the most ruined. France can of course engage in piratical exploits in the Black Sea, but only in so far as these do not affect England. France can dictate to little Belgium, which has become a French province, but, France itself, in relation to Great Britain, is nothing but a Belgium on a larger scale. Without the assistance of England and America, the outlook of France is hopeless, economically as well as militarily, but with its petty bourgeois stupidity France suffers even now from a swelled head and thinks that she will act as chairman in the court of arbitration between the United States and England. The United States however has not even joined the League of Nations, and France is obliged to go cap in hand begging for economic favours and for guarantees for its independence.

And the small nationalities, the petty states? They were promised freedom and independence, but everywhere England has put its thieving hand upon them: upon Finland, White Esthonia, White Lettland, etc. What has been left of Sweden's and Norway's independence? What is the Baltic? It is now a British lake. What is the North Sea? It belongs to England. What is the Indian Ocean fringed by a chain of peoples subject to England: Egypt, Persia, Afghanistan, Baluchistan, India? It is an inner English Sea. Out of the body of Austro-Hungary, of the old Tsarist Russia a number of small states have been cut which have no vitality, but the Entente, the League of Nations, (that is, Great Britain) do not for the time being permit them to die. Austria is crucified and torn to pieces. Hungary made an heroic attempt to raise central Europe from chaos and entered upon the great path of Soviet Federation, that is, on the path of brotherly union between the victorious Labour Republics, a union embracing the economic, military, cultural and every other aspect of their life. Soviet Hungary was, however, crushed and thrown back. We have Bohemia where there is a "union sacré" with the social patriots; and it is the same in miserable Poland, the liberation of which was advocated from the very first by the First International.

It [Poland] was created by dying imperialism to serve its base aims and objects. The democratic Polish Republic, for which a generation of Polish revolutionary patriots have been fighting, many having to flee from autocracy westward, many dying upon the barricades in the revolutionary upheavals of Europe; this democratic Poland is now the most dirty and bloody weapon in the hands of French capital. Whilst the First International inscribed the cause of independent Poland against autocracy in its first pages, Russia, free from autocracy, is now accomplishing the great mission of handing back crucified and violated Poland to the Polish workers and peasants.[5]

From all the parliamentary tribunes we hear talk about the economic regeneration of Europe. There is no greater deception than this. Europe has not regenerated during the eighteen months that have elapsed since our first Congress; on the contrary, it has become incomparably poorer and its prospects more hopeless than before. Not only Europe, but the whole world is in the same condition. How can Europe be regenerated without Russia's raw materials, without Russian corn [i.e., grain]? How can Europe be regenerated without German technique, without the German working class? Now the representatives of the workers of all countries on their return home from this Congress will say to the workers of Europe and of the whole world: "On the basis of what little we saw in Soviet Russia, we can bear witness that if the imperialists leave Soviet Russia in peace, and we offer her some assistance, however small, in the matter of technique, Soviet Russia will, within three or at the utmost five years, offer the European working class five times as much corn and raw materials as old Autocratic bourgeois Russia ever gave before, and that will be only because Russia is a Soviet Republic based on the principles of Communism." . . . We have passed through eighteen months of bitter fighting, and we can tell our West-European comrades with legitimate pride: "Your bourgeoisie has not overpowered us, here we stand, we receive you here in Moscow."

Now if this has come to pass, it is not only because of the mighty efforts of the Russian working class and of the army created by it. We know our strength, we know our sacrifices, and now the envoys of the world's proletariat have come to know more about it. We must however say, that if we withstood it all, it was mainly because we knew and felt the coming help gathering in Europe, America and in all parts of the world; every strike of the Scottish workers on the Clyde; every movement in the towns and villages of Ireland, over which not only the green banner of Irish nationalism, but also the Red banner of the proletarian struggle is waving; every protest; every rising in any of the towns of Europe, America and Asia; the mighty movement of the Hindoos—the colonial slaves of England—and the general growth of class consciousness, the spreading far and wide of the one general cry for a Soviet Federation of the world,—it was this that gave us the confidence that we were on the right path, that gave us strength during the darkest and blackest hours when we were surrounded on all sides, and it seemed that we should be crushed. It enabled us to breathe again and say: "We are not alone, the workers of Europe and Asia and of the whole world are with us. We shall not surrender, we shall hold out." And we did hold out. Without Russia and without Germany, Europe cannot be regenerated. To regenerate Germany it is necessary to let her live, eat and work; but if crucified and crushed Germany is allowed to live, eat and work it will rise against French imperialism. That is why French imperialism, which knows but one commandment, "thou shalt pay"—Germany must pay, Russia must pay—is ready to set the whole world in flames in order that French capital may regularly get its interest. They cannot allow Germany to work in order that she might be able to pay, because a working, rising Germany means an independent Germany opposed to them [i.e., to French imperialism]. . . .

Take any parliamentary report of any country, and you will see that any petty

---

[5] This refers to the Red Army's advance into Poland and the organization of Polish soviets with Russian Communists' help.

bourgeois minister, any third rate official who wishes to carry the bourgeois majority with him and raise a storm of cheers, shakes his threatening fist at the revolutionary proletariat. The bourgeoisie demands from its hirelings, agents, and ministers, blood and iron, because it has grasped the fact that we, the whole world, have entered a stage when there can be no parliamentary mediation between the classes, but bitter, ruthless and deadly struggle. . . . Comrades, there is not the slightest doubt that the proletariat of all countries would have been in power today if between the revolutionary masses and the advanced groups of communist revolutionaries there were not the barriers of the Second International and of the Trade Union International, still large, strong, and complex, which have placed their machinery at the service of the bourgeoisie at the moment of its decline, at the moment of its death . . . They have led the workers for decades, inspiring them with confidence, giving them an organization, wielded authority over them, and then, at the moment when all their energy should have been directed to the liberation of the workers from the yoke of capitalism, they used their machinery for the purpose of binding the workers hand and foot, making them not only physical but also moral slaves of international capital. Now, whilst we are assembled here at the Second Congress at Moscow, the Congress of the Second International, which in program and spirit is opposed to our International, the International of the Red World Commune, is in session in Geneva. From today, from this Congress, from these two Congresses, the division in the ranks of the international working class will proceed with tenfold rapidity. Program against program, tactics against tactics, method against method. . . .

Our Congress coincides with the Congress of the Second International and what is for us and the workers of the whole world important and significant, it coincides with the bitter struggle which the Entente is carrying on against the Soviet Republic through the medium of White Poland; it coincides with the victories of the Red Army on the Western and South-Western fronts. Our Congress was a great landmark in the development of the proletarian world revolution . . . Comrades of Moscow and workers of other parts of Russia, we are filled with pride and joy that for the second time we have been able to call together the best fighters of the international working class, that we could by our experience help them to forge their weapons. Comrades, proletarians, in our Moscow forge we have blown the flames that brought the proletarian steel to red heat, forging it with the hammer of our proletarian Soviet Revolution, tempering it with our experience of civil war, hammering it into an incomparably excellent sword to be used by the International proletariat. With this steel we arm ourselves and others. We say to the workers of the whole world: "In the Moscow forge, on the Moscow anvil, we have hammered out a sharp sword, take it in your hands and strike international Capital to the ground."

3

Lenin on Foreign Trade and the Advantages Inherent in the Policy of Concessions

[Report on Concessions to the Communist Party Faction at the Eighth Congress of Soviets of the R.S.F.S.R., December 1920][6]

Comrades, the question of granting concessions [to foreign countries] has created considerable excitement and even apprehension not only in party circles and among

---

[6] Lenin, *Sochineniia*, XXVI, 5–15, 23. On November 23, 1920, a decree of the Council of People's Commissars had defined "the general economic and political conditions for concessions" to foreign enterprises and individuals. This decree appeared in *Izvestiia*, No. 265, November 25, 1920.

the workers, but also among the peasant masses. All comrades have pointed out that since the publication of the decree of November 23, questions have often been raised at meetings, and written inquiries have expressed the fear that, having driven away our own capitalists, we are now proposing to let in foreign ones. . . .

I believe, however, that we cannot be guided here by revolutionary instinct alone. Weighing all sides of the matter, we shall become convinced of the correctness of the policy we have adopted—our offer of concessions.

. . .

If, in evaluating the present international situation of the Soviet republic, we go back over the past three years, we shall see clearly that we have been able to hold on and to win victories over the tremendously strong alliance of the Entente powers, supported by our White Guards, only because unity has never existed among those powers. We have been able to win so far only because of the serious disagreements among the imperialist powers, only because these disagreements have not been accidental party and domestic disagreements but the result of deep-rooted, permanent differences in economic interests. While upholding the principle of private ownership of land and capital, these powers inevitably pursue a policy of robbery, thus destroying any chance of success for their attempts to join forces against Soviet Russia.

Let us take Japan as an example. She held almost all of Siberia and, of course, could have helped Kolchak whenever necessary. She did not do so, however, because her interests differed radically from America's interests and she did not want to draw chestnuts out of the fire for American capital. This being clear, we had only to make full use of these differences between America and Japan to strengthen ourselves, and also to delay the possibility of Japanese-American agreement to launch joint action against us. . . .

Our [general] policy is to use the differences among the imperialist powers in such a way as to make it difficult for them to reach an agreement, or to make such an agreement at least temporarily impossible.

This has been the basic line of our policy for the past three years. This made it necessary to sign the Brest peace and an agreement with Bullitt concerning the peace and the armistice, both of which were extremely disadvantageous to us. The same line of policy has determined our decision to use the plan of concessions. We are giving America [concessions in] Kamchatka, which is actually not ours because at present Japanese troops occupy it. At this moment we are unable to fight Japan. We are giving America a territory that is useless to us because of our absolute lack of naval and armed forces. By doing so we set American imperialists against the Japanese bourgeoisie in particular, which is the nearest to us and which still holds the Far Eastern Republic under its thumb.[7]

Thus, in negotiating concessions, our chief interest is political; the economic importance of this question is but secondary.

. . .

We have information to the effect that some capitalist countries are taking steps preparatory [to launching an attack on us], while one might say that the White Guards are conducting preparatory work in all countries. Therefore, our main task

---

[7] The Far Eastern Republic, made up of what are now the Maritime and Khabarovsk territories of the U.S.S.R., existed from April 6, 1920, to November 14, 1922; its capital was Chita. It had a democratic form of representative government, but was actually controlled by the Communist Party. Its purpose was to serve as a buffer state between communist Russia and the noncommunist states, especially Japan and the United States. When there was no longer any need for the fiction of an independent democratic republic in Eastern Siberia, the Far Eastern Republic was dissolved and its territory was taken into the R.S.F.S.R. as an oblast.

is to re-establish trade relations; and to do this we must have at least some of the capitalists on our side.

In England, a struggle has been going on for a long time. We are already the winners, because [some] representatives of that country, known for its capitalist exploitation of the people, now favor a trade agreement with Russia. . . . Our direct interest and our direct duty lie in supporting by every possible means the parties and groups that desire the conclusion of this agreement.

[Speaks again about the American concessions and the growing enmity between America and Japan.]

After speaking of this at a meeting in Moscow, I was questioned during the discussion period. It appears, as one comrade put it, that we are inciting Japan and America to war. Actually such a war would be fought by the workers and peasants, and although both these countries are imperialistic powers, we, the socialists, should not incite the two countries against each other, and thus indirectly bring about the shedding of the workers' blood. To this I replied that if we were actually inciting the workers and peasants to war, this would indeed be a crime. But our entire policy and propaganda are directed not to inciting peoples to war, but to putting an end to war.

Experience has shown that only a socialist revolution can end this state of eternal wars. Thus, our policy is not to incite to war. We have done nothing, either directly or indirectly, that would justify a war between Japan and America. Instead our entire propaganda and all our newspaper articles continually reveal the truth—that is, that war between America and Japan will be an imperialist war, similar to the 1914 war between the English alliance and the German alliance; and that therefore the socialists should be concerned not with the defense of the fatherland, but with overthrowing capitalist rule and with the workers' revolution.

But since we, who are doing everything we can to hasten this revolution, are a weakened socialist republic attacked by robber-imperialists, is it not correct to use the differences among the capitalists to make it difficult for them to unite against us? Of course such a policy is correct. We have pursued it for the last four years. And the Brest treaty was the main application of this policy. As long as German imperialism was fighting, we made use of the conflicts among the imperialists; it was for this reason that we were able to hold on even though the Red Army had not then been created.

. . . Our purpose at present is to arrange a trade agreement with England and start regular trade, so as to be able to purchase as soon as possible the machinery required for our extensive plan to re-establish our national economy. The sooner we do this, the better basis we shall have for becoming economically independent of the capitalist countries. Now, having burnt themselves during their military invasion of Russia, they cannot at once think about war. We must utilize the moment, and direct all our efforts toward obtaining trade relations, even at a very high price.

We do not for a moment believe in lasting trade relations with the imperialist powers; what we shall obtain will be simply a breathing space. The history of revolutions, of large-scale conflicts, teaches us that wars, series of wars, are inevitable. A Soviet republic existing side by side with the capitalist countries, surrounded by capitalist countries, is so inadmissible from the capitalist viewpoint that these countries will seize the first opportunity to resume the war. At present, people are tired of the imperialist war; they threaten to revolt when war is suggested. Nevertheless, the capitalists may well resume their plan within a few years. This is why we must do our best to use the chance given us, and to obtain a trade agreement.

In July, when the Red Army was threatening the Polish army with complete rout, England offered the full text of an agreement in which it was demanded that we agree in principle not to carry on official propaganda or to undertake measures directed against British interests in the East. Later on, a political conference was to work out the details of this point, but at the time we were to conclude a trade agreement. They asked us if we wished to sign it. We replied: We want to sign it. We say now also that we are ready to sign it. The political conference will define British interests in the East precisely. We too have interests in the East, and when the time comes, we shall outline them in detail.

At present, England cannot say openly that she is withdrawing her July proposal. Therefore, she delays and conceals from her own people the truth about the negotiations. The negotiations are in an unsettled state, and we cannot be absolutely sure that an agreement will be signed. . . . The policy of our Central Committee is that of maximum concessions to England. And if these gentlemen think they can catch us up on promises, we declare that no official propaganda will be conducted by our government, and that we have no intention of interfering with British interests in the East. . . .

I now approach the question of the relations between England and France. These relations are complicated. On one hand, England and France are both members of the League of Nations and must co-operate; on the other hand, any time the situation is aggravated, they do not act together. . . . In this connection, we must make use of the differences between England and France; we must offer concessions to England as a political expedient. . . . In this situation, with no political unity between England and France, we must take risks to make a military alliance of England and France against us more difficult. A new war against us supported by England and France would mean to us . . . colossal difficulties, would delay our economic development, would undermine the position of our workers and peasants. Therefore, we must be ready to do anything that would be less harmful to us. Clearly the losses from concessions are nothing beside the damage from delay in our economic development and the destruction of thousands of our workers and peasants that will occur if we are unable to ward off the alliance of the imperialists.

Our own way of offsetting this alliance is the negotiations with England over concessions. Herein lies the political aspect of the question.

Finally, let us take the relations of England, and of the Entente as a whole, with Germany. [Industrially] Germany is the most advanced country, with the exception of America. In the matter of electrical development, she stands even much higher technically than America. Yet this country, tied hand and foot by the Versailles treaty, finds itself facing conditions that make its very existence impossible. Under such circumstances, Germany naturally is inclined toward an alliance with Russia. . . .

Our foreign policy, while we are alone and the capitalist world is strong, consists of making use of existing antagonisms (to win over the imperialist powers would be still better, of course, but we shall not be able to do that for quite a while). Our existence depends on two facts: (1) that there exist basic differences among the imperialist powers, and (2) that the victory of the Entente and the Versailles treaty have thrown back the great majority of the German people into a situation in which they cannot survive. Because of the Versailles peace, Germany cannot even dream of a time when she will no longer be plundered of the very means of her existence, when her population will not be condemned to starvation and death. Germany cannot dream of this, and therefore, naturally, her only means of saving herself is an alliance with Russia, toward whom she turns her gaze. They [the Germans] hate Soviet Russia and the Bolsheviks; they shoot their own Communists as the White Guards would shoot us. The German bourgeois government also hates the Bolsheviks, but its foreign situation prompts it to live in peace with Soviet Russia, even against its own wishes.

And here, comrades, we come to the second basis of our foreign policy. We must prove to the peoples who feel bourgeois oppression that there is no salvation for them apart from the Soviet republic. The Soviet republic has repulsed the imperialists' attack for three years; clearly no other country in the world can parry imperialist oppression. Let it be the country of "robbers," of "bandits," of Bolsheviks, and so forth; let it be so, but without this country no improvement in the economic situation is possible.

· · ·

The position of our peasants and workers remains very difficult. We must improve it. No one can question this. I think that we shall all agree that the policy of concessions is also the policy of the continuation of the war, that our task is to maintain the existence of our isolated socialist republic surrounded by its capitalist enemies; to protect the republic, which is so much weaker than the capitalist enemies who surround it; to remove the opportunity for the enemies to create an alliance among themselves for a struggle against us; to keep on interfering with their policies; to prevent them from winning. Our task is to get Russia the machinery and means she needs to re-establish her economy; once this is done, we shall stand firmly on our feet, and the capitalist enemies will no longer be formidable to us. This is the point of view that guides us in our policy regarding concessions.

PEACE WITH THE BALTIC STATES

4

Lenin on Peace with Estonia

[Speech Delivered at the First Session of the All-Russian Central
Executive Committee, February 2, 1920][8]

Peace with Estonia was signed yesterday.[9] This means that in our direct struggle against the counterrevolution supported by the imperialists of the world, and in our efforts toward peace, which again the entire capitalist world tried to prevent, we have proved stronger than the whole world of vultures. This miracle could have happened only because we actually had the majority of the world's population on our side. We have been victorious over Denikin, Kolchak, and Yudenich, not because we had better ammunition, but because the forces hostile to us failed to provide the men to use the perfect weapons of the capitalist world against us. We have forced Estonia to conclude peace with us because we have shown by our actions and by our peace policy that our true desire is to live in peace with everyone. We have shown, too, that we can resist force, but that we also know enough, once we are victorious, to give up the use of force. . . .

5

Ioffe Interprets the Significance of the Treaty of Peace with Latvia of August 11, 1920[10]

One more link has been knocked out of the iron chain with which international imperialism has tried to encircle the workers' and peasants' Russia.

After four months of negotiation, first in Moscow and then in Riga, a Russian-Latvian peace treaty has finally been signed. . . .

[By this treaty] Russia has acquired a wide-open gate to Europe and not just a small back door. Through the splendid ports of Riga, Libava, and Vindava [in

---

[8] Lenin, *Sochineniia*, XXV, 21.
[9] Full text of the treaty appears in Shapiro, I, 34–38.
[10] *Izvestiia*, No. 179, August 14, 1920, p. 1. Text of the treaty appears in Shapiro, I, 54–58.

Lettish, Liepaja and Vente] she will be able to export and import her goods freely.

But Russia has done even more. She has reduced the number of her enemies by one more state, and has instilled into hundreds of thousands of confused minds the idea that all stories about "Soviet imperialism and aggressiveness" are impudent slander and lies, because in both favorable and unfavorable circumstances the Soviet government has maintained its original policy and has remained true to its principles.

The oppressed peoples and states have been given another opportunity to become convinced that the workers' and peasants' Russia is their only defender and savior. Herein lies the main political significance of the Russo-Latvian peace treaty.

6

Soviet Policy of "Peaceful Advance"

[Ioffe's Statement in 1921 on Peace with the Baltic States][11]

.   .   .

By entering into negotiations with the Soviet government [in 1919] during the period of the international economic and political blockade of Russia, a state as small as Estonia made, in its own way, a heroic decision. Without outside aid Estonia could not exist. It could not then count upon Russian support, for at that time Soviet Russia was thought of as a collection of malicious agitators who thought of nothing but revolutionary conflagration instead of being concerned with and guided by the real interests [of the people]. . . .

On the other hand, the entire bourgeois world had begun little by little to doubt the usefulness of military intervention under the leadership of the old tsarist generals, and had begun to see the necessity for economic contact with Russia. Therefore it looked upon the Russian-Estonian negotiations as a test of the realism of Soviet policy and of the possibility of peaceful agreement with that country. This fact made Soviet diplomats particularly cautious. Therefore, the Russian delegation in its first statements [during the peace conference] outlined the essential points that were later to serve as the foundation for all the peace treaties Russia signed with her immediate neighbors.

While conducting the negotiations with Estonia, Russian delegates openly declared that "war between Russia and the republics which sought independence, and which were created on the territory of the former Russian Empire, was a crude misunderstanding. Irrespective of the close economic and historic ties [between Soviet Russia and these countries], the war of liberation from the people who were the first to declare the principle of the right of nations to self-determination and who were struggling for this principle, should never have taken place."

The possibility of co-operation between Russia and bourgeois-democratic republics was noted for the first time during the Russian-Estonian negotiations. The Russian peace delegation asserted that: "The difference in the internal policies, the profound chasm that exists between the principles upon which the life of the peoples inhabiting the Russian Socialist Federated Soviet Republic is founded and the methods with which all other governments of large and small states achieve their rule, must not provide a basis for armed conflict, because, being firmly convinced that the moment is not far off when all peoples will understand the advantage of a soviet socialist regime for them, the Russian revolutionary proletariat is calmly awaiting this moment, and does not press its own principles upon anyone."

In that way the actual foundation for peaceful coexistence with Soviet Russia was provided, but under the circumstances that then existed, that was not sufficient,

[11] A. A. Ioffe, *Mirnoe nastuplenie*, pp. 16–23.

because real guarantees for peaceful coexistence must be supplied by the other party as well. The guarantees provided by international law, which obligate every state that signs a peace treaty honestly to adhere to it, did not appear sufficient, because in its short experience Soviet Russia had met new paradoxes in which a state of war was not admitted but armed clashes actually took place and blood was shed in profusion. It was necessary, therefore, to say directly that the peace which Russia wanted must be a true peace, and that Soviet Russia would not tolerate armed adventures under different pretexts after the conclusion of peace. Soviet Russia needed guarantees that her foes would not try to use peaceful negotiations for the preparation of a new attack. Therefore the Russia delegation declared from the start that hostilities would not cease and an armistice would not be signed until so-called "war guarantees" were given by the other party.[12]

.   .   .

The [proposed] agreement expressed in a certain sense [Soviet] distrust of the old international law, which has been sanctified by tradition and international custom, and thus created a new precedent. The clauses in question have been repeated in one form or another, not only in all treaties that Soviet Russia has since concluded with other states, but also in treaties between other states, for example the treaty between Germany and Latvia. The policy of permitting armed action in a period of legal peaceful relations, the policy of carrying on undeclared war, found legal condemnation in this treaty [i.e., the Soviet-Estonian treaty]. On one hand, Soviet peaceful intentions were specially emphasized; on the other hand, only a peace that was an actual peace was recognized as real.

The Soviet-Estonian peace negotiations brought no immediate results, but nevertheless they had influence. First of all, the bourgeois states began to change their estimate of Russia. The weak and oppressed peoples began to understand that the Soviet government was not their enemy but their friend. The nature of Soviet foreign policy was clearly revealed in the peace negotiations with Estonia.

These were the first negotiations in which the Soviet government could truly reveal its sincere adherence to the principles it proclaimed.

Previously Soviet Russia had met in the international arena only foes that were stronger than she. Her principles were those of self-defense. At Brest-Litovsk, when the Russian delegation energetically and stubbornly defended for some months the right of peoples to self-determination, it might have looked as if Russia was actually defending the right of the Ukraine, Lithuania, Belorussia, Estonia, Latvia, Georgia, Armenia, and Azerbaijan to remain within the limits of Russia; in other words, one might have assumed that Russia was defending her own imperialist advantages, just as Germany was defending hers. Therefore, it might have been said that Russia was basing her arguments on such principles of self-determination of peoples as would permit her to annex territories she needed. But in the negotiations with a weaker adversary there could no longer be such doubts. Every piece of ground ceded to Estonia was cut from the territory of the former Russian Empire; every pound of gold passed over to Estonia was extracted from the coffers of the former Russian state bank. If Soviet Russia on this occasion also remained true to her principles, she proved in practice that a new government has appeared in the world for which justice remains justice even under disadvantageous and harsh conditions. It goes without saying that if Soviet Russia had hesitated she might have appeared to the world no better than any imperialist state acknowledging the right of self-determination of peoples it cares nothing about, as Britain has done with the

---

[12] These guarantees included, among other things, provisions against the presence within the territory of a signatory state of troops of a third power hostile to Russia, and a cessation of hostilities by the signatory state itself during the period of peace negotiations.

Irish. Remembering well that the salvation of Soviet Russia lay in the sympathy and support of the toilers of the whole world, Soviet diplomacy was duty-bound to use its first happy moments in the world arena to reveal its true face and to prove that Soviet Russia differs from all other great states.

It should be remembered that the world bourgeoisie has fought the Soviet regime not only by armed intervention and economic blockade, but also by an artful campaign of lies and diplomacy. The entire bourgeois world has howled about Bolshevik agitation and propaganda, but actually the anti-Bolshevik agitation and propaganda have been and are being conducted on a much wider scale. Not only are Russian goods being blockaded, but Russian literature [is being suppressed], and it is not for nothing that Soviet Russia has been constantly encircled by a ring of White Guard buffer [states], the basic means of the struggle of the bourgeoisie against "Bolshevik infection." The only true propaganda for Russia has been, therefore, a propaganda of action, i.e., by a peaceful foreign policy that could not be concealed by any literary efforts. Peace with Estonia was part of this propaganda, and its influence was, therefore, tremendous. This influence affected not only the toiling masses, who had already refused to believe the bourgeois lies about the Soviet government and continued to sympathize with it, but also the bourgeois classes of small and oppressed peoples. The struggle for national liberation, the right of people to free self-determination, had long ago become the signs of new times, and although not one government risked openly coming out against these principles, sharp claws were often seen under the velvety paws of the imperialists. The small peoples who needed support and help were often obliged to pay for the slightest help with their bodies and blood. In the world of capitalist exploitation and enrichment it could not be otherwise. In the search for additional profits, the economically stronger bourgeoisie oppressed and suppressed the weaker ones. The small and recently created republics were destined to a starvation existence, and were ruined and impoverished, being merely tools for the enrichment of the bourgeoisie of states that are older and capitalistically stronger.

But Soviet Russia, which had destroyed capitalist competition at home, could not of course be directed by considerations of competition in its foreign policy. The economic proximity and connection of territories which only recently were parts of the Russian Empire, and which in the course of centuries were not only politically but also economically one with it, could not be annulled simply by one signature, by a mere declaration of political independence.

The new republics, which were at first orientated toward Germany, and then passed into the sphere of influence of the Entente, soon became convinced that in either sphere their independence was illusory, that in both systems they received nothing and gave everything. In Soviet Russia, they found the only country that required nothing from them and could give them everything, the only country that could lead them out of the deadlock in which they found themselves. Thus despite the class hatred for the proletarian government that the bourgeoisie of any state inevitably feels, the hard position of the small republics forced them to try to orientate themselves toward Soviet Russia.

Of course all this was understood with difficulty, but the Estonian example was too attractive, and following peace with Estonia, peace was also signed with Latvia, Lithuania, Finland, and Georgia. . . .

OVERTURES FROM THE WEST

7

Reply of the All-Russian Central Executive Committee to the League of Nations' Proposal to Send a Commission of Inquiry to Russia, May 14, 1920[13]

The All-Russian Central Executive Committee welcomes every indication that those governments which have been waging war against Soviet Russia, and which have tried to cut her off from other countries by means of barbed wire and a *cordon sanitaire*, have now realized the hopelessness of their attempts to strangle the great Russian people.

The League of Nations' decision to send a delegation to Russia to study the present situation here is considered by the Central Executive Committee as an indication that some members of the League are now trying to give up the policy of struggle against the Russian people. The Central Executive Committee welcomes this decision, even though up to now the League has not even tried to inform the Russian people of its existence.

At the same time, the Central Executive Committee wishes to state that a member of the League of Nations, the government of Poland, having declined a proposal for peace negotiations in neutral or even in Allied territory, has forced a war upon the Russian people. The Polish government is trying to seize lands that belong to Soviet Russia and to the Ukraine. This criminal policy not only has been left unhindered by the League of Nations, but has even received active support from those member powers which regularly support all revolts against Soviet Russia led by the deposed exploiting class.

The Soviet government, which has done everything possible to have the blockade of Russia lifted, is deeply interested in having the representatives of all nations acquaint themselves with the situation in Russia. Consequently, the Soviet government admits to Russia all newspaper correspondents who provide even a small guarantee that they will not abuse the hospitality of the Russian people.

The Soviet government will receive the delegation of the British Trades Union Congress, which is to be a guest of the Russian trade unions, and will give the delegation every opportunity to become thoroughly acquainted with the situation in Russia.

In view of this, the Central Executive Committee agrees in principle to the visit of the delegation of the League of Nations, and will make it possible for the delegation, while on the territory of Soviet Russia, to examine the situation freely, just as do the representatives of other powers on the territory of every sovereign state. It is presumed that the League, as guardian of international law and of the norms of relations between civilized nations, will not send to Russia, as its representatives or experts, persons who are connected with conspiracies against the Russian government.

However, since some of the League's members are actively supporting Poland's war against Soviet Russia and are supplying her with ammunition and instructors, and owing to military considerations, the Central Executive Committee cannot now grant a permit to enter Russia to representatives of the League, some of whom would certainly represent nations that have failed to maintain active neutrality in the war that has been forced upon Soviet Russia.

Firmly believing that the Red Army will soon prove to Poland the advantage of peace with Soviet Russia, and therefore that Soviet Russia . . . soon [will be] in a position to return to peaceful labors and to remove the restrictions of a state of

13 Kliuchnikov and Sabanin, III, 23–24.

war, the Central Executive Committee has appointed a special commission consisting of [names given] who, jointly with the People's Commissar of Foreign Affairs, G. V. Chicherin, will have the authority to permit the visit of the representatives of the League of Nations in due time, and without the necessity of convening a special session of the Central Executive Committee.

8

Lenin Criticizes British Labor Leaders and Defends the Red Terror

[Letter to the British Workers, May 30, 1920][14]

Comrades: First of all permit me to thank you for sending your delegation to acquaint itself with Soviet Russia. When your delegation proposed that I send through its intermediary a letter to the British workers and perhaps also a proposal to the British government, I replied that I would gratefully accept the first proposal, but that I would address myself to the government not through the Labour delegation but directly on behalf of our government through Comrade Chicherin. We have addressed ourselves in that way many times to the British government with the most formal and solemn proposals to start peace negotiations. These proposals are still being made intermittently by Comrade Litvinov and Comrade Krasin, and all our other representatives. The British government has stubbornly refused to accept our proposals. It is, therefore, not surprising that I should want to speak with the delegates of the British workers solely as with a delegation of workers, not as a representative of the Soviet government but as an ordinary Communist.

I was not surprised to find that some members of your delegation have the viewpoint not of the working class, but of the bourgeoisie, the exploiter class, since in all capitalist countries the imperialist war exposed a chronic abscess, namely, the passing of the majority of the workers' parliamentary and trade union leaders to the side of the bourgeoisie. Under the false excuse of the "defense of the fatherland," they actually defended the robbers' interests of one of the two groups of world bandits, i.e., the Anglo-French-American or the German group; they allied themselves with the bourgeoisie against the revolutionary struggle of the proletariat; they covered up this treason with vulgar sentimental reformist and pacifist phrases about peaceful evolution, constitutional methods, democracy, and so forth. Since this happened in all countries, including England, it was not surprising that this tendency was reflected in the composition of your delegation.

Shaw and Guest, members of your delegation, were obviously surprised and hurt by my statement that England, despite our peace proposals and the declaration of her government, continues her intervention, and is carrying on a war against us, helping Wrangel in the Crimea and the White Guards in Poland. They asked me to prove this, to state how many munition trains have been delivered by England to Poland, etc. I replied that in order to have access to the secret agreements of the British government it would be necessary to overthrow that government by revolutionary means, and to seize all the documents connected with its foreign policy, as we did [in Russia] in 1917. . . . Those leaders or representatives of the British proletariat—whether they are members of Parliament, trade unionists, journalists, or other people—who pretend not to know of the existence of secret treaties between Britain, France, the United States, Italy, Japan, and Poland for plundering of other countries and dividing the spoils, and who do not carry on a revolutionary struggle for the exposure of such treaties, demonstrate over again thereby that they are the faithful servants of the capitalists. We knew this long ago. We are exposing this both here and

14 Lenin, Sochineniia, XXV, 262–65.

throughout the world. The visit of a delegation of British workers to Russia will hasten the exposure of such leaders in Britain also.

I had a talk with members of your delegation on May 26. A day later, telegrams were received stating that Bonar Law had acknowledged in the British Parliament that military assistance had been rendered to Poland in October "for defense against Russia." (Of course, only for defense, only in October!) There are still "influential labor leaders" in England who are helping the capitalists deceive the workers, even though *The New Statesman,* one of the most moderate of all moderate middle-class newspapers or periodicals, has written about the delivery to Poland of tanks more powerful than those used during the war against the Germans. Is it possible after this not to laugh at these "leaders" of the British workers who, with an air of hurt innocence, ask what "proof" there is that England is making war on Russia and is helping Poland and the White Guards in the Crimea?

Members of the delegation asked me which I believe to be of the greater importance, the formation in England of a consistent revolutionary communist party or immediate aid by the working masses in England to the cause of peace with Russia. I replied that this is a matter of conviction. Sincere partisans of the liberation of the workers from the yoke of capital cannot possibly oppose the foundation of a communist party, which alone is able to educate the working masses (and not after the bourgeois and vulgar fashion), which alone is actually able to expose, deride, and disgrace "leaders" who are capable of doubting whether England is helping Poland, etc. It need not be feared that there will be too many Communists in England, for there is not even a small communist party there. . . .

Some members of your delegation asked me with surprise about a Red terror, about the lack of freedom of the press and freedom of assembly in Russia, about our persecution of Mensheviks and Menshevik workers, and so forth. I replied that the real culprits of the terror are the imperialists of Britain and their "allies," who have been and are conducting White terror in Finland and Hungary, in India and Ireland, who have been and are supporting Yudenich, Kolchak, Denikin, Pilsudski, and Wrangel. Our Red terror is a defense of the working class against the exploiters; it is the suppression of the resistance of the exploiters . . . Freedom of the press and of assembly in a bourgeois democracy are tantamount to a conspiracy against the toilers; they are the freedom of capitalists to bribe and to buy up newspapers. I have so often explained this in the press that it is not very entertaining to me to repeat myself. . . .

In conclusion, I once more thank you, comrades, for sending us your delegation. The fact of their having become acquainted with Soviet Russia, despite the hostility of many of them toward the Soviet system and the dictatorship of the proletariat, despite their extraordinary subjection to bourgeois prejudices, will inevitably result in speeding up the collapse of capitalism throughout the world.

THE END OF THE WAR WITH POLAND

9

Peace Negotiations Between Soviet and Polish Delegations at Minsk

[First Meeting, August 17, 1920][15]

DANISZEWSKI (*Soviet delegate*) : . . . The Russian government comes here with peaceful intentions and it desires, as it did before, a settlement of ethnographic

[15] Full text in Jan Dąbski, *Pokój Ryski,* pp. 42–44; also *Izvestiia,* No. 183, August 19, 1920, p. 1, and No. 184, August 21, 1920, p. 1.

and territorial problems favorable to the Polish state. The policy of Soviet Russia and the Ukraine,[16] i.e., the policy of the toilers who live by their own labor and do not exploit others, has always been a policy of peace, of the friendly settlement of all conflicts with other peoples. We are not conquerors; we are defending ourselves against an enemy who attacked us; and we shall leave Polish territory as soon as we are given guarantees that the [Polish] leaders have abandoned their policy of conquest. . . .

Reply of the Polish delegation, August 19, 1920: The delegation of the Polish republic has come to Minsk to establish conditions of an armistice and peace, and thus to end the centuries-old Russo-Polish dispute, into which both peoples were drawn by the aggressive policies of the tsarist governments.

The Polish people did not desire and did not start this war against the R.S.F.S.R. It was thrust upon Poland when the Soviet government, having occupied at the close of 1918 the territories of Lithuania and Belorussia, and having forced a soviet regime upon these countries, advanced its troops to the ethnographic boundaries of Poland with the definite intention of marching on Warsaw, overthrowing the democratic regime of the Polish republic, and establishing, against the wishes of the population, a soviet order in Poland. The young Polish republic . . . was obliged, because of the danger threatening her and her liberties, to repel the attack of the Soviet government. . . .

As far as purely Russian territories are concerned, the Polish republic has never revealed any imperialist designs, because no Polish soldier has ever entered such territories, while it is hardly possible to suppose that the government of the R.S.F.S.R. considers itself the legal heir to the robberies committed by the tsarist government in the period of the partition of Poland. . . .

[A lasting peace is possible only if a just agreement is reached in the interests of both states.] . . .

The complete sovereignty and independence of the Polish republic within the territories needed by her for her economic and political development, absolute non-interference in her domestic affairs—these are the fundamental requirements for our peaceful coexistence in the future. Poland, on her part, fully accepting the prinicple that each people should have the form of government it chooses, does not intend to interfere in the affairs of other peoples. . . .

[Second Meeting, August 21, 1920][17]

DANISZEWSKI: . . . Citizen-representatives of the Polish republic! We declare before you, as we have already declared before the world, that we recognize the complete independence and sovereignty of the Polish state. We have actually proved by our policy toward the smaller states that what we say is not mere words. The recent occurrences in the relations between the R.S.F.S.R. and the Lithuanian republic[18] can serve as the best confirmation of this policy. The troops of the R.S.F.S.R. did not interfere with the self-determination of that country; on the contrary, they made this self-determination possible. The troops of the R.S.F.S.R. and the Ukrainian S.S.R. do not use their bayonets to force their own political regime and their own economic and social way of life, i.e., communism, upon other peoples. These peoples themselves must freely choose their own destiny, and we declare that in Poland also we do not intend to establish soviet order and communism with Russian bayonets.

---

[16] The Soviet delegation included representatives from the R.S.F.S.R. (i.e., Russia proper) and the Ukrainian S.S.R.

[17] *Izvestiia*, No. 184, August 21, 1920, p. 1; full text is also given in Dąbski, *Pokój Ryski*, pp. 48–51.

[18] This refers to the signing of a peace treaty between Soviet Russia and Lithuania on July 12, 1920. By this treaty, the city of Vilna, taken from the Poles by the Red Army, was returned to Lithuania.

A communist order is possible only when the large majority of the toilers fully accept the idea of establishing it by their own efforts. Our heroic army has but one task: to defend its toilers' republic. . . . We do not desire to continue the war . . . , we want peace . . . , and we wish to safeguard ourselves from new attacks. In order to achieve this end, we propose that the Polish republic's armed forces and armament be reduced. We do not wish to weaken the internal power of the Polish toiling people . . . ; we believe that the armed forces of the Polish republic can be strengthened by a civil militia made up of workers, which would give stability to the foreign policy of Poland. . . .

In order to re-establish the national economy ruined by war, and to make possible the closest co-operation between the neighboring peoples . . . , we propose that the R.S.F.S.R. and the Ukrainian S.S.R. be granted free transit through Poland. We are convinced that the Polish government will satisfy this fair request, and we declare that immediately upon the conclusion of an armistice, we shall withdraw our army into the interior [of Russia], leaving not more than 200,000 armed men in the regions adjoining the central zone . . .

[Our] general proposals can be formulated as follows:

1. The R.S.F.S.R. and the Ukrainian S.S.R. recognize the independence and sovereignty of the Polish republic, and they solemnly affirm the absolute right of the Polish people to organize their lives and their form of political government as they choose.

2. The R.S.F.S.R. and the Ukrainian S.S.R. renounce any form of indemnity.

3. The final [eastern] frontier of Poland shall run approximately along the line indicated by Lord Curzon in his note of July 11, with changes in favor of the Polish republic to the east [of that line] in the Bialystok and Chelm regions.

4. The Polish republic must reduce all its armed forces, without exception, to 50,000 men as an annual contingent, . . . while the officer personnel must not exceed 10,000 men. The Polish armed forces will be strengthened by the addition of civil militia recruited from among the workers and charged with safeguarding the order and security of the population. The conditions of the organization of this militia will be outlined during the examination of the details of the peace treaty.

5. Immediately after the signing of the treaty, Poland will start to demobilize her forces. Demobilization must be accomplished within a month in accordance with rules and dates to be fixed in the treaty.

6. Poland will retain such firearms and war matériel as may be required by the armed forces mentioned in Paragraph 4 above. The remaining ammunition, including arsenals, must be handed over to the Russian and Ukrainian authorities within a month after the signing of the preliminary peace treaty. . . . From this matériel, Russia and the Ukraine will supply the necessary quantity to the civil militia. . . .

7. Poland will cease the production of ammunition and will start the demobilization of her war industries, in order to have this task completed by a date to be fixed by a mixed commission.

8. Poland will not permit troops, horses, firearms, or war matériel from other states and governments to enter her territory. Likewise, she will not permit any organizations hostile to Russia and the Ukraine on her territory.

9. Hostilities will cease seventy-two hours after the signing of the treaty. The Russian and Ukrainian armies will remain on the line they hold on that date, but not to the west of the line indicated in Lord Curzon's note of July 11. The Polish army will move back [until it is] fifty versts west of the Russian and Ukrainian armies. . . .

10. After the demobilization [of the Polish army], [and the relinquishing of war matériel] to Russia and the Ukraine by the Polish authorities, . . . only 200,000 Russian forces will remain on the line of the neutral zone.

11. Poland must make restitution to the regions that it occupied of such railway stock, postal and telegraphic matériel, and agricultural and industrial machinery as Polish authorities removed to their own regions. Poland must also reconstruct destroyed bridges by dates to be fixed in the peace treaty. . . .

12. Poland must pass a law by which land will be distributed gratis to the families of Polish citizens killed or wounded during or in connection with armed hostilities.

13. Poland will give Russia and the Ukraine the right of free transit for passengers and goods, and the Wolkowysk-Bialystok-Grajewo railway line will remain in the possession and under the control of the Russian republic.

14. Poland must grant complete amnesty to political and military offenders.

15. Immediately upon the signing of the peace treaty, Poland must make public this treaty, and also other documents and materials dealing with the war . . .

10

New Peace Proposals by the Soviet Government

[Declaration of the All-Russian Central Executive Committee, September 23, 1920, Signed by Kalinin, Its Chairman, and Chicherin, People's Commissar of Foreign Affairs][19]

The war between Poland and Russia, caused by Poland's attacking Russia and the Ukraine at a time when the toiling people of Russia were beginning to demobilize their armies and to direct all their energy to peaceful and constructive work, continues. This war, which is being supported by the Entente in its own imperialistic interests, threatens a hard winter campaign, extremely cruel, ruinous, and bloody. Its continuation can be desired by the Entente imperialists only because they wish to profit by the exhaustion of the vital forces of Poland and Russia.

. . . [Consequently,] the Soviet Russian government and the highest legislative body of the republic, the All-Russian Central Executive Committee, consider it their duty to take all possible measures to attain peace and prevent the shedding of blood in a winter campaign that would prove exceedingly hard for both sides.

The All-Russian Central Executive Committee believes that a desirable agreement can be reached in the shortest time possible by applying the principle of self-determination to all regions whose territorial frontiers have been disputed during the present war.

Starting with the principle of self-determination, the R.S.F.S.R. recognized as early as 1917, and continues to recognize fully and absolutely, without any reservations, the independence and sovereignty of the Polish republic. The R.S.F.S.R. likewise recognized the independence and sovereignty of the Ukraine and Belorussia in 1918, and in 1920 signed a peace treaty with the independent and sovereign Lithuanian republic.

In pursuance of this same policy, the All-Russian Central Executive Committee believes that the basis of peace should be expressed first of all by an immediate and solemn confirmation, by both Russia and Poland, of the independence of the Ukraine, Lithuania, and Belorussia, and by recognition of the independence of Eastern Galicia. Second, both Poland and Russia should recognize immediately and officially the governmental bodies of these states (be they Sejm, Parliament, or Congress of Soviets), which already exist and which express the will of the people of these states. On its part, the R.S.F.S.R. recognizes that a soviet regime has not yet been established in Eastern Galicia, and agrees to a plebiscite in this region to be carried on according

[19] *Izvestiia,* No. 213, September 25, 1920, p. 1.

to the soviet principle, i.e., by the vote of those who toil and not on the general bourgeois-democratic basis.

The All-Russian Central Executive Committee, however, must note that certain leading Polish public circles, political parties, and statesmen differ basically from the R.S.F.S.R. in their views on self-determination. If the Polish delegates in Riga agree with those parties, groups, and persons who, in spite of the evidence, deny what happened in 1918, i.e., deny the self-determination of the Ukraine and Belorussia, then no agreement based on self-determination can be reached and negotiations concerning the manner of self-determination will be useless. . . .

Consequently, in order to avoid ambiguity or delay in regard to the main problem that concerns the toilers, i.e., the possibility of a winter campaign, the All-Russian Central Executive Committee instructs its peace delegation to request the Polish peace delegation, if no agreement can be reached immediately on self-determination, to conclude an agreement on the basic principles of peace, temporarily postponing the settlement of disputed points on the following basis:

1. The government of the R.S.F.S.R. takes into account the declaration of the Polish delegation that Poland cannot accept the Russo-Ukrainian delegation's preliminary conditions concerning the reduction of the size of Poland's army, the demobilization of her war industries, the surrender by her of arms, and the transfer of the Wolkowysk-Grajewo railway line to the R.S.F.S.R. The government of the R.S.F.S.R. now withdraws these conditions, and expresses its willingness to propose that the allied Ukrainian republic do the same.

2. The R.S.F.S.R. is ready to sign an armistice and preliminaries of peace immediately, based on recognition of a frontier between Poland and Russia considerably east of the line established by the Supreme Allied Council on December 3, 1919, so that Eastern Galicia would remain west of this line.

The R.S.F.S.R. believes that this proposal clears the way to the quickest possible peace, a peace that will release the Russian, Polish, Belorussian, and Ukrainian toilers from the burden of a new winter campaign.

The repudiation of this offer by Poland would mean that Poland had decided, probably under pressure of the imperialists of France and other countries of the Entente, to conduct another winter campaign. Therefore, the All-Russian Central Execctive Committee is obliged to state that the above proposal is valid for only ten days [after this declaration is made known to the Polish delegation]. If at the end of this period, i.e., before October 5, 1920, the preliminaries of peace have not been signed, the Council of People's Commissars reserves the right to change its conditions. . . .[20]

[20] In replying on September 24 to this new Soviet proposal, the Polish government outlined its conditions for the cessation of hostilities. The first two points of the Polish proposal read as follows:

"1. The contracting parties mutually guarantee to respect each other's political sovereignty, and to abstain from interfering in each other's internal affairs.

"2. The delimitation by the contracting parties of the territories of the Polish republic which were included in the former Russian Empire must be based on the following principles: (a) . . . the frontier line will be established not upon some historical claim but on the basis of a just consideration of the vital interests of the agreeing parties; (b) the national problems in the above territories must be settled justly and in accordance with democratic principles; (c) a durable security for each of the contracting parties from possible attack by the other party must be provided.

"Desiring peace and not wishing to press her own conditions for it, Poland invites the other party to outline the frontiers jointly on the basis of the above-stated principles." (Izvestiia, No. 214, September 26, 1920, p. 1; full text appears also in Dąbski, Pokój Ryski, pp. 83–86.)

11

Statements on the Conclusion of the Soviet-Polish Treaty

[1. Jan Dąbski, Head of the Polish Delegation][21]

The peace treaty we have just signed marks the beginning and the foundation of a new period in the life and development of the Polish and Russian nations. After more than a century of the Polish nation's struggle for independence, after two years of a severe and bloody war, there follows a period of peace and mutual co-operation. The eastern half of Europe, hitherto shaken by war and confusion, will return to normal conditions. Hundreds of thousands of people on both sides who have had to fight or be kept under arms will be able to return to their work, and as before, the soil, drenched with blood, will start to feed the tormented masses of Europe.

Here in this hall we have worked out between Poland and Russia and the Ukraine a peace of understanding. Following the principle of self-determination of nations, [acting] together and out of our free will, we have recognized the independence of the Ukraine and of Belorussia. By mutual agreement we have drawn the frontiers and have decided not to interfere in each other's domestic affairs; we have established the widest rights for national minorities; we have granted the amplest possible rights of option in favor of either of the two sides; we have reached agreement concerning many intricate economic and financial problems; and we have laid the foundations for future economic and political relations. We have endeavored to settle all problems in a fair and righteous way; we have made mutual concessions not only in order to reach agreement, but also to facilitate our future relations. However, the peace treaty, until carried out, remains a dead letter. Only its execution can determine the actual relations between the contracting nations. I can state categorically that the Polish republic will loyally carry out all the obligations this treaty imposes upon it. I am confident the other party will do the same, and for these reasons I believe in the permanence of this peace.

Poland, maintaining an independent policy of sincere peace and co-operation with her eastern neighbors, wants to be a bridge, not a barrier, between the East and the West. Thus she wants close economic relations with Russia, the Ukraine, and Belorussia, because mutual economic interests are the most durable foundation of peace. Such is not only the sincere intention, but also the positive program of the Polish government. Its execution will depend on mutual good will and on mutual understanding of common interests.

The treaty of peace, which we have concluded after long and painstaking work, exists mainly because the nations concerned saw the imperative need for such a peace, both for themselves and for the world at large; but also because of the good will both nations brought to their work. On behalf of the Polish delegation, therefore, I express my sincere thanks to the honorable Russian-Ukrainian delegation for its desire for peace and for its work to attain this peace. First of all, I address my thanks to the honorable president of this delegation, who, by his realistic approach, by his knowledge of affairs, by his diplomatic talent and ability to find a compromise in most difficult situations, did so much to make the peace negotiations successful. In bidding you farewell, gentlemen, now that our difficult and responsible work is over, I want to assure you on my own and my colleagues' behalf, that despite numerous and inevitable frictions, we shall retain forever the memory of our common work. I hope the Russian, Ukrainian, and Belorussian nations will come to see that the Polish nation

[21] Dąbski, *Pokój Ryski,* pp. 187–89.

desires to live with them in sincere, neighborly, and fraternal concord and peace; that it desires economic co-operation with them, in order both to reconstruct its own country and to help—according to its ability—its neighbors in their work of reconstruction. . . .

[2. Adolf Ioffe, Head of the Soviet Delegation][22]

Despite the attempts made by the enemies of the soviet republics, who—after the complete failure of armed intervention—are trying to start a new intervention against Russia and the Ukraine by discrediting them in the eyes of nations desiring peaceful co-operation with them, the language of facts is plain. While a skillful campaign of slander and lies is being carried on to convince people that Soviet Russia and the Ukraine are weak, the soviet rule is being consolidated not only where it has flourished before, but also in areas to which it has not hitherto extended. While the same enemies of the soviet republics tried to use the same slander to intimidate the neighbors of Russia and the Ukraine with rumors about "soviet aggressiveness" and with reports about strong forces of the Red Army concentrated on the frontiers, we here in Riga have been calmly negotiating a peace. Not only have we displayed no aggressiveness, but we have signed a peace treaty that gives satisfaction to the vital, legitimate, and essential interests of the Polish nation.

Thanks to the peaceful policy of Russia and the Ukraine, the old maxim *si vis pacem para bellum* is gradually becoming obsolete and passing into the sphere of legends, while another axiom is triumphant, the axiom I have mentioned so often: namely, that peaceful relations between nations are inaugurated and not terminated by the conclusion of a peace treaty.

None of the peace treaties concluded by Russia and the Ukraine permits preparations for a new war, because none of these treaties leaves any problems unsolved, nor are any solved simply on the basis of a relationship of forces [of the contracting parties], as was formerly done at the expense of some of the nations concluding such treaties. Nations which receive all that is essential to them will themselves take care to see that such a peace is permanent.

By the conclusion of the peace treaty with Poland a series of arrangements have been set for peaceful relations between all the states that belonged to the former Russian Empire, and the tsarist regime of violence has been ended; the nations that have separated without hate or ill-feeling, and are animated by sincere friendship, can and should now develop on the basis of good neighborly relations those bonds of economic rapprochement and community which exist among them as the result of belonging for some centuries to the same state.

I have heard here with deep satisfaction the words spoken by the president of the Polish delegation, who presented the positive program of the Polish government with his characteristic statesmanship. I am happy to declare on behalf of Russia and the Ukraine that if Poland's policy is really not inspired by any interests alien to the Polish nation, the relations of friendship and good neighborliness mentioned by the president of the Polish delegation will certainly be established between the countries concluding the present peace treaty. The establishing of close economic relations with a free Poland, with an independent policy of her own, is the aim the governments of Russia, the Ukraine, and Belorussia have in view; these countries are and will be willing to help their neighbors economically as much as they can.

The peace negotiations lasted several months and often encountered considerable difficulties, especially over economic and financial problems. I must state, however, that both while guns were firing along the front line and blood was being shed, and during the period of calmer conditions [i.e., negotiations], the practical knowledge

[22] *Ibid.,* pp. 190–92.

and tact displayed by the Polish delegation and particularly by its president have greatly assisted both the progress of the negotiations and the possibility of their successful conclusion.

In closing my address, I should like to express on behalf of the Russian-Ukrainian peace delegation our gratitude to the Polish delegation, and particularly to its president.

12

Lenin on War with Poland

[Speech at a Congress of Leather Industry Workers,
October 2, 1920][23]

. . .

The Poles thrust the war upon us, but we know that the main instigators of this war were neither the Polish landlords nor the Polish capitalists because the situation in Poland has been, and still is, much too shaky. Yet in their desperation they [the Polish landlords and capitalists] were willing to try a venture against us. The main force that incited the Poles into war against us was, of course, international capital, and first of all French capital. We have discovered that hundreds of French officers have been and still are active in the Polish army, that all Poland's ammunition, her financial aid, and her military help have come from France.

This accounts for the beginning of the Polish war. Essentially it was a new attempt by the Allies to destroy the Soviet republic.

. . .

I believe (and this is very important) that the present Polish war is the last attempt on Soviet Russia [by the Entente]. . . . You know that the Allied imperialists— France, England, America, and Japan—after defeating Germany forced the Germans to sign the Versailles treaty, a treaty even more brutal than the notorious Brest treaty about which everyone cried so much. . . . One reason this monstrous peace is maintained is that Poland splits Germany into two parts, as the Polish state now has an outlet to the sea. . . . The Versailles treaty has made Poland a buffer state, a state designed to safeguard Germany from Soviet communism, and which the Entente regards as an instrument to be used against the Bolsheviks. With Polish help, the French hope to regain the billions of rubles they loaned the tsarist government. That is why, when the war against Poland broke out . . . it proved to be a war against the Entente more than did the earlier [interventionist] wars. . . .

When we advanced victoriously on Poland, a scream for peace rose from all Europe: It was shouted that the world was tired of war, that the time had come to make peace. But did the scream continue when the Poles advanced? No, Europe was no longer tired of war. What caused the mood to change so rapidly? It is this: When we won over Yudenich, Kolchak, and Denikin, we still could not break the Versailles treaty, . . . but in advancing against Poland we were really advancing against the Entente; in destroying the Polish army we were really destroying the Versailles treaty, upon which the entire structure of present international relations rests.

If Poland had become a soviet country, if Soviet Russia had given the Warsaw workers the help they expected and wanted, the Versailles treaty would have been destroyed and the whole international system established by the [Allies'] victories over Germany would have been destroyed along with it. France would have had no buffer state to separate Germany from Soviet Russia, no battering-ram to use against

[23] Lenin, *Sochineniia*, XXV, 399, 401–2.

the Soviet republic. France would have had to abandon the hope of being paid billions of rubles. . . . France is now heavily in debt, whereas before she was a rich moneylender. She now owes America three times as much as the other countries owe America. She is not far from bankruptcy, and her situation is truly hopeless. You can perhaps understand now why the march of the Red troops to Warsaw precipitated an international crisis, and why it was that the bourgeois press was so alarmed. Briefly the situation was this: If the triumphant march of the Red Army had continued a few more days, not only would Warsaw have been taken (which is not so important), but the Versailles treaty itself would have been smashed. . . .

13

The Failure to Establish Soviets in Poland

a

[Statement by Trotsky, October 20, 1920][24]

. . .

I believe that everyone now agrees that the outcome of the war with Poland did not satisfy our expectations and our hopes.

If we had not been hindered by the necessity of assigning forces to Wrangel's front, we would have been very strong on the Polish front. Then the war would have ended quite differently. We also had to consider to what extent our advance on Warsaw would meet with fighting revolutionary co-operation from the Polish proletariat. [Actually] instead of the revolutionary working class, we found in Poland splendidly armed counterrevolutionary detachments.

. . . In our advance on Warsaw, we carried on an attack on a world-wide scale. We were defeated. Nevertheless, the results of this attack can be seen already in the growth and development of the revolutionary communist movement in Western Europe. Even in our defeat at the Warsaw front we won a momentous victory from the standpoint of the general strategy of both the war and the revolution. We have given impetus to the development of the revolution in Germany. Does this mean that we are not interested in peace with Poland? Nothing of the kind! We wanted peace, but we were obliged to fight, and while fighting we sought the maximum of success, but it escaped us, and we agreed to hard conditions of peace. Are we going to break this peace, as France and other countries are predicting, in order to intimidate Poland? No. They lie. We now want peace most of all, so that we can continue our peaceful labors. . . .

b

[Statement by Julian Marchlewski][25]

. . . The establishment of a soviet order in Poland as a result of the Red Army's victory would undoubtedly have considerably advanced the development of the revolutionary movement in Europe. But as this goal was not reached, we are apparently entering a somewhat quieter period in the development of the revolution. Peace will make it possible for Soviet Russia to grow stronger and, at the same time, will revolutionize bourgeois Poland.

[24] *Izvestiia,* No. 236, October 22, 1920, p. 1.

[25] Julian Marchlewski, "Mir s Polshei," *Kommunisticheskii Internatsional,* No. 14, 1920, p. 2754.

C

[Statement by D. Z. Manuilsky][26]

. . . Our defeat at the front was primarily a strategic defeat. Our army moved forward so quickly that it left behind it hundreds of kilometers with no reserves, no supplies. . . . The opinion of some silly heads that we advanced into the interior of Poland against the will of the Polish proletariat, or even the Polish Communists, is such a mean lie that we do not even think it necessary to repudiate it. . . .

What caused the difficulty in Riga [during peace negotiations] was that we actually had at our diplomatic table the Entente, whose eastern outpost is Poland. In negotiating with Poland we were actually negotiating with the Allied powers, which were standing behind the Polish delegates. And the fact that in Riga the soviet republics, while defending themselves from the European vultures, succeeded in obtaining conditions much more favorable than those which Soviet Russia and the Ukraine were obliged to sign in Brest, shows that the international position of the Soviet government has been consolidated. . . . In Riga we did not and could not consider ourselves defeated, for the Polish army did not stand outside the walls of Kharkov or Moscow; instead, not so long ago, our own Red Army approached the walls of Warsaw. [The other factor was the pressure of the international proletariat.] . . . We can definitely say that if the Italian events[27] had developed into open class war . . . we would have had a much more advantageous peace treaty. . . .

14

The End of Proletarian and Imperialist Offensives

[Ioffe's Statement in 1921 on the Significance of Peace with Poland][28]

The Soviet government, born under the sign of a struggle for peace, was obliged from the moment of its birth to pass to a "peaceful offensive" against the bourgeois order because an armed offensive was not possible, while the coexistence of a soviet government with the imperialistic ones appeared unthinkable. Imperialism, however, proved stronger than one might have supposed, and the revolutionary proletariat was exhausted by the four years of slaughter and the continuous betrayals by its old leaders. The world revolution was delayed. In that way the peaceful offensive of the Soviet government became a means of self-defense. However, the Soviet government actually transformed this defensive action into victory over all its enemies.

Nevertheless, the hard struggle so weakened both contending parties that they can no longer crush and destroy one another immediately, and are now obliged to coexist for a time. What appeared impossible is actually taking place: soviet republics remain within the limits of an imperialist world. . . .

The conclusion of peace with Poland marks the beginning of these new relations between the two contending forces. The Riga peace treaty ends the period of intervention and the period of an open armed struggle by the world imperialists against

[26] *Kommunisticheskii Internatsional*, No. 15, 1920, pp. 3076–79.

[27] In the autumn of 1920, workers in the north of Italy occupied some six hundred factories and held them for several weeks. The government took no action against them, but since they were unable to procure raw materials or sell products, they were obliged to return the seized factories to their owners.

[28] A. A. Ioffe, *Mirnoe nastuplenie*, pp. 3–4. Full text of the treaty between Poland and the R.S.F.S.R., the Belorussian S.S.R., and the Ukrainian S.S.R. appears in Shapiro, I, 105–16.

the soviet republics. . . . The bourgeois world has been bound, and has actually passed to new tactics in its struggle.

Thus the Riga treaty, by marking a turning point in this struggle, acquires particular significance. . . .

THE TRADE AGREEMENT WITH BRITAIN

15

Criticism of the British Draft of the Trade Agreement
[Editorial by Iu. M. Steklov][29]

Since the very first day of the October Revolution the Soviet government has never stopped proposing peace to the British government. For three years the British government has seized every possible excuse to postpone its answer, at the same time continuing its hostile actions against Soviet Russia. Last summer, after a long series of procrastinations and postponements, there appeared some hope that an agreement was about to be concluded. In its note of July 7 [1920], the Soviet government declared its readiness to accept the principles put forward by the British government on June 30 as a basis for an agreement between the two countries. Our government, moreover, at that time as well as later, emphasized that it considered the plan suggested by the British government a kind of armistice between Russia and Great Britain, a preparation for a final peace to be negotiated later. Besides, the Russian government has always maintained that negotiations for a commercial agreement should be accompanied by political negotiations, or that political negotiations should begin immediately after the conclusion of a commercial agreement.

For almost six months the British government has been protracting negotiations, and now at last it has produced a commercial agreement. But the Soviet government can hardly consider this commercial agreement acceptable and in the interests of both parties. First of all, most striking in this draft is the absence of the basic characteristic of similar international agreements, namely, reciprocity. The British draft imposes upon the Soviet government a great number of one-sided obligations, and on such obligations as *are* reciprocal it consistently intensifies the Russian government's responsibility in contrast to that of the British government. Moreover, in violation of the spirit and the letter of the preceding negotiations, the British draft bears a kind of final character and says nothing of the peace conference which, according to the Russian proposals, was to follow the trade agreement and settle all questions at issue between the two governments. Apparently the British government does not want this peace conference, but does not dare to say so openly.

. . .

Such one-sided obligations could only be imposed by a victorious country on a conquered country. But Soviet Russia does not consider herself a conquered country at all, and much as she desires a speedy conclusion of peace, she feels no inclination to humbly accept ultimatums that are dictated to her. For three years Britain has been fighting Soviet Russia; for three years she has been arming our enemies, killing our citizens in the north, the east, and the south; yet she has not been victorious in this conflict. On the contrary, since all her agents have been crushed, since her undertakings against the Soviet republic have been failures, and since the Soviet government, after a three years' war and after having recovered almost all Russian territory, has concluded peace with almost all of its recent adversaries and is now

[29] *Izvestiia,* No. 295, December 30, 1920, p. 1.

much stronger than ever before—it is clearly the British government that has suffered defeat. Soviet Russia does not believe this gives her the right to impose one-sided obligations upon anyone for her own benefit, but at the same time she is firmly determined to reject any attempts to impose such obligations upon herself.

Humanity needs peace. Soviet Russia also needs peace, in order to begin peaceful reconstruction. To obtain this peace, the Soviet government has repeatedly shown its readiness to make concessions. But it has always emphasized that its yielding has certain limits and that it will never permit anybody to treat Russia as a vanquished country.

16

Shortcomings and Advantages of the Anglo-Soviet Trade Agreement

[Krasin's Comments][30]

. . .

I shall not give a detailed history of all the negotiations, but shall only state that the final reason the signing of the treaty was hastened was, very likely, that in March 1921 the Soviet government placed a big order with German factories for 600 locomotives. Quite possibly it was the fear of losing this large order that forced the British government to instruct the British Minister of Trade, Sir Robert Horne, to sign with me on March 16, 1921, a Russo-British agreement, even though guns were still firing around Kronstadt and the Kronstadt revolt had not yet been liquidated. . . .

The treaty signed by us with Britain has serious defects. First, despite our often repeated offer to sign a peace treaty, the British government agreed to conclude only a trade agreement, which does not provide for *de jure* recognition of the Soviet government and the full re-establishment of diplomatic relations between the two countries. The treaty we signed is only a trade agreement, and in it the Soviet Russian government is recognized only as a *de facto* government, i.e., as the actually existing government. Second, with only a year's notice this treaty can be declared invalid by either of the contracting parties. In addition, each of the countries (here I must note that the entire agreement was concluded on the principle of reciprocity, i.e., all our guarantees to England carried reciprocal guarantees from England to Russia), each of the contracting parties can declare the treaty null and void if it finds the other party guilty of hostile propaganda or of supporting some action hostile to it. Obviously, since many possibilities arise for a conflict of interests between such large countries as Russia and Britain, an excuse can be found at any moment for terminating the agreement. [Goes on to describe Soviet efforts to avoid these conditions.] . . .

The next shortcoming of the treaty is that it does not officially safeguard the inviolability of Soviet property in England. True, the British government has promised not to arrest [Soviet] officials or to confiscate goods and ships belonging to the Soviet government, but it did not guarantee that British courts would not attach Russian property upon suit by a third party with claims against the Soviet government. . . .

Since we concluded the trade agreement with Britain our losses on gold, which until then we had sold exclusively at Reval [Tallinn], have diminished to approxi-

---

[30] L. B. Krasin, *Vneshtorg i vneshniaia ekonomicheskaia politika sovetskogo pravitelstva*, pp. 11–16.

mately 6 per cent . . . The gold blockade has gradually been lifted. At the present moment, with the American charity organization[31] working in Russia, and its chairman, American Secretary of Commerce Hoover, having offered to carry on our purchases of food supplies in America through his mediation, I believe that we can consider the gold blockade finally broken, since it is hard to believe that the Americans, when buying food supplies for our starving population, would venture to reduce the price of gold artificially. And if America accepts our gold coin at its full value, we may be sure that other powers, and consequently all European banks, will do the same. This break in the gold blockade, which has cost us several months of stubborn and persistent struggle, is a characteristic example of the methods and means by which we are obliged to defend, step by step, our commercial interests and to insist on normal conditions of work.

Despite its shortcomings, the Russo-English agreement is a very important step toward liberating our foreign trade. . . . We can consider our import trade practically free of restriction. We are not tied down by any restrictions aside from those which apply to all other countries. . . .

THE SEARCH FOR RECOGNITION
BY OTHER STATES

17

The Absence of Rapprochement Between Soviet Russia and the United States

a

[American Policy Toward Soviet Russia Defined by Bainbridge Colby, United States Secretary of State, in a Letter to the Italian Ambassador, August 10, 1920, Usually Spoken of as "the Colby Note"][32]

Excellency: The agreeable intimation, which you have conveyed to the State Department that the Italian Government would welcome a statement of the views of this Government on the situation presented by the Russian advance into Poland, deserves a prompt response, and I will attempt without delay, a definition of this Government's position not only as to the situation arising from Russian military pressure upon Poland, but also as to certain cognate and inseparable phases of the Russian question viewed more broadly.

This Government believes in a united, free and autonomous Polish State and the people of the United States are earnestly solicitous for the maintenance of Poland's political independence and territorial integrity. From this attitude we will not depart, and the policy of this Government will be directed to the employment of all available means to render it effectual. The Government therefore takes no exception to the effort apparently being made in some quarters to arrange an armistice between Poland and Russia, but it would not, at least for the present, participate in any plan for the expansion of the armistice negotiations into a general European conference which would in all probability involve two results, from both of which this country strongly recoils, viz., the recognition of the Bolshevist regime and a settlement of Russian problems almost inevitably upon the basis of a dismemberment of Russia.

[31] The American Relief Administration. The story of the use of Russian gold for relief is told in H. H. Fisher, *The Famine in Soviet Russia, 1919–1923,* pp. 154–59.

[32] *Foreign Relations of the United States, 1920,* III, 463–68.

From the beginning of the Russian Revolution, in March, 1917, to the present moment, the Government and the people of the United States have followed its development with friendly solicitude and with profound sympathy for the efforts of the Russian people to reconstruct their national life upon the broad basis of popular self-government. The Government of the United States, reflecting the spirit of its people, has at all times desired to help the Russian people. In that spirit all its relations with Russia, and with other nations in matters affecting the latter's interests, have been conceived and governed.

The Government of the United States was the first government to acknowledge the validity of the Revolution and to give recognition to the Provisional Government of Russia. Almost immediately thereafter it became necessary for the United States to enter the war against Germany and in that undertaking to become closely associated with the Allied Nations, including, of course, Russia. The war weariness of the masses of the Russian people was fully known to this Government and sympathetically comprehended. Prudence, self-interest and loyalty to our associates made it desirable that we should give moral and material support to the Provisional Government, which was struggling to accomplish a two-fold task, to carry on the war with vigor, and, at the same time, to reorganize the life of the nation and establish a stable government based on popular sovereignty.

Quite independent of these motives, however, was the sincere friendship of the Government and the people of the United States for the great Russian nation. The friendship manifested by Russia toward this nation in a time of trial and distress has left us with an imperishable sense of gratitude. It was as a grateful friend that we sent to Russia an expert commission to aid in bringing about such a reorganization of the railroad transportation system of the country as would reinvigorate the whole of its economic life and so add to the well-being of the Russian people.

While deeply regretting the withdrawal of Russia from the war at a critical time, and the disastrous surrender at Brest-Litovsk, the United States has fully understood that the people of Russia were in no wise responsible.

The United States maintains unimpaired its faith in the Russian people, in their high character and their future. That they will overcome the existing anarchy, suffering and destitution we do not entertain the slightest doubt. The distressing character of Russia's transition has many historical parallels, and the United States is confident that restored, free and united Russia will again take a leading place in the world, joining with the other free nations in upholding peace and orderly justice.

Until that time shall arrive the United States feels that friendship and honor require that Russia's interests must be generously protected, and that, as far as possible, all decisions of vital importance to it, and especially those concerning its sovereignty over the territory of the former Russian Empire, be held in abeyance. By this feeling of friendship and honorable obligation to the great nation whose brave and heroic self-sacrifice contributed so much to the successful termination of the war, the Government of the United States was guided in its reply to the Lithuanian National Council, on October 15, 1919, and in its persistent refusal to recognize the Baltic States as separate nations independent of Russia. The same spirit was manifested in the note of this Government, of March 24, 1920, in which it was stated, with reference to certain proposed settlements in the Near East, that "no final decision should or can be made without the consent of Russia."

In line with these important declarations of policy, the United States withheld its approval from the decision of the Supreme Council at Paris recognizing the independence of the socalled republics of Georgia and Azerbaijan, and so instructed its representative in Southern Russia, Rear-Admiral Newton A. McCully. Finally, while gladly giving recognition to the independence of Armenia, the Government of the United States has taken the position that the final determination of its boundaries must not be made without Russia's cooperation and agreement. Not only is

Russia concerned because a considerable part of the territory of the new State of Armenia, when it shall be defined, formerly belonged to the Russian Empire: equally important is the fact that Armenia must have the good will and the protective friendship of Russia if it is to remain independent and free.

These illustrations show with what consistency the Government of the United States has been guided in its foreign policy by a loyal friendship for Russia. We are unwilling that while it is helpless in the grip of a non-representative government, whose only sanction is brutal force, Russia shall be weakened still further by a policy of dismemberment, conceived in other than Russian interests.

With the desire of the Allied Powers to bring about a peaceful solution of the existing difficulties in Europe, this Government is of course in hearty accord, and will support any justifiable step to that end. It is unable to perceive, however, that a recognition of the Soviet regime would promote, much less accomplish this object, and it is therefore averse to any dealings with the Soviet regime beyond the most narrow boundaries to which a discussion of an armistice can be confined.

That the present rulers of Russia do not rule by the will or the consent of any considerable proportion of the Russian people is an incontestable fact. Although nearly two and a half years have passed since they seized the machinery of government, promising to protect the Constituent Assembly against alleged conspiracies against it, they have not yet permitted anything in the nature of a popular election. At the moment when the work of creating a popular representative government based upon universal suffrage was nearing completion the Bolsheviki, although, in number, an inconsiderable minority of the people, by force and cunning seized the powers and machinery of government and have continued to use them with savage oppression to maintain themselves in power.

Without any desire to interfere in the internal affairs of the Russian people, or to suggest what kind of government they should have, the Government of the United States does express the hope that they will soon find a way to set up a government representing their free will and purpose. When the time comes, the United States will consider the measures of practical assistance which can be taken to promote the restoration of Russia, provided Russia has not taken itself wholly out of the pale of the friendly interest of other nations, by the pillage and oppression of the Poles.

It is not possible for the Government of the United States to recognize the present rulers of Russia as a government with which the relations common to friendly governments can be maintained. This conviction has nothing to do with any particular political or social structure which the Russian people themselves may see fit to embrace. It rests upon a wholly different set of facts. These facts, which none dispute, have convinced the Government of the United States, against its will, that the existing regime in Russia is based upon the negation of every principle of honor and good faith, and every usage and convention, underlying the whole structure of international law; the negation, in short, of every principle upon which it is possible to base harmonious and trustful relations, whether of nations or of individuals. The responsible leaders of the regime have frequently and openly boasted that they are willing to sign agreements and undertakings with foreign Powers while not having the slightest intention of observing such undertakings or carrying out such agreements. This attitude of disregard of obligations voluntarily entered into, they base upon the theory that no compact or agreement made with a non-Bolshevist government can have any moral force for them. They have not only avowed this as a doctrine, but have exemplified it in practice. Indeed, upon numerous occasions the responsible spokesmen of this Power, and its official agencies, have declared that it is their understanding that the very existence of Bolshevism in Russia, the maintenance of their own rule, depends, and must continue to depend, upon the occurrence of revolutions in all other great civilized nations, including the United States, which will overthrow and destroy their governments and set up Bolshevist rule in their stead. They have made it quite plain that they intend to use every means, including of course, diplomatic agencies, to promote such revolutionary movements in other countries.

It is true that they have in various ways expressed their willingness to give "assurances" and "guarantees" that they will not abuse the privileges and immunities of diplomatic agencies by using them for this purpose. In view of their own declarations, already referred to, such assurances and guarantees cannot be very seriously regarded. Moreover, it is within the knowledge of the Government of the United States that the Bolshevist Government is itself subject to the control of a political faction, with extensive international ramifications through the Third Internationale [sic], and that this body, which is heavily subsidized by the Bolshevist Government from the public revenues of Russia, has for its openly avowed aim the promotion of Bolshevist revolutions throughout the world. The leaders of the Bolsheviki have boasted that their promises of non-interference with other nations would in no wise bind the agents of this body. There is no room for reasonable doubt that such agents would receive the support and protection of any diplomatic agencies the Bolsheviki might have in other countries. Inevitably, therefore, the diplomatic service of the Bolshevist Government would become a channel for intrigues and the propaganda of revolt against the institutions and laws of countries, with which it was at peace, which would be an abuse of friendship to which enlightened governments cannot subject themselves.

In the view of this Government, there cannot be any common ground upon which it can stand with a Power whose conceptions of international relations are so entirely alien to its own, so utterly repugnant to its moral sense. There can be no mutual confidence or trust, no respect even, if pledges are to be given and agreements made with a cynical repudiation of their obligations already in the mind of one of the parties. We cannot recognize, hold official relations with, or give friendly reception to the agents of a government which is determined and bound to conspire against our institutions; whose diplomats will be the agitators of dangerous revolt; whose spokesmen say that they sign agreements with no intention of keeping them.

To summarize the position of this Government, I would say, therefore, in response to your Excellency's inquiry, that it would regard with satisfaction a declaration by the Allied and Associated Powers, that the territorial integrity and true boundaries of Russia shall be respected. These boundaries should properly include the whole of the former Russian Empire, with the exception of Finland proper, ethnic Poland, and such territory as may by agreement form a part of the Armenian State. The aspirations of these nations for independence are legitimate. Each was forcibly annexed and their liberation from oppressive alien rule involves no aggressions against Russia's territorial rights, and has received the sanction of the public opinion of all free peoples. Such a declaration presupposes the withdrawal of all foreign troops from the territory embraced by these boundaries, and in the opinion of this Government should be accompanied by the announcement that no transgression by Poland, Finland or any other Power, of the line so drawn and proclaimed will be permitted.

Thus only can the Bolshevist regime be deprived of its false, but effective, appeal to Russian nationalism and compelled to meet the inevitable challenge of reason and self-respect which the Russian people, secure from invasion and territorial violation, are sure to address to a social philosophy that degrades them and a tyranny that oppresses them.

The policy herein outlined will command the support of this Government.

Accept [etc.]

BAINBRIDGE COLBY

b

[A Circular Letter from the People's Commissar of Foreign Affairs
of the R.S.F.S.R., G. V. Chicherin, to the Russian Plenipotentiaries
Abroad, September 10, 1920][33]

The note of the American Secretary of State, Bainbridge Colby, . . . transmitted
by radio cable and addressed to the Italian ambassador, presents a polemical attack
without precedent in diplomatic practice. Since it is directed against the policies and
the political regime of Soviet Russia, Soviet Russia cannot ignore it.

Try to explain to the public in general, and to the toiling masses in particular,
the falsity and the unfairness of the American government, and, especially, pass on
your opinion [of the attack] to the representatives of the Italian government to whom
Mr. Colby's note was addressed. Develop the following thesis in your argument:
that in criticizing the policy of the governments of Great Britain and Italy, the American government (1) supports the principle of the indivisibility and territorial integrity of the former Russian Empire, and (2) considers it possible to enter into
relations, or even to establish friendly relations, only with a nonsoviet Russian
government.

In advancing his principle of the indivisibility of former Russian territory, Mr.
Colby makes exceptions only of Poland, Finland, and Armenia. Since they were
forcibly annexed to Russia, and since Russian territorial rights are not involved in
their separation from Russia, he considers the desires of these nations for independence to be legal. Mr. Colby appears to believe that other nationalities oppressed by
tsarist Russia were not annexed by force; [therefore] he regards as illegal Georgian,
Azerbaijani, Lithuanian, Latvian, Estonian, and Ukrainian desires for independence, either in the form of complete separation from Russia or in the form of federative relationships. These distinctions drawn by the American government among
the different nationalities ruled by the former Russian Empire appear incomprehensible, probably owing to that government's ignorance of the actual facts of
national interrelationships in Eastern Europe.

The American government's list of exceptions clearly emphasizes its desire to
support the territorial integrity of the former tsarist empire, and to condition its
friendly relations with Russia upon the demand that her government be nonsoviet.
However, at the present time, any other government would be a bourgeois government—i.e., a capitalist government—and, in view of the present co-ordination of
economic relations in the world, it would also be a government connected with the
interests of the dominating international financial groups. Among these groups, as
a consequence of the World War, the financial groups . . . of the United States of
America play the most important role. Thus, Mr. Colby conditions his country's
friendly relations with Russia upon the existence in Russia of a political regime subservient to the interests of financial groups in the United States of America.

An object of Mr. Colby's specially warm feelings, he points out, was the Russian
government of 1917—which forced the toiling masses in Russia to sacrifice their
lives to carry on the war on the side of the coalition of which the United States was
a member (to protect the interests of the ruling financial groups in that country),
and which, under the pretext of a democratic regime, actually supported bourgeois
rule in Russia (i.e., supported the capitalist regime, and, in the final reckoning, the
rule of the dominating international financial groups).

As long ago as 1905, when the weakness of tsarist Russia was revealed for the
first time, as was her actual dependence on the leading Western European capitalist
groups, Maximilian Harden[34] wrote that Russia was actually a colonial country,

---

[33] Kliuchnikov and Sabanin, III, 56–60.
[34] Maximilian Harden (1861–1927) was an influential German publicist.

which should be governed by trading-company methods, with the help of stewards and industrial and commercial agents. On this outspoken statement were based all the plans worked out by the Entente governments during their intervention against the Soviet regime in Russia, and it also explains the animosity toward the Soviet order of the North American financial groups represented by Mr. Colby.

It is remarkable, however, that in his desire to retain the territorial integrity of the tsarist empire, Mr. Colby not only deviated sharply from British policy, but even definitely opposed it. Evidently the financial groups represented by Mr. Colby are convinced that in the new states that have been created from former Russian territory, the influence of other financial groups (namely those of England) has been established so thoroughly that the only way to defeat these groups is to abrogate the independence of these states. . . .

The Soviet government undeviatingly supports the right of the toilers of all races to self-determination, including the right to separate and the right to create independent states. On this principle is based the undeviating desire of the Soviet government to establish and to maintain friendly relations with the border states that have separated from Russia.

At the same time, the regime represented by the Soviet government, under which the toiling masses become masters of their own fate once the authority of the exploiters is removed, is the only guarantee against and the only check on exploitation by leading international financial groups, especially the American groups. Hence Mr. Colby's irreconcilable animosity toward the Soviet regime, and his absolutely false picture of it, which disagrees fundamentally with existing facts. Mr. Colby supposes that the Soviet regime is based not on the representation of the great masses but on crude force. Yet in no other regime are the toiling masses independent of the privileged minority of exploiters and of finance capital, whose power is itself actually based on crude force.

Crude force rules supreme and despotic everywhere a parliamentary regime exists, yet according to Mr. Colby a parliamentary regime is the only regime worthy of recognition. In every parliamentary regime the toiling masses, themselves unorganized, are subordinated firmly to organized political parties, which in turn are completely controlled by the country's ruling financial groups. These financial groups maintain their own unlimited power by means of a perfected organization with many branches connected with numerous local interests. They control the minds of great masses by means of the press, which they control; by means of literature, which they inspire; and through the church, which acts jointly with them. Under the so-called democratic regime, the apparent freedom of the press, of meeting, of union, and of opinion is actually a staging of the domination of the ruling financial groups performed by the mercenary press, mercenary politicians, mercenary courts, and mercenary men of letters and clergymen, and controlled by the leading financial groups.

The Soviet regime alone represents a permanent organization of the toiling masses; in it the local soviets are the true bearers of supreme authority and also of local executive authority. These soviets are the permanent institutions of the toiling masses in each given locality. Where the toiling masses are given such power, and are drawn into daily administrative work to such an extent, it is absurd to suppose that a central authority can govern contrary to their will.

But the toiling masses themselves, faced by a bloody civil war that threatens all their achievements, acknowledge the expediency of a strong centralized revolutionary authority to conduct the civil war, to suppress the last resistance of the exploiting classes, and to conduct a hard struggle against the capitalist governments of the world, which have united to strangle the revolution in the country in which the toiling masses have won power. At this moment, when all the capitalist governments of the world have united to suppress Soviet Russia's resistance by force of arms, by a blockade resulting in starvation and cold, by organizing continuous conspiracies within the country, and by supporting the exploiting classes in the struggle against the toiling masses now in power—at such a time the great masses of the toilers realize very clearly that only a merciless dictatorship of the proletariat can save their revolutionary achievements and defend them from the attack of capital and its agents, both outside and at home.

The Communist Party, which is carrying on a merciless struggle against the exploiters of the world, is predominant in Soviet Russia only because the toiling masses themselves realize that its rule provides the only reliable means for a successful struggle against the deadly menace of world capitalism.

The Communist Party is faced by an irreconcilably inimical attitude on Mr. Colby's part because it heads the revolutionary movement of the toiling masses in all other countries, and in particular in America itself. This universal struggle is an actual fact, but Mr. Colby tries to explain it as propaganda by agents of the Soviet Russian government. This is not the first time that American financial groups have attempted to discredit the Soviet government by defamatory accusations. We remember very well the publication in America of forged documents[35] so crude that even a little serious study would have sufficed to expose them. These documents were intended to prove the absurd theory that the Bolsheviks were agents of the German government. In countries governed by parliamentary regimes, including America, where the press both serves the interests of financial groups and dominates public opinion, defamation of Soviet Russia is one of the chief weapons in the struggle against the revolutionary movement of the toiling masses. Consequently, in his note to the Italian government, Mr. Colby showers upon the Soviet government crude and defamatory accusations.

The representatives of Soviet Russia are instructed to publish their strong and decisive protest against the false accusation that the Soviet government breaks its promises and concludes treaties with the intention of violating them. Not a single example can be produced to prove this defamation. Even the Brest treaty, which was forced upon the Soviet government, was adhered to most scrupulously.[36] Although a box belonging to the Russian embassy was broken open in a Berlin railway station and was found to contain leaflets against the Brest treaty, it was later proved that these leaflets were not put in the box by officials of the Russian government. Similarly with all other "violations" of diplomatic agreements alleged against the Soviet government. When the Soviet government promises to abstain from disseminating communist literature, all its representatives undeviatingly keep this promise, and they are now instructed to make this fact known in a most categorical manner.

[35] Edgar Grant Sisson, special representative of the United States Committee on Public Information, collected a number of documents in Russia in the winter of 1917–18; they were published by the Committee in 1918 under the title *The German-Bolshevik Conspiracy*. For a recent evaluation of these documents, see George Kennan, "The Sisson Documents," *Journal of Modern History*, Vol. XXVIII, No. 2, June 1956, pp. 130–54.

[36] This statement conflicts with Ioffe's report on subversive work in Berlin during his time as Soviet plenipotentiary there in 1918–19. According to Ioffe:

"The famous Paragraph 2 of the Brest peace treaty bound revolutionary Russia with an iron chain, and at first seemed to make her very existence meaningless. The Brest treaty, or rather the above-mentioned paragraph, forbade agitation against the military and political institutions of Germany. Yet the whole significance of the Russian revolution was that it represented the vanguard of the world socialist revolution, and that it could be victorious only as a world revolution. Therefore, it was clear from the start that this paragraph could not be adhered to. For the Russian revolutionaries who had been accustomed for scores of years to revolutionary work in spite of all shackles, the way out was clear: What could not be done openly and legally had to be done conspiratorially and illegally. Therefore, what had to be done was done in the tried and true manner: (1) by making use of all legal possibilities, (2) by illegal secret agitation and propaganda." (A. A. Ioffe, "Germanskaia revoliutsiia i rossiiskoe posolstvo," *Vestnik Zhizni*, No. 5, 1919, p. 35.)

The Soviet government realizes quite clearly that the revolutionary movement of the toiling masses in every country is the task of these masses themselves. Therefore the Soviet government believes that the communist regime cannot be forced upon another people, and that the struggle for it must be conducted by the toiling masses themselves in each country. Because in America and many other countries the toiling masses have neither won power nor even come to believe in the necessity of winning it, the Soviet Russian government believes it necessary to establish and maintain undeviatingly peaceful and friendly relations with the existing governments in these countries.

The Soviet government realizes very clearly that the elementary economic requirements of the peoples of Russia and of other countries demand the establishment among them of normal relations, [based on] the regular exchange of commodities . . . and noninterference in domestic affairs. Mr. Colby is deeply mistaken in supposing that normal relations between Russia and North America would be possible only if Russia were governed by a capitalist regime. The Soviet Russian government believes, on the contrary, that the absolutely correct, loyal, and friendly relations required for the development of trade and for the satisfaction of the economic needs of both countries should be established now, despite social and political differences between the two countries.

The Russian government is convinced that the more farsighted representatives of North American business circles, as well as the toiling masses, will repudiate the narrow-minded policy expressed in Mr. Colby's note—a policy harmful to America herself—and that, in the near future, in spite of the differences in their respective political regimes, normal relations will be established between Russia and North America, as well as between Russia and England.

THE FAMINE

18

Maxim Gorky's Appeal to the American People, Moscow, July 13, 1921[37]

The corn [grain]-growing steppes are smitten by crop failure, caused by the drought. The calamity threatens starvation to millions of Russian people. Think of the Russian people's exhaustion by the war and revolution, which considerably reduced its resistance to disease and its physical endurance. Gloomy days have come for the country of Tolstoy, Dostoyevsky, Meneleyev [Mendeleev], Pavlov, Mussorgsky, Glinka and other world-prized men and I venture to trust that the cultured European and American people, understanding the tragedy of the Russian people, will immediately succor with bread and medicines.

If humanitarian ideas and feelings—faith in whose social import was so shaken by the damnable war and its victors' unmercifulness towards the vanquished—if faith in the creative force of these ideas and feelings, I say, must and can be restored, Russia's misfortune offers humanitarians a splendid opportunity to demonstrate the vitality of humanitarianism. I think particularly warm sympathy in succoring the Russian people must be shown by those who, during the ignominious war, so passionately preached fratricidal hatred, thereby withering the educational efficacy of ideas evolved by mankind in the most arduous labors and so lightly killed by stupidity and cupidity. People who understand the words of agonizing pain will forgive the involuntary bitterness of my words.

[37] *American Relief Administration Bulletin,* Second Series, No. 16, September 1, 1921, p. 2. No Russian text is available to check this translation.

I ask all honest European and American people for prompt aid to the Russian people. Give bread and medicine.

MAXIM GORKY

19

Mr. Hoover's Reply to Maxim Gorky's Appeal, July 23, 1921[38]

I have read with great feeling your appeal to Americans for charitable assistance to the starving and sick people of Russia, more particularly the children. To the whole American people the absolute *sine qua non* of any assistance must be the immediate release of the Americans now held prisoners in Russia and adequate provision for administration. Once these steps have been taken the American Relief Administration, a purely voluntary association and an entirely unofficial organization of which I am chairman, together with other cooperating charitable American organizations supported wholly through the generosity of the American people, have funds in hand by which assistance for the children and for the sick could be undertaken immediately. This organization previously during the last year intimated its willingness to undertake this service as one of simple humanity, disengaged absolutely from any political, social or religious motives. However, for obvious administrative reasons it has been and is compelled to stipulate for certain undertakings. Subject to the acceptance of these undertakings we are prepared to enter upon this work. We are today caring for three and one half millions of children in ten different countries and would be willing to furnish necessary supplement of food, clothing and medical supplies to a million children in Russia as rapidly as organization could be effected. The administrative conditions that we are obliged to make are identically the same as those that have been established in every one of the twenty-three countries where operations have been conducted one time or another in care of upwards of eight million children.

The conditions are that the Moscow Soviet authorities should give a direct statement to the Relief Administration representatives in Riga:

A.   That there is need of our assistance.

B.   That American representatives of the Relief Administration shall be given full liberty to come and go and move about Russia.

C.   That these members shall be allowed to organize the necessary local committees and local assistance free from governmental interference.

D.   That they shall be given free transportation, storage and handling of imported supplies with priority over other traffic, that the authorities shall assign necessary buildings and equipment and fuel free of charge.

E.   That in addition to the imported food, clothing, and medicines the children and sick must be given the same rations of such local supplies as are given to the rest of the population.

F.   That the Relief Administration must have the assurance of non-interference of the government with the liberty of all of its members.

On its side the Relief Administration is prepared as usual to make a free and frank undertaking:

First.   That it will, within its resources supply all children and invalids alike without regard to race, creed or social status.

Second.   That its representatives and assistants in Russia will engage in no political activities.

[38] *Ibid.,* pp. 3–4.

I desire to repeat that these conditions are in no sense extraordinary but are identical with those laid down and readily accepted by the twenty-three other governments in whose territories we have operated.

HERBERT HOOVER[39]

20

Official Soviet Appreciation of American Help

[Resolution of the Council of People's Commissars, Moscow, July 10, 1923][40]

In the trying hour of a great and overwhelming disaster, the people of the United States, represented by the A.R.A., responded to the needs of the population, already exhausted by intervention and blockade, in the famine-stricken parts of Russia and Federated Republics.

Unselfishly, the A.R.A. came to the aid of the people and organized on a broad scale the supply and distribution of food products and other articles of prime necessity.

Thanks to the enormous and entirely disinterested efforts of the A.R.A., millions of people of all ages were saved from death, and entire districts and even cities were saved from the horrible catastrophe which threatened them.

Now when the famine is over and the colossal work of the A.R.A. comes to a close, the Soviet of People's Commissars, in the name of the millions of people saved and in the name of all the working people of Soviet Russia and the Federated Republics, counts it a duty to express before the whole world its deepest thanks to this organization, to its leader, Herbert Hoover, to its representative in Russia, Colonel Haskell, and to all its workers, and to declare that the people inhabiting the Union of Soviet Socialist Republics will never forget the help given them by the American people, through the A.R.A., seeing in it a pledge of the future friendship of the two nations.

L. KAMENEV,
Acting President of the Council of People's Commissars

N. GORBUNOV,
Chief of the Administrative Department of the Council of People's Commissars

L. FOTIEVA,
Secretary of the Council of People's Commissars

21

Lenin's Appeal to the International Proletariat, August 2, 1921[41]

In several provinces in Russia there is a famine which, apparently, is hardly less intense than the calamity of 1891.

This famine is the serious legacy of Russia's backwardness and of seven years

---

[39] On July 28, 1921, the Soviet government accepted Mr. Hoover's conditions as a basis for negotiation and proposed a meeting of representatives to draw up an agreement. The text of the relief agreement is given in H. H. Fisher, *The Famine in Soviet Russia, 1919–1923*, pp. 507–10.

[40] Fisher, *op. cit.*, p. 398.

[41] Lenin, *Sochineniia*, XXVI, 477.

of war—first imperialist, then civil—which were imposed upon the workers and peasants by the *pomeshchiks*[42] and capitalists of all countries.

Help is needed. The Soviet republic of workers and peasants expects that help from the toilers, from the industrial workers, and from the small-scale farmers.

These masses are themselves oppressed by capitalism and imperialism in all countries, but we are convinced that, in spite of their own hard situation caused by unemployment and rising prices, they will answer our call.

The people who have themselves been experiencing all along the oppression of capital will understand the position of the workers and peasants of Russia; they will realize, with the instinct of the toiling and exploited people, the necessity for helping the Soviet republic, which was obliged to assume first the joyful but hard task of overthrowing capitalism. The capitalists of all countries are taking revenge for this on the Soviet republic. They are making new plans for another intervention and for counterrevolutionary conspiracies.

We are convinced that [on this account] the workers and small farmers who live by their labor will come to our rescue with still greater energy.

CHARGES AND COUNTERCHARGES

22

Soviet Suspicion of the Little Entente

[Iu. M. Steklov's Comment][43]

From Rumania comes information that a Little Entente has been formed. It includes Czechoslovakia, Rumania, Yugoslavia, and Poland. These are known to be agents of the Large Entente, and it is clear that Poland, the strongest and most imperialistic of them, will play the leading role. They will all serve the Large Entente, but at the same time the three [others] will serve the interests of Polish imperialists as well, when Poland tries to make its position secure. Since it is a child of the Large Entente, the Little Entente bears, from the moment of its birth, the same mark of Cain as its parent. . . .

The purpose of the new international formation (so the rest of the world is told) is the defense of Eastern Europe and the maintenance of peace. . . .

"The defense of Eastern Europe!" That sounds very noble. But the question then arises: From whom is it to be defended? And the answer is clear: From Soviet

---

[42] Members of landed class and land proprietors.

[43] *Izvestiia*, No. 137, June 26, 1921, p. 1. As early as October 1918, tentative negotiations were opened between M. Beneš representing Czechoslovakia and MM. Pašić and Trumbić representing Serbia and the newly liberated Yugoslavs. Similar negotiations were opened on December 30, 1920, between Prague and Rumania. The following conventions resulted: (1) *Convention of Alliance between the Kingdom of the Serbs, Croats, and Slovenes and the Czechoslovak Republic,* signed at Belgrade, August 14, 1920; (2) *Convention of Alliance between the Kingdom of Rumania and the Czechoslovak Republic,* signed at Bucharest, April 23, 1921; and (3) *Convention of Alliance between the Kingdom of the Serbs, Croats, and Slovenes and the Kingdom of Rumania,* signed at Belgrade, June 7, 1921. Article One of all three conventions stated: "In case of an unprovoked attack . . . against one of the two High Contracting Parties . . . the other Party agrees to assist in the defence of the Party attacked. . . ." Article Three: "Neither of the High Contracting Parties shall conclude an alliance with a third Power without preliminary notice to the other." (*League of Nations Treaty Series,* Vol. VI, 1921, No. 154, pp. 209–13; *ibid.,* No. 155, pp. 215–19; and Arnold J. Toynbee, *Survey of International Affairs, 1920–1923,* pp. 507–8, respectively. See also Albert Mousset, *La Petite Entente, ses origines, son histoire, ses connexions, son avenir.*)

Russia. But in that case it becomes the defense not of Eastern Europe but of Western Europe; not against attempts by Soviet Russia, who does not even think of attacking anyone, but against the so-called penetration of Bolshevik ideas. But this, too, is a *façon de parler* because everyone knows that no diplomatic combination can prevent the "penetration of ideas," especially when those ideas, the hateful ideas of communism, arise everywhere and quite independently of any "intrigue" or "attempts" on the part of Moscow. This means that the question is not of defense, but of attack. Does the Little Entente itself wish to attack? That is hardly likely. But attack is required by its masters, and when they need that attack, immediately the Polish *zolnierzy* [soldiers], the Rumanian lancers, the Czech legionnaires, and even the Hungarian *honvéds* [home defenders] will go into action, as well as other soldiers who will be sold to the Entente by the small governments who seek subsidies, just as, once upon a time, the German princes sold their "faithful Hessians" and other grenadiers to old England.

As to "the maintenance of peace," we know very well what that means in the language of the imperialists. But a certain grain of truth can be found in this case. The members of the Little Entente need peace in order to retain their conquests and seizures. But this is a kind of peace that does not depend on them. Created by the grace of the Large Entente and also living by its grace, they are fully dependent upon it and simply execute its will. And when the Large Entente gives orders, the Little Entente will launch a war. Again: Against whom? Austria or Hungary? But they are unimportant units at the moment. Against Germany? Germany is hardly about to present any threat to Eastern European peace. . . . Then against whom? Clearly against Soviet Russia. This is particularly clear with Rumania and Poland, whose anti-Russian designs happily agree with the anti-Bolshevik antipathies of France and England. . . .

[But] parallel to this Little Entente of the imperialist vultures, there is being created another entente—that of the workers, i.e., the Communist International. This proletarian entente is taking deep root in the countries from which French diplomacy formed a creature of its own, i.e., the Little Entente. In Czechoslovakia the Communists represent an important proletarian force; in Yugoslavia this force is also significant; in Poland it is already quite considerable; and what is especially important is that it is an ever-growing force. Only in Rumania is it still weak, but there, too, it can grow rapidly if it succeeds in reaching the countryside. . . . In the Baltic countries it is not a negligible force either. . . .

Therefore, in registering the new enemy, Soviet Russia can remain calm. The Little Entente no more represents the last word in history than the Large Entente that gave birth to it. The last word belongs to the toiling masses. We hope that the present [Third] Congress of the Communist International will bring together the vanguard of these masses, making them such a powerful proletarian entente that they will be able, at the decisive moment, to repulse all attempts by vultures large and small on the citadel of international socialism.

23

The Soviet Government Charges That France Incites Poland and Rumania to New Anti-Soviet Activity

[Declaration by the People's Commissariat of Foreign Affairs, Moscow, September 13, 1921][44]

In its reply to Noulens on September 7 of this year, the People's Commissariat of Foreign Affairs expressed a supposition *en passant* that in [proposing to] send

[44] *Sovetskaia Rossiia i Polsha,* pp. 49–50.

a commission, allegedly to study the famine conditions, France might have been attempting to camouflage a reconnoitering plan. This supposition was soon confirmed. The People's Commissariat of Foreign Affairs now has very exact and reliable information about the diplomatic steps taken by the French government during the last few weeks to draw Poland and Rumania into war with Russia.

A note of September 3 handed to the Polish government by the French ambassador in Warsaw suggests that the Soviet government's concentration on efforts to overcome the famine gives Poland and Rumania a convenient opportunity to present Russia with their maximum demands in the form of an ultimatum of their own. In its note [to the Polish government] the French government also demands, on the basis of the military convention signed between France and Poland, that the army and the supreme leadership of the Polish General Staff be handed over to the French military mission in Poland. The ultimatums of France, Poland, and Rumania would be presented [to the Soviet government] just as soon as the Polish and Rumanian armies were put into battle readiness.

The French note states further that Paris considers Poland's position hopeless without considerable French assistance, and that to get this assistance Poland must follow French policy on the Russian question when France, after settling the German problem, is in a position to change its Russian policy radically. On its part, France would demand in its ultimatum [to the Soviet government] the liberation of hostages and civil war prisoners, and the liquidation of organizations engaged in communist propaganda in France.

In order to pacify the Polish cabinet members who are against war, the French note assures them that the Soviet government would most probably comply with the ultimatum and would agree to serious concessions; that in case war did break out, France would render Poland extensive military and financial assistance; and that Rumania has already agreed to the French policy. A similar note was sent to Rumania.

According to information at the disposal of the People's Commissariat of Foreign Affairs, the French proposal, although approved by the Polish cabinet, the highest leaders of Polish policy, was declined by the Polish government (and also by Rumania). Poland agreed to resort to threats, but not to go as far as armed conflict. Simultaneously, however, the Polish government is sounding out Germany to see if by making concessions in Upper Silesia it can procure Germany's favorable neutrality in case of a Polish-Russian war.

In making known these facts, the authenticity of which has been confirmed by many sources, the People's Commissariat of Foreign Affairs presents for the judgment of the toiling masses and honest citizens of the world the diabolic machinations being resorted to by France. While adorning herself with the toga of a benefactress of the Russian people, France at the same time tries to bring upon these people—already deeply affected by one disaster, famine—a new calamity, war. While preparing for this war, she tries to send spies to Russia under the cloak of charity. And to achieve her mercenary ends, she is prepared to draw into a new and disastrous war the Polish people, who have already been ruined by a previous one.

24

Proposed Warning to Soviet Russia's Neighbors

[Lenin to the Politburo, December 22, 1921][45]

Please discuss whether a special resolution of the [Ninth] Congress of Soviets should be taken against the adventurous policy of Poland, Finland, and Rumania (Japan should not be mentioned for a number of reasons).

[45] *Leninskii Sbornik*, XXXV, 304.

State in detail in the resolution how we have proved by [our] actions that we value both the self-determination of peoples and peaceful relations with the states that were formerly parts of the Russian Empire. State in detail that we rely fully on the peaceful intentions not only of the workers and peasants of all enumerated countries but also of the majority of sensible bourgeoisie and government representatives. As for the adventurers, end with the strongest threat that if the adventurous pranks of bands like Savinkov's are not put to an end, if our peaceful work is interfered with, we shall rise to a patriotic war, so that those who now take part in adventure and banditry shall be absolutely crushed.

The resolution of the congress will be all the more useful if worded in such a way that we can circulate it in all languages among the masses.[46]

25

The Soviet Government Calls for an International Conference to Settle Outstanding Problems Between Russia and the Allies

[Official Note of the People's Commissar of Foreign Affairs to the Governments of Great Britain, France, Italy, Japan, and the United States, October 28, 1921][47]

According to the Western European press, the representatives of the powers conferring at Brussels insisted that the Russian government recognize the debts of the preceding [i.e., tsarist] governments before credits are offered the Russian government to help the famine-stricken population.

So far, the Russian government has not been officially informed of the decisions of this conference. However, because of the famine, which has afflicted masses of people, the Russian government has decided not to heed the usual rules of diplomatic etiquette, since it believes it should make known at once its opinion of the Brussels decision. . . .

In pointing out to the working masses of all countries and all other citizens to whom the interests of humanity are dear the attitude taken by the Brussels Conference, the Russian government declares that the proposal to recognize the old debts under certain conditions corresponds with its own intentions at the moment. . . .

Obviously complete peace cannot be re-established if Russia and her 130 million people are excluded [from the general efforts]. Economic collapse cannot be prevented without the revival of Russia, and the question of relations between Russia and other countries, which is a world problem of the first magnitude, cannot be settled except by an agreement with the Soviet government.

In view of the permanent interests and ever-present needs of all states and all peoples, the economic restoration of Russia is an absolute necessity, not only for herself but for the other states as well. . . .

Having as its aim the interests of all the working people of Russia, the workers' and peasants' government, which has emerged victorious from unparalleled ordeals of civil war and foreign intervention, is offering private enterprise and capital the chance to co-operate with it in developing the natural wealth of Russia.

The Soviet government has re-established private trade and private ownership for small business enterprises, and concessions and leases for large-scale under-

---

[46] In accordance with Lenin's recommendation, the Ninth Congress of Soviets issued a declaration on the international position of the R.S.F.S.R. on December 28, 1921, which duly appeared in *Izvestiia*, No. 1, January 1, 1922, p. 1.

[47] *Izvestiia*, No. 243, October 29, 1921, p. 1; also Kliuchnikov and Sabanin, III, 140–42.

takings. It gives foreign capital legal guarantees and a margin of profit sufficient to satisfy its interests and to induce it to take part in the economic work of Russia.

In this way the Soviet government aims at establishing economic agreements with all powers, and for this purpose at concluding first of all a definite peace between Russia and the other states.

The Soviet government finds its pursuit of this objective blocked by the demand that it recognize the old debts of the tsarist government.

Although firmly convinced that no people is obliged to pay the cost of chains riveted on them through long centuries, the Soviet government, in its unshakable determination to come to a full agreement with the other powers, is inclined to consent to several essential concessions in this highly important matter. . . .

For these reasons the Russian government declares itself ready to recognize the obligations toward other states and their citizens which arise from state loans concluded by the tsarist government before 1914, on the express condition that there shall be special conditions and facilities that make it possible to carry out this undertaking.

Obviously we cannot possibly grant this recognition unless the Great Powers undertake simultaneously to put an end to every action that threatens either the security of the Soviet republic and of the friendly Far Eastern Republic, or their sovereign rights and the inviolability of their frontiers; and to observe scrupulously the sovereignty and territorial integrity of these republics.

In other words, the Soviet republic can assume these obligations if the Great Powers conclude a definite peace with it and recognize its government.

For this purpose the Russian government proposes as a matter of urgency the convocation of an international conference to deal with these questions, to examine the claims of other powers against Russia, and the claims of the Russian government against other powers. Only a conference of this kind can bring about general peace. . . .

This proposal is the best proof of the Russian government's desire for peace with all states and for economic relations that nothing can disturb. The carrying out of this proposal is in harmony with the interests of all governments and all peoples.

The Russian government expresses the sincere hope that this proposal will be speedily followed by the definite establishment of economic and political relations between Russia and other states.

G. Chicherin,
People's Commissar of Foreign Affairs.

THE THIRD CONGRESS OF THE COMINTERN

26

On the Eve of the Third Congress of the Communist International

[Editorial by Karl Radek][48]

·   ·   ·

As the Third Congress convenes, a great world-wide economic crisis is clearly demonstrating the inability of capitalism to organize the world anew. The congress meets at a moment when millions and millions of workers in the wealthiest capitalist countries are without work, when not a single important political crisis has yet been

[48] *Pravda*, No. 133, June 22, 1921, p. 1.

solved, when [the final outcome of] all these crises is simply delayed. Furthermore, there remains unsolved that task for which the Communist International was formed—namely, the task of leadership of the advancing world revolution. The communist parties, the instruments of this leadership, are still being formed in many countries. Here the task of the Comintern will be first of all to spur the Communists to increase their efforts tenfold in order to infiltrate the masses and to influence them in the communist direction.

Such is the actual situation in Britain and in the United States of North America. In other countries, such as Italy, Sweden, Czechoslovakia, and France, the communist parties are more or less at the Comintern's disposal, but these mass parties, thanks to the "centrist" tendencies still prevalent among their leadership, and to a certain amount of passiveness, are unable either to impress the masses with truly communist agitation or to direct the struggle. [Gives examples in Italy and Germany.] . . .

In discussing the question of partial demands and partial action, the Comintern will demonstrate very clearly to the communist parties, on the basis of its own practice, that they should never consider agitation and propaganda alone as sufficient, but that they must take part in all aspects of the proletarian struggle, that they must develop their own organizations within the ranks of the struggling proletariat, proceeding progressively from the mere strike to insurrection.

To support the Red Trade Union International[49] in its struggle against the Amsterdam lackeys of world capital is a supplementary organizational task of the partial struggle, i.e., the movement toward the seizure of power. The Third Congress of the Communist International will lay the groundwork for the congress of the Red Trade Union International that will immediately follow.

The agenda of the congress includes two "foreign" problems: Russia and Eastern. The leading party of the Comintern [i.e., the Russian party] will report to the congress on its policy for retaining and co-ordinating the power of the working class in a country that is mainly agricultural and that is in a difficult period of transition from war to peace. The congress must make clear its attitude to the

---

[49] Prior to World War I there were two international labor organizations: the Second International, political in aim but admitting trade unions, and the International Federation of Trade Unions (I.F.T.U.).

Both organizations were weakened and divided by the stresses of the war. In order to preserve some measure of contact between the trade unions of the belligerent countries, the I.F.T.U. established a temporary bureau in Amsterdam. After the war, at a congress in Amsterdam in 1919, the I.F.T.U. was reconstituted—hence the title "Amsterdam International."

A year later, in 1920, a minority of trade union representatives from various countries participated in the founding of a new international trade union movement sponsored by the Third or Communist International—the Profintern, also known as the Red Trade Union International.

With the exception of a brief period during which the British Trades Union Congress attempted a rapprochement with the Russian trade unions, the relations between the I.F.T.U. (Amsterdam) and the Profintern (Moscow) were marked by extreme hostility.

During World War II, this hostility was suspended, and at the end of the war the I.F.T.U. and what remained of the Profintern merged and formed the World Federation of Trade Unions, an organization which included representatives of most unions throughout the world, with the exception of the American Federation of Labor. But this war-born alliance proved short-lived; in 1949 the World Federation split on the issue of communist control. In November of that year representatives of nearly fifty million trade unionists of the noncommunist world—including the A.F.L. and the C.I.O.—founded a new international body, the International Confederation of Free Trade Unions. The constitution and decisions of the First World Congress of the I.C.F.T.U. are given in *For Bread, Peace, and Freedom,* I.C.F.T.U. Pamphlet No. 1 [1950].

policy of this first isolated proletarian state. At the same time the congress will be asked to decide how the struggle of the world proletariat for power can be hastened by means of an upsurge and increase in the revolutionary movements in the East.

Hundreds and hundreds of delegates and visitors from all countries of the world hasten to take part in the congress of the Communist International. Already a powerful organization representing the masses, the Comintern will be consolidated still further by the work of this congress. And if certain signs do not deceive us, it will soon be called upon to prove its strength in great revolutionary battles.

Revolutionary passion is needed for these battles. But it must be accompanied by cold farsightedness and an accurate estimate of the situation. The Russian Communist Party, under whose banner the congress is meeting, has proved by all its past actions that a union of these two traits is possible. The Russian Communist Party greets the delegates to the Third Congress of the Communist International with a call: Forge your arms for victory, which we shall win not by the heroic effort of one moment, but by a struggle that grows in intensity from day to day.

27

Lenin's Estimate of the International Situation, July 5, 1921[50]

. . .

In order to outline the tactics of our party, it is necessary, it seems to me, to begin with a study of the international situation. We have already discussed in detail the economic position of capitalism internationally, and this congress has passed definite resolutions concerning it. In my theses[51] I referred to this economic position very briefly, and exclusively from the political viewpoint. I shall not [now] deal with economic problems, but I would stress that as regards the international political situation of our republic, a certain equilibrium of forces has undoubtedly been established. These forces [only recently] conducted open warfare among themselves for leadership by this or that class. This equilibrium between bourgeois society (i.e., the international bourgeoisie as a whole) and Soviet Russia is, of course, only relative. I speak of equilibrium in the international situation in a military sense only. . . . Sufficient inflammable material has accumulated in the capitalist states and in those countries which so far have been considered the objects and not the subjects of history, i.e., the colonial and semicolonial countries; it is quite possible, therefore, that in these countries, sooner or later and quite unexpectedly, revolts will flare up, as well as great battles and revolutions.

Throughout the last few years we have witnessed an actual struggle of the international bourgeoisie against the first proletarian republic. The whole international political situation centered around this struggle . . . and it is in this situation that a change has now occurred. Inasmuch as the attempt of the international bourgeoisie to throttle our republic has not succeeded, a certain equilibrium, of course a very unstable one, has come to exist.

Of course we realize very well that the international bourgeoisie is at present much stronger than our republic, and that only a peculiar set of circumstances prevents it from continuing the war against us. In the past few weeks we again saw

---

[50] Lenin, *Sochineniia*, XXVI, 450–53.

[51] For Lenin's theses, see *ibid.*, pp. 427–35.

an attempt to renew intervention in the Far East.[52] There is not the slightest doubt that similar attempts will be made in the future. What is important is that an unstable equilibrium, a breathing spell, exists; we must make use of it, taking into account its characteristics and its peculiarities, always remembering that the necessity for armed struggle may again arise, and suddenly. Organizing and consolidating the Red Army remain our task as before. In our food policy, too, we must think first of our Red Army. In the present international situation, when we must still expect new attacks by the international bourgeoisie and new attempts at invasion, we can follow no other path. But practically speaking, the equilibrium shows us not only that the revolutionary movement has somewhat advanced, but that its advance has not proceeded along the straight line we expected.

When we started the international revolution, we did it not from the conviction that we could force its development, but because a number of circumstances impelled us to begin this revolution. We thought: Either the international revolution will come to our assistance, and then our victories will be fully secured, or we shall do our modest revolutionary work with the clear understanding that if we are defeated we shall nevertheless have contributed to the cause of the revolution and that our experience will be of value to other revolutions. It seemed clear to us that without the support of the international revolution the victory of the proletarian revolution was impossible. Even before the revolution and also after it, we thought: Either now, or at least very soon, revolution will take place in other countries, in the more advanced capitalist countries, or we shall perish. But in spite of this belief, we did everything we could to retain the soviet system under all circumstances and at any cost, because we realized that we were working not only for ourselves but also for the international revolution. We knew this, and we often said it before the October Revolution, as well as directly after it and during the signing of the Brest-Litovsk treaty. All this was in general correct.

Actually, however, the movement did not proceed along the direct line we anticipated. The revolution has not as yet come about in other large countries with advanced capitalist development. It is true the revolution is developing—and this we can affirm with pleasure—throughout the world; it is for this reason only that the international bourgeoisie cannot throttle us, although it is a hundred times stronger than we are both economically and militarily.

I mentioned in Article II of the theses how this situation came about, and what conclusions can be drawn from it. My final conclusion is this: The international revolution we predicted is developing, but not along the straight line we expected. We have clearly not brought about revolution in other capitalist countries since the conclusion of the [Versailles] peace, although it was a bad peace. But the revolutionary symptoms in those countries, as we know, are considerable and numerous, more considerable and numerous, in fact, than we had thought. Leaflets are now beginning to appear telling us that during the last years and months these revolutionary symptoms have been much more serious in Europe than we had suspected.

What must we do now? We now need a thorough preparation for the revolution and a thorough study of its actual development in the advanced capitalist countries. This is the first lesson we must draw from the present international situation. As far as our Russian republic is concerned, we must use this short-lived lull to adapt our tactics to the zigzag line of history. Politically this equilibrium is very important; it shows us clearly that in many Western European countries where the large masses of the working class, and very likely the large majority of the popu-

---

[52] Anti-Bolshevik forces that had seized the Maritime Province in March 1921 were at this time forming a new government, the so-called National Government, in Vladivostok with the help of the Japanese. This government lasted until October 25, 1922, when the army of the Far Eastern Republic recaptured Vladivostok.

lation, are organized, the main support of the bourgeoisie is the hostile organizations of the working class that have joined the Second and Second-and-a-Half Internationals. I speak of this in Article II of my theses, and I believe that here I should mention only two points, which have already been clarified in our discussion of tactics. First, the conquest of the majority of the proletariat. The more organized the proletariat in a capitalistically developed country, the more thorough the measures history expects from us in the task of preparing the revolution, and the more thorough our conquest of the majority of the working class must be. Second, the main support of capitalism in the industrially developed countries is provided by the working class members of the Second and Second-and-a-Half Internationals. Without support from this section of the workers, from counterrevolutionary elements within the working class, the international bourgeoisie would have been absolutely unable to hold out.

I would also like to emphasize here the significance of the movement in the colonies. In this respect the old parties, in all the bourgeois and petty bourgeois workers' parties of the Second and Second-and-a-Half Internationals, retain remnants of the old sentimental conceptions, namely, a deep sympathy for the oppressed colonial and semicolonial peoples. However, they still consider the movement in the colonial countries an insignificant national and absolutely peaceful movement. But this is not so. From the beginning of the twentieth century, a very important change has taken place in this regard, namely, millions and hundreds of millions—actually the vast majority of the population of the globe—now are becoming independent active revolutionary factors. And it is absolutely clear that in the future decisive battles of the world revolution, the movement of the majority of the population of the globe, although aimed first at national liberation, will [in the end] turn against capitalism and imperialism, and will perhaps play a much greater revolutionary role than we expect. It is important to stress that we, for the first time and in our International, have taken into consideration the preparation for that struggle. It goes without saying that there are great difficulties in this huge task. Nevertheless, the movement is progressing . . .

28

The Third Congress of the Communist International on the World Situation

[Excerpts from the Theses Adopted by the Third Congress of the Communist International, July 4, 1921][53]

THE WORLD SITUATION AND OUR TASKS

I. *The Essence of the Problem*

. . .

The first period of the revolutionary movement following the end of the war, which has been characterized by the elemental nature of its onslaught, by considerable lack of cohesion in method and aim, and by the extreme panic of the ruling classes, may now be regarded as having reached its almost complete termination. The class self-confidence of the bourgeoisie and the apparent stability of its government machinery have undoubtedly been consolidated. The [bourgeoisie's] fear of communism has not disappeared, but has undoubtedly relaxed. The leaders of the bourgeoisie are now even boasting of the power of their governmental machinery, and

[53] *Kommunisticheskii Internatsional v dokumentakh*, pp. 166–83, 197–99, 207–8.

have passed to the offensive against the working masses everywhere, both economically and politically.

3. In view of this situation, the Communist International brings to the attention of and places before the entire working class the following questions:

To what extent does this new relationship between the bourgeoisie and the proletariat correspond to the actual balance of the [contending] forces? Is it true that the bourgeoisie is about to restore the social balance that was upset by the war? Is there any reason to suppose that the period of political upheaval and of class wars is going to be superseded by a new and prolonged period of the restoration and growth of capitalism? Does this necessitate a revision of the program or tactics of the Communist International?

. . .

V. *International Relations*

27. The economic situation of the world in general and the decline of Europe in particular presage a long period of extremely serious economic difficulties, disturbances, and crises . . . The international relations that have grown out of the war and the Versailles treaty render the situation still more hopeless. . . .

31. The last great war, in both its original causes and its chief combatants, was a European war; its crux was the hostility between Britain and Germany. The intervention of the United States simply widened the scope of the struggle; it did not deflect it from its original course. The European conflict was settled by world-wide means. The war, having settled the British-German and American-German quarrel in its own way, not only did not solve the problem of the relations between the United States and Britain, but put that problem for the first time prominently forward as one of the first magnitude in world politics, and the American-Japanese question as one of the second magnitude. Thus the last war was in reality only a European prelude to a genuine world war to solve the problem of imperialist autocracy.

32. This, however, represents only one aspect of international policy, which has yet another aspect—the Russian Socialist Federated Soviet Republic and the Third International, brought about by the war. All the forces of the world revolution are arraying themselves against all the imperialist combinations. . . .

The fact that some of the capitalist governments have concluded peace and commercial treaties with Soviet Russia does not mean that the bourgeoisie of the world has given up the idea of destroying the republic of soviets. What we are witnessing is nothing but a change, perhaps a temporary change, of the techniques and methods of struggle. The Japanese *coup d'état* in the Far East may serve as an introduction to a new period of armed intervention.

It is altogether obvious that the longer the revolutionary movement of the world proletariat takes, the more inevitably the contradictions of the international economic and political situation will impel the bourgeoisie to force another bloody denouement on the world-wide scale. . . .

33. Even though the last war confirmed with terrible conviction that "wars are unprofitable"—a truth underlying both bourgeois and socialist pacifism—the processes of economic, political, ideological, and technical preparation for a new war proceed at full speed throughout the entire capitalist world. Humanitarian antirevolutionary pacifism has become an auxiliary to militarism.

The Social Democrats of every variety and the Amsterdam trade unionists, who are exhorting the workers of the world to adapt themselves to the economic and political conditions resulting from the war, are rendering the imperialist bourgeoisie most valuable service in the matter of preparing the new slaughter, which threatens to annihilate civilization completely.

. . .

VII. *The Prospects and Problems Involved*

37. The war did not have a proletarian revolution as its immediate consequence, and the bourgeoisie has some ground for registering this fact as a great victory for itself.

Only petty bourgeois dullards, however, see the European proletariat's failure to overthrow the bourgeoisie during the war or immediately after it as an indication that the program of the Communist International has failed. The Communist International bases its policy on the proletarian revolution, but it neither dogmatically fixes any definite calendar date for the revolution, nor pledges to bring it about mechanically at a set time. Revolution has always been, and is today, a struggle of living forces carried out under given historical conditions. The war, by upsetting the capitalist equilibrium all over the world, provided favorable conditions for the proletariat, which is the basic force of the revolution. The Communist International has been exerting all its efforts to take full advantage of this situation.

The difference between the Communist International and the Social Democrats . . . is not that we are trying to time the revolution for a definite date while the Social Democrats are opposed to any utopian and putschist action. It is rather that the Social Democrats hinder the actual development of the revolution by striving, both in the government and when in opposition, to restore the equilibrium of the bourgeois state, while the Communists do their utmost to overthrow and destroy the bourgeois state, and replace it with the dictatorship of the proletariat.

But during the two and a half years since the war, the proletarians of various countries have exhibited enough self-sacrifice, energy, and readiness for the struggle to have made the revolution triumphant had there been a strongly centralized international communist party on the scene ready for action. But during the war and immediately thereafter, by force of historical circumstance, there was at the head of the European proletariat the organization of the Second International, which was and remains an invaluable political weapon in the hands of the bourgeoisie.

38. . . .

It is absolutely beyond dispute that the open revolutionary struggle of the proletariat for power has been temporarily delayed everywhere. But it was not in the nature of things that the postwar revolutionary offensive, not having resulted in immediate victory, would go on developing without deviation along an upward curve. Political development proceeds in cycles and has its ebbs and flows. The enemy does not remain passive, but struggles. If the offensive of the proletariat does not lead to direct victory, the bourgeoisie uses the first opportunity for a counteroffensive. The loss by the proletariat of some of the positions it had won too easily leads to a temporary depression in its ranks. However, it remains indisputable that in the present epoch the curve of capitalist development proceeds, despite temporary rises, constantly *downward*, while the curve of revolution proceeds, despite some ebbs, constantly *upward*. . . .

39. The fundamental task of the Communist Party in the current crisis is to conduct, extend, widen, and unite the present defensive struggle of the proletariat, and, as it develops, to transform it into the final political struggle. Should the pace of development slacken, however, and should the present [economic] crisis be followed by a period of upsurge in some countries, this would by no means be an indication of the beginning of a stable epoch. So long as capitalism exists, periodic vacillations are inevitable. These vacillations are going to accompany capitalism in its death agony as they did during its youth and maturity. If during the present crisis the proletariat is pushed back under the onslaught of capitalism, it will immediately resume the offensive as soon as a more favorable combination of circumstances arises. . . .

40. Whether the revolutionary movement progresses quickly or slowly, the Communist Party must remain the party of action. This party stands at the head of the struggling masses. It firmly and clearly formulates its slogans, and it exposes the equivocal slogans of the Social Democrats, which always tend toward compromise. Whatever the turns in the course of the struggle, the Communist Party should always strive to fortify its contested positions by accustoming the masses to active maneuvering, by arming them with new methods calculated to lead to an open conflict with the enemy forces. Using every lull to capitalize upon the experience of the preceding phase of the struggle, the Communist Party should strive to deepen and widen class conflicts, to combine them nationally and internationally by unity of goal and practical activity, and in this way, at the head of the proletariat, to shatter all resistance on the road to its dictatorship and the socialist revolution.

THESIS ON TACTICS

I. *Definition of the Problems*

"The new international labor organization is established for the purpose of arranging for united action by the proletariat of different countries who aspire toward the same goal, i.e., the overthrow of capitalism, the establishment of the dictatorship of the proletariat and of an international soviet republic, and the complete elimination of classes and the realization of socialism, which is the first step toward the communist society." This definition of the aims of the Communist International, laid down in its statutes, clearly defines all the tactical problems of our struggle for the proletarian dictatorship. How are we to convert the majority of the working class to the principles of communism? How are we to organize the most active section of the proletariat for the coming struggle? What attitude should the proletariat take toward the proletarianized petty bourgeois groups? What are the best and quickest ways to demoralize and destroy the organs of bourgeois power, and to prepare for the final decisive international battle for the dictatorship? The problems of the dictatorship itself, as the only way to victory, call for no argument. The development of the world revolution has absolutely proved that there is only a single alternative in the given historical situation: either capitalist or proletarian dictatorship. . . .

II. *On the Eve of New Battles*

The world revolution, i.e., the decay of capitalism and the organization of the revolutionary proletariat into an aggressive, victorious power, will require a prolonged period of revolutionary struggle. Variations in the sharpness of [social] conflicts in different countries, the difference in the social structures and the obstacles to be overcome, the high degree of organization of the bourgeoisie in the capitalist countries of Western Europe and North America—all these have kept the inevitable victory of the world revolution from coming right after the World War. The Communists were therefore right in declaring during the war that the period of imperialism would pass on to the prolonged period of social revolution, i.e., to a long series of civil wars within capitalist countries, and of wars between the capitalist states on one side and proletarian states and exploited colonial peoples on the other. . . .

The universal economic crisis that began in mid-1920 and has since extended over the entire world, creating and increasing unemployment everywhere, has proved to the international proletariat that the bourgeoisie is powerless to lead the world out of ruin. . . . The working class is beginning to free itself from the illusion that if it were to give up its intention of wresting political power by revolutonary methods, it could attain political and economic power by gradual and peaceful means, i.e., the illusion by which the Social Democrats and the trade union bureaucracy have kept the working class from participating in the revolutionary struggle. . . .

. . . What we are confronted with, then, is not the delay of the world revolution, not its ebb, but on the contrary, the aggravation of social antagonisms and social struggle and the transition to open civil war.

III. *The Important Task of the Present*

Obtaining decisive influence over the majority of the working class and drawing its most active elements into a direct struggle are the most important tasks now confronting the Communist International. Despite the present objectively revolutionary economic and political situation, wherein the most acute revolutionary crisis may arise suddenly (a big strike, a colonial upheaval, a new war, even a severe parliamentary crisis), the majority of the working class is not yet under the influence of communism. . . .

In the very first year of its existence, the Communist International disavowed all sectarian tendencies. It called upon all the parties affiliated with it, however small, to enter the trade unions, overcome from within the reactionary trade union bureaucracy, and transform the trade unions into revolutionary mass organizations of the proletariat, into organs of the struggle. In the very first year of its existence the Communist International called upon the communist parties not to confine themselves to propaganda, but to utilize . . . every opening bourgeois society offers: freedom of the press, freedom of association, and all forms of bourgeois representative institutions, however distorted they might be. At its Second Congress the Communist International publicly repudiated sectarian tendencies in its resolutions on trade unionism and the utilization of parliamentarianism.

The experience gained in the two years' struggle of the communist parties has completely corroborated the correctness of this decision of the Communist International. . . .

. . .

X. *International Co-ordination of Action*

In order to break the front of the international counterrevolution, in order to make use of the combined forces of the Communist International and to hasten the victory of the revolution, it is necessary to strive, with all energy, for united international leadership in the revolutionary struggle.

The Communist International imposes on all communist parties the duty of supporting each other most energetically in the struggle. The growing economic conflicts demand the immediate intervention of the proletariat of other countries. The Communists must carry on diligent propaganda in the trade unions to prevent not only the importation of strikebreakers but also the exportation of the goods of those countries where a considerable section of the proletariat is engaged in struggle. In cases where the capitalist government of one country perpetrates outrages against another country by trying to plunder or subjugate it, the communist parties must not only protest, but do all in their power to prevent such a pillaging campaign by their government. . . . [Outlines the tasks of Communists in various countries.]

. . . The unconditional support of Soviet Russia has been and still is the main duty of the Communists of all countries. Not only must they act resolutely against any attacks on Soviet Russia, but they must also struggle to do away with all the obstacles placed by capitalist states in the way of Soviet Russia's communication with the world's markets and with all other nations. Only if Soviet Russia succeeds in reconstructing its national economy, in mitigating the terrible misery caused by three years of imperialist war and three years of civil war, and in raising the efficiency of its masses, will it be able in the future to assist the victorious proletarian states in the West with food and raw material, and to protect them against being strangled by American capital.

The world-wide political task of the Communist International is not to arrange demonstrations to protest particular events, but to increase international solidarity among Communists, and to guide their joint and ceaseless struggle in closed formation [against capitalists]. It is impossible to foretell on what front the proletariat will succeed in breaking the capitalist lines. Perhaps it will be in capitalist Germany, whose workers, cruelly oppressed by the German and Entente bourgeoisie, must either win or die; or perhaps in the agrarian southeastern countries, or in Italy, where the decay of the bourgeoisie has reached an advanced stage. The Communist International must therefore intensify its efforts on all sectors of the workers' world front. Every communist party [belonging to the Communist International] is duty-bound to do its utmost to help every other section of the Communist International that might be waging a decisive battle. Whenever a serious domestic conflict develops in one country, the communist parties of other countries must stage similar conflicts in their own countries and develop them into an open struggle.

THE WORK OF ORGANIZING THE COMMUNIST PARTIES
AND THE METHODS AND SCOPE OF THEIR WORK

· · ·

IV. *On Propaganda and Agitation*

20. Our chief general duty to the open revolutionary revolt is to carry on revolutionary propaganda and agitation. . . .

21. The principal forms of communist propaganda and agitation are: individual verbal propaganda, participation in the trade union and political workers' movement, and influence through the party press and party literature. Every member of a legal or illegal party must participate regularly in one or another of these forms of activity.

Individual propaganda must take the form of systematic house-to-house canvassing by special groups of agitators. Not a single house within the area of local party influence must be omitted from this canvass. In larger towns a specially organized outdoor campaign with posters and the distribution of leaflets usually produces results. In addition, the cells and factions should carry on regular personal agitation in workshops and institutions, accompanied by distribution of literature.

In countries whose population contains national minorities, the party must devote the necessary attention to propaganda and agitation among the proletarian strata of these minorities. The propaganda and agitation must, of course, be conducted in the languages of the respective national minorities, for which purpose the party must create the necessary special party organs.

22. In capitalist countries in which a large majority of the proletariat has not yet reached revolutionary consciousness, the communist agitators must constantly seek new and better forms of propaganda, in order to meet the nonrevolutionary workers halfway and thus facilitate their entry into the revolutionary ranks. The communist propaganda, with its slogans, must foster the budding, unconscious, incomplete, vacillating, and semibourgeois revolutionary tendencies that are struggling for supremacy in the minds of the workers against the bourgeois traditions and conceptions. . . .

23. The communist agitation among the proletarian masses must be conducted in such a way that our communist organizations will be recognized by the struggling proletarians as the courageous, farsighted, energetic, and ever-faithful leaders of their own common movement.

In order to achieve this, the Communists must take part in all the elementary struggles and movements of the working class, and they must defend the workers' cause in all conflicts between them and the capitalists over hours and conditions of labor, wages, etc. The Communists must also study the concrete problems of working-class life. They must help the workers to arrive at a correct understanding of these problems. They must draw the attention of the workers to the most flagrant abuses and must help them to formulate their demands to the capitalists in a practical and concise form. They must awaken in the workers the spirit of solidarity, the consciousness of the community of interests among all the workers of the country as a united working class, which, in its turn, is a section of the world army of the proletariat.

Only by the everyday performance of such elementary duties, and by continuous and selfless participation in all the struggles of the proletariat, can the "Communist Party" develop into a real communist party. Only by adopting such methods will it be distinguished from the outlived, socialist, pure propagandist parties whose duty is limited to recruiting new members, talking about reforms, and making use of all parliamentary "impossibilities." The self-sacrificing and conscious participation of all party members in the daily struggles and controversies between the exploited and the exploiters is essentially necessary not only for effecting the dictatorship of the proletariat, but for carrying it out. It is only by leading the working masses in the daily warfare against the onslaughts of capitalism that the communist party will become the vanguard of the working class, will acquire the capacity for systematic leadership of the proletariat, and will become fully prepared [for the struggle] for the complete elimination of the bourgeoisie. . . .

THE OBJECTIVES OF COMMUNIST FOREIGN POLICY

29

Lenin on a Dual Policy to Take Advantage of the Weakness of Capitalist States

[Excerpts from the Stenographic Notes on Lenin's Speech at a Meeting of the All-Russian Central Council of Trade Unions, April 11, 1921][54]

. . .

The future is highly promising. We must, however, on no account mix two kinds of activities: One is the work of agitation which brings that future nearer; the other is knowing how to manage [our affairs] in such a way that we shall be triumphant in the capitalist encirclement. If we cannot do this, we may have the misfortune of applying to ourselves the saying "Before the sun rises, the dew will ruin your eyes." We must be able, by making use of the peculiarities of the capitalist world, and also by taking advantage of the eagerness of the capitalists for raw materials, to derive advantages that will consolidate our economic position (this may sound very strange) among the capitalists. The task appears somewhat odd: How can a socialist republic improve its position while leaning on capitalism? But we had this experience during the war [i.e., the war against intervention]. We were victorious in that war not because we were stronger, but because, although weaker, we made use of the enmities that existed among the capitalist states. Now, too, we shall either utilize the enmity that exists among the various trusts, or show ourselves unable to adapt to capitalist peculiarities; and in that case we shall be unable to exist in the capitalist environment. . . .

[54] *Leninskii Sbornik*, XX, 169.

30

Kamenev's Estimate of the World Situation and the Objectives of Communist Foreign Policy

[Speech at the Tenth Party Congress, Moscow, March 15, 1921][55]

We must seriously and thoroughly discuss our relations with the capitalist states at this moment. Our expectations of immediate assistance from Western Europe in the form of revolution in at least one or two capitalist countries—which would have considerably eased our own task—have not been realized as quickly as we had desired.

Had the rising of the proletariat on a world-wide scale overthrown the rule of the bourgeoisie in at least one or two of the largest capitalist countries, then the question of capitalist encirclement would no longer confront us, nor would there be any problems about treaties, loans, concessions, and all the other questions connected with them.

While continuing to rely on this rising, we must at the same time so map out our practical policy as to be fully prepared if the world situation should require us to struggle for the existence of the isolated and only socialist republic in the world. Therefore, we must take into serious consideration the world situation as it exists today.

When the World War started, the revolutionary Marxists diagnosed the ensuing slaughter as a struggle among the largest imperialist powers for the redistribution of the world. Two years have now passed since the official end of the war; peace treaties have been signed. It would be hard, however, to find any hypocrite who would say that Europe is now in a state of peace. . . . At any moment, the old slaughter may bring forth its natural offspring—i.e., some new, still more monstrous, and still more destructive imperialist war.

If we examine the situation in Europe, we see that the imperialists of the Great Powers have attained their goal; they have redistributed the world among themselves. They have divided it into two unequal camps. On one side we have the largest victor-powers, England, France, America, and Japan; on the other side we have a motley of countries—colonies in the full sense of the word, countries that were colonies before the war, and semicolonial countries that were granted independence during the war but are actually toys in the hands of the victor-powers. Finally, we have allegedly independent countries, the old cultural and industrial countries, such as Germany and Austria, which actually have been made into vassals and placed in a state of bondage to the victor-powers.

The position of Germany and Austria is unique. One cannot consider them as colonies, because they are industrial countries. Neither can one consider them independent, because in their foreign policies, in their economic activities, and, above all, in their domestic policies, they are obliged to follow the directives, often accompanied by threats, of the victor-powers. . . .

If I had more time, I would give you an economic analysis of the position of the European countries, and I would construct for you the true hierarchy of dependencies. We would then see that America, which is seemingly holding aloof from the coming bloody encounter in Europe (and we are nearing this encounter), America, which is standing aside with folded arms and letting the European gentlemen fight among themselves, has actually reaped the richest harvest for herself. By entering the war at the last moment, she succeeded, both by her financial measures and by provisioning the fighting forces, in profiting . . .

[55] *Desiatyi sezd R.K.P.,* pp. 454–69.

Next comes England, the richest of the European countries, which actually controls Europe's entire economy. Then comes France, which, although seemingly in the camp of the victors such as England, is at the same time so exhausted economically and so weakened by the war that she cannot possibly be put on a par with England as an economic, military, or political force. So we have a number of gradations among the victors, as well as among the vanquished. As a result, international relations resemble a powder keg ready to explode at any moment. . . .

What does this situation actually portend? First, a new imperialist war. Those of us who study world policies know that the Pacific will undoubtedly be the center of the new world war. It is here that a clash is possible between the former allies— i.e., England and America, with Japan on the English side. The struggle for the Pacific, for Asia, is the basic question of the day in both England and America. No one in America denies that the future struggle will be a struggle for control of the world between the two most important victors, the former allies—i.e., England and America, with Japan on the English side. Presumably, then, in the new world war, as in the last one, no country will remain neutral, and the two largest powers will draw all the remaining powers into economic, political, and financial dependency.

This new destructive war can be prevented (and we hope we can prevent it) only by the revolt of the proletariat in one country or the other. Clearly, then, under present circumstances the position of the Soviet republic is quite special. . . . For one thing, the Soviet republic no longer participates in the division of the world; for another, thanks to its three years of struggle, it has won its right to an independent existence. If we analyze our struggle against foreign intervention, against foreign interference, objectively and historically, we see that the basic issue in this war was whether or not the Soviet republic, this huge territory with a population of millions, would become a colony of one or another capitalist group. There was not the slightest doubt that whether Russia continued the war in alliance with England and America or made a separate peace, whether she triumphed with England and America or was vanquished with the other coalition, she would have had to serve as a colony, as a source [of raw materials], as a market for the goods exported from one or another of the capitalist countries.

Our three years of war won independence for us. This is a very important fact. What we have won cannot be taken from us; thanks to the Soviet government, and thanks to the heroic struggle of the workers and peasants, Russia has saved herself from being made into a colony. Thanks to our independent position, we are able to take a definite place in the historical process of development.

At the same time, the relations between us and the capitalist powers are also changing. Three years ago there could have been only one kind of relations between us: the relations of people fighting on opposite sides of a barricade, the relations of two armies, relations entirely those of war.

And yet, as you know, comrades, throughout this period other new relations were developing. . . . Now we seem to be approaching a turning point—treaty relations are being substituted for purely war relations. We are on the eve of signing an agreement with England.

. . . But does this mean that we are on the way to making peace with the capitalist world? It would, of course, be the greatest illusion on our part to think so; and, of course, none of the representatives of the world bourgeoisie who are conducting negotiations with us in one form or another are counting on such a reconciliation. Still less can we expect these relations to lead to some reconciliation. No, our agreements represent only a new form of struggle, the struggle to establish communism in one isolated country. This task is, of course, a difficult one, one we had never contemplated. Yet in our present situation it is imperative for us to retain the basis of the communist regime, the basis of the socialist state—i.e., the Soviet proletarian republic—which is surrounded on all sides by capitalist states.

Shall we be able to accomplish this task? I think that this is an academic question to which no direct answer can be given. The real question at present is as follows: In view of existing conditions, how can we retain the soviet government, and retain it until such time as the proletariat in one country or another comes to our rescue?

Therefore, we cannot possibly regard our [new] relations [with the capitalist countries] as the beginning of a reconciliation with the capitalist powers by means of trade agreements. We have no doubt that the bourgeois capitalist states desire trade relations with us, and that they are coming to us because they need us. If they resort to this policy of agreement, it means that their other policy has failed—the policy they practiced for three years, the policy by which they tried to force us into submission. . . . Have they given up their plan? Of course not. And, of course, any time they find it convenient and suitable to give up their policy of signing agreements, the policy of buying and selling, they will again resort to armed struggle against us.

[Speaks of the Kronstadt revolt, then in progress, and incited, in his opinion, by anti-Soviet forces in Paris to delay the signing of the Anglo-Soviet trade agreement.] . . .

This agreement [with England] is very important, not [only] because England can supply us with much that we need at present—i.e., machinery, raw material, and so forth—but because once England enters into a trade agreement with us, a number of other countries will feel free to do the same thing—especially the vanquished countries, which are afraid to move a step without England. . . . Furthermore, an agreement with England opens the possibility of trade with America and an agreement with Canada, which is actually an independent English colony. Through this agreement, the entrance of the North American states into trade relations with us is inevitable. These are the vistas opened to us by an agreement with England. Unquestionably those who realize that this agreement would be both a diplomatic and a military victory for Soviet Russia, as well as a consolidation of our international position, will make every possible effort to prevent its passage.

[Speaks of the need of the European countries to utilize the economic forces of Soviet Russia.]

.   .   .

The disintegration of the capitalist economy in Western Europe is so advanced that our raw materials, which will bring us into the world economy, cannot delay the revolutionary process there even for a day, not for an hour. Moreover, the development of the productive forces of the world economy does not contradict the proletarian revolution, but, on the contrary, only stimulates its development, because it intensifies [class] differences.

. . . If the capitalists had succeeded in tying Russia hand and foot, together with all her natural wealth, [and thus in] placing the toiling masses of workers and peasants in servitude, then the collapse of world capital could, very likely, have been delayed. . . .

Comrades, during the last three years we needed an army to defend the existence of Soviet Russia. Now we can say boldly: In order to defend her existence, Soviet Russia must develop her productive forces with the greatest possible speed, and on a gigantic scale. Once we enter the arena of world economic competition, two possibilities confront us: Either by developing our productive forces we shall be victorious in this economic arena as we have been in our military efforts, or we shall be overtaken by the capitalist countries. We dare not shut our eyes to this fact. When we went to war we knew our adversary was stronger than we were, both numerically and in the superiority of his training, equipment, ammunition, tanks, guns, and planes. So now, too, we must say to ourselves: The capitalist countries are at present more powerful than we are economically; they have more engines, more machinery, more equipment, and a better organization, and they know how to manage their economy better than we do.

We must acknowledge this fact. They are stronger than we are. However, we are now in a position to prevent them from forcing us to give in to their strength. How can we do this? By developing our productive forces. This means that we must start to develop our natural resources with unheard-of rapidity.

I am now approaching a question that has worried the party: While developing our natural resources, can we save and develop our economy without the help of foreign capital? . . . Our answer is no. We can, of course, restore our economy by the heroic effort of the working masses. But we cannot develop it fast enough to prevent the capitalist countries from overtaking us, unless we call in foreign capital. We must realize this clearly; we must also explain it to the workers. . . .

. . . In developing our natural wealth, we cannot receive help from foreign capital unless we pay for it. We shall have to pay a tribute.

. . . We are paying for our economic backwardness; and, in addition, we are paying a percentage to foreign capital because the world revolution is not advancing as rapidly, not taking over control of the means of production in Western Europe as quickly, as desirable.

. . .

But we are convinced that the foreign capitalists, who will be obliged to work on the terms we offer them, will dig their own grave. Without them we cannot rearm ourselves [economically]; this is the dialectic of history; we cannot rearm ourselves [economically] without the electrification of Russia. But while strengthening Soviet Russia, developing her productive forces, foreign capital will fulfill the role Marx predicted for it when he said that capital was digging its own grave. With every additional shovel of coal, with every additional load of oil that we in Russia obtain through the help of foreign technique, capital will be digging its own grave.

Therefore, without pessimism, but with full confidence and a firm conviction that we must, at any cost, preserve the principles of socialist economy in Soviet Russia until such time as our poor and devastated country is joined by the proletarian soviet republics of other more industrially and economically advanced countries, we can resort to new measures, [the right to] which we won as the result of three years of war—i.e., to attracting the assistance of foreign capital.

We are half encircled by capitalists: one half of the circle [around us] is made up of capitalists, and the other half by rising Asia, revolutionary Asia, which is non-capitalist. If we are able to hold on, it is because a certain equilibrium has come to exist between Europe and the Asia which is already raising its head. Historically, geographically, and politically, we hold a pivotal position. It is not without reason that in the first clause of the English treaty the English included the following: "We shall trade with you if you give up your propaganda in Egypt, India, Afghanistan, and so forth."

In spite of the capitalist encirclement, we shall defend Soviet Russia.

PART II

The Beginning of "Peaceful Coexistence"
1922–1923

PART II

By 1922 Soviet leaders had altered to some extent their timetable for revolution. They continued to view as inevitable the extension of revolutionary upheaval throughout other parts of the world, but while waiting hopefully for that to happen, they devoted most of their energy to strengthening the Russian state and the soviet system within Russia. The necessity of temporary coexistence and of economic exchange with the nonsoviet world had by this time been officially incorporated into communist doctrine. Thus Lenin could report to the Ninth All-Russian Congress of Soviets, December 23, 1921 : "I must state something that I have already had occasion to say, and that is that a certain, although highly unstable, equilibrium in international relations has been reached." The menace from the West had not been overcome, however, for Russia was "surrounded by people, classes, and governments that openly profess the greatest hatred for us."[1]

But that these people and governments nevertheless could and should be dealt with through the normal channels of trade and diplomacy had become the prevailing Soviet view. As previously noted, the realities of the Russian Communists' situation—their evident and desperate need for Western goods and techniques—had compelled them to rationalize the desirability of trade with the West. Kamenev, for example, had discovered that such trade would neither "delay the revolutionary process" nor "contradict the proletarian revolution," but would "stimulate its development, because it intensifies [class] differences."[2]

At the same time the Western Allies had rediscovered what the members of another alliance had learned in the days of the French Revolution, that is, how difficult and hazardous it is to intervene against a revolutionary regime in a country possessing great manpower, great spaces, and other resources for resistance. The economic troubles in the West, the desire to recoup some of the losses of war by trade with Russia, and the hope of recovering the value of foreign investments expropriated by the Communists, combined to make it about as easy for the Western European governments to accept Lloyd George's formula for curing anarchy by abundance as it was for the Communists to accept the formula of peaceful coexistence. As the first consequence of these rationalizations, provisional agreements were signed between individual powers and the new Soviet state. Several of these bilateral arrangements were made during 1920–21 as we have seen. During the next two years, 1922–23, attempts were made to enlarge the field of Soviet Russia's international relations. In this diplomatic move the Communists' chief assets were the lure of the Russian market and the rivalries of the Allies. For their part the Allies were in a position to give Russia what it most wanted, now that world revolution had been postponed—*de jure* recognition and technical aid.

During these years Soviet Russia took part in a number of international

[1] Lenin, *Sochineniia,* XXVII, 113, 117; see Document 31.
[2] See our p. 93.

conferences convened for the settlement of outstanding issues. Part II will be concerned with these various general conferences, Part III with Soviet diplomatic relations with individual Western powers.

The Genoa Conference Preliminaries

When the Allied Supreme Council met at Cannes, January 6, 1922, Lloyd George recommended that a general economic reconciliation with Russia be attempted. Accordingly, the Supreme Council decided to call an economic and financial conference the following March in Genoa, to discuss measures for the "economic reconstruction of Central and Eastern Europe." Both Russia and Germany would be invited to take part. In a resolution adopted January 6, the Council declared:

The Allied Powers consider that the resumption of international trade throughout Europe and the development of the resources of all countries are necessary to increase the volume of productive employment and to relieve the widespread suffering of the European peoples. A united effort by the stronger powers is necessary to remedy the paralysis of the European system. This effort must include the removal of all obstacles in the way of trade, the provision of substantial credits for the weaker countries and the co-operation of all nations in the restoration of normal prosperity.[3]

This Supreme Council resolution, which came to be known as the Cannes Resolution, also included the following statement of the terms upon which the Allied powers were willing to undertake the proposed discussions:

1. Nations can claim no right to dictate to each other regarding the principles on which they are to regulate their system of ownership, internal economy and government. It is for every nation to choose for itself the system which it prefers in this respect.

2. Before, however, foreign capital can be made available to assist a country, foreign investors must be assured that their property and their rights will be respected and the fruits of their enterprise secured to them.

3. The sense of security cannot be re-established unless the Governments of countries desiring foreign credit freely undertake—

(a) That they will recognize all public debts and obligations which have been or may be undertaken or guaranteed by the State, by municipalities, or by other public bodies, as well as the obligation to restore or compensate all foreign interests for loss or damage caused to them when property has been confiscated or withheld.

(b) That they will establish a legal and juridical system which sanctions and enforces commercial and other contracts with impartiality.

4. An adequate means of exchange must be available, and generally, there must be financial and currency conditions which offer sufficient security for trade.

5. All nations should undertake to refrain from propaganda subversive of order and the established political system in other countries than their own.

6. All countries should join in an undertaking to refrain from aggression against their neighbors.

Also included was an indirect offer of official diplomatic recognition for the Soviet government provided it would agree to the foregoing stipulations.[4]

[3] *The Genoa Conference for the Economic and Financial Reconstruction of Europe. April 10 to May 19, 1922. Joint Report of the Canadian Delegates,* p. 23. (Hereafter cited as *Genoa Conference . . . Report of the Canadian Delegates.*)

[4] *Ibid.,* pp. 23–24.

As soon as it was informed of the proposed conference, the Soviet government announced that it would send representatives.[5] The possibilities opened by the conference, however, were viewed with somewhat mixed feelings by various Soviet leaders. Karl Radek welcomed it as recognition of Soviet authority. He said that the demand for Soviet recognition of tsarist debts was simply a tactical move on the part of the Allies, and predicted—somewhat overoptimistically as it turned out—that the principal tasks of the conference would be to decide what loans would be placed at Russia's disposal, what organizations would advance them, and under what conditions they would be raised. Radek may have been intimating to the Allies what Soviet Russia wanted from the conference. In any case, he also sounded a warning that the Soviet government would go only so far. Of the Cannes Resolution's implication that foreign business would require special legal guarantees in Russia, he wrote: "Capitalism is capable of adapting itself to [varied] conditions; if political conditions in Russia are impregnable, and if at the same time the capitalists are guaranteed some profit, they will toe the line."[6]

Chicherin was somewhat more skeptical. He called the Cannes decision a political triumph for the British tradition and English business interests, and an attempt at a peaceful penetration into Russia necessitated by Russia's growing economic significance, military power, and political influence in the East. France, so he reasoned, had gone along with the British policy for fear that otherwise Britain would skim the cream off of trade with Russia. He saw the new attempt at international rapprochement as a chance for Russia to get the economic collaboration she wanted, but he warned that economic collaboration might become economic enslavement:

We have business aims; we desire the economic restoration of Russia; we wish to participate through it in regulating the economic relations of the world; we want to carry out economic tasks jointly with Western business circles in a purely business-like manner; but with all that, we must guard Russia's independence, permitting neither the violation of her sovereign rights nor interference in her domestic affairs.[7]

Lenin, too, joined in the comment on the forthcoming conference. In speaking before the communist section of a congress of metalworkers in Moscow, March 6, 1922, he said:

We need to trade with the capitalist countries as long as they exist as such. We are negotiating with them as merchants, and the fact that we can achieve our ends is being proved by the ever-increasing number of our trade agreements with capitalist countries, as well as by the number of transactions carried out. . . . All attempts to impose terms upon us as if we were vanquished are outright nonsense and not worth answering. We are entering relations as tradesmen, and we know what they owe us, and what legitimate and even high profit they may derive from us.[8]

Nor did Lenin share Radek's optimism. Believing that because of political unrest among the inviting powers the conference might never be held, he emphasized in this speech the continuing danger of foreign intervention and the dangers from within arising out of the economic conditions within Russia.

[5] Translations of Chicherin's telegrams addressed to the Allied Supreme Council, January 8, 1922, and to the Italian premier, January 10, 1922, appear in Degras, I, 287–89.
[6] *Pravda,* No. 6, January 10, 1922, p. 2; see Document 32.
[7] *Materialy genuezskoi konferentsii,* p. 19; see Document 33.
[8] Lenin, *Sochineniia,* XXVII, 170, 173.

Lenin further believed, apparently, that the powers that had called the conference might themselves try to break it up. This notion appeared in his report
to the Eleventh Party Congress on March 27, when he stated:

There exists in the bourgeois camp a group that is extremely strong and much more
powerful than any other single group, and whose aim is to break up the conference.
There are other groups that insist on its convocation. These latter groups are now
dominant. . . . It is not immaterial to us whether we deal with representatives of
the militant group or the pacifist groups. . . . We go to Genoa with a practical purpose—to widen our trade and to create conditions under which this trade can develop
best and most successfully. But we are far from being sure of the success of the
Genoa Conference.[9]

Despite these particular doubts, Lenin remained optimistic about the future
of Soviet trade with the West, taking the line that it was bound to increase regardless of Genoa. His report to the Eleventh Party Congress, March 27, 1922,
said:

Do not forget that in recent years the most urgent, daily, practical, and obvious
interests of all the capitalist powers have demanded the development, consolidation,
and expansion of trade with Russia. And since such interests exist, we can argue,
quarrel, and break off negotiations on some issues (it is quite possible that there will
be a break-off), but in the end basic economic necessity will force its way. We are
quite sure on that score. We cannot be sure of the time [it will take], we cannot be
sure of [immediate] success; but we can confidently predict here that progress will
be made toward developing normal trade relations between the Soviet republic and
the rest of the capitalist world.[10]

Meanwhile the Western powers had been having trouble getting the conference under way. In January 1922, French reaction to the decision to hold
the conference had overthrown the Briand government that had sponsored it,
and the much less conciliatory Poincaré had taken over. A month later there
was also a cabinet shake-up in Italy.

On February 8 Poincaré sent a memorandum to London proposing extensive
revision of the Anglo-French plans for the conference. He insisted that the
question of German reparations be dropped, which left for consideration only
the Russian problem. He further requested a preliminary agreement among the
Allied governments on the economic plans that might be presented during the
discussions, and asked, in addition, that the conference be delayed for three
months.

As a compromise the British proposed that an Allied commission of experts
draw up the economic and financial proposals to be presented. In accord with
an agreement to this effect reached by Lloyd George and Poincaré at Boulogne,
such a commission met in London, March 20–28, and drafted a series of proposals, known as the London Memorandum of Experts, which were in due
time presented for the consideration of the Genoa Conference.

The Soviet government interpreted the French cabinet crisis and the Poincaré note to London as new evidence of the desire of certain bourgeois circles
to break up the conference. Rakovsky, one of the Soviet delegates to the conference, predicted that the conference would make outrageous, unacceptable

[9] *Ibid.*, pp. 225–26.
[10] *Ibid.*, p. 226.

demands of Russia. Speaking of press reports that restitution of private property to foreigners would be demanded, he said: "We shall sign no promissory notes that would enslave our government; we shall sign no commitments that would violate the basic laws of the Soviet republic—the laws nationalizing the land and giving the state monopoly of industry and foreign trade." Like Lenin he was pessimistic about the possible outcome of the conference, but optimistic about the eventual resumption of full-scale trade:

[Our] whole problem is to hold on, not to count on a loan, on credits that might come after the Genoa Conference. We must not forget that we are still passing through a phase of a revolutionary epoch; we must look to ourselves for remedies for our own ills; we ourselves must fight the famine and the breakdown of our transportation system; and we must make our Red Army even stronger, because this army is our only support. If this opinion, if this realization, supports us as well in the future as in the past, then economic agreement will soon be reached.[11]

The Genoa Conference finally opened April 10, 1922. With the delegates of thirty-four states participating and seven hundred news correspondents watching them, this promised to be one of the most important meetings of the powers, second only perhaps to the Paris Peace Conference. The United States was conspicuously absent, but by no means indifferent.

Lenin did not go to Genoa. The Soviet leaders apparently decided that any prestige the Soviet government might gain through having its head sit down with other heads of state and any added strength to the Soviet delegation because of Lenin's presence were offset by other considerations. Two public explanations were given for keeping Lenin at home: He had to help combat the famine, and he would not be safe in Genoa. Resolutions adopted by various groups of workers, soldiers, and students dwelt on the second point: "We ask the All-Russian Central Executive Committee," said one, "not to send our beloved Ilich to Genoa and London. Protect Ilich."[12]

Lenin's absence also increased the bargaining maneuverability of the Soviet delegation. Chicherin, when he did not want to say either yes or no, could say that he had to refer to his government. He could also indicate that an answer was not final by saying he would refer the matter to his government for further instructions. With Lenin at the conference, there would have been no one in Moscow to refer to. In using this method Soviet Russia was reverting to the ways of traditional diplomacy and only partially adopting the method of "diplomacy by conference" that the Allies had found useful during and immediately after World War I.

The Genoa Conference

From the first it was apparent that the inviting powers—Britain, France, Italy, and Belgium—would take the leading role in the deliberations. It was apparent also that the inviting powers' objectives differed widely from those of the Soviet representatives. Essentially, the Soviet government hoped to obtain through the conference loans with which to rebuild the Russian economy ac-

[11] Kh. G. Rakovsky, *Nakanune Genui*, pp. 30, 32; see also Document 34.

[12] N. L. Rubinshtein, *Sovetskaia diplomatiia v borbe protiv izoliatsii SSSR i ustanovlenie diplomaticheskikh otnoshenii s kapitalisticheskimi stranami*, p. 17. (Hereafter cited as *Sovetskaia diplomatiia v borbe protiv izoliatsii SSSR.*)

cording to their own designs. The European powers, on the other hand, hoped by means of the conference to force the Soviets to recognize past liabilities and to restore the rights of private enterprise, at least for foreigners, within the Russian state.

After Premier Facta of Italy had been elected chairman of the conference, Lloyd George took the floor to deliver the first speech. After the usual pleasantries required on such an occasion, he raised the difficult question of Russian debts. "We meet," he said, "on equal terms, provided we accept equal conditions. . . . These conditions the inviting powers laid down at Cannes. . . . They are the only conditions upon which we can consent to deal with others. . . . The first is that when a country enters into contractual obligations with another country or its nationals for value received, that contract cannot be repudiated, whenever a country changes its government, without returning the value." He then went on to summarize the other conditions laid down in the Cannes Resolution and to state that "if any people reject these elementary conditions of civilized intercourse between nations, they cannot be expected to be received into the comity of nations." Lastly he pointed to the need for peace and economic reconstruction in Europe and expressed his hopes that these ends might be met by the work of the conference.[18]

When Chicherin, as head of the Soviet delegation, took the floor, he emphasized the need for economic collaboration between what he described as the "old social order and the new one now being created." He stated that the coexistence of these two orders was quite possible and announced his government's willingness to open its frontiers to the creation of international communication routes; to make available millions of desiatinas of soil for cultivation; and to grant forest and mining and other concessions to foreigners. But in regard to past debts and claims he warned that "the task of ending European economic chaos will be attempted in vain . . . if the economically more powerful nations, instead of fostering Russia's economic revival and facilitating her future progress, crush her under the weight of demands that not only are beyond her strength but are survivals of a past that is odious to her." While the Soviet delegation was willing to accept the Cannes Resolution in principle, he said, it reserved the right to present supplementary articles and amendments. Of these he suggested three in the course of his speech, the first being a general limitation of armaments:

The Russian delegation wish to propose to the Conference the general limitation of armaments. Russia will support all measures tending to lighten the burden of militarism, on condition that the limitation be applicable to the armies of all countries, and that the rules of war include the absolute abolition of the most barbarous methods of warfare, such as the use of poison gas, aerial warfare, and in particular the destruction of peaceful populations. Russia, for her part, is prepared to limit her armaments on condition of full and complete reciprocity, and on condition that she be given the necessary guarantees against any kind of attack upon her or interference in her domestic affairs.

Next he proposed that a series of international conferences be convened periodically, to include representatives of workers' organizations as well as governments. For this purpose he recommended that the League of Nations

[18] *Les Documents de la Conférence de Gênes*, pp. 12–17.

be made "a true union of all peoples without the domination of some over the others, without the present division into victors and vanquished." Lastly he suggested, as a step toward financial stabilization in the world, that the existing reserves of gold be redistributed (by long-term loans) among all countries to match the prewar apportionment, and that the products of industry be redistributed on the same basis. In concluding, he reiterated the communist view that the causes of war and of economic crisis could not be effectively suppressed under the existing world order, but added that the Soviet delegation was willing to agree to any measures to this end, "even though they be merely palliatives."[14]

Chicherin's suggestions are an excellent example of the Communists' use of conference diplomacy to appeal to the people of the world over the heads of the delegates to whom the suggestions are ostensibly addressed. Chicherin's first proposal—disarmament and the abolition of "barbarous methods of warfare"— would appeal to the people of all countries; the reorganization of the League would appeal to those who were not members, especially Germany and other defeated nations; and the redistribution of gold reserves would interest the "poor" nations, i.e., all except the United States and perhaps Britain. Chicherin's last observation on the inevitability of war and economic crises under capitalism was a bow to Marxist dogma calculated to appeal to the Social Democrats, collectively the largest political party in Western Europe.

The French representative, M. Barthou, immediately protested that the delegates were expected to stick to the agenda outlined at Cannes, which had not included a universal conference or a series of conferences. His most emphatic protest, however, he reserved for Chicherin's attempt to introduce the question of disarmament into the deliberations. "This," he declared, "is not on the agenda, and I say simply but clearly that when and if Russia wants to examine this question she will be faced not only with the reserve of France, but with her protest and absolute final and decisive refusal to discuss it."[15]

Chicherin replied that the Russian delegation had not been officially informed of the agenda, but had learned of it only through the press. Although the agenda included certain other questions that had not been contained in the Cannes Resolution, he said, the Russian delegation would nevertheless bow to the collective will of the conference in the matter. As for disarmament:

I am not aware of the official position taken in this respect by the governments of the powers who have convened this conference. The point of view of France was known to us from statements made by M. Briand at Washington in the debate on the limitation of armaments: that armaments could not be limited by France because of the state of armament in Russia. We were therefore led to suppose that if Russia consented to disarm, the cause invoked by M. Briand would *ipso facto* disappear.[16]

Thus having made it appear that the French government was the foe of disarmament, which practically everybody in the world wanted, while Russia was the champion of disarmament and peace, Chicherin sat back and waited for his next opportunity.

[14] *Materialy genuezskoi konferentsii*, pp. 78–82; also *The Soviet Union and Peace . . .*, pp. 82–86. See also Document 35.

[15] *Les Documents de la Conférence de Gênes*, p. 32.

[16] *Materialy genuezskoi konferentsii*, p. 84.

On the second day the conference broke up into four commissions, but almost immediately it became apparent that the inviting powers expected many of the decisions to be reached outside the commissions, through personal negotiations among the delegates. Accordingly, although the Report on the Reconstruction of Russia (part of the London Memorandum of Experts) was given to the Soviet delegation at the first meeting of the political commission, discussion of it was reserved for an extracurricular meeting at the Villa Albertis, where the British delegation was staying.

The Report called upon the Soviet government to accept absolute responsibility for paying debts incurred by its predecessors, and for paying the claims of foreign owners of property in Russia who had suffered losses because of nationalization or other Soviet practices. This second demand soon became the principal obstacle to agreement. The Report specified detailed means by which these Russian debts and liabilities could best be met, chief among them being the creation of a Russian debt commission and mixed arbitral tribunals to determine the amount and method of payment.

Annexes to the Report further defined the Allied terms. The Soviet government was expected not only to restore the property formerly owned by foreigners in Russia, but also to pay compensation for losses suffered by the owners during the period in which the property had provided no profits. Further, any owner not desiring restitution was to have the right to claim monetary compensation. Property no longer in existence or unidentifiable was covered by other clauses.

The scope of the annexes extended to holdings that had previously belonged to Russian citizens and not to foreigners. Annex II, Article 9, specified that where interest in former private enterprises in Russia had been used as collateral in obtaining an unpaid loan, whether by a Russian or by a foreigner, the creditor could apply directly to the Soviet government to obtain satisfaction:

Where a debtor is entitled, or, if he had been a national of one of the other Powers, would have been entitled, to claim compensation . . . the creditor may . . . make a direct claim against the Soviet Government in respect of the loss arising from his unpaid debt instead of against the debtor.

Annex III dealt with the means by which monetary claims of former owners would be met. Its first article stated: "All accepted claims for monetary compensation against the Russian Soviet Government will be met by the issue of new Russian bonds up to the amounts fixed by the Mixed Arbitral Tribunals." Its second article provided that the bonds "shall be free both as to interest and capital from all Russian taxation, both present and future, and shall be subject to redemption by annual drawings."

On the other hand, Annex I contemplated granting the Russian debt commission the power "to determine, if necessary, among the revenues of Russia those which should be specially assigned to the service of the debt, for example, an allocation of certain taxes or of royalties or dues upon undertakings in Russia," as well as the power, if necessary, "to control, if the commission thinks fit, the collection of all or part of these assigned revenues, and to deal with the proceeds. These assignments and this control (if imposed) should cease as soon as the Russian debt service appears adequately assured by the inclusion of the appropriate sums in the Russian budget."

The Russian debt commission itself, according to the Report (Annex I), would consist of "members nominated by the Russian Government and members nominated by the other Powers, together with the independent chairman chosen from outside, by agreement among the other members, or, in default, by the League of Nations through the Council or through the Permanent Court of International Justice." The functions of the commission would be three: to constitute and prescribe the procedure of the mixed arbitral tribunals; to issue new Russian bonds to cover the debts and liabilities; and to determine all questions arising out of the issue, rates of interest, and terms of redemption of the new bonds.[17]

From the various provisions set forth in the Report, it was clear that what the Allied powers contemplated was the restoration of private property in Russia. That they also expected extraterritorial privileges was equally evident from detailed provisions for the administration of justice in Russia, including the following:

No domiciliary search may be made in the residence or establishment of a foreigner settled in Russia, nor may his arrest be carried out without the assistance or consent of his Consul. In the case of an appearance before a Russian court on a criminal charge, judgment can only be carried out with the consent of the Consul concerned. The only punishment that may be inflicted as a result of a prosecution on political grounds is expulsion, subject to the above condition.[18]

Some years later a Soviet writer analyzed the terms of the Report as follows:

The London Memorandum expected the Soviet government to give up its right to deal independently with the country's budget, placing it under the control of the Entente. . . . Extraterritoriality was proposed for foreigners in Russia . . . and, finally, the Soviet government was expected to give up its monopoly of foreign trade. Thus actually the regime of capitulations, similar to the one that had been applied by Britain and France to Turkey and other dependent and semicolonial countries, was to be applied to Soviet Russia, and the latter was actually to become a semicolony of Britain and France.[19]

During the discussions of the Report at the Villa Albertis, Soviet representatives replied to the demands made upon Russia by outlining counterclaims based upon losses and damages sustained by the Russian state as a result of the Allied intervention and blockade. On April 20 the Russian delegation addressed a memorandum to the members of the conference branding the demands of the Report "equivalent not only to the exploitation of the toiling population of Russia, but to their total enslavement by foreign capital," and declaring that the Report ignored the "essential question of the means necessary to obtain the . . . economic reconstruction of Russia." Russia's economic restoration could be achieved only by generous long-term credits in money and merchandise, and "not by plundering Russia and retarding Russia's economic development for the sake of satisfying the interests of foreign capitalists."

Following the line of Soviet diplomacy, the Soviet delegation delegation argued that the best way to protect the interests of foreign capital in Russia

[17] *Genoa Conference . . . Report of the Canadian Delegates*, pp. 27–31.
[18] *Ibid.*, p. 34.
[19] N. L. Rubinshtein, "Sovetskaia Rossiia na genuezskoi konferentsii," *Voprosy Istorii*, No. 2–3, 1946, p. 8.

would be by *de jure* recognition of the existing Russian government. The proposed Russian debt commission was unthinkable; it would "change into an organ of foreign control over the whole economic life of the Russian Republic." Responsibility for Russian war debts was disclaimed, and the inviting powers were bluntly informed that the Soviet government would accept neither the principle of restitution of industries to private titles nor "even obligatory leasing to their ex-proprietors." Moreover, it was declared that "if the obtaining of new credits destined for the economic reconstruction of Russia is subordinated to the payment of foreign obligations, and if all the positive results of the new loans and the economic recovery resulting from them are devoted to the payment of old debts, these new credits will lose all sense for the Russian people, and Russia will be obliged to continue the work of her economic reconstruction by her own means and without hoping for the help of foreign capital." Yet the memorandum wound up on a somewhat conciliatory note, calling upon all countries to recognize their public debts and declaring that while the Soviet government considered losses of foreign citizens due to acts of the Soviet government to be offset by the losses suffered by Russia from the intervention, it was willing to discuss both and to compensate the foreign owners if the balance was not in its favor.[20]

The Allied delegates promptly refused to recognize liability for the intervention, but agreed to ignore the tsarist war debts. Thereupon the Soviet delegation announced that it would have to consult its government for further instructions.

At this point the two powers that occupied a somewhat inferior status at the conference—Russia and Germany—announced that they had settled their differences independently of the conference in a treaty, signed April 16 at Rapallo.[21] This announcement created great excitement and annoyance among the delegations of the inviting powers, particularly as it was generally assumed that the treaty included secret clauses in addition to its published text, a belief that persisted in spite of Chicherin's quick denial.[22] Moreover, by the published terms of the treaty, Germany dropped all claims against the Soviet government— a fact that further complicated the Allies' efforts to get their claims recognized.

Soviet leaders and communist historians have claimed, with justice, that the Rapallo treaty was a great diplomatic gain. It did not, of course, "split the anti-Soviet united front" or reflect "the contradiction between Germany and the Entente."[23] It probably widened the split already existing between France and Britain and deepened the abyss between Germany and the Allies because it established an entente between two potentially great powers which had been, for different reasons, ostracized from the concert of the victorious Great Powers.

As the sensation created by the announcement of the Rapallo treaty died down, the deliberations at Genoa continued. The Allies retaliated against the Germans for Rapallo by excluding them from further participation in the dis-

[20] For text see *Materialy genuezskoi konferentsii*, pp. 127-39.

[21] For details see Part III, pp. 168-70.

[22] No text of the alleged secret clauses to the Rapallo treaty is yet available. The text of the alleged military convention between Germany and the R.S.F.S.R., dated April 3, 1922, is given in Shapiro, I, 383. The authenticity of the document has not been definitely established.

[23] N. L. Rubinshtein, *Sovetskaia diplomatiia v borbe protiv izoliatsii SSSR*, p. 21.

cussions of the Russian question on the ground that German-Russian affairs had been settled. The Soviet delegation, after consulting its government, delivered on April 24 a series of counterproposals to the Report of the experts. The Soviet government would give preference to former foreign owners of enterprises in Russia in the granting of concessions, but only if (1) Russia were granted credits for economic reconstruction, and (2) the Soviet government received *de jure* recognition. Further, the offer would apply only to persons who legally owned property in Russia before March 1917, a provision included to offset the speculation abroad in Russian securities.

In regard to the property rights of foreigners, these Soviet counterproposals stated:

> The Russian government declares that it is prepared to restore the rights of foreigners to the use of their former and now nationalized or requisitioned property when it is found possible in virtue of the social and economic system and the basic laws of the Russian republic, i.e., that it is prepared to grant them the most favored right to their property in the form of concession or lease. . . .
> The Russian government is also disposed to satisfy those claims of former owners which it finds just and which do not disagree with the aforementioned conditions. This will be accomplished by means of a free agreement between the government of Russia and the former owners, or by some other way that the conference may choose.[24]

On May 3 the Allies presented a new memorandum to the Soviet delegation, offering the desired credits, but demanding in return that the Soviet government accept a number of conditions similar to those put forward in the original Report of the experts. The major European powers would create an international corporation with an initial capitalization of 20 million pounds sterling to finance reconstruction and other undertakings in Europe "which, without assistance, would have difficulty in procuring the necessary funds." The various countries would make available further aid to Russia by certain other methods. In return, the Soviet government was to (1) "refrain from any action that might disturb the territorial and political status quo in other states"; (2) "suppress all attempts in its territory to assist revolutionary movements in other states"; (3) "use all its influence to help restore peace in Asia Minor"; and (4) "adopt an attitude of strict neutrality between the belligerent parties."[25] The Soviet government was also to recognize tsarist debts and obligations to foreign nationals, as per the experts' Report, and to abandon its claims to damages for losses incurred during the civil war and intervention. The Allies did, however, agree that for the present they would make no claims against the Soviet government for Russian war debts.

With regard to compensation of foreign nationals, this new memorandum stipulated that "the Russian Soviet Government recognises its obligation, in accordance with the said [Cannes] Resolution, to restore or compensate all foreign interests for loss or damage caused to them when property had been con-

[24] For counterproposals of the Russian delegation to Articles 1–7 of the London Memorandum of Experts, see *Materialy genuezskoi konferentsii*, pp. 148–49. An English translation appears in Degras, I, 301–3.

[25] This referred to the hostilities in Anatolia, where Kemal's Turkish forces had received aid and encouragement from Russia in their spectacular defeat of the Greek invasion.

fiscated or withheld."[26] This phraseology marked a new Allied approach; in effect, the Allies tacitly accepted the principle of compensation in lieu of restitution. In consequence the Belgian and French delegations, still holding out for absolute restitution, refused to sign the new memorandum. Also in this memorandum the demands for extraterritorial rights for foreigners were dropped.

The Soviet delegation found this second Allied memorandum no better than the first, and they complained that their counterproposals had been ignored. The lack of a spirit of compromise they attributed to the influence of certain oil magnates who had combined forces, so they declared, in order to apply greater pressure upon Russia.

On May 11 the Soviet delegation replied, condemning the introduction of political questions into the discussion, reasserting claims arising out of the intervention and blockade, calling the demand for restitution of or compensation for nationalized private property of foreign nationals a violation of the Cannes Resolution (which acknowledged the right of nations to organize their economic systems to suit themselves), and repeating their offer of preference in concessions in lieu of restitution or compensation. Lastly, and as a new element, they proposed that the financial disputes between the Allies and themselves be turned over to a mixed commission of experts, to be appointed by the conference.[27]

On May 19 it was decided to refer the still unresolved Russian problem to such a commission of experts, to convene at The Hague. Thus the Genoa Conference drew to a close with no settlement having been reached.

B. E. Shtein, general secretary of the Russian delegation to the Hague Conference, later attributed the failure of both the Genoa Conference and the Hague Conference primarily to differences over restoring foreign private ownership in Russia. He said the question of debts and credits was secondary: "There is no doubt . . . that a compromise could have been reached on these two problems if the third problem, that of private property, had been settled." As for debts, "one party did not refuse to pay, but insisted on a moratorium, [while] the other party insisted on immediate payment, but agreed to talk about a moratorium." Of credits he wrote that the Russian delegation insisted on government credits to the Russian government, while the opposition favored private credits or government credits to private individuals. Shtein further declared that the non-Russian point of view regarding private property underwent considerable revision during the Genoa Conference, at least so far as Great Britain and Italy were concerned, for although France and Belgium continued to demand outright restitution, Britain and Italy were willing to discuss what forms compensation in lieu of restitution might take.[28]

Shtein's analysis of the differing points of view of Britain and France was essentially correct. On June 2, before the opening of the Hague Conference, Poincaré sent the United States and the Allied governments a memorandum insisting upon the need for a preliminary agreement for co-ordinated action at The Hague. In reply, Britain refused not only to draft a preliminary agreement, but even to declare that the Russian memorandum of May 11 to the Genoa Conference was unacceptable. As a result it appeared for a time that France would

---

[26] *Genoa Conference . . . Report of the Canadian Delegates*, pp. 48–55.

[27] For text see *Materialy genuezskoi konferentsii*, pp. 230–41. An English translation appears in Degras, I, 308–18.

[28] B. E. Shtein, *Gaagskaia konferentsiia*, pp. 3, 5.

not go to The Hague. On June 19, however, Lloyd George and Poincaré met in London, and the next day they issued a statement that their two governments had reached complete accord regarding the forthcoming conference.

The Hague Conference

At the Hague Conference, as at Genoa, the problem of foreigners' compensation for losses arising out of the Russian revolution proved an insurmountable barrier to agreement. The Western representatives again refused to accept the Soviet plan of concessions in lieu of restitution, while the Soviet delegates refused to agree to restitution.

At the Hague Conference there were two commissions: the non-Russian commission, divided into subcommissions on private property, credits, and debts; and the Russian commission, which participated as a body in working with all three subcommissions.

Russia's representatives told the subcommission on private property that whereas the Soviet government felt the same as ever about concessions in lieu of restitution, it was now willing to go further and to compensate those former owners who would not agree to concessions—but only if the Soviet government were given a definite commitment on credits. As for the concessions, only those industries would be available in which concessions would fit in with the over-all plans of the Soviet government for the development of Russian industry.[29]

It soon became evident that the European experts were unwilling to accept the Soviet scheme. Whole industries, some of which had been developed largely by foreign capital, were absent from the Soviet list of available concessions, and at the same time the European powers expected complete restitution of nationalized property. When it became apparent that the conference was about to bog down, Litvinov, in a last-ditch effort to reach some sort of settlement, asked for a plenary session of the non-Russian commission. But two days before this session was held, its futility was underscored by the subcommission on private property, which adopted a report stating that "it is plain that no satisfactory arrangement on the subject of private property can be recommended at the present Conference."[30] This report listed the reasons for the failure to reach agreement: the Russian government's refusal to acknowledge its obligation to meet claims; the lack of assurance that previous owners of Russian property would be given preference in concessions; the absence, from the list of available concessions, of many industries previously owned by foreign nationals; the Russian experts' refusal to provide specifically for restitution of possession; and the Russian failure to give practical assurances of compensation unless credits were previously promised. The report concluded: "The Sub-Commission was . . . asked seriously to entertain the proposal that in effect foreign countries should themselves pay for the compensation of their own nationals, while the Russian Government refused to discuss even the possibility of guaranteeing the one form of compensation which lay within their competence [i.e., restitution]."[31]

[29] *Conference at The Hague. 1. Non-Russian Commission. 2. Russian Commission. June 26–July 20, 1922. Minutes and Documents*, pp. 43–44, 68–69.
[30] *Ibid.*, p. 206.
[31] *Ibid.*, p. 208.

The plenum for which Litvinov had asked was held July 19. There he declared that since no credits to the Soviet government had been forthcoming, one of the cardinal conditions of agreement as contemplated at Genoa had been removed, and that the Russian commission could make no further proposals because their instructions had been based upon the assumption that credits were to be given. He thereupon offered to sound out his government on the possibility of recognizing liability for nationalized property without a guarantee of credits, provided the other delegations would ask their governments whether an affirmative Soviet reply would be an acceptable basis for an agreement.[32]

The other delegations did not act on Litvinov's proposal, and the next day, July 20, the non-Russian commission adjourned the conference.

The Hague came no closer than Genoa to accomplishing the announced purposes of the conferences, but from the Soviet point of view the time and effort had by no means been wasted. On the contrary, the conferences had given Soviet diplomats an excellent chance to use the tactics of international class struggle. The Soviet negotiators had put Russia ostensibly on the side of the pacifists and the war-weary against the militarists, of the defeated and humiliated against the proud victors, of the poor against the rich, and of the socialists against the capitalists.

The Communists publicly interpreted the abrupt termination of the Hague Conference as a maneuver of the European states to avoid revealing, as they had at Genoa, their differences in regard to Russia. The Soviet leaders believed that Great Britain and the states of the Little Entente actually wanted to continue negotiations, which France and Belgium opposed. The Russian suggestion that new instructions be obtained was rejected, they felt, because it would have exposed "contradictions" among the Western powers. The existence of these disagreements or "contradictions" was an article of communist dogma which Soviet diplomats were bound to reiterate and exploit. The Soviet diplomats made the most of such opportunities for getting publicity and gaining prestige as were offered by international conferences, but in actual negotiations it was obviously more to their advantage to deal with the capitalist governments individually and play one off against another.

According to the official Soviet view, the capitalist powers at The Hague "formed a united front in presenting impudent demands and in categorically denying Russian claims."[33] Steklov wrote in *Izvestiia* that the Allied attempts to recover tsarist debts and to get compensation for foreign losses were merely the latest attempt of the wealthy bourgeoisie to lay their hands on Russian national wealth. He also explained why the Western powers tried to get Russia to agree at The Hague to meet the claims of private owners without themselves being willing either to guarantee credits to Russia or to specify the extent of the claims that would be made. Capitalist syndicates, he said, had been buying up shares of enterprises formerly owned by Russian capitalists with the intention of claiming compensation for them. The Soviet leaders were very sensitive on this point. After the Brest-Litovsk treaty with the Central Powers, the Communists suspected that German capitalists were up to the same game. It was to frustrate this capitalist stratagem, so it was said, that the Soviet government

[32] *Ibid.*, pp. 193–94.
[33] *Izvestiia*, No. 162, July 22, 1922, p. 1.

nationalized enterprises sooner than it had intended (or was prepared) to nationalize them.

As for the future, Steklov explained that the Soviet government, having been able to maintain its rights, would in the long run be able to work out amicable economic agreements with the capitalist powers, agreements to the advantage of both sides. He suggested that the bourgeois governments had probably entered into a general pact not to make individual agreements with the Soviets, but he predicted that individual capitalist governments and business syndicates would not be able to withstand the temptation. This, he declared, would prove to be the vulnerable spot in what he called the "capitalist world conspiracy against Soviet Russia."[34]

According to the Communists, offstage maneuvering by oil magnates had added to the difficulties at Genoa and The Hague. These magnates, they believed, were behind the attempts to get Soviet Russia to agree to prohibit the use by one group of foreigners of industries developed by another. Failing this, they worked for a general agreement among the non-Russian powers to the same effect.

Many years later, when Soviet diplomatic history had to be rewritten in order to make the United States the chief villain, N. L. Rubinshtein claimed that although the American government did not formally participate at The Hague, it intervened at the last moment to break up the conference in order to protect Standard Oil interests against Royal Dutch Shell.[35]

Disarmament

Meanwhile, Soviet diplomats had also been busy with another project, a peace program. The Soviet government had issued a Proclamation on Peace on November 8, 1917, the second day of its existence, and its diplomats had assiduously promoted peace ever since. The Communists did not expect to abolish war until they had abolished capitalism, but in the meantime the advocacy of disarmament might lessen the danger of war. It also had other advantages: It was a popular cause, especially in countries that had been involved in World War I; it was attractive to the weak or disarmed powers; and it brought out the contradictions and rivalries of the Great Powers. It was admirably suited to the purposes of Soviet diplomacy.

On March 29 and 30, 1922, on their way to the Genoa Conference, Soviet delegates stopped over in Riga long enough to hold a conference with delegates of Latvia, Poland, and Estonia. Finland was represented only by an observer, and Lithuania had refused to participate because of the Polish-Lithuanian conflict. The resulting Riga Protocol proposed closer commercial relations among the governments represented, affirmed their desire for peace and their support of the principle of limitation of armaments by all states, and recommended that neutral zones be established along the frontiers of the signatory powers. It also contained the interesting statement that "each government bears the responsibility for the formation on its territory of armed bands, as well as for the passage of those bands into the territory of the neighboring states." Lastly, the Protocol said that "it will be useful for the parties represented at the meeting to draw up

---

[34] *Ibid.*; see Document 36.
[35] N. L. Rubinshtein, *Sovetskaia diplomatiia v borbe protiv izoliatsii SSSR*, p. 22.

at Genoa definitive proposals aiming at the realization of the above-mentioned principles."[36]

Although, as previously noted, Russia failed to get disarmament on the agenda at Genoa, the governments of Poland, Finland, Estonia, Latvia, and Lithuania accepted a Soviet invitation of June 12[37] for a regional discussion of the problem. The Moscow Conference on the Limitation of Armament was accordingly convened in December 1922.

At the first plenary session Litvinov introduced the Russian proposals: (1) that the land forces of each participating state be proportionally reduced on the basis of a reduction of the Russian army to one-quarter of its then total number (i.e., to 200,000 men); (2) that maxima be fixed for the army budgets of each state; (3) that irregular military formations be dissolved; and (4) that neutrality be introduced in frontier zones. No reductions of naval strength were proposed, Litvinov explained, since naval matters did not involve Russia and her neighbors so much as the stronger sea powers. Lastly, he told the delegates that in the Soviet view moral disarmament was no substitute for the Russian proposals.

Litvinov emphasized that the elimination of every possibility of armed conflict was impossible so long as capitalism survived in the majority of the countries, but added that the Russian government was fully convinced that "even partial disarmament would greatly diminish the possibility of armed conflict."[38]

The delegates of Poland, Estonia, Latvia, and Finland did not agree that a proportional reduction of land armies would guarantee peace, unless it were accompanied by binding guarantees of a political nature, particularly in view of the Soviet preponderance in war potential. They argued that the effect of the Russian proposals would be merely to reduce the defensive capacity of the Baltic states and Poland. They maintained that the principle of moral disarmament should be accepted first, and that military reductions could be discussed later. First set up machinery for settling disputes amicably, they said, and then work on material disarmament. Tension between Lithuania and Poland, however, prevented a united front of the Polish-Baltic bloc. Lithuania did not join in pressing this point of view, and even occasionally sided with the Soviet delegation.

Specifically, the Polish-Baltic bloc proposed that members of the conference (1) sign a treaty of nonaggression and arbitration; (2) specify the maximum number of effective forces proposed by their respective governments for 1923; and (3) refer the problem of limitation of land and naval forces to a com-

---

[36] *Materialy genuezskoi konferentsii*, pp. 51–53; also *Conférence de Moscou pour la limitation des armements, 1922*, pp. 239–41 (cited hereafter as *Conférence de Moscou*). English text appears in Degras, I, 296–98.

It is of some interest that twenty-eight years later the five communist-ruled states in the United Nations voted against (5–50) Resolution 380 (V) of November 17, 1950, of the General Assembly, which declared that "fomenting civil strife in the interest of a foreign power" constituted aggression. In 1951 two societies, the Lithuanian Council and the Polish-American Congress, opposed the following draft of a paragraph of a Declaration on Rights and Duties of States prepared by the International Law Commission, on the ground that it would "outlaw" Western support of anticommunist underground movements: "Every state has the duty to refrain from fomenting civil strife in the territory of another state, and to prevent the organization within its territory of activities calculated to foment such strife."

[37] English text of this invitation appears in Degras, I, 320–22.

[38] *Conférence de Moscou*, pp. 46–51; see Document 37.

mission of military experts, to meet after ratification of the treaty of nonaggression and arbitration. This commission would consider not only proportional reduction, but war potential and political and strategic position as well.[39]

The Soviet delegation reminded the delegates that the conference had been called chiefly to discuss the reduction of armaments on a proportional basis. Moral disarmament, said the Russians, was meaningless unless accompanied by actual material disarmament. The Russian government had agreed to a treaty of nonaggression and arbitration—upon which the conference had been simultaneously working—but only on the condition that a general disarmament treaty also be prepared. The Russians could not ratify a nonaggression treaty under the conditions proposed by the Polish-Baltic bloc, and they made it clear that insistence upon this point of view would end the conference.[40]

Poland and the Baltic states held to their position, and the conference came to an end, its only achievement having been the draft of a declaration, dated December 8, 1922, advocating a treaty of nonaggression and arbitration along the following lines: The signatories would desist from armed attack upon each other's territories; they would agree to withhold aid from any nonsignatory state that might commit an act of aggression upon any of them; infringement of the agreement by any signatory would automatically release the other signatories from all obligations to that state arising out of the agreement; the signatories would solve by peaceful means all conflicts that might arise among them; and such future controversies as could not be resolved through the usual diplomatic channels should be resolved by arbitration.[41]

The Lausanne Conference

In the course of 1922 and 1923 the Soviet government was invited to send representatives to two other international governmental conferences—the Lausanne Conference on Near Eastern Questions and the Rome Conference on the Limitation of Naval Armament.

The Lausanne Conference sat from November 20, 1922, to July 24, 1923, with an interruption from February 4 to April 23, 1923. It had been convened by Great Britain, France, and Italy for the purpose of negotiating a settlement with Turkey to replace the Treaty of Sèvres, which the Turkish nationalists could not be persuaded or forced to accept.

Although the Soviet government had not been officially recognized by the Western powers, it was nevertheless invited to participate in such sessions of the Lausanne Conference as related to control of the Straits. Previously, as early as September 1922, the Soviet government had itself proposed that a conference on Near Eastern problems be convened by the interested powers. In proposing this conference, the Soviet government had at the same time accused Great Britain of refusing "to return to Turkey the Straits and the lands that unquestionably belong to her, allegedly in order to defend the Straits, but actually

[39] *Ibid.*, pp. 205–7; see Document 38.
[40] *Ibid.*, pp. 215–23; see Document 39.
[41] *Ibid.*, pp. 152–53. Later Soviet disarmament proposals will be discussed in Part V of this volume, as well as Soviet parallel efforts in the twenties to build up a strong Soviet defense in accordance with the plan outlined by M. V. Frunze, who took Trotsky's place as People's Commissar for Military and Naval Affairs in 1925.

in order to dominate them." The Soviets had also demanded the right to full participation in any conference that might be called, observing that the Straits question was primarily the concern of the littoral powers, which did not, of course, include any of the Allies or the United States.[42]

At Lausanne, Soviet exclusion from non-Straits sessions was justified on the grounds that those discussions were to be concerned only with a peace settlement. The People's Commissariat of Foreign Affairs vigorously protested this arrangement, charging the inviting powers with attempting to keep the peoples of the East in a state of dependency, and demanding full participation for Soviet Russia, the Ukraine, and Georgia.[43]

Once the discussions of the Straits settlement were opened, it became apparent that Russia and Britain were diametrically opposed, each having espoused the reverse of its traditional position. Thus Soviet Russia, anxious above all to keep the British fleet out of the Black Sea and having no fleet of consequence, demanded that the Straits be closed to all warships. Britain, on the other hand, no longer worried by Russian naval strength and determined to keep open the sea lanes to the Caucasus, had no intention of surrendering the right to send the British fleet through the Straits.

At the first meeting of the Straits commission of the Lausanne Conference, December 4, 1922, over which Lord Curzon of Great Britain presided, Ismet Pasha of Turkey outlined the general views of the Turkish government, as proclaimed two years previously in the National Pact:[44] to wit, the establishment and maintenance of the security of Constantinople and of the Sea of Marmora. Otherwise, he said, the Turkish government was ready to conclude international agreements opening the Straits to the commerce of all nations.

Chicherin, the second speaker, listed Russia's two goals: equality with the other powers in all matters before the conference; and the preservation of peace and security in the territories of Russia and the republics allied with her, and freedom in their economic relations with other countries. To these ends he declared that the Straits should be closed in peace and war to military vessels and military aircraft of all countries except Turkey (which should have the right to fortify the coasts of the Straits), and that permanent freedom for commercial navigation should be guaranteed. In support of his position he argued that "the closing of the Straits to warships is also in accordance with the principle of equality between all States, whereas the opening of the Straits to warships would confer a preponderant position on the strongest sea Power." Lastly, stressing the importance of the Straits to the economic life of the Soviet federation, he said:

Any solution based on the presence in the Straits of forces belonging to certain Powers, and tending to create a preponderant situation for one Power or group of Powers, will encounter determined opposition not only from Russia and her allies,

[42] Kliuchnikov and Sabanin, III, 201–2; see Document 40.

[43] *Ibid.*, pp. 203–5; see Document 41. On February 22, 1922, Georgia, the Ukraine, and several other Soviet republics had agreed that Russia should represent their interests at the proposed conference.

[44] During 1919 Mustafa Kemal Pasha organized a Turkish National Assembly with a program of resistance against both the Sultan and the Allied plans for partition and a control of Turkish lands. On January 28, 1920, the Assembly adopted a "National Pact," virtually a declaration of Turkish national integrity.

but from public opinion in all countries which desires to eliminate those causes of conflict in the Near East which constitute a permanent menace to the cause of peace . . .[45]

The Rumanian and Bulgarian delegates spoke next. The Rumanian delegate proposed that the Straits be open at all times to war vessels as well as commercial vessels, and that the territories adjacent to the Straits be demilitarized. The Bulgarian delegate proposed that the Straits be closed at all times to all but commercial vessels.

The Soviet delegation demanded that the views of the Western powers be made known immediately, but the conference was adjourned for the day after Ismet Pasha stated that although the Russian proposals corresponded most closely to Turkey's point of view, the Turkish position would not be elaborated until after the demands to be made of Turkey had been presented.

At the second meeting of the commission, December 6, Lord Curzon outlined the proposals of the Western powers. They were in direct opposition to the Soviet position: (1) complete freedom of passage through the Straits for warships in peacetime, the same in wartime if Turkey was neutral, and freedom of passage for neutral warships if Turkey was a belligerent; (2) demilitarization of certain zones of the European and Asiatic shores of the Dardanelles and the Bosporus, with an international commission to supervise and inspect the demilitarization; and (3)—like the Soviet proposals—freedom of commercial passage.

The Russian plan for closing the Straits to warships, said Curzon, not only represented a reversal of the traditional Russian policy but violated "the principle of international law that the passage between the two seas should be regarded as an international highway." Moreover, the closing of the Straits "would, if adopted by this conference, give to Russia a position of exceptional and indefensible advantage within the Black Sea." While Chicherin had contended that opening the Straits to warships would benefit the strongest naval powers, closing the Black Sea would place the other littoral countries at the mercy of "the littoral Power possessing the strongest land forces, in other words, Russia herself." The over-all Soviet objective, Curzon concluded, was "to convert the Black Sea into a Russian lake with Turkey as the faithful guardian at the gates."[46]

Two days later, December 8, at the third meeting of the Straits Commission, Ismet Pasha proposed that the number of warships permitted to enter the Black Sea be limited. He also urged a guarantee securing the Straits, Constantinople, and the Sea of Marmora against surprise attack, and declared that Turkey favored freedom of passage for commercial vessels in both peace and war.

Chicherin immediately took the floor to defend the original Soviet proposals. He argued that international law supported not the British but the Russian point of view. The Black Sea, he said, should be regarded as a *mare clausum*, and hence should not be subject to laws pertaining to passages between seas. He charged the British with attempting to set up a regime in the Straits directed toward war, not peace; and he reiterated the Russian position that the Straits

---

[45] *Lausanne Conference on Near Eastern Affairs, 1922–1923. Records of Proceedings and Draft Terms of Peace* (Cmd. 1814), pp. 128–31.

[46] *Ibid.*, pp. 140–41.

should be closed to warships and that freedom and sovereignty should be retained by Turkey.

On December 14 the British delegation introduced a draft proposal on passage through the Straits, based, like previous Western proposals, upon the principle of freedom of passage for warships as well as commercial vessels, but incorporating the Turkish proposal to limit the tonnage of warships entering the Black Sea. According to this draft, which was eventually adopted by the conference, each of the nonlittoral powers should have the right to send three warships, each not in excess of 10,000 tons, into the Black Sea in times of peace, except that the total tonnage of any one power should not exceed the total Black Sea tonnage of the strongest littoral power. Moreover, a commission would be created to check the number of war vessels passing through the Straits, relieving Turkey of the responsibility.

Further, during a war in which Turkey was neutral, the tonnage limitation would not apply "to any belligerent Power to the prejudice of its belligerent rights in the Black Sea." Turkey, as a neutral power, was not to interfere with navigation through the Straits, "the waters of which, and the air above, must remain entirely free in the case of neutrality, just as in ordinary times of peace," but no belligerent power was to be allowed to carry out any hostile act within the Straits. In a war in which Turkey was a belligerent, neutral ships were to have complete freedom of passage within the aforesaid limitations, as in time of peace, and Turkey was not to take any action against enemy ships which would prevent the free passage through the Straits of neutral ships and aircraft.

The draft proposed complete freedom of passage for nonmilitary vessels, both in peacetime and in wartime if Turkey was neutral. With Turkey belligerent, the same rule was to apply, but Turkey was to have the right to search neutral vessels and aircraft for evidences of assistance to her enemies. Turkey was further permitted to prevent enemy vessels from using the Straits, but only by such measures as would not impede the free passage of neutral vessels.[47]

Chicherin promptly condemned this British draft proposal as threatening the vital interests of Russia, violating the most elementary requirements of Turkish safety and independence, necessitating further naval armament, and placing an obstacle in the way of general peace.[48] The Russian delegation followed with a draft proposal of their own, which declared the Black Sea a *mare clausum* of the littoral powers. By this proposal no war vessels (including submarines) or military aircraft except those of Turkey would be permitted through or over the Straits. Turkey was to have full sovereignty over the Straits, including permission to fortify them; and commercial vessels and aircraft were to have freedom of passage through the Straits.

As spokesman for the Western powers, Lord Curzon in turn branded the Soviet proposals unacceptable, particularly the designation of the Black Sea as a *mare clausum*, and declared that the Allied powers could not recede from the position outlined in the British draft. Chicherin thereupon charged that the British proposal amounted to the creation of a stronghold in the Straits against Russia and her allies. All the statements of Lord Curzon, he said, had but a single object: "to render the defense of the Straits and Constantinople impossible, and expose Russia to attacks by the great fleets."[49]

[47] *Ibid.*, pp. 243–46.   [48] *Ibid.*, pp. 236–38.   [49] *Ibid.*, pp. 263, 274.

But in spite of the heated Soviet opposition, the Turkish government accepted the British draft, which was thereupon adopted as the draft of the Straits convention, with the Soviet delegation abstaining.

Some months later, however, during the course of the Rome Conference on the Limitation of Naval Armament, the Soviet government reversed its stand, and Soviet representatives added the signature of Russia to the Lausanne draft, with certain reservations.

In summing up the Lausanne Conference and its relationship to the general world situation, Chicherin described Britain's tactics as "complicated in application, but simple in meaning. She first tried to bargain and to obtain from Turkey what she wanted. After that she left France to dabble in further negotiations while she herself, in turn, either aggravated the situation or played the role of a peacemaker between France and Turkey." According to Chicherin, whereas Great Britain had succeeded at Lausanne in reaching her main goal—a treaty opening the Straits to naval vessels—the economic and financial decisions of the conference (in which Russia did not participate) represented a great victory for Turkey. The British, said Chicherin, hoped to offset this victory by a skilled penetration into Turkey and by drawing to the British side the upper circles of Turkish bourgeois society, but they would fail because of the irreconcilable interests of the two powers. "Opening the Straits to foreign men-of-war," he said, "places the most important regions of Turkey under a continuous threat. The Turkish people's independence and their right to self-determination are not yet completely secure. . . . Turkey's only true and constant friend remains, as before, the soviet republics."[50]

The Rome Conference

Some months later the Soviet government was invited to send representatives to the Rome Conference on the Limitation of Naval Armament. The League of Nations called the Rome Conference to discuss applying the principles of naval limitation worked out during the Washington Conference in 1922 to those states which had not been represented at Washington.

Soviet leaders seized the occasion of the invitation to denounce the League again, but nonetheless saw it as a step toward recognition of the Soviet government. Thus Steklov wrote in *Izvestiia*:

Whether it is agreeable to the League and its affiliated imperialist powers or not, Soviet Russia has already attained such international significance, its prestige in international politics has so increased, that the present lords of the world have to include it in their reckoning. . . . We have a right to regard this step [the invitation] as a mild preparation for the general recognition of Soviet Russia. We may go even further . . . and say that this step taken by the League of Nations is synonymous with an actual recognition of Soviet power . . .

We have made no secret of the fact that we regard the League of Nations as an alliance of bourgeois states in which a few great imperialist nations wield the real power for their own purposes, granting the League far-reaching powers in so far as these are advantageous to them. From this standpoint, we regard the League of Nations as an instrument of the imperialist policy of the largest bourgeois states— of the so-called Entente.

[50] G. V. Chicherin, "Lozanskaia konferentsiia i mirovoe polozhenie," *Mezhdunarodnaia Zhizn*, No. 2, 1923, pp. 4, 6; see Document 43.

ПУТЬ В МОГИЛУ.

"WHAT NEXT?!" "Imperialism" plods on past the tombstones of past conferences (right to left: The Hague, Brussels, Sèvres, Versailles, Washington, Genoa, Lausanne, Locarno, Geneva). The legend beneath reads "The Way to the Grave." Pravda, No. 122, May 29, 1926.

As to the possibilities inherent in the Rome Conference, Steklov reasserted the Soviet distrust of such gatherings:

But, can one expect that any conference convened by the League of Nations, or by any other grouping of bourgeois powers, is capable of solving to any great extent the question of the limitation of armament and the problem of preventing war and of alleviating military burdens, to say nothing of the fundamental question of universal peace? This is another question. Our answer to this is a secret to nobody. But this does not imply that no action will be taken by the Soviet government in defense of its political principles wherever and whenever such opportunity may arise.[51]

The Soviet "action in defense of its political principles" at the Rome Conference consisted in arguing for limitation of tonnage on its own terms; for neutralization of the Bosporus and the Dardanelles; for prohibition of the entry of nonlittoral powers' war vessels into the Baltic; and for demilitarization of the Korea Strait. None of these Soviet proposals was adopted; nor did the Soviet government agree to the plan for limitation of naval armament as advocated by the Washington signatories. According to the Soviet delegate, E. A. Berens, the Washington agreements had been arrived at only after suitable political guarantees had been agreed upon; by the same token, unless the Baltic and Black seas were closed to warships of nonlittoral powers, the Soviet Union could not agree to limit her navy. Since the other powers represented were disinclined to turn the Baltic and the Black seas into giant Soviet lakes, the conference ended in failure and Soviet Russia was left free to build up her naval forces as she might see fit.

The Congress on War Against War

Still another international conference occupied the attention of Soviet leaders during the period under consideration, a conference of socialist organizations throughout the world for the purpose of preventing future wars. In April 1922 the Congress of the International Federation of Trade Unions instructed its executive body to do its utmost to promote a campaign on behalf of peace and disarmament. In December 1922 the executive body summoned a world peace congress at The Hague, known as the Congress on War Against War. Although the composition of the congress was in general unfriendly to the Soviet government, and although the Russian Mensheviks were represented, nevertheless the Soviet Russian Council of Trade Unions sent Karl Radek, A. Lozovsky, F. A. Rotshtein, and A. A. Malinovsky as its representatives.

Lenin himself outlined the tasks of the Soviet delegates. They were to condemn as sterile the Amsterdam International's decision, adopted at its Rome congress, to call a general strike in the event of the outbreak of war. Instead, they were to advocate "the maintenance and formation of illegal organizations made up of all the revolutionaries [drawn into] participation in the war, for the purpose of carrying on a prolonged struggle against war . . ."[52]

At the conference Soviet delegates called for a "united front of the working class against the whole of bourgeois society" and recommended that repre-

[51] *Izvestiia*, No. 57, March 15, 1923, p. 1.
[52] Lenin, *Sochineniia*, XXVII, 372-75; for excerpts see Document 44.

sentatives of the Eastern revolutionary movement be included within the international socialist movement. The Soviet scheme for a united front, said Lozovsky, would involve establishing international committees of action in every country. All working class organizations would be represented on these committees and subject to the committees' directions in the fighting. Lozovsky called also for abolishing and preventing splits in the mass trade union movement, "on condition of the preservation of freedom of propaganda, and of campaigning against the theory and practice of defending the bourgeois fatherlands." In short, the Soviets would co-operate with the united front provided they retained freedom of action within it. Understandably, this plan was more attractive to the politically less sophisticated revolutionary peoples of Asia than to the European socialists. The fourteen Soviet points also demanded an end to class co-operation and coalition with the bourgeoisie; opposition to bourgeois pacifism; the establishment of legal and illegal organizations to dispense propaganda and train leaders for a potential soldiers' revolt; a campaign for the abrogation of the Treaty of Versailles; a campaign for recruiting workers and peasants in the colonial areas; a campaign to get the Allies to evacuate German and mandated territories; a campaign to disarm bourgeois organizations and arm the working class; and a campaign for the establishment of labor governments "whose duty shall be to carry out the above demands even against the will of the capitalist classes."[53]

The congress showed little enthusiasm for this Soviet bid for general socialist support of the communist program. The representative of the Russian Mensheviks, R. A. Abramovitch [Abramovich], had the following to say:

The Bolshevists are not in earnest when they make these attempts at reconciliation; they seek, not to build an iron wall, but by all available means, even the most unscrupulous, to follow the example of the Jesuits in days gone by, who held that the end justifies the means. Instead, therefore, of building an iron wall, they seek to undermine the foundations of the present wall which you here represent . . . and since we know this, this very knowledge prevents us from responding with enthusiasm to the appeal made to us . . .

Is it Radek's idea to establish a united front as he has already done in Russia, that is to say, by shutting us up in prison and locking the prison door himself? . . . Or does Radek perhaps mean the unity which has been re-established in Russia by dissolving, with the aid of the police and the Red Guards, those trade unions in which we had a majority, and casting our old trade union leaders into prison, where they have been languishing for the past two years?

. . . In spite of our heavy toll of sacrifices, in spite of all the bloodshed of which these gentlemen have been guilty, in spite of all we are prepared to forgive everything. One condition only we must insist on . . . and this condition is that the system of police and military despotism shall be brought to an end in Russia and that the same freedom shall be restored, not to the bourgeoisie . . . but to the working classes as is the case in the capitalist states of Europe.[54]

Vandervelde of Belgium also spoke out emphatically against the Soviet proposals, calling upon the Communists themselves to start the move for a united front of socialists by granting socialist Georgia the right to self-determination and by pardoning the condemned Russian socialists. Vandervelde further de-

[53] *Report of the International Peace Conference* . . . , pp. 143–45; see Document 45.
[54] *Ibid.*, pp. 146, 148.

clared: "We shall do well to remember that neither is a united front possible, nor any effective action, unless there is a [certain] minimum of agreement regarding the aim, and the means to be employed in order to attain it. . . ."[55]

The conference eventually adopted five resolutions—(1) On the Task of the Labor Movement in the War Against War; (2) On Imperialism, Militarism, and the Transformation of the League of Nations; (3) Against the Policy of Sanctions and the Threatened Occupation of the Ruhr Basin; (4) On Education; and (5) On the Task of the Pacifist Organizations[56]—each of which the Soviet delegation opposed.

Thus the Soviet government and the Russian Communists who headed it had no better success at coming to terms with the European socialists than with the capitalist governments. Little progress resulted from the attempts at general international governmental settlements, and less from the attempt at international socialist co-operation. The Russian Communists seem not to have been disturbed by failures they must have anticipated. More positively, they had used the conferences to stress the differences between the capitalist powers, to try to undermine the position of European socialist leaders, and to present Russia as the friend of all nations and groups with grievances.

The Soviet Attitude Toward the League of Nations

In its drive for security and *de jure* recognition, Soviet diplomacy again and again came up against the League of Nations. Here, as in other areas of diplomacy, the Russian Communists followed a dual policy: On one hand they denounced the League as a coalition of predatory imperialist powers; on the other, they demanded the right to take part in such conferences of the League as affected Russian interests.[57]

The Soviet attitude toward the League was influenced by the fact that Soviet Russia had not been invited to become a member, by the communist theory of capitalist encirclement, by the fear of any coalition or alliance of which Russia was not a member, and by the Communists' own plans for developing the "camp of socialism" headed by Soviet Russia into a real league of the toilers of all countries. These plans, as sketched by Stalin and later embodied in the structure of the Union of Soviet Socialist Republics, provided for a complex centralized federation of the nationalities formerly in the Russian Empire, plus a confederation in which new, non-Russian soviet republics might become close allies of Soviet Russia within the camp of socialism. As faithful Communists saw it, the Soviet multinational state would solve both the national question and the problems of international co-operation.[58]

Pending the revolutionary transformation of foreign governments into soviet socialist republics, the Communist International—founded in 1919, the same

---

[55] *Ibid.*, pp. 118–24.

[56] Full texts, *ibid.*, pp. 201–6.

[57] The Soviet attitude toward the League or Nations was clarified in Lenin's speech to the party executives, October 15, 1920 (Lenin, *Sochineniia*, XXV, 414–16) and in Chicherin's note to the Secretary General of the League, March 15, 1923 (Kliuchnikov and Sabanin, III, 238–39); see Documents 47 and 50.

[58] Stalin, *Sochineniia*, V, 138–55, and Kliuchnikov and Sabanin, III, 225–26; see Documents 48 and 49.

year as the League of Nations—was the agency through which the Communists promoted their idea of a real league of peoples, united and harmonious, in place of the so-called "League," divided by the ambitions and contradictions of its greedy imperialist members.

Soviet Leadership in the World Revolution

The Soviet government did not abandon either its long-range revolutionary goals or its short-term plan to build the power of the Soviet state. But since neither recognition nor loans had been forthcoming on an international scale, there remained only the policy of working for *de jure* recognition from and trade agreements with individual bourgeois governments. That such recognition would be forthcoming the Communists remained confident, pointing to the increasing prominence of the Soviet government in world affairs.

The Communists continued to reiterate their faith in the eventual world revolution. The Fourth Congress of the Comintern, November 5–December 3, 1922, passed a resolution which, like others issued by the Comintern, was a kind of declaration of an international class war under Russia's leadership:

. . . The proletarian revolution will never be victorious within the limits of one country only, . . . it can only be victorious on an international scale, as a world revolution. All activities of Soviet Russia, its struggle for its own existence and for the realization of the revolution, are at the same time a struggle to free the oppressed and exploited proletarians of the world . . . In all countries the workers, the poor, and the oppressed must actively display their moral, economic, and political solidarity with Soviet Russia. . . . The workers and the oppressed must advance the following slogans in all countries: Hands off Soviet Russia; *de jure* recognition of Soviet Russia; general and real support to the economic restoration of Soviet Russia. . . . The Fourth Congress calls upon the proletariat of all capitalist countries to follow the example of Soviet Russia—to launch a decisive attack on capitalism, and to devote all its energy to the world revolution![59]

With reference to the world situation, Karl Radek told the Fourth Congress: "The Communist International must reckon with the possibility of a slow advance of the world revolution . . . This implies temporary defeats and retreats. This requires the employment of all sorts of means in the struggle, and first of all a thorough preparation for the struggle." Consequently, said Radek, the political changes that were taking place in the world must be constantly watched: "The struggle of the Communist International becomes, therefore, more and more closely bound up with all fluctuations and changes in the world situation."[60]

Bukharin was even more doctrinaire. "The Communist Manifesto says that the proletariat must conquer the world," he reminded the Congress. Socialism could be attained only by the use of bayonets and guns, i.e., by Red intervention: ". . . The expansion of the Red Army is also the expansion of socialism, of the proletarian authority, of the revolution."[61]

[59] Lenin, *Sochineniia*, XXVII, 489; see Document 53.

[60] Karl Radek, *Likvidatsiia versalskogo mira* . . . , p. 64. Radek's report appears also in English under the title *The Winding-up of the Versailles Treaty*; see Document 51.

[61] *IV Vsemirnyi Kongress Kommunisticheskogo Internatsionala, 5 noiabria–3 dekabria 1922 g.; Izbrannye doklady, rechi i rezoliutsii*, p. 196 (hereafter cited as *IV Vsemirnyi Kongress*); see Document 52.

DOCUMENTS

THE INTERNATIONAL SITUATION ON THE EVE
OF THE GENOA CONFERENCE

31
Lenin on Domestic and Foreign Policies of the Republic

[Report of the All-Russian Central Executive Committee and the Council
of People's Commissars to the Ninth All-Russian
Congress of Soviets, December 23, 1921][1]

.   .   .

Speaking first on the international situation of our republic, I must state something
that I have already had occasion to say, and that is that a certain, although highly
unstable, equilibrium in international relations has been reached. We are actually
witnessing it now. It is extremely strange for those of us who have lived through
the revolution from the time of its inception, and for those who have known and
directly witnessed the unheard-of difficulties that confronted us when we broke up
the imperialist front, to see the present situation. Probably no one expected, or could
have expected, things to happen as they did. . . .

When we ask ourselves how one of the most definitely backward and extremely
weak countries, treated with hostility by the most powerful countries of the world,
has succeeded in warding off an attack, we see clearly that we were right on the basic
point. We were right in our suppositions and in our calculations. Although we did
not receive the immediate, direct support from the toilers of the world on which we
based our whole policy, we had support of another kind—their sympathy, even in the
countries most hostile to us. This support and sympathy served as the final and most
decisive factor, in that all invasions directed at us ended in failure because the union
of the toilers of all countries, which was proclaimed, consolidated, and applied within
our republic, had such influence everywhere. . . .

If we very calmly weigh the sympathy toward Bolshevism and the socialist revolution, if we take stock of the international situation simply from the standpoint of
forces, regardless of whether they support the toiling masses or the exploiting class,
it is clear that capitalism is decaying, and that since the war, which was ended first
by the Brest-Litovsk treaty and later by the Versailles treaty (I do not know which
is the worse), hatred of war has steadily increased in the victorious countries. The
farther we proceed from the war, the clearer it becomes—not only to the toilers, but
to many of the bourgeoisie of the victorious countries—that capitalism is disintegrating, that the world economic crisis has created an unbearable situation from
which there is no escape, despite the victories that have been won. This is why we,
who are immeasurably weaker, economically and militarily, than other powers, are
stronger than they, because we have foreseen and correctly estimated what has
already resulted and is bound to result from the imperialist confusion, from the bloody
entanglement and the antagonisms [now manifesting themselves] . . .

[1] Lenin, *Sochineniia*, XXVII, 113–19.

Here is the essence of the international situation: We have before us an extremely unstable, but nevertheless a certain and indisputable equilibrium. For how long? I do not know, and I do not think anyone else knows either. Therefore, we must practice extreme caution.

The first commandment of our policy, the first lesson drawn from our government's activity during this year, the lesson that must be learnt by all workers and peasants, is to be on guard; we are surrounded by people, classes, and governments that openly profess the greatest hatred for us. We must remember that we are always only a hair's breadth from some invasion. We shall do our utmost to avoid this calamity. . . . We know very well what unheard-of calamities war brings to the workers and peasants. Therefore, we must be very careful and very cautious. We are prepared to make the greatest concessions and sacrifices to retain the peace we have purchased so dearly, but not endless sacrifices. . . .

There is a limit beyond which we will not go. We shall not permit playing with peace treaties; we shall not allow attempts to interfere with our peaceful work. We shall stand as one man to defend our existence.

Comrades, what I have said must be quite clear. You could not expect any other statement from anyone reporting to you on our policy. You know our policy. Unfortunately, there now exist two worlds: the old world, capitalism, which has become entangled but which will not give in; and the new world, which, though still very weak, is growing and is invincible. . . .

32

Radek on the Invitation to the Genoa Conference[2]

The conference of the Allied prime ministers at Cannes decided to call an international conference for March to discuss the reconstruction of the world economy. Soviet Russia has been officially invited to this conference. Neither France nor the United States of America, whose representative, Colonel Harvey, was present at the Cannes Conference, made any protest against this decision.

The decision signifies a great shift in the international situation. The Supreme Council of the Entente has now officially approved the opinion of the greatest economists of the bourgeois world: There is no possibility of reconstructing the world economy without Russia's participation. But this decision means more; it shows that the Allies, who were hoping that famine might overthrow the Soviet power, have seen that their hopes are futile and that the Soviet power is the only possible authority in Russia. . . . This does not mean that the Allies will make no further attempts to overthrow us by armed force; it simply means that they have seen the futility of their past plans and [now] want peace with us.

The Allies' decision follows three years of struggle and a year of watchful waiting, arms in hand, in hopes of a forceful change from within; it is the most important event in current world politics. It means that despite the incredibly sluggish pace of the world revolution, it has been impossible to destroy Soviet Russia; that the break we cut in the system of capitalist nations in 1917 remains unhealed. An unstable equilibrium now ensues. . . .

The British government's telegram notifying the Soviet government of the decision to invite its representatives to the international conference stated that should the Soviet government so desire, conditions for its recognition would be discussed at the conference. This formulation is merely a subterfuge. The invitation itself

[2] *Pravda*, No. 6, January 10, 1922, p. 2.

. . . with the proviso that before Russia can enter the active system of international economy, the Soviet government must assume certain obligations considered essential by the capitalist powers, is recognition of the Soviet government. . . .

The Soviet government has not applied for a certificate of morality from the government of Lloyd George, Briand, or Harding; we feel no desire to have our virtue acknowledged by governments that are oppressing the masses of their workers. What we need are real, businesslike relations with them—and these relations will force the capitalist governments to drop their persecution of Soviet Russia. . . .

The discussion in the last few weeks of what debts we are ready to recognize is merely an attempt to force us to recognize all sorts of debts that may now exist anywhere on earth—this attempt is simply a tactical move. It is absolutely pointless to set up a classification of debts. But one thing is important: Will the Allies place credits at Russia's disposal in order to guarantee the rehabilitation of the Russian economy? Even if the Soviet government should be ready today to recognize Russian national debts to the extent of one hundred billion gold rubles—no man on earth knows the precise figure of Russia's indebtedness—the Allies would not obtain the slightest advantage from this recognition, for it would remain a scrap of paper. . . .

But the [official] recognition of debts [by the Soviet government] is supposed to lead to the granting of concessions for exploiting Russian resources, concessions which in turn are to insure the concessionnaire country's loans to Russia. The principal task of the conference will be to determine the proportions of the loans, who will advance them, and under what conditions they are to be raised. Everything else will be mere diplomatic byplay.

Soviet Russia's return to participation in world economy, her readmission to the present comity of nations, involves a number of general and specific questions. The general questions concern our domestic policy. Can capitalists operate in the territory under the workers' dictatorship? At first the Allies proposed conditions. They wanted to dictate changes in Soviet Russia's system of government. Soviet Russia declared that she would not tolerate such interference. The Allies no longer speak of these conditions, an admission that 150 million Russians are not in the position of Negroes in the Congo or of defenseless China. The Entente is beginning to understand that once the use of foreign capital ceases to be a matter of newspaper discussion and becomes an actual fact, the Soviet government and the Russian working class will establish the legal forms and institutions required to raise Russia's productive forces. Capitalism is capable of adapting itself to [varied] conditions; if political conditions in Russia are impregnable, and if at the same time the capitalists are guaranteed some profit, they will toe the line. On the other hand, the New Economic Policy and the legal norms of Soviet Russia are not rigid. In Russia there will be no pure capitalism so long as the soviet power of the workers and peasants exists; there will be no pure communism unless the international working class is victorious after a prolonged period of struggle, and unless it can bring real advantages to the peasants, thus proving to them the value of the communist system of economy.

Another general question: What about those enterprises whose powers transcend those of a [particular] capitalist group, and for which united action is necessary? When such enterprises are actually launched, the Soviet government will not, of course, oppose them. The essence of the question is this: Under what conditions may such enterprises be formed, and of what character are they? Do they threaten the independence of Russia, do they mean the enslavement of Russia? . . .

The international conference must take place as soon as possible; but it must be very carefully prepared if it is not to fail. All its delegates must know just what the negotiations will be about, and must guide public opinion in their countries accordingly. The Versailles negotiations—that Tower of Babel—produced such results that the Allies, after only three years, must again discuss the reconstruction of world economy. The lesson of Versailles will be the more important since Russia is not a disarmed nation, as Germany was at Versailles.

33

Chicherin's Pre-Genoa Report on the International Situation to the All-Russian Central Executive Committee, January 27, 1922[3]

More than once during the discussion of our foreign policy before the All-Russian Central Executive Committee, we have pointed out the special role played by England [in international affairs]. When I introduced our first peace treaty, the treaty with Estonia, for the ratification of the Central Executive Committee, I spoke of the serious differences between England and France over the Baltic states and Russia. On the banks of the Thames, I said, can be found the entire political wisdom of the capitalist world. The statesmen of the Thames can look far ahead and know how to sense rising new historical forces. To conclude an agreement with such a force and thus disarm it—that is the summit of traditional British political art. Witness the present prime minister, Lloyd George, who is pliable and understands the political and social forces that surround him, and who is ready to compromise. Representing as he does the serious business circles in England, he has to overcome the strongest opposition by narrow chauvinistic elements, private mercenary groups, and English military and court circles. This opposition is the reason the policy of compromise toward the Soviet Russian government has developed so slowly and with such long interruptions. . . .

One idea that prompted leading capitalists to seek economic rapprochment with us at this time was the idea that they could more suitably consolidate their economic position in Russia in a time of famine.

Lloyd George made use of this capitalist conception to carry out his policy of compromise. His continual refrain was that trade with the Bolsheviks is the best way to disarm them and to reduce the danger from them. Lloyd George's project and our theory of historical development are diametrically opposed, but our practical policies coincide in the desire to establish full peaceful relations and mutual economic collaboration. We understand this collaboration differently, of course, but we both want to remove the barriers that interfere with it.

Both the Brussels Conference delegates and the Great Powers' international commission to help the starving Russians demanded that we recognize the debts. We went halfway to meet this demand in our note of October 28,[4] agreeing in principle to recognize the prewar debts on condition that an international conference be convened to study the claims of both sides, to settle the differences finally, and to establish full accord between Russia and the other powers, thus guaranteeing that the endless attempts at intervention and the continuous attacks on the Soviet frontiers would be finally and absolutely ended. . . .

When an attempt to regulate international relations without us at the Washington Conference clearly proved inadequate, the English press pointed out three basic reasons necessitating an agreement with Soviet Russia: (1) Russia's economic significance, an essential factor in regulating world economy; (2) Russia's military power, without which general peace cannot be established; and (3) Russia's po-

[3] *Materialy genuezskoi konferentsii*, pp. 15–20; also Degras, I, 289–92.
[4] See Document 25.

litical influence in the East, a factor of world significance. These three reasons prompted the decision of the Supreme Council at Cannes to invite us to an international conference, a political triumph for the British tradition. The policy of English business interests, aimed at peaceful penetration into Russia, has won.

We desire economic collaboration too; but we shall not let it take the form of economic rule over Russia. . . . The business point of view won because it coincided with a parallel, although somewhat different, desire among the leading groups of our irreconcilable enemy, France. . . . French policy has been dictated by the desire to have Russian loans paid, and by constant fear of the rebirth of German military might. But French policy just after the war was a kind of new Napoleonism, an attempt at a continental hegemony in Europe.

The French continental military policy, which is both deeply personal and abstract, in practice became entangled in its own contradictions. . . . Many French business interests began to talk about an agreement with Soviet Russia. In August of last year, when the West's business interests forcefully carried out their famine policy in order to penetrate Russia by peaceful means [i.e., by bringing in food supplies], the French press expressed the fear that England would get the best out of this measure. . . .

We face the realization of our desires, but we also face a new and serious danger, an attempt to unify all economic interests so as to turn economic collaboration with us into economic enslavement. It is here that our struggle will take place. We have business aims; we desire the economic restoration of Russia; we wish to participate through it in regulating the economic relations of the world; we want to carry out economic tasks jointly with Western business circles in a purely businesslike manner; but with all that, we must guard Russia's independence, permitting neither the violation of her sovereign rights nor interference in her domestic affairs.

Our interests coincide with Italy's. Had Italian policy been more independent, had Italy not yielded to the pressure of the Great Powers, our political and economic relations with her would have been better long ago. . . .

Similar lack of independence has been shown, unfortunately, by the most powerful of the modern states, the United States of America. In regard to the international conference and the various plans for economic collaboration with Russia, America is a question mark . . . False information about the situation in Russia, which is cultivated with particular success by the old tsarist diplomatic circles and by the bourgeoisie who left Russia for the United States, has had all along too strong an influence in the American political world, and still prevents American political and business circles from seeing that their true interests are in meeting us halfway . . . Many American journalists are in our country, and we hope soon to break down the thick wall of prejudice and false information that separates so much of American society from us and prevents the rapprochement that is in our mutual interest.

America did not participate in the Supreme Council, which made the decision concerning the international conference. Its representative, Harvey, was at Cannes only as an observer. The documents upon which today's report to the Extraordinary Session of the All-Russian Central Executive Committee are based come from the Great Powers of the Entente, excluding America and Japan.

The People's Commissariat of Foreign Affairs believes that the Extraordinary Session of VTSIK[5] must send to the conference a delegation with broad powers. It also recommends that the allied soviet republics and the Far Eastern Republic act jointly with the Russian republic. We have already had a preliminary agreement on that point.[6] We believe that today's session of VTSIK, at which the delegation

[5] Vserossiiskii Tsentralnyi Ispolnitelnyi Komitet (All-Russian Central Executive Committee).

[6] The text of the final agreement appears in Kliuchnikov and Sabanin, III, 168–69.

to the international conference will be decided upon, will mark a memorable day in the history of Soviet Russia.

THE GENOA CONFERENCE

34

A Member of the Soviet Delegation on the Genoa Conference

[Rakovsky's Forecast][7]

What is the purpose of the Genoa Conference, what is its goal, and what possible results can we expect from it? One paragraph of its agenda calls for the "establishment of international peace on a firm basis." The same paragraph, however, states that "existing treaties should be left unchanged," leaving us skeptical about the European diplomats' wisdom and intentions. Can peace on a firm basis be legally founded on the treaties that followed the last imperialist war—on treaties drafted when the victors, unopposed by the vanquished, were in a position to dictate whatever they wished? (At the international conference where these treaties were outlined, the vanquished did not even have the right to vote.)

A number of problems, all dealing with "world economic reconstruction," have been outlined for discussion at the Genoa Conference. Nothing interests the masses in the workers' and peasants' republic more deeply than economic reconstruction, both in our own country and in the world in general, and nothing will be given more businesslike and serious consideration. But, we may ask, can we expect lasting economic recovery while we live under capitalist conditions of production on a world-wide scale, with the contradictions of class struggle, exploitation, opposition, and imperialism that they entail? No, of course not. Under such conditions we can speak only of a palliative, of some provisional settlement of the problem.

Here, too, we must ask ourselves whether or not the delegates to the Genoa Conference will actually discuss world economic reconstruction in a businesslike manner. Is anything concealed behind the attractive slogans they advance? . . .

Keeping in mind the ordeal brought upon us by European diplomacy, and passing to the Genoa Conference, we wonder if its agenda does not express two things: the conditions that prompt the governments to call the conference, and the desire of these governments to kill it. . . .

The War Party and the Genoa Conference

The Genoa Conference was not conceived in the chancelleries of the diplomats; it is not an expression of their good will. The idea of a conference to discuss world economic recovery was advanced and insisted upon partly by the workers (who for the past four years have continually said "Hands off Russia"), but mainly by industrial firms interested in markets abroad and in a large trade turnover. . . .

The Tactics of Breaking off the Conference and Launching an Intervention

The Western press—the French, the Czech, and the Polish press, the press of the Big and the Little Entente—warns not to expect much from the Genoa Conference. What does this actually mean? It means that France and her satellites are trying to disrupt the conference. At the start the French government insisted on delaying the conference for three months, after which it published the famous French Memorandum. The general consensus is that France does not want the Genoa Con-

[7] Kh. G. Rakovsky, *Nakanune Genui*, pp. 3–32.

ference; she was obliged to agree to it partly by her commercial and industrial circles, and partly by England and Lloyd George, who, for his part, is being spurred on by the workers and by the strong wave of English pacifism. . . .

By way of creating a congenial atmosphere and justifying themselves to their working masses and to such of their bourgeoisie as want to start trade relations with us, the capitalists have launched in their press a systematic campaign against the Soviet republic. They say that we have called more men to arms, and that we have sent abroad what was left of our gold (including Rumanian gold) to carry on agitation and to undermine the armies of other countries, especially France. They say that we go to the Genoa Conference, not with businesslike intent, but to carry on communist propaganda. Finally, they say that our domestic situation is such that we may surrender our power any day. Such is their preliminary work upon public opinion—lies, distortions, and vulgar inventions.

Meanwhile, their conference tactics have already been planned. They will present us with outrageous demands. We shall naturally be unable to accept these demands, because in their basic conception they defy the revolutionary masses of the Soviet republic; because such demands can be imposed only upon slaves, and not upon citizens, not upon the workers and peasants of the Soviet repulic who have emerged victorious after four years of civil and international war.

Old Tsarist Debts—Our Counterclaims

We are told to pay the tsarist debts. Everyone knows that we have already agreed in principle to pay them, though with the following reservation:

Let them pay us, too, for the four years of civil war that they directed (as we can prove with innumerable clear examples). . . . Yes, there [at Genoa] we shall present them [the Allies] with the bill. We shall show them.

We cannot allow relations between states to be based on the will of one state. No, if this is really to be an agreement, if it is to be a compromise, then the interests of both sides must be considered.

But the Allies say beforehand: "We do not intend to pay you for Kolchak or Denikin." At least that is what the French press has said, and that is what Lloyd George and Poincaré decided at their last meeting at Boulogne.

War Debts—the Brest Peace

But they go even further. They say that we must pay them war debts, that we must pay for the war that gave them—France, England, and Italy—huge territories and enormous wealth. . . .

All these facts reveal the absence not only of good will in convoking the conference, but also of elementary commercial honesty and willingness to co-operate on the capitalists' part. Still another circumstance makes their usurious claims ridiculous. In the end, they realize perfectly well that the payment of any debt is simply an abstract wish.

·   ·   ·

Private Claims

But France and England take up still another aspect of the problem. They say: "They [the Russians] have no money, it is true, and therefore, even if they sincerely wished to pay, they could not. But they have enterprises that belonged to foreigners before the revolution, which were later nationalized. Let them be good enough to return those enterprises."

In this way the question of private claims comes to the fore. They [France and England] now insist in their press that we return these factories, these mines, and this land.

Behind them, we hear the whisper of the Russian capitalists, the Russian land-lords, the owners of houses, factories, and mines, who are now abroad: "If you return their property to them, then return ours also. Why should you make a distinction between the two groups? . . ."

Meanwhile, not being sure of the future, they sell their [former] possessions to foreign capitalists. . . .

Nationalization and Confiscation

Now let us consider the legal aspect of the question from the standpoint of bourgeois civil law. Does this law prohibit a state from nationalizing property, if such a step is necessary to the state's preservation and defense? In such circumstances, nationalization is an indisputable right of every bourgeois state. Every bourgeois constitution gives the state the right to expropriate property and nationalize it, provided the owner is indemnified. And when property is taken away as punishment, bourgeois law applies quite a definite term, "confiscation."

Did not the bourgeois states confiscate the property of the subjects of the Central Powers for the debts of their governments?

When an intervention was started against us . . . had we not the right, by bourgeois law, to confiscate the property of the Allies' citizens? What does bourgeois law say to this? And if, in addition, we consider that in our country the Allies were dealing not with an ordinary state, but with a state different from all others—a state that creates its own laws—then it would appear that what was done was logical, absolutely legal, and absolutely judicious. . . .

What We Are Offering

. . .

Now we are going to Genoa with a businesslike plan for economic reconstruction, and we shall tell them point-blank: "We do not intend to offer you a communist program. We do not intend to make Communists of you; and we suppose that you do not wish to make us adhere to capitalist forms of exploitation and bourgeois forms of administration. Did not you, yourselves, state at Cannes: 'No nation can claim the right to dictate the principles by which another nation must regulate its system of ownership, internal economy, and government'? . . .

"In this huge country of ours, which possesses the greatest wealth of resources in the world, there is plenty to be gained by capitalists. You will have your profit. We guarantee to you that the Soviet government will abide by whatever obligations it assumes.

"We did not sign the obligations that the tsarist government assumed; but to refuse to recognize these obligations is not to deny other norms of obligation. To us, the obligations assumed by the workers' and peasants' government are sacred. We carry on our work in a businesslike manner. We declared the New Economic Policy not because we grew tired of being Communists, not because we decided to give up even an inch of our communist plans, but because, after we emerged from the long war period, we were obliged to adapt our economy to the new and peaceful conditions. The best guarantee that we shall live up to obligations that we voluntarily assume is our interest in the working of your capital. If we do not abide by our obligations, then the capitalists will not come to us. We are interested in being honest businessmen and tradesmen." . . .

If they [the capitalists] think they can use the Genoa Conference to compromise the Soviet government, . . . they fail to consider the political maturity of both their own workers and peasants and ours. We go to the Genoa Conference with open and honest intentions; we go there to give and to receive in order to reach agreement; but we shall sign no promissory notes that would enslave our government;

we shall sign no commitments that would violate the basic laws of the Soviet republic—the laws nationalizing the land and giving the state monopoly of industry and foreign trade. We shall not assume any obligation that would violate the sovereignty of the government of the workers and peasants.

We Must Hold On to the End

Our delegation will find itself in an extremely difficult situation. We are already faced with a bloc of states antagonistic to us. There is no doubt, however, that they do not all think alike. Conditions differ: Some are anxious to start trade with us immediately; others are more interested in various reparations. Most important of all, two systems of government, differing in principles and aims, will face each other at Genoa. The soviet republics will face the greatest trials. And here every worker, Communist, and Red soldier must consider how he can help the Soviet government in its difficult task.

What do our enemies count on? . . .

They say: "There is famine [in Russia] that has overpowered the workers and the peasants; they need help; they must give in." . . . Yes, they expect to win because of famine, ruin, and a probable new intervention. But . . . if they do, they will go against their own workers and their own peasants; they will antagonize the bourgeois elements that are trying to reach our market; they will meet distrust and opposition. And if, at this time, when we approach them with a desire to come to an honest agreement, they indicate that they do not wish such an agreement, we shall say to them: "If you interfere with the conclusion of peace at this conference which you yourselves convened, then we shall have new allies from your own ranks."

[Our] whole problem is to hold on, not to count on a loan, on credits that might come after the Genoa Conference. We must not forget we are still passing through a phase of a revolutionary epoch; we must look to ourselves for remedies for our own ills; we ourselves must fight the famine and the breakdown of our transportation system; and we must make our Red Army even stronger, because this army is our only support. If this opinion, if this realization, supports us as well in the future as in the past, then economic agreement will soon be reached. The whole question rests on self-restraint, on continuing the struggle, on keeping up our fighting mood. He who holds on during the last quarter-hour wins in the end.

. . .

35

Soviet Policies on Coexistence of Old and New Systems, Economic Concessions, Peace, Disarmament, Equality of All Peoples, Participation of Workers' Organizations, Reform of the League of Nations

[Chicherin's Speech at the Genoa Conference, April 10, 1922, Delivered in French][8]

The Russian delegation, representing the government that has always sustained the cause of peace, receive with particular satisfaction the declarations of the preceding speakers, who have proclaimed the eternal necessity for peace. The delegation associate themselves especially with the Italian prime minister's declaration that neither victors nor vanquished are gathered here, and the British prime minister's assurance that we are all here upon an equal footing.

[8] *Materialy genuezskoi konferentsii*, pp. 78–82, also *The Soviet Union and Peace* . . . , pp. 82–86.

The Russian delegation desire to declare above all that they have come here in the interest of peace and of the general economic reconstruction of Europe, which has been ruined by the prolonged war and the postwar policies.

While remaining faithful to communist principles, the Russian delegation recognize that in the present period of history—a period that permits the parallel existence of the old social order and the new one now being created—economic collaboration between the states representing these two systems appears essential to world economic reconstruction. The Russian government, consequently, attaches special importance to the first clause of the Cannes Resolution, which calls for the reciprocal recognition among nations of existing systems of property and political and economic systems. The Russian delegation have come here not to disseminate propaganda for their own theoretical point of view, but rather to establish practical relations with the governments and with the commercial and industrial circles of all countries on a basis of reciprocity, equal rights, and full recognition. . . .

With a view to world economic needs and to the development of the world's productive forces, the Russian government is prepared to open its frontiers voluntarily to international communication routes. It is prepared to deliver for cultivation millions of desiatinas of the most fertile soil in the world. It is prepared to grant forest concessions, mining concessions of infinite richness for coal and other minerals—particularly in Siberia—and concessions of all kinds throughout the territory of the Russian Socialist Federated Soviet Republic. [Elaborates on concessions.]

. . .

Meanwhile, the economic reconstruction of Russia, and with it the task of ending Europe's economic chaos, will be attempted in vain . . . if the economically more powerful nations, instead of fostering Russia's economic revival and facilitating her future progress, crush her under the weight of demands that not only are beyond her strength but are survivals of a past that is odious to her. . . .

All efforts directed toward reconstructing world economy will be in vain so long as threats of new wars, perhaps even more devastating than the last war, hang over Europe. Russia is prepared to help consolidate peace as far as this can be done within the limits of the social and political order still existing in most countries.

The Russian delegation wish to propose to the conference the general limitation of armaments. Russia will support all measures tending to lighten the burden of militarism, on condition that the limitation be applicable to the armies of all countries, and that the rules of war include abolition of the most barbarous methods of warfare, such as the use of poison gas, aerial warfare, and in particular the destruction of peaceful populations. Russia, for her part, is prepared to limit her armaments on condition of full and complete reciprocity, and on condition that she be given the necessary guarantees against any kind of attack upon her or interference in her domestic affairs.

In welcoming with satisfaction this first European conference, and also the British prime minister's proposal that similar conferences be convened periodically in the future, the Russian delegation desire to emphasize that these conferences must be enlarged to include all peoples. In our view, universal peace can only be established by an international congress in which all peoples have equal status and their right to determine their own destinies is recognized. We also believe that the method of representation at these conferences should be modified. The official participation of the workers' organizations is indispensable. The decisions of the congresses must be applied not by force or by pressure upon minorities, but by the free will of all participants.

The Russian government is even willing to adopt as its point of departure, subject to certain necessary modifications, the old agreements regulating international relations among the powers, and to participate in revising the statutes of the League of Nations, so as to transform it into a true union of all peoples without the domination of some over the others, without the present division into victors and vanquished.

The international congress of which I speak should appoint technical commissions to outline and elaborate a program for the economic reconstruction of the world. This program must not be imposed by force; it must appeal to the interests of every participant. The international routes—the railways and river and maritime routes that will in time be internationalized—must be mapped out. [Gives more details] . . .

If the desire of all peoples for economic collaboration is sincere, if they will strive to end the world economic crisis by common effort, if they will agree to make sacrifices, it will not be difficult, so the Russian delegation believe, to find means for the gradual stabilization of the financial situation in most states and for the stabilization of exchanges. One way might be to redistribute, by means of long-term loans, the existing reserves of gold among all countries in the same proportion as existed before the war, without prejudice to the interests of the countries now actually possessing this gold. This redistribution should be combined with a rational redistribution of the products of industry and commercial activity, and with a distribution of fuel (naphtha, coal, etc.) according to a definite plan.

I have merely outlined the fundamental points of the proposals the Russian delegation hope to put forward. I wish to repeat that as Communists we do not believe that war and economic crisis can be effectively suppressed under the world order as it now exists. Nevertheless, in the interest of Russia and of all Europe, in the interest of tens of millions of people upon whom the existing economic chaos has been inflicting superhuman privation and suffering, we are ready to contribute our aid to all measures—even though they be merely palliatives—calculated to improve the world economic situation and remove the threat of new wars. We are prepared to support all progressive proposals advanced by other countries in this respect.

In greeting once more the European conference at Genoa, and in expressing sincere thanks to the Italian government for its hospitality, the Russian delegation solemnly proclaim their resolve to contribute with all their strength to the success of the conference's work.

THE HAGUE CONFERENCE

36

"Finita la Commedia!" Says Steklov

[Soviet Explanation of the Failure of the Hague Conference][9]

The inglorious end of the Hague Conference has come. It dies unnoticed, and actually it has been dead for some time. At least we ceased to expect anything from it long ago. At any rate, the worst that was expected has actually happened.

What happened behind the scenes is still not quite clear. But one thing is more or less evident: Unlike the Genoa Conference, this conference saw the Entente powers try to conceal their differences and to stand as one bourgeois front against the Soviet republic. If the conference has broken down stupidly and quickly, its breakdown is due, to a great extent, to the desire [of the bourgeois states] not to display their differences again before the world.

Thus the largest bourgeois states, which previously had disagreed, now look to be strongly united. True, at the July 18 session, the Little Entente (and apparently England also) favored continuing the negotiations with Russia, thus leaving France and Belgium seemingly isolated. However, it was soon clear that the cleavage was to be covered up; and the representatives of the bourgeois states declined unanimously, but tacitly, the Russian delegation's suggestion that they clarify obscure points by

[9] *Izvestiia*, No. 162, July 22, 1922, p. 1.

approaching their respective governments, thus providing new grounds for further discussions.

The bourgeois states formed a united front in presenting impudent demands and in categorically denying Russian claims. Yet the Russian claims were no more than natural. Soviet Russia agreed to recognize old debts, and expressed her readiness to compensate in one form or another the former foreign owners who had suffered from the revolution, on condition that the Soviet government be granted definite credits. Meanwhile, the bourgeois states wished to obtain satisfaction on the first two points, but refused to assume any obligations toward Russia. Furthermore, it was even clearer at The Hague than at Genoa that the bourgeois governments had transferred their emphasis to getting the property of former private owners [in Russia] restored to them. Herein lies the key to the secret of the Hague Conference.

The European governments, who act on the instructions of influential bourgeois circles, wish to lay their hands on the basic sources of Russian national wealth. They intend to do this on the basis of old rights, annihilated by the revolution, and not by means of new sacrifices. But what is remarkable is that all the efforts of the Russian delegation to get specific data on the claims of foreign capitalists and governments against Soviet Russia met definite refusal. The international bourgeoisie does not wish to lay its cards on the table. While concealing the size of the cudgel with which it intends to deal a blow to the Russian toiling masses, it is suggesting that they bend their necks meekly to the blows.

What is the sense of this secrecy? A corner of the curtain is lifted by news of the systematic buying of Russian oil shares by foreign capitalist syndicates. Although the October Revolution annulled all the rights of the former private owners, during the last few years foreign capitalist companies (with their governments' help and sometimes on government instructions) have been buying shares of enterprises in Russia, both those which were owned jointly by Russian and foreign capitalists, and those which belonged to Russian capitalists alone. And we know that not only oil shares, but also shares in mines, metallurgical works, country estates and individual property in towns, forests, and so forth have been bought.

And now the foreign capitalists wish us to accept their claims on presentation, based though they are on illegal transactions. It is natural that they do not wish to declare this openly, and consequently they refuse to define the actual amount of their claims against Russia. That is why they consistently desire a preliminary agreement from the Soviet government to meet the claims of private owners without providing, on their part, guarantees of credits to Russia. Obviously the Russian government would not agree to such an approach even if the foreigners' claims against Russia were limited to transactions that were, from the bourgeois point of view, quite legal. The position of the bourgeois states becomes still more unacceptable to us when we have reason to believe that the foreign capitalists intend to present to us bills that are definitely sham and false.

Under such circumstances, the Hague Conference was doomed to failure. But what will follow? The road is clearly being chosen, i.e., the road of separate agreements. To insure themselves against the possible weakness of any single government, the bourgeois governments have secretly formed a bloc of common interests, bound together by a mutual agreement not to seek privileges in Russia that might be detrimental to their allies. Apparently the various capitalist syndicates and companies have formed a similar bloc, so as not to damage each other's interests.

But will the bourgeois governments and the capitalist syndicates withstand this temptation? We have our doubts. As we have noted, the press in the various countries insists on separate agreements with Russia. The liberal English press, for example, speaks for separate agreements, and at the last plenary session [of the conference] the Little Entente countries also showed signs of vacillation. We have reason to suppose that many, if not all, of these states will sign separate agreements with the Soviet republic. Italy may, too, and separate groups of financiers and industrialists undoubtedly will. This is the most vulnerable spot in the capitalist world conspiracy against Soviet Russia, as we can see from the unprecedented behavior of the non-Russian delegations at the Hague Conference. Separate groups of capitalists will be even less able than states to hold out.

Therefore, the results of the Hague Conference do not grieve us very much. Soviet Russia will be able to maintain her rights. She will force the bourgeois countries, after some waiting, to take the only possible course—amicable agreement with the Soviet republic on conditions of mutual advantage, and on a basis acceptable to both sides.

THE MOSCOW DISARMAMENT CONFERENCE

37

Soviet Proposals for Reducing Armies by Two-Thirds and Limiting Military Budgets

[The First Session of the Moscow Conference on the Reduction of Armaments, December 2, 1922][10]

LITVINOV: In its invitation of June 14 of this year, the Russian government outlined the main problems confronting the conference and laid down its general principles for the mutual reduction of armaments. Noting with profound satisfaction that this invitation received a favorable response from Russia's western neighbors, the Russian government believes that these problems and principles can serve as guides in the work of the conference.

[Mentions unsuccessful attempt to introduce question of disarmament at Genoa.] . . . Forced by this refusal to narrow its goal and to limit itself provisionally to the reduction of armaments only, and that only between Russia and her neighbors, the Russian government is nevertheless convinced that the solution of this problem—given good will and complete mutual confidence—will lead to results of sufficient value for all the interested nations, and will strengthen the bonds of peaceful collaboration between Russia and her western neighbors.

From this standpoint, the Russian government invites the conference delegates to formulate a precise plan for the common reduction of land forces, based on a reduction of the existing Russian army to one-quarter of its present dimensions (to 200,000 men) during the next eighteen months to two years, and on a corresponding reduction of the armies of the states on Russia's western frontiers. [Stresses reciprocity.] . . .

Meanwhile, the actual reduction of existing armed forces, even if pursued to the extreme, will not in itself mean effective mutual limitation of armament unless, at the same time, precise limits are set for the military budgets of the contracting parties. Only by strictly limiting total military expenditure can the contracting powers abate the danger of rivalry in making technical improvements in war matériel. . . . Assuming that such financial disarmament can best be achieved by establishing maximum figures for necessary budgetary expenditures for the army, figures to be identical for all the contracting parties, the Russian government empowers its delegation to establish a final figure, after the commission has thoroughly discussed the problems and considered all the determining factors.

While proposing that the maximum figures for land forces and military budgets

---

[10] *Conférence de Moscou*, pp. 46–71; Litvinov's speech also appears in *The Soviet Union and Peace* . . . , pp. 115–18.

be fixed by agreement, the Russian government considers that the simultaneous dissolution of irregular military formations, forces recruited from particular groups
of the civil population, would be the best guarantee of the real and loyal execution
of this measure. . . . The Russian government declares itself ready to proceed with
this dissolution, on condition that analogous measures be taken by the governments
of all the contracting parties. . . .

As to secondary questions, the Russian government believes it would be useful to
make a special point of neutrality in frontier zones. . . . The agreement recently
concluded between Russia and Finland can serve as an example for the general
regulation of relations along most of Russia's western frontier. . . .

The Russian government, to its profound regret, is unable to make any proposals
regarding the reduction of naval forces. [States Russia's need for naval forces in
view of naval armament of other powers.] . . .

The Russian government hopes that the conference, although thus limited in
scope, will take decisive steps to reduce land forces and military budgets, as well as
dissolve irregular military formations, alleviate border conflicts, and strengthen the
bonds of peaceful economic collaboration between the Russian people and their
nearest western neighbors.

The Russian government fully realizes that the present socio-economic structure
of most countries, based on the exploitation of man by man and of some peoples by
others, makes it impossible to eliminate every last possibility of armed international
conflict. The tentative attempts of the Great Powers to regulate international relations, while removing some of the former injustices, have created new and worse
ones, and have opened the way to new wars in the future. The Russian government is fully convinced, however, that even partial disarmament would greatly
diminish the possibility of armed conflict, as well as provide immediate relief. The
proposals advanced by the Russian government are perfectly concrete and realizable.
Talk of so-called "moral disarmament"—so often heard at international conferences as a pretext for avoiding real disarmament—is no substitute.

. . . This conference will open the way to general disarmament—to the goal
which, in the interests of the toilers in its own country and those of all humanity,
the government of the workers and peasants of Russia has set for itself.

J. SELJAMAA: [Affirms the pacific intentions and desires of the Estonian people
and emphasizes the importance of armament reductions.] I wish especially to draw
your attention to the conviction of several noted minds that material disarmament
must be preceded and accompanied by political disarmament.

[Other delegates follow, expressing their pacific intentions and their serious interest in peace and in settling disagreements peaceably.

[Enckell, the Finnish representative, states among other things that partial disarmament will not in itself provide security, since the resulting strengths will still
be unequal. . . . At a meeting later in the day, he asks the conference to settle the
conflict between Russia and Finland before taking up the question of disarmament. . . .

[Wesmanis, the Latvian delegate, states that Latvia agrees with Finland's views;
he declares that an army of 200,000 is as great a danger to an army of 5,000 as an
army of 800,000 to one of 20,000, and that machinery for settling disputes amicably
should be set up before armament reductions are discussed.] . . .

LITVINOV: . . . It would be illogical to reject the Russian proposal on the
pretext that it is first necessary to examine the different means of controlling conflict. The court of arbitration, the so-called League of Nations, the Council of
Ambassadors, the Supreme Council of five or seven—have they prevented wars?
Have they ever contributed anything to allay serious conflicts?

Since the last great European war, the belligerent states have been placing all their differences before the court of arbitration. Though the Russian delegation do not reject the newly formulated plan, and though they are disposed to discuss it either during this conference or later, they insist that this proposal cannot replace their own.

[Speaks of militarism as a cause of war.] . . .

Obviously each state is surrounded by other states. Witness Russia, which is menaced from the south and east. Only recently the Japanese menace was quite real. Nevertheless, Russia is ready to reduce her effective forces to a strict minimum, without even considering the possibility of aggressive action by distant countries. Russia must watch over the safety of her coast lines. Frontier questions and coastal questions cannot be placed in the same category; moreover, Russia's western neighbors have fewer coastal questions than Russia has. While by no means intending to reject the newly formulated proposal, the Russian delegation are bound to declare that this proposal must not be considered before the preceding problem, which is of essential interest to the countries represented at this conference. It is inadmissible to assume that one of the questions can be supplanted by the other.

PRINCE RADZIWILL: [Agrees with most of the reasoning of the chairman of the Russian delegation, but declares that if militarism is a great evil, war is a still greater one.] . . . Our chief objectives are to create an atmosphere of confidence that will allow us to prevent the outbreak of new wars in the future, and to accomplish the technical task of disarmament. Russia proposes to reduce her effective forces by three-quarters. The Polish government, for its part, is prepared to discuss the reduction of armaments. Meanwhile, it wishes to have real guarantees of a general nature. We must first examine certain political problems, the solution of which will serve as the basis for technical discussions.

The Polish delegation propose that two commissions be formed, one political, the other technical. The decisions of the first will serve as the basis for the work of the second. Since the Bureau [of the conference] can take charge of all political questions, there will be no need to create a special political commission.

[The Latvian delegate states that without the distrust among states there would be no militarism and declares political disarmament essential. . . .

[Saunus, of the Lithuanian delegation, then proposes that present and future conflicts be submitted to international arbitration as provided for by the Covenant of the League of Nations. He stresses that political disarmament must precede material disarmament. . . .

[The delegates of Estonia and Finland emphasize the necessity of creating an atmosphere of confidence among the nations.]

38

The Reply of the Delegations of Estonia, Latvia, Finland, and Poland to Soviet Proposals, Read by the Polish Delegate, Prince Radziwill

[Session of the Military and Technical Commission of the Conference, December 11, 1922][11]

Having taken into account the state of work of the conference, caused by the attitude of the Russian delegation, whose point of view differs essentially from that

---

[11] *Conférence de Moscou*, pp. 205–7.

of the majority of delegations present at the conference, the delegations of Estonia, Finland, Latvia, and Poland believe it their duty to state the following:

The work of the League of Nations—in which more than fifty states have been participating for two years (including all the states represented at the Moscow Conference except Soviet Russia)—and the discussions here have shown clearly that universal limitation of armament can only be achieved by establishing a principle (1) that can be carried out exactly, and (2) that will safeguard the security of the different countries.

The work of the League of Nations has shown that merely reducing effective forces, military budgets, and the reserves of war matériel is not enough—it is also necessary to create political guarantees of peace and security for the respective countries.

Although Russia is not a member of the League of Nations, and although according to the declarations of the Russian delegation she has no intention of becoming affiliated with it, the governments of Estonia, Finland, Latvia, and Poland hoped to serve the general cause and hasten settlement of the armament question by accepting the Russian invitation and thus enlarging the circle of states working on this serious problem. . . .

The Russian delegation's proposal that the armies of all states represented at the conference be reduced to one-quarter of their effective forces in 1922, and that a fixed maximum budgetary expense be established for the army, not only is inequitable so long as Russia possesses greater war industries and more material resources than other countries, but tends to maintain Soviet Russia's military power intact while reducing the total defensive capacity of the neighboring countries to a level far below their minimum security requirements. . . .

The delegations of Estonia, Finland, Latvia, and Poland propose that the conference:

1. Sign a treaty of nonaggression and arbitration, by which a common agreement would be established [among the states];

2. Register the figures communicated by the delegates concerning the maximum number of effective forces proposed for 1923 by their respective governments;

3. Convoke a commission of military experts, after ratification of the above treaty, to work out the limitation of land and naval forces, taking into account such conditioning factors as the manpower, financial expense, war industry, war matériel reserves, and political, strategic, and geographical position of each country. . . .

39

Soviet Rejection of Counterproposals by Poland and the Baltic States

[Declaration of the Russian Delegation at the Final Session of the Military and Technical Commission, December 12, 1922][12]

Having acquainted themselves with the collective declaration of the combined delegations of Estonia, Finland, Latvia, and Poland, the Russian delegation believe it their duty to give the following reply:

The declaration of the united delegations contains, in addition to a refusal to continue the work of the conference, a summary of the principal stages in its convocation and its subsequent activities. The Russian delegation feel bound to submit their own exact interpretation of this summary, so as to forestall the legends to which certain statements in the united delegations' declaration could easily give rise.

---

[12] *Ibid.*, pp. 215–23; also *The Soviet Union and Peace* . . . , pp. 119–25.

The Russian government's note of invitation of last June 14 proposed that the conference should concentrate chiefly on the mutual reduction of armament on a proportional basis. This proposal was not rejected by any of the governments invited. Furthermore, the governments whose delegations have now united in a common declaration organized several conferences between June 14 and December 1 to consider the Russian government's invitation and the questions connected with it. During this period they could have considered (indeed the Russian delegation have every reason to believe that they did consider) those very questions whose complexity and difficulty they now use as an excuse to give a new direction to the conference. Following the example of Rumania, the united delegations have now made preliminary conditions. The inconsistency of the united delegations' declaration that they cannot continue considering armament reductions owing to insurmountable complexities is further demonstrated by their military experts' active examination of this very question. These experts have shown themselves adequately informed on armament matters, especially as affecting the six countries represented at the conference.

Finally, the Russian delegation did not limit or intend to limit the time for the work of the conference. Expecting to encounter difficulties on certain questions, they did not expect the conference to end in a few days. The delegations have had, and still have, full opportunity to put before the conference any and every question connected with the actual reduction of armament. . . .

Thus, neither the course of events during the preparatory period, nor the organization of the work of the conference itself, nor the prospects for its work in the future have been such as to give the united delegations the slightest right to demand changes in the course of the conference, let alone to refuse to consider the most important question because it is extremely complex and because discussions on it to date have not produced unanimity of opinion. The Russian delegation can only regard such implications as an attempt by the united delegations to conceal the real motives underlying their behavior. . . .

The Russian delegation are aware that the League of Nations, led by the Great Powers of the so-called Entente, has systematically rejected and continues to reject all proposals, however modest, for actually reducing armaments. It even rejects analogous resolutions, preferring palaver about so-called "moral disarmament." France plays the most prominent role in these discussions, although she is not decreasing, but increasing her armed forces. . . .

[Reiterates Russian position that resolutions concerning moral disarmament are meaningless unless accompanied by material disarmament.] . . .

Although true to this point of view, the Russian delegation have nevertheless actively joined in discussing the united delegations' draft proposal for the agreement on nonaggression and arbitration, and have introduced several important amendments, being convinced that this treaty is fundamentally connected with effective armament reductions. [Points out that certain clauses introduced by the Russian delegation were rejected as going too far.] . . .

Furthermore, despite the resistance of the authors of the draft treaty of nonaggression and arbitration to transforming the purely political discussion into a real instrument for consolidating and developing peaceful relations, and despite their evident preference for hazy and dubious phrases, the Russian delegation, recognizing the urgency of the matter, agreed to subscribe to this treaty, on condition that it embody also the decisions of the conference on the actual reduction of armaments.

Proceeding to this vital matter, and bringing to the attention of the conference their project for the mutual reduction of armament based on a decrease of the Russian army to 200,000 (one-fourth of its present strength), the Russian delegation immediately met unanimous opposition from the united delegations.

The united delegations declared categorically that at the present time their governments could consider only an insignificant reduction of their armies, and the fixing of military budget norms for 1923 only. The opposition forced the Russian delegation to limit the scope of their original proposal to what had been designed as its first stage, namely that reductions be based on the establishment for 1923 of Russian army budget norms of 600,000 men, with corresponding reductions of the armies of other countries. Thereupon the united delegations communicated the figures proposed for their armies for 1923, observing that these figures were on almost the same scale as the proposed Russian reduction from 800,000 men in 1922 to 600,000 in 1923. The Polish delegation in particular stated that by this proportion the effective forces of the Polish army in 1923 would not exceed 280,000. Further discussions, however, revealed that the figures quoted by the united delegations did not actually represent any reduction compared with 1922, i.e., that the delegations had misrepresented the actual facts. On the basis of the Polish government's reply to the League of Nations' questionnaire of June 28, 1922, it was established that Poland had an army of 293,744 men in 1922. In comparing this figure with the one of 280,000 supplied by the Polish delegation for 1923, one must conclude that no serious reduction has been made.

By now it was obvious that the governments of Poland, Finland, Latvia, and Estonia were not in the least disposed to reduce their armies in 1923, and that their delegations, by making statements to the contrary and using incorrect figures, were merely covering up their true feelings. The Russian delegation state that only at this point did the united delegations remark upon the insurmountable complexity of the question and the impossibility of discussing it further.

This simple fact established, the Russian delegation need not investigate in detail the occasional arguments by which the united delegations endeavored to conceal their views. It is only in the interest of re-establishing the truth that the Russian delegation consider it necessary to repeat that the proportional reduction of the armed forces of Russia and her western neighbors, especially at the modest rate suggested at this conference, not only would fail to change the balance of power in favor of Russia, but would, on the contrary, considering the extent of her territory and the length of her western and southwestern frontiers, place her in a much less advantageous situation. The Russian delegation consider the reference to a supposedly powerful war industry in Russia particularly strange, coming as it does from a group of powers headed by Poland, who have at their disposal the incomparably greater war industries of France, with whom Poland is bound not only by the theoretical ties of close friendship, but also by the quite real ties of a military convention. . . .

Turning to the practical proposals made in the declaration of the united delegations, the Russian delegation can be brief, for these proposals have already occupied the attention of the conference, and the Russian delegation have already given them an exhaustive reply.

If the Russian delegation cannot sign a nonaggression and arbitration treaty with the countries represented by the united delegations, it is not because they find the provisions of this treaty and the arrangements arising therefrom unacceptable. On the contrary, the delegation endeavored to extend these mutual obligations and to make them more exacting.

However, the delegation believe that signing simple formal declarations cannot create an atmosphere of mutual confidence until the states represented here prove that they have no individual or joint aggressive intentions toward Russia by the only convincing means, namely, by revealing their willingness to reduce their regular armies and to dissolve their irregular armed forces. The Russian delegation do not want to affix their signatures to phrases that conceal the absence of true effort and the obstinate desire to evade it.

The Russian delegation note the figures quoted by the united delegations for armies in their countries in 1923, and state that these figures are very little or no lower than those for 1922. In other words, the governments of these countries, for their part, actually reject the idea of reducing armaments.

As for the third proposal of the united delegations—that a commission of military experts be set up to discuss practical measures for reducing armaments—the Russian delegation state that a similar commission already exists within the framework of the conference and has already begun to work. The proposal to interrupt its work for several months and resume it only after the signature and ratification of simple declarations that are nothing unless they relate specifically to results obtained at the conference is, in the opinion of the Russian delegation, a poorly concealed attempt to sabotage the present conference by creating the empty appearance of achievement. This would simply mislead the masses, who aspire to peace, and who are being ground down by the burden of military taxation.

In conclusion, the Russian delegation consider it necessary to ask the united delegations this question once more: Do they wish to continue further joint work on armament reduction along the lines of this conference, and within the framework already established?

The Russian delegation feel obliged to warn the united delegations that insistence on their point of view would make continuation of the conference impossible, for it would show that the majority of the conference's participants are pursuing aims radically opposed to its principal purpose. If the Russian delegation are to consider as final the Estonian, Finnish, Latvian, and Polish delegations' declaration ending the work of this commission, and consequently the Moscow Conference, the delegation will feel bound to regard this declaration as a refusal to accept the Russian government's proposal for actual disarmament and will, without the least apprehension, appeal to the masses all over the world, and especially in the countries represented at the conference, to draw their own conclusions from this refusal.

THE LAUSANNE CONFERENCE

40

The Soviet Government's Offer to Convene a Conference on the Problems of the Near East

[Telegram of the Assistant Commissar of Foreign Affairs, L. M. Karakhan, to Great Britain, France, Italy, Yugoslavia, Bulgaria, Rumania, Greece, and Egypt, September 24, 1922][13]

The Russian government believes that but one problem is responsible for the events in the Near East, and that is recognition of the Turkish people's right to full sovereignty over Turkish lands, and primarily over Turkey's capital, Constantinople, and the Straits.

The Western powers, especially the most irreconcilable of them, Great Britain, refuse to return to Turkey the Straits and the lands that unquestionably belong to her, allegedly in order to defend the Straits, but actually in order to dominate them.

The freedom of the Straits concerns primarily the littoral powers, [i.e.] Russia, her allies, and Turkey, whose possessions encircle the greater part of the Black Sea coast.

In 1920 Turkey proclaimed in her national slogan, which she is now struggling to realize, the freedom of the Straits for peaceful commerce and navigation, on condition that the security of the Straits be guaranteed by the interested powers.

[13] Kliuchnikov and Sabanin, III, 201–2.

The principle of the freedom of the Straits for merchant ships was confirmed by Russia in Article 5 of the Russo-Turkish treaty of March 16, 1921, which stated that the international status of the Straits would be guaranteed by the littoral powers.

Meanwhile, official Western statements about the Straits refer to the great victor powers of the war of 1914 as the only interested powers, ignore Russian interests altogether, and see Turkey simply as the object of negotiations.

This attitude was made particularly clear in the British government's communiqué of September 16, stating that, next to Great Britain, France and Italy were the powers most interested in the Straits.

The Russian government must categorically protest the Western powers' usurpation of the rights of Russia and the republics allied to her.

Next to Turkey, Russia and her allies, the Ukraine and Georgia, are the countries most interested in the freedom of the Straits. Historically, the European powers have recognized Russia's interest in the Eastern problem, and in all international treaties dealing with the regime of the Straits they have even acknowledged Russia's preponderance. The recognition of Russian interests went so far in 1916 that the powers of the Entente, allied to tsarist Russia, promised in a special agreement to give Russia both the Straits and Constantinople.

The Soviet government does not consider that Russia's interests require the enslavement of part of the Turkish people. Therefore, the Russian government has annulled the old treaties of the tsarist government.

The far-reaching [Western] recognition of Russian interests in the recent past permits us to hope that the Western powers will not now deny Russia's primary interest in the settlement of the future of the Straits.

The Soviet government again repeats its earlier declaration that Russia will not accept any decision arrived at without her participation, and against her interests.

Russia and Turkey have agreed on a plan for applying the freedom of the Straits, and Russia warns the Western governments not to repeat the mistakes made when the interests of the powers concerned were ignored.

No decision on the Straits without Russia's participation can be final or lasting. Any such decision will simply provide ground for further conflicts.

Great Britain's views on the freedom of the Straits reflect the desire of a strong naval power to control a route that is vitally important to other powers, and so to hold these powers under a continuous threat. This threat is directed primarily against Russia and Turkey.

Great Britain is sending her armed forces to the Near East, and she is trying to draw France, Italy, Yugoslavia, and Rumania into this war with Turkey. According to the official communiqué of the British government, the planned war would be to defend Constantinople and the neutral zone, and also to defend Europe from the aggressive and hostile advance of the Turks. But this latter consideration deserves no attention whatsoever; no government could take it seriously. As for the defense of the Turkish capital undertaken by Great Britain and her allies against the Turkish people, their national army, and the Turkish government, which wishes only to be left alone in its effort to return to its legal place of sojourn, this is a claim that can only arouse the greatest possible astonishment. . . .

The Russian government believes that some powers' separate efforts to end the Near Eastern crisis by a mutual agreement, but without the participation of the interested peoples, can neither bring positive results nor prevent the threat of a new war.

In view of Russia's special position in the East and on the Black Sea, and in the interests of the peoples most concerned with the peaceful settlement of the Near Eastern problem, the Soviet government proposes that a conference of all interested powers, and primarily of the littoral powers, be convened immediately.

The Russian government hopes that its voice will be heard by all who seek true peace, peace based on the equality of all parties concerned and on complete respect for Turkish sovereignty over all Turkish lands.

41

Russia's Reply to the Allied Proposal of Limited Participation at the Lausanne Conference

[Chicherin to the Soviet Official Agent in London, Krasin, November 2, 1922; Copies Directly to the Foreign Ministers of France and Italy][14]

Please communicate to the British government as follows:

The Russian government has received the communiqué of October 27 from the governments of Great Britain, France, and Italy inviting Russia to send representatives to the Near Eastern Conference at Lausanne to discuss the regime of the Straits.

The Russian government finds it quite inadmissible and absolutely inexcusable to exclude Russia from the discussions of all the other questions before this conference. The Russian government wishes to note first of all that the proposed Lausanne Conference differs entirely in composition from the conference that signed the Treaty of Sèvres. Thus the discussions of Near Eastern problems on the agenda of the conference can in no way be considered a belated liquidation by the participants in the great European war [of the problems arising therefrom]. Besides, such a liquidation has now become impossible, owing to the brilliant victories won by the Turkish people. Consequently [it appears that] the new conference will attempt a general settlement of all Near Eastern problems. This supposition is confirmed by the fact that some Lausanne participants have already concluded separate agreements with Turkey. Therefore the Russian government cannot consider this conference as a meeting of parties who are in a state of war, and who seek to end their military activities. The majority of the invited powers do not represent belligerent powers.

Assuming [therefore] that the object of the Lausanne Conference will be, as it appears, to effect a general settlement of all Near Eastern questions, the Russian government cannot possibly agree to participate only in the discussions on the Straits. The Russian government finds absolutely incomprehensible the absence not only of Russia, but of Bulgaria, which adjoins Turkey, while Yugoslavia and Rumania and even Japan are invited.

The Russian government regards such an artificial selection of participants as an attempt by the inviting powers to determine arbitrarily the rights and degree of participation of every state in the settlement of Near Eastern problems. The inviting powers, who are letting some states participate and excluding others, have no legal basis whatsoever for such action.

As a result of the inviting powers' action, the strong powers will inevitably violate the legal rights of weaker states and aim at an arbitrary settlement at the weaker states' expense. One fears that the inviting powers intend to restore neither the Turkish people's full rights nor their sovereign authority over their own territory and waters. The arbitrary composition of the Lausanne Conference, and the stubborn refusal of the inviting powers to permit Russia to participate fully in it, make it very unlikely that the Turkish people's vital interests will be completely satisfied, and that the principle of their sovereignty will be properly applied. . . .

Soviet Russia, which is the friend of all oppressed peoples, and which proclaims the right of all nations to self-determination, has established friendly relations with the peoples of the East, and has thus brought about a stable state of affairs in the

East. Soviet Russia believes it her duty to continue to apply these principles at the Lausanne Conference.

The Russian government is alien to every desire to renew the methods of the old tsarist government, and of other governments who pretended to act as guardians of Turkey. Therefore, the Russian government believes it necessary to be present at the conference for the special purpose of insisting on the restoration of the full sovereign rights of the Turkish people, which is essential to a stable peace in the Near East, in which Russia is directly interested. From the military point of view, this move would guarantee peace on the Black Sea and the security of the Russian, Ukrainian, and Georgian coast.

The inviting powers have shown by their actions that they desire to keep the peoples of the East in a state of dependency. Their refusal to let Russia participate in the conference except in the discussions on the Straits is also an attempt to violate Russia's rights and interests in the domain of foreign policy, and to worsen the international situation.

. . .

In view of its interest in general peace, its belief in the right of peoples to self-determination, and its own duty to safeguard the legal rights, prestige, and vital interests of the Soviet republic, the Russian government must insist most emphatically on the full and unlimited participation of Soviet Russia and the Ukraine and Georgia in the Near Eastern conference, on the basis of absolute equality with the other participants.

The Russian government asks the inviting powers of the Lausanne Conference to reply at the earliest possible moment, so as to permit the Russian delegation to arrive for the opening of the conference.

42

Lenin on the Straits

[Lenin Interviewed by a British Journalist, October 27, 1922][15]

. . .

Question 3: Is Russia's demand to participate in [the settlement of] the Near Eastern problem only a question of prestige? Would you consent to the French proposition that Russia should participate only in the second part of the conference, when the Straits question is discussed?

Reply: Russia's participation in the settlement of the Near Eastern problem is by no means a matter of prestige. I hope our international policy during the past five years has proved that we care very little about prestige and never make any demand or jeopardize peace merely for the sake of prestige. No nation is so indifferent to prestige or so ready to meet the claims of prestige with hearty ridicule as Russia. I believe that modern diplomacy is speedily approaching a time when it will treat the question of prestige the same way we do.

Our Near Eastern policy is of most concrete, immediate, and vital interest to Russia and the federated states. If these states are not allowed to participate in the Near Eastern conference, any number of animosities, conflicts, and differences will arise. Difficulties will be created in trade relations between Eastern countries and [Western] European countries, difficulties that will seriously interfere with, and even obviate, the peaceful coexistence of these countries.

That is why the Russian government is not content with the Paris suggestion

[15] Lenin, *Sochineniia,* XXVII, 312-14; also *The Observer* (London), October 29, 1922, p. 13.

that Russia participate only in the question of the Straits. We believe that such a limitation would inevitably cause France and England some very practical and immediate economic difficulties in the near future.

Question 4: What is Russia's program for the settlement of the Straits?

Reply: Our program in its general outlines contains the following points: First, satisfaction of the national aspirations of Turkey. We consider this necessary not only on behalf of national independence. Our experience during the last five years in settling national problems . . . has convinced us that the best method is to give maximum satisfaction to national aspirations, and to provide conditions that will eliminate conflicts among different national elements within a state. . . . Second, the closing of the Straits to all armed ships in peace as well as in war. This is to the immediate commercial interest of all the powers, not only the ones adjacent to the Straits, but the others also. It must be remembered that although there is much pacifist phrase-making . . . and even condemnation of war, the readiness to take real steps, even the most preliminary, to a guarantee of peace is almost entirely lacking. We need fewer general declarations, solemn promises, and flashy formulas, and more simple, clear decisions and actions leading toward real peace, not to speak of the entire abolition of the danger of war. Third, full freedom for commercial shipping. . . .

Question 5: Do you agree to leave the control of the Straits to the League of Nations if Russia, Turkey, Germany, and the United States become members, or would you advocate a special commission for this purpose?

Reply: We are, of course, opposed to the League of Nations, not only because of our special economic and political regime, but also . . . [from the point of view of international peace]. The League of Nations bears the birthmark of its war origin; it is so enmeshed in the Versailles treaty, and is so completely inadequate as regards the equality of nations and the peaceful coexistence of peoples, that our negative estimate of it seems to me quite understandable and in need of no further comment.

43

Soviet Interpretation of the Significance of the Turkish Nationalist Movement

[Excerpts from Chicherin's Article on the Lausanne Conference and the World Situation][16]

The World War has revealed two tendencies in the treatment of the Eastern peoples and of colonial countries in general. First, the war led to new seizures by the world imperialists—new aggressions on their part and the creation of new protectorates, spheres of influence, and mandated territories—and finally to attempts to put down the Eastern peoples who have been defending their independence. Persia was actually occupied by England; the Near East was divided among the Western powers; Turkey was pillaged and then converted by the Sèvres treaty into a miserable scrap of an independent country. Simultaneously, however, the war initiated a reverse process. The weakening of imperialist Europe has made it easier for the colonial people to fight for their freedom. These two tendencies, imperialist aggression and imperialist disintegration, have prompted the Eastern peoples to start a struggle against imperialist oppression.

The soviet republics, which have become an ideological and actual embodiment of the principle of self-determination, provide a historical precedent for the struggle

[16] G. V. Chicherin, "Lozanskaia konferentsiia i mirovoe polozhenie," *Mezhdunarodnaia Zhizn*, No. 2, 1923, pp. 3–6.

of the Eastern peoples for liberation. The existence of the soviet republics has led to a complete redistribution of world power, and has made it possible for the peoples of Asia, step by step, to carry on their victorious struggle.

This process has affected Turkey's destiny more obviously than any other country's. No Asiatic people has fought so heroically and energetically as the Turkish people. No Eastern people has been subjected to such terrible destruction as Turkey was at the time the Central European coalition was broken up. No Asian country revived its power so rapidly as Turkey, or launched such a victorious struggle as the one resulting, at Lausanne, in the capitulation of the world powers to small Turkey, weakened by twelve years of *war*.

Turkey's victory was the result of the heroic struggle of the Turkish people, of the Turkish peasants and artisans who took up arms at the time of the foreign seizure of their country. But Turkey's victory is at the same time our victory. For, in the struggle against foreign invasion, when the remnants of Turkish statehood (the members of Parliament who fled Constantinople, the democratic-minded officers, and so forth) met in the cities of eastern Turkey and re-created a national government, and when a great political tide brought Mustafa Kemal Pasha to national leadership, the Soviet republic served as a political and moral beacon in the life-and-death struggle of these people. . . .

After this, the Turkish liberation movement entered a new phase. The complete routing of the Greeks cleared Asia Minor of the enemy, except in areas adjoining the Straits. Then came a new struggle, or rather, a new form of struggle—struggle at the green table—first at Mudania [in Turkey], and later at Lausanne. The specter of Soviet Russia haunted that green table. Under these circumstances, Turkey's victory in this new phase is also our victory.

Why did the world powers agree to grant the greatest possible concessions to little Turkey? Because they feared Soviet Russia. At the moment of greatest tension between Turkey and the West, and particularly while the Lausanne Conference was recessed, why was the war not renewed, and why were the huge forces of England not unleashed upon little Turkey? Because of Soviet Russia.

The internal distintegration of imperialist Europe also worked to this end. The Anglo-French conflict was revealed to be especially sharp during the Lausanne Conference. The forces of these two colossi were not equal. France, tied up in the Ruhr, was helpless against England; involved elsewhere, she was at the mercy of her rival. At the Paris meeting before the opening of the [Lausanne] conference, Poincaré actually capitulated to England and sold out the Franco-Turkish friendship. Having thus committed himself beforehand, Poincaré was doomed to political impotency. England's tactics were complicated in application but simple in meaning. She first tried to bargain and to obtain from Turkey what she wanted. After that she left France to dabble in further negotiations while she herself, in turn, either aggravated the situation or played the role of a peacemaker between France and Turkey.

England succeeded first of all in reaching her main goal—a treaty opening the Straits to the naval vessels of other countries. This, the greatest victory of English imperialism, was sanctioned by the conference. Turkey tried to obtain only a certain modification of the rule for opening the Straits. Mustafa Kemal Pasha had already committed himself on the essential point of this decision during the preconference negotiations with the Western powers; his categorical statement to that effect is found in an early-September newspaper interview. The Turkish government apparently wished to rid itself at any cost of England's presence in Constantinople and the Straits. That this agreement concerning the opening of the Straits will be short-lived, even the most Anglophile section of the French press has recognized.

The procedure of the Lausanne Conference itself seems to have passed through several stages. First, from mid-November to mid-December, it worked partly on a preliminary study of the various Near Eastern problems and partly on settling basic principles pertaining to the Straits. From mid-December to mid-January, while the ghost of the unsettled Mosul problem hovered over all its work, the conference was occupied with a detailed examination of economic and financial questions.

England was principally interested in two questions, the Straits and Mosul. In mid-December, during a preliminary examination of all the problems on the agenda, the conference reached the Turkish-Mesopotamian boundary problem, and the Mosul question was withdrawn from the agenda. France and Italy stepped aside and allowed England to bargain alone with Turkey. Turkey needs Mosul, because her trade routes to Persia pass through the Mosul vilayet. The transfer of Mosul to the imaginary kingdom of Iraq (i.e., to the English protectorate) cuts off Turkey from Persia. For England, the Mosul question is a matter first of oil policy, second of Arabian policy. If she is to play the role of patron of the Arabs, and in particular of the imaginary kingdom of Iraq, England must be particularly anxious to retain the Mosul vilayet for Iraq. The negotiations between the English and the Turkish experts were absolutely fruitless. To transfer the entire question to the League of Nations, as the Entente decided to do without Turkey's consent, would make it easier for England's will to prevail. Thus the nine months' delay in settling the problem is actually a serious concession by England, because Turkey, once peace is concluded, will be in a much stronger position with regard to Mosul than she was at the Lausanne Conference.

The conference discussions of economic and financial questions revealed England's conciliatory spirit even more clearly. English capital evidently hopes to compensate itself for losses resulting from international decisions and regulations by a skilled penetration into Turkey. The pioneer of England's capitalistic influence, Urquhart,[17] has tried with remarkable energy and artfulness to tie up English and Turkish interests in a mixed trading company. This policy of drawing to her side the upper bourgeoisie of Turkey is now England's chief instrument in this field, and her compliance at the Lausanne Conference was directed to this end.

French capital has not been able to compete with English in this field. The French usurers and petty businessmen have lost their base in the liberated Turkish state. They oppose the existence of free Turkey more violently than the more pliant large-scale English capitalists. Petty businessmen who have been [financially] injured, and usurers who are anxious for every cent, have always interfered with the policy of the active French capitalists, whose intentions toward Turkey have found clearest expression in the friendly policy of Franklin-Bouillon[18] and certain elements of the French press. The radical duplicity of France's policy has done her very great harm by making French action [in this matter] appear continually vacillating and by undermining confidence in French diplomacy.

One of the basic characteristics of Turkish policy is preference for America and American capitalists. Turkey does not fear aggressive action from America as she does from the Western European countries. The Chester concession,[19] which makes

---

[17] John Leslie Urquhart was a British industrialist who negotiated with the Soviet government for mining concessions in the Urals and what is now Kazakhstan. The project was declined by the Soviet government October 6, 1922, as unsatisfactory.

[18] Henri Franklin-Bouillon, a Radical Socialist politician, was head of the Commission of Foreign Affairs in the French Chamber of Deputies, and in charge of France's negotiations with Turkey.

[19] The Chester concession was an extensive railway concession in Turkey negotiated before World War I by an American group headed by Admiral C. M. Chester, a retired U.S. Navy officer. After World War I and the nationalist revolution, the Ottoman-American Development Company, successor to the Chester group, obtained a concession to build a railway and exploit all mineral resources found within twelve miles on either side of the right of way. The concession caused some friction at the Lausanne Conference. The Ottoman-American Development Company was unable to carry out its agreement and the concession

American capital more influential than European in Turkey, loomed large at the Lausanne Conference, and contributed considerably to the remarkable compliance of the Western powers.

Relinquishing the national home of the Armenians; equalizing the Turks and European nationals in the question of minorities; exchanging (i.e., forcefully banishing from Turkey) all the Greek population except in Constantinople; relinquishing all privileges for foreigners including the right to pursue liberal professions in Turkey in the future; liquidating capitulations; equalizing the rights of Turkish and foreign societies; allowing foreign legal advisers consultative functions only, without any juridical or other rights—all these represent a tremendous diplomatic victory for Turkey. More important, they are the first examples of the retreat of imperialist powers before the oppressed peoples of the East.

No matter how many points the Western imperialists yield to Turkey, however, their interests and Turkey's remain irreconcilable. Western imperialistic capital is bound by its very nature to aim at exploiting Turkey. Opening the Straits to foreign men-of-war places the most important regions of Turkey under a continuous threat. The Turkish people's independence and their right to self-determination are not yet completely secure. The struggle still goes on; it has but assumed different forms. Turkey's only true and constant friend remains, as before, the soviet republics.

THE HAGUE CONGRESS ON WAR AGAINST WAR

44

Lenin Outlines the Tasks of the Soviet Delegation at the Hague, December 4, 1922[20]

In connection with the conference at The Hague, I believe the greatest difficulty in combating the danger of war is that of overcoming the false opinion that this problem is simple, clear, and comparatively easy to solve.

"We shall reply to war with a strike or a revolution" — this is what the most important reformist leaders customarily tell the workers. And often enough these seemingly clear-cut words satisfy and pacify the workers and peasants and the members of the co-operative movement.

Actually, perhaps, it would be best to begin by rejecting such a plan altogether. [Instead] it should be stated that especially now, since the recent war, only the most stupid and deceitful people could suppose such a formula to be of any use whatever. It should be explained that one cannot "reply" to a war by a strike or a revolution, in the simplest and most literal sense of the word.

It must be definitely explained how great the secrecy is that surrounds the birth of war, and how helpless an ordinary workers' organization, even though it calls itself a revolutionary one, is in the face of a really impending war.

What happened during the last war, and why it could not have been otherwise, must be explained over and over again.

Special attention must be given to explaining why the "defense of the fatherland" question will inevitably be advanced and will inevitably be resolved by the overwhelming majority of the workers in favor of their own bourgeoisie.

---

passed into the hands of Canadian interests, which could not find funds in time to meet the deadline for starting operations. The Turkish government thereupon canceled the concession. Leland J. Gordon, *American Relations with Turkey, 1830–1930*, pp. 278–82.

[20] Lenin, *Sochineniia*, XXVII, 372–73; also *International Press Correspondence*, No. 32, June 5, 1924, pp. 322–23.

Therefore, elucidation of the following points should be emphasized: first, the "defense of the fatherland"; second, and connected with the first, "defeatism"; and finally, the only possible means of combating war—the maintenance and formation of illegal organizations made up of all the revolutionaries [drawn into] participation in the war, for the purpose of carrying on a prolonged struggle against war . . .

45

Fourteen-Point Program Proposed by the Russian Delegates and Rejected by Noncommunist Delegates

[Excerpt from Rotshtein's Speech at the Sixth Session of the International Peace Congress, December 13, 1922][21]

"That the present International Peace Congress, being firmly of the opinion that only the abolition of the capitalist system which generates wars will put a stop to them, and that the first condition of any effective struggle against imperialist wars is the creation of a united, purely working-class front, resolves:

"(1) To establish an international Committee of Action consisting of representatives of the International Federation of Trade Unions, the Second International, the International Working Union of Socialist Parties, the Communist International, the Red Trade Union International and the International Co-operative Alliance for the purpose of fighting war;

"(2) To establish similar committees of action in every country, consisting of the representatives of the above-enumerated Internationals;

"(3) To draw into the said committees of action all labour organisations not belonging to any above-mentioned Internationals, provided they are earnestly willing to fight war;

"(4) To charge these committees of action with the task of taking measures to do away with the splits in the mass trade union movement, and to prevent new splits among the trade unions on the condition that freedom of propaganda is preserved, combined with unity of action against the capitalist class;

"(5) To charge these committees and organisations affiliated to them with the duty to carry on a systematic campaign against the theory and practice of defending the bourgeois fatherlands, calculated as it is to deliver the working class, bound hand and foot, into the hands of the international bourgeoisie;

"(6) To recognise that in order to secure maximum results for the struggle of the working class for peace it is necessary to break with the system of co-operation of classes, of coalition with the bourgeoisie, and to draw a sharp line between the labour organisations and the capitalist Governments;"

I may say there are 14 points altogether. [Laughter.]

"(7) Considering that the bourgeoisie is chasing after the illusion of establishing peace on the basis of capitalism, the nursing ground of wars, to recognise as part of the successful struggle against war the necessity of exposing those pacifist illusions and, while not declining the assistance of pacifist organisations in the fight against war, to proclaim its opposition to the bloc with bourgeois pacifism as a form of co-operation of classes;

"(8) To accept as part of the programme for preparing the army and the labouring masses for decisive action against war the necessity of establishing among the soldiers of the armies legal as well as illegal organisations which, after persistent and systematic propaganda in the army, should at the critical moment place themselves at the head of a soldiers' revolt against the bourgeoisie;

[21] *Report of the International Peace Congress* . . . , pp. 143–45.

"(9) To initiate and carry on a determined mass campaign for the abrogation of the monstrous Treaty of Versailles and others of this kind, against the international league of Imperialist Powers acting in the guise of a League of Nations, against the enslavement of the labouring masses of Germany, Austria, Bulgaria, and other countries by means of so-called reparations, and for the imposition of the entire liability for making good the devastation of war upon their authors, the capitalist classes;

"(10) To expose all conspiracies of international Imperialism against the interests of the labouring masses and to demand the immediate publication of all secret treaties;

"(11) To draw into the struggle against war the workers and peasants of the colonies and semi-colonies which are exploited by various Imperialist bandits;

"(12) To carry on a campaign for the immediate evacuation by the Allied troops of German provinces and, generally, for the withdrawal of troops from all territories and countries (including those of Asia and Africa) occupied by the Imperialists in virtue of League of Nations mandates, that is, by right of might;

"(13) To carry on a campaign for disarmament of the white organisations of the bourgeoisie and for the arming of the working class and the establishment in all countries of Labour Governments whose duty shall be to carry out the above demands even against the will of the capitalist classes;

"(14) To organise on January 8 to 15 an international War-against-War week, to end on January 15 in a one-day strike of protest against war, against the Treaty of Versailles, against Imperialism and the dictatorship of Capital, and for the power of Labour."

INTERNATIONAL SIGNIFICANCE OF THE LEAGUE OF NATIONS AND THE SOVIET UNION

46

Stalin on the Need of Confederation as Well as Federation of Soviet Republics

[Stalin's Remarks on the Theses on the National and Colonial Questions Drafted by Lenin and Adopted by the Second Congress of the Communist International, July–August, 1920][22]

On June 11, I received your draft of the theses on the national and colonial questions for the Second Congress of the Communist International. I am not able (have no time) at the present moment to comment on the theses in detail, but I would like to comment briefly on one weakness. I mean the absence of any mention of confederation in the theses—confederation as a transition step toward bringing together the toilers of all countries.

For the nations which were a part of old Russia, our (soviet) type of federation can and must be considered as expedient and as leading toward international unity. The reasons for this are self-evident: those nationalities either had no statehood of their own in the past, or lost it long ago, and therefore can be grafted to the soviet (centralized) type of federation without particular difficulties.

This cannot be said, however, of those nationalities which were not a part of the old Russia but existed as independent entities and developed their own statehood, and which, if they become soviet, will be obliged to adopt one or another type of political relations (connections) with Soviet Russia. For example, consider the future soviet Germany, Poland, Hungary, Finland. It can hardly be expected that

[22] Lenin, *Sochineniia*, XXV, 624.

these nations, which have their own sovereignty, their own military and monetary systems, will immediately agree, once they become soviet, to enter into a federation with Soviet Russia on the same basis as the Bashkirs or Ukrainians. In your theses, by the way, you note a difference between the Bashkir and the Ukrainian type of federated connection, whereas actually there is no such difference, or it is so insignificant that it amounts to nothing. But the others [i.e., the formerly independent states] would be inclined to consider a federative union as belittling their political independence, as a threat to that independence.

I have no doubt that for these latter nationalities a confederation (that is, an alliance of independent states) will be the most acceptable form of union. I do not even mention the backward nationalities, such as, for example, Persia or Turkey, to whom soviet federation, and federation in general, is still less acceptable.

In view of all this, I believe that the paragraph of your theses concerning the means of bringing together different nations must also include (along with federation) *confederation*. Such a correction would make the theses more elastic, and would provide still another transitional step toward bringing together the toilers of different nations. It would also help the nationalities that were not part of old Russia to form a political connection with Soviet Russia.[23]

47

Lenin on the Disunity and Ineffectiveness of the League of Nations

[Excerpt from Speech at a Conference of the Members of the Local Party Executive Committees of the Moscow Province, October 15, 1920][24]

· · ·

How could it have happened that Soviet Russia, which was exhausted by the imperialist and civil wars, surrounded by enemies, cut off from its sources of equipment and ammunition, that this Soviet Russia was victorious? This is indeed something we must consider seriously. If we do so, we shall begin to understand the mechanism of both the Russian and the international revolutions. We shall see that the Russian revolution is only a link in the chain of the international revolution, and that our cause is firmly established and invincible. . . . Three Allied powers conducted a war against us. One would expect these three Allies to have no trouble uniting their aims. But . . . they could not form an alliance against us; with every step they took, disagreements appeared. This was particularly clear during the Polish

---

[23] The points in Lenin's theses to which Stalin specifically refers are as follows:

"6. . . . We must not content ourselves now with a mere recognition or declaration of the unity of the workers of different nations; we must carry out a policy designed to bring about the closest union between Soviet Russia and all the national and colonial liberation movements. We must determine the structure of this union in accordance with the stage of development of the communist movement among the proletariat of each country, or of the revolutionary liberation movement of backward countries and backward nationalities.

"7. Federation is a transitional stage toward the complete union of the toilers of all nations. Federation has already proved its efficacy in practice in the relations of the R.S.F.S.R. and the other soviet republics (Hungarian, Finnish, and Latvian in the past, and Azerbaijani and Ukrainian at present). Within the R.S.F.S.R. federation has also been effective with regard to those nationalities which had neither national existence nor autonomy (for example, the autonomous republics of Bashkirs and Tatars, which were formed within the R.S.F.S.R. in 1919 and 1920)" (*Vtoroi Kongress Kominterna*, p. 492).

[24] Lenin, *Sochineniia*, XXV, 414–16.

war that has just ended. Our march on Warsaw . . . showed us just what relations existed among our enemies. On July 12, when the Red troops were approaching the Polish frontier, we received a telegram from the British foreign minister, Curzon, on behalf of the League of Nations, that "famous" league, that union which was allegedly unifying Britain, France, the United States, Italy, and Japan—the powers that possess gigantic military strength and all the naval forces of the world, the powers against whom [our] military resistance would prove to be quite senseless and impossible. Curzon, in the name of the League of Nations, proposed that we end the war and enter into negotiations with the Poles in London. . . . Our reply was interpreted by France as insolent. The League of Nations might have been expected to take appropriate measures against us. But what actually happened? The League of Nations was powerless, while Britain and France acted at cross purposes.

. . . After our reply Britain immediately steered an independent course opposed to that of France. France needed the forces of the Russian White Guards for defense against Germany; Britain did not, because it is a naval power and does not fear an attack that its fleet can ward off. The League of Nations, which tried to threaten Russia, was powerless. The interests of the League's separate members have been shown to be mutually opposed; France wishes Britain's defeat, and vice versa. When Comrade Kamenev, negotiating with the British government in London, asked whether such-and-such an action was permissible against France's wishes, the British prime minister was obliged to say that France would pursue its own course, and that "we cannot go with France."

It has been proved, therefore, that the League of Nations actually does not exist, that the union of capitalist powers is simply a deception, and that it represents two vultures trying to tear the prey from each other. When we signed the peace treaty in Riga,[25] we knew what really kept Poland, Britain, France, and Wrangel from joining forces [against us]—to wit, the fact that Britain aims at bringing under its influence the new small states, such as Finland, Estonia, Latvia, and Lithuania, and is absolutely unconcerned with re-establishing tsarist, White Guardist, or bourgeois Russia. Britain, therefore, acts against the wishes of France and cannot support the cause of Poland and Wrangel. France, on the contrary, would sacrifice every last Polish soldier to recover the money it once loaned [to tsarist Russia]. . . .

48
Stalin on the Socialist and Capitalist Camps

[Excerpts from Stalin's Statements in Connection with the Formation of the Union of Soviet Socialist Republics, November 18 and December 26, 1922][26]

. . .

The initiation of the movement [to unify the independent soviet republics] belongs to the republics themselves. . . .

[25] The armistice with Poland and preliminary conditions of peace, signed on October 12, 1920.

[26] Stalin, *Sochineniia*, V, 138–41, 142, 146–51, 154–55. After much agitation and considerable pressure from Moscow, the congresses of soviets of the Ukraine, Belorussia, and Transcaucasia adopted resolutions in favor of joining the R.S.F.S.R. in a union of soviet socialist republics. At the first session of the Tenth Congress of Soviets of the R.S.F.S.R., December 23, 1922, these resolutions for union were received and the project of union was approved. One week later the First Congress of Soviets of the U.S.S.R. met, elected a Central Executive Committee, authorized the drafting of a constitution for the U.S.S.R., and decided on the organization of the new government. At the Second Congress of Soviets of the U.S.S.R. the constitution was approved, January 31, 1924.

The movement for the unification of the independent republics is not new, sudden, or unusual. It has its own history. It has already passed through two phases and has now entered a third one.

The first phase, 1918–21, was the period of intervention and civil war, when these republics were threatened with terrible danger, and when they were obliged to unite for war purposes in order to defend their own existence. This phase led to the military unification, to a military alliance of the soviet republics.

The second phase, late 1921 and early 1922, was the period of the Genoa and Hague conferences, when the Western capitalist powers (having lost hope of success in intervention) tried to reintroduce the principle of capitalist ownership in the soviet republics. Their efforts to that end were not military but diplomatic. Whereupon all soviet republics were joined in a diplomatic coalition; had this not been done, they could not have withstood the Western powers' [political] pressure. On the eve of the Genoa Conference, a well-known agreement was signed by the eight independent friendly republics,[27] thus effecting what can be called a diplomatic union of the soviet republics. So ended the second phase, the phase of the union of our republics.

The unification movement has now entered a third phase, the economic one. Obviously, the third phase completes the two preceding ones.

.   .   .

The unification [of the soviet republics] must be voluntary, absolutely voluntary, providing the right of each national republic to secede from the union. The voluntary principle must, therefore, be laid down as fundamental . . .

.   .   .

What reasons, what circumstances have led the [soviet] republics to form a union?

There are three reasons . . .

The first is the domestic economic conditions of these republics. . . .

The second . . . is connected with our foreign situation, by which I mean our military position, our relations with foreign capitalists through our Vneshtorg [Commissariat of Foreign Trade], and our diplomatic relations with the bourgeois states. We must remember, comrades, that despite our success in ending the civil war, the danger of an attack from outside still exists. This danger calls for an absolute unification of all military matters, for one absolutely united army. . . .

In addition to the military danger, there is also the danger of the economic isolation of our federation. You must realize that after the Genoa and Hague conferences, and the Urquhart affair, we cannot expect a great inflow of capital from abroad. It is true that the attempted boycott of our republic has failed, but the danger of economic isolation remains. This new form of intervention is no less dangerous to us than the military one; we can avoid it only by creating a single economic front to meet the capitalist encirclement.

Finally, there is our diplomatic position. We have witnessed quite recently, on the eve of the Lausanne Conference, the Allies' efforts to isolate our federation. These efforts failed, and the organized diplomatic boycott directed against us was broken. The Entente had to back down and take our federation into account. However, we may expect new attempts to isolate our federation diplomatically. Hence the necessity of a united front along the diplomatic line also. . . .

[27] Stalin refers to the agreement signed in Moscow on February 22, 1922, by the plenipotentiary representatives of the so-called independent republics of Azerbaijan, Armenia, Georgia, Belorussia, the Ukraine, Khorezm, Bukhara, and the Far East, whose independence had been recognized by the R.S.F.S.R. By this treaty the R.S.F.S.R. was vested with the power to represent all these republics at the Genoa Conference.

Finally, the third reason for unifying our republics comes from the character of our Soviet government and the class nature of the Soviet power. Essentially the Soviet government is an international organization; it calls upon the masses to unite and it helps to unite them. Capitalist order—private ownership and the exploitation of man by man—divides the peoples, breaks them up into separate and hostile camps; consider Great Britain and France, and even such small multinational states as Poland and Yugoslavia, which are known for irreconcilable national internal contradictions. These contradictions undermine the very foundation of such states. The Western states, where capitalist democracy rules and the principle of private ownership prevails, are known for national animosities and struggle within their borders. But here in the world of soviets, authority is based not on capital, but on labor; not on private ownership and exploitation, but on collective ownership and the struggle against exploitation. Such an authority by its very nature inclines the toiling masses toward a union of the socialist family.

It is significant that in the West, in the world of bourgeois democracy, we see a gradual decline, a disintegration of the multinational states into separate political entities (for example, Great Britain, which does not know how to settle matters with India, Egypt, and Ireland; or Poland, which cannot come to an agreement with the Belorussians and the Ukrainians). But in our federation, which unites no fewer than thirty nationalities, we see the opposite process: the consolidation of a political alliance among independent republics, a continually growing rapprochement among independent nationalities for the purpose of forming an independent state! Thus we see two types of political coalition: the capitalist type, which leads to disintegration of the state, and the soviet type, which gradually and permanently brings together formerly independent nationalities into one independent state.

.   .   .

Since the formation of the soviet republics the states of the world have been divided into two camps: the camp of socialism and the camp of capitalism. In the camp of capitalism we find imperialist wars, national differences, oppression, colonial slavery, and chauvinism. In the camp of the soviets, in the camp of socialism, we have, on the contrary, mutual trust, national equality, peaceful coexistence, and fraternal co-operation among the peoples. Capitalist democracy has tried for scores of years to solve the national contradictions in such a way as to support simultaneously both the free development and the systematic exploitation of nationalities. It has failed in these efforts, and it will fail in the future. As a matter of fact, the entanglement of national differences grows continuously and threatens capitalism with destruction. It is only here, in the world of soviets, in the camp of socialism, that we have succeeded in eradicating completely all national oppression and establishing mutual trust and fraternal co-operation. Only after the soviets had succeeded in these endeavors could we organize our federation and defend it against domestic and foreign foes.

Five years ago the Soviet government successfully laid the foundation for peaceful coexistence and fraternal co-operation. Now we see the desirability and necessity of unifying [our republics]. We have before us the task of erecting a new edifice, a new, powerful, unified toilers' state. The will of the peoples of our republics, whose recent congresses have unanimously resolved to form a union of the republics,[28] definitely shows that the task of unification has been correctly conceived, and that it is based on the great principle of the consent and equality of peoples. Let us hope, comrades, that our Union republic will be both a true bulwark against international capitalism and a decisive step toward unifying all the toilers of the world into a World Soviet Socialist Republic.

[28] The reports of the Twelfth Party Congress, April 17–25, 1923, reveal that considerable disagreement was expressed before the unanimous resolution was adopted.

49
Toward a World Soviet Socialist Republic

[Excerpts from the Declaration Concerning the Formation of the
Union of Soviet Socialist Republics, Adopted at the First Congress
of Soviets of the Union, December 30, 1922][29]

. . .

For many decades the capitalists have attempted to settle the problem of minorities
and to combine the free development of peoples with the exploitation of man by man;
but their attempts have failed. Instead the web of national contradictions has grown
more tangled and now threatens the very existence of capitalism itself. The bourgeoisie has been proved incapable of organizing international co-operation.

Only in the Soviet camp, only under the dictatorship of the proletariat, which the
majority of the population support, have we seen national oppression uprooted,
conditions of mutual trust created, and a foundation laid for fraternal co-operation
among the peoples. . . .

The peoples of the soviet republics met recently in the congresses of their respective soviets and unanimously adopted resolutions to form a Union of Soviet
Socialist Republics. Their decision, as peoples exercising equal rights, is conclusive
proof of the voluntary nature of this unification. The resolutions give every republic
the right to secede from the Union, and allow all other soviet socialist republics, both
present and future, to join it if they choose. To judge from the unanimous decision
of the people, the new Union state will be a worthy expression of the basic principles
of peaceful coexistence and fraternal co-operation laid down in October 1917. It
will be a true bulwark against world capitalism and a new and decisive step toward
the unification of the toilers of all countries into a World Soviet Socialist Republic. . . .

50
Soviet Attitude Toward the League of Nations

[Excerpt from the Note of the People's Commissariat of Foreign
Affairs of the R.S.F.S.R. to the Secretary General of the League of
Nations Stating Russia's Willingness to Participate in the Conference
on the Limitation of Naval Armament, March 15, 1923][30]

The Soviet government's attitude toward the so-called League of Nations has
been expressed more than once by responsible Soviet leaders. The Soviet government adheres steadfastly to this attitude. It finds in the League a coalition of some
states that are trying without any ground whatsoever to usurp the authority of the
other states, at the same time camouflaging with nonexistent legality their own
inroads into the rights and independence of other peoples. . . .

The Soviet government still believes that this quasi-international institution
actually serves as a screen to conceal from the masses the predatory imperialist
purposes of some Great Powers and their vassals. It is confirmed in its view every
time the state that has assumed the leading role in the League of Nations passes a
resolution on international problems in which the soviet republics are interested.

. . .

Without in the least deviating in principle from its attitude toward the League
of Nations, the Soviet government is nevertheless ready to consider the proposed

[29] Kliuchnikov and Sabanin, III, 225–26.
[30] *Ibid.*, pp. 238–39.

conference [on naval disarmament] as an assembly of the representatives of separate states, even though some of these states are members of the quasi–League of Nations.

The Soviet government therefore expresses its readiness to participate in this conference, whether it is convened by the government of the U.S.A., which initiated the first conference on naval disarmament, or by some other group of powers. Moreover, the Soviet government believes that without the participation of Russia and her allies, this conference will prove fruitless, for the measures its initiators contemplate can be carried out only if all states participate in it. Therefore, although the agenda of the conference mentions only the members of the so-called League of Nations, the Soviet government believes it desirable and necessary that Russia and her allies participate also.

THE FOURTH CONGRESS OF THE COMMUNIST INTERNATIONAL AND SOVIET RUSSIA'S INTERNATIONAL REVOLUTIONARY TASKS

51

Russia, the Great Powers, and the World Revolution

[Radek's Report on the International Situation to the Fourth Congress of the Communist International, October 28, 1922][31]

The year that separates us from the Third Congress marks the beginning of the liquidation of the Versailles peace and of the treaties connected with it. . . . From the conferences at Washington, Genoa, and The Hague and the present victory of the Turkish army, it is clear that the pillars on which the Versailles treaty was erected are breaking one after another. That treaty is being liquidated in Eastern and Southeastern Europe and Asia Minor by the Red Army and the Turkish national forces, in the Far East by the American dollar, and in Central Europe by the collapse of the German mark. . . .

The Correlation of Forces of the Versailles Peace

The peace treaties signed after the Allied victory over Germany, Austria-Hungary, Bulgaria, and Turkey in Europe indicate not an all-round victory of Allied capitalists, but rather the establishment of a balance of power among the member states of the Entente. These treaties established the hegemony of French imperialism in Europe and of Britain in the Near East and on the seas, and they gave Japan an exceptionally privileged position in her struggle for supremacy in the Far East.

A close look at the Versailles peace [shows that] the creation of Poland and the French occupation [of the Rhine provinces], the pushing of the French frontiers to the left bank of the Rhine, have made France absolutely supreme on the European continent. . . .

[31] Karl Radek, *Likvidatsiia versalskogo mira; doklad IV Kongressu Kommunisticheskogo Internatsionala*, pp. 3–5, 21–29, 62–64; also appeared in English under the title *The Winding-up of the Versailles Treaty. Report to the IV Congress of the Communist International.*

In the Far East the Allies have abstained from defending [the interests of] China, contrary to that country's expectations; Shantung has remained in Japanese hands, thus opening the way to the Chinese coal and ironworks that are so important to the consolidation of Japanese militarism. Besides, Japan has received important naval bases in the southern parts of the Pacific. [Goes on to speak of the Allies' plan to destroy Germany.]

The Capitalist World and Soviet Russia

Viewed chronologically, the liquidation of the Versailles peace began not in Germany, but in Russia. When the Allies signed the Versailles treaty, which mentioned Russia only in certain supplementary clauses, their policy was based entirely not only on destroying Soviet Russia, but on destroying Russia as a great power.

In fact, the policy of strangling Germany, of destroying her as an international factor, implied the destruction of Russia as a great power. Even if the Whites had won, they would have been affected by the destruction of Germany, since irrespective of who governs Russia, her interests require at least the existence of Germany. . . . However, not only the Allies' German policy but their decisions on the Near East question implied the elimination of Russia. . . . The victorious Allies looked upon Russia as a sphere for exploitation; that is, they regarded her as their prospective colony, like Turkey and Persia. In fighting Soviet Russia, the Allies not only made war against the first proletarian state, but tried to destroy Russia [as an independent power], which could have presented them with a bill to pay. Their aim was to crush Soviet Russia and to put in her place a weak White [i.e., anti-Bolshevik] Russia. . . .

. . . Even at the beginning of 1921 the Allies generally expected Soviet Russia's ultimate defeat. Nonetheless Britain was ready to enter into a commercial treaty with Soviet Russia.

There were two reasons for this. First, the unemployment in Britain after mid-1920 proved to the Allies, and especially to the British industrial bourgeoisie, that the Versailles policy could not be continued, and that new markets were necessary, for Germany as well as themselves. At that time British capitalists saw only one way out of the reparations maze: to let Germany develop Russian economic resources and reconstruct her economic life at the expense of the Russian peasantry and workers. The second reason looked further into the future. When in 1921 the rivalry between Britain and France was aggravated by the reparations problem and the Near East question, Britain began to wonder whether France was not presuming too much on the strength of its victory [in the war]. Some farsighted British capitalists suggested a policy of counterbalancing France by strengthening Russia and Germany, at least by making use of a Germany based on Russian resources.

The New Economic Policy [in Russia] convinced Britain that communism in that country was bankrupt, and that the Soviet government and Soviet Russia were heading back toward capitalism. . . . [Lloyd George] pointed out that Soviet Russia needed credits for economic reconstruction. He declared that "the leading men of Soviet Russia, who understand the international situation very well, see the impossibility of achieving communism, but they are under pressure from a workers' oligarchy. The Soviet government cannot, therefore, give up at once their [old] convictions, but they will do so eventually and will take the road to capitalism." That was unquestionably the general view of the bourgeois politicians who convened the Genoa Conference.

They were convinced that once the demands for restoring capitalism were sufficiently well camouflaged, the Soviet government would restore all property to the former foreign capitalists. Then private foreign capital would resume its development in Russia, and the insignificant remnants of nationalized industries still in the hands of the Soviet government, unable to compete with private industry, would be transferred to the Russian bourgeoisie. . . . The practical mind of the Briton [Lloyd George] was prepared to let the Russian government call itself a soviet and to let Russian schools continue teaching communism, if only Soviet Russia would surrender her industries to foreign capitalists. At the very moment that the Allies were discussing reductions in Germany's reparations payments, they presented Soviet Russia with tremendous claims due them from the prewar period, as well as war debts. By these demands, they hoped to compel Soviet Russia, which was not able to pay, to hand over to the Allied capitalists old industries, huge concessions, the income from customs duties, and perhaps also the railways, as security for reimbursement at a later date. This was the plan the Allies took to Genoa, where they virtually declared to Soviet Russia: "While we have proved unable to conquer you with the sword and have therefore let you remain in power, we want to turn you into a colony of the Allies."

Soviet Russia flatly rejected that proposal. She refused to hand over her industries or even to farm them out as private property to private capitalists. The Soviet government, in order to restore the country's devastated economy, and because of the slow development of the world revolution, is still prepared for a compromise, but only a compromise that further develops the achievements of the October Revolution. Therefore, the Soviet government refused to restore private property. . . . The conference at Genoa, and the one at The Hague that followed, were failures, for the Allies were evidently not inclined to recognize the existence of a country that is taking the first steps toward establishing socialism. . . .

The failure at Genoa and The Hague by no means proves that an agreement between Soviet Russia and the capitalist world is impossible; it shows only that the time has not yet arrived for such an agreement. The question of whether a *modus vivendi* between capitalism and proletarian dictatorship or between capitalism and socialism is possible—this question is incorrectly formulated. A *modus vivendi* has existed for the last five years, an unstable equilibrium characterized by a series of transactions between us and the capitalist world. The real question is this: On what basis are these transactions to be effected?

For the time being, the capitalist world is still convinced that Soviet Russia, owing to economic pressure, will eventually capitulate, and that it will merely try to mask its transactions. The continued existence of the Soviet government, the growth, even at a slow pace, of Russia's productive forces, and a policy of waiting are the preliminary conditions of these transactions. On the whole we may say that the Versailles treaty, as far as it relates to Russia, has been liquidated, since the hope of victory by force of arms has been abandoned. But no definite compromise between the old capitalist world and the new proletarian world has yet been effected. The capitalist world expects to dictate terms to Soviet Russia. However, time—in the course of which Soviet Russia will not be alone in her sufferings— . . . time works for Russia. The whole international situation, in creating new alignments of forces and further straining international relations, increases Soviet Russia's prestige. [As a consequence of Soviet Russia's growing power] its business transactions with the outside world will be based not on capitalist interests only, but on the principle of mutual concessions, concessions determined by the nature of the Soviet Russian [state] and by the international situation. . . .

It cannot be said definitely whether or when the existing antagonistic tendencies will . . . become sufficiently acute to result in a new world war.

The bourgeoisie of the world have been so shaken by the last world war, the effects of which are not yet overcome, that they are in mortal fear of a new world war, which would bring the final victory of the world revolution. Therefore, they seek feverishly for new compromises. But split up in hostile capitalist groups, unable to subordinate their respective special interests to the general interests of world capital, they are continually doing Penelope's work. . . . Therefore, the bankruptcy of the Versailles treaty, instead of relaxing tensions and bringing about an agreement between the Great Powers that could secure peaceful progress, will lead to new conflicts for the repartition of the world. [Discusses the failure of Europe's working class to pursue the correct course.] . . .

The Communist International is the only section of the international proletariat that is carrying on an active revolutionary world policy. By daily mobilizing the working masses for the struggle against the economic consequences of the war, by mobilizing these masses for the revolutionary struggle, the Communist International is becoming a proletarian factor in world politics. Its policy of supporting Soviet Russia is a part of its gigantic struggle against imperialist war and imperialist peace, and for the proletarian reconstruction of the world.

In Soviet Russia the working class possesses a politically organized center of revolutionary struggle. When the sycophants of the Second and Second-and-a-Half Internationals accuse the Communist International of defending the interests of the Russian state, the Communist International calmly replies: The interests of the Russian proletarian state are the interests of the Russian working class organized into a state, of the first victorious section of the world proletariat; therefore, they coincide with the interests of the working class of the world. . . . The Communist International must reckon with the possibility of a slow advance of the world revolution, just as Soviet Russia does. This [delay of the world revolution] implies temporary defeats and retreats, and requires the shifting of tactics. If the working class wishes to play its full historical role, it must continually study political changes in the world. The struggle of the Communist International becomes, therefore, more and more closely bound up with all fluctuations and changes in the world situation. The Communist International must consequently impress upon all its sections in various countries the need to interpret in a uniform manner every separate event in world politics, as well as the general trend of events; it must awaken [in these sections] a passionate desire not only to understand and interpret events but also to hasten the historic process and to change the whole social complexion of the world. This is the will to world revolution, the instrument of which is the working class.

52

The Right of Red Intervention to Extend Socialism

[Bukharin's Explanation of the Russian Party's Position on This Issue at the Fourth Congress of the Comintern, 1922][32]

· · ·

Another tactical problem must be made clear [in our program], and that is the right of Red intervention. This question seems actually to be up to each individual communist party. Word comes from everywhere about Red militarism. We must point out in our program that every proletariat has a right to have recourse to Red intervention. . . .

The Communist Manifesto says that the proletariat must conquer the world. But this cannot be done simply by snapping one's finger. For this we need bayonets and guns. Yes, the expansion of the Red Army is also the expansion of socialism, of the proletarian authority, of the revolution. It is on this ground that the right of Red intervention is justified, when it technically simplifies the realization of socialism. . . .

· · ·

[32] *IV Vsemirnyi Kongress K.I.*, p. 196.

53

Soviet Russia's Leadership in the World Revolution and the Duty of All Workers to Support Russia

[Resolution of the Fourth Congress of the Communist International
on the Russian Revolution][33]

. . .

The Fourth World Congress reminds the proletariat of all countries that the proletarian revolution will never be victorious within the limits of one country only, that it can only be victorious on an international scale, as a world revolution. All activities of Soviet Russia, its struggle for its own existence and for the realization of the revolution, are at the same time a struggle to free the oppressed and exploited proletarians of the world from the chains of slavery. The Russian proletariat has fully fulfilled its duty to the world proletariat by acting as advanced fighter for the revolution. The world proletariat must now do its own duty. In all countries the workers, the poor, and the oppressed must actively display their moral, economic, and political solidarity with Soviet Russia. It is not only their international solidarity, but also their own interests that must spur them on to launch a violent struggle against the bourgeoisie and the capitalist states with this aim [the revolution] in view. The workers and the oppressed must advance the following slogans in all countries: Hands off Soviet Russia; de jure recognition of Soviet Russia; general and real support to the economic restoration of Soviet Russia. Every growth in Soviet Russia's strength further weakens the world bourgeoisie. The very fact that Soviet Russia has existed for five years is the heaviest and most decisive blow to world capitalism.

The Fourth Congress calls upon the proletariat of all capitalist countries to follow the example of Soviet Russia—to launch a decisive attack on capitalism, and to devote all its energy to the world revolution!

[33] Lenin, *Sochineniia*, XXVII, 489.

Part III

Diplomatic Triumphs and Revolutionary Failures, 1922–1924

In the several international conferences of 1922–23 Soviet diplomacy did not gain its principal short-range objectives of *de jure* recognition and the settlement of the debt question, but it made gains nevertheless. The Rapallo treaty, the establishment of full-scale diplomatic relations, and the beginnings of open economic and secret military relations with Germany greatly strengthened the Soviet position in respect to the Western powers, who could no longer negotiate with the ostracized Germans and the ostracized Russians separately. On the other hand, the Soviets could deal with the Allies individually since their not quite united front disintegrated after the Genoa and Hague conferences. Moreover, from the long-range point of view, both the imperialist powers and the colonial and semicolonial peoples were behaving as they were supposed to behave according to Marxist-Leninist theory. Britain and France were at odds over Germany and the Near East. Japan and the United States were at odds over the Far East. The Turks, the Egyptians, the Syrians, the Iraqis, the Persians, the Indians, and the Chinese were in their several ways trying to rid themselves of foreign rule or foreign influence and thus realize the inspiring aim of national self-determination so eloquently proclaimed by Woodrow Wilson. The Communists saw in these events not the ferment of Mr. Wilson's idealism, but another kind of ferment caused by the contradictions of capitalism in the epoch of imperialism.

Nationality Relations—The Union of Soviet Socialist Republics

At home, meanwhile, the Soviet leaders were carrying through a program of centralization which, since it concerned several soviet republics, had an international significance as suggesting the presumable pattern of relationship between all possible soviet republics of the future.

By the end of the civil war and the war with Poland—i.e., during 1920–21— the Ukrainian S.S.R. and the Belorussian S.S.R. were established as communist-ruled soviet republics with close military and economic ties with the R.S.F.S.R. Communist-ruled republics were also established along the southeastern border of Soviet Russia in 1920 and 1921 when communist pressure from the inside, supported by Red Army pressure from the outside, brought about the overthrow of the national governments of Azerbaijan, Armenia, and Georgia. As soon as soviet republics were established in these Transcaucasian states, Stalin, with the approval of Lenin, began a campaign to unite them into a single Transcaucasion Federation. The unification took place in 1922.

In Moscow, meanwhile, the Communists had begun to urge that the soviet republics form a union with the R.S.F.S.R. As the first step in this direction, the communist governments of the smaller republics signed treaties of alliance or military and economic co-operation with the communist government of the

R.S.F.S.R.[1] Within the same period, 1920–21, the R.S.F.S.R. also signed treaties of alliance and economic agreements with the Khorezm People's Soviet Republic (September 13, 1920) and the Bukhara People's Soviet Republic (March 4, 1921).[2]

A further step toward the union of all the soviet republics was taken when representatives of the Ukraine, Belorussia, Georgia, Azerbaijan, Armenia, Bukhara, Khorezm, and the Far Eastern Republic empowered the R.S.F.S.R. to act for all of them at the Genoa Conference of 1922.[3]

In the "Theses on the Current Tasks of the Party in Regard to the National Question" adopted by the Tenth Party Congress, March 8–16, 1921, Stalin stated the party line on unification:

Not one soviet republic taken separately can consider itself safe from economic exhaustion and military defeat by international imperialism. Therefore, the isolated existence of separate soviet republics has no firm basis in view of the threats to their existence from the capitalist states. The common interests of the defense of the soviet republics on one hand, the task of reconstructing the productive forces destroyed by the war on the other, and the necessary help with food for the nonproductive soviet republics from the productive ones—all strongly call for a political union of the separate soviet republics, which alone can save them from the imperialist yoke and national oppression. The national soviet republics, which have freed themselves from their "own" and from "foreign" bourgeoisie, will be able to defend their existence and conquer the united forces of imperialism only by joining in a close political union. Otherwise they cannot achieve victory.[4]

Following the party line, local communist leaders in each of the allegedly independent republics introduced resolutions urging union. Finally at the first session of the Tenth Congress of Soviets of the R.S.F.S.R., December 23, 1922, the Russian Communist leaders took note of these resolutions and then adopted their own resolution favoring the unification of the R.S.F.S.R., the Ukrainian S.S.R., the Belorussian S.S.R., and the Transcaucasian S.F.S.R. On December 29, a conference of the plenipotentiary delegates of these soviet republics drafted a declaration and a treaty to establish the Union of Soviet Republics; the two acts were signed the next morning, December 30. On the same day, the First Congress of Soviets of the Union met in a one-day session and accepted the two acts as provisional until a Second Congress was held.[5] The Congress also elected a Central Executive Committee, which was instructed to draft a constitution and work out the organization of the new government. Work on this task continued throughout the entire year 1923. On January 31, 1924, the Second Congress of Soviets of the Union adopted the proposed constitution and thereby formally established the Union of Soviet Socialist Republics.

Apart from the proclaimed advantages of internal and external security, there was the further fact, according to the treaty signed on December 30, 1922, that under the dictatorship of the proletariat in Soviet Russia, it had been pos-

---

[1] The texts of these treaties are given in *Obrazovanie S.S.S.R. Sbornik dokumentov, 1917–1924*, pp. 247–50. (Hereafter cited as *Obrazovanie S.S.S.R.*)

[2] *Obrazovanie S.S.S.R.*, pp. 241–47 and 251–57 respectively.

[3] *Ibid.*, p. 259.

[4] Stalin, *Sochineniia*, V, 21–22.

[5] Texts appear in *Obrazovanie S.S.S.R.*, pp. 332–37.

sible to destroy national oppression at its very roots and to form a union of the peoples inhabiting the former Russian Empire on an equal basis. The treaty finally implied that since the soviet regime of the Union was international by its nature, it was actually impelling the toiling masses of all soviet republics to seek amalgamation in one big socialist family.

The Communists claimed that this act had international significance since it created a voluntary union of equal peoples from which each member had the right to withdraw freely and into which all soviet socialist republics "both now existing and which may come to exist in the future" had the privilege of entering. This new united state, it was alleged, would serve both as a "bulwark against world capitalism," and as a new and decisive step toward unifying the toilers of all countries in a "World Soviet Socialist Republic."[6]

The establishment of the Union of Soviet Socialist Republics, like so many communist moves, purported to be one thing, but actually was another. Far from a voluntary union of equals, which all members were free to enter or to leave, the Union actually represented a centralization of power in the hands of the Moscow Politburo through its control of the communist parties that ruled the constituent republics. The establishment of the Union also meant the consolidation of economic power.

Meanwhile Russia was recovering from the devastation of war and famine. In June 1923, the American Relief Administration closed its relief operations to the tune of warm tributes from Chicherin and others. "The American nation," said Chicherin, "which but yesterday took possession of a virgin continent and turned it into a miracle of the most perfect technique of production and culture," could understand better than anyone else the aspirations and hopes of the peoples of Russia. He hoped that the American nation, "possessed of the incalculable technique and accumulated fruit of its gigantic production," would enter into close economic co-operation with Russia, and promised that the Soviet government would "do its utmost to remove all obstacles to a close and durable co-operation between America and Russia."[7]

During the period under review Soviet Russia strengthened both its economic and diplomatic position but suffered a severe loss in the illness of Lenin, who had a stroke in 1922 and thereafter took less and less part in communist leadership until his death in January 1924.

The Party's Estimate of the International Situation, 1922–24

Throughout the period 1922–24, the Communists continued to regard the international political and economic situation as unstable and full of contradictions and conflicts of interest. At the same time they believed that the coexistence of the communist and capitalist systems was inevitable, at least for some time to come.

Chicherin, analyzing the international situation in February 1923, declared

---

[6] Kliuchnikov and Sabanin, III, 226; see also Document 49. For more information on the communist nationalities policy, see the companion volume, *Soviet Russia and the East, 1920–1927*, and Richard Pipes, *The Formation of the Soviet Union: Communism and Nationalism, 1917–1923.*

[7] H. H. Fisher, *The Famine in Soviet Russia, 1919–1923*, p. 397.

the triangular relationship between Britain, France, and Germany to be the determining factor in the international relations of the period. In his view, the most pressing test of the Soviet government was

the liquidation of the blockade against the soviet republics, which has not yet been completely raised, and the complete clearing of the way to unhampered economic relations with all countries. While being constantly on guard, we dare not let a single detail of the daily play of world antagonisms escape us, for there can be no world politics without Russia and her allies, and there is no longer a single international problem toward which Russia and her allies can adopt a neutral attitude.[8]

Extension of the Breathing Space: Coexistence and Revolution

One of the chief aims of Soviet foreign policy at this time was to lengthen the "breathing space"—to gain time to build the power of the Soviet state. This was the objective of Soviet peace propaganda, always, of course, with the proviso that the Communists had no intention of buying peace at the price of capitulation to foreign interests. This attitude was made clear at the Genoa and Hague conferences of 1922, as noted in the preceding chapter. In May 1923, Trotsky spelled it out again:

We desire peace above all things, naturally not at the price of capitulation, not at the price of converting the Soviet Union into a vassal state of foreign capitalists. We know that the governments of the Entente, since the war and the Versailles peace, have not dealt with other states and nations in any manner other than that of order or command. But let them know that their command does not reach Red Moscow.[9]

The Communists were not sure the peace they wanted could be had. Steklov, writing in *Izvestiia*, expressed this Soviet fear of new outbreaks when he declared that although the soviet republics wanted peace,

Soviet Russia does not intend to let herself be attacked without retaliation, nor is she incapable of returning blow for blow. It is precisely with the desire to preserve peace that we issue this warning to the treacherous elements so anxious to utilize the present moment for new war adventures, for new threats against our internal and external interests. We hope that our warning will be heard and understood. If not, so much the worse for those who do not want to hear![10]

But despite their professed belief in the possibility of coexistence and their oft-proclaimed desire for peace, the Communists continued to work toward the supreme objective of extending the revolution into other parts of the world. The Third Congress of the Communist International in 1921 had adopted the slogan "To the Masses." At the Fourth Congress, November-December, 1922, this slogan was again emphasized, along with tactics for implementing it—i.e., for creating a united front with the working masses throughout the world. The Fourth Congress's "Theses on the Tactics of the Communist International" declared the task of the Communist International to be "to get hold of the majority of the working class in America and Europe."

[8] *Pravda*, No. 34, February 15, 1923, p. 1; see Document 54.
[9] *Pravda*, No. 105, May 13, 1923, p. 3. Trotsky was speaking on the need for peace at an extraordinary plenary session of the Moscow soviet, May 12, 1923.
[10] *Izvestiia*, No. 14, January 21, 1923, p. 1; see Document 55.

The Congress also stressed the importance of creating throughout the colonial and semicolonial areas "a center for the communist parties which will represent the interests of the world proletariat as a whole." It emphasized the need of supporting "by every available means the national-revolutionary movement directed against imperialism." These tasks, according to the theses, were all the more necessary since "in view of the present temporary stabilization of bourgeois society an intense crisis may arise quite unexpectedly in connection with a large-scale strike, a colonial uprising, a new war, or even a parliamentary crisis," the idea being that a trained, class-conscious proletariat could capitalize on any such upheaval, as the Bolsheviks had done in Russia in 1917. The tactics of the united front were described as "no less than an offer by the Communists to struggle jointly with workers who belong to different parties or groups, and with the nonparty workers, to defend the daily interests of the working class against the bourgeoisie."[11]

Zinoviev threw further light on the purposes of the united front in 1924 when he declared:

The Communist International must explain to the masses systematically and persistently, taking advantage of every suitable example, every important episode in the civil war, and especially such important events as those in Germany, that it is useless to expect a peaceful transition to a workers' (or workers' and peasants') government within the framework of democracy. We must explain to the workers that the united front of the entire proletariat will make the struggle considerably easier and will ensure victory, but that it will on no account substitute peaceful, democratic, and painless evolution for revolutionary struggle. The tactics of the united front are tactics of revolution and not of evolution. The advantage of these tactics is that by substituting peaceful evolutionary methods for the revolutionary ones, they guarantee success to the revolution.

Obviously, the united front tactics, as a method of agitation among large working masses, are adapted to a definite epoch, namely to the epoch when Communists in nearly all the most important countries are a minority in the workers' movement, and when definite revolutionary battles do not as yet take place.[12]

German Rapprochement and the German Revolution

During this period of increasing contact with the West—a period which in fact was highlighted by the granting to the Soviet Union of full *de jure* recognition by the chief European powers—Soviet leaders were also busy attempting to bring about a revolution within the domains of one of these powers, Germany. Thus in Germany the simultaneous pursuit by Moscow of two seemingly incompatible policies—rapprochement and revolution; legal, above-ground, friendly diplomatic and economic overtures and illegal, underground, subversive activities—was outlined with unusual clarity. The dual policy led, naturally enough, to contradictions and rivalry between the Commissariat of Foreign Affairs and the Comintern.

Diplomatic relations between Germany and Soviet Russia had been terminated late in 1918 when the German socialist government had ordered the Soviet diplomatic mission out of the country. For several months, while the Soviet government was fighting the civil war and the German government was de-

---

[11] *Kommunisticheskii Internatsional v dokumentakh*, pp. 299–300; see Document 56.
[12] *Kommunisticheskii Internatsional*, No. 1, 1924, p. 522; see Document 73.

fending itself against both the Right and the Left, there was practically no official contact between the two countries. The new German republic, however, had refused to join the Allied blockade of Russia. Relations were resumed late in 1919 when a Soviet representative, V. L. Kopp, arrived in Berlin to negotiate two agreements, signed in April and July, 1920, on the repatriation of war prisoners. Kopp remained in Berlin as an unofficial Soviet representative, and the German government sent an unofficial representative of its own to Moscow. The next Soviet-German agreement, that of May 6, 1921, was known as the *Provisional Agreement Regarding the Extension of the Sphere of Activity of their Mutual Delegations Engaged in the Assistance of Prisoners of War*.[13] Article I of this agreement stated that "commercial representatives shall be attached to the delegations of both Parties for furtherance of economic relations," and significantly added that "the representatives of the R.S.F.S.R. in Germany shall be recognized as the only body representing Russia." New representatives were soon exchanged between the two countries, with N. N. Krestinsky representing Soviet Russia in Berlin. During the winter of 1921–22 commercial activities between the two countries continued to grow.

During the Genoa Conference, as noted on the preceding pages, the Soviet and German delegations signed the Rapallo treaty re-establishing full diplomatic relations between their governments.

This agreement, signed at Rapallo, a few miles from Genoa, on April 16, 1922, had apparently first been conceived as early as December 1921. In the course of 1921 and 1922, such Soviet representatives as Radek, Rakovsky, and Krasin had conducted negotiations with the German government and with certain German trusts, among them Krupp, Stinnes, and Allgemeine Elektrizitäts-Gesellschaft, directed by Walter Rathenau. In March 1922, when the Soviet delegation had passed through Berlin en route to Genoa, further discussions concerning a treaty had taken place, but no decision had been reached. Finally, while the unofficial negotiations between the Allied and Soviet delegations at Genoa were under way at the Villa Albertis, Germany and Russia had come to terms and signed the Rapallo treaty. The British ambassador to Berlin, Viscount D'Abernon, reports in his memoirs that when the moment finally came, Rathenau hoped to use the threat of agreement with Russia to force concessions from the British, but was dissuaded by Baron Adolf von Maltzan, his secretary of state for eastern affairs, who argued that it would be "behaving monstrously to Tchicherin."[14]

As finally agreed upon, the treaty restored normal diplomatic relations, provided for full *de jure* recognition of the Soviet government by the German government, and set Russo-German trade upon a most-favored-nation basis. Most important from the standpoint of the Allied powers' relations with Russia and Germany, the signatories mutually renounced compensation for war damages or for civil damage arising out of the war, and Germany renounced all claims, national or private, arising out of Soviet legislation, provided the Soviet government would recognize no similar claims of other governments. Moreover, in a separate clause the two governments agreed to help supply each other's economic requirements, while the German government declared itself ready to support

---

[13] Shapiro, I, 119–20.
[14] Edgar Vincent D'Abernon, *An Ambassador of Peace; Pages from the Diary of Viscount D'Abernon*, I, 321.

the agreements with the Soviet government contemplated by private German firms.

As mentioned earlier, the Allied representatives at Genoa were profoundly shocked by the news of the treaty. The German renunciation of claims against the Soviet government was a blow to their effort to force the Russians to recognize liability for foreign losses. But even more unsettling, perhaps, were the persistent rumors of secret clauses of a military nature, rumors that continued to circulate despite denials by both signatories. Chicherin, in a note to M. Barthou of the French delegation, made a blanket denial of secret military clauses and also denied the French charge that the treaty was directed against France. "From the Russian government's point of view," said Chicherin, "the treaty is simply the first of a series of individual agreements which, in the opinion of the Russian delegation, should complement the general agreement toward which the powers assembled at Genoa are striving."[15]

That the Soviet government considered the Rapallo treaty a model treaty the All-Russian Central Executive Committee left no doubt. The resolution of May 18 on the work of the Russian delegation at Genoa and the treaty with Germany stated:

The true equality of the two systems of property [communist and capitalist], and a co-ordination between them, even though it be a temporary condition until the world in general passes from the system of private property and the crises it produces, economic chaos, wars, etc., to the higher system of property, has found its expression only in the Rapallo treaty. . . .

. . . The All-Russian Central Executive Committee welcomes the Russo-German treaty concluded in Rapallo as the only correct way out of the difficulties, chaos, and threats of wars; accepts this treaty as a normal form for treaties in the relationship between the R.S.F.S.R. and the capitalist states; and instructs the Council of People's Commissars and the Commissariat of Foreign Affairs to pursue their policy in the future in a similar vein, and to allow deviation from the format of the Rapallo treaty only under exceptional circumstances when a compromise would be compensated for by some exceptional advantage for the toiling masses of the R.S.F.S.R. and its allied republics.[16]

The Soviet government viewed the successful negotiation of this treaty with Germany as a great diplomatic success for both signatories and as a complete defeat for Entente policy. According to *Istoriia Diplomatii*:

The Treaty of Rapallo blocked the attempt of the Entente to create a united capitalist front against Soviet Russia. The plan for reconstructing Europe at the expense of the defeated countries and Soviet Russia collapsed. Soviet diplomacy won a victory because it followed the direct instructions of Lenin, who said: "It is necessary to be able to make use of the contradictions and differences among the capitalists. If we had not followed this plan, we would have been hanged long ago on separate trees, much to the enjoyment of the capitalists."[17]

The storm of protest and indignation aroused by the treaty gave the Communists considerable pleasure, and they took pains to emphasize how greatly

---

[15] Chicherin to M. Barthou, April 29, 1922, *Materialy genuezskoi konferentsii,* p. 327.

[16] Kliuchnikov and Sabanin, III, 191–92.

[17] V. P. Potemkin (ed.), *Istoriia diplomatii,* III, 181; see Document 58.

the agreement had increased the capacity of each of the signatories to resist the Allies. In this regard one Soviet commentator wrote in *Izvestiia:*

> True enough, the alliance between the two countries, one a boundless source of raw material, and the other the most industrially advanced country in Europe, such an alliance, of course, opens wide vistas for both countries. And the signing of this alliance on the basis of reciprocity, without the suppression of one by the other, ensures the peaceful and friendly coexistence of both countries, making each much more capable of resisting the predatory attacks of capitalist robbers.
>
> In addition to the industrial outlook, our enemies are also alarmed over military possibilities. Their frightened imagination is already confronted with a picture of a military alliance between the two most powerful states in Europe, an alliance that would cut to size their military victory and their aggressive imperialism. They recollect how Wilhelm once wrote to Nicholas: "Let us unite, and then the whole world could not frighten us!" . . .
>
> Since the consummation of the Russo-German treaty we can remain calm. Irrespective of the turn of events, we already have a serious achievement on our side: We will be considerably helped in our economic reconstruction by one of the world's most industrially developed countries.[18]

Poland and France were the powers most disturbed by the Rapallo events, Poland going so far as to withdraw from the political commission of the Genoa Conference as a result. As punishment for signing the treaty, Germany was excluded from further participation in any conference work concerned with the Russian problem, ostensibly on the ground that Germany's relations with Russia were settled by the treaty. As noted in Part II, the Russian delegation protested this action bitterly. In a note to the chairman of the Polish delegation, Chicherin termed it an attempt to deprive the Soviet government of the right to conclude agreements with other states; he further branded it a violation of the Riga peace agreement of March 1921 between Russia and Poland, and a violation of the Riga Protocol, signed March 30, 1922, by Russia, Poland, Estonia, and Latvia. Finally, he asserted that the Riga Protocol had obligated Poland to help the Soviet government obtain *de jure* recognition at Genoa, an assertion the Polish government was quick to deny.

Poland's reply to the Russian note denied any attempt to deprive Russia of the right to sign treaties. As for the Riga Protocol,

> the very title of the document repudiates the definition you give it in interpreting it as a treaty and speaking of the obligations such a treaty would involve. It is necessary to note that, contrary to your statement that Poland assumed an obligation, among other things, to make every effort possible that the Russian government be given *de jure* recognition, the delegates who signed the Riga Protocol actually expressed only their conviction that *de jure* recognition of the Russian government would be in the interests of the economic reconstruction of Eastern Europe.[19]

Through Steklov, writing in *Izvestiia,* Moscow warned Poland, as well as the world in general, that the pressure being applied to Germany and Russia as a result of the treaty would only bring them closer together.[20]

[18] N. Semashko, "Pochemu oni vzbesilis," *Izvestiia,* No. 93, April 28, 1922, p. 1.

[19] *Materialy genuezskoi konferentsii,* pp. 316–17.

[20] *Izvestiia,* No. 97, May 4, 1922, p. 1.

Soviet Relations with German Nationalists, Militarists, and Industrialists

A period of rapprochement did indeed follow. Although the Soviet government insistently proclaimed that the Rapallo treaty included no secret military clauses (and although it appears that such proclamations were literally true), the Rapallo policy nevertheless led to increasing contact, secret in nature, between Soviet and German military and industrial interests. At the same time certain Russian Communists, notably Radek, encouraged the idea of an alliance within Germany between the militant nationalists and the Communists.

During the period 1919–20, when there had been little direct contact between Russia and Germany, Karl Radek, from his cell in Moabit prison, had managed to play a guiding role in the development of the German Communist Party.[21] His contacts had not been limited to Communists; among his visitors had been German nationalists, General Staff officers, and prominent industrialists.[22]

A number of German nationalists, many of them ex-officers in the German army and all of them animated by a desire to revenge Germany's humiliation, were in the process of forming semiofficial secret organizations. Then, as later, Russian Communists appeared to find it easier to work with these extremists of the Right than with their fellow Marxists of the German Social Democratic Party. They took easily to the idea of a national front of all classes in Germany against the Entente. They based their proposal upon a theory that the Versailles policy had forced the German bourgeoisie into a revolutionary role. The German Communist organ, *Die Rote Fahne,* put it this way:

The German bourgeoisie, in view of the hopelessness of its attempts at compromise [with the Entente], is compelled to carry on a . . . revolutionizing policy, but is unable in its struggle against the Entente to rely on the masses of the people. On the contrary it is doomed by history to repel the masses. . . . For this reason, the national and nationalist sentiments let loose by it are bound in the long run to turn against it. The Communist Party of Germany must make it clear to the nationalist masses of the petty bourgeoisie and the intellectuals that the working class alone, once it wins victory, will be able to defend German soil, the treasures of German culture, and the future of the nation.[23]

A month later, Radek spoke before the Executive Committee of the Comintern on Schlageter, a young German nationalist who opposed the French occupation of the Ruhr and was shot on orders of the French command:

The story of this martyr of German nationalism should not be forgotten nor passed over with a mere phrase. It has much to tell us, and much to tell the German people. . . . If Germany wants to be in a position to fight, it must create a united front of workers, and the brain workers must unite with the hand workers, and form a solid phalanx. The condition of the brain workers cries out for this union. Only old prejudices stand in the way . . . We believe that the great majority of the na-

---

[21] See above, p. 25.

[22] See Document 59.

[23] Excerpts from the resolution on the settlement of the differences within the German Communist Party, signed by the Executive Committee of the Comintern, representatives of the Central Committee of the German Communist Party, and representatives of the opposition within this party. *Die Rote Fahne,* No. 107, May 13, 1923, p. 7.

tionalist-minded masses belong not to the camp of capitalists but to the camp of the workers. We want to find, and we shall find, the path to these masses.[24]

Early in July of the same year, 1923, exploring the possibilities for a communist-nationalist agreement, Radek wrote:

Let the Social Democrats and the bourgeois press—those organs of German decay—rave about a fascist-communist bloc; it will not deter me from trying to clarify the position of the German fascist elements, which, I assume, do not *consciously* intend to serve the interests of German reaction and of German capitalism, but are trying to find a way to a new concept, without which the collapse and decay of the German people cannot be prevented . . . Fascism does not represent a clique of officers but a broad, even though contradictory, movement of the people. It rests upon the broad masses sunk in social misery, which are abused by feudal and capitalistic society for purposes which, if ever achieved, would spell the destruction of these masses by office-holders, intellectuals, and artisans. The Communist Party is now a well-established party of the masses. It not only can but must assume a stand toward another mass movement such as fascism.[25]

Little actually came of the attempt at rapprochement between the German Communists and the German nationalists at this time, beyond some sympathetic interchanges between Communists and nationalist leaders. But the rapprochement between Soviet and German military and industrial leaders produced considerably more substantial results. By this means Germany was able to circumvent the Versailles prohibition of German rearmament, and Russia, in return, gained technical and military assistance.

In 1922 Radek, who had returned to Russia in 1920, went back to Germany, where he was admitted (if not welcomed) into German military and industrial circles, and where he conducted personal negotiations with no less a figure than General von Seeckt, commander-in-chief of the German Reichswehr. General von Seeckt was intent upon rebuilding the German army and the German nation. To this end he was willing to negotiate even with such a radical, exotic person as Radek—who in his appearance, opinions, and disrespectful wit offended all the canons of the military caste—and to regard Russia as a potential ally. Of this possibility he wrote:

It [the Rapallo treaty] is the first, though very considerable, strengthening of German prestige in the world at large. This is so because more is read into the document than actually is warranted. No politico-military agreements exist, but the possibility of their existence is believed in. . . . The very fact that the Rapallo treaty has placed us under suspicion of having achieved this accretion of power, without commitments on our side, is the paramount and inestimable value of this agreement. . . . We are striving for two things: (1) to strengthen Russia economically and politically, and thereby indirectly strengthen ourselves by building up a potential ally; and (2) to strengthen ourselves directly, at first cautiously and with circumspection, by helping Russia build an armament industry that would be useful to us in case of need. The German government cannot participate in or even officially recognize all these still largely preliminary transactions; they can only be conducted through military channels. That they [military authorities] should not reach agreements binding for the Reich without the knowledge of the politically responsible offices is, of course, a

---

[24] Radek at the Third Enlarged Plenum of the ECCI, June 21, 1923, *International Press Correspondence,* No. 49, July 12, 1923, pp. 502–3.
[25] *Die Rote Fahne,* No. 156, July 10, 1923, p. 1.

foregone conclusion. . . . Germany will not be bolshevized, not even by an understanding with Russia in foreign affairs.[26]

To solve the problem of providing war matériel for the German army he was rebuilding behind the backs of the Inter-Allied Commission of Control, General von Seeckt planned to build prototypes abroad, principally in Russia, beyond the range of the Commission. He argued that it would not be in the interest of future armies to accumulate stocks of matériel that would become rapidly obsolete; that it would be sufficient to make a few prototypes and arrange for their mass production, the factories being organized for a rapid switchover from peace to war production. This task would have to be accomplished by close co-operation between soldiers and economists. Naturally, it would necessitate state subsidies for the maintenance of the machines and the purchase of raw materials. But on the whole, such a system would be preferable to producing and storing large quantities of matériel of questionable wartime value.[27]

The story of the secret military rapprochement between the German Reichswehr and Moscow did not come to light until a few years after the first steps in this direction were made. On December 3, 1926, the *Manchester Guardian* broke the story. According to the *Guardian,* in the summer of 1921 (presumably after the Soviet-German agreement of May 6, 1921) the German War Ministry had asked the German Junkers-Werke to construct on foreign territory ammunition works that could be used by Germany if necessary. The War Ministry had agreed to finance the plan, and negotiations were soon opened. The Junkers-Werke were instructed to build planes in Russia, some to be sold to the Soviets, the majority to be retained by Germany. The Junkers management at first vacillated, "in view of the violation of the Treaty of Versailles involved," but the War Ministry insisted, offering them twenty-one million gold marks on condition the plan remained secret. In December 1921, a delegation including two Junkers men and two representatives of the War Ministry went to Moscow under assumed names to conduct negotiations with the Soviet government. The Soviet government reportedly acted with caution, but in February 1923 a satisfactory agreement was reached by which the Junkers management would begin constructing planes in Moscow—300 a year at first—the majority of which would be sent to Germany. On May 5, 1924, the German War Ministry, the Junkers firm, and the Soviet government entered a new agreement, by which the Junkers management received four million gold marks, and were to receive an additional eight million, as well as a loan of twelve million. However, said the *Guardian,* a conflict developed between the Junkers-Werke and the War Ministry, and although General von Seeckt attempted arbitration, the disagreement was not settled.[28]

On December 6, 1926, the *Berliner Tageblatt* confirmed the *Guardian's* story. Recalling that in 1921 the Soviet government had offered the German government a defensive alliance, which the German government had declined on the ground that Germany was not in a position to render military assistance to the Soviets, the *Tageblatt* stated that thereupon the question of building German

[26] Friedrich von Rabenau (ed.), *H. von Seeckt, aus seinem Leben, 1918–1936* . . . , pp. 313, 317–18; see Document 61.

[27] H. von Seeckt, *Gedanken eines Soldaten,* pp. 99–100.

[28] *Manchester Guardian Weekly,* No. 23, December 3, 1926, p. 447, and No. 24, December 10, 1926, p. 468.

war planes on Soviet territory had been raised, and that over the objection of Germany's President, Ebert, German engineers had built three factories in Russia.[29]

Later on, in the course of debates in the German Reichstag in 1926 and 1928, frank admissions of the German-Soviet military and industrial alliances were made. A special company, the Gesellschaft zur Foerderung gewerblicher Unternehmungen, so it was stated, had been set up in 1923 to manage the German factories in Russia and supervise the delivery of war matériel to Germany. In the spring of 1926 the name of this company was changed to Wirtschaftskontor. In 1928 War Minister Gessler, speaking in the Reichstag, admitted that preliminary negotiations for German-Soviet co-operation had begun as early as 1921, and in May 1928, a spokesman for the German government admitted before the Reichstag foreign affairs committee that this co-operation had been steadily in effect.[30]

Further evidence of collaboration between Soviet Russia and Germany in the production of war materials is found in the memoirs of Professor V. N. Ipatieff, who participated in the construction of poison gas plants in Russia for Germany and Russia.[31]

Nor did the Soviets themselves deny the collaboration when evidence of it came out. Shortly after the appearance of the *Manchester Guardian*'s story, a *Pravda* editorial shrugged it off: "Supposing this information to be correct, it is in itself of little significance."[32]

Moreover, Bukharin had conveniently evolved a theory to justify military alliances with bourgeois states. According to his view the proletarian state was justified in entering into military alliances with bourgeois states whenever such alliances would further the destruction of other bourgeois states. Thus he declared November 18, 1922, before the Fourth Congress of the Communist International:

... there is no difference in principle between a loan and a military alliance; and I affirm that we have already grown up enough to conclude a military alliance with the bourgeoisie of one country so as to be able, with its help, to crush the bourgeoisie of another country. One can always take into account the consequences of this or that correlation of forces. This is purely a question of strategic and tactical expediency.

Bukharin further declared it the duty of Communists in every country to assist such blocs.[33]

Not all Communists accepted Bukharin's views. In reply to French critics he wrote the following to Boris Souvarine, a member of the French Communist Party in Paris:

[29] *Berliner Tageblatt* (evening ed.), Jhg. 55, No. 575, Dec. 6, 1926, p. 1.

[30] See the speech of P. Scheidemann (German Social Democrat) on December 16, 1926 (*Verhandlungen des Reichstags stenografische Berichte*, III. Wahlperiode 1924. Band 391, pp. 8578–84). See also W. M. Knight-Patterson (Wladyslaw Kulski), *Germany from Defeat to Conquest, 1913–1933*, pp. 402–3. For later elucidation of the Soviet-German military agreement, see J. Epstein, *The Seeckt Papers,* and George W. E. Hallgarten, "General Hans von Seeckt and Russia, 1920–1922," *Journal of Modern History*, XXI, No. 1, March 1949. Both of these writers base their statements on Seeckt's personal papers.

[31] V. N. Ipatieff, *The Life of a Chemist*, pp. 382–88, 399, 423, 468; see Document 62.

[32] *Pravda*, No. 291, December 16, 1926, p. 1; see Document 63.

[33] *IV Vsemirnyi Kongress K.I.*, p. 196; see Document 64.

Some French opportunists, in order to demonstrate their radicalism, have been fastening on . . . my declaration that under certain circumstances a proletarian government may enter into an agreement with a bourgeois state, and that such a temporary agreement, in so far as it represents the interests of revolution and is carried out under the control of the International, is of course to be supported by the International. . . .

The social revolution in Europe will still require many years, and its completion many decades. During this time many proletarian states may find themselves obliged to make temporary agreements with subjugated or semisubjugated bourgeois states, with weak and threatened states against strong and threatening ones. Each such agreement must be carefully weighed, and thoroughly evaluated and deliberated.

It goes without saying that no agreement is permissible by which workers' states could be made directly or indirectly into the tools of imperialism, tools for the oppression of other people. Agreements of the nature mentioned above must be evaluated, not in the light of the superficially interpreted and actually nonexistent interests of one workers' state, but in the light of the world proletarian movement as a whole. The Communist International is the organ of such international control. . . .[34]

During the period of the military rearmament negotiations the Germans and the Russians made some progress in economic collaboration. With the support of German credits German-Soviet mixed companies were established, such as "Derutra" (Deutsch-Russische Transport Aktiengesellschaft) and "Deruluft" (Deutsch-Russische Luftverkehrsgesellschaft), and a large number of concessions were negotiated with German firms for manufacturing, mining, and other activities in Russia.

At the same time, however, that the Soviet government was building up military and industrial relations with the German War Ministry and with German military and industrial circles, Soviet leaders were also pursuing quite a different line in Germany.

The terms of the Versailles peace had brought satisfaction to neither the victors nor the vanquished. One of the chief objectives of the Poincaré government, which had come to office in France in 1922, had been to force Germany to meet her reparations obligations, a policy motivated primarily by a determination to make French heavy industry securely predominant over German, and by fear of German revenge. The reparations payments themselves were to have been used to restore war-devastated regions. But on May 31, 1922, the reparations commission granted Germany a moratorium on payments for the rest of the year, in spite of French protests, for it had become clear that the payments were causing the collapse of the mark. On August 1, Lord Balfour, the British foreign secretary, proposed the abandonment of all inter-Allied debts and reparations claims, adding that if the United States should insist on the payment of the British debt to her, Britain would have to insist on receiving enough to cover these payments. The United States, however, took the line that inter-Allied debts and reparations were separate problems and that the German default on reparations would therefore not excuse default on Allied payments to the United States.

On December 26, 1922, the reparations commission, on a motion by France, again declared Germany in default. On January 9, 1923, after a last-minute

---

[34] *Izvestiia*, No. 6, January 11, 1923, p. 3; also *International Press Correspondence*, No. 3, January 26, 1923, p. 39.

attempt at dissuasion by Britain and Italy, Germany was declared in default on coal deliveries. The next day, January 10, France and Belgium sent a note to Berlin informing the German government that owing to Germany's violation of Paragraphs 17 and 18 of the Eighth Section of the Versailles treaty, the French and Belgian governments were sending a commission (La Mission Internationale de Controle des Usines et Mines) to the Ruhr region to assume control of the German coal syndicate as a guarantee of Germany's reparations pledges. The next day, January 11, French and Belgian troops marched into the Ruhr region and began an occupation of Essen and its vicinity. The Essen city government immediately proclaimed a state of siege, and on January 13 the central German government recommended passive resistance. Soon thereafter a reckless policy of inflation of the mark was undertaken to finance the passive resistance. By way of retaliation, the French increased the army of occupation.

The Poincaré policy was indirectly assisted by events in the Near East, for after the Kemalist victory over the Greeks in September 1922, French diplomacy had been able to dissuade the Turks from occupying Constantinople, and in return Poincaré appeared to expect a free hand from the British in the Ruhr. The resignation of the Lloyd George cabinet as a result of the Near Eastern crisis had also strengthened Poincaré's hand.

The Soviet government characterized the occupation of the Ruhr as a new threat to peace, inspired by the desire of French iron interests to gain control of German coal resources. A Soviet commentator predicted in *Pravda* that "negotiations between the industrialists of both countries with regard to the division of the shares will now be reopened," and that Britain "will only interfere to make sure that neither one party nor the other acquires 51 per cent of the shares in the Franco-German iron-coal syndicate."[35]

The Ruhr events were further pictured as new evidence of the inevitability of the collapse of capitalism, and as steps toward hastening this end. In *Izvestiia* Steklov put it this way:

The world is facing a dilemma: Shall it expose itself at regular intervals to the risks of new wars and universal slaughter; or shall it put an end once and for all to the rule of the capitalist cliques, and thus enter the road of the socialist revolution? Since there is no other way, and since mankind does not want to and cannot perish, the days of capitalism are numbered. Every armed adventure undertaken by the ruling classes will only bring closer the moment of this historic decision.[36]

In the *Pravda* article previously quoted, Lozovsky spoke of how the Ruhr occupation increased the number of adherents to communism:

Every new conflict opens the eyes of new hundreds of thousands of proletarians. What neither the Comintern nor the Red Trade Union International could accomplish has been effected by Poincaré and Lord Curzon. Lausanne and the Ruhr are stages on the road to the liquidation not only of the Versailles treaty, but of the whole system that gave it birth. Go on as you have begun, Messrs. Poincaré, Curzon, Stinnes. Divide up the world; quarrel over who is to have the greatest number of shares; the revolutionary proletariat will soon find a way to unite you on the same gallows.[37]

[35] A. Lozovsky, "Lozanna i Rur," *Pravda*, No. 35, February 16, 1923, p. 1; also in *International Press Correspondence*, No. 10, March 15, 1923, p. 148.

[36] *Izvestiia*, No. 5, January 10, 1923, p. 1.

[37] Lozovsky, *op. cit.*, p. 1.

Another editorial writer in *Pravda* felt that an alliance with Soviet Russia was the only hope for the German government, but noted that "in view of its class instinct, the German government deliberately avoids this path," and that the German Social Democrats were playing a similar passive and shameful role. According to this writer:

The worse the German economic situation becomes under the influence of the French robbers' pressure, the lower the German mark's value will sink, and the worse the economic position of the German worker will become. Germany will then conclude that there is only one way out of the existing situation, that is, an alliance with Soviet Russia and a merciless struggle against French imperialism and Germany's own bourgeoisie.[38]

The belief that the Ruhr events would help the spread of communism was further emphasized by Bukharin in a speech to the Fourth All-Russian Congress of Press Workers:

We ought to be grateful to M. Poincaré, because the Ruhr events constitute a powerful aid to [our] propaganda against the further development of imperialist and bourgeois tendencies. . . . This confusion and aggravation of the situation is of advantage to the proletariat, because the restoration and establishment of the capitalist order in Western Europe would have been most dangerous to us. The starving working class would have been made more passive by some slight alleviation of their situation, and this would have inevitably resulted in reformist tendencies [among them]. Under the present circumstances there can be no such prospect . . . Whatever happens, our forces will be relatively strengthened, because the total forces opposed to us will be weakened. . . .[39]

Soviet leaders blamed Britain, Italy, and Japan for the invasion of the Ruhr, as well as France and Belgium, on the theory that they could have prevented the action had they so desired. Thus in an "Appeal to the Peoples of the World in Connection with the Occupation of the Ruhr Basin by the FrenchTroops," on January 13, 1923, the Soviet government asserted:

But imperialist France is not alone. Her allies could have prevented her from committing this crime, but they did not. They either actually participated in the seizure of the Ruhr region or treacherously washed their hands of it by limiting themselves to verbal protests and fruitless demonstrations. Therefore, they are also guilty of crime. The responsibility for what is being done and will be done rests not only with the Paris rulers, but also with London, Rome, Brussels, and Tokyo.

Nor was the possibility of a general war overlooked. The same appeal went on to declare: "Once more the world has been plunged into a state of prewar fever. Sparks are flying in the powder keg into which Europe has been turned by the Versailles treaty."[40]

Furthermore, Soviet leaders displayed apprehension that Poland or Czechoslovakia, particularly Poland, might use the occasion of the French action in the Ruhr to strike at Germany. It is not clear whether real or pretended fears led the Russians to "play the Polish card" (Lenin's term) as a way of drawing Ger-

[38] *Pravda*, No. 6, January 11, 1923, p. 1; see Document 65.

[39] *Izvestiia*, No. 28, February 8, 1923, p. 3; see Document 66.

[40] *Izvestiia*, No. 9, January 14, 1923, p. 1; also Kliuchnikov and Sabanin, III, 228.

many closer to Russia. It is clear, however, that they saw such an attack as a direct threat to themselves. Thus an editorial in *Pravda* declared:

. . . if the Polish bourgeoisie imitates the example of its patron and guardian, i.e., France, sends its troops to the German front, and invades a country that is already being robbed, then a European storm is inevitable. In that storm the white wings of the rapacious Polish eagle will be broken. In the final analysis, the proletariat, and not the bourgeoisie, will win.[41]

Meanwhile, Moscow, in an effort to make the best possible propaganda use of the Ruhr situation, directed that shipments of flour be offered the Germans in the Ruhr, and called upon the workers of the world to follow the Russian example and make needed supplies available to the Ruhr workers. In an "Appeal of the All-Russian Central Council of Trade Unions to the Workers of the Ruhr Coal Basin, to the Workers of the World, and to the Workers of Russia," the following declaration was made:

The more you, the proletarians of England, France, Italy, Poland, and Czechoslovakia, struggle against your own robbers' governments, the more the German proletarians will know that they are not alone; the more they will be able to stand up and struggle with intensified energy for a workers' government in Germany, which will then stretch its hand to help the workers of all countries begin the joint task of reconstructing the world and freeing it from the yoke of international capital.[42]

In August 1923, while the French occupation of the Ruhr was still in progress, the Cuno cabinet in Germany resigned following a no-confidence vote in the Reichstag. A new middle-of-the-road government was thereupon formed by the leader of the People's Party, Gustav Stresemann, with the support of the Social Democratic, Center, and Democratic parties. The immediate heritage of the new Stresemann government, however, was economic ruin. Many factors, among them the policy of passive resistance in the Ruhr, the devaluation of the mark (which had been undertaken in order to finance this resistance), and the general reparations burden, had brought Germany to a state of imminent collapse. The whole of Germany was soon gripped by strikes and general political and social unrest.

Indecision and Failure of the German "October," 1923

Yet in spite of the Russian Communists' long-held belief that such a revolutionary situation would sooner or later develop in Germany, the Comintern leaders were not ready when the time came. Not the least of the reasons for their indecisiveness was the struggle for power then in progress to determine who should succeed the ailing Lenin as top man.

Throughout the summer of 1923 and into the fall, Stalin, Radek, and the German party leader, Brandler, were all advocating caution. In a letter to Zinoviev and Bukharin, written in the summer of 1923, Stalin said: "If today in Germany the power, so to speak, falls, and the Communists seize hold of it, they will fall with a crash. That [will happen] in the 'best' case. And at the worst,

[41] *Pravda*, No. 13, January 19, 1923, p. 1.
[42] *Pravda*, No. 49, March 4, 1923, p. 1; see Document 67.

they will be smashed to pieces and thrown back. . . . In my opinion, the Germans must be curbed and not spurred on."[43]

At about the same time, Radek declared: "Not only must we not yet advance to the decisive battle, but we must avoid everything that could give the enemy an opportunity to defeat us in separate attacks." Nonetheless, said Radek, he saw signs that the time was approaching for a general attack. The German bourgeoisie could not solve the crisis in Germany; the power of German Social Democrats was decaying while that of the German Communists was growing. He instructed the German party to strengthen its forces, to seek allies among the proletarianized petty bourgeoisie, and "to combine the maximum strength of our clear communist policy with a deliberate acceptance of such compromises as are necessary for broadening our bases and such as coincide with the line of historical development."[44]

Meanwhile the Social Democrats had come into control of the governments of Thuringia in March and of Saxony in September. In Bavaria nationalists were busily agitating and planning for the famous "Beer Hall Putsch" of November. The government of the Reich, pressed by the French from abroad and by the Right and the Left parties from within, held on precariously. Under orders from the Comintern, the German Communists did not make a bold strike for power. But in September Brandler and other party leaders were called to Moscow, where they remained until nearly the middle of October. Brandler was then ordered back to Berlin with instructions to enter the Thuringian and Saxon governments as a step toward preparing for an armed uprising. Radek and other experts in revolutionary tactics, well supplied with funds, went along to give professional direction to the enterprise.

Walter Krivitsky, former chief of Soviet intelligence in Western Europe, reports as follows:

When news reached our department of the French occupation of the Ruhr, a group of five or six officers, including myself, were ordered to leave at once for Germany. Within twenty-four hours all arrangements were made. Moscow hoped that the repercussions of the French occupation would open the way for a renewed Comintern drive in Germany. . . . We at once created three types of organizations in the German Communist Party: the Party Intelligence Service working under the guidance of the Fourth Department of the [Russian] Red Army; military formations as the nucleus of the future German Red Army, and *Zersetzungsdienst*, small units of men whose function was to shatter the morale of the Reichswehr and the police. . . . We Soviet officers organized German Communist Military formations, the foundation of the German Red Army that was never to be, in a very systematic fashion, dividing them into units of one hundred men, *Hundertschaft*.[45]

Moscow's abrupt about-face in deciding to make a revolutionary drive for power in Germany was due to news that seemed to portend better relations between Germany and the Allies. Franco-German negotiations to end the Ruhr occupation and Stresemann's earlier decision to call off the German policy of passive resistance might mean a German decision to move away from Russia toward the West. About this time the British prime minister, Stanley Baldwin,

[43] *Arbeiterpolitik* (Leipzig), February 9, 1929, p. 78, as given in Leon Trotsky, *The Third International After Lenin*, p. 323; see Document 68.

[44] *Pravda*, No. 171, August 1, 1923, p. 2; see Document 69. See also Document 70.

[45] W. G. Krivitsky, *In Stalin's Secret Service*, pp. 38–39, 41.

had secured a promise of American aid to avert the complete economic and financial collapse foreshadowed by the devaluation of the mark and the repercussions of this devaluation throughout the world. The eventual outgrowth of the promised American aid was the Dawes Plan.[46]

Once the decision to undertake an uprising in Germany had been made, the Soviet propaganda machine went into high gear to inform the world that the long-awaited day was at hand. Appropriate slogans were devised: "Workers' Germany and Our Workers' and Peasants' Union Are the Bulwark of Peace and Labor," "German Steam Hammer and Soviet Bread Will Conquer the World," etc.[47] The Soviet press told Russian peasants that if the German workers were to win, the new German government would immediately join with Soviet Russia and so "unite in Europe the tremendous power of 200 million people, against which no war in Europe will be possible . . . because no one would be able to face such a force."[48]

At the same time Soviet leaders warned of the danger of foreign intervention to throttle the revolution. An article in *Izvestiia* said:

Now when events in Central Europe are developing with dazzling rapidity, when a hard class struggle is unfolding in Germany, when the greatest economic crisis of Central Europe is threatening to spread to Poland and to a number of other states, we must be prepared more than ever before for any plot on the part of our enemies. . . . The struggle in Germany will lead either to the victory of the revolution or to its defeat. If the German revolution is victorious, capitalist Europe will probably launch a violent struggle against the victorious German revolution. . . . If the violent class struggle in Germany should end with the defeat of the working class and the triumph of monarchy, we have no guarantee that triumphant reaction will not turn its bayonets against the first republic of soviets. Who knows whether or not this will be a starting point for the advance of world reaction against our country of peaceful labor?[49]

In this article, and again in a speech by Trotsky the next day, the point was made that Russian forces were not expected to be needed in the German revolution. According to the article:

We do not aim at interference in Western European events as our enemy likes to proclaim. We maintain that if Germany is destined to have a revolution, the victory of the revolution will depend on the correlation of the domestic forces that are now waging a violent struggle within Germany. According to all information, the working class of Germany, which is struggling at present against German fascism, is sufficiently strong to be the victor in the present conflict.[50]

Trotsky, while speaking on the broader subject of Poland's role, said in this regard:

As for victory within Germany itself, no help is needed there. German workers themselves will win, and the revolution is poor indeed if it is not able to deal with its own bourgeoisie. No assistance with manpower is needed for the German revolution.[51]

[46] See our pp. 262–64, 296–98.
[47] *Izvestiia,* No. 244, October 25,1923, p. 1.
[48] *Pravda,* No. 233 (Supplement), October 14, 1923, p. 2.
[49] V. D. Vilensky (Sibiriakov), "Politika mira," *Izvestiia,* No. 240, October 20, 1923, p. 1.
[50] *Ibid.*
[51] *Izvestiia,* No. 241, October 21, 1923, p. 1 ; see Document 72.

Zinoviev, who had long been arguing that the time was at hand for revolution in Germany, declared that the German "worker-giant is now convinced that the country and the working class can be saved only by revolution." He argued that in Germany there would be no need to send armed workers to the countryside, because the "agricultural workers themselves will do most of the work necessary to reduce to nought (or better to destroy) the counterrevolution of the estate owners and the rich peasants. The majority of the agricultural workers sympathize with communism."[52]

Following the communist notion of the "hegemony" of the proletariat, Zinoviev emphasized that "the German revolution will operate from a powerful industrial base." The petty bourgeoisie in the cities would lend a hand: "One can say that the role of the peasants in Russia . . . will be played in Germany by the middle class in the towns."[53] Other favorable factors were the availability of Russian revolutionary experience, which the Germans could draw upon; the Communist International and the sympathy for communism it had stirred up throughout the world; and the dissensions among the Entente powers, which, so Zinoviev asserted, would keep them from taking joint action to put down the German revolution.

Zinoviev listed in some detail his reasons for thinking that foreign intervention, although undoubtedly the dangerous factor in the German situation, might not prove formidable. Britain might attempt a blockade, but she did not have a land force strong enough to constitute a decisive menace; the morale of France's troops would be poor; in Czechoslovakia the multiplicity of nationalities would render action difficult; Hungary's domestic crisis would preclude action; and in Austria a German revolution would simply provoke strong sentiment for union with Germany. "Certain groups of the Polish bourgeoisie may be the most dangerous and the most desperate enemy of the German revolution," he thought, but even Polish intervention could not be successful, since "contact with the German proletariat would disperse the nationalism that still influences a considerable fraction of the Polish proletariat.[54] In conclusion, Zinoviev made the following optimistic assertion:

If, in spite of everything, the international bourgeoisie risks an outright immediate war against the revolution, it may at first have some success, but in the end it will break its neck. Germany's sixty million men and women will, under the proletarian rule, repulse the invaders, and in spite of all obstacles the German proletarian revolution will triumph.[55]

Poland's role in the event of revolution in Germany was viewed with particular apprehension not only to Zinoviev, but by all Russian Communists. The Russians feared actual armed intervention by Poland less than they feared Polish interference with free transit between Russia and Germany, which would scotch the Soviet plan to supply food to the German revolutionary forces. Trotsky warned the Poles that they would regret such a move:

Poland can be either a bridge between Germany and us, or a barrier. If she is a bridge, we shall pay her cash. We need direct transit to Germany. . . . Without

[52] G. E. Zinoviev, *Les problèmes de la révolution allemande*, pp. 10–11; see also Document 71.
[53] *Ibid.*, p. 13.
[54] *Ibid.*, pp. 43–44.
[55] *Ibid.*, p. 46.

this transit our rural economy will suffocate. Poland must decide whether she will be a bridge or a barrier . . . We do not want war; we shall pay for peace, but not by isolating ourselves from the European market.[56]

The Soviet government sent a special emissary, V. L. Kopp, to Poland to negotiate for Polish neutrality in the event of uprisings in Germany, and transit for Russian goods across Poland. Kopp also discussed these matters with the other Baltic states. According to a later report:

There was every reason to fear Polish action against revolutionary Germany. . . . Our special envoy for the negotiations with Poland and the border states, Comrade Kopp, insisted on one thing only, i.e., the maintenance of mutual neutrality in case of decisive events in Germany, and the transit of our grain across Poland "irrespective of the internal political conditions in the countries of our export." These last words were taken from our government communiqué and they mean that, together with guarding the German revolution from armed intervention from outside, we wished to help Germany with food. The right of this huge agricultural country [the U.S.S.R.] to an exit to the world market was so elementary and indisputable that the Polish government did not dare to decline our legal demand openly. But it revealed its true intentions by its refusal to confirm its oral agreement in writing and in a clear statement.[57]

The Soviet communiqué referred to in the quotation was issued November 17, 1923. It declared the Soviet government was mainly concerned with "ensuring the political relations of the eastern sector of Europe against any unexpected upheaval, and in this way . . . fully assisting in the maintenance of peace throughout Europe." But the Polish government had been unwilling to guarantee free transit irrespective of conditions in the countries to which the goods might be directed, and the negotiations broke down.[58]

Communist Reasons for the Failure of the German "October"

Meanwhile, the October revolution in Germany failed to come off as ordered. Although the German Communists entered the local governments of Saxony and Thuringia, they failed to obtain socialist support in the plan for insurrection. When the central German government threatened to use the Reichswehr against the Thuringian and Saxon Social-Democratic opposition, the German Communists could not persuade the socialist leaders to agree to armed resistance. At a conference of the Saxon Industrial Councils at Chemnitz, October 21, Brandler asked for a general strike and participation by the Saxon government in armed resistance to the Reichswehr, but the socialists ignored the request. As a result the German Communist Party was obliged to call off the armed resistance to the Reichswehr, and the plans for the revolution in Thuringia and Saxony collapsed.

Communists in Hamburg, however, unaware of what had taken place at the Chemnitz conference, went ahead with their revolution in that city the next day, October 22. They seized police stations and supplies of arms, but they were easily defeated by government forces. The following day, October 23, units of the Reichswehr occupied Dresden, the capital of Saxony; the Saxon socialist

[56] *Izvestiia*, No. 241, October 21, 1923, p. 1; see Document 72.
[57] M. Tanin, *Mezhdunarodnaia politika SSSR (1917–1924)*, p. 17.
[58] Kliuchnikov and Sabanin, III, 291–92.

government ceased to exist, and the Communists were forced underground. Within a month the Thuringian socialist government met a similar fate, and the German revolution, to which the Russian Communists had looked forward with such enthusiasm, came to an end without having actually started.

The failure in Germany caused a great deal of soul searching, scapegoat hunting, and explaining in the higher circles of the Comintern. Stalin, as was his custom in those days, did not commit himself. Brandler and Radek were especially blamed for their handling of the operations in Germany.

Zinoviev, anxious to turn the blame away from himself, argued that although revolution had been expected, no revolutionary situation had arisen. In analyzing what had happened, or rather failed to happen, he said:

The German Communist Party revealed many weaknesses and made a number of serious mistakes during these critical weeks, but we do not consider it mistaken in not bringing out the proletariat into a general struggle in October. . . . The retreat should have been less passive. But the abstention from fighting a decisive battle was inevitable under the circumstances . . . The big wave of political strikes in August 1923 led us to believe that the German Communist Party already had the majority of the proletariat behind it, or at least the social[ist] sections of it, which are most important. This proved to be a mistake. The German Communist Party was then (as it is now) only on the way to conquering this majority.

Zinoviev went on, in a characteristically neat about-face that failed to mention his own earlier attitude, to charge the German Communist Party with failure to understand that September and October were suitable for organizing demonstrations designed to attract more followers, but were not suitable for an uprising. "There was no justification," he declared, "for some comrades' hopes of rousing the masses to an armed rising 'suddenly' by one bold action." He further charged the German Communists with inadequate technical preparation and with failure to estimate the enemy's strength properly.[59]

Yet Zinoviev remained optimistic about the future of the revolution in Germany, maintaining as much as a year later that it was going to come. On the anniversary of the Hamburg uprising the following year, 1924, he characterized that event as Germany's 1905, a rehearsal for battles to come, and went on to declare:

It is a mistaken idea that in October 1923 a revolutionary opportunity, unique of its kind, was let slip. The defeat of October 1923 was no more decisive than the defeat of the Spartakus revolt in January 1919. The decisive main battles, the battles that decide the fate of a country for decades, have not yet taken place in Germany. These struggles, however, will come before very long.[60]

Trotsky, on the other hand, maintained that the revolutionary situation had been present in Germany, but that Moscow, by acting too slowly and too late, had failed to take advantage of it. Moreover, unlike Zinoviev, he conceded the seriousness of the defeat and that the German revolution would be long delayed.

Bukharin had still another explanation. Analyzing the lessons of the German events before the Thirteenth Party Congress in May 1924, he attributed the failure to the leaders of the German Communist Party, and especially to their belief that "with the use of the means and methods of bourgeois democracy, of

[59] *Kommunisticheskii Internatsional*, No. 1, 1924, pp. 501–2; see Document 73.
[60] G. E. Zinoviev, "K godovshchine gamburgskogo vosstaniia," *Pravda*, No. 242, October 23, 1924, p. 1; see Document 74.

bourgeois state machinery, [after] once passing through a considerable period of development, it would become possible to proceed more or less painlessly to the higher stage [of political development]."[61]

Bukharin also declared that the German party leaders had apparently interpreted the tactics of the united front in Germany as giving the go-ahead for political co-operation with the Social Democrats—even for forming a long-term bloc with them—rather than as a mere maneuver aimed at snatching from the Social Democrats their influence upon the masses, and leading the latter in an attack against the bourgeoisie.

The failure of the German October Revolution was examined in detail at the Fifth Congress of the Comintern, June 17–July 8, 1924. When Radek's old sin of favoring co-operation with the German nationalists and his praise of the German extremist Schlageter were brought up, Radek replied:

I wish to correct a legend that has been spread here . . . Now there was no Radek standpoint, but there was the standpoint of the Comintern, which was stated in the resolution published by *Die Rote Fahne* on May 13 [1923]. . . . I beg leave to quote Comrade Zinoviev's letter to me of July 20 [1923], in which he wrote: "Your articles about Schlageter are correct and good." This proves once more that Comrade Zinoviev was fully in agreement with the whole Schlageter campaign.[62]

Finally, April 4, 1925, at a meeting of the Fifth Enlarged Plenum of the Executive Committee of the Communist International, the blame for the German failure was again fixed on Radek, Brandler, and Thalheimer. A resolution adopted by the Executive Committee charged:

The faction headed by Radek, Brandler, and Thalheimer tried to convert the revolutionary tactics of the united front into tactics of coalition with the Social Democrats. . . . The Thirteenth Congress of the Russian [Communist] Party unanimously declared that the policy of Comrade Radek, who at that time was trying to speak in the name of the Russian Communist Party, had nothing in common with the real policy of the party. The Frankfurt Congress of the German Communist Party, with equal determination, condemned the policy of Brandler and Thalheimer.[63]

Thus in 1923 one phase of Soviet foreign policy, the promotion of revolution abroad, had failed completely in Germany, while the other phase, the promotion of ordinary diplomatic and economic intercourse, not only had succeeded with Germany, but had increased the prestige and the diplomatic bargaining power of both nations.

During 1923 communist revolutionary policy had also affected adversely the somewhat ambiguous relations of Soviet Russia and Great Britain. For a brief time the tension between these two states threatened to put an end to the limited British recognition of the Soviet government implied by the trade agreement of March 1921.

The Anglo-Soviet Crisis, 1923

The crisis in Anglo-Soviet relations came on May 8, 1923, when a memorandum was presented to the Soviet government by the official British repre-

[61] *Trinadtsatyi Sezd Rossiiskoi Kommunisticheskoi Partii (Bolshevikov). Stenografi-cheskii otchet, 23-31 maia, 1924*, p. 337.
[62] *Piatyi Vsemirnyi Kongress K.I.*, pp. 680, 682.
[63] *Kommunisticheskii Internatsional v dokumentakh*, p. 523; see Document 75.

sentative in Moscow. Lord Curzon, who signed this memorandum, charged that Russia had violated the trade agreement by continuing her propaganda activities in Asia, and demanded that these activities be ended and apologized for, on threat of abrogation of the agreement.

A month earlier, on March 30, the British representative in Moscow, Mr. Hodgson, had appealed to the People's Commissariat of Foreign Affairs to stay the execution of a Catholic priest, Mgr. Butkiewicz (Butkevich), who had been sentenced to death for political activity. In reply, the Commissariat of Foreign Affairs called the British action an unwarranted intervention in Russian affairs, and accused Great Britain of doing worse things, such as assassinating political prisoners in Ireland, India, and Egypt. Mr. Hodgson, the British representative in Russia, declared the Soviet note unacceptable:

No one has questioned the right of the Russian Government to exercise jurisdiction within its own territory, so that I intend to make no observations on your first paragraph.

When, however, you impugn the sincerity of the British Government in its appeal for clemency on behalf of condemned persons, and adduce, in support of this charge and as representing facts, the irresponsible utterance of some individual in France whom you style "the representative of the Irish Republic," and who, *inter alia,* accuses the British Government of being responsible for the murder in cold blood of political prisoners, the position is different, and I must ask you, if you wish me to accept this note, to couch it in such terms as will make it possible for me to do so.

The Commissariat of Foreign Affairs thereupon reiterated that as the "note of 30th March cannot be qualified otherwise than as an entirely inadmissible attempt at interference in the internal affairs of the independent and sovereign R.S.F.S.R., the People's Commissariat of Foreign Affairs cannot acknowledge that the expressions employed in its answering note were inapt or not suitable to the circumstances of the case."[64]

It was at this point that Lord Curzon sent the Soviet government his memorandum of May 8, reviewing the entire course of Anglo-Soviet relations and threatening their termination unless certain conditions were met.

The memorandum began as follows:

The tone and character of the notes recently received by the British agent at Moscow from the Russian Commissariat for Foreign Affairs . . . have imposed upon His Majesty's Government the duty, which has perhaps been already too long delayed, of considering carefully, and *seriatim,* in relation to a large number of similar incidents, whether it is desirable, or indeed possible, that the relations of the two Governments should remain any longer upon so anomalous and indeed unprecedented a footing, and whether His Majesty's Government can with due self-respect continue to ignore the repeated challenges which the Soviet Government has thought fit with apparent deliberation to throw down.

Curzon then charged the Soviet government with flagrant violation of the provisions of the trade agreement of 1921 requiring abstention from hostile action or propaganda, and quoted communications between the Soviet government and its agents in Persia, in Afghanistan, and along the Indian border to substantiate his charges. After describing the anti-British operations of the Soviet minister in Teheran, and of the Soviet consul in Kermanshah, Curzon declared:

[64] *Correspondence between His Majesty's Government and the Soviet Government respecting the Relations between the two Governments* (Cmd. 1869), pp. 3–4.

That these activities are well known to, and have been authorized by, the Soviet Government at Moscow is demonstrated by a report from M. Shumiatsky, the Russian representative at Teheran to the Commissariat for Foreign Affairs, in February 1923, which contains the following interesting paragraph: "Our mission, in carrying out the instructions which your telegram amplifies, had decided on this political line of action, especially in North Persia and Teheran; a good group of workers has been organized who can act in an anti-British direction with real activity . . . If the Commissary for Foreign Affairs will agree to the plan of the mission, for the first expenditure 300,000 *tomans* will be necessary as a credit to enable us to work."

In describing the activities of F. F. Raskolnikov, the Soviet representative in Kabul, Curzon said that on February 17, 1923, Raskolnikov "informed the Soviet authorities in Tashkent that every possible means should be used 'to aggravate the undoubted existing crisis by making a breach between Afghanistan and the English,' and that 'the immediate delivery of arms and money would have an immense significance.'" The memorandum then detailed other subversive activities of Raskolnikov's and quoted the following communication of March 16, 1923, from L. M. Karakhan, the Assistant People's Commissar of Foreign Affairs, to Raskolnikov: " 'Bring with you a concrete proposal with regard to the form the co-operation in assisting the tribes should take. On the settlement of this question will depend the question of the delivery of arms. Please inform us of your ideas as to the form of co-operation necessary to ensure local supervision in the distribution of the arms.' "

With regard to Soviet activities in India, Curzon cited certain communist activities in training and financing Indian elements,[65] and then declared:

In their note of the 27th September, 1921, the Soviet Government indignantly repudiated any connection between themselves and the mischievous body known as the Third International. It is singularly unfortunate, if this be the case, that a member of the Soviet Government, M. Sokolnikov, People's Commissary for Finance, and presumably a responsible official, should at a meeting of the Financial Commission of the Fourth Congress of the Third International held at Moscow on the 25th November, 1922, have been one of the body of three by whom the sums of £80,000 and £120,000 were allotted to the British and Indian Communist parties respectively. Of this sum £75,000 had arrived in England by the beginning of January, 1923. A little earlier, in September, 1922, the Soviet Government had borne the expense of equipping and despatching to India and other Eastern countries sixty-two Oriental students trained in propaganda schools under the Third International. . . .

The above paragraphs contain but a few selected examples among many scores of similar incidents, covering in their wide ambit Egypt, Turkey, the British Dominions, and even Great Britain, which testify to the consistent manner in which the Soviet Government has flouted and infringed the preliminary condition upon which the Trade Agreement was signed. It is clearly impossible that an arrangement should be perpetuated which is faithfully observed by one party and as systematically violated by the other. Unless such acts are repudiated and apologized for, and unless the officials who have been responsible for them are disowned and recalled from the scene of their maleficent labours, it is manifestly impossible to persevere with an agreement which is so one-sided in its operation.

Also included in Curzon's note were claims for compensation for certain outrages committed upon British citizens in Russia and for redress of grievances

[65] See the companion volume, *Soviet Russia and the East, 1920–1927.*

in connection with three British trawlers attacked by Soviet ships while fishing outside the three-mile limit near Murmansk. Two of these trawlers had been seized by the Soviet government and their crews detained; the third had been wrecked in the course of the attempted seizure, and its crew had drowned.

Lastly, Curzon demanded of the Soviet government a cessation of propaganda and other activities hostile to Great Britain; compensation of British subjects and for British ships as mentioned above; and withdrawal of the two Soviet communications in the Butkiewicz affair, all within ten days. Curzon concluded:

His Majesty's Government have no desire or intention to enter into a prolonged and possibly acrimonious controversy on any of these subjects; but, unless, within ten days of the receipt of the above communication by the Commissariat for Foreign Affairs, the Soviet Government has undertaken to comply fully and unconditionally with the requests which it contains, His Majesty's Government will recognise that that Government does not wish the existing relations between them to be maintained. In that case His Majesty's Government, on their part, will, in view of the manifest infringement of the Trade Agreement by the Soviet Government, as set forth in the earlier part of the present memorandum, consider themselves immediately free from the obligation of that agreement, in accordance with the provisions of the third paragraph of its thirteenth article.[66]

The Curzon memorandum produced great excitement and indignation within Russia. The Soviet leaders diverted attention from Curzon's charges by suggesting that this was possibly a renewed threat of war and intervention. Speaking before the Moscow soviet on May 13, Trotsky declared: "We do not know whether Lord Curzon's act is an isolated one on the part of Great Britain, or whether there are also others, nearer home or equally distant, collaborating with Lord Curzon in the same diplomatic—and perhaps not merely diplomatic— plans." In any case, the Soviet Union was anxious for peace: "[Despite Curzon's note] we shall not take a single step or utter a single word that might tend to render the situation more acute, or close the path to a peaceful solution through negotiations."[67]

Along this same line Bukharin told the same meeting of the Moscow soviet:

Comrades! The situation is pretty critical just now. Anything might happen. But this is what we say: If fate calls us to struggle instead of settling matters through diplomatic negotiations, we all, as one man, with arms in our hands, will march on to this struggle! The British government must understand that if it wants to talk to us, it must speak as an equal to an equal, because the Soviet republic is not the Ruhr zone of occupation, nor is it India, the colony of the British King . . .[68]

The Petrograd soviet followed the same line, adopting a declaration, addressed to the workers of the world, branding the Curzon ultimatum "either an attempt to institute a new blockade of the Soviet country . . . or the precursor of an open declaration of war," and calling upon the Council of People's Commissars to reject the ultimatum. The Petrograd document declared:

We appeal to the workers of all countries. A new campaign is being opened against Soviet Russia. In this campaign the victory, or even the semi-victory, of world

[66] *Correspondence between His Majesty's Government and the Soviet Government respecting the Relations between the two Governments* (Cmd. 1869), pp. 5–13.
[67] *Pravda*, No. 105, May 13, 1923, p. 3.
[68] *Ibid.*

imperialism would signify the annihilation of the workers' movement for many years, and the establishment of blackest reaction.[69]

On the diplomatic level, the Commissariat of Foreign Affairs, anxious to retain trade relations with Britain, was as conciliatory as possible. It denied most of the charges relating to propaganda against Britain, countering with its own charges of anti-Soviet activities by British agents in the Caucasus and the Near East. It pointed also to British disregard of Russian interests in the Dardanelles, Eastern Galicia, the Memel district, Bessarabia, and elsewhere. It reiterated its stand that the Soviet government could not assume responsibility for the activities of the Third International. To the demand for compensation of British nationals it counterposed similar demands of its own. On the other hand, it pointed the way to an amicable settlement of the fishing boat dispute; it apologized, in effect, for the tone of the Butkiewicz notes; and, lastly, it suggested that the establishment of normal diplomatic relations would smooth out difficulties between the two governments, and proposed a conference to settle all issues in dispute.[70] Equally conciliatory in tone was the Soviet note of June 4 to the British government which finally led to a settlement.[71]

Communist Interpretation of the Anglo-Soviet Crisis

Certain Soviet leaders, among them Trotsky and Bukharin, asserted that the Curzon ultimatum had been designed to provoke Soviet Russia into war. At a congress of metalworkers on June 6, Trotsky said: "Lord Curzon worded his note in very strong language, expecting to receive a discourteous and offensive reply from us, and thus to be able to arouse British public opinion against us."[72]

Radek, in his report on the international situation to the Third Enlarged Plenum of the Executive Committee of the Communist International, June 15, 1923, embroidered upon the provocation theory:

It is perfectly clear that even if Soviet Russia were prepared not only to renounce propaganda, but even to raise two fingers and swear that Lord Curzon was the greatest friend of the Eastern peoples, economic developments would nevertheless strengthen the position of Soviet Russia in the East. This, in Curzon's opinion, represents a menace to the policy he doggedly pursues in accordance with the whole of the past, namely, the consolidation of relations with the colonies and with India in particular. . . .

Accordingly, Lord Curzon said: "Either we succeed in forcing Soviet Russia to her knees now, in drawing her into the channels of British policy and eliminating her from the list of decisive factors in the East, or we provoke a war before Soviet Russia becomes too dangerous for us. . . ."

British policy counted upon provoking us into a war with Poland . . .[73]

Radek warned that the Soviet republic was in danger and that the Curzon ultimatum was a symptom of the danger, although "in spite of the capitalist offensive, there are no grounds for believing in the possibility of capitalist re-

[69] *Pravda*, No. 107, May 16, 1923, p. 3; see Document 76.

[70] Kliuchnikov and Sabanin, III, 250–56; see Document 77.

[71] Text of this note appears in *ibid.*, 261–64; an English translation appears in Degras, I, 399–403.

[72] *Izvestiia*, No. 134, June 19, 1923, p. 4.

[73] *Kommunisticheskii Internatsional*, No. 26–27, 1923, pp. 7108–10.

construction; on the contrary, we are on the threshold of acceleration in the destruction of Europe . . ." In fact, said Radek,

Soviet Russia is in danger just because we are becoming stronger and because the capitalists are losing hope of our destruction. . . . Soviet Russia is strong, and will defend herself and not allow herself to be defeated, even if she is compelled to rely upon her own strength. But it will depend upon the international proletariat whether a new attack upon Soviet Russia is to be fended off by Soviet Russia alone, or whether the whole proletariat will assume a counteroffensive.[74]

At the Second Congress of Soviets of the U.S.S.R., January 30, 1924, Kamenev encouraged his audience to believe that Soviet Russia's growing strength and the general disintegration of capitalist civilization would bring de jure recognition at a price the Soviets were willing to pay:

We see in the general [world] situation the beginning of the end of the first period, the period when the Soviet government was obliged to struggle for recognition. We are definitely on the threshold of a new period, a period that will undoubtedly present some definite dangers, dangers of capitalistic pressure that we must overcome, and that we shall have to oppose by economic methods. It is clear that we stand at a turning point in our international position. The power of the U.S.S.R., its continuous economic growth against a background of general disintegration and the breaking up of capitalist civilization, can no longer be concealed or disputed. Those who think that de jure recognition is something for which we are prepared to pay, even at the cost of our own advantages, are mistaken.[75]

De Jure Recognition by the British and Other Governments

Speaking of the advantages of recognition, Kamenev said:

De jure recognition means for us, first of all, the legalization of our trade relations. This is necessary to us, but it is also necessary to those who want our bread, our lumber, and our oil, and who want us to buy their machinery and cotton. . . . De jure recognition is the recognition of our laws and of our legislature, which is obligatory for those who wish to maintain business and commercial and economic relations with us. That is de jure recognition, and such recognition we need.[76]

Meanwhile, the Soviet government had not retreated from its adamant refusal either to pay the debts of preceding Russian governments or to restore nationalized property to foreign claimants. Nevertheless negotiations with private concerns were going on. Once the breakdown of the general economic conferences at Genoa and The Hague had revealed the inability of the Western European powers to deal as a united group with the Soviets, they began to move toward recognition separately. The race for trade with Russia was on, stimulated by unfavorable economic conditions throughout Europe. The Russian "window to Europe" was about to be thrown wide open.

Although Soviet negotiations with Italy had been under way for some little time, Great Britain, as it turned out, was actually the first of the powers—after

---

[74] Ibid., pp. 7122–23.

[75] Vtoroi Sezd Sovetov Soiuza Sovetskikh Sotsialisticheskikh Respublik. Stenograficheskii otchet, pp. 68–69 (cited hereafter as Vtoroi Sezd Sovetov S.S.S.R.); see Document 78.

[76] Ibid.

Germany—to accord the Soviet government full *de jure* recognition. In the British election of January 1924, Stanley Baldwin's Conservative Party failed to win a majority over its Labour and Liberal rivals, and the Labour Party (with Liberal acquiescence) took office for the first time. The British election was fought chiefly over the domestic matter of tariff policy, but since the Labour Party had included in its platform recognition of the Soviet government, Soviet leaders immediately branded recognition the deciding factor in the election.

On February 1, 1924, shortly after the Labour cabinet took office, the British government offered to recognize the U.S.S.R. "as the *de jure* rulers of those territories of the old Russian Empire which acknowledge their authority," and proposed that the Soviet government send to London "representatives armed with full powers . . . to draw up the preliminary bases of a complete treaty to settle all questions outstanding between the two countries." Further, the offer proposed the exchange of chargés d'affaires pending the appointment of ambassadors.[77]

The Soviet government promptly replied, welcoming the British action and stating that it would shortly send plenipotentiaries to London to discuss "the settlement of outstanding claims and obligations of one party against the other, as well as the determination of means for the restoration of Russia's credit in Great Britain."[78]

A week later, on February 8, 1924, Italy followed Britain's lead. Although the preliminary Italo-Soviet economic and political agreement, which had been signed more than two years earlier, on December 26, 1921,[79] had not been ratified by the Italian Parliament until early in 1923, Mussolini, almost immediately after gaining power in 1922, had expressed a desire for trade with the U.S.S.R., and on November 30, 1923, he officially stated his intention to recognize the Soviet government. Negotiations had therefore been resumed, and were under way when news of the British move arrived.

Radek interpreted the Italian recognition according to the theory of the inevitable contradictions between capitalist states, reinforced by economic necessity:

> Italy can view even less indifferently than England the breaking up of the Entente and must seek support, contacts, and help wherever she can. . . . Italy's chief competitor in the Mediterranean is France. . . . The struggle with France forced Italy to come to an agreement with Yugoslavia in order to secure her Adriatic rear. The Soviet Union is the neighbor of Rumania and the strongest naval power on the Black Sea. This ensures its influence in the Balkans, an influence that will increase with the growth of the U.S.S.R. as a world power. Already these purely political reasons have forced Mussolini, this counterrevolutionary realist, to abandon the legitimist game, and to seek a rapprochement with the Soviet government.
>
> But the main reason for the recognition is economic conditions. Italy needs grain, oil, and coal from abroad. . . .[80]

De jure recognition of the Soviet government by other governments soon followed the British and Italian action. On February 13, 1924, the Norwegian government presented to the Soviet representative in Norway a note granting

[77] *Daily Herald,* February 2, 1924, p. 1.
[78] Kliuchnikov and Sabanin, III, 296; also *Daily Herald,* February 3, 1924, p. 3.
[79] See p. 24.
[80] *Pravda,* No. 32, February 9, 1924, p. 1; see Document 80.

„Эх, тяжела ты, шапка наркоминдела!"

"'AH, WHAT A BURDEN FOR YOU . . .'" Chicherin, People's Commissar of Foreign Affairs, is weighed down by recognitions. French premier Edouard Herriot is adding France's recognition to the stack. Izvestiia, No. 250, October 31, 1924.

recognition, and on February 24 the Austrian government informed the People's Commissariat of Foreign Affairs of its desire to renew normal relations with Russia. On March 8 Greece extended recognition; on March 15 Sweden did the same, and added a trade agreement for good measure. Denmark followed on June 17, Hungary on September 5, and Mexico on August 4. Somewhat earlier, on May 31, China and Soviet Russia signed *An Agreement on the General Principles for the Regulation of the Problems Arising between the Soviet Union and the Chinese Republic.*[81]

France acted somewhat more slowly than Britain and Italy. On December 22, 1923, the Poincaré government had proposed (through the medium of the newspaper *Le Temps*) an agreement establishing normal Franco-Soviet diplomatic relations, on the condition that Russia recognize prewar debts and compensate French citizens holding Russian bonds or owning property in Russia that had been nationalized. This offer, however, had provided for the annulment of the Russian war debts to France if Soviet Russia, on its part, renounced its claims for compensation for the damages suffered by Russia through the Allied intervention. However, there were two conditions attached to this offer: (1) that Russia should support the French government every time the opportunity arose, in its efforts to get inter-Allied debts annulled or postpone paying them, and (2) that Russia treat its other creditors in a similar manner. A mutual guarantee of nonaggression between the U.S.S.R. and its neighbors had also been suggested. Upon publication of the offer, the press of both France and Russia began to discuss the proposal; but after the French parliament ratified the Bessarabian protocol of 1923,[82] sanctioning the annexation of Bessarabia by Rumania, relations between the two governments deteriorated. On April 9, 1924, the question of recognizing the Soviet government again came before the French Chamber of Deputies, but no decision was taken. A month later, in May, the Left bloc won the elections and Herriot succeeded Poincaré as premier. Some months later, on October 28, 1924, France too gave *de jure* recognition to the Soviet government.

The telegram by which Herriot informed the Commissariat of Foreign Affairs of the French decision proposed the immediate exchange of ambassadors and the initiation of negotiations of "a general character, and especially of an economic nature," but reserved the claims of the French state and its citizens pending an economic settlement.[83]

In interpreting the French action, Steklov noted in *Izvestiia:*

It has been remarked in the foreign press, especially the French press, that the French government's moves toward establishing normal relations with the Soviet republic seem to indicate that France desires to occupy the "vacant place" temporarily created by the [Soviet-]English political crisis.[84] If so, it would only prove the keen discernment of the French politicians, and also that they have finally fully realized the importance to France of renewing friendly relations with the Soviet Union.[85]

[81] For texts see Shapiro, I, under respective countries.

[82] This was the treaty of October 28, 1920, between the principal Allied powers and Rumania by which Rumanian sovereignty in Bessarabia was recognized. For details on the earlier Bessarabian situation, see our p. 33 n.

[83] *L'Humanité,* No. 7611, October 30, 1924, p. 1; see Document 82.

[84] A reference to the crisis caused by the Zinoviev letter; see our pp. 264–66.

[85] *Izvestiia,* No. 248, October 29, 1924, p. 1; see Document 83.

Another Soviet commentator interpreted the recognitions according to the dogma of capitalist antagonisms:

This means that in the future we shall be even better able than before to use, in the interests of the toilers of our Union and the world in general, the antagonisms among the imperialist powers. We have done this in the past, and not without success. It also means that now, advancing as a full-fledged member [of the international community] on the chessboard of international diplomacy, we shall be even better able than before to contrast, as events occur, our own political line of struggle with the imperialist line . . .[86]

Aloofness of the United States

The United States not only did not follow the European powers in recognizing the Soviets, but continued to criticize Soviet methods and practices. An official American proposal in August 1922, that an American Statistical Commission be sent to Russia to ascertain the possibility of negotiations, came to nothing when the Russian representative in the Far East, L. M. Karakhan, told the *New York Times* that the American government was sufficiently acquainted with conditions in Russia through the staff of the American Relief Administration, and that a visit of the nature proposed could only be acceptable on the basis of reciprocity.

On March 21, 1923, Secretary of State Hughes, in discussing recognition with a delegation of the Women's Committee for the Recognition of Russia, gave the State Department's position in these words:

As I said to the representatives of your organization a year ago, the fundamental question in the recognition of a government is whether it shows ability and a disposition to discharge its international obligations. Stability, of course, is important; stability is essential. Some speak as though stability was all that was necessary. What, however, would avail mere stability, if it were stability in the prosecution of a policy of repudiation and confiscation? In the case of Russia, we have a very easy test of a matter of fundamental importance, and that is of good faith in the discharge of international obligations . . . This is not a question of the rich or of the poor. It is a question of principle. . . .

Not only would it be a mistaken policy to give encouragement to repudiation and confiscation, but it is also important to remember that there should be no encouragement to those efforts of the Soviet authorities to visit upon other peoples the disasters that have overwhelmed the Russian people.

Hughes went on to quote statements made by Zinoviev, Lenin, and Trotsky the preceding fall in regard to world revolution, upon which he observed:

Now I desire to see evidences of the abandonment of that policy. I desire to see a basis for helpfulness. We want to help. We are just as anxious in this department and in every branch of the administration as you can possibly be, to promote peace in the world, to get rid of hatred, to have a spirit of mutual understanding, but the world we desire is a world not threatened with the destructive propaganda of the

---

[86] F. A. Rotshtein, "Kakaia polza ot priznaniia," *Pravda*, No. 59, March 12, 1924, p. 1; see Document 81.

Soviet authorities, and one in which there will be good faith and the recognition of obligations and a sound basis of international intercourse.[87]

On July 19, 1923, in a letter to Samuel Gompers, Hughes made the same points. He pointed out that the "legitimacy of a government as judged by former European standards" was not the issue, since "We recognize the right of revolution and we do not attempt to determine the internal concerns of other States." Calling recognition "an invitation to intercourse," he went on to say:

While this spirit of destruction at home and abroad remains unaltered the question of recognition by our Government of the authorities at Moscow cannot be determined by mere economic considerations or by the establishment in some degree of more prosperous conditions, which, of course, we should be glad to note, or simply by a consideration of the probable stability of the regime in question. There can be no intercourse among nations any more than among individuals except upon a general assumption of good faith.[88]

Speaking in the same month President Harding expressed a similar point of view:

International good faith forbids any sort of sanction of the Bolshevist policy. The property of American citizens in Russia, honestly acquired under the laws then existing, had been taken without the color of compensation, without process of law, by the mere emission of countless decrees. Such a policy challenges the very groundwork of righteous intercourse among peoples and rends the basis of good faith everywhere in the world.[89]

In December 1923, President Coolidge, in his message to the Congress, said of Russia:

Whenever there appears any disposition to compensate our citizens who were despoiled, and to recognize that debt contracted with our Government, not by the Czar, but by the newly formed Republic of Russia; whenever the active spirit of enmity to our institutions is abated; whenever there appear works mete [sic] for repentance; our country ought to be the first to go to the economic and moral rescue of Russia.[90]

On the basis of this speech by Mr. Coolidge, the Soviet government again suggested negotiations with the United States.[91] But Secretary Hughes rejected the suggestion, pointing out that if the Soviet government intended to comply with the American conditions, nothing prevented it from doing so, and that in the meantime no reason for negotiation existed.[92] Thereafter, Mr. Hughes became one of the favorite targets of Soviet jests and denunciations.

By way of reply to this American position, Chicherin declared Hughes to be simply the representative of "world reaction and world imperialism in the struggle against the colonial peoples." After excoriating Hughes for his "imperialist machinations," Chicherin concluded:

[87] *Foreign Relations of the United States, 1923,* II, 756–58.

[88] Full text, *ibid.,* pp. 760–64.

[89] *Speeches and Addresses of Warren G. Harding, President of the United States,* p. 377.

[90] *Foreign Relations of the United States, 1923,* I, ix; see Document 84a.

[91] Kliuchnikov and Sabanin, III, 294; see Document 84b.

[92] *Foreign Relations of the United States, 1923,* II, 788; see Document 84c.

New imperialist attempts at an international economic blockade of the U.S.S.R. in one or another form are quite possible in the near future. . . . Therefore, the Soviet government foresees the possibility of a new aggravation of international relations and a new threat to peace. The people must take the cause of peace into their own hands and bridle the audacious imperialists.[93]

This belief that new attacks against the Soviet Union might be forthcoming was also voiced by Zinoviev in a speech on Soviet foreign policy delivered at a meeting of the communist faction of the Second Congress of Soviets of the U.S.S.R. in February 1924:

I think that a combination of these two attitudes, i.e., of the greatest caution and maneuvering within the bourgeois encirclement, and of readiness for a sharp turn of events when the time comes and the struggle begins, . . . will provide the basis for our future international policy, and will correspond with what Vladimir Ilich taught us. . . . I believe that the Central Committee, which must now work without Vladimir Ilich, will continue to maneuver cautiously as regards the bourgeois encirclement, in order to prevent a war that we cannot possibly afford. At the same time, we must be quick to act and to attack when serious changes take place, changes such as we have already seen in Germany, Poland, Bulgaria, and such as may occur tomorrow in other countries, since the political and economic situation is unstable.[94]

The Soviet Government and the League of Nations

While seeking recognition from individual states, the Communists avoided even the appearance of recognizing what Chicherin called the "bourgeois consortium of capital," the League of Nations. The Soviet government went even further than the United States. In 1921 two members of the League's health commission established contact with the Soviet Commissariat of Health, which led to the participation of a Soviet representative in an All-European Sanitary Conference in Warsaw, March 20–28, 1922. The Soviet objection to recognizing the League was met by the pretense that a "special international commission" was meeting in the same place at the same time and with the same members as the League's health organization. The Soviet representative could participate in such a commission and the Soviet Health Commissariat could collaborate with representatives of the League so long as they were considered private persons.

The Communist Estimate of the Situation in 1924

Stalin, reviewing the Soviet international situation in June 1924, saw the period marked by the failure of attempts to isolate the Soviet Union and by an enormous increase in Soviet prestige. He attributed these developments to the impotence of the imperialist powers and their conflicts among themselves; the consolidation of Soviet power within Russia; and the increasing influence of the Soviet Union among the masses in the capitalist countries.[95]

[93] *Izvestiia*, No. 220, September 26, 1924, p. 2; see Document 85.
[94] *Pravda*, No. 29, February 6, 1924, p. 4. Zinoviev apparently referred to the changes following the German events of 1923 described above, the assassination of the newly elected President of Poland in December 1922, and the popular disturbances and subsequent assassination of Premier Stamboliisky in Bulgaria in 1923.
[95] Stalin, *Sochineniia*, VI, 235–39; see Document 86.

In a speech delivered on the tenth anniversary of the outbreak of World War I, Trotsky summed up the Soviet attitude toward the international situation as follows: The defeat of the German revolution marked the opening of a new period in which democratic-reformist-pacifist elements in bourgeois society had temporarily assumed leadership in Western Europe. These elements were themselves but the servants of the new "masters of capitalist humanity"—the United States of America. America would attempt to place Europe on a "ration" in order to maintain the privileged position of its own workers, and thus "every success of Americanism . . . will prepare the ground for the growth of Bolshevism in a more centralized and more revolutionary form, and on a tremendously large scale."[96]

[96] Trotsky, "K voprosu o perspektivakh mirovogo razvitiia," *Izvestiia*, No. 177, August 5, 1924, pp. 3–4; see Document 87.

DOCUMENTS

THE INTERNATIONAL SITUATION AND THE NEED TO WIN THE MASSES

54
Chicherin on the International Situation

[Speech at an Improvised Meeting at the Station of Sebezh on His Way to Moscow from the Lausanne Conference, February 1923][1]

The Concentration and Cartelization of Capital

If I am to sum up the results of my recent observations abroad, speaking generally I must say that the most important feature of the present period is the concentration and cartelization of capital on an international scale. In some countries the process of concentration had already been greatly advanced. Now we find behind the scenes, as a constant motive force, a struggle for an international alliance of the national trusts and for their growth beyond national frontiers. . . .

The ruined middle and petty bourgeoisie and the increasingly impoverished bourgeois intelligentsia plunge into the extremest chauvinism, and create a heated political atmosphere. . . . Their furious activity creates an impression that war is ever near, and, within certain limits, may even lead to direct military action. But there is no immediate danger of a new world war. The motive power for a world war can only be a fundamental antagonism between leading economic groups, and these groups are as yet a long way from being that antagonistic.

The situation was different before the last war. At that time, large industry supported militarism while the petty bourgeoisie supported pacifism; but now, as a rule, large industry is the upholder of pacifism, and the petty bourgeoisie, at least its ruined section, has become the main prop of militaristic and ultra-chauvinistic tendencies.

Relations Between France and Germany

Diplomatic life in Western Europe is based on the triangular relations of England, France, and Germany. The Anglo-French world antagonism is by no means fully developed. And yet this antagonism permeates all current diplomatic relations. Among the most important questions between France and Germany is that of their economic rapprochement, of the agreement to be reached between the industrial capitalists of the two countries. This interesting example of a tendency toward international cartelization deserves close attention. In reparations, it has meant economic agreements regarding payments in kind. But it goes much further. The France of today differs considerably from prewar France; her developed industrial capital is gaining ever-increasing influence over her politics. . . . [This capital] requires markets; it requires economic relations with other countries. The Treaty of Versailles gave France a surplus of iron; she needs Germany for working up this iron. Negotiations with regard to contracts, trusts, and cartels have already been

---

[1] *Pravda*, No. 34, February 15, 1923, p. 1; also *International Press Correspondence*, No. 8, March 1, 1923, pp. 113–14.

carried on between a number of French and German industrial concerns. These efforts, and the growing influence of industrial capital, were the cause of the French attempt, particularly toward the end of last year, to resume official commercial relations with Russia. . . .

The Ruhr Adventure

The Ruhr adventure, which has shaken all Europe's political and economic life to its foundation and has thus been extremely harmful to the soviet republics, which need economic relations with other countries, is bound up in a most complicated manner with various tendencies within French industry itself. The bourgeoisie, of course, preserves the customary sacred unity against the national enemy, but the industrial periodical, *Journée Industrielle*, is already openly expressing its dissatisfaction with the Ruhr policy. This policy, which is impoverishing Germany, brings no advantage to France, for France cannot utilize the wealth of the Ruhr area without German aid. Thus the policy leads indirectly to the further impoverishment of France, and injures her industry. . . .

The Ruhr question is at the same time bound up with one of the most important points of contact between French and German industry. It is a well-known fact that French heavy industry, possessing the ore [of Lorraine], requires the coke of the Ruhr; and that German heavy industry, if to a lesser degree, requires French iron. Many people have been inclined to attribute the long-planned occupation of the Ruhr to France's desire to lay her hands on needed coke, which—it may be observed—she cannot produce without the organizational help of the Germans. However, even the secret report of Dariac, the chairman of the finance committee of the Chamber of Deputies, which created such a sensation when it was published by the *Manchester Guardian* in November, being regarded as the clearest expression of French aggressive designs, recommended nothing more than preparations to separate the left bank of the Rhine from Germany. But while urging French heavy industry to form a cartel with German heavy industry, this report goes no further than to demand the retention of the bridgeheads occupied in 1921 (Düsseldorf and Duisburg).

It is known that shortly before the Ruhr adventure the Poincaré government prevented previously planned negotiations between representatives of French and German heavy industry, apparently for fear that control of reparations might slip out of government hands. Despite this, industrial magnates of the two countries opened communication with one another, and the demands from the French side were spoken of as too high. But though the formation of a cartel with German industry could be enormously profitable to the industry of eastern France, it might wreck other undertakings—those in Normandy, for example.

It is possible that this mutual tendency toward a peaceful understanding [between France and Germany] will not gain the upper hand at once; it is extremely difficult to find a way out of the crisis while the French government insists on its reparations demands and the German government insists on the evacuation of the Ruhr before opening negotiations. But it is highly probable that the Ruhr adventure will form only an episode in the cartelization of the two countries' industries. So long as the suffering German masses are given to nationalist feelings, so long will the Right gain advantage from the extremity of the crisis. At the same time, the whole of Europe is suffering from the consequences of this adventure.

The Waiting Policy of England and America

English intervention, or rather joint intervention by England and America, would lead to an immediate reconciliation; but both powers continue to watch and wait. The political and economic rapprochement of these two states is one of the most important political facts of today. Under the leadership of the present Conservative government, England is taking a much greater interest in her colonies and dominions than in the past, and is investing capital in them. However, a great number of English banks are still closely connected with the Continent, and a considerable section in German economic circles still follows England. Many Frenchmen believe that England, by a variety of skillful maneuvers, forced France to take the Ruhr plunge, and is now gaining time (and amusement) by leaving France in this difficult situation. The same Frenchmen would not be at all surprised to hear that England simultaneously instigated Germany's resistance.

The Antagonism Between England and France

The Ruhr question, like the Lausanne Conference, increased the tension between England and France to actual hate, although these world competitors are at the same time highly dependent on one another. The interrupted Lausanne Conference is bound to be followed by a period of very active secret diplomacy and an increased struggle between France and England. . . .

Soviet Russia Is the Only True Friend of the Oppressed Peoples

Simultaneously with the international cartelization of capital, but poles apart from it, an emancipation of the peoples oppressed by capitalism is proceeding. The numerous delegations of the Eastern nations at Lausanne saw in the soviet republics their sole true friend, and this alliance became closer and closer in the course of the conference. Many of the native newspapers in the East traced Turkey's diplomatic success at Lausanne to the diplomatic support of the soviet republics, the presence of whose delegates lent firm security to Turkey up to the end of the conference. The soviet republics played their historic part as the friends of all oppressed peoples, all peoples whose existence is in danger, or who are threatened by attack.

The Straits Question Remains Unsolved

The continuous vacillation of French policy at Lausanne was doubtless the result of Anglo-French conflicts on the Ruhr question. Thanks to our attitude, the conviction spread in French political circles during the conference that opening the Straits to foreign warships—that is, the surrender of the Black Sea to England— would be disadvantageous to France. France, Italy, and Turkey are all still bound by their previous agreements on this question. But even should the diplomatic negotiations with Turkey lead to a general treaty, and should the Straits convention worked out at Lausanne, which is unacceptable to us, actually be signed, this convention will not exist for long. This is openly stated not only by some Turkish journalists, but also by the French and the Italians.

Without Russia There Is No World Politics

The situation is thus one of unheard-of complexity, and the position of Soviet diplomacy is, as a consequence, also very complex. While being especially concerned with the security of our frontiers, our coasts, and the means of access to our coasts, and while at the same time opposing everything that might endanger general peace, and while also defending the oppressed and threatened peoples, we must not for a moment forget our most pressing actual task—i.e., the liquidation of the blockade against the soviet republics, which has not yet been completely raised, and the complete clearing of the way to unhampered economic relations with all countries. While being constantly on guard, we dare not let a single detail of the daily play of world antagonisms escape us, for there can be no world politics without Russia and her allies, and there is no longer a single international problem toward which Russia and her allies can adopt a neutral attitude.

55

The Threat of a New War

[Editorial by Iu. M. Steklov in *Izvestiia*][2]

. . .

There are at least four inflammatory points from which a world conflagration may be kindled. They are: the Balkans again—the eternal Balkans, which have served as material for conflicts since the nineteenth century; the Ruhr basin, occupied by the French; the Memel territory seized by Lithuania; and finally, Poland, which has added new fuel to the old embers scattered by the world vultures, embers ready to catch fire at any moment.

So far we have spoken only of immediate causes of conflicts. We have not mentioned the underlying factors, continually at work, which tend toward future world wars. We have not named the old competitive quarrel between Japan and the United States, the similar competition between England and the United States, the increasing antagonism between France and England, and so forth, and so forth. . . . Under certain circumstances these causes of conflict can remain under the surface for a long time yet, and need not necessarily exercise a destructive force. But for these factors to suddenly display their full force, and quickly transform a local conflict into a world-wide conflict, only some trivial incident in one of the areas mentioned is required.

The fire in the Balkans has not yet burned out. The Lausanne Conference failed to solve the Near Eastern question. The danger of new conflicts in the Balkans continues to exist. In addition, the conflagration has recently spread over a larger area. Aside from the campaign against Turkish emancipation, we see fresh flames springing up on the Hungarian frontier. Making full use of the confusion created by the French occupation of the Ruhr, the Hungarian White Guard has decided that the moment for revenge has arrived, and consequently the possibility of armed conflict in Central Europe has arisen. Rumania has already declared that a state of war exists on the Hungarian frontier. The states of the Little Entente are mobilizing their troops. A conflict is developing into which Czechoslovakia, Yugoslavia, Hungary, Rumania, Poland, and perhaps Italy, which is anxious for an opportunity to settle with Yugoslavia, may be drawn.

But of all the recent events, the occupation of the Ruhr basin by the French militarists is the most likely to unleash the hounds of world war. This occupation has created the utmost tension everywhere. And should this dangerous situation lead to a serious struggle, the struggle will affect the interests of the soviet republics to the greatest extent.

Germany's complete suppression would clearly constitute the greatest danger for Soviet Russia. It would have the effect (1) of rendering French imperialism the immediate neighbor of Soviet Russia (and it must be remembered that the hostile activity of French imperialism toward Soviet Russia has never abated), and (2) of increasing the possibility of a new war of intervention, which would find willing and malicious support from our nearest neighbors, White Poland and Rumania.

The political equilibrium of Eastern Europe depends upon the attitude adopted by Poland in the approaching conflict. . . . The Polish imperialists do not attempt to conceal their plans to seize Russian as well as German soil. Furthermore, they are endeavoring to break up the united federation of soviet socialist republics into states at odds with one another, and to place some of these states, such as Belorussia and the Ukraine, under their direct influence . . .

[2] *Izvestiia*, No. 14, January 21, 1923, p. 1; also *International Press Correspondence*, No. 6, February 15, 1923, p. 83.

It is now clear why the Polish delegates at the Moscow Conference on Disarmament[3] (with the support of the Baltic states, it may be observed) rejected our peace motion and refused to adopt a policy for a real reduction of armaments. Leaving the limitation of armaments solely to Soviet Russia, her neighbors, especially Poland, think of nothing but how to increase their armed forces for aggressive purposes. The Polish militarists, while making belligerent plans that may once more plunge Eastern Europe into bloody chaos, are taking into consideration the reduction of the Red Army.

We have actually reduced our army very considerably, and we are continuing to reduce it. According to the decision of the last congress of soviets, the standing workers' and peasants' army is to be reduced to 600,000 men. It is unnecessary to remark, however, that the Soviet power, while reducing its armed forces, has not for a moment lost sight of the possibility that its enemies might start a war. The reduction of the army has naturally been accompanied by various measures for mobilizing the required armed forces at any time. Thus [we have] available a force capable of repulsing any attack. . . .

The Soviet republic wants peace. This it has proved not by words alone, but by deeds. But Soviet Russia does not intend to let herself be attacked without retaliation, nor is she incapable of returning blow for blow. It is precisely with the desire to preserve peace that we issue this warning to the treacherous elements so anxious to utilize the present moment for new war adventures, for new threats against our internal and external interests. We hope that our warning will be heard and understood. If not, so much the worse for those who do not want to hear!

56

Moscow's Determination to Win the Masses

[Excerpts from the "Theses on the Tactics of the Communist International" adopted by the Fourth Congress of the Communist International, November 5–December 5, 1922][4]

. . .

Now, even more than at the time of the Third Congress, it is necessary to state that in view of the present temporary stabilization of bourgeois society an intense crisis may arise quite unexpectedly in connection with a large-scale strike, a colonial uprising, a new war, or even a parliamentary crisis. Consequently the "subjective factor," i.e., the degree of class-consciousness and readiness for the struggle of the working class and its vanguard, as well as their degree of organization, acquires a tremendous significance.

To get hold of the majority of the working class in America and Europe—that has been and is the task of the Communist International. As far as the colonial and semicolonial countries are concerned, the Communist International must fulfill the following two tasks:

1. To create a center for the communist parties which will represent the interests of the world proletariat as a whole;

2. To support by every available means the national-revolutionary movement directed against imperialism, to become a vanguard of this movement, and to awaken and develop within this national movement a social movement also.

All these enumerated points go to show that united-front tactics must be adopted. The slogan of the Third Congress, "To the Masses," is more relevant now than ever

[3] See Part II, p. 112.
[4] *Kommunisticheskii Internatsional v dokumentakh*, pp. 299–300.

before. In many countries the struggle to form a proletarian united front is just beginning. . . .

Reformists need a schism. But the Communists are interested in unifying all the forces of the working class against capital.

The communist vanguard must apply united front tactics to the everyday struggle of the masses for their closest daily interests. To carry on this struggle, the Communists are even prepared to negotiate with the traitor leaders of the Social Democrats and the Amsterdamians. . . .

The tactics of the united front are no less than an offer by the Communists to struggle jointly with workers who belong to different parties or groups, and with the nonparty workers, to defend the daily interests of the working class against the bourgeoisie.

Every action undertaken for the sake of some insignificant daily need will promote revolutionary enlightenment and revolutionary education, because it is this experience gained in the struggle that will convince the toilers of the inevitability of the revolution and of the significance of communism. . . .

RELATIONS WITH GERMANY: RAPALLO AND THE SECRET AGREEMENTS

57
Soviet Denial of Secret Clauses
[Chicherin to M. Barthou, April 29, 1922][5]

Sir,—In the comments of the French press, and in the declarations of the heads of the French government, the treaty between Russia and Germany, which was negotiated several months ago at Berlin and was signed at Rapallo, is interpreted as an act directed against the interests of France. The assumption has been repeatedly expressed that the Treaty of Rapallo was supplemented by secret clauses of a military and political nature, clauses that would reveal Russia's aggressive intentions toward France or her allies.

The Russian delegation declares in the most categorical manner that the Rapallo agreement contains no secret military or political clause and is accompanied by no such clause, and that the Russian government is not engaged in any undertaking whatever directed against the interests of the French or any other nation.

The sole purpose of the Rapallo treaty was to liquidate questions pending between two states that have been at war, both of which feel the need to re-establish peaceful relations in their own interests and in the interests of the whole of humanity.

Far from being directed against France or any other power, this treaty is from the Russian government's point of view simply the first of a series of individual agreements which, in the opinion of the Russian delegation, should complement the general agreement toward which the powers assembled at Genoa are striving. These agreements should serve as a basis for peace and equilibrium in the world. So far as France in particular is concerned, the Russian government considers that there are many points of contact between the interests of the two countries which will facilitate agreement on all the questions at issue between them. . . .

Believe me, this letter is only dictated by a sincere desire to dissipate any misunderstandings that might have impeded the normal progress of the Genoa Conference.

Please accept (etc.)

CHICHERIN

[5] *Materialy genuezskoi konferentsii*, pp. 327–28.

58

Soviet Evaluation of the Rapallo Treaty a Quarter of a Century Later[6]

The Treaty of Rapallo blocked the attempt of the Entente to create a united capitalist front against Soviet Russia. The plan for reconstructing Europe at the expense of the defeated countries and Soviet Russia collapsed. Soviet diplomacy won a victory because it followed the direct instructions of Lenin, who said: "It is necessary to be able to make use of the contradictions and differences among the capitalists. If we had not followed this plan, we would have been hanged long ago on separate trees, much to the enjoyment of capitalists." [Lenin, *Sochineniia*, XXV, 498.]

The diplomacy of the Entente, which was directed toward bringing Soviet Russia to her knees, and which removed the question of German reparations from the agenda [of the Genoa Conference], considering it already settled, suffered complete defeat, while both the signatories of the Rapallo treaty derived considerable political advantage from it. The treaty put an end to the disputed questions of the past. In place of the Brest-Litovsk treaty, based on violence, the Rapallo treaty created new relations, which ensured to both states complete equality and a chance for peaceful economic co-operation.

The political significance of the Rapallo treaty was defined in three basic points: first, the mutual annulment of all claims; second, the re-establishment of diplomatic relations between Germany and Russia (next to the Baltic states and the Eastern powers, Germany was the first power to enter into normal diplomatic relations with Soviet Russia); and third, the economic rapprochement between Russia and Germany, which ended their isolation. This last point both broke the economic blockade around Soviet Russia and gave Germany a chance to develop her commerce.

59

Radek's Contact with the German Nationalists During His Imprisonment in Berlin in 1919–20

[Excerpt from Radek's Reminiscences][7]

. . . [Walter] Rathenau came without any preliminary warning. I knew him only by his books and by his activity as chairman of the board of the Allgemeine Elektrizitäts-Gesellschaft, and as an organizer of the supply of raw material for Germany during the war. Later on, when he was Germany's foreign minister, I had occasion to meet him many times and had a chance to form an opinion of his exceedingly complicated nature. . . .

[Radek was also visited by his old friend Mur, a socialist who came from an aristocratic Austrian family and had maintained old connections with the German military and other influential people.]

Old Mur brought to me Baron Reibnitz, a fellow student of Ludendorff's at the Military Academy. Reibnitz was the first representative from the group later known as "national Bolsheviks," with whom I was to deal. In officers' circles he advocated not only an alliance with Soviet Russia, but also the so-called peaceful revolution. He believed that Germany could not re-establish its productive forces without na-

---

[6] V. P. Potemkin (ed.), *Istoriia diplomatii*, III, 181.

[7] *Krasnaia Nov*, No. 10, October 1926, pp. 164–66, 169–71.

tionalizing its industries and setting up factory committees to draw the proletariat into the task of organizing the industries. While the workers were helping organize production, the organized proletariat and intelligentsia were to launch a moral revolution, aimed at forcing the owning classes to give up their property in return for a certain remuneration. He implored me to write in this vein, referring to Lenin's April 1918 speech to the Soviet government dealing with its tasks of the day. This speech, which had appeared in Germany, had greatly affected one section of bourgeois public opinion. I pointed out to Baron Reibnitz that Lenin had made his speech after power had been assumed [by the Bolsheviks], and suggested that he keep on persuading the bourgeoisie that it should capitulate, while we, the Communists, would take charge of providing the "pressure" by the working class. . . .

Soon Comrade Kopp arrived in Berlin, and in the guise of a [Soviet] plenipotentiary to conduct negotiations regarding war prisoners, he settled down as a semilegal [Soviet] ambassador . . . Kopp began to look for a way of releasing me. . . .

Meanwhile our negotiations with Estonia had been started, and I was appointed by the Soviet government a member of the peace delegation to Estonia. But how was I to get there? . . . Suddenly I received information from a Jesuit priest, who had been released from prison together with Archbishop Kropp, that Pilsudski and we [the Soviet government] had signed a secret agreement on the basis of which Poland promised to let me through. But the Germans did not believe it until they received an appropriate telegram from Warsaw. I was then allowed to move on to the private apartment of Baron Reibnitz, from which I was to start on my journey. . . .

When Baron Reibnitz asked me the next morning whether I had any objection to having Colonel Bauer, the chief of German artillery in the war and first adviser to Ludendorff, breakfast with us, I naturally replied that I had not. In the dining room I met a man who moved like a cat and was absolutely lacking in military bearing. We began to talk about the internal and foreign situation in Germany. A few days before, the parliamentary commission of the Reichstag had discussed the reasons for the delay [in the peace negotiations]. Ludendorff had cursed the parliamentarians. Referring to Ludendorff's attack, I told Bauer that I was under the impression that a *coup d'état* was being engineered [in Germany]. Bauer replied that they had not even thought of it. Ludendorff thought it would be very easy to get hold of the government, but then the railways would stop functioning. It was impossible now to rule against the will of the workers of Germany. One had to wait until bourgeois democracy had disillusioned the workers and convinced them that the "dictatorship of labor" in Germany was possible only if an agreement were made between the working class and the officers. He gave me to understand that on this basis a business agreement was possible between the officers, on one hand, and the Communist Party [of Germany] and Soviet Russia, on the other. They [the officers] realized that we were invincible, and that we were Germany's allies in the struggle against the Entente. . . . I pointed out to Bauer that only the German Central Committee could speak for the German Communist Party, and that negotiations with the Soviet government could be carried on only in Moscow. Bauer left.

[Radek was then visited by Ernst Heilman, one of the leaders of the German Socialist Party, and also by Stampfer, editor of *Vorwärts*.]

The technicalities regarding my transit through Poland dragged on. In order not to abuse the hospitality of Baron Reibnitz, who was not used to such disarrangement in his apartment as I had made, I was obliged to move to the apartment of the police commissar, Gustav Schmidt, where I stayed for several days. There in the hall sat a detective chewing pastilles made of potato. I began to talk to him about his financial situation, which was naturally very bad, and soon I had the fellow in my pocket; he brought me a leather suit and a large Mauser from the police supplies.

He was obliged to put down the names of my visitors, but was satisfied with the list that I myself gave him. He was very much shaken when my first visitor in the new apartment proved to be the former foreign minister, Rear-Admiral Hintze.

Hintze is a man of small stature, elegant, and with the immovable face of a Chinese. He made a strong impression upon me. Here was a man who was deeply shaken by the situation in Germany. He told me at length about the mood of the workers in Silesia, where he had an estate. He had talked to the men there, and he interpreted the revolution in terms of workers merely refusing to work for the capitalists. The Catholic workers told him about the injustices of the capitalist system and about the necessity of organizing life anew. They hated the bourgeoisie. Germany [he said] would hardly rise to her feet again unless she changed her political system. He favored an agreement with Soviet Russia and declared that he would like to see our present conditions with his own eyes. . . .

Rathenau brought the chief director of the Allgemeine Elektrizitäts-Gesellschaft, old and intelligent Felix Deutsch, who had old connections with Russia and knew the Russian industrial world very well. Deutsch was very skeptical about the possibility of any regime except the capitalist one.

60

Secret Transactions Between German and Soviet Representatives in the Early Twenties

[Account Based on General von Seeckt's Personal Papers][8]

By the end of September, 1921, on the basis of the trade agreement, confidential negotiations were begun with Krasin concerning the reconstruction of the Russian armament industry with German co-operation. The negotiations, even though rather open, were, as a rule, conducted in private residences, at first also in the home of [General] von Schleicher. The actual transactions lay essentially in the hands of [General] von Hasse. They were the result less of a Russian predilection for Germany than of Russia's aversion to letting England interfere in her economic life.

.   .   .

The year 1921 had not brought the Russians as much progress as they might have hoped for. Relief undertakings against the famine had not proved very successful. A committee of the League of Nations made up by England and France conferred on the extension of credit to Russia. However, it never got beyond conferring. The motives prompting a quest for suitable trade relations with Berlin were therefore strengthened. In a personal interview between Seeckt and Radek a remarkable discussion ensued. Radek, undoubtedly acting upon instructions, tried to bargain with Seeckt for German participation in an attack on Poland. Seeckt refused unequivocally, because such co-operation would necessarily bring about an immediate war with France and Czechoslovakia. He recommended, however, to the Chancellor, as he had before in the Russo-Polish war, a neutrality friendly to Russia. Radek, on the other hand, was obviously striving for a more narrowly defined military agreement. In Moscow great attention was centered on the reconstruction of the army; assistance was hoped for not only in rebuilding the armament industry but also in strengthening and improving the officers' training corps. To this Seeckt frankly replied that the common purposes of Germany and Russia lay only in the future.

.   .   .

[8] Hans von Rabenau (ed.), *H. von Seeckt, aus seinem Leben, 1918–1936,* pp. 308–9, 319.

During an interview on June 19, 1922, Chicherin calmly declared, with what one might be tempted to call naïve outspokenness, that Russia had ratified the Treaty of Rapallo so readily because of her designs on Poland. Conferences between the high command and Russia were prolonged into the closing months of 1922. When Cuno succeeded Wirth, Seeckt, on November 23, acquainted the new Chancellor very candidly with his Eastern projects. Perhaps he did this because already in the first week of September he had made a report to Ebert on his transactions with the Russians. Moreover, Cuno had promised collaboration in the spirit of the Treaty of Rapallo.

Radek's view of the world differed radically from Seeckt's; yet in a discussion on December 19—again in Schleicher's home—he held forth on the possibilities of aligning the most heterogeneous elements of the entire world for the benefit of Russia and Germany.

In 1925 Seeckt conferred personally with Chicherin once more.

61

Seeckt on the Russian Problem

[Excerpts from Letters to General von Hasse and Chancellor Wirth, 1922][9]

. . . It seems to me that in Berlin a belated fear of the Rapallo agreement is rising. I am less concerned with its material aspects than with its moral effect. It is the first, though very considerable, strengthening of German prestige in the world at large. This is so because more is read into the document than actually is warranted. No politico-military agreements exist, but the possibility of their existence is firmly believed in. . . .

The very fact that the Rapallo treaty has placed us under suspicion of having achieved this accretion of power, without commitments on our side, is the paramount and inestimable value of this agreement. . . . We are striving for two things: (1) to strengthen Russia economically and politically, and thereby indirectly strengthen ourselves by building up a potential ally; and (2) to strengthen ourselves directly, at first cautiously and with circumspection, by helping Russia build an armament industry that would be useful to us in case of need. The German government cannot participate in or even officially recognize all these still largely preliminary transactions; they can only be conducted through military channels. That they [military authorities] should not reach agreements binding for the Reich without the knowledge of the politically responsible offices is, of course, a foregone conclusion. As long as the German government does not act officially, the German embassy in Moscow is not the proper place for transactions. The embassy, of course, is not to counteract the efforts outlined; it should secretly be in harmony with the adopted policy. Anyone who is still rooted in the days of Versailles and clings to the idea that Germany has foregone all "imperialistic and military" aspirations—that is to say, without demagogic verbiage, that she has forever renounced an active policy— is not suitable to represent German interests in Russia, or perhaps anywhere else. It is obvious that Germany today is not in a position to offer resistance to France. Our policy is to pave the way for a future chance of doing so. France's crossing Germany to come to the assistance of Poland remains a military monstrosity so long as Germany does not voluntarily co-operate. That concept stems from the trend of our diplomatic thought of 1919; since then three years have passed. A Franco-Russian war on the Rhine is a political bugaboo for children. Germany will not be bolshevized, not even by an understanding with Russia in foreign affairs.

[9] *Ibid.*, pp. 313, 317–18.

62
Soviet-German Co-operation in Producing Poison Gas
[General V. N. Ipatieff's Recollections][10]

. . . During the summer [1923] we learned that the German government had sent to the U.S.S.R. a special commission composed of experts on military supplies and armaments, officers of the General Staff, and representatives of the Commissariat of Finance, to study Russian munition factories and to work out satisfactory agreements on the co-operative manufacture of guns and poison gases. A special commission headed by Rosengolts, who was head of the Aviation Administration, was set up in Moscow to confer with the German delegation. . . .

I heard of the German commission's arrival when I was called to a meeting of the Chief Committee on Concessions and there met the entire delegation. Those of us who were connected with war supplies were to inform the German delegates of Russian developments in this field. As I remember it, Bittker, who spoke German, was chairman. The Germans had elected Dr. Stolzenberg, a member during the war of a German war chemical organization headed by Professor Haber, to supervise construction of plants for producing poison gases. . . . After the meeting, Bogdanov asked me to work on this mixed commission on the production of poison gases . . . I received further orders to join a commission to inspect the Samara plant, about thirty miles from the city of Samara. This factory, though started during the war, had never been operated. If possible it was to be used for the production of chlorine and, later, for phosgene. It had been built by the Ushkov Company, whose chief director was Schein. . . . The commission [was] sent to inspect it . . .

Our problem was the serious one of appraising the factory building and equipment and estimating how they could be put into operation. The War Technical Administration needed the information before the Russian and German governments could decide the amount of money required for their joint project. The greater the value of our original investment, the more the Germans would have to invest. They were, therefore, on the commission to check our estimates and to determine operating costs for Germany . . . Our final total appraisal [was] approximately 6,000,000 rubles . . . but Stolzenberg's figure was considerably less.

[Ipatieff was sent to Germany to see Stolzenberg's plant.] . . .

During this visit to Germany, I was invited by the War Ministry to meet certain high military officials. . . . My visit to it [the War Ministry] was very secret, and I went there and back in a closed military car. . . .

Back in Moscow . . . the conferences with the German delegates continued for some months before the final contract was signed, the major cause of delay being the relative sums to be furnished by each government. Besides reconstructing the plant proper, an additional one had to be built and the German-supplied equipment installed. The German government awarded Stolzenberg the contract for rebuilding the Samara plant, and a special technical-economic commission subordinated to the Revolutionary War Council was formed to supervise the construction. Its members were Galperin, another Party member, myself, and two German military representatives. . . .

Before Dr. Stolzenberg was given the contract to erect the plant, he wrote me a letter saying that after the ratification of the agreement he would donate 500,000 marks to establish a fund, which might be deposited in Sweden, for scientific investigation in the field of poison gases and gas masks. . . . He never mentioned the 500,000-mark donation again, though his contract was most favorable.

· · ·

[10] V. N. Ipatieff, *The Life of a Chemist,* pp. 382–88, 399, 423, 468.

Most of my time in 1924 was spent on the Russian-German Commission constructing poison-gas factories . . .

In 1926 . . . the Russian-German Commission on the production of poison gases was very time-consuming. . . .

Toward the end of 1928 our negotiations with the Germans finally broke down. As I had long suspected, Stolzenberg's method of making yperite and phosgene was very doubtful, and it proved impossible to put the plant into operation. With the departure of the Germans the responsibility of the work fell to the Russian members of the commission. . . .

63

Soviet Explanation of Soviet-German Military Co-operation[11]

Through the efforts of the German Social Democratic lackeys of the Entente, an important English liberal news organ let out a fat newspaper canard which, having visited the backyards of different European editorial offices, flopped down heavily at some unknown place, and, so it seems, breathed its last. The sensation was short-lived, but we must say it was brilliant while it lasted, because there were some feathers on this bird which could provide an illusion of truth.

It seems that on the territory of our Union, and in accordance with an agreement between our war ministry and the German war ministry, some German firms constructed some works three years ago that now produce material needed for our defense. This material includes aeroplanes, poison gas, ammunition, and so forth.

We are not admitted into the secrets of our war ministry, and we do not know whether this information agrees with the actual facts. Supposing this information to be correct, it is in itself of little significance.

If we give foreigners concessions to construct factories and produce articles needed by our consumers, why should we forbid, or even fail to encourage, foreigners to open factories and works that we need for our defense? On the other hand, as far as we can ascertain from the Versailles treaty, Germany is forbidden to produce munitions at home or import them, but her firms are not forbidden to open factories or works abroad, including those which produce aeroplanes and munitions.

However, if the bird in question had been dressed up [only] in the colors described above, perhaps she would not even have been able to fly, and could only have aroused general mirth. This fact being fully noted by those who created the bird, they added to its decoration something else: Only a fraction of the ammunition that has been and is still being produced by the works in question goes to the defense of the Soviet Union; the large part of it is sent to Germany!

Not long ago, so it is said, six ships fully loaded with these nice things went from Leningrad to Stettin. In other words, these factories work for the German Reichswehr and German Black Hundreds, circumventing in this way the Versailles restrictions, and actually serving the cause of the monarchist and nationalist reactionaries of Germany!

The venerable *Vorwärts* reprints this nonsense from the English newspaper . . . and pathetically questions the Communists and workers: "Do you realize where the bullets and the guns that are used against you come from?" So it comes about that it is not "bloodhounds" such as Noske, not the Social Democrats, but the U.S.S.R., the country of the victorious revolution, that is the ally and the helper of the reactionary forces who are strangling the [German] workers' movement.

"Refrain from laughter, friends," said a certain Roman poet. However, considering these communications copied from the English newspaper not sufficiently

[11] *Pravda*, No. 291, December 16, 1926, p. 1.

significant, the organ of the [German] Social Democrats provides additional data, borrowed from the "report" of the Soviet ambassador in Berlin, Comrade Krestinsky, who said [according to *Vorwärts*] that the two delegates coming to Moscow from Königsberg should be given specially cordial attention because they belonged to the conservative and nationalist group, and that the rest of the delegates should be treated with corresponding and gradually lessening attention.

We have always supposed that German Social Democrats, and in particular their leaders, had a certain connection with the artists who specialize in the fabrication of anti-Soviet falsifications. Now *Vorwärts* has proved it. . . .

The disgusting position taken by these slanderers against their own fatherland, which they so enthusiastically defended during the imperialist slaughter, does not interest us at this point. What concerns us at present is the accusation directed against us: that we are helping German reaction and German chauvinists; that we are helping Germany to arm herself for revenge, and for future war against yesterday's victors. In a word, that we are the most dangerous foe of democracy and European peace.

These new "proofs" of our "Red imperialism" and our treacherous attitude are actually needed at present by the bourgeois governments because of the feverish armament of our own neighbors, and because a special effort is being made to isolate and to weaken us.

[*Pravda* then refers to a press report of the shipping of munitions from Italy to Rumania and from Greece to Poland.]

But when it becomes necessary to disguise these activities as a bugaboo of Soviet imperialism, the thief's method is resorted to—namely, [his] participation in the efforts of others to catch him. Thus the obliging *Vorwärts* proves through fabrications (and perhaps a number of fabrications) that it is the Soviet Union that is threatening the peace by constructing ammunition works with the help of German firms, and in collusion with the German Reichswehr . . . and by having almost signed a secret military alliance with the German government. The English paper, which we mentioned earlier, actually states that a secret military convention exists between our government and the German war ministry.

Meanwhile, the *Berliner Tageblatt*, which has undertaken to deny the allegations, has found nothing better to say in defense of its own government than an equally untrue statement—namely, that a few years ago the Soviet government offered a military alliance [to Germany]. Of course there is no such alliance, either planned or actual; but one had to be invented to support the lie about the mutual services rendered by our war ministry and the German war ministry.

All in all, we believe that German democracy has well earned its bread from the Entente, and that it deserves a Nobel prize next year, since this year the prize has already been awarded to someone equally deserving.[12]

64
Bukharin on Military Alliance with Bourgeois States

[Excerpt from Speech at the Fourth Congress of the Communist International on Its New Program, November 18, 1922][13]

. . .

The question is this: From the standpoint of strategic usefulness to the proletariat as a whole, can a proletarian state sign military alliances with bourgeois states?

[12] Stresemann and Briand were awarded the Nobel Peace Prize in 1926.
[13] *IV Vsemirnyi Kongress K.I.*, pp. 195–96.

Here there is no difference in principle between a loan and a military alliance; and I affirm that we have already grown up enough to conclude a military alliance with the bourgeoisie of one country so as to be able, with its help, to crush the bourgeoisie of another country. One can always take into account the consequences of this or that correlation of forces. This is purely a question of strategic and tactical expediency. That is how we should present it in our program.

If the defense of the country and military alliance with bourgeois states are presented in this form, then the duty of the comrades in every country will be to assist the success of such a bloc. If, in the future, the bourgeoisie of an allied country is itself defeated, then new tasks will arise. (Laughter.) However, there is no need for me to outline them here; you will understand them yourselves without difficulty. . . .

THE RUHR OCCUPATION AND THE GERMAN "OCTOBER"

65

Soviet Reaction to the Occupation of the Ruhr[14]

Radio communiqués from various places describe the beginning of the occupation of the Ruhr region by French troops. . . .

A long occupation is unthinkable, since it would mean both the complete economic breakdown of Germany and a tremendous strengthening of France, both politically and economically. Britain and America do not want France strengthened, and because of the correlation of forces and interests among these countries, they will have their way.

Hence there can be only a temporary occupation, to put pressure on Germany. Moreover, if the French government were to succeed in carrying out its threat [of occupation], it would mean a complete shake-up of German economic life, a catastrophic new fall of the German mark, and also a fall of the French franc, which has been falling recently along with the mark. Therefore, it is very doubtful that France would gain anything from the occupation.

Politically, the provisional occupation of the Ruhr should further strain the relations between France and England, increase the general ill-feeling in Germany toward France, and strengthen the position of the monarchists [in Germany]; but it will hardly lead to any active opposition in German bourgeois circles. . . . Only a close economic and political alliance with Soviet Russia might enhance the position of the present German government. But, in view of its class instinct, the German government deliberately avoids this path, and therefore must become reconciled to its present degrading role. The German Social Democrats are playing a similar passive and shameful role. . . . The worse the German economic situation becomes under the influence of the French robbers' pressure, the lower the German mark's value will sink, and the worse the economic position of the German worker will become. Germany will then conclude that there is only one way out of the existing situation, that is, an alliance with Soviet Russia and a merciless struggle against French imperialism and Germany's own bourgeoisie.

14 *Pravda*, No. 6, January 11, 1923, p. 1.

66

Bukharin on the Occupation of the Ruhr

[Speech Delivered at the Fourth All-Russian Congress of Press Workers][15]

The events in the Ruhr indicate that the European situation is far more disastrous than it seemed in the past months. The Ruhr events have done much to shake the belief that international stability has been secured, both between states and between the various social forces of Europe. . . .

We ought to be grateful to M. Poincaré, because the Ruhr events constitute a powerful aid to [our] propaganda against the further development of imperialist and bourgeois tendencies. . . . Thus the chief significance of the Ruhr occupation is that it permits us to launch a campaign of exposure, and that it provides us with a great political asset upon which we can rely in the future, upon which we can already rely today, to dispel the illusions of the working class.

The Ruhr events are even more important from the standpoint of their ultimate results. . . . The main question, upon which depends the future destiny of the whole of humanity, is whether the bourgeoisie will succeed—on the basis of the victory of one bourgeois coalition over another—in healing the wounds made by the war and restoring political balance. . . .

If, hitherto, it was believed (we ourselves did not believe it) that equilibrium would be restored among the powers of Europe, any such prospect has now completely vanished. Political relations have reached a most critical point, so that the political equilibrium, one may say, has been completely overthrown. . . .

This confusion and aggravation of the situation is of advantage to the proletariat, because the restoration and establishment of the capitalist order in Western Europe would have been most dangerous to us. The starving working classs would have been made more passive by some slight alleviation of their situation, and this would have inevitably resulted in reformist tendencies [among them]. Under the present circumstances there can be no such prospect—the events in the Ruhr have helped us very much. Whatever happens, our forces will be relatively strengthened, because the total forces opposed to us will be weakened. . . .

67

Communist Propaganda on the Ruhr Occupation

[Appeal of the All-Russian Central Council of Trade Unions to the Workers of the Ruhr Coal Basin, the Workers of the World, and the Workers of Russia][16]

Comrades! The All-Russian Central Council of Trade Unions and the proletariat of Russia are following with the greatest interest the hard struggle being conducted by German workers against the French occupation of the Ruhr basin. The Russian workers know what an imperialist occupation means. . . .

. . . Every class-conscious worker knows that it is you, the workers of the coal basin, who will suffer and go hungry. . . .

The All-Russian Central Council of Trade Unions and the Russian proletariat

[15] *Izvestiia*, No. 28, February 8, 1923, p. 3; also *International Press Correspondence*, No. 8, March 1, 1923, p. 115.

[16] *Pravda*, No. 49, March 4, 1923, p. 1.

cannot look indifferently upon your struggle and your suffering. The Russian proletariat knows what hunger means. Only a year ago we asked the workers of all
countries to help us in the struggle against famine and destitution caused by the
imperialist war and intervention in [our] country. The position of Russia is improving. . . .

Defended by their army, the toiling masses of Russia began to work. And now,
although Russia is still poor, and although she is just starting to rebuild her economy,
the Russian proletariat feels itself duty-bound to remember not only the starving
and suffering proletariat of Russia [but also others]. It also feels duty-bound to
pay back as much as possible of its debt.

From a collection made among the workers throughout Russia, the All-Russian
Central Council of Trade Unions is sending one-half million *puds* of flour, i.e., about
800 carloads, to the starving and struggling proletariat of the Ruhr basin in the hope
that its example will be followed by the workers of other and wealthier countries. . . .

Proletarians of France, England, Italy, Poland, and Czechoslovakia! The German proletarians have proved by years of hard struggle that they are fighting against
their own bourgeoisie. If they have not yet succeeded in freeing themselves from
the yoke, it is primarily because the scourge of the Versailles treaty is driving the
petty bourgeoisie, and the workers who lack class-consciousness, into the arms of
German nationalism. The more you, the proletarians of England, France, Italy,
Poland, and Czechoslovakia, struggle against your own robbers' governments, the
more the German proletarians will know that they are not alone; the more they will
be able to stand up and struggle with intensified energy for a workers' government
in Germany, which will then stretch its hand to help the workers of all countries
begin the joint task of reconstructing the world and freeing it from the yoke of
international capital. . . .

68

Stalin's Ideas on Help to the German Revolutionaries

[Stalin's Letter to Zinoviev and Bukharin in the Summer of 1923][17]

Should the Communists (at the given stage) strive to seize power without the
Social Democrats; are they mature enough for that? That, in my opinion, is the
question. When we seized power, we had in Russia such reserves as (*a*) peace, (*b*)
the land to the peasants, (*c*) the support of the great majority of the working class,
(*d*) the sympathy of the peasantry. The German Communists at this moment have
nothing of the sort. Of course, they have the Soviet nation as their neighbor, which
we did not have, but what can we offer them at the present moment? If today in
Germany the power, so to speak, falls, and the Communists seize hold of it, they
will fall with a crash. That [will happen] in the "best" case. And at the worst, they
will be smashed to pieces and thrown back. The whole thing is not that Brandler
wants to "educate the masses," but that the bourgeoisie plus the Right Social Democrats will surely transform the lessons—the demonstration—into a general battle
(at this moment all the chances are on their side) and exterminate them. Of course,
the Fascists are not asleep, but it is to our interest that they attack first; that will
rally the whole working class around the Communists (Germany is not Bulgaria).
Besides, according to all information, the Fascists are weak in Germany. In my
opinion, the Germans must be curbed and not spurred on.

[17] *Arbeiterpolitik* (Leipzig), February 9, 1929, p. 78, as given in Leon Trotsky, *The
Third International After Lenin,* pp. 322–23.

69

The Time to Provoke Communist Action in Germany
Is Not at Hand

[Radek's Statement in the Summer of 1923][18]

[Speaks of the necessity of capturing the German petty bourgeoisie, e.g., engineers, officers, bank employees, in order to win the revolution.]

The time has not yet come for a general attack. But it is approaching. Its approach is heralded by the following signs: (1) the hopeless prospects of the German bourgeoisie, which is not able to solve the crisis in Germany; (2) the growing confusion among the German bourgeoisie; (3) the decay of the power of the Social Democrats; and (4) our growth.

The strategic tasks of the German Communists are to accelerate the revolution by organizational efforts; to strengthen our forces; to draw into the struggle the reserves of the working class; to seek allies among the proletarianized petty bourgeoisie; to combine the maximum strength of our clear communist policy with a deliberate acceptance of such compromises as are necessary for broadening our bases and such as coincide with the line of historical development; and to make the Communist Party the living conscience of the suffering German people, that it may be the leader of these people.

We must fight the battles with which history confronts us, never forgetting that we are still the weaker side. Not only must we not yet advance to the decisive battle, but we must avoid everything that could give the enemy an opportunity to defeat us in separate attacks. The days of such a defeat as we suffered in March [1921]—the defeat of an army unaware that the time for a new offensive had not yet come—are now past. But the defeats that an army suffers when it begins an offensive without sufficient artillery preparations are still possible. It bleeds to death against the barbed wire entanglements of the enemy. Should the enemy take the offensive, he would find himself in an untenable position. The party must be ready not only to repulse the attack of the enemy, but also to pass to the counterattack after a victorious defense. But we, on our part, must not yet provoke the decision. . . .

70

Zinoviev on the United Front with the Saxon Government,
October 1923[19]

· · ·

The entry of German Communists into the Saxon government can be justified only if sufficient guarantees are given that the Saxon state will truly serve the working class, that it will truly begin to arm tens of thousands of workers against Bavarian and Pan-German fascism, that it will truly undertake to eliminate from the government machinery the bourgeois elements inherited from the government of Wilhelm II, and that it will immediately take revolutionary economic measures against the bourgeoisie.

If the present Saxon government will really make Saxony a Red country, capable (at least to some extent) of becoming the rallying point for all the revolutionary

---

[18] *Pravda*, No. 171, August 1, 1923, p. 2; also *International Press Correspondence*, No. 56 (34), August 16, 1923, p. 602.

[19] G. E. Zinoviev, *Les problèmes de la révolution allemande*, p. 29. A seventy-two-page pamphlet, originally published in German.

proletarian forces of Germany, the German proletariat will support its efforts. If the Saxon government does not do this, then German Communists must use the Dresden episode only to demonstrate to the masses that [their] leaders lack character. We repudiate the united front if it is used to conceal revolutionary objectives. . . .

71

Zinoviev on the Problems of the German Revolution, October 1923[20]

German events are developing with the certainty of fate. . . .

. . . Soon everyone will see that the autumn months of 1923 mark a turning point not only for Germany, but also for the world in general. . . .

The social basis of the coming revolution is absolutely clear. In the cities the workers are definitely numerically superior [to the rest of the population]. These workers have followed the counterrevolutionary German Social Democrats in one way or another . . . [but] this worker-giant is now convinced that the country and the working class can be saved only by revolution.

From the moment the German working class turns its back upon the German Social Democrats and follows the Communist Party, the fate of Germany is sealed. . . .

In the forthcoming decisive events, seven million agricultural workers will exercise a very great influence on the countryside. . . . There will be no need to send armed workers to the countryside. The agricultural workers themselves will do most of the work necessary to reduce to nought (or better to destroy) the counterrevolution of the estate owners and the rich peasants. The majority of the agricultural workers sympathize with communism. Of course Germany's prosperous peasants, that is, small landowners, are splendidly organized; and they will meet the proletarian regime with furious resistance. But let us return to figures, because the outcome of the struggle is certain.

The forthcoming German revolution will be a proletarian class revolution. The twenty-two million German workers who make up its army represent the cornerstone of the international proletariat. They will meet the capitalists with an international revolution. According to the highest estimates, in 1917 Russia had eight to ten million workers among a population of 160 million. Germany, with a population of sixty million, has more than twenty million workers. With us, the working class was only a small minority; in Germany it is the principal element, the majority of the population. . . .

Most important of all, the German revolution will operate from a powerful industrial base. It is true that German industries are in a very difficult position . . . But even so, German industries represent a formidable power. In that sense, Lenin was correct when he said: "In Western Europe, and especially in a country such as Germany, it will be much more difficult to start a proletarian revolution than in Russia. But it will be much easier to continue and to finish it." The German proletariat has preponderance both in industry and in agriculture. . . .

The German revolution will be a proletarian class revolution. Not that the rest of the German population should be considered a single reactionary mass—quite the contrary. The proletarian revolution in Germany will be characterized precisely by the role played in it by urban petty bourgeois elements: by clerks, petty officials [etc.]. One can say that the role of the peasants in Russia, war-weary, exhausted by continued ravages and devastation, and pushed to the abyss by the actions of capitalists,

[20] *Ibid.*, pp. 9–13, 41–46.

will be played in Germany by the middle class in the towns. The middle class will naturally vacillate between the proletariat and the bourgeoisie. It may even support the enemies of the revolution more often than not. But in the end it will provide [us with] auxiliary forces. The urban and rural proletariat will under no circumstances abandon revolutionary ideas. Today it has succeeded, and in a truly short time, in neutralizing the petty bourgeois elements and in gaining the sympathy of some of them. . . .

The attitude of the German petty bourgeoisie in the cities is due partly to the brutal policies of the Entente . . . and partly to the egotism of the German capitalist bourgeoisie, which has been ruinous to the middle classes. We, the Marxists, know that industrial capital destroys the petty bourgeoisie, and consequently proletarianizes most of them. But it is in Germany that we see for the first time that process being accomplished on a considerable scale. . . .

Foreign Difficulties

All the difficulties [of the German proletarian revolution] in achieving a domestic correlation of forces are secondary to the difficulties from the outside that will come into being the day after victory is won. The threat of an immediate war on the part of the French, Czech, and Polish bourgeoisie, the possibility of an English blockade—these are the main international political difficulties that will confront the German revolution.

. . . Foreign danger is the vulnerable point in the German revolution.

The advantages Soviet Russia had in October 1917, when she appeared in the world arena, were as follows: First, the war was in progress. International imperialism was split into two camps fighting a life-and-death struggle, and thus could not immediately unite against the Russian soviets. The newly-born Soviet republic had time to breathe. Second, the enormous size of Russia's territory served it well. We could yield space to gain time. The bourgeois encirclement inflicted considerable damage, of course, upon the young proletarian state: intervention, blockade, and so forth. Nevertheless, this encirclement was much less definite, and therefore much less dangerous, than it might prove to be for the German revolution.

On the other hand, the Russian revolution lacked certain advantages that the German revolution will have. The Russian revolution was first, while the German revolution will have before it the experience of the workers' state for six years. . . . The German revolution begins at a time when the Communist International has already been in existence for five years, when the communist movement has spread all over the world, and when the Communists constitute a considerable force in the most important countries of Europe. Both parties, the international bourgeoisie and the international proletariat, have acquired experience. Therefore, the struggle will be more intense.

In 1923–24, there are not, as there were in 1914–17, two imperialist camps—the Entente and the Central Powers—in a state of war. However, dissensions within the Entente begin to look increasingly serious. If there is no war between the imperialists, there is an increasingly deep animosity. . . .

Imperialism will undoubtedly attempt to organize an international front against the German proletarian revolution. But its success is doubtful. Six years of struggle against the Russian revolution have shown that to erect a united front is no easy matter. There is bound to be a struggle in the camp of the imperialist bourgeoisie between two types of policy: an imperialist policy of conquest, and a social-class policy in the broad sense . . .

It goes without saying that the German proletariat must prepare for the worst, that is, it must expect international imperialism to interpret its revolution not as an isolated episode but as affecting the fate of all European bourgeoisie. It must make its plans accordingly.

France, England, Poland, and Czechoslovakia—these are the countries that might intervene immediately in the German revolution. The future of the revolution will be decided not only in Germany, but in England, in France, in Poland, and in Czechoslovakia.

England. The English press already sees the British fleet occupying the Baltic ports to safeguard "the interests of Great Britain." The bourgeois elements that propose such a plan will probably be sufficiently influential. But even if England decides to blockade proletarian Germany, this blockade would not play a decisive role. In other words, England today is in no position to advance a strong territorial force.

France. Imperialist France has enormous military strength. She is vastly superior in her air fleet, technology, and armament. But if she decides on a large-scale occupation of Germany, she will need hundreds of thousands, perhaps a million, soldiers. In the end, this army will experience the fate of Wilhelm II's army in the revolutionary Ukraine. Morale will be the decisive factor, and the superiority in this respect belongs to the German proletariat and its allies. To conquer the German revolution by using colonial troops exclusively, as certain leading circles of the French bourgeoisie are contemplating, is impossible. The many thousands of colonial workers employed in the factories of Paris have already participated in economic strikes.

If imperialist France immediately declares war on revolutionary Germany, she will face not only formidable resistance in Germany but revolutionary counteraction at home.

Poland. Certain groups of the Polish bourgeoisie may be the most dangerous and the most desperate enemy of the German revolution. If the French imperialists decide not to risk their troops, they will not hesitate to send bourgeois Poland to battle. There is no reason whatever for France to spare her own vassal. But if the Polish bourgeoisie decided to act as an agent of counterrevolution, it would sign its own death warrant. Contact with the German proletariat would disperse the nationalism that still influences so much of the Polish proletariat. The greater the equivocal opposition of the P.P.S. [Polska Partja Socjalistyczna] to the German revolution and the more the P.P.S. is disposed to support the adventures of the Polish bourgeoisie, the more the Polish proletariat will tear itself away from nationalism and the P.P.S. The Polish bourgeoisie oppresses the Ukrainians, the Lithuanians, the Germans, and the Jews. From the moment it enters a war of conquest against the German revolution (or against Soviet Russia) it will find itself on a volcano, and the nationalities question will give it a great deal of trouble at home.

Czechoslovakia. By its geographical position, Czechoslovakia could help greatly to suppress the proletarian revolution in Germany. Its covering troops could reach Dresden in a few hours. But in Czechoslovakia, likewise, the multiplicity of nationalities will render unity of action difficult. There may even be among its bourgeoisie some people who understand that a White Germany constitutes a serious danger to their country, while a Soviet Germany at least would not threaten them. As to the powerful Czech proletariat, directed by the Communist Party, it will perform its historic mission.

The victory of the German revolution will truly provoke in Austria a strong movement for union with Germany. The Austrian workers can play an important role in the struggle against the Fascists of Bavaria, the German Vendée.

Reactionary Hungary, in the throes of a domestic crisis, cannot possibly play an active role in repressing the German revolution or in a war against the allies of Soviet Germany.

A victorious revolution in Berlin will provoke tremendous enthusiasm among the immense forces of the French, Polish, and Czech proletariat. A task of tremendous gravity will fall upon the communist parties of France, Poland, and Czechoslovakia: to organize direct aid to the German proletarian government. The latter will not decline, of course, under certain conditions, to buy the neutrality of the Entente. It may even consent to satisfy the French government in regard to the clauses of the Versailles treaty, if by so doing it can avert war, obtain the evacuation of the Ruhr, etc.

Perhaps the German revolution, too, will be obliged to sign a Brest-Litovsk treaty. This possibility is not excluded, at least not by the Communist Party (which is the principal force in the imminent revolution). We can imagine the march of the German revolution regardless of a Brest treaty. Such a treaty would in no way lower our morale, or clip the wings of the revolution. Its force of attraction will not suffer in the least. We are no longer so naïve and inexperienced as we were at the time of the revolution of October 1917. We know very well the strength of the international bourgeoisie; it is even more dangerous and more redoubtable for the German revolution than for the Russian revolution. We know that the millions of workers who will take part in the revolution do not want war, but peace, even at a high price.

If, in spite of everything, the international bourgeoisie risks an outright immediate war against the revolution, it may at first have some success, but in the end it will break its neck. Germany's sixty million men and women will, under the proletarian rule, repulse the invaders, and in spite of all obstacles the German proletarian revolution will triumph.

72
Poland: Bridge or Barrier?

[Trotsky Speaking on the International Situation at the Moscow Province Congress of Metalworkers, October 1923][21]

· · ·

Five years ago the victorious German revolution failed to justify the hopes of the German working class. The Social Democrats, who then led the working class, shared the power with the bourgeoisie, later passing the authority entirely to them. Now Germany must make a choice: either complete disintegration or a social revolution. . . .

The question of Poland interests not only the German workers, but also you and me. . . . Already some impatient comrades are saying that war with Poland is inevitable. (Commotion in the hall.) I do not believe it. There are many indications that there will be no war with Poland. What should we fight for? We do not want a war, and we do not say this simply so that the world may hear us. Our economic achievements are not very great as yet. We have not yet learned to close the scissors, that is, to close the gap between the [price of] produce in the countryside and that in town. We have just started to heal our wounds. Under these circumstances, war would be tremendously harmful to our economy. . . .

As for victory within Germany itself, no help is needed there. German workers themselves will win, and the revolution is poor indeed if it is not able to deal with its own bourgeoisie. No assistance with manpower is needed for the German revolution.

Some Polish bullies say that Germany and Russia can be compared to pincers as far as Poland is concerned. I do not agree with this point of view. . . .

Poland can be either a bridge between Germany and us, or a barrier. If she is a bridge, we shall pay her cash. We need direct transit to Germany. . . . Without

[21] *Izvestiia*, No. 241, October 21, 1923, p. 1.

it our rural economy will suffocate. Poland must decide whether she will be a bridge or a barrier.

If Poland wants to be a barrier, she will find herself in the pincers of which the Polish chauvinists are in the habit of speaking. We do not want war; we shall pay for peace, but not by isolating ourselves from the European market.

Poland, of course, must assure us also that her armed forces will not interfere in the European civil war.

Is this program realizable? Why not? . . .

It is evident to everyone that Europe is on the eve of great upheavals. We must take every possible measure to avoid war, and that means first of all that we must intensify our present work tenfold. [Speaks further on the need of building up the Soviet economy.] . . .

73

Analysis of the Failure in Germany

[Zinoviev on the Lessons of German Events and United Front Tactics][22]

What has happened in Germany in the last few weeks and what the Communist Party has done during these events must be made clear to all sections of the Communist International. . . . We shall deal more fully in a separate document with the concrete practical tasks now confronting the German Communist Party. Here we shall only take up questions of definite international significance.

In October 1923 the German Communist Party and the Executive Committee of the Comintern believed that the revolutionary crisis in Germany had reached a stage at which an armed rising would be only a question of weeks. Events have shown that our calculations were exaggerated. Some comrades explain things as follows: The revolutionary crisis in Germany was ripe for a victorious armed rising in October, but the German Communist Party missed the right moment; hence the present state of affairs. We consider such a diagnosis utterly wrong. In any case, it is a definite mistake to speak merely of an error of judgment in timing preparations for an armed rising [or to say that] the tasks facing the German Communist Party were of a purely technical nature. The German Communist Party revealed many weaknesses and made a number of serious mistakes during these critical weeks, but we do not consider it mistaken in not bringing out the proletariat into a general struggle in October.

In its retreat, the party could and should have mobilized the masses for separate big actions—demonstrations, strikes, etc. The retreat should have been less passive. But the abstention from fighting a decisive battle was inevitable under the circumstances.

As is quite clear today, not only the technical but even the political preparations for decisive battles were inadequate. The big wave of political strikes in August 1923 led us to believe that the German Communist Party already had the majority of the proletariat behind it, or at least the social[ist] sections of it, which are most important. This proved to be a mistake. The German Communist Party was then (as it is now) only on the way to conquering this majority. At that time it certainly had not done so. The second half of September and the beginning of October were particularly suitable for organizing a series of demonstrations and other actions aimed at drawing large sections of workers into the active struggle. But the German Communist Party failed to do this. At that time a wrong notion became manifest within the party that the crisis had reached the stage of a rising and that partial

[22] *Kommunisticheskii Internatsional*, No. 1, 1924, pp. 501–3, 522–23; also *Communist International*, No. 2, 1924, pp. 84–102.

actions were impossible. . . . The party had in the factory committees a proletarian mass organization. With the support of these factory committees, the party should have agitated energetically for the establishment of soviets of workers' deputies and at the same time prepared the factory committees to act as soviets temporarily. The party did not do the first, and did the second very badly. As a result, workers who were not yet in the Communist Party, but had already severed all connection with the bourgeoisie and the Social Democrats, were left without an authoritative center.

There was no justification for some comrades' hopes of rousing the masses to an armed rising "suddenly" by one bold action. The technical preparation (we mean the organizational machinery of the party, the arming of workers, the rallying together of the Red hundreds,[23] etc.) proved very inadequate.

At the same time, the enemy's technical and political strength was underestimated. It is now clear that our opponents have at least half a million armed men. The enemy also showed much greater political elasticity and adaptability than anticipated, while the German Social Democrats have shown themselves much closer to the counterrevolutionary camp than before the September events.

Mistakes in fixing dates and estimating the tempo of revolutionary events are bound to happen. But we must do our utmost to correct these mistakes as rapidly as possible and to prevent their repetition in the future.

In this case, too, the tempo of events was miscalculated.

But nevertheless, the fundamental estimate of the German situation made in October remains correct. The German Communist Party must on no account remove armed risings and the conquest of power from its program. On the contrary, these matters are as concrete and urgent as ever. No matter how important the partial victories of the German counterrevolution were, they cannot solve the problem.

The arming of workers and the technical preparation for decisive struggles must continue. Red hundreds can be maintained not only on paper but in reality if they have the sympathy and the support of the working class as a whole. To obtain this support and sympathy, they must be linked with the everyday partial struggles of the proletariat. These Red hundreds can depend on the wholehearted support of the masses in the matter of arming, training, and scouting, provided the masses can depend on the Red hundreds in their demonstrations, strikes, and other collisions with the bourgeois authorities. Only then will the masses look upon them as their shock battalions. The Hamburg example has shown the great significance of a heroic fight put up by communist shock troops—although in Hamburg, too, the support of the masses was very inadequate. . . .

A proletarian revolution in Germany is inevitable. The revolutionary crisis in Germany is bound to become still more acute in the near future. The objective tasks of the revolution are not yet solved. All the important factors that brought Germany to the brink of proletarian revolution are not only continuing in force, but becoming more acute.

. . .

The Communist International must explain to the masses systematically and persistently, taking advantage of every suitable example, every important episode in the civil war, and especially such important events as those in Germany, that it is useless to expect a peaceful transition to a workers' (or workers' and peasants') government within the framework of democracy. We must explain to the workers that the united front of the entire proletariat will make the struggle considerably easier and will ensure victory, but that it will on no account substitute peaceful, democratic, and painless evolution for revolutionary struggle. The tactics of the united front

[23] See p. 179.

are tactics of revolution and not of evolution. The advantage of these tactics is that by substituting peaceful evolutionary methods for the revolutionary ones they guarantee success to the revolution.

Obviously, the united front tactics, as a method of agitation among large working masses, are adapted to a definite epoch, namely to the epoch when Communists in nearly all the most important countries are a minority in the workers' movement, and when definite revolutionary battles do not as yet take place. As the situation changes, the application of united front tactics will have to change also. Even now these tactics are applied differently in different countries; the united front tactics recommended for Germany, for instance, would not be suitable at all for Poland. The sections of the Communist International must learn, under the general guidance of the Executive Committee, to adapt united front tactics to the specific situations in their countries.

The events of September-November, 1923, in Bulgaria, Poland, and Germany apparently mark the beginning of a new chapter in the history of international revolution. As the struggle grows more intense and more decisive, we shall have to modify more than once the application of the united front tactics in the various countries. . . .

74

Zinoviev Does Not Abandon Hope for the German Revolution

[Description of the Hamburg Uprising][24]

The brightest spot in the workers' movement in Europe in 1923, and perhaps in the last few years, is the October revolt of the Hamburg proletarians. The movement of the Bulgarian and Polish insurgents in the autumn of 1923 contains much that is great and heroic, but the Hamburg movement stands on a far higher level. The Hamburg revolt was a movement with a clearly defined aim, with a definitely formulated program, that is, the dictatorship of the proletariat. In the composition of its participants, in the clearness of its program, and in its leadership, which was in the hands of the Communist Party, the Hamburg revolt was a purely proletarian class movement. Under the organized leadership of the communist vanguard, the revolt without doubt saved the honor of Germany's working class. It is the precursor of far more powerful battles, which will decide the fate not only of Germany, but of the working class of all Europe. The Hamburg revolt, which was on a relatively small scale, has shown us what the near future will bring to the European proletariat on a far more imposing scale. A mere handful of the Hamburg proletariat, with a heroism reminiscent of the finest moments of the Paris Commune and the Russian revolution, fought like lions under the banner of the proletarian dictatorship, and with courageous hands tore aside the curtain from the future and pointed out to the great masses of European workers, who are still groping for a way to end the rule of the bourgeoisie and their Social Democratic lackeys, the highway of the proletarian revolution.

The revolt of the Hamburg workers was crushed, but its defeat, like many another, has had greater results than many a "victory." The December uprising of the Moscow workers in 1905 was also defeated, but it nevertheless played a powerful part in the later history of the Russian proletariat. The revolt of the Hamburg work-

[24] G. E. Zinoviev, "K godovshchine gamburgskogo vosstaniia," *Pravda*, No. 242, October 23, 1924, p. 1; also *International Press Correspondence*, No. 76, October 29, 1924, p. 844.

ers will play a similar role in the future history of the German revolutionary proletariat.

Comrade Lenin characterized the events of 1905 as the "dress rehearsal" for the revolution of 1917. Similarly, the Hamburg revolt of 1923 was a "rehearsal" for the decisive battles that are to come.

The revolutionary is not the man who decides to take up arms only when the victory is 99 per cent won. On very few occasions in history could victory be regarded as absolutely certain. The revolutionary and the Communist is the man who takes up arms when reasonable chances of victory exist, and when it is the duty of the vanguard to show the way to the whole class. Such revolutionaries and such heroic Communists, in the true sense of the word, were the Hamburg proletarians in 1923.

The proletarian revolution in Germany is approaching ever nearer, in spite of all the Daweses, Eberts, and Noskes. It is a mistaken idea that in October 1923 a revolutionary opportunity, unique of its kind, was let slip. The defeat of October 1923 was no more decisive than the defeat of the Spartakus revolt in January 1919. The decisive main battles, the battles that decide the fate of a country for decades, have not yet taken place in Germany. These struggles, however, will come before very long. The glorious fight of the Hamburg vanguard constitutes a guarantee that in due time the German Communist Party will be capable of fulfilling its historic task.

The Communist International sends warmest greetings to the Hamburg communist proletarians, to the glorious detachments of proletarians who stood amidst the powder smoke in 1923, and who fought in the front line of all the most advanced elements of the European working masses. It is with special affection that the Russian workers, who in 1917 experienced the joy of victory over the enemy, but who in the past had also experienced the bitterness of heavy defeats in the struggle against the malicious bourgeoisie and their Social Democratic hirelings, greet the Hamburg proletarians. Everyone who was present at the Fifth Congress of the Communist International will remember with what enthusiasm the Moscow workers received the representatives of the Hamburg proletariat, and what response every account of the class struggle in Hamburg found among the best workers of the Soviet Union.

The revolt in Hamburg is a powerful episode in the civil war in Germany. The experience of the Hamburg insurgents must be studied with love and attention by the international proletariat, just as in its time the Russian proletariat studied, on instructions from Comrade Lenin, the December revolt of 1905.

Hamburg is a watchword and a slogan. Hamburg constitutes an entire program for the German (and not only the German) proletariat. Hamburg is the symbol of civil war in tomorrow's Germany. Hamburg is the banner of the Communist International.

75

Mistakes Made in Germany in 1923

[Resolution of the Fifth Enlarged Plenum of the Executive Committee
of the Communist International, April 4, 1925][25]

. . .

Radek, Brandler, and Thalheimer share the greatest responsibility for the Social Democratic distortions of the tactics of the German Communist Party, which caused such damage to the German revolutionary movement in 1923. The faction headed by Radek, Brandler, and Thalheimer tried to convert the revolutionary tactics

---

[25] *Kommunisticheskii Internatsional v dokumentakh*, p. 523; also *International Press Correspondence*, No. 47, June 4, 1925, p. 634.

of the united front into tactics of coalition with the Social Democrats. By means of the "Saxony" policy (the conditions upon which Brandler joined the government of Saxony, his "work" in it, etc.) this "faction" converted communist tactics into a banal parliamentary farce that revealed the utter political impotence of these three comrades.

The Thirteenth Congress of the Russian [Communist] Party unanimously declared that the policy of Comrade Radek, who at that time was trying to speak in the name of the Russian Communist Party, had nothing in common with the real policy of the party. The Frankfurt Congress of the German Communist Party, with equal determination, condemned the policy of Brandler and Thalheimer. Finally, the Fifth Congress of the Comintern, in the name of the communist parties of all countries, severely condemned the Menshevik deviations of these three comrades. . . .

RECOGNITION AND NONRECOGNITION: THE UNITED KINGDOM, EUROPE, AND THE UNITED STATES

76

The Petrograd Soviet on the War Danger

[A Declaration of the Petrograd Soviet to the Workers of All Countries, May 1923][26]

The Petrograd soviet has discussed the ultimatum sent by Lord Curzon to the Soviet government, and declares:

The workers of Petrograd, and—we are convinced—the working masses of all other peoples of Russia as well, have read the ultimatum of the English imperialists with indignation. . . . The ruling circles of British imperialism have forgotten that Soviet Russia does not permit herself to be addressed in the language of ultimatums, that the Union of Soviet Socialist Republics is no Ruhr area, and that our workers' and peasants' government is not at the mercy of foreign governments, which have done their best to ruin our country, but is founded solely on the united efforts and the determined will of the working masses of the great Soviet federation.

Of what does Lord Curzon accuse our country? In the eyes of the imperialists the blackest crime is the friendship between the first victorious workers' and peasants' state and the oppressed peoples of the East. Stricken blind, they cannot see that just as no one can prevent plants from turning to the sun, so nothing can prevent the East's oppressed millions, exploited by world imperialism and degraded by financial capital, from striving toward alliance and friendship with the only soviet country, a country that greets them not treacherously, but fraternally; not with egotistic aims, but in a spirit of equality.

Lord Curzon further accuses our country of not refraining from determined measures of self-defense against spies, even when these hide their real calling under priestly garb. In Lord Curzon's words, this is not persecution of spies, but persecution of religion. An insignificant occurrence, the fining of fishing vessels that illegally entered our waters, has been shamefully exaggerated into a hostile act. The real import of the ultimatum is clear. It is either an attempt to institute a new blockade of the Soviet country, just as she is beginning to recover from the injuries caused by the first, or the precursor of an open declaration of war. To this irrecon-

---

[26] *Pravda,* No. 107, May 16, 1923, p. 3; also *International Press Correspondence,* No. 41, June 7, 1923, pp. 386–87.

cilable representative of imperialism, our mere existence is a crime. And our greatest crime is that we are mastering all our difficulties, that we have begun to improve our economy, that we have not let Russia be converted into a colony or a semicolony, and that we have successfully resisted the excessive appetite of Urquhart and other "concessionaires."

The shots fired at Comrade Vorovsky[27] light up the situation. What the most irreconcilable sections of international imperialism are now planning is nothing less than a new campaign against the Russian revolution. The Ruhr events, the ultimatum sent by Curzon, the murder of Comrade Vorovsky, the triumphal visit by General Foch to Poland, the provocative preparations of the Polish government, the ceremonious visit of an English mission to Rumania, the increasing onslaught of world capitalism against the workers of all countries . . .—all these are links in the same chain.

Let the imperialists of England and the world learn that there is no power capable of overcoming our Soviet country. We fear the threats of no imperialist government whatever. We laugh at attempts to frighten a country that has been the object of so many attacks during the past five years, and that has repulsed them all successfully. We declare that any attempt to threaten us with war or intervention will be the signal for ten millions of our adult population to spring to arms ready to fight to the last drop of blood against the foreign invader. . . .

From the Council of People's Commissars we categorically demand the absolute rejection of Lord Curzon's ultimatum.

We appeal to the workers of all countries. A new campaign is being opened against Soviet Russia. In this campaign the victory, or even the semi-victory, of world imperialism would signify the annihilation of the workers' movement for many years, and the establishment of blackest reaction.

We appeal to the English workers, upon whose shoulders an immense historical responsibility rests. We most firmly hope that the English workers will do their utmost to prevent the present rulers of Britain from again unleashing the dogs of war in Europe.

Russia's toiling workers and peasants will do their duty to the utmost. This we guarantee to the English workers. We demand that they too do their duty. Down with the instigators of new imperialist wars! Long live the struggle of the international proletariat for peace and the workers' government!

ZINOVIEV,
Chairman of the Petrograd Soviet of
Workers' and Peasants' Deputies

77

The Soviet Government Replies to the British Ultimatum

[Note of the Assistant People's Commissar of Foreign Affairs of the
R.S.F.S.R., Litvinov, to Mr. Hodgson, May 11, 1923][28]

1. Although the increasing reaction in Europe against the working class in recent months, which is inevitably accompanied by increased enmity toward the soviet republics, gave reason to fear that steps would be taken against the workers' and peasants' republics, nonetheless, the memorandum of the British government, which

[27] V. V. Vorovsky, representing the Soviet government at Lausanne, was assassinated by one M. Conradi on May 10, 1923.

[28] Kliuchnikov and Sabanin, III, 250–56; also *Reply of the Soviet Government to His Majesty's Government respecting the Relations between the two Governments* (Cmd. 1874), pp. 2–8.

in its sharpness and hostility bears the nature of an ultimatum, and which threatens to rupture the peaceful economic relations between two countries equally interested in the development of peaceful co-operation, has been a great surprise to the government of the R.S.F.S.R. To use ultimatums and threats is by no means the way to settle separate and secondary disputes among states. In any case it is not the way to attain normal relations with the soviet republics.

2. The Russian republic has by no means failed to consider the fact that, of all the Great Powers, Great Britain was the first to conclude with it an agreement, however provisional and insufficient. The Russian government, in its relations with Great Britain, as well as in its negotiations with other countries, has taken this fact into consideration. At the same time it is fully aware that this agreement has not been advantageous to itself alone, Great Britain having derived both political and economic advantages from it, and that the establishment of peaceful relations with the soviet republics is the most essential factor for peace and for the restoration of economic well-being of all the countries of Europe, in which Great Britain herself is considerably interested. . . .

3. The Russian government does not endeavor to dispute the abnormal condition of present-day relations, or the defectiveness of the present basis of the agreement mentioned in the British memorandum. The Russian government, for its part, has steadfastly striven for a complete regulation of relations, for an open discussion of all questions dividing the two states from one another, and for the creation of a more durable basis for eliminating disagreement and conflicts. It is, however, obliged to state that the present unsatisfactory basis of agreement has been chosen by Great Britain herself. And even within the confines of the present agreement, the British government unfortunately has invariably refused to subject the whole complex of conflicting interpretations between the two states to businesslike consideration, and has thus rendered the satisfactory solution of the conflicts that arise from time to time exceedingly difficult, in many cases impossible.

4. The memorandum sent us by the government of Great Britain speaks of repeated challenges issued to Great Britain by Soviet Russia, even of deliberate challenges. The Soviet government takes the liberty of stating that such an assertion is entirely unfounded, and regrets that the government of Great Britain has not found it possible to name a single instance of such a challenge. The Soviet government is prepared, for its part, to recount the actual challenges thrown down by the government of Great Britain to the Soviet government within the last two years, directed not only against the Soviet government, but against the whole Russian people, for whom the government of Great Britain saw fit to express sympathy in its ultimatum. It suffices to mention Great Britain's universally acknowledged disregard of the soviet republics' interests in a number of international questions, for example the Dardanelles, East Galician, Memel district, and Bessarabian questions.

5. The Russian government sent no notes protesting these violations of the Anglo-Russian agreement, not because it could not substantiate such protests, but because it still hoped for a mutual settlement of all contested and unsolved questions. The Russian government, however, must state that it has numerous statements and documents relating to extremely intense anti-Soviet activity by British government agents in the Caucasus and especially in districts adjoining Soviet Central Asia, in the support lent to the Basmachi bandit movement[29] in Turkestan and in eastern Bukhara. And then there was the support not so long ago given to White Guard generals by English consuls in enlisting officers and sending them to Vladivostok when that town was occupied by the Whites. The Soviet government, being anxious to maintain friendly relations with Great Britain and to provoke no conflicts, now points out

---

[29] For information on the Basmachi, a group of Muslim insurgents, see the companion volume, *Soviet Russia and the East, 1920–1927*.

these facts not as an indictment of the government of Great Britain, but to prove that the Soviet government does not believe in basing its protests on statements of informers and on intercepted documents, the reliability of which is invariably doubtful in such cases. All governments have such material at their disposal; should they use it not merely for information purposes, but to bring about conflicts and as a foundation for protests, no friendly relations could exist between any two states whatever.

6. Unfortunately, the British government has seen fit to use such doubtful materials against the Soviet government in an official exchange of notes. It must be mentioned that the Foreign Office, as early as 1921, scarcely five months after the conclusion of the Anglo-Russian agreement, published a lengthy memorandum containing accusations against the Russian government, and based solely on information of this character. The Russian government at that time succeeded in proving that the British government had been misled by prejudiced, irresponsible, and malicious informers, and was able to point out the dark sources from which the apocrypha compromising the Russian government had been brought to the government of Great Britain.

The British memorandum anticipates that we may reject the new material upon which it bases its new indictments, and thus deprives the Russian government of the chance to analyze that material in detail. Since the Russian government does not wish its silence to be interpreted as a recognition, even indirectly, of the credibility of these statements, it is obliged to declare that the extracts and quotations cited by the British government are a combination of fiction and portions of deciphered telegrams, altered to accord with desired tendencies, and supplemented at will. The Russian government categorically declares that the quotation referring to Persia is pure invention, and bears no relation whatever to any official documents known to the Russian government. A characteristic example of intentional misrepresentation of information is the reference to Raskolnikov's telegram in the matter of aiding Vaziristan with 3,000 rubles and ten cases of cartridges. If the British government really has this telegram in its hands, and not in a maliciously distorted form, it should know that the aid in question was rendered not by Raskolnikov but by another person in no way connected with the Soviet government, whose name the Soviet government cannot disclose, being bound by the generally recognized rules of international forms of intercourse. These examples throw a bright light on the remainder of the information.

7. To pass on to lesser matters, the Soviet government does not consider it necessary to deny that it actually sent money to its representative in Persia, quite openly, through London banks. The government of Great Britain must be extremely suspicious if it thinks that the Soviet government spends its money in the East only on anti-British intrigues. The British government knows better than anyone else, if it is correctly informed, that the Soviet government is not trying to attain and does not attain good relations with the Eastern peoples by money and intrigues, but by really disinterested and benevolent actions.

8. It would be useless to discuss in detail the memorandum's accusations with regard to so-called propaganda in the East. The essential error of these accusations lies obviously—apart from their groundlessness—in a misapprehension of the duties assumed by Russia in the East. These accusations appear to reflect the British government's assumption that the Russian republic is not to pursue a policy of its own in the East, but must everywhere support British undertakings. The Soviet government has never undertaken any such engagement or concluded any agreement with Great Britain on this point, nor can it regard the maintenance and development of friendly relations with the peoples of the East, based on a sincere respect for the rights and interests of these peoples, as a violation of the Anglo-Russian agreement. If the British government considers such a policy to be inevitably anti-British, then

the misunderstandings that have arisen are fully comprehensible. Regrettably, the government of Great Britain never specifies its demands of the soviet republics with respect to Eastern policy, and has not answered the Russian government's note of September 27, 1921, proposing a friendly conference on ways and means to avoid further misunderstandings of this sort. Even when a favorable opportunity for such a conference occurred, when the leaders of the foreign offices of both countries met in private at Lausanne, Lord Curzon only repeated general reproaches, and refrained from explaining and discussing these.

9. The government of Great Britain has deemed it necessary to refer in its memorandum to the activity of the Third International, despite the Soviet government's frequent declarations that it cannot by any means be identified with the Third International. The Soviet government, which has explained this matter more than once, has no desire to return to it, just as it does not wish to discuss the declarations and actions of certain political parties and other organizations whose members are in the British government. As to the reference to the participation of the People's Commissar of Finance, Mr. Sokolnikov, in some financial commission of the Third International, which is alleged to have subsidized communist parties, the Soviet government declares this report untrue from beginning to end, and the work of malicious informers.

10. As to so-called propaganda, the Soviet government can state with satisfaction that the British government has brought forward no concrete accusations of propaganda in Great Britain itself, despite recent allegations in the British press that the Soviet government is carrying on propaganda through its commercial delegates and other representatives.

11. The government of Great Britain has seen fit to substantiate its ultimatum to the Soviet government and its threat of breaking off relations by pointing out instances in which the Russian government violated the interests of British subjects. To this the Soviet government can only reply that the British government, apart from the fishing boats to which we refer later, cannot prove a single violation of British subjects' interests during the whole period of the Anglo-Russian agreement. The shooting of the engineer Davison, mentioned in the memorandum, in connection with the activity of the spying organization of the notorious Paul Dukes[30] in Russia, took place in January 1920, that is, sixteen months before the conclusion of the agreement, and before the end of the period of English intervention and blockade. The arrest of Stan Harding,[31] accused of spying, partly on the information of the American journalist, Miss Harrison, also fell within this period. It would be futile to repeat all the explanations given by the Russian government in the prolonged exchange of notes. It must be mentioned, however, that during this period an incomparably larger number of Russian subjects had to suffer physically and morally from British actions in the north and south of the soviet republics, and within Great Britain's sphere of influence. One such case, mentioned during the exchange of notes, is the shooting of the twenty-six Baku commissars.[32] If compensation is mentioned at all, justice demands that it apply to all cases that occurred at that period, and thus to the Kolomiitsev family, Babushkin, Karakhanian, and other citizens imprisoned for years in English and Indian prisons without trial. It is not right to

---

[30] A British secret agent active in Soviet territory, author of *Red Dusk and the Morrow*.

[31] A British journalist in Soviet Russia.

[32] Twenty-six commissars representing the Soviet government in Baku surrendered their authority and fled Baku before the occupation of the city by the Turks in August 1918. Upon their arrival in Krasnovodsk, they were arrested by the local antisoviet authorities and sentenced to exile in India. The train that ostensibly was to carry them to India was stopped soon after it left Krasnovodsk; the commissars were ordered from the train and murdered on the spot. The Russian Communists have since claimed that the British authorities in Transcaspia at that time were responsible for the murders. (See V. A. Chaikin, *K istorii rossiiskoi revoliutsii.*)

measure similar cases by dissimilar measurements. The Russian government is ready to provide compensation for the family of Davison, and for Mrs. Stan Harding, if the English government does the same for the above-mentioned Russian subjects.

12. The question of territorial waters was exhaustively dealt with in the Russian government's note [of May 7], which pointed out that no international standards imposing obligations now exist, that different countries take different courses in this matter, and that it is entirely unjustifiable to demand that Russia accept a British regulation that is not even applied throughout Britain's entire empire. The Russian government again declares its readiness to take part in an international conference on this matter, and to submit to its decisions. The note mentioned above states that the affair of the arrested fishing boat, the *James Johnson*, has been passed on to the Supreme Court, which has annulled the verdict of the Murmansk court of justice, and that the arrest and the confiscation of the vessel have been canceled. Although the fishing boats had entered territorial waters, violating the laws of the country, the Russian government, wishing to avoid increased friction in its relations, has taken steps to free all British fishing boats, even the *Lord Astor*, held up a few days ago within the four-mile zone. The Russian government cannot hold itself responsible for the fishing boat that was sunk by a storm, together with the Russian guard, but it is willing to place this matter before a board of arbitration.

13. Although the position of the Church in the soviet republics has nothing whatever to do with the relations of these republics with Great Britain, the Soviet Russian government deems it necessary, in the interests of correctly informing the public, to categorically deny the assertion that there is any religious persecution in Russia. Soviet justice is applied solely to those clerics who misuse their ecclesiastical position to subvert the internal or external security of the soviet republics. The Soviet government is ready to acknowledge the unaccustomed tone of Mr. Weinstein's first note. It is nevertheless necessary to recollect the indignation and excitement called forth among the working and peasant population of Russia by the attempt, made by a neighboring country, to interfere in this internal affair of Soviet Russia's, for the purpose of utilizing the trial of the Catholic prelates for aggressive political aims. The excitement aroused must be known to the British mission. The British representative, Mr. Hodgson, tried to negotiate privately on this matter with the Assistant People's Commissar, Mr. Litvinov, who replied categorically that he did not think it possible to negotiate with Mr. Hodgson on this subject either officially or unofficially. This should have shown Mr. Hodgson what the Soviet government's attitude would be toward an official step on his part; unfortunately, he was not restrained by this circumstance from sending off his note, which was regarded by the Commissariat of Foreign Affairs as a direct challenge. In referring to the representative of the Irish republic in his note, Mr. Weinstein intended merely to show how very inconvenient it is for both parties when there is interference in internal affairs, and that Russia would regard interference in the Cieplak affair[33] just as Great Britain would regard Russian interference in the Irish question. Except for the above-mentioned neighbor and Great Britain, no other government made any official application to Russia in this affair. In these circumstances, the unusual tone of Mr. Weinstein's note is easily comprehensible. In any case, this note was returned by Mr. Hodgson; it has not been handed to the British government a second time and can therefore be regarded as nonexistent, just like the second note that followed it, which contained nothing offensive.

14. The Soviet government believes that one of the chief causes of the constantly recurring misunderstandings between Soviet Russia and the British government is

---

[33] Archbishop Cieplak and Mgr. Butkiewicz were the two leading Roman Catholic prelates in Soviet Russia. In July 1922 they were tried for alleged acts of treachery against the Soviet government and were sentenced, Cieplak to ten years of solitary confinement and Butkiewicz to death. The British protested the sentences to the Soviet government.

that certain Entente states decline to negotiate with other states on an equal footing—a result of the Versailles peace. Noting that during the last few years many states have actually become completely or partially dependent upon the Entente countries, the Russian government feels obliged to declare that the soviet republics are not dependent, will not and cannot be dependent, on the will of any foreign government. If Great Britain's ruling circles would recognize this fact, the chief obstacle to the restoration of normal peaceful relations, such as are in the interest of both states, would be removed.

15. Despite the repeated misunderstandings, the soviet republics hold the present relations with Great Britain in high esteem, and are anxious to maintain these in the interests of general peace, of the economic restoration of devastated Europe, and of the peoples of the Soviet Union and the British people alike, and therefore are willing to enter into the friendliest and most peaceful settlement of the existing conflicts.

16. The step taken by the British government has obviously been prompted by an incorrect estimate of the position of the soviet republics, an estimate formed under the visible influence of White emigrés, who never distorted reality so much as at the present time. The Russian government takes into consideration the international situation, the events in Central Europe, the growing activity of militarists in countries adjacent to the soviet republics, the journeys of Entente generals to these countries, and in particular the recent inspection of the Rumanian frontiers by the British military mission; it is fully aware that a breach of relations would involve new dangers and new complications threatening to peace, and that by causing such a breach the British government would take upon itself an immense responsibility in the eyes of history. The Russian government declares that no reason exists for a rupture of relations, that most points of dispute between the soviet republics and Great Britain are insignificant compared with the possible consequences of a rupture, and that with good will on both sides satisfactory solutions would be reached quickly and without great difficulty at a conference of competent representatives of both states. The Soviet government, for its part, sincerely desires to arrive at an understanding, and it is convinced that the British government will express the same desire.

17. The Soviet government therefore proposes to the government of Great Britain that it accept the proposal for a conference, and arrange the time and place for this conference, in order that the authorized representatives of both parties may not only consult on and solve the secondary questions in dispute, but also fully settle the problem of Anglo-Russian relations.

78

A Communist Analysis of the World Situation at the Beginning of 1924

[Excerpts from Kamenev's Speech at the Second Congress of Soviets of the U.S.S.R., January 30, 1924][34]

. . .

The present international situation is characterized by the definite collapse of all the basic forces which were instrumental in drafting the Versailles treaty, and which tried to impose upon mankind the standards of the Versailles treaty as a guarantee of peace, freedom, and material well-being. . . .

[34] *Vtoroi Sezd Sovetov S.S.S.R.*, pp. 61–69.

A few years have been sufficient to fully prove the correctness of our position. We said that the Versailles treaty was a continuation of war, and therefore that it could not result in freedom, peace, economic well-being, or the development of the world economy.

Upon what, then, were the Versailles standards based? Upon the victors' mutual responsibility for exploiting the vanquished. This conception has suffered a complete defeat from two points of view. Whereas it has been possible to destroy the economy of defeated countries, to turn the great economy of the German people into a scrap heap, to interfere with the further development of economic relations between Central and Eastern Europe, it has been impossible to rebuild the world economy on the ruins of formerly economically powerful and technically developed countries. Germany lies in a heap of ruins, but she is dragging down with her the entire capitalist civilization of Europe.

Similarly, the old policy of jointly exploiting the vanquished and weak has proved absolutely incapable of withstanding the onslaught of time. Only a few years ago the victors made professions of eternal friendship and permanent unity. But what do we see now?

In England, the collapse of the national Conservative-Liberal bloc, which represented one of the basic forces in the Versailles peace. In France, the certain decline of the imperialist and militarist policy that gained dominance almost the day after the victory. There is a complete conflict of interests between England and France, and a violent and hardly concealed struggle between them. . . .

Finally, there is Italy. She has clearly abandoned the principle of mutual responsibility and is clearly unable to follow the road of France, because her Mediterranean and African interests differ from those of the French capitalists. She is trying to devise a national policy of her own.

All the small states grouped around these large states are naturally considerably shaken . . . We see totally chaotic political relations, the complete disintegration of the world economy, and an actual clash among the contending forces. New conflicts and new imperialist wars cannot be prevented on the bases of capitalist competition and imperialist development.

In the background . . . [we observe] the increasing power of the one state that alone, owing to the revolutionary energy of its workers and peasants, has succeeded in tearing itself away from the clutches of the imperialist war, neither sharing the fruits of victory nor joining the ranks of the vanquished (who were equally responsible for the war). Our policy of peace and of waiting, based on our conviction that the world economy cannot be restored without the co-operation of the 130 million people united under the Red flag of the U.S.S.R.—this policy of patience, self-control, and strength has borne fruit. We now see all countries interested in our Union, seeking agreement with us and political co-operation from us.

Britain's attitude is of great interest in the current phase of world history. The English people have rid themselves of the Conservative-Liberal bloc, which entered wars at a nod from the British capitalists, and which, under Lloyd George, has tried for several years to consolidate its [most recent] victories. This conservative bloc has suffered defeat, and we now observe the so-called Labour Party coming to power.

Comrades, we are realists. We know the British Labour Party's policy too well to have any illusions about it. However, we must remember that at present millions of English workers, millions of organized English workers trained in the prolonged struggle with capitalists, are approaching the power of government. Under MacDonald, Webb, Snowden, and Thomas [Tom] Shaw, the problem of workers' government will be given the most serious consideration [by the workers]. For the first time, England's working class will be able to examine their leaders not only in opposition, but in office.

We may rest assured—and the Labour Party leaders themselves say—that they are not taking office with any idea of satisfying the legal class demands of the proletariat to any considerable extent.

However, even this [limited Labour program] is bound to influence the English proletariat. The workers will now be able to watch their leaders in the seat of the government. If they do not satisfy the workers' minimum demands, they will be held accountable to the masses.

We are absolutely convinced that whatever the leaders do, the increased class-consciousness of the British workers will lead to increased class solidarity, greater political strength, and a growing conviction of the necessity of assuming political power. British imperialism, which will now be directed—we do not know for how many days, weeks, or even months—by the leaders of the so-called Labour Party, is a basic force of bourgeois-capitalist civilization. We, as well as the English proletariat, will do well to watch quietly the new and so-called workers' government, and to see how much the increase in demands placed before it helps to clarify the needs of the working class.

As to our relations with Britain, you know that the present prime minister of Britain won the trust of the [English] people partly because he made his first and most outstanding campaign slogan the complete *de jure* recognition of the U.S.S.R.

We do not doubt, and the prime minister, MacDonald, is well aware, that while voting for the workers' government the working masses of England were also voting for full recognition of the U.S.S.R.

But because MacDonald owes his position not only to the working class, but also to the Liberals, we already see attempts to delay carrying out the promise . . . [of] full recognition. It will be interesting to see whether, under Liberal pressure, the campaign promises are withdrawn. We hope they will not be, and that MacDonald will do what the working class empowered him to do—grant full recognition to the Soviet government.

Even after recognition, certain controversial problems will require conferences, explanations, elucidations, perhaps even debate, but it is just these methods, in our opinion, that offer the best possibility of general agreement.   Therefore, we have already informed England that we are prepared, once recognition is granted, to create an Anglo-Russian commission to study all the economic problems in dispute between us. We would like to hope that with MacDonald's government (more so than with Curzon's, or even Lloyd George's) we can agree on measures to safeguard general peace, settle the antagonisms now tearing the entire world asunder, and open friendly negotiations toward limiting the burden of war expenditures that weighs so heavily upon Europe, and also upon the working class of England. The present British government must decide whether Curzon's May ultimatum was truly the last convulsive attempt of English conservative circles to create a new period of tension between the two countries. . . .

As for Italy, here, comrades, we witness a rare frankness. I shall not remind you of Mussolini's speech in Parliament, in which (with, I repeat, laudable frankness) he stated what prompted him to recognize and come to an agreement with Soviet Russia. Negotiations became possible on that basis and have proceeded so quickly and so favorably that a treaty granting full recognition may be signed by the Italian government any day.

The third Great Power, which so far we have met only on the field of battle, is France. We are realists, and thus we need not always confine ourselves to diplomatic documents. We can allow ourselves the luxury of analyzing the actual motives [of governments]. And I think that behind the French government's re-examination of French policy toward the U.S.S.R. lies the fact that the French bourgeoisie recognizes the U.S.S.R.'s growing strength and does not wish to be the last to come round; that is, it does not wish to lag behind England and Italy in recognizing and consequently trading with the U.S.S.R. This explains the change we have noticed in the French government's attitude.

We are ready to welcome these steps by the French government. We know from the newspapers that M. Beneš, the foreign minister of Czechoslovakia, a state that is friendly with France and only recently signed a special agreement with her, has offered to clear the way for negotiations between France and Russia. We think that M. Beneš does the right thing, in his own way, of course, and in so far as he considers his action the right one for his own country. On the other hand, we would think it much more rational and fruitful if [our] inevitable negotiations [with France] were conducted directly. . . .

You know that we were recently obliged to transfer part of our trading machinery from France to Berlin. I fear we shall have to go on doing so, since without a trade agreement our trading organs face an absolutely impossible situation. We naturally prefer to establish our trading centers in the countries with which we have normal relations. . . .

I turn now to Germany. We are connected with Germany more closely than with any other country, by our geographical position and our common economic interests, and because Germany, which had been crushed by triumphant imperialism, found at the required moment sufficient courage and foresight to sign the Rapallo treaty. Our German policy, therefore, has been and remains to consolidate friendly relations and increase economic contacts.

But during the period upon which I am reporting, other things have also become evident. The Soviet government could not ignore the October–November crisis that shook Germany. The proletarian conscience cannot ignore some other country's proletariat when it is straining all its forces to win better living conditions. Our soviets serve as a loudspeaker that announces the mood, the interests, and the enthusiasm of the large proletarian masses; this is their duty and their obligation. But also, comrades, we could not overlook it [the German crisis] because of business and political considerations. Germany's foreign minister, Stresemann, declared that during the crisis of October–November, Germany's fate and Soviet Russia's were linked. We agree absolutely with the German foreign minister. Like Stresemann, we see the victory of fascism, the victory of military reactionary circles in Germany, as opening the door of the Soviet republic to world imperialism. The advance of the French troops from the Rhine region—where they were firmly established on the shoulders of the victorious German counterrevolution—further into Germany would have rocked the very foundation of the world situation upon which the Soviet republic rests. It would have been very strange to demand at that moment, with events presaging the overthrow of the entire system of Central Europe, that we take no preventive measures.

To protect our national security and safeguard the achievements of the October Revolution, we had to act. Our policy was best expressed during those months by Comrade Kopp's trip to Latvia, Lithuania, and Poland. What did Comrade Kopp go there for? What did we trust him to achieve? We tried to achieve two things: guarantees of nonintervention in German affairs and agreements assuring us free transit between the U.S.S.R. and Central Europe, irrespective of political and social changes there. . . .

Thus, comrades, everything shows us that the U.S.S.R. has long since crossed the European Rubicon; it no longer needs to seek or buy recognition. The situation is different now, and woe unto the government that fails to notice the great changes in the Soviet government's position.

. . .

We see in the general [world] situation the beginning of the end of the first period, the period when the Soviet government was obliged to struggle for recognition. We are definitely on the threshold of a new period, a period that will undoubtedly present some definite dangers, dangers of capitalistic pressure that we must overcome, and that we shall have to oppose by economic methods. It is clear that we stand at a turning point in our international position. The power of the U.S.S.R., its continuous economic growth against a background of general disintegration and the breaking up of capitalist civilization, can no longer be concealed or disputed.

But in entering the new period, we must repeat Lenin's statement of a few years ago, which has remained a leading principle in our foreign policy: "The later the recognition, the harder our conditions."

We do not insist; we do not hurry. We have already passed the most difficult period, the period of intervention and blockade. We have become a factor in world economic development; without us it is impossible. And, therefore, those who think that *de jure* recognition is something for which we are prepared to pay, even at the cost of our own interests, are mistaken. *De jure* recognition means for us, first of all, the legalization of our trade relations. This is necessary to us, but it is also necessary to those who want our bread, our lumber, and our oil, and who want us to buy their machinery and cotton.

We do not seek *de jure* recognition as a means to international rank. *De jure* recognition is not a favor. The great peoples who have created under a great leader a Union of Soviet Socialist Republics do not need any legal anointment by the priests of capital.

But the legalization of our business, industrial, and commercial relations includes the recognition of our legal system and our legal institutions. *De jure* recognition is the recognition of our laws and of our legislature, which is obligatory for those who wish to maintain business and commercial and economic relations with us. That is *de jure* recognition, and such recognition we need.

Comrades, you can see from the outline I have given you that there are no storm clouds on our horizon directly threatening our independence and our territory. But let us not flatter ourselves. Remember the past year, remember the last nine months, and you will see that during that period imminent misfortune twice knocked at our gate. In May, that typical representative of world imperialism and conservatism, Curzon, knocked at our door and made us all spring to our feet as one man. In October and November new events knocked at our door, and we again had to jump to our feet.

Do not think that what I have told you—although it undoubtedly indicates the consolidation of our international position, the growth of our prestige, and an increased desire to trade and to make political agreements with our proletarian workers' republic—precludes new crises. The world is in chaos. Hostile feelings are boiling as in a caldron. All other governments see us as some mad daredevils who have ventured to go against those governments' principles, against their civilization, against the foundation of their economic order. Therefore, we must be ready at any moment for a new challenge. We must be ready not only to sign treaties and accept recognition, but also to face any day new events which, like those of last May and last October, will make us concentrate all our forces, and which will test our capacity for self-defense and our readiness for battle. . . .

. . . And if some madman's hand tries to disturb our peace and our constructive economic work, the workers and peasants of all the nationalities of the Union will stand as one man to defend the independence of our country, our territory, our state.

79

Soviet Explanation of the Significance of British Recognition

[Resolution Adopted by the Second Congress of Soviets of the
U.S.S.R., February 2, 1924][35]

Having heard the communication concerning the full *de jure* recognition of the U.S.S.R. by Great Britain, and the establishment of full normal diplomatic relations between the two states, the Second Congress of Soviets of the U.S.S.R. notes with satisfaction that this historic step was one of the first acts of the first government of Great Britain representing the working class.

The workers' and peasants' government of the U.S.S.R., which originated in the great revolution, has made the struggle for peace its foremost objective, and throughout its existence has worked persistently for the re-establishment of normal relations between all peoples. Unfortunately no previous British government came to meet the government of the U.S.S.R.; as late as last May, British diplomats sent the U.S.S.R. an ultimatum threatening to interrupt trade relations, an ultimatum pregnant with a direct threat to European peace.

Throughout this period the British working class has been the true ally of the working masses of the U.S.S.R. in their struggle for peace. The peoples of the U.S.S.R. remember the efforts of the British working masses and the advanced section of the British public to end the boycott, the blockade, and armed intervention. They realize that recognition was effected by the unfaltering will of the British people, who unanimously demanded it as necessary to the establishment of universal peace, to world economic reconstruction after the ruin caused by the imperialist war, and, in particular, to Great Britain's own successful struggle against industrial stagnation and unemployment.

The Soviet government's pacific policy, under the guidance of V. I. Lenin, and the loudly proclaimed determination of the British people have at last established normal relations between the two countries, relations that are worthy of the great peoples of both countries and that lay the foundation for their friendly co-operation.

In the tense atmosphere of contemporary international relations, fraught with the danger of new world conflicts and justly disturbing the working people of all countries, this step by the British Labour government acquires special significance.

The Second Congress of Soviets of the U.S.S.R. declares that co-operation between the peoples of Great Britain and the U.S.S.R. remains as before one of the first cares of the Soviet government. Following its policy of peace, the Soviet government will make every effort to settle all controversial questions and misunderstandings, and to develop and consolidate the economic relations so necessary for the economic and political progress of the peoples of both countries and of the whole world.

The Second Congress of Soviets of the U.S.S.R. stretches out its friendly hand to the British people, and empowers the Union government to undertake with the British government whatever proceedings the recognition has made possible.

M. KALININ,

Chairman of the Second Congress of Soviets
of the Union of Soviet Socialist Republics

[35] *Vtoroi Sezd Sovetov S.S.S.R.,* Appendix, pp. 16–17.

80

A Communist Interpretation of Russia's Recognition by Italy

[From an Article by Karl Radek in *Pravda*][36]

The example of the British government was followed by the Italian government. The example of the leader of the Second International, Ramsay MacDonald, was followed by Mussolini, the leader of Italian fascism, the ideological inspirer of the international counterrevolution.

In the interest of historical truth it should be noted, however, that M. Mussolini "did not follow" MacDonald, for he had already been conducting negotiations for many months past concerning the recognition of the Soviet government. He simply delayed recognition too long, hoping that the English would not be able to turn the rudder so quickly.

If one puts side by side the recognition of the Soviet government by the so-called labor government of Britain and by the truly counterrevolutionary government of Italy, one can see how little ground the Second International has for special laurels. Both MacDonald and Mussolini pursue through the recognition of Soviet Russia definite economic and political aims, the result of the international situation and their own countries' positions.

Just a few days ago we discussed why the so-called "Labour government" of Britain recognized the Soviet government. But what are the special motives of Mussolini? First, Italy can view even less indifferently than England the breaking up of the Entente and must seek support, contacts, and help wherever she can. Italy is a Mediterranean power. Italy's chief competitor in the Mediterranean is France. Therefore, at Washington Italy insisted on equalizing her naval power with France's. Italian emigration to America and to the French colonies goes on, causing many difficulties between Italy and France. The struggle with France forced Italy to come to an agreement with Yugoslavia in order to secure her Adriatic rear. The Soviet Union is the neighbor of Rumania and the strongest naval power on the Black Sea. This ensures its influence in the Balkans, an influence that will increase with the growth of the U.S.S.R. as a world power. Already these purely political reasons have forced Mussolini, this counterrevolutionary realist, to abandon the legitimist game, and to seek a rapprochement with the Soviet government.

But the main reason for the recognition is economic conditions. Italy needs grain, oil, and coal from abroad. She imports her grain and oil from America. What can she pay in return? Industrial products. But the tariff policy of the United States makes Italian industrial export particularly difficult. England did not adopt the most-favored tariff policy as the Conservatives wished, but the Conservatives might return to the helm, and besides, Italian industry finds it difficult, in general, to compete with English and American production. The U.S.S.R., on the contrary, can give Italy grain, oil, and some coal in return for finished goods. Cheap freight makes this exchange easier. This is why Mussolini recommended recognition of the Soviet Union.

Just as the pressure of the English workers on MacDonald helped the English Labour government to overcome the bourgeois prejudices that were interfering with the recognition of Soviet Russia, so this step of the Italian bourgeoisie was facili- tated by the fascist shamelessness, which precludes any sentimentality and definitely sides with the strong. Only poor M. Poincaré still plays the role of Buridan's ass, unable to choose between the hay of old debts and the oats of new profits. The petty

[36] Karl Radek, "Posle Anglii-Italiia," *Pravda*, No. 32, February 9, 1924, p. 1.

bourgeoisie, even though they are fond of the clatter of arms, belong to the breed of the most indecisive people.

81

A Communist Interpretation of the Role of Soviet Diplomacy After Recognition

[From an Article by F. A. Rotshtein in *Pravda*][37]

We have been recognized by those who wished to strangle us. It is not we who have changed, for we continue to emphasize our revolutionary origin. It is our enemies who have changed. Our international significance will be tremendously increased by this recognition. Our work in the international arena will become even more active and more fruitful. . . .

[Says the bourgeois world has admitted its own inefficiency, and has thus lost the game to revolutionary Russia. Emphasizes the advantages therefrom for Russia.] . . .

But standing above all the direct advantages to us of our recognition by the bourgeois governments is the tremendous increase in our international prestige. Russia, this huge country of 130 million people, possessing boundless natural wealth, was very important and influential in world politics even in tsarist times, although her internal weakness caused her to be spoken of as "the colossus with feet of clay."

Our new Soviet state, our union of the republics, which was born on the ruins of tsarist Russia and which has been powerfully welded in foundation and in composition as no other state in modern history has been, is now called upon to play a still more decisive role in international relations. It was this indisputable fact that chiefly prompted the bourgeois governments to recognize the Soviet government, hateful to them as it still is. Europe is again breaking up into two camps, and neither of these camps can allow itself to ignore the position the Soviet state might choose to take.

This means that in the future we shall be even better able than before to use, in the interests of the toilers of our own Union and the world in general, the antagonisms among the imperialist powers. We have done this in the past, and not without success. It also means that now, advancing as a full-fledged member [of the international community] on the chessboard of international diplomacy, we shall be even better able than before to contrast, as events occur, our own political line of struggle with the imperialist line—our policy of disarmament, of the true self-determination of peoples, and of the true liberation of the oppressed nationalities from foreign exploitation, against the hypocritical, rapacious, and at best halfway policy of the capitalist powers. There were times when we joined bourgeois parliaments[38] to contrast our program to theirs. We believed revolution by parliamentary methods impossible, but we believed in using the parliamentary tribune to denounce our class enemies and to educate and organize our toiling masses.

The international arena, which we now enter as a generally recognized power, can be compared in some respects to the past bourgeois parliaments. Once in it, we shall advance our demands; we shall struggle to get them realized; we shall force the other party to remove its mask and show its true face. Then the peoples will be able to distinguish among the governments and the political and public regimes which these governments support; they will see who is their friend and who is their enemy. In Genoa, in Lausanne, we have already crossed swords with the international policy of the imperialist powers, and the impression produced on the toilers by these conflicts has been far from advantageous to those powers. We can expect a still stronger

[37] F. A. Rotshtein, "Kakaia polza ot priznaniia," *Pravda*, No. 59, March 12, 1924, p. 1.
[38] The reference is to Bolshevik members in the tsarist Duma.

impression in the future when we participate much more actively in international affairs and in settling international problems, for we shall be able to speak not only as a large state, but also as a generally recognized power. Only then will the full significance of what now appears harmless, being called officially *de jure* recognition, become evident.

82

Notes Exchanged Between the French Premier and Chicherin Concerning the Recognition of the U.S.S.R. by France

a

[The Telegram of the Chairman of the Council of Ministers and Foreign Minister of France, Herriot, to the Chairman of the Council of People's Commissars of the U.S.S.R., Rykov, and the People's Commissar of Foreign Affairs of the U.S.S.R., Chicherin, Paris, October 28, 1924][39]

Following the minister's declaration of June 17, 1924, and your communication of July 19, 1924,[40] the government of the Republic, true to the amity that unites the Russian and French peoples, recognizes *de jure,* and from this date on, the government of the Union of Soviet Socialist Republics as the government of the territories of the former Russian Empire where its authority is recognized by the people, and as the successor within these territories of the preceding Russian governments.

The government of the Republic is prepared, therefore, to engage in regular diplomatic relations with the government of the Union by means of the reciprocal exchange of ambassadors.

In communicating to you this recognition, which must not violate any of the obligations assumed and treaties signed by France, the government of the Republic wishes to believe in the possibility of general agreement between our two countries, of which the renewal of diplomatic relations represents the beginning. In view of the above, the government of the Republic intends to reserve especially the rights of French citizens based on the obligations contracted by Russia and her subjects under the preceding governments, the keeping of which is guaranteed by the general principles of law which remain for us the basis of international relations. Similar reservations apply to the responsibilities assumed by Russia since 1914 in regard to the French state and its citizens.

In this spirit, and desiring to serve once more the interests of peace and the future of Europe, the government of the Republic is anxious to find, jointly with the Union, a just and practical arrangement that would permit the re-establishment between the two nations of normal diplomatic and commercial relations, once the confidence of France is restored. As soon as you announce your agreement to begin negotiations of a general character, and especially of an economic nature, we shall welcome your plenipotentiary delegates to Paris.

Until the successful outcome of these negotiations, the treaties, conventions, and agreements that existed between France or French citizens and Russia will remain in abeyance, and individual legal relations contracted prior to the establishment of the power of the soviets will continue to be regulated by the old rules. Likewise the settlement of all transactions between the two states will be fully postponed, while the measures to safeguard [them] in France have already been or will be taken.

39 *L'Humanité,* No. 7611, October 30, 1924, p. 1.
40 This was the correspondence between the two governments regarding delays in granting visas to the representatives of their respective countries. Chicherin stressed that such difficulties were due to the lack of normal diplomatic relations between the two countries.

Finally, it should be understood that from now on, noninterference by each state in the other's internal affairs is taken to be a rule guiding the relations between the two states.

b

[Telegram of the Chairman of the Central Executive Committee of the U.S.S.R., Kalinin; the Chairman of the Council of People's Commissars of the U.S.S.R., Rykov; and the People's Commissar of Foreign Affairs of the U.S.S.R., Chicherin, to Herriot][41]

Heartily welcoming the offer of the French government to re-establish full normal diplomatic relations between the U.S.S.R. and France, with the immediate exchange of ambassadors, and the immediate beginning of negotiations directed toward the re-establishment of friendly relations between the peoples of the U.S.S.R. and France, the Central Executive Committee of the U.S.S.R. expresses its conviction that an agreement can be reached between the states in regard to all questions mentioned in the telegram of the Chairman of the Council of Ministers of the French republic of today's date, an agreement that will be enormously advantageous for the peoples of the U.S.S.R. and of France, provided there is good will on both sides and an absolute respect for their reciprocal interests.

The Central Executive Committee of the U.S.S.R. attaches the greatest significance to the removal of all misunderstandings between the U.S.S.R. and France, and the conclusion of a general agreement providing a durable basis for friendly relations between them. [In these considerations] the U.S.S.R. is guided by its ever-present desire to truly secure a general peace in the interests of the toiling masses of all countries, and to establish friendship with all peoples. In particular, the Central Executive Committee of the U.S.S.R. emphasizes the considerable advantage to both parties of creating between themselves close and durable economic relations, relations that would enhance the development of their productive forces and commerce, as well as their closer economic co-operation. The Central Executive Committee of the U.S.S.R., like the French government, considers mutual noninterference in internal affairs essential to relations with other countries in general, and with France in particular. It welcomes [therefore] the declarations of the French government on this question.

While agreeing to the negotiations between the U.S.S.R. and France in Paris, the Central Executive Committee of the U.S.S.R. wishes to inform the French government that it has instructed the Council of People's Commissars and the People's Commissariat of Foreign Affairs to take all necessary measures for immediately opening such negotiations, expressing its firm hope that all questions confronting the two countries will be fully settled in the interests of both states and of world peace.

83

A Communist Interpretation of French Recognition

[Iu. M. Steklov in *Izvestiia*][42]

The French government has at last decided to take the step that both its friends and its enemies have long been expecting it to take. On October 28 there arrived the *de jure* recognition of the Soviet Union by France.

France is the last of the so-called great European powers . . . to recognize the

---

[41] Kliuchnikov and Sabanin, III, 330.
[42] *Izvestiia*, No. 248, October 29, 1924, p. 1.

Soviet republic. Germany, Italy, and England already recognized us some time ago. With the decision of the Herriot government there is completed the ring of diplomatic recognition of the Soviet Union in Europe. Hereafter recognition by small European states will not be especially significant, and some of them will perhaps even regret that they have so delayed their decision and have thereby placed themselves in a less favorable position.

In a word, in Europe the fundamental cycle is completed. Among the non-European Great Powers who have not granted us recognition, there now remain only the United States and Japan. Both these powers may have to follow suit before long, and Japan may well be compelled to do so under special circumstances, that is to say, as a state which, in the new European-Asiatic political combination, is seeking to defend its interests in the Far East from the onslaughts of world imperialism, which has commenced an offensive.

Thus the decision of the French government has, in a certain respect, a historical significance. It marks the conclusion of an entire phase in the international relations of the Soviet Union and the opening of a new phase, the establishment of mutual relations between the Soviet state and the capitalist states under the conditions of so-called normal diplomatic relations.

Like every document of this character, the Paris cabinet's note is couched in general and sometimes vague terms, allowing the widest interpretation. We shall probably be obliged to return to its interpretation more than once, and many of its clauses will become precise only during the approaching negotiations between representatives of the two countries. But its main outlines can be seen quite clearly at first glance.

On the whole, we must acknowledge that this historic document is drawn up in a form acceptable to the Soviet republic. It has been drafted in a spirit approximating the ideas that have been repeatedly developed in the columns of *Izvestiia*.

On one point the French government has proved more decisive and more logical than MacDonald; that is, it at once appointed an ambassador to Moscow, and proposed that the Soviet government appoint an ambassador to Paris. This shows (1) that the deficiencies of the English method, which deferred the exchange of ambassadors to the indefinite future, have been proved by experience, and (2) that the French government is ready to clear the ground for a genuine understanding with the Soviet Union, and to eliminate beforehand the trifling formal hindrances that could only arouse mistrust and create justifiable dissatisfaction.

It has been remarked in the foreign press, especially in the French press, that the French government's moves toward establishing normal relations with the Soviet republic seem to indicate that France desires to occupy the "vacant place" temporarily created by the [Soviet-]English political crisis.[43] If so, it would only prove the keen discernment of the French politicians, and also that they have finally fully realized the importance to France of renewing friendly relations with the Soviet Union.

One clause that might arouse some objections is the one that formulates the extent to which France recognizes the Soviet Union. Unlike the document submitted by MacDonald, which refers to the *territories* that recognize the Soviet's government's rule, the French document refers to the *inhabitants* who recognize it. This is perhaps a slight modification of the English document and constitutes its improved edition. A better formulation might perhaps have been found, one that would eliminate any doubts regarding hidden intentions on the part of the other party. But partly basing ourselves on official French explanations, and partly starting with the logical assumption that the French government—which knows our attitude toward any attempt to challenge the unity and indivisibility of the Soviet Union—hardly desired to create misunderstanding between the two countries at the very outset, we are prepared not to see in this phraseology any hidden intent until the contrary has been proved;

---

[43] A reference to the crisis caused by the Zinoviev letter; see our pp. 264–66.

the more so as this formula, under certain conditions, can also be interpreted in a sense particularly favorable for the Soviet Union. Thus, for instance, the *inhabitants* of Bessarabia, which has been illegally taken from the Soviet Union, without doubt acknowledge as *their* sovereign, not the Rumanian oligarchy, but the Soviet government. And in certain circumstances this formula could be used to defend their right to self-determination, and as an argument against the ratification of the Bessarabian Protocol,[44] which has been duly acknowledged by the French parliament.

It is only natural that the French government carefully and definitely reserves all its rights, leaving ours in the shadow and passing over them in silence. It goes without saying that we, on our part, will formulate our point of view, which in a number of questions may not be opposed to the French, but in others will unavoidably differ from theirs. For if M. Herriot emphasizes that the recognition cannot violate any of the obligations and agreements accepted and signed by France, so we on our part will be compelled to consider whether among those obligations and agreements there are not some that clearly infringe on our interests and were concluded to the detriment of our inalienable rights. And if M. Herriot expresses the hope that French confidence will find itself justified, we also should like to hope that our confidence in the good will of France will not meet with any sharp disillusionment.

M. Herriot intends to seek a just and practical way out of the situation that has been created. We seek the same, and we presume that with good will, and having regard to mutual interests, it will be possible, though not without pain, to find such a way out. But it will clearly be necessary to *seek* such a way.

However this may be, now at last the ground has been laid and the soil prepared for an agreement between the two governments. From now on there will be negotiations between them to sift and settle all the disputed questions that divide them. It may be assumed that these negotiations with France will proceed more rapidly and smoothly than our negotiations with other states. . . .

84
The Soviet Government's Failure to Re-establish Friendly Relations with the American Government

a

[Excerpt from President Coolidge's Message to Congress, December 6, 1923][45]

Our diplomatic relations, lately so largely interrupted, are now being resumed, but Russia presents notable difficulties. We have every desire to see that great people, who are our traditional friends, restored to their position among the nations of the earth. We have relieved their pitiable destitution with an enormous charity. Our Government offers no objection to the carrying on of commerce by our citizens with the people of Russia. Our Government does not propose, however, to enter into relations with another régime which refuses to recognize the sanctity of international obligations. I do not propose to barter away for the privilege of trade any of the cherished rights of humanity. I do not propose to make merchandise of any American principles. These rights and principles must go wherever the sanctions of our Government go.

But while the favor of America is not for sale, I am willing to make very large concessions for the purpose of rescuing the people of Russia. Already encouraging evidences of returning to the ancient ways of society can be detected. But more are needed. Whenever there appears any disposition to compensate our citizens who

[44] For text see *Treaty between the Principal Allied Powers and Roumania signed at Paris, October 28, 1920.*

[45] *Foreign Relations of the United States, 1923,* I, VIII–IX.

were despoiled, and to recognize that debt contracted with our Government, not by the Czar, but by the newly formed Republic of Russia; whenever the active spirit of enmity to our institutions is abated; whenever there appear works mete [sic] for repentance, our country ought to be the first to go to the economic and moral rescue of Russia. We have every desire to help and no desire to injure. We hope the time is near at hand when we can act.

b

[Chicherin, People's Commissar of Foreign Affairs, to President Coolidge][46]

It has been the constant endeavor of the Soviet government to bring about the resumption of friendly relations with the United States of America based on mutual trust. With this end in view the Soviet government has repeatedly announced its readiness to enter into negotiations with the American government and to remove all misunderstandings and differences between the two countries.

Having acquainted ourselves with your message to Congress, and being sincerely anxious to establish at last a durable friendship with the people and the government of the United States, the Soviet government wishes to inform you of its complete readiness to discuss with your government all problems mentioned in your message, these negotiations being based on the principle of mutual noninterference in the internal affairs of each party. The Soviet government will continue to steadfastly adhere to this principle, and it expects the same attitude from the American government.

As to the question of claims mentioned in your message, the Soviet government is fully prepared to negotiate with the view of reaching a satisfactory settlement, and assuming, of course, that this settlement will be based on the principle of reciprocity. On its part, the Soviet government is prepared to do all that is in its power, and in so far as the dignity and interests of the U.S.S.R. permit, to bring about the desired end of renewal of friendship with the United States of America.

c

[American Reply to Chicherin's Note: Instructions from Secretary of State Charles Evans Hughes to the American Consul at Tallinn, December 18, 1923][47]

Hand to the Soviet representative at Reval [Tallinn] for communication to Tchitcherin the following:

"With respect to the telegram to President Coolidge from Tchitcherin of December 16th, the Secretary of State today made the following statement in reply: 'There would seem to be at this time no reason for negotiations. The American Government, as the President said in his message to the Congress, is not proposing to barter away its principles. If the Soviet authorities are ready to restore the confiscated property of American citizens or make effective compensation, they can do so. If the Soviet authorities are ready to repeal their decree repudiating Russia's obligations to this country and appropriately recognize them, they can do so. It requires no conference or negotiations to accomplish these results which can and should be achieved at Moscow as evidence of good faith. The American Government has not incurred liabilities to Russia or repudiated obligations. Most serious is the continued propaganda to overthrow the institutions of this country. This Govern-

[46] Kliuchnikov and Sabanin, III, 294; also *Foreign Affairs of the United States, 1923,* II, 787.
[47] *Foreign Relations of the United States, 1923,* II, 788.

ment can enter into no negotiations until these efforts directed from Moscow are abandoned.' "

HUGHES

85

A Soviet Interpretation of American Refusal to Recognize the Soviet Government

[Statement by Chicherin in a Newspaper Interview][48]

The American Secretary of State, Mr. Hughes, has made another statement against the renewal of relations with the U.S.S.R. This last statement by Mr. Hughes crowns his policy as revealed in the course of the last few weeks, during which Mr. Hughes, and the Right wing of the American Republican Party represented by him, have acted invariably as a major force of world reaction and world imperialism in the struggle against the colonial peoples, and have acted directly or indirectly against the Soviet republic.

Many times since coming to office, Mr. Hughes has made statements directed against the Soviet republic. His arguments have varied, but his unquestionable enmity toward the workers' and peasants' Russia has remained unchanged. At first his chief argument was that Soviet Russia represented, as he put it, a vacuum from an economic point of view. The development of our exports, especially of grain, and also our imports of raw material, such as cotton, have been sufficient evidence to refute this argument.

Mr. Hughes's other argument was the alleged absence of a guarantee of the safety of life and property of foreigners on Soviet territory. This argument has long ago been repudiated by facts, which have been confirmed by representatives of the A.R.A., by American senators and journalists, and by other visitors to our republic.

In Mr. Hughes's last diplomatic document refusing our offer of negotiations, two arguments were advanced: First, we annulled debts; second, we carry on agitation against the existing regime in America.

Mr. Hughes's reference to the activity of the Comintern, for which he calls the Soviet government responsible, is an inexcusable exaggeration and falsification of facts. Do Mr. Hughes and others hold Mr. MacDonald, for example, whose party is now at the helm in Britain, responsible for all the actions of the Second International, of which his party is a member? . . . The Communists in the government occupy themselves with the government's business and serve the government's needs, while the party organizations are engaged in party work, just as the Republican Party of America engages in government work without reducing its party work outside the government. The analogy is complete. . . .

Still more forceful is the division between the Communist Party and the government in regard to the Comintern, which is an international organization, and in which the Russian [Communist] Party is only one of many parts. Thus every attempt to call Soviet political organs and their foreign representatives organs of the Comintern is an obvious and international attempt to deceive the poorly informed public.

It is true that the workers' and peasants' Soviet government expresses the will of the toilers and of their party. Here it differs radically from the Right-wing Republican Party of America and its leader, Mr. Hughes, now at the helm and expressing the will of large-scale American bankers and trusts. But the fact that the Soviet government serves the workers' interests and Mr. Hughes and his gov-

[48] *Izvestiia*, No. 220, September 26, 1924, p. 2.

ernment serve the capitalists' interests does not mean that these two governments cannot reach a compromise. On the contrary, innumerable facts show that if there is a will, such a compromise is quite possible.

As to Mr. Hughes's second argument, regarding the R.S.F.S.R. decree annulling foreign debts, it was precisely on this question that our government offered to negotiate with the American government. Did not the recently signed general treaty with Great Britain prove that on this point mutually advantageous agreements between the Soviet Union and other states are possible?

Mr. Hughes's recent arguments are just as groundless and senseless as his earlier ones, and they show that he wishes to pursue at any cost a policy of irreconcilable hostility to the Soviet republic. While the Anglo-Soviet treaty bases the relations between a bourgeois state and the Soviet republic on equality and mutual recognition of each country's [political] system, Mr. Hughes's declaration is permeated from beginning to end with the idea of the impossibility of relations on such a basis, and with the desire to destroy the Soviet order, to wipe it off the face of the earth. It does not even occur to Mr. Hughes that equality is possible; and, therefore, his activity is a continual hindrance to any compromise between the U.S.S.R. and America, and is false propaganda against the Soviet regime. . . .

Two years ago, in the autumn of 1922, upon returning from abroad, I gave our press a long interview on the general world situation at that time, pointing out the Anglo-French antagonism as one of the mainsprings of world relations. I also described America's isolation as one of the chief phenomena of the then existing foreign situation. Now this situation has radically changed. We see a very active Anglo-American bloc as the chief force in the policy of the bourgeois states. We also see France weakened and reduced to a secondary position by the senseless policy of Poincaré, whom the powerful Anglo-American bloc hardly takes into consideration. From the unification of the capitalist world reached at the London Conference,[49] it is clear that France has ceased to be an important and decisive factor in regard to reparations, and that the Anglo-American bloc will now become such a factor.

When I gave that interview two years ago, the attention of the political world was centered upon Germany and upon the Mediterranean with North Africa and the Near East. At the present moment, we have suddenly had opened before us a huge panorama of the advancement of world imperialism. . . .

The Anglo-Soviet treaty aroused the indignation of the reactionary crust of the capitalist world, who are now seeking revenge. It was at that time that the active American policy made its appearance in the world arena, closely connected with Great Britain's policy in an all-round joint action. The provisional and alleged settlement of the important differences in European policy at the London Conference permitted the imperialist powers to come out in a united front against the colonies, which are liberating themselves, and against the Soviet republic.

These and similar facts concerning the reactionary aggressive policy scarcely correspond to the well-known pacifist speeches of Herriot and MacDonald in the League of Nations on disarmament, or to the pacifist interview given by Hughes recently in Paris.

So far the imperialist machinations of Mr. Hughes and his allies have produced very poor results. . . .

Nevertheless, new imperialist attempts at an international economic blockade of the U.S.S.R. in one or another form are quite possible in the near future. . . . Therefore, the Soviet government foresees the possibility of a new aggravation of international relations and a new threat to peace. The people must take the cause of peace into their own hands and bridle the audacious imperialists.

[49] The Inter-Allied Conference on Reparations and Inter-Allied Debts held in London, July 16–August 16, 1924.

THE CONSOLIDATION OF SOVIET POWER AND THE AIMS OF THE "AMERICAN CAPITALISTS"

86

Review of the International Situation in 1924

[Stalin's Report on the Results of the Thirteenth Congress of the Russian Communist Party to the School of Secretaries of the County Committees of the Central Committee of the Party, June 17, 1924][50]

. . .

What has occurred in the international situation this year in regard to Soviet Russia? What new and fundamental characteristic in the international world was the Thirteenth Congress bound to take into account when passing to the new year?

The past year may be characterized, first, by the failure of several attempts to make Western Europe's international policies openly fascist. If we ignore Italy, where fascism is deteriorating, we note that in the principal European countries, France and England, attempts to promote fascist policies have definitely failed, and the promoters of these policies, to speak crudely, have gone overboard. This, first, is what the year has given us.

Second, this year has seen a number of attempts by militant imperialists in England and France to isolate our country. These attempts, too, have completely failed. Without any doubt Poincaré's numerous machinations against the Soviet Union and Curzon's well-known ultimatum were designed to isolate our country. But what were the results of these attempts? Instead of isolating the Soviet Union, they led to its *de jure* recognition. Moreover, instead of the isolation of the Soviet Union, we have the isolation of Poincaré and Curzon.

The prestige of our country has proved to be more significant than some of the old imperialist politicians expected. This is a second characteristic of the past year. How has this come about? Some people attribute it to the wisdom of our policy. . . . But to explain it by our wisdom, or by the correctness of our policy, is not sufficient. We are confronted here, not so much with the fact of a correct policy, as with a situation that has recently developed in Europe and determined the success of our policy. In this connection we note the following circumstances:

First, the inability of the imperialist powers to capitalize on their victories in the war, and to establish a more or less bearable peace in Europe—their inability to carry on their own development without further plundering the conquered countries and colonies, without conflicts and clashes among themselves over the division of their spoils. Hence the new efforts to arm. Hence the danger of a new war.

But the masses do not want a new war, for they have not forgotten the sacrifices they had to bear for the sake of the capitalists' profits. Hence their growing displeasure with the policy of militant imperialism. Here lies the weakness of imperialism. Why were Poincaré and Curzon driven away? Because among the people it is said that they are the instigators of new wars. Because their openly militant policy has aroused the displeasure of the masses with imperialism in general, and thus has created a threat to imperialism itself.

Second, the consolidation of Soviet power at home. The capitalist states have plotted the downfall of the Soviet government. . . . Through him [Beneš] the imperialists announced that there should be no hurry to recognize the Soviet republics, since the Soviet regime was unstable and the Soviet government would soon be swept aside by a new bourgeois-democratic government. . . . For a number of states the

[50] Stalin, *Sochineniia*, VI, 235–39.

policy of "abstention" has [now] changed into a policy of "recognition." . Why? Because it is difficult to argue against the obvious—that is, against the fact that the Soviet government is as solid as a rock. First, the man in the street, naïve though he may be, is bound to see that the Soviet government may be stronger than the bourgeois governments, for these governments have come and gone during the seven years of the dictatorship [of the proletariat], while the Soviet government has remained. Second, the man in the street realizes that our country's economy is developing and our exports are continually increasing. . . .

We are accused of carrying on propaganda against capitalism in Western Europe. It must be said that we do not need such propaganda—that we do not require it. The very existence of the Soviet state, its consolidation, and its material prosperity serve, among the European workers, as the best propaganda for the Soviet government. Workers who come to the Soviet country and see how the proletarian rule works learn what a Soviet government is, and what the working class is capable of when it is at the helm. This is true propaganda—a proof with facts; and it impresses the workers far more than any propaganda by word of mouth or in print.

We are blamed for spreading propaganda in the East. This is also nonsense. We do not need propaganda in the East. Let any citizen of a dependent or colonial country come to the Soviet Union and see how the people are governing their country; let him see the white and dark races, the Russians and the non-Russians, the peoples of all colors and nationalities pulling together in harness, directing the administration of this great country. Let him see this and he will see that this is the only country where the fraternity of the peoples is not a phrase, but an actuality. . . .

Third, the Soviet government's increasing influence and popularity among the masses in the capitalist countries. Our country is the only country in the world capable of pursuing a policy of peace, and this policy is not pharisaical, but is being pursued honestly, openly, decisively, and systematically. Now, this is recognized by all; our enemies and our friends alike recognize that only our country can rightly be called the bulwark and the torchbearer of world peace. . . . Have you noticed that some rulers in Europe are trying to build their careers on the basis of "friendship" with the Soviet Union—that even such a ruler as Mussolini is not completely averse to "earning" [advantages] from this "friendship"?

These facts indicate above all that the Soviet government has become truly popular among the masses in the capitalist states. Nothing has contributed more to this popularity than the policy of peace, pursued honestly and courageously under the difficult condition of capitalist encirclement.

Such are the general trends that have contributed to the success of our foreign policy during this year. . . .

87

Trotsky on the Chances of American Domination in Europe During the Pacifist-Reformist Era

[Speech Delivered on the Tenth Anniversary of World War I at a Meeting of the Society of Friends of the Physics and Mathematics Faculty, July 28, 1924][51]

The absolute impossibility of future human progress [under capitalism] has been revealed very definitely in the last ten years . . . We have entered the epoch of revolution.

Considered in this light, the past ten years can be broken up into several distinct

[51] Trotsky, "K voprosu o perspektivakh mirovogo razvitiia," *Izvestiia*, No. 177, August 5, 1924, pp. 3–4.

periods. First, the imperialist war, which lasted four years—and for us a somewhat shorter time. Next, beginning with February, and especially October, 1917, the period of revolutionary payment for the war. The history of 1918, 1919, and to some extent 1920, at least for some countries, is totally and entirely the history of the liquidation of imperialist war, and of the immediate expectation of proletarian revolution in all Europe. . . . The last steps of the postwar ascent were the September 1920 revolt in Italy and the March 1921 days in Germany. Almost corresponding with September 1920 in Italy was the Red Army advance on Warsaw, which was also an integral part of the powerful revolutionary tide and which also receded. One can say that this period of direct postwar revolutionary attack ended with the formidable upheaval of March 1921 in Germany. . . . After that it might have seemed, and actually did seem to our enemies and foes, that an epoch of the restoration of capitalist equilibrium, of the healing of the wounds inflicted by the war, and of the consolidation of bourgeois society was actually beginning.

From the viewpoint of our revolutionary policy, this new period began with retreat. We announced this officially, though not without a serious internal struggle, at the Third Congress of the Communist International in mid-1921. We stated that the first powerful attack following the imperialist war had not been sufficient to win victory because there had been no leading party capable of ensuring victory, and that the last important event of this three-year period, the March movement in Germany, was pregnant with great danger: If that movement continued along the road it had taken, it threatened to destroy completely the young parties of the Communist International. The Third Congress issued an order: "Step back; do not assault the battle lines to which postwar events have permitted our parties in Europe to advance."

A period of struggle to win influence over the masses then began, that is, a period of systematic and persistent agitational and organizational work under the slogan of a united proletarian, later a workers' and peasants', front. This period lasted about two years. . . . Toward the end of this short period, Europe was shaken once more, by the powerful convulsions of the Ruhr occupation.

. . . Actually the Ruhr occupation was a short repetition of the imperialist war . . . As a result, Germany, and with it to some extent the rest of Europe, again lived in an atmosphere of war. Germany's economy was disrupted, and, on the rebound, the French economy was also disrupted. History, so it seemed, repeated itself . . . In the course of 1923 things in Germany moved suddenly and radically toward revolution. Bourgeois society was deeply shaken. The bourgeois prime minister, Stresemann, said openly that he was heading the last bourgeois government in Germany. The Fascists said, "Let the Communists come to the helm; we shall follow them." The national and political existence of Germany became entirely and irrevocably dislocated. You remember the state of the German mark and of the German economy during that period. The masses were joining the Communist Party in great numbers. The Social Democrats, the chief element of stagnation and a servant of the old society, were split, weakened, and lost their self-confidence. The workers were leaving their ranks. Looking back at this period, which covers almost the entire year of 1923, especially its second half (starting from June, after passive resistance had been abandoned), we say: History never before provided and will never again provide conditions more favorable to the revolution of the proletariat and the seizure of power. . . . Yet one thing was lacking. The [German] Communist Party had not sufficient hardening, foresight, courage, and battle readiness to ensure timely action and victory. This example teaches us once again—especially the many young people among us—the importance of correct leadership by the Communist Party . . .

The defeat of the German revolution opened a new period in the development of Europe and probably of the world in general, the period of rule by the democratic-pacifist elements of bourgeois society. In the place of Fascists come pacifists, demo-crats, Mensheviks, radicals, and other Philistine parties. . . .

At present the reformists are at the helm in the most important European coun-tries. . . . But there is, of course, one practical question that is closely related to "reforms," a question of life and death for the workers of Europe, especially in Germany, the territories of former Austria-Hungary, Poland, and France. That is the question of the stabilization of currency. . . . This is the central question in the life of the continental European proletariat. The current reformist-pacifist era was unquestionably made possible by certain successes in stabilizing currency. However, these successes are far from reliable or steady.

The new reformism we face must, therefore, be evaluated first of all as follows: What hope is there that economic equilibrium, be it even relative and temporary, will be achieved, and in particular what is the hope for the stabilization of currency and wages? What are the chances of success, and how well founded are they?

When approaching this problem, we come face to face with the central figure in the current history of mankind, with the United States of North America.

Comrades, to consider the fate of Europe or of the world proletariat without taking into account the strength and significance of the United States of North America . . . [is to ignore] the master. Because—and let us remember it well!—the masters of capitalist humanity are New York and Washington . . . We see this even in the plan of Experts.[52] . . .

In the past, the development of Europe, and of the world in general, pretty well followed the movement of the British baton. . . . Britain's predominance over Europe and over the world in general at the time of her greatest flowering is nothing to the present predominance of the United States over the world, including Britain. This is the central problem of European and world history. Without understanding it, no understanding of the current chapters of modern history is possible. . . .

America has assumed fully and finally and for some time past a policy of active world imperialism. . . .

American imperialism is in essence mercilessly savage, rapacious, and brutal, yet thanks to America's special situation American imperialism can cloak itself in a mantle of pacifism, thus differing from the ways of the imperialist rascals of the old world. . . . This is not accidental; it has been made possible by geographic and historical circumstances. The United States does not require territorial armed forces. Why? Because no one can reach it: to the right, there is the Atlantic; to the left, the Pacific (even the ocean is "pacific"!). Let anyone try to reach it.

Britain is an island; this partly explains her peculiarities and also her advantages. The United States, likewise, is a gigantic island in regard to the old countries. . . . It is an island, moreover, with all the advantages of Russia, that is, gigantic distances. Even without a fleet, the United States would be almost impregnable to European or Japanese attack because of these great distances. Here you have the basic geo-graphical reason for this pacifist mask that has become America's second face . . .

The other reason for [America's] pacifist piety is, as mentioned earlier, historical. The United States arrived in the world arena late in history, when the entire world had already been seized, divided, and oppressed. The imperialist advance of the United States takes place, therefore, under the banner of "freedom of the seas," the "open door policy," etc. Hence, when America is forced to resort to an open militarist crime, the responsibility for it, in the eyes of its own population, and to a certain degree of the rest of mankind, falls upon the other citizens of the world, not on America itself.

.   .   .

[52] The Dawes plan.

What does American capital want? What is it seeking? It seeks, so people say, stability; it wishes to restore the European market; it wishes to make Europe capable of paying up. But by what means? And within what limits? American capital is not going to make Europe strong enough to become a competitor. It cannot permit Britain (let alone Germany and France, primarily Germany) to regain its prewar world markets, because American capital finds itself crowded; because it is now exporting capital, that is, it exports its products, and it exports itself . . . At present American capital commands [American] diplomats. It is quite ready, and it intends, to run the European banks and trusts as well, and the European bourgeoisie as a whole . . . In the final analysis, the question concerns not only Germany, but France, and also Great Britain. . . . People often say that America goes with Britain, that an Anglo-Saxon bloc has been formed. People often talk about Anglo-Saxon capital, Anglo-Saxon policy. The basic world antagonism, they say, is the enmity between America and Japan. But those who say this do not understand the situation. The basic world antagonism is found in the conflict of interests between the United States and Great Britain. And this will be revealed more and more . . .

[But] what are the German and French Social Democrats doing, what are the socialists now doing in Europe? . . . They are educating themselves and trying to educate the working masses in the religion of Americanism. That does not mean, of course, that they have all become Presbyterians or Quakers; it means that they are preparing a new political religion out of Americanism and American capital. They teach and try to teach the toiling masses that without the pacifist role of American capital and its loans to Europe, Europe cannot exist . . . This [teaching] is now the core of political life in Europe, especially in Germany. In other words, the European Social Democrats have become before our very eyes a political agent of American capital. . . . The Social Democrats accept this program [the Dawes Plan] as the basis of all their activity; it unifies the French, German, British, Dutch, and Swiss Social Democrats . . . In short, the Second International now has a unifying program, a program brought from Washington by General Dawes.

Again we see the same paradox. While perpetrating the greatest robbery, American capital has full opportunity to behave as an organizer, a peacemaker, imbued with humanitarian principles, and at the same time it gives the Social Democrats a platform that is much more advantageous for them than yesterday's national platform. . . .

America has not yet learned to realize its power. But it is learning on the body and bones of Europe. For a little while America will need Britain as a guide along the road of world politics. But that time will be short. . . . The world position of the United States is expressed in figures against which one cannot argue. [Quotes figures of American production.] . . .

A few days ago Britain gave up her plan to fortify Singapore. . . . Britain can pursue her policy in the Pacific either with Japan against America, or with America against Japan. . . . MacDonald was called upon to decide: with America against Japan or with Japan against America? And he gave up the fortification of Singapore. This, of course, is not the last word in British imperialist policy. The decision may be made anew. But at the moment Britain has begun to withdraw from an independent policy—or an alliance with Japan—in the Pacific. . . . [Goes on to speak of the possibility of a war between America and Britain.] Just as America, in order to sap the very life of Europe, comes out in the mantle of pacifism, so, during the war with Britain, it will come out as a great liberator of colonial peoples.

Old grandmother history is telling fortunes to American capital: For each plundering act, a slogan of liberation is prepared. In China, it is the policy of the "open door." Japan wants to break up China and, because Japan has no iron, coal, or oil, and China has them all, to conquer by armed force certain Chinese provinces.

Japan cannot live or fight without coal, iron, and oil—these three colossal require-
ments in her [forthcoming] struggle against the United States. Therefore she is
trying to safeguard herself by seizing the riches of China. But what about the United
States? They say "Open door policy in China." What does America say about the
oceans? "Freedom of the seas." That sounds good, but what does it actually mean?
"British fleet, move aside and give way to us." The open door of China means
"Japanese, move aside and let us pass." The real issue is economic seizures, robbery.
But thanks to certain conditions in the United States this work assumes either a
pacifist or a liberating aspect. . . .

Unlike Britain, America does not intend to build an American army for [her]
colonies, including Europe, or establish American administration there. It will
"allow" them to maintain at home a toothless reformist-pacifist order, backed by
Social Democrats, radicals, and other vulgar parties, at the cost of their own peoples,
and it will make them bless America (for the time being) for not threatening their
"independence." Such is the plan of American capital, and such is the program upon
which the Second International is being resurrected!

This American "pacifist" program of universal enslavement is far from peaceful.
On the contrary, it is pregnant with the greatest revolutionary wars and upheavals.
It is not in vain that America continues to build its navy. . . .

Let us return to an earlier question, the chances of the present European reformism. They are directly proportionate to the chances of American imperialist
"pacifism." If the work of turning Europe into a new type of American dominion
has a certain success, that is, does not meet within the next few years with popular
resistance, war, or revolution, then the European Social Democrats, this shadow of
American capital, will to a certain extent retain their influence, and a rotten balance
will be maintained in Europe, made up of what remains of the old power and the
embryo of new and weak life sustained by meager rations contributed [indirectly]
by America. . . . The question must, therefore, be asked: What power have the
European Social Democrats? Or rather, what chance has American capital, by a
meager financing operation, of supporting the new regime in Europe?

No definite prediction can be made; still less can the time be indicated. It is sufficient to understand the new mechanics, the basic factors that will determine the
position of Europe. Thus prepared, we can follow the development of events, weigh
the successes and failures of the chief master of the present epoch, the United States
of America, understand the political zigzags of the European Social Democrats,
and in this way increase the chances for proletarian revolution. The contradictions
that prepared the imperialist war and plunged Europe into it ten years ago, and that
were then consolidated diplomatically by the Versailles treaty and still further by
the development of class war in Europe—these contradictions indisputably continue
to exist as large open wounds. The United States will be confronted by them in their
most desperate form. To put a strong starving country [indirectly] on a ration is
a hard task. . . . America does not intend to increase the German ration, especially
the ration of the German workers. The same goes for the French and British
workers, as second and third. Because what does America need? It needs to ensure
its profits at the expense of the toiling masses of Europe and the world in general,
and by this means to ensure also the privileged position of the upper crust of the
American working class. Without the American workers' aristocracy American
capital cannot hold on; without Gompers and his trade unions, without qualified
workers who are well paid, the American political regime will collapse. But the
American workers' aristocracy can be maintained in a privileged position only by
placing the European "plebs," the proletarian "mob," on a hungry and cold ration,
cruelly, measuredly, and avariciously.

The further things go along this line, the harder it will be for European Social
Democrats to support the gospel of Americanism before the European workers, and

the more centralized the European workers' resistance to the master of masters, American capital, will become. The slogan of the European general revolution and its political form, the Soviet United States of Europe, will become increasingly direct, practical, and significant. What does the Social Democratic Party offer the European workers? It tells them: We in Europe who are broken up and ruined by the Versailles treaty cannot live without America. But the European Communist Party will say: You lie; we shall be able to if we wish; there is no need for us to be broken up. We can become a united Europe, a proletarian United States of Europe. . . . Every success of Americanism, in so far as the Americans succeed, will prepare the ground for the growth of Bolshevism in a more centralized and more revolutionary form, and on a tremendously large scale. The future is ours!

As I am speaking at a meeting convened by the Society of Friends of the Physics and Mathematics Faculty, allow me, comrades, after having given this revolutionary Marxist criticism of Americanism, to say that in so doing we do not wish to pass judgment on Americanism as a whole. We intend to learn from the Americans and from Americanism whatever is worth learning. We need American techniques and American working efficiency. . . . Americanized Bolshevism will conquer and destroy imperialistic Americanism.

PART IV

"Socialism in One Country" and the Pacifist-Reformist Interlude
1924–1926

Part IV

"Socialism in One Country" and the
Pacifist-Reformist Interlude
1924–1926

PART IV

The Soviet leaders showed great elation over the *de jure* recognitions that "rained down as from the Horn of Plenty," as one European foreign office after another hurriedly followed the example of the first British Labour government. By interpreting this rain of recognitions as reluctant admission by the capitalists of Soviet Russia's growing power, and as further evidence of the fatal contradictions and weaknesses of the capitalist states, the Communists compensated, in some measure, for the failure of the German "October" of 1923.

The year 1924 marked the beginning of a new phase of Soviet foreign policy. The change was neither so sudden nor quite so radical as the change from War Communism to N.E.P. on the home front, but it was comparable in direction and significance. The revolutionary foreign policy reflected in the encouragement of revolutionary movements in Germany, the Baltic regions, and the Near and Far East had had results only in Turkey and China, and even in these countries the results were due more to nationalist than to communist leadership or inspiration.[1] In the West the policy of revolutionary incitement had failed, while the policy of peaceful coexistence had been remarkably successful in cementing both economic and diplomatic relations. The lesson was clear. The Communists did not, of course, give up their world revolutionary objectives any more than they gave up their social revolutionary objectives when they adopted the N.E.P., but they made a strategic retreat or at least a strategic pause on the international front.

This strategic retreat meant different policy trends and new rationalizations of those trends in Marxist-Leninist terms. The new focus of the revolution was the Soviet Union and not the world revolutionary movement. Communist leaders generally agreed that bourgeois society had entered an era of temporary stabilization, but they did not agree on how long the "pacifist-reformist" period, as they called it, would last. This indefinite extension of the breathing space gradually became the policy of "socialism in one country," accompanied by disarming propaganda to the effect that Russian Bolshevism was not exportable, and that peaceful coexistence was possible and advantageous to all regardless of political and economic differences.

---

[1] One of the least-known successes of Soviet foreign policy was the signing of two agreements with the Mongolian People's Republic, by which Soviet Russia acquired control over the finances and communications of Outer Mongolia. One agreement was for establishing a Mongolian Industrial and Commercial Bank under Russian management, the other for building a Chita-Urga railway line, also under Russian management. The first Russian ambassador, A. N. Vasilev, enjoyed much authority in Mongolia, and took active part at the sessions of the Mongolian People's Party. "The international respect that the U.S.S.R. enjoys," Vasilev said at the Third Congress of the Mongolian People's Party in 1925, "reflects upon you also. It is no mere words to say that you have been able to gather here only because the Communist International made it possible for you to work freely. Therefore, remember well: The stronger the U.S.S.R., the stronger you will be also." *3-i sezd Mongolskoi Narodnoi Partii*, p. 3. See also the companion volume, *Soviet Russia and the East, 1920–1927*.

Stalin and the Party Machine

Within the communist hierarchy itself, 1924 saw the end of an era. On January 24, after some two years of illness during which he had more and more withdrawn from active leadership in the affairs of party and state, Vladimir Ilich Lenin died. The death of this remarkable revolutionary leader, who had so dominated the party and the government, set off a desperate struggle for succession, the reverberations of which were for many years to rend both the Russian party and the whole international communist movement. By the end of 1924, the new leader had emerged. He was Iosif Vissarionovich Dzhugashvili, the Georgian revolutionary, who as Stalin, the colorless but faithful party worker, had risen unobtrusively to the post of General Secretary of the party. From that strategic post he moved cautiously to establish himself as Lenin's heir, and as the only true interpreter of the word of the departed master. Leon Trotsky, whose name was publicly and continuously linked with Lenin's throughout the revolution and the civil war, lost the battle for succession to this patient, ruthless, determined party manipulator; along with others of Stalin's more eminent and more brilliant rivals, Trotsky made the fatal mistake of underestimating him. By the end of 1924 the era of Lenin had ended, and the era of Stalin had begun.

The Eighth Congress of the Russian Communist Party, in March 1919, had set up three new directing organs, a Political Bureau, known as the Politburo; an Organizational Bureau, known as the Orgburo; and a Party Secretariat. This reorganization soon further centralized the already highly centralized Communist Party, and correspondingly decreased the influence of the once-powerful Central Committee. By 1919, when these changes were introduced, Stalin had so established himself as an organizer and administrator that he was the only communist leader appointed a member of all three organizations. When the Party Secretariat—which had originally been composed of a Responsible (*otvetstvennyi*) Secretary and five technical or administrative secretaries—was reorganized in 1922 and placed under the jurisdiction of a General Secretary, Stalin was given that position. From it he was able to bring pressure to bear upon the Central Control Commission, an adjunct of the party's Central Committee that supervised the loyalty and activities of party members. Moreover, at the Eighth Party Congress he had also been appointed Commissar of Workers' and Peasants' Inspection, a post from which, in theory, he was to work for the elimination of bureaucratic tendencies within the government. In fact, however, Stalin used these strategic positions to place his own men in key positions in the party and the government, and thus built up a personal political machine that far surpassed the creations of the most famous machine politicians in the Western democracies.

Although strong differences of opinion of both a theoretical and a practical nature had long divided communist leaders, Lenin, by the force of his own personality, had usually succeeded in carrying his comrades with him and imposing his own concepts upon the party. With his death, the differences came to the fore.

Lenin's Testament

Lenin, in his illness, worried about the struggle between Trotsky and Stalin, which he foresaw and feared might lead to a fatal split in the party. In his famous testament, he wrote that Stalin might misuse the great power he had acquired as General Secretary, and that Trotsky had too much self-confidence and was too much of an individualist. Lenin had no clear-cut solution to recommend, and his advice to increase the number of members of the Central Committee from fifty to one hundred neither lessened the power of the Politburo or the General Secretary, nor diminished the ambition of the principals. A week later Lenin added a postscript to the will. He proposed that Stalin be replaced as General Secretary by someone more patient, more loyal, more polite, and more considerate of his comrades. This famous and controversial document was not published in Russia until many years later, but it was soon published abroad[2] and it was read at a plenary session of the Central Committee in May 1924, four months after the death of its author. It seems to have been circulated among individual members of the party and among the delegates to the Thirteenth Congress, May 23–31, 1924. Although this famous episode does not relate directly to Soviet foreign policy, it suggests how the party reached a decision that in turn had far-reaching effects on Soviet foreign policy.

Interestingly enough, in 1925 Trotsky himself denied that Lenin's will had been written for publication in the press. He contradicted Max Eastman's statement in *Since Lenin Died* that the document had been concealed, and accused Eastman of vilifying the Central Committee and the party:

The Thirteenth Party Congress, which received this letter with the greatest attention as it did all the other letters, drew from it the conclusions appropriate to the situation and the moment. Any suggestion that the "Testament" was kept secret or distorted is a malicious invention directed fully against Lenin's intention and against the interests of the party he created.[3]

Socialism in One Country *vs.* Permanent Revolution

The story of how Stalin, in alliance with Zinoviev and Kamenev until the early months of 1925 and later by himself, defeated Trotsky, removed him from his post as Commissar of War in 1924, expelled him from the Politburo in 1926 and from the party in 1927, exiled him to Alma-Ata in 1927, and expelled him from Russia in 1929, is outside the scope of this narrative. We are concerned only with what appear to have been the effects of these events in Soviet foreign policy.

There was one key theoretical difference between the two groups. Stalin and his supporters favored "socialism in one country"—temporarily. The opposition bloc, represented by Trotsky, Zinoviev, Kamenev, and other prominent Bolsheviks—now usually known as the Trotskyites—favored "permanent revolution." Actually the two contending groups agreed on a number of crucial points, and disagreed chiefly on methods and tactics. On these points they agreed: (1) the international character of the Russian revolution; (2) the need of building socialism in Russia; (3) the existence of domestic contradictions and conflicts within Russia; (4) the revolutionary role of the proletariat of other countries.

Trotsky's main argument was that Soviet society could not possibly become economically self-sufficient, and that only socialist revolutions in other coun-

[2] Lev Trotsky, *The Real Situation in Russia*, pp. 320–21.
[3] *Bolshevik*, No. 16, September 1, 1925, p. 68.

tries—that is permanent revolution—could solve Russia's problems. Stalin, however, insisted that the chief obstacle to building socialism in Russia was Russia's bourgeoisie, and that their resistance could be overcome by Russia's own forces. To this end, it was imperative for Soviet Russia to prolong the breathing space—the *peredyshka*—that is, to keep the capitalists from war and intervention. It was necessary to cultivate peaceful relations with these states at any cost, particularly since a temporary stabilization of capitalism was evident.

Stalin did not give up the idea of world revolution; he argued only that new circumstances made new methods necessary. What he proposed was to count less on the increasing weakness of capitalism and more on the growing strength of the first land of socialism. To support this view, he drew upon Lenin's theory of revolution:

The revolution that has been victorious in one country must regard itself not as a self-sufficient entity, but as an aid, a means for hastening the victory of the proletariat in all countries. For the victory of the revolution in one country, in the present case Russia, is not only the product of the uneven development and progressive decay of imperialism; it is at the same time the beginning of and the prerequisite for the world revolution.[4]

From this Stalin argued that "the more effective the assistance rendered by the first socialist country to the workers and toiling masses of all other countries, the more rapidly and thoroughly the world revolution will develop." He quoted Lenin to the effect that the victorious proletariat in one country should "stand up . . . against the rest of the world, attracting to its cause the oppressed classes of other countries against the capitalists, raising revolts in those countries against the capitalists, if necessary even coming out with armed force against the exploiting classes and their states."[5]

Stalin closed his argument with a remark calculated to show that he was as much of a revolutionary as the next man. "Actually," he wrote, "the October Revolution not only needs support from the revolution in other countries, but must itself support the revolution in those countries in order to accelerate the overthrow of world imperialism."[6]

Stalin followed Lenin in stressing the importance of the conflicts among the bourgeois states and of knowing when to make a strategic retreat,

when the enemy is strong, when retreat is inevitable, when it is obviously disadvantageous to accept battle forced upon us by the enemy, when, with the given alignment of forces, retreat becomes the only way to ward off a blow against the vanguard and to keep the reserves intact. . . . The purpose of this strategy is to gain time, to demoralize the enemy, and to accumulate forces in order to assume the offensive.[7]

Stalin adopted Lenin's view that the world revolution would develop out of "contradictions within the world system of imperialism," citing Lenin's *Imperialism, the Highest Stage of Capitalism* to support his predictions. The next

---

[4] Stalin, *Sochineniia*, VI, 396.

[5] *Ibid.*, pp. 399–400; Lenin, *Sochineniia*, XVIII, 232–33.

[6] Stalin, *Sochineniia*, VI, 401. The above passages are quoted from Stalin's introduction to his book *Na putiakh k Oktiabriu*. The introduction, entitled "Oktiabrskaia revoliutsiia i taktika russkikh kommunistov," was published separately as a leaflet; it also appeared in all editions of Stalin's *Problemy Leninizma* and finally in his *Sochineniia*, Vol. VI.

[7] Stalin, *Sochineniia*, VI, 160; see Document 89.

break in the chain of world imperialism, he said, would come in its weakest link, possibly India or Germany.[8]

Later, in December 1925, the Fourteenth Congress of the Russian Communist Party adopted a resolution incorporating the theory of socialism in one country into the general body of communist doctrine. The resolution stated:

In the realm of *economic* construction, the Congress starts with the fact that our country, the country of the dictatorship of the proletariat, possesses "all that is necessary to build a fully socialist society" (Lenin). The Congress believes that the primary task of our party is the struggle for the victory of socialist reconstruction in the U.S.S.R.

This resolution then went on to take note of

the partial stabilization of capitalism and the relative consolidation of the political power of the bourgeoisie in Europe; the vast expansion of the role of the United States of America . . . ; the gradual decline of the British Empire as a world power; the contradictions in the camp of the victors themselves; the contradictions between the United States of America and Europe; the uprooting of the entire imperialist system by the colonial and semicolonial peoples of China, India, Syria, and Morocco, who are now being politically awakened . . . ; and finally, the growth—in new forms—of the workers' movement in Europe and its close connection with the proletariat of the U.S.S.R. . . .

Lastly the resolution instructed the party's Central Committee to base its policy upon strengthening the alliance between the proletariat of the U.S.S.R. and the Western European proletariat and the oppressed peoples, aiming at the development and victory of the international proletarian revolution; upon a policy of peace; upon economic reconstruction within the U.S.S.R., aimed at making the U.S.S.R. economically independent of its capitalist neighbors; upon consolidation of the country and an increase in the power of the Red Army, the Red Navy, and the Soviet air fleet.[9]

The argument over "socialism in one country" versus "permanent revolution" flared up once more in 1926–27 when the opposition, in addition to criticizing the thesis of socialism in one country, also condemned Stalin's policy in China.

In his later writings Trotsky maintained that he had been opposed from the beginning, i.e., from 1923, to the Communist-Kuomintang alliance in China, which Stalin and his supporters approved. As a matter of fact, the opposition openly opposed Stalin's policy in China only in 1926, after the first coup by Chiang Kai-shek in Shanghai in March of that year. From that date on, the opposition demanded that the Communists withdraw from the Kuomintang and set up soviets in China. Stalin, on the other hand, continued to maintain for some months that the Communist-Kuomintang alliance should be continued, and that it was too soon to organize soviets in China. Later, when Trotsky's opposition was practically eliminated, Stalin reversed himself on the Chinese situation and adopted Trotsky's point of view.

The final threshing out of the differences between Stalin's group and Trot-

---

[8] *Ibid.*, p. 98; also Stalin, "The Foundations of Leninism," in *Problems of Leninism*, p. 21. See Document 88.

[9] *Vsesoiuznaia Kommunisticheskaia Partiia (Bolshevikov) v rezoliutsiiakh i resheniiakh sezdov, konferentsii i plenumov Ts.K. (1898–1935)*, II, 48–49 (hereafter cited as *V.K.P. v rezoliutsiiakh*).

sky's took place when the two groups stated their views before the Executive Committee of the Communist International in December 1926. Stalin opened the discussion by restating the meaning of the principle of socialism in one country. "Is the proletariat of the U.S.S.R. capable of overcoming its own Soviet bourgeoisie?" he asked. The party, he said, had answered this question in the affirmative: "If this is incorrect, if the party had no grounds for asserting that the proletariat of the U.S.S.R. was capable of constructing socialist society in spite of the relative technical backwardness of our country, then our party would have no justification for remaining in power." According to Stalin, the party believed that Russia's own forces would provide the economic bases of socialism; he conceded, however, that "the proletariat of a single country is incapable of overcoming the world bourgeoisie by its own efforts." In conclusion, he repeated the old communist thesis that the necessary respite from war and intervention, the *peredyshka*, could be best gained by exploiting the antagonisms between capital countries.[10]

In his reply, Zinoviev ridiculed Stalin's interpretation of Lenin's views. It was wishful thinking, he said, to believe that the capitalists would agree to wait a decade while the Communists organized and developed socialist production in one country. Moreover: "For the proletariat to recognize that the question of world revolution is for us a question of life and death, is entirely different from its believing that it is building socialism independently of the course of world revolution."[11]

Trotsky, in this debate, stressed Russia's economic weakness and the difficulty of overcoming that weakness in isolation and in the face of the hostility of world capitalism. Russia could build a socialist society only if its productive forces were stronger than those of capitalism, which they were not. "The issue does not rest with the struggle of the proletariat against its own bourgeoisie, but on the life-and-death struggle of an isolated socialist agency against the capitalist world system."[12]

Bukharin, supporting Stalin, argued that the opposition had not specified whether they could build socialism under the existing conditions or were doomed to destruction unless a world revolution enabled the Western European proletariat to come to their aid. He said Trotsky was taking the line of the Social Democrats, that Russia's backwardness made a socialist revolution in Russia impossible.

D. Z. Manuilsky also condemned the pessimism of the opposition. If Soviet Russia was economically dependent on world capitalism, the world capitalists

---

[10] *Puti mirovoi revoliutsii; sedmoi rasshirennyi plenum Ispolnitelnogo Komiteta Kommunisticheskogo Internatsionala, 22 noiabria–16 dekabria, 1926. Stenograficheskii otchet,* II, 10–12 (cited hereafter as *Puti mirovoi revoliutsii*). Speaking ten months later before the Central Committee and the Central Control Commission (October 23, 1927), Stalin discussed how Russian industrial development, and particularly that of the shipbuilding industry, could be achieved. After dismissing capitalist methods, he concluded: "There remains to us only one way, that indicated by Lenin; raising our industry, the re-equipment of our industry, on the basis of means accumulated at home." He denied the opposition's claim that such domestic means could not bring about socialism in Russia, and once again emphasized that the basic aim of Soviet foreign policy was to have peace in order to go ahead with industrialization (Stalin, *Sochineniia,* X, 198–99).

[11] *Puti mirovoi revoliutsii,* II, 74.

[12] *Ibid.,* p. 103.

were even more dependent on Russia, since Russia was the only market that offered any solution for the capitalist problem of overproduction.

Whether it was Stalin's arguments or Stalin's control of the party machine or a combination of these factors that determined the result, the outcome of the long debate was a foreign policy that gave priority to strengthening the "first land of socialism" over promoting revolution abroad. The world revolution was still to come, but later. The contradictions of capitalism would insure its ultimate triumph, but in the meantime peace and trade with the West were necessary to make a strong Soviet state capable of playing the important part assigned to it under this theory.

The theory of socialism in one country may have been primarily a rationalization forced on the Communist Party and the Soviet government by the unlooked-for stabilization of the capitalist countries in the 1920's, or it may have been a reflection of Stalin's characteristic caution. In either event, world revolution received less emphasis and the Comintern declined in importance. Peace and peaceful coexistence were played up; diplomatic, cultural, and particularly commercial relations were developed.

Had Trotsky won the contest with Stalin, he too might have been forced to make a strategic retreat on the revolutionary front, but it is unlikely that he would have retreated so soon or so far.

Anglo-Soviet Treaties of August 8, 1924

As mentioned in the preceding chapter, the instrument by which the British Labour government had extended *de jure* recognition to the Soviet government had also proposed a conference to draw up "the preliminary bases of a complete treaty to settle all questions outstanding between the two countries." Accordingly, on April 14, 1924, negotiations began in London to draft a treaty embodying a general settlement between Great Britain and the U.S.S.R.

Before and during these negotiations the British and Soviet press hotly debated the issues of claims and counterclaims. The British claims were estimated by some at almost a billion pounds sterling; the Soviet counterclaims were more indefinite, based as they were upon injury to Russian citizens and damage to Russian property resulting from the intervention and blockade. Soviet representatives estimated—and certain representatives of the British Labour Party agreed—that the damage done by the British more than equaled Russia's prewar debts to Britain and that one set of claims should cancel the other.

British creditors, owners of property in prerevolutionary Russia, and business and financial interests generally gave the British government some very stiff prerequisites for British loans and credits to Russia, which, from the Soviet point of view, were the main purpose of the negotiations.

Late in February, 1924, the Federation of British Industries formally stated that "at the coming conference the Soviet Government should recognize without qualifications its liability to discharge in full its debts. The Soviet Government should also make suitable provision for the payment of interest and arrears of interest on these debts." Moreover, the Federation expressed a desire to have its own delegates at the forthcoming conference.[13]

On the eve of his first meeting with the Soviet delegation, Prime Minister

[13] *The Times* (London), February 21, 1924, p .11.

Ramsay MacDonald was handed a memorandum listing the British bankers' conditions for the restoration of Russian credit in Great Britain. These conditions included : restoration by Russia of private property rights for foreigners; recognition by Russia of public and private debts; drastic changes in judicial procedure within Russia, including restoration of the sanctity of private contract; a guarantee against state confiscation of private property; restoration of the right of private trade between foreigners and Russia; and the abandonment by the Russian government of propaganda against foreign governments.[14]

When Rakovsky, head of the Soviet delegation, saw the bankers' memorandum, he denounced it as an attempt to interfere in the internal affairs of the Soviet state. He emphatically declared that the Soviet government would never give up its monopoly of foreign trade or change its juridical codes. He added, however, that although the Soviet government would not restore property rights to former owners, it was willing to grant them compensatory concessions to operate such of the former foreign-owned properties as the Soviet government desired to lease.[15]

Prime Minister MacDonald opened the conference on April 14 by emphasizing the need to liquidate past differences, to agree on the mutual rights and obligations of the two countries, and to state them clearly. He said that both British and Russian claims should be considered.[16]

In his reply, Rakovsky repeated that the Soviet government had no intention of giving up the nationalization of land and property or the monopoly of foreign trade, but expressed his conviction that even so a way would be discovered to rapprochement and collaboration. As for political questions, said Rakovsky, "in so far as the British and Soviet governments adopt as a starting point the principle of respecting the independence and sovereignty of the Eastern states, we shall not find it difficult to settle all the questions pertaining to the interests of Great Britain and the Soviet Union in the East." He urged limiting armaments, reorganizing the League of Nations, and revising the Treaty of Versailles. Lastly, he reiterated the communist line: "The Soviet government, guided by the Communist Party, considers the elimination of war possible only on the condition of a socialist organization of [national] economy. We are, however, ready to collaborate in any serious attempt by any government to reduce the danger of war."[17]

In spite of this official optimism, the negotiations dragged on for a number of months, and finally, on August 5, the official British communiqué stated :

The Anglo-Soviet Conference, after having sat in Committee the whole of Saturday and Sunday, met in full session on Monday at noon, and sat till 7:15 this morning. As the Soviet Delegation was unable to accept amendments and concessions offered in regard to Article 14 of the Draft treaty, no agreement was reached. Negotiation broke down and the Treaty will not be signed.[18]

[14] Complete text of the above memorandum appears in *The Times* (London), April 14, 1924, p. 11.
[15] *The Times* (London), April 26, 1924, p. 9; also appeared in abbreviated form in *Izvestiia*, No. 98, April 30, 1924, p. 1. See Document 93.
[16] *The Times* (London), April 15, 1924, p. 9.
[17] *Izvestiia*, No. 88, April 16, 1924, pp. 1–2; *The Times* (London), April 15, 1924, p. 9. See Document 92.
[18] *The Times* (London), August 6, 1924, p. 10. The article in question concerned British claims and appeared as Article 11 in the draft of the general treaty as finally adopted.

On the following evening, however, Arthur Ponsonby, representing the British in the negotiations, announced to the House of Commons that "complete agreement" had been reached, and that the drafts of a general treaty and a treaty of commerce and navigation would be signed. The two treaties, often spoken of as one, were in fact signed on August 8, 1924.

The treaty of commerce and navigation provided for the restoration of normal trade relations. British goods were to get most-favored-nation treatment in Russia, and Russia was to get the benefits of the export credit system and also (since the Soviet government had nationalized foreign trade) diplomatic immunity for her trade representative in England and his assistants.

The general treaty provided for a British loan to the Soviet government after claims of British subjects against Russia were settled, and for the appointment of a commission representing the two countries "to consider the validity and to ascertain the amount of the claims." That is, the two really troublesome questions of claims and a loan were actually not settled at all but left for future settlement. On the other troublesome issue, propaganda, both signatories agreed

to respect the undoubted right of a State to order its own life within its own jurisdiction in its own way, to refrain and to restrain all persons and organizations under their direct and indirect control, including organizations in receipt of any financial assistance from them, from any act overt or covert liable in any way whatsoever to endanger the tranquility or prosperity of any part of the territory of the British Empire or the Union of Soviet Socialist Republics or intended to embitter the relations of the British Empire or the Union with their neighbors or any other countries.[19]

Both of these Anglo-Soviet treaties—and particularly the section of the general treaty that dealt with the provisions for a loan to Russia—were bitterly condemned in Great Britain by the Association of British Creditors, by chambers of commerce, and by the Federation of British Industries, as well as by prominent Conservatives and Liberals. In Parliament Lloyd George expressed a widely held opinion when he criticized the undersecretary of state because he was "going to guarantee a loan upon a security of which he does not even know the conditions."[20] Furthermore, the belief that the treaties provided no real compensation to British creditors and that the satisfaction of the British claims depended on the will of the Soviet government caused widespread British opposition to the treaties.

But the Soviet government was pleased. Chicherin said the treaties recognized "the October Revolution as the basis of the Soviet state," and that they gave the Soviet Union "an advantage that overbalances the sacrifices we shall have to bear as a result of our partial recognition of old debts."[21]

Further insight into the Soviet attitude toward the British claims was provided by a comment in *Izvestiia,* the official government organ:

There can be no reason to become excited and to lose one's temper over such typical businessmen as the [British] bankers. They must realize that no one will pay the debts of such corpses as the [Russian] autocracy, and also that every business agreement must be based on the consideration of mutual claims. We can hardly suspect

[19] *General Treaty between Great Britain and Northern Ireland and the Union of Soviet Socialist Republics. Signed at London, August 8, 1924* (Cmd. 2260).
[20] *Debates 1924* (Great Britain, House of Commons, Fifth Series, Vol. 176), p. 3036.
[21] *Izvestiia,* No. 189, August 21, 1924, p. 3; see Document 94.

the British bankers of ignorance. They understand very well. But the Anglo-Soviet negotiations have passed through only a first stage, and they are now entering the second stage in which British claims will have to be co-ordinated with practical discussions concerning the loan to the Soviet Union . . .[22]

Moreover, although the Communists accepted the negotiations and the treaties as conciliatory gestures by the British Labour Party, their general attitude of hostility toward that party remained. In a speech at the Fifth Congress of the Comintern in June 1924, while the negotiations were still going on, Zinoviev described the Communists as "the only force that has no illusions about the 'Labour' government," and quoted Lenin to the effect that while the Communists should support the Labour government, their support should be "the support the rope gives to the person on the gallows."[23]

The Soviet Government and the Dawes Plan

Elsewhere in the West, meanwhile, France had failed to secure reparations from Germany by her occupation of the Ruhr. The repercussions of Germany's threatened bankruptcy which were making themselves felt throughout Europe, had led to negotiations, which in turn led to the appointment of two international committees of experts to study the German situation and to work out a schedule of reparations payments that would permit the stabilization of Germany currency and the balancing of the German budget.

The larger international committee of experts, under the chairmanship of the American financier Charles G. Dawes, held its first meeting in Paris in January 1924, and in April of that year submitted a report known as the Dawes Plan. By this plan, German reparations would be scaled to fit Germany's capacity to pay, and reparations payments would be based on trade. Further, a large loan was to be floated to set German finances in order.

Although the report did not mention the occupation of the Ruhr directly, it did state that success in stabilizing German currency and balancing the German budget could be attained only if Germany had control of and free economic activity in all the territory defined as German by the Treaty of Versailles. The German government accepted the Dawes Plan and the Allies adopted it at a conference in London on August 30. The French agreed to end the occupation of the Ruhr within a year. Since the effect of the Dawes Plan would be to lessen the tensions among the capitalist states, it is not surprising that the Communists condemned it as simply another and more effective method of exploiting Germany. They turned on the full pressure of their propaganda machine to discredit both the plan and its originators. *Izvestiia* termed it "a plan for the most cruel exploitation of the German worker . . . an agreement among separate factions of world capital which are preparing a bankers' advance in a joint effort to make the German worker pay tribute to the world money exchange." The plan really meant "peace among the capitalists and war against the working class," but the capitalists would fight over the spoils, and the resulting war "will fall as a heavy burden on the shoulders of the working class."[24]

[22] V. D. Vilensky (Sibiriakov), "Dva soglasheniia," *Izvestiia,* No. 192, August 24, 1924, p. 1.
  [23] *Piatyi Vsemirnyi Kongress K.I.,* I, 444–45; also G. E. Zinoviev, *Speech in Reply to Discussion of Report on the Work of the E.C.C.I.,* p. 14. See Document 97.
  [24] Vilensky, "Dva soglasheniia."

Капиталистическая Европа идет вперед.

НА ЗОЛОТОЙ ЦЕПИ...

"ON A GOLDEN CHAIN . . ." America leads capitalist Europe by a chain attached to an American dollar round her neck. Izvestiia, No. 19, January 24, 1926.

According to Radek, the plan meant that the United States had decided to return to Europe and enrich itself "from the blood of the German people," with the Americans capitalizing on their "unprecedented power and domination over a capitalist Europe weakened by the war." He also charged the Second International, as represented in the British Labour government and the French Left bloc, with "responsibility before history for this modernized Versailles system."[25]

The manifesto of the Fifth Congress of the Comintern, adopted in July of 1924, called upon the Communists to "struggle against that conspiracy of the capitalist violators which goes by the harmless name of the Experts' plan," and advocated instead the creation of a "Workers' and Peasants' United States of Europe," which was to be set up "by fierce struggle in each country against the national bourgeoisie, by combining the proletarian forces of all countries to seize power and establish the proletarian dictatorship."[26]

In a speech in September 1924 devoted to an analysis of the international situation, Stalin said that the Allies' adoption of the Dawes Plan had replaced French hegemony with American, and thus added new contradictions without solving any of the old ones. "Future world events," he said, "will be determined by these hostilities, and not by the 'pacifist' speeches of such gallows-birds as Hughes or the loquacious Herriot. . . . The London Conference [at which the Dawes Plan was adopted] has simply masked the hostilities in a way that will provide new reasons for their extreme aggravation."[27] Stalin noted optimistically that the Soviet government was becoming more popular among the masses abroad—as evidence of which he pointed to the political victories of MacDonald in Britain and Herriot in France, two men in whom the Communists found little indeed to admire. This increasing popularity of the Soviet Union he attributed to the hatred of the working class for capitalism, the hatred of war by the masses, and the hatred of imperialism by the oppressed in the dependent countries and colonies. From this he reasoned: "One can hardly doubt that these three kinds of hatred will contribute to the undermining of the 'pacifist-democratic regime' of the present imperialistic rule. . . ."[28]

The Zinoviev Letter

Meanwhile, the British Labour government had run into serious opposition from Liberals as well as Conservatives on the issue of the Anglo-Soviet treaties. So serious was the opposition that the MacDonald cabinet—governing as it was by grace of coalition with the Liberal Party—would probably have succumbed to a vote of censure on the treaty issue, had it not first been censured on a different matter, the so-called Campbell affair. John Rich Campbell, an acting editor of the *Workers' Weekly*, had allegedly called upon British troops to mutiny; the MacDonald cabinet had started to prosecute and then reversed itself and dropped the case. On this issue, on October 8, 1924, Great Britain's first Labour cabinet fell.

New parliamentary elections were called for October 29. On October 25,

[25] *Izvestiia*, No. 154, July 9, 1924, p. 1.
[26] *Piatyi Vsemirnyi Kongress K.I.*, II, 200–201; see Document 95b.
[27] Stalin, "K mezhdunarodnomu polozheniiu," *Bolshevik*, No. 11, 1924, p. 14; see Document 96. For more on Soviet attitude toward the Dawes Plan, see X. J. Eudin, "Moscow's Views of American Imperialism," *The Russian Review*, October 1954, pp. 276–84.
[28] Stalin, "K mezhdunarodnomu polozheniiu," *loc. cit.*, pp. 18–20.

in the midst of the campaign, the British press published a letter purportedly written by the Soviet Comintern leader, Zinoviev, to British communist leaders, telling them how to build up a British Red Army and outlining plans for a communist insurrection in Britain.[29] The British press also printed a copy of the official British Foreign Office protest to the Soviet government regarding the letter. Coming as it did at a time when bitter feeling toward the Soviet government was running high in Britain as a result of displeasure over the treaties, the Zinoviev affair unquestionably influenced the elections. The Conservative Party gained an overwhelming majority—winning over 400 seats, while the Liberal and Labour parties won fewer than 200.

One of the first acts of the new Tory cabinet was to reverse the previous Labour Party decisions in regard to the Anglo-Soviet treaties; it informed the Soviet government that it could not recommend either that Parliament consider the agreements or that the King ratify them. The Anglo-Soviet treaties therefore failed to come into force. Britain's *de jure* recognition of the Soviet government remained in effect, however, along with the Anglo-Soviet trade agreement of 1921.

Soviet officials, meanwhile, had denied the authenticity of the Zinoviev letter, claiming that it was a forgery perpetrated to influence the British elections. The British Communists said the Russians were concerned with more urgent matters than the creation of a British Red Army. Moscow proposed that the entire matter be investigated by a commission to be appointed by the General Council of the British Trades Union Congress.[30]

A commission appointed by the British government did in fact establish that no department of the British government had at any time seen the original of the document, but a thorough investigation was never made. Whether the letter was a forgery or not, however, its spirit was in harmony with any number of other communist pronouncements.

Even while the Soviet negotiations with Great Britain for establishing normal political and economic relations were in progress, Bolshevik leaders were speaking of the approaching collapse of the capitalist order and of Russia's need for military and economic strength to defend herself against possible attacks during the period of collapse. The Executive Committee of the Communist International, jointly with the Red Trade Union International, addressed the Red Army upon the occasion of its sixth anniversary in the following words:

The task of the Red Army is not yet accomplished. Its struggle is not yet over. The soviet socialist republics are surrounded by a ring of capitalists and landowners who are forever plotting attacks against them, forever ready to pounce on them and to demolish the cradle of the world revolution. Always be on guard! Always be ready to defend the Soviet government. A universal struggle of the working classes and enslaved peoples against their enslavers and oppressors is brewing. At any moment the workers and peasants of a given country may rise in arms, and the final battle between capital and labor flare up throughout the world. . . .[31]

A resolution of the Fifth Congress of the Communist International, June 17–July 8, 1924, stressed the particular importance of the British Communist Party and outlined a number of its immediate tasks, among them

[29] See Document 99a.
[30] See Documents 99 and 100.
[31] *Izvestiia*, No. 45, February 23, 1924, p. 1.

to support and encourage the growth of the Left-wing group in the Labour Party
. . . ; to oppose the so-called "Labour government" of MacDonald by exposing
clearly to the masses its bourgeois and anti-labor nature . . . ; to carry out an
active campaign for the organization of committees of action . . . ; to begin a
particularly careful campaign for bringing the unemployed under the party's influence . . .[32]

Bukharin also underlined communist policy in Britain in a speech in Moscow
reported in *Pravda* on October 24, one day before the British press published the
Zinoviev letter:

The British Labour Party is an opportunist party, not a communist one, and it is
even hostile to communism. But as the development of the British working class
proceeds step by step, the British workers advance to the revolutionary point of
view very slowly. Because of this we must be extra-cautious in our policy. We must
gently push the working class, and thus help it abandon more and more of its illusions,
its desires, its hopes and beliefs in the value of peaceful reforms. It will then pass
on from this peaceful opportunist method to the revolutionary method: the overthrow of the bourgeoisie.

Broadly implying that Soviet support of the Anglo-Soviet treaty was simply
a matter of expediency, Bukharin went on to say:

Inasmuch as the British working class supported the treaty, we had to support it too.
The workers of all shades are in favor of the treaty, and almost all the bourgeoisie
is against it. If we came out against the treaty now, our stand would be absolutely
incomprehensible to England's working masses. If the British government would
admit twenty or thirty of our first-class agitators, we could very likely succeed in
making the masses see things correctly. But since this is impossible, and since visas
are obtained with great difficulty, especially when they are wanted for the purpose
of interpretation [of the situation], we are obliged to take into account our communist weakness in the Great Britain of King George. We do not say that we
shall not sign the treaty; neither are we in raptures over it. But if in the struggle
for this treaty, the British proletariat intensifies its pressure upon the bourgeoisie,
we shall be the winners. . . .[33]

United Fronts

The Soviet leaders did not allow their contempt for the British Labour Party
or their hostility toward reformist socialists in general to prevent them from
trying to incorporate these groups in their united front policy. The aims and
meaning of that policy had been fully endorsed in a resolution adopted by the
Eleventh Party Congress, December 19–22, 1922, after receiving the report of
the party's delegation to the Comintern; specifically, the party expressed "its
solidarity with the tactics of a united front finally formulated by the [Second]
Enlarged Plenum of the Executive Committee of the Comintern."[34]

The ECCI decision in question read in part as follows: "The party must do
everything it can to continue and intensify communist work in the trade unions
in order to win them; it must organize factions in all trade unions, even those
that already have communist leadership. This must be done in order to increase
communist influence in them and to capture the majority in other unions."[35]

[32] *Piatyi Vsemirnyi Kongress K.I.*, II, 48–49; see Document 98.
[33] *Pravda*, No. 243, October 24, 1924, p. 5.
[34] *V.K.P. v rezoliutsiiakh*, I, 426.
[35] *Kommunisticheskii Internatsional v dokumentakh*, p. 282.

In line with this policy, the Fifth Congress of the Communist International (June 17–July 8, 1924) emphasized that the Comintern was "to remain an irreconcilable mass communist party of the proletarian revolution, which attracts the masses and trains them for the revolutionary struggle for power."[36]

Earlier, to implement the slogan "To the Masses," the Communist leaders had set up two special sections of the Comintern, the International Women's Secretariat and the Co-operatives' Section, and four "internationals" affiliated with, and, of course, controlled by the Comintern: the Red Trade Union International or Profintern; the Communist Youth International or KIM; the Red Sport International or Sportintern; and the Peasants' International or Krestintern. Since these institutions in different ways served the aims of Soviet foreign policy, a word should be said about each of them.

The International Women's Secretariat. In November 1920, communist women of various countries held a conference at which it was decided to organize the International Women's Secretariat as a branch of the Comintern. Klara Zetkin was appointed secretary, and Moscow was chosen as the permanent seat of the new organization. According to a decision of the ECCI in the spring of 1921, a publication, *Die Kommunistische Fraueninternationale,* edited by Klara Zetkin, was started, and March 8 was declared to be official Women's Day. In June 1921, the second conference of the International Women's Secretariat met simultaneously with the Third Congress of the Communist International. Eighty-two women representing twenty-eight countries participated in this conference, including women from Eastern countries. It was decided to form a special Women's Secretariat for the Eastern countries. At the fourth conference of the International Women's Secretariat, May 29–June 10, 1926, important resolutions, a thesis, and other directives were adopted on work among women.[37]

The Co-operatives' Section. The Third Congress of the Comintern (June 1921) recognized the importance of the co-operative movement as a means of influencing a section of public opinion in favor of the communist program and the policies of Soviet Russia. In November 1922, the first international conference of communist members of co-operative organizations met in Moscow and outlined tactics for winning over the co-operative organizations then not under communist influence. Final decisions on this task were made by the Fourth Congress of the Comintern in 1922. At the second conference of communist members of co-operative organizations, held in Moscow in June 1924, L. M. Khinchuk, head of the Russian Trading Corporation (Arcos) in London, was the chief speaker. A "Manifesto Addressed to All Co-operators; to All Workers and Peasants; to All Proletarian Housewives" was adopted. This stated, among other things, that the co-operative organizations "will fulfill the historic tasks they are called upon to perform when they become a component part of the proletarian movement and take an active part in the fight of the working class, and in this manner help to establish a united front between the revolutionary workers and peasants."[38]

[36] *Piatyi Vsemirnyi Kongress K.I.,* II, 47.

[37] *International Press Correspondence,* No. 69, October 26, 1926, pp. 1195–1210.

[38] *International Press Correspondence,* No. 40, July 10, 1924, p. 394. See also the resolution on the "Role of Co-operative Organizations and the Tasks of Communist Members in the Present Period of the Proletarian Revolution," adopted at the Fifth Congress of the Comintern (*Piatyi Vsemirnyi Kongress K.I.,* II, 135–37).

The Profintern. The Profintern, or Red Trade Union International, originated in Moscow in July 1920, at a conference of Russian Communists and delegates from revolutionary unions in Italy, Yugoslavia, Bulgaria, Spain, and France. An International Council of Revolutionary Trade Unions was created at this conference and placed under the authority of the Communist International. At the first congress of this new organization, held in Moscow July 3–19, 1921, it changed its name. At its second congress in 1922 and its third in 1924, the Profintern established its organization and worked out a program. The latter congress adopted a resolution similar to one taken at the Fifth Congress of the Comintern: "The Congress expresses its conviction that . . . the slogan of the unity of the international movement will create the necessary prerequisites . . . for the organizational consolidation of a united workers' front against international capital."[39]

The Communist Youth International. According to the Soviet Encyclopedia, this was "an international nonparty organization of youth working under the ideological and organizational leadership of the Communist International."[40] Its first congress was held in Moscow, July 9–22, 1920. One of the important tasks of this group was to conduct revolutionary propaganda in the armies of all countries. A resolution of the Executive Committee of the Communist Youth International (March 17, 1924) described this task in these words: "The anti-military work must in no case be confined to a general agitation among the workers; it must be carried on among the soldiers of the standing armies as well as among the professional armies."[41]

The Sportintern. The predecessor of the Sportintern was the Soviet *Vseobuch* ("Universal Training"), an organization for paramilitary training created during the civil war in Russia. The Red Sportintern was founded on the initiative of Soviet and foreign promoters of physical culture in July 1920, in Moscow. Like similar organizations, it had its own executive committee and presidium elected at the congress, and it served as a means for class education. The Sportintern soon had branches in various countries. The largest were in the U.S.S.R., Czechoslovakia, and the United States; others were in Sweden, Great Britain, Uruguay, Argentina, Canada, India, Cuba, Algeria, Denmark, Holland, and elsewhere. The chairman of the Sportintern, Podvoisky, speaking at the Seventh Enlarged Plenum of the ECCI, on November 27, 1926, summarized his group's tasks as follows:

(a) to propagandize among the broad proletarian and peasant masses the idea that the workers' and peasants' sport movement should have revolutionary aims only; (b) to use the revolutionary sport organizations for the purpose of revolutionizing the masses; (c) to exercise a revolutionary influence upon the bourgeois armies through the workers' sport organizations; (d) to outline an organizational plan for the purpose of drawing together the existing organizations of defense, as well as those to come, and the workers in the revolutionary sport movement . . .[42]

The Krestintern. The Krestintern was created by representatives of different peasant parties and organizations who attended the Moscow Agricultural Expo-

[39] *Resolutions and Decisions. Third World Congress of the Red International of Labor Unions Held in Moscow, July 1924,* p. 16.
[40] *Bolshaia Sovetskaia Entsiklopediia,* XXXIII, 826.
[41] *International Press Correspondence,* No. 26, April 24, 1924, p. 250. See also the resolution of the Fifth Congress of the Comintern (*Piatyi Vsemirnyi Kongress K.I.,* II, 143–49).
[42] *Puti mirovoi revoliutsii,* I, 357.

sition in 1923, and held their first International Peasant Conference in the autumn of that year. According to the Soviet Encyclopedia, the Krestintern aimed at "unifying under its leadership the struggle of the revolutionary peasant organizations of all countries";[43] its slogan was "Peasants and Workers of All Countries, Unite!" The 1923 congress of the Krestintern elected a presidium and a general secretary to act *ad interim*. A. P. Smirnov, who later became Commissar of Agriculture of the R.S.F.S.R., was the first general secretary of Krestintern, holding this position until March 1928. A special International Institute of Agriculture, under the Krestintern's supervision, was founded in Moscow to study agricultural problems and the peasant revolutionary movement all over the world. Its official organ was *Agrarnye Problemy*. On the tenth anniversary of the beginning of World War I (July 1924), the Krestintern appealed to the peasants of the world for action, warning that "if the masses of the people remain passive, we shall witness in the not distant future a new war even more terrible than the past one."[44]

The holding company for these organizations, the Comintern, at its Fifth Congress in 1924 heard Zinoviev speak on the necessity of capturing the masses through the trade unions. According to Zinoviev,

no one who thinks seriously of the proletarian revolution, or of winning a majority of the working class, can treat the question of the unity of the trade unions lightly. The bolshevization of the parties is the tactic of true struggle for unity within the trade union movement, and the incessant struggle for communism within the unions. The more the Social Democrats provoke [us], the more we must maneuver, the closer we must unite our ranks in the trade unions, the harder we must work within the unions.[45]

The Congress supported Zinoviev's stand in a resolution, which stated that "the trade unions play a tremendous role during the preparatory period for the revolution, and will play an exceptional role when the social revolution occurs, for when they become the organs of proletarian dictatorship after the victory of the proletariat, the trade unions will be charged with the most important task of social reconstruction."[46] Speaking on the same problems, A. Lozovsky, a member of the presidium of the All-Russian Central Council of Trade Unions and secretary of the Profintern, explained to the Congress that "the trade unions are the natural link between the party and the working class. It is only through their medium that the party can set into motion the working class as a whole. That is why the Communist International has always paid great attention to the trade union movement."[47]

The united front program had some strange results. The American Communists, for example, were encouraged to support the presidential campaign of Senator La Follette's farmer-labor party, and the British Communists sought co-operation with the British trade unions affiliated with the Amsterdam International.

In November 1924, a delegation of British trade union officials, headed by the president of the British Trades Union Congress, A. A. Purcell, visited Moscow and upon its return reported favorably on the achievements of the Soviet

---

[43] *Malaia Sovetskaia Entsiklopediia*, V, 29.
[44] *International Press Correspondence*, No. 44, July 19, 1924, p. 440.
[45] *Piatyi Vsemirnyi Kongress K.I.*, I, 872.
[46] *Ibid.*, II, 115.
[47] *Ibid.*, I, 801.

government. A Russian trade union delegation paid a return visit to England in April 1925. An outcome of these visits was a joint declaration, drawn up by British and Soviet trade union leaders, establishing an Anglo-Russian Trade Union Committee, one purpose of which was to influence the Amsterdam International toward co-operation with the Red trade unions.[48]

Within Russia the Left-wing Communists opposed the organization of this Anglo-Russian Committee, but such Soviet leaders as M. P. Tomsky, A. I. Rykov, and Bukharin supported it, and it had Stalin's blessing. It did not, however, survive the British general strike of 1926, of which many Soviet leaders expected great things, but which only embittered relations between the official trade union organizations.

Meanwhile, the Soviet government kept pressing the British for a regulation of relations and for a loan, but the British government refused to talk about such matters until the Soviets stopped their anti-British propaganda. In a report to the Third Congress of Soviets of the U.S.S.R. in May 1925, Chicherin said that this British stipulation amounted to a demand that "the Communist Party cease to be a communist party."[49]

In the meantime, the Western European powers were trying to supplement the League of Nations with some sort of security system that would satisfy French demands for protection against a renewal of German aggression.

Locarno

At the fourth assembly of the League of Nations in September 1923, the temporary commission appointed to deal with the reduction of armaments presented a draft treaty of mutual assistance, based upon British and French proposals and modified by long negotiations. The draft treaty declared aggressive war to be an international crime; the signatories pledged themselves not to commit this crime, and to assist any of their number against whom it was committed. The League Council was given wide powers in case of threats of aggression.

The response of both members and nonmembers of the League was mixed and predominantly unfavorable. Latvia and Estonia, both exposed to the power of the U.S.S.R., approved, as did Czechoslovakia, Belgium, and France. The Eastern European allies of France neither approved nor disapproved. The United Kingdom and the British Dominions disapproved, largely on the ground that the draft treaty meant too great an extension of international obligations. Italy and Japan did not reject the draft but filed reservations; only one Latin-American state responded at all; the United States gave a categorical no; and the Soviet Union maintained its customary negative attitude toward anything connected with the League of Nations as then constituted.

The governments that criticized the draft treaty most severely tempered their rejection by insisting that limitation of armaments was necessary, but observed that the League had been unable to formulate practical proposals without dealing with the problem of security, and that the problem of security concerned not only League members but some nonmembers, notably the Soviet Union and the United States. These considerations seemed to confirm the communist diagnosis that the contradictions of capitalism were too fundamental to be overcome by negotiations. But at its Fifth Assembly, in September 1924, the League

[48] *Izvestiia*, No. 87, April 16, 1925, p. 3; see Document 102.
[49] *Izvestiia*, No. 110, May 16, 1925, p. 5; see Document 103.

tackled the problem again and made exceptionally rapid progress. On October 2, the Assembly unanimously recommended that the governments then represented accept a draft protocol for the pacific settlement of international disputes, a document later known as the Geneva Protocol.

The new proposal, like its predecessor, was designed to preserve peace and lessen the burden and danger of armaments, but its emphasis was slightly different. The 1923 draft treaty of mutual assistance had tried to make sure that a state that had reduced its armaments should receive immediate and effective aid if attacked. The Geneva Protocol provided so thoroughly for compulsory settlement of all international disputes that no "private" war between states would be possible without one or the other belligerent's being stigmatized as an aggressor. The Protocol also provided for an economic boycott against an aggressor and for participation in a disarmament conference.

Smaller states approved the Geneva Protocol, as they had the draft treaty, but some of the League members outside of Europe had not lost faith in geographical isolation. As a Canadian delegate explained, in "this association of mutual insurance against fire, the risks assumed are not equal. We live in a fire-proof house, far from inflammable materials. A vast ocean separates us from Europe."[50] The newly installed Conservative government in the United Kingdom was also unwilling to assume the commitments of the new proposal, and the Protocol did not come into effect. But the search for security went on.

On various occasions during 1923–24 the German government had suggested to France frontier guarantees, pledges to renounce war, and schemes for arbitrating disputes. The French government, under the cold and unyielding guidance of Raymond Poincaré, had not encouraged these suggestions, but early in 1925 Gustav Stresemann tried again. He proposed to the French government a pact by which Britain, France, Italy, and Germany would guarantee the existing German territorial status on the Rhine and pledge themselves to abstain from war. This time Aristide Briand for France and Austen Chamberlain for Great Britain responded favorably, and negotiations followed. Britain and France made three conditions: (1) Germany should become a member of the League of Nations, and thereby assume responsibility for upholding the Treaty of Versailles and other obligations incumbent upon League members; (2) Belgian frontiers should be discussed; and (3) Poland and Czechoslovakia should take part in the negotiations.

Delegates of Britain, France, Germany, Belgium, Italy, Poland, and Czechoslovakia met on October 5, 1925, at Locarno to discuss the proposed security pacts and the admission of Germany into the League of Nations. Also on the agenda were German participation in League sanctions and the passage of French troops across German territory in the event of war in the East. The conference ended on October 16, when the following agreements were signed: a five-power treaty of mutual guarantee of the Franco-German and Belgo-German frontiers, signed by France, Belgium, and Germany, with Italy and Great Britain as the guarantors; treaties of arbitration between Germany and France, Germany and Belgium, Germany and Poland, and Germany and Czechoslovakia; and Franco-Polish and Franco-Czech treaties of mutual assistance in the event of a breakdown of the five-power guarantee pact or of some other attack upon the signatories.

[50] A. J. Toynbee, *A Survey of International Affairs: 1924*, p. 63.

Выдвиженцы в Европе.

ГЕРМАНИЯ «ВЫДВИГАЕТСЯ» В ЛИГУ НАЦИЙ.

"A PROMOTION IN EUROPE." A British bobby leads Germany, in a dunce cap reading "Treaty of Locarno," to the League's doorstep. The legend beneath reads "Germany Promoted to the League of Nations." Izvestiia, No. 271, November 27, 1925.

In February 1926, in accordance with her undertaking at Locarno, Germany applied for admission to the League of Nations. But as a result of pressure by Spain and Brazil for seats on the League Council, Germany was not admitted until the following September, at which time she was assigned a permanent seat on the Council.

The Soviet government took no pleasure whatever in this evidence that Germany and the Western Allies were becoming more friendly. Soviet diplomacy then, as later, sought to block all efforts to smooth out the capitalistic contradictions on which communist theory put such great hopes. Reading sinister meaning into moves aimed at working out the reparations problem, Soviet leaders bitterly condemned the Locarno agreements in general and the provision for German entry into the League of Nations in particular. The Allied powers, they said, were trying to entice Germany into a struggle with the U.S.S.R.; Germany had signed away her right to an independent foreign policy. "If this plan materializes," said an editorial writer in *Izvestiia*, "if this intention of the frightened and shortsighted vulgar Social Democrats is carried out, Germany will cease for a long time to be an independent international entity."

Soviet Suspicions About the League of Nations

The chief Soviet objection was that by joining the League Germany would assume an obligation to uphold Article 16 of the League Covenant, which pledged League members to render all possible aid to any member state that might become a victim of aggression, and specifically to permit the passage through their territory of the armed forces of any other member engaged in upholding the Covenant. The *Izvestiia* editorial quoted above said of this:

The pacifist façade of the League of Nations covers its most unattractive imperialist character. Essentially it is a coalition of victors who guarantee each other the stability of their achievements. The vultures not only divided their spoils, but also formed an alliance to protect them. The League of Nations is an international institution to safeguard the frontiers that resulted from the imperialist war. It guarantees existing territorial relations. Anyone who wishes to change these relations is considered a violator. Joint action must be taken against violators of peace; at the League's call its members must rush to the armed defense of the existing frontiers and the consolidation of the status quo. The League of Nations has two faces: a pious hypocritical face for the masses, who are being deceived, and a brutal military face for all the adversaries of the military acquisitions of the imperialist victors . . . If Germany joins the League of Nations, she will surrender her own future, in so far as there is a future within the bourgeois order.

Izvestiia added that by joining the League, Germany would assume a number of obligations that were of concern to the U.S.S.R. "Any day a situation may arise in which, in accordance with the constitution of the League of Nations, Germany will be obliged to be in a camp hostile to the Soviet Union."[51]

Rykov emphasized this Soviet concern about the obligations of Article 16 in a report to the Fourteenth Moscow Province Party Conference:

In the present international situation and in the present relation of forces, we can be sure from the beginning that if any bourgeois country belonging to the League of Nations begins a war against the Soviet Union, the League will find the necessary

[51] "Pered opasnostiu nepopravimogo shaga," *Izvestiia*, No. 218, September 24, 1925, p. 1.

formula for representing us, and not its member, as the attacking party. Through her membership in the League of Nations, Germany will automatically be under obligation to carry out the League's resolutions, even if they be directed against us.

Rykov denied rumors, which he said were circulating in the West, that Soviet Russia was to join the League:

As a matter of principle, we support the view that the League of Nations is an instrument not of peace but of war, not of liberation but of oppression; we consider the propaganda that capitalist society might furnish a remedy for war to be a crime, and not an error, on the part of the Second International. In our opinion, war was, is, and will be, inevitable under capitalism; war is insolubly bound up with capitalism and is part of its very nature.[52]

Rakovsky added his voice to the party-line interpretation of the Locarno agreements. He wrote: "Every state that has undertaken certain obligations and has made certain sacrifices, whether real or fictitious, will, of course, try to use these groupings to its own advantage against us."[53] Both Rykov and Rakovsky feared that Locarno would further complicate the relations of the Soviet Union and Great Britain. Rykov branded Locarno as evidence of a "regrouping of powers in Europe under British leadership," and found cause for concern in "Britain's endeavors to keep a free hand for herself in the solution of various questions concerning Eastern Europe, and her antagonism to the Soviet Union."[54]

Rakovsky, as negotiator of the Anglo-Russian treaty, expected that Locarno would further delay the renewal of negotiations with Britain:

After this conference, which made Britain the heroine of the day, she will maintain her former position with still greater obstinacy. . . . The fact that our offers to negotiate have been declined gives us every reason to suppose that Britain is waiting for an advantageous moment when she can gather all her forces against us and bring special pressure to bear upon us with the greatest chance for success.

Giving a foretaste of future moves in Soviet diplomacy, Rakovsky declared that the Locarno powers could prove that the pacts were not directed against the Soviet Union only by signing agreements or treaties with the Soviet Union containing mutual guarantees to "abstain from attack, blockade, or intervention." Although he hoped that the Soviet Union might eventually negotiate such pacts, he saw in conflicts of interest among the Locarno powers "the germ of a development in international relations that would paralyze the aggressive efforts of separate states against us."[55]

It is interesting that Litvinov, who was soon to play such an active role in League councils, used the occasion of an interview with the foreign press in Moscow on November 23, 1925, to deny that the U.S.S.R. would join the League. He said that the Soviet government was more interested than any other government in peace based on the independence and self-determination of all peoples, and that it would welcome the creation of an international organization in which nations could settle their disagreements in a friendly way. The

[52] *Izvestiia*, No. 280, December 8, 1925, p. 5; see also Document 108.
[53] Kh. G. Rakovsky, *Liga natsii i S.S.S.R.*, p. 47; see Document 107.
[54] *Izvestiia*, No. 280, December 8, 1925, p. 5.
[55] Rakovsky, *op. cit.*, pp. 50–53; see also Document 107.

present League, however, was not that kind of an organization. It had neither protected weak nations against oppression by stronger ones, nor done anything serious about disarmament. On the contrary, it was a screen for military preparations against weak nations, and "a diplomatic stock exchange at which the strong powers carry on their business behind the backs of and at the expense of smaller and weaker nations."[56]

Communist Theory of International Law

Although the Communists held that there could be no permanent peace between the communist and noncommunist worlds, and although they continued to regard the League of Nations as likely to take hostile action against them at any time, they admitted that the temporary coexistence of the two worlds was a fact and to their advantage. They set out to devise new methods for maintaining peaceful relations and preserving Soviet security. These new methods required a theoretical basis, an interpretation of the principles of international law compatible with communist theory.

The first period of Soviet relations with the outside world, from October 1917 to the end of 1919, was a period of *rubashka* diplomacy. Appeals to the masses were made over the heads of their governments; civil wars and revolutions were expected almost immediately everywhere. Trotsky used the negotiations at Brest-Litovsk more for waging political warfare than for reaching agreements. From his explanation of his "no war—no peace" declaration as a maneuver to expose the aggressive aims of the Central Powers, and from Lenin's references to the Brest-Litovsk treaty as a "Tilsit peace" that must be accepted because of Russia's weakness and need for a *peredyshka,* it is clear that the Bolshevik leaders based their hopes of survival more on the destruction of the capitalist enemy governments through revolution than on treaties and agreements based on international law. Stuchka's observation that his government considered international law relatively unimportant reflects this point of view.[57]

But by 1920 Soviet leaders had come to realize that the period of coexistence meant renewing diplomatic relations, taking part in international conferences, and negotiating treaties and trade agreements, not as maneuvers in political warfare but to establish international commitments with binding force. The Soviet experts, therefore, needed a formula by which they could both repudiate tsarist commitments and maintain that commitments negotiated by them would be binding on all concerned.

According to traditional Marxism, the state was an emanation of the class struggle and an instrument of class rule. Did it follow, then, that these class instruments were subject to international law? If revolutions had given rise to other proletarian class states, the Russian state could have carried on international relations with such states without theoretical complications. But this had not happened. The other countries were still ruled by enemy classes which, in theory, could never recognize the proletarian state as legitimate. In theory, therefore, these class instruments could not carry on relations with each other on the basis of international law, but could only carry on the class struggle in

[56] Kliuchnikov and Sabanin, III, 334–35; also *Izvestiia,* No. 268, November 24, 1925, p. 1.

[57] *P. I. Stuchka, Revoliutsionnaia rol prava i gosudarstva,* p. 49.

the international sphere. The problem was how to reconcile with Marxism the necessities of the *peredyshka* and the theories of socialism in one country and peaceful coexistence.

E. A. Korovin undertook to make this reconciliation in his *Mezhdunarodnoe pravo perekhodnogo perioda* ("International Law of the Transition Period"), published in 1925. First he reaffirmed that neither complete intellectual nor complete material community could possibly exist between socialist and bourgeois states:

Is it necessary to prove that the very existence of the Soviet state, its flag, its hymn, and its seal represent the strongest rejection of the bourgeois regime, as such, and a permanent threat to its security? Need we refer to the international solidarity of the toiling masses everywhere, to the existence of the toilers' international, to the factual and economic impossibility of a prolonged existence of a socialist oasis, and to our certainty of a world revolution—these cornerstones of our domestic and foreign policies?[58]

Having reaffirmed the inevitability of international class war, Korovin postulated a twilight zone, a period of transition from the socialist oasis encircled by an imperialist desert to the all-encompassing, luxuriantly blooming communist paradise. During this transition period relations between proletarian and non-proletarian states required certain rules or norms. Since the proletariat "has never aimed at mere negation and destruction for the sake of destruction" of such cultural assets as science, art, and law, certain norms of existing international law could and should be retained. Others should be repudiated and still others modified.

On the basis of the theory that the state was the instrument by which one class maintained its rule over other classes, Korovin denied the continuity of the legal personality of a state in which there had been a change in the ruling class, as had occurred in Russia. To be sure, state obligations are binding on the state that made them, but a new ruling class need honor only such obligations and rights of its predecessors as do not conflict with its own principles. Thus the proletarian state could both repudiate the financial obligations of the tsarist and Provisional governments, and retain such rights as territorial possessions, whose membership in the Soviet Union presumably reflected the will of the masses and hence was consistent with the principles of the proletarian class organization.

This theory was vague enough to give latitude in dealing with situations as they arose, without any formal abandonment of Marxist theories. For example, in surrendering tsarist extraterritorial rights in China and capitulations in Turkey and Persia by special agreements, the Soviet government seemingly endorsed the principle of a continuity of state personality, since it merely repudiated the policies of its predecessor state. Likewise, while repudiating in theory the principle of special privileges for citizens of one state residing on the territory of another, the Soviet government, when confronted with the famine disaster, made a special agreement granting diplomatic immunities and other privileges to the American Relief Administration, a private organization from a state that did not even recognize the Soviet government.

The status of trade delegations in foreign countries raised several problems.

[58] E. A. Korovin, *Mezhdunarodnoe pravo perekhodnogo perioda,* p. 13.

One incident, which occurred in Berlin, is described below. The Soviet government claimed for these Soviet state organs the rights of extraterritoriality customarily granted to diplomatic missions. But the trade delegations performed two kinds of functions. They regulated foreign trade, which was generally recognized as a state function justifying extraterritoriality, but they also carried on business, a function for which extraterritoriality was not customarily granted. The usual compromise gave the premises and a few designated members of the trade delegations the status and privileges of diplomatic missions, but made the delegations' operations and funds subject to the laws of the place of domicile.

Soviet leaders never departed from Marxist theory so far as to accept the use of arbitration in settling international disputes. Korovin quoted Litvinov as declaring at The Hague (July 12, 1922) that because of the abyss of hatred between the capitalist and socialist worlds, it would be impossible to find anywhere in the universe an impartial judge. Perhaps only an angel could pass impartially on the Russian question.

Chicherin at Genoa (April 10, 1922) supported the principle of unanimity and opposed the principle of majority decisions in the work of international conferences. In other words, he and his delegation upheld the right of the veto.[59]

Bilateral Neutrality and Nonaggression Pacts with Turkey, Afghanistan, and Persia

As an alternative to multilateral procedures such as those of the League, in which the Soviet Union was bound to be in a minority, the Soviet leaders worked out a network of bilateral neutrality and nonaggression pacts to regulate relations with neighboring states.

In September 1925, Chicherin went to Poland and Germany to explore the chances of negotiating bilateral treaties of neutrality, nonaggression, and nonintervention acceptable to both these countries and Russia. The only immediate outcome of his trip was a commercial treaty with the German government which in effect reorganized the trade relations between the two governments, relations that had been temporarily disrupted as the result of a German police raid on the premises of the Soviet trade delegation in Berlin the preceding year.

This raid was the final act of a comic opera incident that began when the Berlin police took into custody a German Communist named Bozengardt, who had formerly been an employee of the Soviet trade delegation. As they were passing the delegation's premises on foot, the policemen allowed themselves to be inveigled into the building by their prisoner. Once inside Bozengardt began to shout for help. Members of the delegation staff rushed to his aid, and locked the two Berlin policemen in a room until Bozengardt made his escape.

The Berlin chief of police was naturally considerably annoyed and retaliated by a search of the trade delegation's premises. The Soviet ambassador, N. N. Krestinsky, protested that this was a violation of the delegation's extraterritoriality. After long correspondence, a temporary recall of the Soviet ambassador, and a brief embargo on the shipment of goods from Germany, both sides cooled off and made verbal amends. An agreement was signed based on the principle already mentioned: Certain officials of the trade delegation en-

[59] *Ibid.*, pp. 47–48; also "La République des Soviets et le droit international," *Revue Générale de Droit International Public*, Tome XXXII, 1925, p. 298.

joyed diplomatic immunities, while others were subject to the jurisdiction of German laws and courts.[60] In addition, on October 12, 1925, the Soviet government signed a treaty with Germany comprising seven separate agreements—(1) an agreement regarding conditions of residence and business and legal protection; (2) an economic agreement; (3) a railway agreement; (4) an agreement regarding navigation; (5) a fiscal agreement; (6) an agreement regarding commercial courts of arbitration; (7) an agreement regarding the legal protection of industrial property—and a final protocol.[61]

Shortly thereafter, however, the Soviet government negotiated the first of the bilateral neutrality and nonaggression pacts by which it hoped to discourage attack, convince the world of its peaceful intentions, and ensure a continuation of the breathing space. The Treaty of Paris was signed with Turkey on December 17, 1925.

Soviet diplomacy in this case, as in others, profited by the diplomatic misfortunes and disappointments of others. The League, on December 16, decided a frontier dispute between Turkey and Iraq in favor of Iraq. The territory in dispute, the Mosul region in northern Iraq, contained great resources in oil, resources of some moment to the British government, which held the mandate for Iraq. The disappointed Turkish government looked for diplomatic consolation from the source that would cause the British the greatest misgivings. The Turkish foreign minister, who had represented his country before the League, signed the Soviet treaty the day after the League's award was made.

The Turkish-Soviet treaty included two provisions that were to appear in subsequent similar treaties: (1) that in the event of "military action being taken against either Contracting Party by one or more other powers, the other Contracting Party undertakes to maintain neutrality as towards the first Contracting Party"; (2) that "each Contracting Party undertakes to abstain from any aggression against the other . . . [and] not to participate in any alliance or agreement of a political character with one or more other powers directed against the other Contracting Party, . . . [and] each of the two Contracting Parties undertakes not to participate in any hostile act by one or more other powers directed against the other Contracting Party." The third and final paragraph of the treaty laid down directions for ratification.[62]

Similar treaties were subsequently signed with Afghanistan and Persia, thus serving the double purpose of consolidating the southern frontiers of the Soviet Union and feeding British apprehensions about England's position and Soviet intentions in the Near East. The treaty with Afghanistan, signed in Paghman on August 31, 1926, included in addition to paragraphs concerning neutrality and nonaggression a third paragraph setting forth mutual recognition of sovereignty, agreement to withhold aid from pretender governments, agreement to desist from subversive propaganda, and refusal to permit transit of foreign armies. According to this provision:

The High Contracting Parties, mutually recognizing the sovereignty and integrity of the other, undertake to abstain from all kinds of armed and unarmed interference

---

[60] For text of the agreement, see Kliuchnikov and Sabanin, III, 313–14. A German documentary account of this episode is given in F. M. Purlitz (ed.), *Deutscher Geschichtskalender* ..., I Band, Januar–Juni 1924, Inland, pp. 186–93.

[61] The text of the treaty appears in Shapiro, I, 288–302.

[62] *Ibid.,* p. 313.

in the internal affairs of the other Contracting Party and also not to join or assist any other state or states which may take steps against or interfere with the other contracting state.

The Contracting Parties will not permit any individuals in their own territories to establish or to prosecute activities detrimental to the other Contracting Party; to take steps for the subversion of the established Government of the other contracting state; to take any action against the integrity of the territory of the other Contracting Party; to mobilize or collect armed forces against the other Contracting Party; and will prevent them from taking said actions. Similarly the Parties will not countenance the transit through their territories of any armed forces, arms, firearms, ammunition or the supply of any kind of war materials intended for use against the other Contracting Party, and likewise will take active steps to prevent the same from passing through its territory.[63]

Here, then, was what appeared to be a clear undertaking by the Soviet government not to interfere in the affairs of Afghanistan either through the Third International or in any other way. At the same time the treaty would prevent the government of Afghanistan from permitting transit of British or other hostile troops across its territory to threaten Russia's southern frontier.

The treaty with Persia, similar to that with Afghanistan, also included an agreement to settle "by a pacific procedure appropriate to the circumstances" any disputes that might arise between the two governments.[64] It was signed October 1, 1927.

The Soviet-German Neutrality and Nonaggression Treaty of April 24, 1926

Shortly after the unsuccessful negotiations of March 1926, concerning German entry into the League of Nations, and during the ensuing delay, Germany responded to new Soviet overtures concerning a neutrality and nonaggression pact, and on April 24, 1926, signed such a treaty. Not only did this new Russo-German agreement reaffirm the old policy of close collaboration between Russia and Germany initiated at Rapallo in the spring of 1922, but to the Western powers it appeared as a threat to the system of agreements achieved at Locarno. In response to Western charges that the treaty undermined Locarno, Litvinov declared before the All-Russian Central Executive Committee that

the answer to this question depends on the purposes of Locarno itself. If Locarno, as its initiators try to convince us, aims at bringing peace to Europe and consolidating the relations between European countries, then the supporters of Locarno, it would seem, should warmly welcome the Soviet-German treaty as a new step toward the consolidation of friendship between two great peoples. But if Locarno, as we have always suspected, has as one of its aims the formation of a single anti-Soviet front, the isolation of our Union, then one must admit that the treaty signed today does contradict the spirit of Locarno, and we can only rejoice that we have succeeded to a certain extent in removing the anti-Soviet sting from Locarno.[65]

The treaty itself reaffirmed the Rapallo policy, called for neutrality if either contracting party were attacked by a third party, and provided that if "a coali-

[63] *Ibid.*, pp. 322–23.
[64] Article V of the Treaty. Complete text in Shapiro, I, 340–41.
[65] *Izvestiia*, No. 95, April 25, 1926, p. 2; see Document 111.

tion will be formed among third countries for the purpose of submitting one of the Contracting Parties to an economic or financial boycott, the second Contracting Party will not join such a coalition."[66]

This effectively cut out German participation in League sanctions. By the treaty, according to Litvinov, "The German government outlined the probable nature of its conduct in the event the League of Nations should reveal intentions that were either against the basic concept of peace or one-sided and directed against the U.S.S.R." :

The German government also outlined its views on Articles 16 and 17 of the Covenant of the League of Nations. As you know, these articles provide for international sanctions and international reprisals against countries named as aggressors by the League. The German government stated that the League can decide whether the U.S.S.R. is an aggressor (in an armed conflict with a third power) only with German consent, as was stipulated in the well-known German declaration at Locarno.[67]

The treaty also reassured the Soviet Union that it need not fear attack by way of Germany. Moreover, Soviet leaders regarded the Turkish and German treaties as a highly satisfactory pattern for treaties between capitalist and socialist countries and hoped to negotiate other, similar treaties. Poland and the Baltic powers, however, toward whom the Russians turned next, were not enthusiastic about bilateral arrangements, and responded with counterproposals of their own for a general settlement based on arbitration. Lithuania, because of her continuing dispute with Poland over Vilna, was the only exception.[68] The Soviet government repeated that it could not accept the principle of arbitration by a third power, since by communist theory there could be no neutral in a controversy between a communist proletarian dictatorship and a bourgeois government.

In a statement to representatives of the German press in December 1926, Chicherin warned the Baltic governments that they needed neutrality and non-aggression pacts more than the Soviet Union, and that sooner or later such pacts would be concluded. In the meantime, he said :

We shall do as much as possible to meet the Baltic states, but we shall not give up the principle that prohibits the signing of treaties of arbitration. I have no doubt whatever that all the Baltic states will sign guarantee pacts with us sooner or later, and that the clause concerning arbitration will be excluded from these pacts.

I cannot help laughing every time some clever person tries to convince us that joining the League of Nations secures a country from isolation and serves as some kind of guarantee. In our opinion it does not decrease isolation. . . . The gradual improvement and consolidation of our relations with other states is our goal. We move toward this goal, and we avoid isolation, by establishing friendly political relations and by steadily consolidating economic relations, not by placing ourselves blindly in the trap of the League of Nations.[69]

Negotiations with Poland and the Baltic States

On January 16–17, 1925, several months before Locarno, a conference called by Poland and attended by representatives of Latvia, Estonia, Finland, and Poland met at Helsinki to discuss the proposed treaty of arbitration. Soviet

[66] Article III. Text in Shapiro, I, 317.
[67] *Izvestiia*, No. 95, April 25, 1926, p. 2.
[68] See Part I, pp. 9–10.
[69] *Izvestiia*, No. 284, December 8, 1926, p. 1.

spokesmen made the familiar accusation that the delegates were really concerned with less innocent matters, in this case a projected military convention directed against the U.S.S.R. The delegates actually completed and signed several documents. One, a convention on arbitration, provided for a court of arbitration, to which the contracting parties agreed to refer any disputes with each other that could not be settled by diplomatic means. Others dealt with passport formalities, communication facilities, and intellectual co-operation.

Since the danger from Russia was never absent from the minds of Baltic statesmen, problems of mutual aid were bound to be considered. Events in Estonia had proved that the danger of Soviet Russian intervention through the communist movement was real. In late 1924 the Estonian government arrested a number of local Communists and charged them with planning to overthrow the government by an armed uprising. It also charged the Soviet legation in Estonia with delivering Comintern funds and instructions to the Estonian Communists. On December 1, 1924, Estonian Communists responded by attacking all important government offices in the capital and managed to seize and hold for several hours the principal railway station, the post and telegraph offices, and the airfield. Estonian authorities soon put down the revolt and arrested more Communists, who were subsequently tried and executed. The Soviet government denied any complicity in the Estonian events.[70]

The Polish and Baltic military experts who met on March 2, 1925, to draft a joint military defense agreement, were undoubtedly influenced by what had happened so recently in Estonia. Great Britain was asked to act as guarantor, but refused, and that plan was abandoned. Thereupon Estonia advanced a new proposal, this time for an agreement between Poland, Estonia, and Latvia, without Finland. Lithuania, as noted above, held aloof from all negotiations that included Poland. Soviet Russia condemned both the conference of military experts and the Estonian proposal, taking her usual line: that they were not what they appeared to be, but were directed primarily against her. Moscow also charged the French General Staff with meddling in the conference of military experts.

After the signing of the Locarno treaties, new proposals for an Eastern European settlement were made. In December 1925, the Finnish representative in the League of Nations proposed a plan for a "Northern Locarno," a non-aggression and neutrality treaty covering the Baltic and Scandinavian countries and Poland. Another proposal, for an "Eastern Locarno," was based on a Polish-Baltic bloc.

The Communists regarded all these efforts as anti-Soviet, and continued to propose their own system of neutrality and nonaggression treaties to their western neighbors. Poland countered with a proposal for a guarantee treaty between Poland, Finland, Estonia, and Latvia on one side, and the U.S.S.R. on the other, a proposal the Soviets rejected as an attempt to establish Polish hegemony in the Baltic region.

At that point the Soviet government offered to sign separate nonaggression and neutrality pacts with Lithuania, Latvia, Estonia, and Finland. According to the Soviet account, Poland and Britain then intervened, with the result that the Baltic governments on May 5 simultaneously declined the Soviet offer.

Negotiations between Latvia, Estonia, and Finland continued, however. On

---

[70] *Izvestiia,* No. 277, December 4, 1924, p. 1.

July 14, 1925, the foreign ministers of those governments met in Tallinn, and ten days later they issued a statement suggesting that the Soviet Union join them in a preparatory commission. When the Soviet government declined,[71] the three Baltic powers withdrew their demand for a preparatory commission and announced that they were willing to open direct negotiations with the U.S.S.R. Such negotiations were started, but broke down when the border states insisted on a provision for arbitration by a special referee or arbiter. In October 1926, Estonia and Finland broke off negotiations; Latvia persisted, and after a Social Democratic cabinet came into office late in 1926, a preliminary Latvian-Soviet neutrality pact was signed on March 9, 1927. This treaty, however, did not come into effect.

With the breaking off of Anglo-Soviet relations in May 1927,[72] relations between the Baltic states and the Soviet Union deteriorated also, and it was not until 1932 that neutrality or nonaggression treaties with Poland, Finland, and the Baltic states were actually signed and ratified. The Lithuanian treaty was an exception.

The Soviet-Lithuanian Neutrality and Nonaggression Pact

As previously noted, Lithuania had been acting independently of the other Baltic states and Poland, because of the Vilna dispute. On September 28, 1926, Lithuania signed the Treaty of Moscow with the Soviet Union. Following the accepted Soviet formula for neutrality and nonaggression treaties, this pact provided for mutual recognition of sovereignty and territorial integrity; guaranteed nonaggression and neutrality in the event of attack by a third party; and provided for "conciliation commissions"—rather than League-sponsored arbitration commissions—made up of members of the interested states, to deal with conflicts diplomacy could not solve.[73]

The rapprochement between Soviet Russia and Lithuania implicit in this treaty led to uneasiness in Poland. Accordingly, on October 20, 1926, Poland raised the Vilna question at the Ambassadors' Conference of that date. The conference confirmed the decision of May 15, 1923, by which Vilna had been recognized as a part of Poland.[74] On the basis of this reaffirmation—and in spite of the Lithuanian protest—the Polish government notified the Soviet government, on October 23, 1926, that the new Soviet-Lithuanian pact violated the Soviet-Polish Riga treaty of March 1921, which obligated the Soviet government to give up all former rights and claims to territories in dispute between Poland and Lithuania. On November 19 the Soviet government replied that the Riga treaty had stipulated that the question of Vilna should be decided by Poland and Lithuania and that the Soviet government would abide by the decision. But since Lithuania did not recognize the decision of the Ambassadors' Conference in regard to Vilna, the U.S.S.R. could not consider the question as finally settled.[75]

[71] For comments of Soviet press, see editorial in *Izvestiia,* No. 208, September 10, 1926, p. 1.

[72] See Part V, p. 344.

[73] Text appears in Shapiro, I, 323.

[74] See Part I, p. 10.

[75] Texts of the Polish note of October 23 and the Soviet reply of November 19, 1926, appear in Kliuchnikov and Sabanin, III, 356–57.

As 1926 drew to a close, the Soviet government had succeeded in working out neutrality and nonaggression pacts with Turkey, Germany, Afghanistan, Persia, and Lithuania, thereby to some degree compensating for its diplomatic setback at Locarno and for what it regarded as the threat to its peace implicit in the Locarno agreements and Germany's entry into the League of Nations.

The Soviet Leaders' Estimate of the International Position of the U.S.S.R. at the End of 1926

In explaining the neutrality and nonaggression pacts to the Fourth Congress of Soviets, April 19, 1927, Rykov said: "The aim of these treaties, so far as we are concerned, is to guarantee real peace, and to assure the neutrality of the two contracting parties in case of military actions." Although Russia's relations with Germany and Turkey were now satisfactory and her relations with France and Japan were likely to improve, said Rykov, the danger of attack had actually increased, because of the general improvement in Russia's economic position:

It must be borne in mind that as the capitalist system's difficulties become more acute, as the so-called stabilization of capitalism becomes more and more doubtful, an endeavor will undoubtedly be made to place the responsibility for all this and for the lack of success both in foreign and home affairs—for the struggle at home with the working class—very largely upon the shoulders of the republic of soviets. . . . The existence side by side of the two systems, of socialism and capitalism, over a long historical period may of course very well lead to armed conflicts between these two systems.[76]

The general position of the U.S.S.R., as the Soviet leaders optimistically viewed it, was about what it had been a year earlier, on March 3, 1926, when Rykov summed it up as being defined by three factors:

First, a definite increase in and consolidation of the economic and political power of the U.S.S.R., the only proletarian country in the world, which builds its economy on a socialist basis; second, repeated crises of European capitalism and an increasing dependence upon ever-expanding American capitalism; and third, the development of the anti-imperialist national movement for liberation in the colonial and semicolonial countries.

On that occasion Rykov reiterated the official line: A period of stabilization was at hand and the Communists were to make use of it to build up socialism at home, thus not only raising the Soviet standard of living but strengthening the revolutionary movement throughout the world. "The strength of the international workers' movement, the strength of the socialist movement, depends to a considerable extent upon the successes we achieve on our domestic front."[77]

The Communist International Party Line in 1926

At the Fifteenth Party Conference, November 1, 1926, Stalin officially explained how socialism in one country was related to the world revolution and the ultimate victory of socialism. Stalin cited numerous passages from Lenin's works to show that "our revolution is a socialist revolution—not only a signal, an

[76] *Izvestiia*, No. 90, April 20, 1927, p. 2; also *Russia's Foreign Policy Outlined by Mr. A. I. Rykov (Chairman of the Council of People's Commissaries) at the Soviet Congress of the Union of Socialist Soviet Republics on April 19th, 1927*, pp. 17–24. See Document 120.
[77] *Izvestiia*, No. 57, March 10, 1926, p. 3.

impetus, and a point of departure for the world revolution, but a necessary and sufficient basis for building a complete socialist society in our country." Socialism in one country would not, of course, be complete and final victory: ". . . in order to win full victory we must see to it that our present capitalist encirclement is supported by a socialist environment; we must see to it that the proletariat is victorious in at least a few other countries. Only then can we consider our victory complete and final." Socialism in one country should be thought of "as a step, as a means, as the way toward the victory of the proletarian revolution in other countries. . . ."

In summing up, he distinguished between the victory of socialism in one country and the final victory of socialism as follows:

If to achieve socialism in one country means to solve the internal contradictions that can be fully solved in one country (we are naturally thinking of our own country), then to achieve the final victory of socialism means to solve the contradictions between the country of socialism and the countries of capitalism, contradictions that can be overcome only by the forces of the proletarian revolution in several countries. . . . That is the basic line of our party.[78]

The Communist International, which reflected the struggles for power within the Russian party, was also brought into line behind the new policy of socialism in one country, in spite of considerable opposition by European communist leaders of the Trotsky persuasion. In 1925 the International had accepted the theory of a partial stabilization of capitalism. In 1926 this view was reiterated, but the Sixth Enlarged Plenum of the ECCI, February 17–March 15, 1926, also stressed the temporary nature of the stabilization and found evidence of what it termed increasingly acute conflicts within the capitalist hierarchy. At the same time the ECCI spread as widely as possible the notion of the "consolidation of the economic and political power of the proletariat" within the U.S.S.R.

According to the ECCI:

The absence of a directly revolutionary situation during the epoch of partial and untenable stabilization of capitalism can and must impel the Communist International to make corresponding changes in the methods of its work, but the aim and the basis of the Comintern's activity remain as of old. . . . [The Comintern must] pay more attention to the political training of communist parties, to their tempering, organizational consolidation, ideological firmness, revolutionary determination, and knowledge of how to approach the masses. . . . [It must] put before the masses more extensively, more decisively, and more persistently than ever before, its program for saving Europe by means of the proletarian revolution, the dictatorship of the proletariat, and the formation of the United States of Socialist Europe . . . and for realizing the slogan "Proletarians of all countries and oppressed peoples of the world, unite!"[79]

The ECCI also noted that

the victorious proletarian revolution in Europe should not necessarily be understood as a simultaneous victory of the proletariat throughout the whole of Europe. Rather,

[78] Stalin, *Sochineniia,* VIII, 261–66; also *Izvestiia,* No. 256, November 5, 1926, pp. 3–4. See also Document 116.

[79] "Proletarians of all countries, unite!" was the old Marxist slogan. The reference to the oppressed peoples was added by Zinoviev at the Baku Congress of the Peoples of the East in 1920.

it should be interpreted as a whole period of revolutionary upheavals, during which the proletarian revolution may be victorious first in separate countries, or in one European country, and only later extend to all the countries of Europe.

The ECCI also re-emphasized the importance of a united front with the working class—the "united front from below"—and urged that the trade union movement, and particularly its Left element, should be the center of the united front agitation. Communists were reminded of the importance of the co-operative movement as a source of allies. Finally, the workers of the world were called upon to support the economic development of the U.S.S.R., and party members were instructed to struggle to win over the middle strata of the population, the peasantry and the urban petty bourgeoisie.[80]

In a report to the Seventh Enlarged Plenum of the ECCI, November-December, 1926, Bukharin again expounded the thesis of a partial and temporary stabilization of capitalism. He saw the rate of development of the U.S.S.R., which he called far greater than that of the capitalist world, as enormously encouraging to comrades in other countries, who would see in it "a mighty lever of the international proletarian revolution, and consequently the most important contributor to the disintegration of the forces of international capital."[81]

---

[80] *Kommunisticheskii Internatsional v dokumentakh,* pp. 537, 547, 548–56; see Document 115.

[81] *Puti mirovoi revoliutsii,* I, 45. For the entire report, see *ibid.,* pp. 30–112. This also appeared as a separate booklet in English, entitled *Capitalist Stabilization and Proletarian Revolution.*

DOCUMENTS

THE STRATEGY AND TACTICS OF THE PROLETARIAN REVOLUTION

88
Stalin on the Theory of the Proletarian Revolution, April 1924

[Excerpts from Lectures on the Foundations of Leninism at the Sverdlov University, April-May, 1924][1]

. . .

In the past the prerequisites for the proletarian revolution were usually discussed in terms of the economic condition of individual countries. This approach is no longer adequate. We must now start with the economic state of all or most countries, with the state of the world economy. Individual countries and individual national economies have ceased to be self-sufficient units, have become links in a single chain called the world economy. The old "cultured" capitalism has grown into imperialism, and imperialism is a world system of financial enslavement and colonial oppression . . .

. . . Now the proletarian revolution must be regarded primarily as the result of the development of contradictions within the world system of imperialism, as the result of the breaking of the imperialist world front in one country or another.

Where will the revolution begin? Where, in what country, can the front of capital be pierced first?

Where industry is more developed, where the proletariat constitutes the majority, where there is more culture, where there is more democracy—that was the reply usually given formerly.

No, objects the Leninist theory of revolution; not necessarily where industry is more developed, and so forth. The front of capital will be pierced where the chain of imperialism is weakest, . . . and it may so happen that the country which starts the revolution, which makes a breach in the front of capital, may be less developed in a capitalist sense than other countries, countries that nevertheless remain within the framework of capitalism.

In 1917 the chain of the imperialist world front proved to be weaker in Russia than in the other countries. It was there that the chain gave way and provided an outlet for the proletarian revolution . . .

Where will the chain break in the near future? Again, where it is the weakest—possibly in India. Why? Because India has a young, militant, revolutionary proletariat, which has as an ally the national-liberation movement—an undoubtedly important and undoubtedly powerful ally. Because there the revolution is opposed by such a well-known foe as foreign imperialism, which lacks all moral credit and is deservedly hated by the oppressed and exploited masses of India.

Or perhaps in Germany. Why? Because the factors operating, say, in India, are beginning to operate in Germany as well; but, of course, the enormous difference

---

[1] Stalin, *Sochineniia*, VI, 95–99; also Stalin, "Foundations of Leninism," in *Problems of Leninism*, pp. 20–21.

between India's level of development and Germany's is bound to stamp its imprint on the progress and outcome of a revolution in Germany.

That is why Lenin said this:

"The Western European capitalist countries will consummate their development toward socialism . . . not by the gradual 'maturing' of socialism, but by the exploitation of some countries by others, by the exploitation of the first of the countries that was defeated in the imperialist war combined with the exploitation of the whole of the East. On the other hand, precisely as a result of the first imperialist war, the East has been definitely drawn into the revolutionary movement, has been definitely drawn into the general maelstrom of the world revolutionary movement."[2]

Briefly, the chain of the imperialist front must, as a rule, give way where the links are weakest, and not necessarily where capitalism is more developed, where there is such-and-such a percentage of proletarians and such-and-such a percentage of peasants, and so on. . . .

89
Stalin on the Strategy and Tactics of the Revolution

[Excerpts from Lectures on the Foundations of Leninism at the Sverdlov University, April-May, 1924][3]

Strategy deals with the main forces of the revolution and their reserves. It changes with the passing of the revolution from one stage to another, but remains essentially unchanged throughout a given stage.

Tactics are the rules for the proletariat's conduct in the comparatively short ebbs and flows of the movement, . . . when old slogans and old methods of struggle and organization must be replaced by new ones, etc. The object of strategy is to win the war against tsarism, let us say, or against the bourgeoisie, to carry the struggle against tsarism or against the bourgeoisie to its end. Tactics are concerned with less important objects, for they aim not at winning the war as a whole, but at winning a particular engagement, or a particular battle, at carrying through successfully a particular action corresponding to the concrete situation in the given period of rise or decline of the revolution. Tactics are a part of strategy, subordinate to it and serving it.

Tactics change according to the ebb and flow. During the first stage of the revolution (1903 to February 1917), while the strategic plan remained unchanged, tactics changed several times. . . .

The reserves of the revolution can be:

Direct: (*a*) the peasantry and in general the intermediate strata of the population within the country; (*b*) the proletariat of the neighboring countries; (*c*) the revolutionary movement in the colonies and dependent countries; (*d*) the gains and achievements of the dictatorship of the proletariat—part of which the proletariat may give up temporarily, while retaining superiority of forces, in order to buy off a powerful enemy and gain a respite; and

Indirect: (*a*) the contradictions and conflicts among the nonproletarian classes within the country, which can be utilized by the proletariat to weaken the enemy and to strengthen its own reserves; (*b*) contradictions, conflicts, and wars (the imperialist war, for instance) among the bourgeois states hostile to the proletarian state, which can be utilized by the proletariat in its offensive or in maneuvering in the event of a forced retreat.

There is no need to speak at length about the reserves of the first category; their

[2] Lenin, *Sochineniia*, XXVII, 415–16.
[3] Stalin, *Sochineniia*, VI, 153–61, 165–67; also Stalin, "Foundations of Leninism," in *Problems of Leninism*, pp. 60–66, 69–70.

significance is understood by everyone. As for the reserves of the second category, whose significance is not always clear, it must be said that sometimes they are of prime importance for the progress of the revolution. . . . It must be presumed that now, when the contradictions among the imperialist groups are becoming more and more profound, and when a new war among them is becoming inevitable, reserves of this description will assume ever greater importance for the proletariat.

The task of strategic leadership is to make proper use of all these reserves to achieve the main object of the revolution at the given stage of its development.

What does making proper use of reserves mean?

It means fulfilling certain necessary conditions, of which the following must be regarded as the principal ones:

First: The concentration of the main forces of the revolution at the enemy's most vulnerable spot at the decisive moment when the revolution has already become ripe, when the offensive is going full speed ahead, when insurrection is knocking at the door, and when bringing the reserves up to the vanguard is the decisive condition of success. The party's strategy from April to October, 1917, well illustrates this manner of utilizing reserves. . . .

Here is what Lenin, paraphrasing the well-known theses of Marx and Engels on insurrection, says about this condition:

(1) Never play with insurrection. When beginning it, firmly realize that you must go on to the end.

(2) You must concentrate a great superiority of forces at the decisive point, at the decisive moment. Otherwise the enemy, who has the advantage of better preparation and organization, will destroy the insurgents.

(3) Once the insurrection has begun, you must act with the greatest determination, and by all means, without fail, take the offensive. "The defensive is the death of every armed rising."

(4) You must try to take the enemy by surprise and seize the moment when his forces are scattered.

(5) You must strive for daily successes, even if they are small . . . and at all costs retain "moral ascendancy."[4]

Second: The selection of the moment for the decisive blow, the moment for starting the insurrection, so timed [as to coincide with the moment] when the crisis has reached the climax, when it is fully apparent that the vanguard is prepared to fight to the end, the reserves are prepared to support the vanguard, and maximum consternation reins in the ranks of the enemy.

The decisive moment, says Lenin, is when

(1) all the class forces hostile to us have become sufficiently entangled . . . ;

(2) all the vacillating, wavering, unstable, intermediate elements, i.e., the democratically inclined petty bourgeoisie as distinct from the capitalist bourgeoisie, have sufficiently exposed themselves before the people, have sufficiently disgraced themselves through their practical bankruptcy;

(3) among the proletariat a mass sentiment in favor of supporting the most determined, supremely bold, revolutionary actions against the bourgeoisie has arisen and begun vigorously to grow. Then, indeed, revolution is ripe; then, indeed, if we have correctly gauged all the conditions indicated above . . . and if we have chosen the moment rightly, our victory is assured.[5]

The manner in which the October insurrection was carried out may be taken as a model of such strategy.

Third: Undeviating pursuit of the course adopted, no matter what difficulties and complications are encountered on the road toward the goal . . .

4 Lenin, *Sochineniia,* XXI, 319–20.
5 *Ibid.,* XXV, 229.

Fourth: Maneuvering the reserves with a view to effecting a proper retreat when the enemy is strong, when retreat is inevitable, when it is obviously disadvantageous to accept battle forced upon us by the enemy, when, with the given alignment of forces, retreat becomes the only way to ward off a blow against the vanguard and to keep the reserves intact. . . .

The purpose of this strategy is to gain time, to demoralize the enemy, and to accumulate forces in order later to assume the offensive.

The signing of the Brest-Litovsk peace may be taken as a model of this strategy, for it enabled the party to gain time, to take advantage of the conflicts in the camp of the imperialists, to demoralize the forces of the enemy, to retain the support of the peasantry, and to accumulate forces in preparation for the offensive against Kolchak and Denkin. . . .

Such are the principal conditions of correct strategic leadership.

. . .

What is the difference between revolutionary tactics and reformist tactics?

Some think that Leninism is opposed to reforms, opposed to compromises and to agreements in general. This is absolutely wrong. Bolsheviks know as well as anybody else that in a certain sense "every little bit helps," that under certain conditions reforms in general, and compromises and agreements in particular, are necessary and useful.

"To carry on a war for the overthrow of the international bourgeoisie," says Lenin, "a war that is a hundred times more difficult, protracted, and complicated than the most stubborn of ordinary wars between states, and to refuse beforehand to maneuver, to utilize conflicts of interest (even though temporary) among one's enemies, to refuse to temporize and compromise with potential (even though transient, unstable, vacillating, and conditional) allies—is this not ridiculous in the extreme?"[6]

Obviously, therefore, it is a matter not of reforms, compromises, and agreements, but of the use people make of them.

To a reformist, reforms are everything; revolutionary work is something incidental, something just to talk about, mere eyewash. That is why reformists under the bourgeois regime inevitably transform reforms into an instrument for strengthening that regime, an instrument for undermining the revolution.

To a revolutionary, on the contrary, the main thing is revolutionary work and not reforms; to him reforms are by-products of the revolution. That is why revolutionaries under the bourgeois regime naturally transform reforms into instruments for disintegrating this regime and strengthening the revolution, into a base for the further development of the revolutionary movement.

The revolutionary will accept a reform and use it as an aid in combining legal work with illegal work; under its cover, he will intensify his illegal revolutionary preparation of the masses for the overthrow of the bourgeoisie.

This is what making revolutionary use of reforms and agreements under the conditions of imperialism means. . . .

90

Stalin on the October Revolution as the Beginning of and the Prerequisite for World Revolution

[Introduction to Stalin's Book *Na putiakh k Oktiabriu*, December 17, 1924][7]

There can be no doubt that the universal theory of a simultaneous victory of the revolution in the principal countries of Europe, the theory that the victory of social-

---

[6] *Ibid.*, p. 210.
[7] Stalin, *Sochineniia*, VI, 395–401.

ism in one country is impossible, has proved to be an artificial and untenable theory. The seven years' history of the proletarian revolution in Russia speaks not for but against this theory. It is unacceptable as a scheme of development of the world revolution, for it contradicts obvious facts. It is still less acceptable as a slogan, for it fetters, rather than releases, the initiative of individual countries which, by reason of certain historical conditions, obtain the opportunity to break through the front of capital alone; it does not stimulate such countries to an active onslaught on capital, but encourages them to wait passively for the "universal climax"; it cultivates among the proletarians of the separate countries not the spirit of revolutionary determination, but the Hamlet-like doubt expressed by the question "What if the others fail to give us support?" Lenin was absolutely right in saying that the victory of the proletariat in one country is a "typical case," that "simultaneous revolution in a number of countries" can only be a "rare exception."[8]

But, as is well known, Lenin's theory of revolution is not limited to this side of the question. It is also a theory of the development of the world revolution. The victory of socialism in one country is not a self-sufficient task. The revolution that has been victorious in one country must regard itself not as a self-sufficient entity, but as an aid, a means *for* hastening the victory of the proletariat in all countries. For the victory of the revolution in one country, in the present case Russia, is not only the product of the uneven development and progressive decay of imperialism; it is at the same time the beginning of and the prerequisite for the world revolution.

Undoubtedly, the paths of development of the world revolution are not as plain as they may have seemed previously, before the victory of the revolution in one country, before the appearance of developed imperialism, which is "the eve of the socialist revolution." For a new factor has arisen, the law of the uneven development of the capitalist countries, which operates under the conditions of developed imperialism, and which connotes the inevitability of armed collisions, the general weakening of the world front of capital, and the possibility of the victory of socialism in individual countries. Another new factor is the vast Soviet country, lying between West and East, between the center of the financial exploitation of the world and the arena of colonial oppression, a country which by its very existence is revolutionizing the whole world.

All these factors (not to mention other, less important ones) cannot be ignored in studying the path of development of the world revolution.

.   .   .

It is true that the final victory of socialism in the first country to emancipate itself is impossible without the combined efforts of the proletarians of several countries. It is equally true, however, that the more effective the assistance rendered by the first socialist country to the workers and toiling masses of all other countries, the more rapidly and thoroughly the world revolution will develop.

How should this assistance be expressed?

First, the victorious country "should do the utmost possible in one country, to develop, support and awaken the revolution in all countries."[9]

Second, the "victorious proletariat" of one country, "having expropriated the capitalists and organized its own socialist production, should stand up . . . against the rest of the world, the capitalist world, attracting to its cause the oppressed classes of other countries, raising revolts in those countries against the capitalists, and if necessary even coming out with armed force against the exploiting classes and their states."[10]

The characteristic feature of the assistance given by the victorious country is not

[8] Lenin, *Sochineniia*, XXIII, 354.
[9] *Ibid.*, p. 265.
[10] *Ibid.*, pp. 232–33.

only that it hastens the victory of the proletarians of other countries but also that, by facilitating this victory, it ensures the final victory of socialism in the first victorious country.

Most probably, as the world revolution develops, alongside the individual centers of imperialism and the capitalist system throughout the world there will arise individual centers of socialism and a system of these centers throughout the world, and the struggle between these two systems will fill the history of the development of the world revolution.

"For," says Lenin, "the free union of nations in socialism is impossible without a more or less prolonged and stubborn struggle by the socialist republics against the [politically] backward states."[11]

The October Revolution is significant not only because it marks a great blow by one country to the system of imperialism, not only because out of it came the first center of socialism in the ocean of imperialist countries, but also because it constitutes the first stage of world revolution and a mighty base for its further development.

If those who forget the international character of the October Revolution, and declare the victory of revolution in one country to be purely national, are wrong, so are those who acknowledge the international character of the October Revolution but nonetheless regard it as something passive, merely destined to accept help from without. Actually, the October Revolution not only needs support from the revolution in other countries, but must itself support the revolution in those countries in order to accelerate the overthrow of world imperialism.

91

Soviet Strength Lies in the Success of Soviet Economic Development

[Kamenev at a Party Conference at Krasnaia Presnia, May 8, 1924][12]

. . .

In the general international situation we see the absolute failure of the economic and political system that resulted from the imperialist war. If we weigh the prospects of the capitalist system objectively, we shall see clearly that the system is already in a state of convulsions. We have patience; we have learned to wait for years for the moment when the world proletarian revolution will break out to help us. We will not say even now that the last and ninth wave[13] of the proletarian advance on the bulwark of capitalism will come tomorrow, or the day after. But we find in every historical occurrence, in every column of the newspapers, in every telegram that comes to us from the center of capitalist civilization and capitalist enslavement, confirmation of our diagnosis when we say "incurably ill." . . .

In view of this disintegration of capitalism and the bourgeoisie, and the growth of the communist forces and the workers' movement all over the world, we must carefully and guardedly make use of every conflict that rends the hostile bourgeois world. Our strength at present lies in the growth of our internal power. We grow with every new economic success within our own country. At present the Red Army's bayonets and Budenny's horsemen mean less to the international proletarian movement than the Soviet government's economic achievements, the achievements of construction. . . .

Since the [last] party conference in January, we have been recognized by Great

---

[11] *Ibid.*, p. 233.

[12] *Pravda*, No. 104, May 10, 1924, p. 4. Krasnaia Presnia is the name of an industrial ward in Moscow.

[13] The most powerful.

Britain and Italy. These recognitions are not accidental; they reveal the tremendous increase in the power of our Union. There is no doubt about this. But you must also remember other facts. During the negotiations with Rumania,[14] the Soviet government was asked to sign treaties legalizing the robbery our neighbors committed while we were fighting domestic counterrevolution. Our government is now carrying on negotiations with MacDonald and Mussolini, since they have recognized us and seem prepared to discuss on a businesslike basis mutual advantages and firm industrial relations. But if any of them demand that we lower our banner even for a moment and sacrifice the honor of our proletarian republic before such usurpers as the Rumanians, the Soviet people will definitely refuse.

As to the negotiations with Britain, our government has discussed and weighed in detail the prospects these negotiations open before us. Relations with the European market, with the European countries, are very desirable for us, but they are desirable for purely business reasons. We know that our country is growing, becoming stronger economically, but this growth is slow. And inasmuch as this economic growth is based on the petty peasant economy that predominates in our country, it will continue to be slow. Therefore, foreign capital will be useful for our economic development and consolidation. We need credits, we need loans. And we are quite willing to negotiate with those who are willing to talk to us on terms of equality about these credits, about these loans. But before we talk, they must recognize that the revolution accomplished by the workers and peasants cannot be turned back, that the October achievements and the achievements won in the struggle against the counterrevolution cannot be crossed out with red ink at some diplomatic round table. Those who hope to force us to give up our basic achievements, that is, the nationalization of industries, the nationalization of land, the annulment of tsarist and war debts, are deeply mistaken. . . .

ANGLO-SOVIET TREATY NEGOTIATIONS

92

Rakovsky Answers MacDonald at the Opening of the Conference in London, April 14, 1924[15]

[Expresses sincere gratitude for the words of welcome.]

The highest governing body of our Union's peoples has declared in its resolution that close co-operation with Britain is one of the foremost aims of the Soviet government. . . .

Today, at the opening of the conference, I consider it my duty to indicate to you the general principles by which the Soviet delegation will be guided in dealing with the problems before us. Despite the complexity and difficulty of these problems, we see no insurmountable obstacles to complete understanding between Great Britain and the U.S.S.R.

[Speaks of the need for economic co-operation between the two countries; calls their economic structures mutually complementary.]

We are ready to do all we can to adjust the economic differences that have here-

---

[14] A conference was held in Vienna in February 1924 to discuss Soviet-Rumanian relations. Agreement on the Bessarabian problem could not be reached, and the conference soon adjourned.

[15] *Izvestiia*, No. 88, April 16, 1924, pp. 1–2; also *The Times* (London), April 15, 1924, p. 9.

tofore been regarded as obstacles to commercial and financial co-operation between Great Britain and the Soviet Union. This range of questions includes the question of prewar debts and private claims. Although with the continuous development of commercial relations between the two countries this question has lost the exceptional importance attached to it at Genoa and at The Hague, we are ready to submit it to detailed discussion, for we believe that if both countries' interests are taken into consideration, nothing blocks its solution.

The British government may also count on our full and sincere good will in solving the political questions that confront us. In our opinion, the obstacles to the solution of these questions can be removed by our common efforts. We have renounced the policy of conquest of the former tsarist government; we have annulled the old tsarist treaties and [repudiated the tsarist practice of] partitioning Eastern states into spheres of influence. The Soviet government has no intention of reverting to that policy. It is absolutely excluded by the socialist organization of our state, which is based on the absolute equality of nationalities.

Other reasons, too, make any return to the old policy impossible. The war has awakened the national consciousness of the peoples of the East, and any attempt on our part to obstruct that legitimate consciousness would be not only a crime against our own interests, but also a piece of folly, because such a policy is bound sooner or later to fail. In consequence, in so far as the British and Soviet governments adopt as a starting point the principle of respecting the independence and sovereignty of the Eastern states, we shall not find it difficult to settle all the questions pertaining to the interests of Great Britain and the Soviet Union in the East.

Although the present conversations are concerned with clarifying Anglo-Soviet relations, we believe that their significance reaches far beyond the borders of our two countries. The program outlined in the notes of the two governments embraces the question of the treaties between Great Britain and the former governments of Russia, and thereby concerns the fundamental problems of the political life of the whole world.

The working masses of the Union acclaimed Great Britain's recognition of the U.S.S.R., above all because they saw in it not merely a diplomatic formality, but an expression of the British people's desire to work in common with us for the consolidation of universal peace. In this, in our view, lies the enormous historic import of the present conversations. Every people, as you have observed yourself, Mr. Prime Minister, is interested in the success of these conversations. The endeavors of the two greatest states in the world not only to iron out their own misunderstandings and their differences, but also to solve problems affecting the peace of the world, may become the starting point of a radical departure in international relations.

The urgency of the problem of establishing a durable peace is becoming more and more obvious to all peoples. Nevertheless, the government of the Union observes with profound regret that in spite of the numerous peace treaties signed after the World War, social and national conflicts of interest have never appeared in so acute a form as at the present time. The means employed by governments to extricate themselves from a situation that the masses find intolerable have only aggravated the antagonisms in question. The assurances freely given during and after the World War that it was the last war and that the development of militarism would be brought to an end, have proved illusory. . . . We consider, therefore, that the question of disarmament should present itself to governments with perfect clearness and in an absolutely imperative manner. Disarmament must be carried to the furthest possible limits.

Although during the last three years we have reduced our army twelve times, from six million men at the beginning of 1921 to 500,000, spread over our immense territory of twenty million square kilometers, the government of the Soviet Union declares its readiness, provided the other states consent to do likewise, to take further decisive steps toward disarmament. Our government is also ready to contribute in every way to a universal decrease in naval armaments, subject, however, to certain political guarantees formulated by our representative [at the recent conference] in Rome. I shall confine myself here to stating our government's general view on this question.

We are aware of the British government's and British people's great interest in the League of Nations. The Soviet government does not share this attitude toward the League of Nations as it now exists, but would be prepared to endorse a plan of international organization that excluded coercion and measures of reprisal, which can only result in serving the selfish interest of certain powerful states. The only international organization now possible, in our view, would be one in which all governments were on a footing of perfect equality. We believe that the principle of international co-operation should be not only honored but extended, particularly to labor legislation.

We consider that governments desiring to create the conditions for a stable peace should try to eliminate, by common efforts, the causes that lead to conflicts among peoples.

The Soviet government has repeatedly declared its profound conviction that the best condition for a stable peace would be the revision of the Treaty of Versailles and the other treaties connected with it. . . .

What I have said is already familiar to public opinion in Great Britain. The same idea has been repeatedly expressed by outstanding British politicians, as well as by Britain's most eminent writers. Obviously, we do not think that the abrogation of the Treaty of Versailles should lead to the re-establishment of states which, like Austria-Hungary, could rest only on violence and feed on the antagonisms that led to the World War.

A reorganization of Europe can be stable only if it is based on the people's will and if it takes into account their aspirations for national independence. The Soviet government, therefore, is prepared to support by common efforts and to pursue—perhaps not at one stroke, but by continued diplomatic efforts—a policy of the revision of frontiers on ethnographic principles, applying a plebiscite wherever necessary, as, for example, we suggested at the Vienna Conference in the case of Bessarabia.

We do not believe that wars can be completely abolished until the social causes that engender them are abolished. The Soviet government, guided by the Communist Party, considers the elimination of war possible only on the condition of a socialist organization of [national] economy. We are, however, ready to collaborate in any serious attempt by any government to reduce the danger of war.

We consider that the differences between the social structures of our two countries need not be an obstacle to political and economic collaboration. The opposite view, which finds an echo in a certain portion of public opinion in England, is absolutely disproved by the progressive development of Anglo-Soviet commercial relations.

I consider it my duty, and particularly after the speech of the Prime Minister, to emphasize today that the Soviet government fully shares the view of the British government that mutual nonintervention in internal affairs is indispensable if there is to be mutual confidence. The principle of nonintervention is for us a guarantee against attempts to make us give up the basis of our socialist organization—the nationalization of large-scale industry, the nationalization of land, the monopoly of foreign trade—or renounce our socialist legislation.

The peoples of the U.S.S.R. are determined to hold onto the conquests of the revolution, which constitute the *raison d'être* of the Soviet government, and for which the toiling masses of the entire Union fought against the coalition of domestic foes and foreign states. With that frankness which must characterize our relations, I must remind you, Mr. Prime Minister, that former British governments also took part in that foreign intervention in Russia. Since you yourself and your party, Mr. Prime Minister, opposed that intervention, it will not surprise you that the sentiments it provoked among our toiling masses have not yet fully subsided. But we have met here to dissipate past sentiments, and, by banishing the distrust that still exists, to provide a basis for lasting friendship.

Returning to our future labors here, the Soviet delegation believes we should strive first to solve all political and economic questions which are of equal interest to both countries, and which, by their very nature, need no preliminary detailed investigation. In this way our conference might yield quick results which, by strengthening mutual confidence, would help us solve more difficult problems.

In conclusion, we express our profound conviction that the government of the British people, who have created by unrelenting toil the greatest industry in the world, will discover the way to rapprochement, to co-operation, and to a stable peace with the toiling masses of the Union, among whom the revolution that liberated them from the oppression of the old regime also awakened a tremendous desire for economic progress and cultural development.

93

Rakovsky's Comment to the Press on the British Bankers' Memorandum, April 25, 1924[16]

Although Paragraph 6 of the British bankers' memorandum gives, as one of the chief conditions for restored confidence between the two countries, mutual non-interference with each other's home affairs, Paragraphs 3, 4, and 5 are an actual attempt to make us renounce the very foundations of the Soviet Socialist organisation. The memorandum demands the re-establishment of private property. The memorandum demands the abolition of the monopoly of foreign trade. The memorandum demands a change of our code. Our answer to such an attempt is a categorical "Never!"

The authors of the memorandum did not try to ascertain the reason why we are asking for a loan nor on what terms we want to get this loan. I must first of all declare that if we raise the question of the loan it is because we consider that that is the only way to solve the question of pre-war debts, and also that such a loan would contribute to the development of trade relations between Britain and the Union of the Soviet Republics. I also must state in all frankness that, should we not be required to pay off certain liabilities, we would not ask for a loan.

It is not true that our Soviet code does not offer guarantees for investors and the capital they invest. It is not true that a loan invested in Soviet Russia runs any risks. I am able to say that these loans, far from having less, will offer more guarantees than other loans contracted here on the English market. It is also false that the monopoly of foreign trade is standing in the way of development of Anglo-Russian trade. On the contrary, it is because of the monopoly that we are such honest payers.

I must firmly declare that we will not restore property to former owners. However, on this point, too, we could make some practical business offers. One of the practical means of compensating the former owners could be to lease to them on a concessionary basis enterprises which had been formerly their own, and which, according to our economic plan, are to be given as concessions.

The question of the liquidation of pre-war debts could be solved satisfactorily

[16] *The Times* (London), April 26, 1924, p. 9; also appears in abbreviated form in *Izvestiia*, No. 98, April 30, 1924, p. 1. Complete text of the British bankers' memorandum appears in *The Times*, April 14, 1924, p. 11.

only subject to a consideration for our counter-claims—that is to say, on condition of real help being extended to us and interested circles taking into account the ruin brought upon us by intervention and which we are now warding off with so much pains.

94

Chicherin on the Anglo-Soviet Treaty, at the Special Plenary Session of the Moscow Soviet, August 20, 1924[17]

". . . Although the treaty supplies only the principle on which the [general] agreement is to be based, its significance is nevertheless tremendous. Even if difficulties over ratification should arise in Parliament, the very signing of the agreement is an immensely important event, being a first step in the development of our international relations. . . .

"Now for the first time we have signed a final peace treaty regulating our relations with the most powerful state among the Great Powers. This treaty gives us an advantage that overbalances the sacrifices we shall have to bear as a result of our partial recognition of old debts.

"By signing this treaty, the British government has recognized that our partial concession on debts is an exception to our decrees. In this way the [political] regime of the U.S.S.R. has acquired international recognition. . . .

"This treaty actually means international recognition of the October Revolution as the basis of the Soviet state. Seven years had to elapse before this could be accomplished. . . .

"The record of the five postwar years of antagonism [between us and the West] shows, on one hand, a deep crisis and disintegration in the West, and on the other, the economic restoration and growth of the U.S.S.R. That was the baggage with which we arrived at the peace conference in London."

Emphasizing the achievements of the Soviet government, such as the agreement with Germany concerning the extraterritoriality of the Soviet [trade] mission, and pointing out that even our exact opposite—Mussolini—is conducting, on the whole, a line of foreign policy favorable to us, Comrade Chicherin declared that we are now also confronted with serious issues in the Pacific. . . .

"The treaty points out the direction and the length of the path of history, along which we shall continue with our old firmness and with our deep conviction that our course is the right one."

THE DAWES PLAN

95

The Dawes Plan and the Communists

a

[The Principles Outlining the Committee of Experts' Plan, known as the Dawes Plan; Letter of Charles G. Dawes, Chairman of the Committee of Experts, to the Reparations Committee, April 9, 1924, Attached to the Report of the Committee of Experts][18]

[17] *Izvestiia*, No. 189, August 21, 1924, p. 3.
[18] Rufus C. Dawes, *The Dawes Plan in the Making*, pp. 299–302.

Your Committee of Experts has unanimously adopted a report upon the means of balancing the budget of Germany and the measures to be taken to stabilize its currency, which I now have the honor to submit.

Deeply impressed by a sense of its responsibility to your commission and to the universal conscience, the committee bases its plan upon those principles of justice, fairness, and mutual interest, in the supremacy of which not only the creditors of Germany and Germany herself, but the world, has a vital and enduring concern.

With these principles fixed and accepted in that common good faith which is the foundation of all business and the best safeguard for universal peace, the recommendations of the committee must be considered not as inflicting penalties, but as suggesting means for assisting the economic recovery of all the European peoples, and the entry upon a new period of happiness and prosperity unmenaced by war.

Since, as a result of the war, the creditors of Germany are paying taxes to the limit of their capacity, so also must Germany pay taxes from year to year to the limit of her capacity. This is in accord with that just and underlying principle of the Treaty of Versailles, reaffirmed by Germany in her note of May 29, 1919, that the German scheme of taxation must be "fully as heavy proportionately as that of any of the powers represented on the commission." More than this limit could not be expected, and less than this would relieve Germany from the common hardship and give her an unfair advantage in the industrial competition of the future. This principle the plan embodies.

The plan has been made to include flexible adjustments which, from the very beginning, tend to produce the maximum of contributions consistent with the continued and increasing productivity of Germany. The conservative estimates of payments to be made in the near future are dictated by business prudence in outlining the basis of a loan, and should not destroy perspective as to the effects to be registered in the aggregate of eventual payments, which will annually increase. With normal economic conditions and productivity restored in Germany, most hopeful estimates of amounts eventually receivable will be found to be justified. Without such restoration, such payments as can be obtained will be of little value in meeting the urgent needs of creditor nations.

To insure the permanence of a new economic peace between the Allied Governments and Germany, which involves the economic readjustments presented by the plan, there are provided the counterparts of those usual economic precautions against default recognized as essential in all business relations involving expressed obligations. The existence of safeguards in no way hampers or embarrasses the carrying out of ordinary business contracts. The thorough effectiveness of the safeguards should not embarrass the normal economic functioning of Germany, and is of fundamental importance to her creditors and to Germany.

Great care has been taken in fixing conditions of supervision over Germany's internal organization so as to impose the minimum of interference consistent with proper protection. This general plan, fair and reasonable in its nature, if accepted, leads to an ultimate and lasting peace. The rejection of these proposals by the German Government means the deliberate choice of a continuance of economic demoralization, eventually involving her people in hopeless misery.

In the preparation of this report, the committee has carefully and laboriously covered the broad field of investigation. It has had the constant co-operation of able staffs of experts, gathering information, digesting it and presenting it. It conducted, on the ground, an examination of the officials of the German Government and its representatives of its labor, agriculture and industry. It received from the German Government and its representatives voluminous and satisfactory answers in response to its written inquiries. In connection with various features of its report, both for gathering information and for advice, it has called to its assistance outside experts of international reputation. The published reports and statements of economists of world-wide standing have been in its hands. It has had the benefit of the accumulated information heretofore gathered by your commission.

In speaking of my colleagues and as bearing upon the value of this report, I feel that I should make it known to your commission and to the world, that their governments have in no case limited their complete independence of judgment and action, either before or after their appointment by you. Limited only by the powers granted by your commission, each has performed his arduous and responsible work as a free agent. These men, searching for truth and advice thereon, were answerable only to conscience. In granting this freedom, the governments have but followed your own spirit and intent in constituting the committee, but in so doing, they have paid the highest tribute which governments can bestow—complete confidence in a time of crisis in human affairs. In their vision, in their independence of thought, and above all, in their spirit of high and sincere purpose, which rises above the small things over which the small so often stumble, my colleagues have shown themselves worthy of this trust. That their work, which I now place in your hands, may assist you in the discharge of your great responsibilities, is their prayer and the knowledge hereafter, that it has done so, will be their full reward.

CHARLES G. DAWES, Chairman.

b

[The Closing Part of the Manifesto of the Fifth Congress of the Communist International to the World Proletariat, on the Occasion of the Tenth Anniversary of World War I, July 5, 1924, Signed by the Presidium of the Congress][19]

.   .   .

Our immediate and pressing task in the struggle against war is the struggle against that conspiracy of the capitalist violators which goes by the harmless name of the Experts' plan. And here, as everywhere, the first blow must be directed against the Social Democrats. They intimidate the workers with the formidable forces of America, and demand their submission and obedience. They predict the ruin of Europe, and first of all Germany, should the latter fail to submit to American capital. We, the Communists, say to the workers of Europe: Your only salvation is in an irreconcilable war against the Experts' plan, against its promulgators and supporters. You must clear the Social Democrats from your path; you must overthrow the bourgeoisie; you must take power into your own hands; you must unite the various sections of the economic structure of Europe, and direct them along the road to socialism. If Soviet Russia has been able to defend herself victoriously for a number of years against the capitalists of Europe and America, surely the European proletariat will be even more secure if, upon seizing power, they unite the European countries into a Soviet federation, a Workers' and Peasants' United States of Europe. By so doing, they will not only rescue European culture from decline and decay and guarantee freedom and independence to the colonial and semicolonial peoples, but deal a mortal blow to American capital's domination of the world. The revolutionary movement in America will receive a great impetus. The European socialist federation will thus become the cornerstone of the world socialist republic. Only then will human beings be able to think and act like real human beings; only then will world economy be organized on a basis of solidarity and reason, and world relations be transformed into the fraternal exchange of material and spiritual wealth between peoples and continents. War will be a thing of the past, since there will be

[19] *Piatyi Vsemirnyi Kongress K.I.*, II, 200–201; also *International Press Correspondence*, No. 43, July 18, 1924, pp. 432–33.

no longer any reason for it. Armies and soldiers will disappear. All the efforts of human beings will be directed toward the enrichment of our earth, toward the improvement and adornment of human life.

Such is the task of the Communist International—a huge task, but not an impossible one. Marx and Lenin showed us the way—by fierce struggle in each country against the national bourgeoisie, by combining the proletarian forces of all countries to seize power and establish the proletarian dictatorship. Whoever tells you there is another way is lying. The Communist International serves the cause of the proletariat by speaking the truth. Let that truth resound throughout the world like the alarm bell of the revolutionary struggle!

Against war, against the bourgeoisie, against socialist traitors!

For the world revolution, for the dictatorship of the proletariat, for communism!

96
Stalin on the International Situation, September 1924[20]

· · ·

2. *The Interference of America in the Affairs of Europe
and the London Agreement of the Entente Powers
Concerning Reparations.*

· · ·

The London Conference of the Entente powers presents the fullest expression of the false and misleading bourgeois-democratic pacificism. As the MacDonald-Herriot rise to power and the loud proclamation of the "establishment of normal relations" with the Soviet Union has served to conceal the current intense class struggle in Europe and the bourgeois states' mortal animosity toward the Soviet Union, so the agreement just reached in London is expected to conceal the intense rivalry between England and France for hegemony in Europe, the steadily increasing friction between Britain and America in their struggle for mastery of the world market, and, finally, the German people's superhuman struggle against Entente oppression. "There is no longer war between the classes, the revolution is at end. Now it is possible to bring about co-operation between all classes," shout MacDonald, Renaudel & Co. "There is no longer any rivalry between France and Britain, between America and Britain, between Germany and the Entente. The war is over; now we can consummate our efforts by proclaiming a universal peace with America at the head"—so shout these people's collaborators in the London agreement, their fellow-betrayers of the working class, the Social Democratic heroes of pacifism.

What, however, actually happened at the London Conference of the Entente powers?

Prior to the London Conference decisions on reparations were made by France alone, more or less independently of the "allies," because France had a majority on the reparations committee. The Ruhr was occupied to disorganize Germany, and to make certain that France would obtain reparations from Germany—i.e., coal and coke for French metallurgy, chemical and semi-manufactured products and dyes for the French chemical industry, and the duty-free import of Alsatian textiles into Germany. This plan was to have provided the material basis for French military and economic hegemony in Europe. But, as is known, the plan did not work; the occupation brought the opposite results. France received practically no deliveries in money or in kind. Finally, the initiator of the occupation, Poincaré, was thrown overboard because his openly imperialistic policy threatened to bring on a new war and revolution. French

[20] Stalin, "K mezhdunarodnomu polozheniiu," *Bolshevik*, No. 11, 1924, pp. 11–20; also Stalin, *Sochineniia*, VI, 286–301.

hegemony in Europe failed not only because French methods of occupation and open plunder made economic co-operation between the French and German industries impossible, but also because England, realizing that the unification of German coal and French metal would undermine the English metallurgical industry, was definitely against such co-operation.

.   .   .

What conclusion, then, can we draw from this conference?

There can be but one conclusion. The London Conference not only settled none of the old European contradictions, but added new ones—between America and England. England, seeking predominance on the Continent, will continue, as heretofore, to increase the hostility between France and Germany. America, seeking predominance in the world market, will work to increase the hostility between England and France. We shall not even mention the strong hostility between Germany and the Entente. Future world events will be determined by these hostilities, and not by the "pacifist" speeches of such gallows-birds as Hughes or the loquacious Herriot. The law of the unequal development of imperialist countries and the inevitability of imperialist wars remains in force now more than ever before. The London Conference has simply masked the hostilities in a way that will provide new reasons for their extreme aggravation.

3. The Growth of Revolutionary Elements in the Workers' Movement in Europe. The Growth of the Popularity of the Soviet Union.

That the "pacifist-democratic regime" is unstable, that it is but foam on the surface of deeply troubled revolutionary processes taking place within the working class movement, is clear from the decisive victory of the revolutionary wing of the communist parties in Germany, France, and Russia; the growth of an active Left wing within the British workers' movement; and, finally, the growth of the popularity of the Soviet Union among the toiling masses of the West and East.

[Discusses the development of the communist parties in the West.] . . .

To sum up: We are witnessing in the West the beginning of the process of the final shaping up of true Bolshevik parties, which will be the pillars of the coming revolution in Europe. [Discusses trade unions in the West.] . . .

Finally, a few words about the increasing popularity of the Soviet Union among the peoples of the bourgeois countries. . . . The "recognition" of the Soviet Union by a number of bourgeois states does not by itself mean anything special. Such recognition is dictated (1) by capitalist competition, with each country trying to take "its place" in the Soviet market; and (2) by the "program" of pacifism, which requires "normal relations" and the signing of some kind of "treaty" with the Soviet Union. What is significant is that the present "democrats" and "pacifists" have defeated their bourgeois competitors in parliamentary elections by recommending "recognition" of the Soviet Union. MacDonald and Herriot have come to the helm and can remain there only because, among other things, they hypocritically talk about "friendship with Russia"; the power of these "democrats" and "pacifists" is a reflection of Soviet authority among the masses. Even such a well-known "democrat" as Mussolini considers it necessary to boast to the Italian workers of his "friendship" with the Soviet government. Even such snatchers of other people's property as the present leaders of Japan do not wish to do without "friendship" with the Soviet Union. We do not even mention the tremendous authority of the Soviet power among the masses in Turkey, Persia, China, and India.

How can one explain the extraordinary power and exceptional popularity of the

Soviet government's "dictatorial" and revolutionary authority among the masses in foreign states?

First, by the workers' hatred of capitalism, and their desire to free themselves from it. The workers of the bourgeois states sympathize with the Soviet government primarily because it is the power that overthrew capitalism. . . .

Second, by the masses' hatred of war and their desire to break up the military preparations of the bourgeoisie. The masses know that the Soviet government was first to launch an attack against the imperialist war, and that by that attack it undermined the war. The masses see that the Soviet Union is the only country that fights preparations for new wars. They sympathize with the Soviet government because it is the bearer of peace among all peoples and a bulwark against wars. . . .

Third, by the hatred of imperialism felt by the oppressed masses of the dependent countries and colonies, and their desire to break away from it. Only the Soviet government has broken the chains of "patriotic" imperialism. Only the Soviet Union builds its life on the basis of equality and co-operation among nations. The Soviet government is the only government in the world that defends to the end the unity, independence, freedom, and sovereignty of Turkey, Persia, Afghanistan, and China, of the colonial and dependent countries of the world. The oppressed masses sympathize with the Soviet Union because they see it as their ally in their struggle to free themselves from imperialism. Conversely, as the international popularity of the Soviet government increases, so does the oppressed peoples' hatred of world imperialism.

Such are the facts.

One can hardly doubt that these three kinds of hatred will contribute to the undermining of the "pacifist-democratic regime" of the present imperialistic rule. . . .

"THE ZINOVIEV LETTER"

97

Zinoviev on the British Labour Government at the Fifth Congress of the Comintern, June 26, 1924[21]

. . .

Objectively, the counterrevolutionary "Labour" government of MacDonald, generally speaking, must be detrimental to the bourgeoisie. Comrade Lenin was a thousand times right when he told the Second Congress that a "labor" government would come into power in Britain. This "Labour" government must be given support by the Communists, but it must be the support the rope gives to the person on the gallows. Since the most farsighted bourgeois find it necessary to support British Menshevism [i.e., the British Labour Party], it becomes evident that these bourgeois can no longer maintain their power by their former methods. Of course, the Menshevik party is not a true workers' party, for it is not a revolutionary party. But Menshevism frequently looks with one eye to the left and with the other eye to the right. Menshevism can help (perhaps against its wishes) to disintegrate and undermine the position of the bourgeoisie.

Therefore, we must have very clear views on this matter, and our agitation must be partially changed, because we are passing through a new democratic-pacifist "era." We must explain to the workers of the world what this "era" means. We must make

[21] *Piatyi Vsemirnyi Kongress K.I.*, I, 444–45; also G. E. Zinoviev, *Speech in Reply to Discussion of Report on the Work of the E.C.C.I.*, p. 14.

them understand that it cannot last, and that the Social Democrats are again deceiving the workers. In the historical arena we are the only force that has no illusions about the "Labour" government—about this screen of "democracy" and "pacifism." And because we are the only force of this kind in the whole world, we must set ourselves the task of finding out and exposing all the concrete characteristics that differentiate the present bourgeois regime from the former. . . .

98

The Concrete Tasks of the British Communist Party Outlined by the Fifth Congress of the Communist International, June 17–July 8, 1924[22]

At present, Britain and its possessions play the principal role in all international questions. Consequently, the Communist Party of Britain has gained tremendously in importance, and to train this party to fulfill its duties has become one of the most important tasks of the Communist International. In its attitude toward the Labour government, the Communist Party of Britain has displayed certain ideological and tactical deviations. In the immediate future, it must concentrate its strength on the following tasks:

(a) To support and encourage the growth of the Left-wing group in the Labour Party so that it may develop into a real revolutionary wing within the Labour Party and launch intensive work within the minority movement of the trade unions.

(b) To oppose the so-called "Labour government" of MacDonald by exposing clearly to the masses its bourgeois and anti-labor nature.

(c) To maintain a clear and distinct communist line during the forthcoming election campaign and in all future elections.

(d) To concentrate on organizing institutions for the united front from below (strike committees, factory councils, and so forth), and to point out to the working masses the political significance of the economic struggle so organized.

(e) To carry out an active campaign for the organization of committees of action in the factories and trade unions, in order to exercise pressure on the so-called "Labour government" to carry out its promises (so far ignored) to nationalize railways and mines, increase unemployment benefits, construct workers' homes, etc. Only by exposing the Labour government's treachery on the basis of the daily needs of the working class, and by getting broad working masses to support these aims, can the Communist Party of Britain destroy the illusions of the working masses about the so-called "Labour government."

(f) To emphasize contact with the colonies, support of colonial national-revolutionary movements, the question of militarism and naval development, disarmament, and the relations of Britain to the Soviet Union, to imperialist France, and to the Experts' plan.[23]

(g) To begin a particularly careful campaign for bringing the unemployed under the party's influence.

(h) To direct its special attention to the internal development of the party, to gaining new working class members, to forming factory cells; to educating party members and instructing them about the international workers' movement.

---

[22] *Piatyi Vsemirnyi Kongress K.I.*, II, 48–49; also *International Press Correspondence*, No. 62, August 29, 1924, p. 653.

[23] The Dawes Plan.

99

"The Zinoviev Letter"

a

[Zinoviev's Alleged Instructions to the British Communist Party][24]

EXECUTIVE COMMITTEE, THIRD COMMUNIST INTERNATIONAL,
PRESIDIUM

Moscow, September 15, 1924

To the Central Committee, British Communist Party.
(Very Secret.)

Dear Comrades,

The time is approaching for the Parliament of England to consider the treaty concluded between the Governments of Great Britain and the S.S.S.R. for the purpose of ratification. The fierce campaign raised by the British *bourgeoisie* around the question shows that the majority of the same, together with reactionary circles, are against the treaty for the purpose of breaking off an agreement consolidating the ties between the proletariats of the two countries leading to the restoration of normal relations between England and the S.S.S.R.

The proletariat of Great Britain, which pronounced its weighty word when danger threatened of a break-off of the past negotiations and compelled the Government of MacDonald to conclude the treaty must show the greatest possible energy in the future struggle for ratification and against the endeavours of British capitalists to compel Parliament to annul it.

It is indispensable to stir up the masses of the British proletariat, to bring into movement the army of unemployed proletarians, whose position can be improved only after a loan has been granted to the S.S.S.R. for the restoration of her economics and when business collaboration between the British and Russian proletariats has been put in order. It is imperative that the group in the Labour party sympathising with the treaty should bring increased pressure to bear upon the Government and parliamentary circles in favour of the ratification of the treaty.

Keep close observation over the leaders of the Labour party, because these may easily be found in the leading-strings of the *bourgeoisie*. The foreign policy of the Labour party as it is already represents an inferior copy of the policy of the Curzon Government. Organise a campaign of disclosures of the foreign policy of MacDonald.

The I.K.K.I. [ECCI] will willingly place at your disposal the wide material in its possession regarding the activities of British imperialism in the Middle and Far East. In the meanwhile, however, strain every nerve in the struggle for the ratification of the treaty, in favour of a continuation of negotiations regarding the regulation of relations between the S.S.S.R. and England. A settlement of relations between the two countries will assist in the revolutionising of the international and British proletariat not less than a successful rising in any of the working districts in England, as the establishment of close contact between the British and Russian proletariat, the exchange of delegations and workers, etc., will make it possible for us to extend and develop the propaganda of ideas of Leninism in England and the colonies. Armed warfare must be preceded by a struggle against the inclinations to compromise which are embedded among the majority of British workmen, against the ideas of evolution

---

[24] *Documents Illustrating the Hostile Activities of the Soviet Government and Third International against Great Britain* (Cmd. 2874).

and peaceful extermination of capitalism. Only then will it be possible to count upon complete success of an armed insurrection. In Ireland and the colonies the case is different; there there is a national question, and this represents too great a factor for success for us to waste time on a prolonged preparation of the working class.

But even in England, as in other countries where the workers are politically developed, events themselves may more rapidly revolutionise the working masses than propaganda. For instance, a strike movement, repressions by the Government, etc.

From your last report it is evident that agitation-propaganda work in the army is weak, in the navy a very little better. Your explanation that the quality of the members attracted justifies the quantity is right in principle, nevertheless, it would be desirable to have cells in all the units of the troops, particularly among those quartered in the large centres of the country, and also among factories working on munitions and at military store depots. We request that the most particular attention be paid to these latter.

In the event of danger of war, with the aid of the latter and in contact with the transport workers, it is possible to paralyse all the military preparations of the *bourgeoisie* and to make a start in turning an imperialist war into a class war. Now more than ever we should be on our guard. Attempts at intervention in China show that world imperialism is still full of vigour and is once more making endeavours to restore its shaken position and cause a new war, which, as its final objective, is to bring about the break-up of the Russian proletariat and the suppression of the budding world revolution, and, further, would lead to the enslavement of the colonial peoples. "Danger of War"; "The *Bourgeoisie* seeks War; Capital, fresh Markets"—these are the slogans which you must familiarise the masses with, with which you must go to work into the mass of the proletariat. These slogans will open to you the doors of comprehension of the masses, will help you to capture them and march under the banner of Communism.

The military section of the British Communist party, so far as we are aware, further suffers from a lack of specialists, the future directors of the British Red army.

It is time you thought of forming such a group, which, together with the leaders, might be, in the event of an outbreak of active strife, the brain of the military organisation of the party.

Go attentively through the lists of the military "cells," detailing from them the more energetic and capable men; turn attention to the more talented military specialists who have, for one reason or another, left the service and hold Socialist views. Attract them into the ranks of the Communist party if they desire honestly to serve the proletariat and desire in the future to direct not the blind mechanical forces in the service of the *bourgeoisie*, but a national army.

Form a directing operative head of the military section.

Do not put this off to a future moment, which may be pregnant with events and catch you unprepared.

Desiring you all success both in organisation and in your struggle,

With Communist greetings,

President of the Presidium of the I.K.K.I.,

ZINOVIEV,

Member of the Presidium,

McMANUS.

Kuusinen, Secretary

b

[Zinoviev's Statement to Representatives of the Foreign Press,
October 27, 1924][25]

The letter of September 15, 1924, that has been attributed to me is a forgery from the first to the last word. Let us first take the heading. The organization of which I am the chairman never describes itself officially as the "Executive Committee of the *Third* Communist International"; the official name is "Executive Committee of the Communist International." Equally incorrect is the signature: "President of the Presidium." The date was likewise very clumsily chosen by the forger. On September 15 I was taking a cure at Kislovodsk, and therefore could not have signed any official letters.

. . .

What, then, is the meaning of this whole sensational event in connection with the alleged "letter" of the ECCI? And who is the chief culprit in this forgery?

Apparently the *Daily Mail* played an important role in this incident. A telegraphic communiqué states that "a copy of the document came into the possession of the *Daily Mail*, and we considered it our duty to publish it. Yesterday afternoon we sent copies to the other London newspapers, and somewhat later the Foreign Office decided to publish the document." It is evident that the *Daily Mail* is not quite innocent in this matter.

Please note how the date was chosen. The "exposure" of the alleged letter of the ECCI was intended to take place in England at a time when there remained only a couple of days before the election, and consequently our reply could not arrive in time.

It is not difficult to understand why some of the leaders of the Liberal-Conservative bloc had recourse to such a method as the forging of documents. Apparently, they seriously thought that they would be able, at the last minute before the election, to create confusion in the ranks of those voters who sincerely sympathize with the Anglo-Soviet treaty.

It is much harder to understand why the British Foreign Office, which is still under the control of the prime minister, MacDonald, did not refrain from making use of such a clumsy forgery.

We, on our part, have proposed that an examination into the whole affair regarding our alleged "letter" be entrusted to the British trade unions, and that a commission appointed by the General Council of the British Trades Union Congress have access to all documents, and pass judgment, which we shall consider as final. Thus, we hope we have proved to all British workers and to all unprejudiced people in Britain that we have nothing to fear from an investigation of this matter, and that the document attributed to us is a forgery.

Today we received news from fairly reliable sources that the forged letter originated in Polish circles. In Poland there apparently exists a permanent group of enterprising people, probably closely connected with the Polish secret service, who supply similar "documents" to those foreign governments which, for one reason or another, require them.

A strange state of affairs! It is sufficient for any bourgeois statesman of Europe or America—let us say, Mr. Hughes—to find himself in a difficult situation, when this or that "letter" of the ECCI, alleged to be signed by us, is immediately placed at his disposal. This "letter" is then solemnly published and the press of a certain camp raises the necessary alarm.

[25] *Izvestiia,* No. 247, October 28, 1924, p. 3.

It would seem, therefore, that the ECCI has been especially engaged in writing letters that are very useful to statesmen of the type of Hughes and Curzon! And in a strange way these alleged "letters"—like Easter eggs—fall into the hands of the respective bourgeois ministers when they need them in a political campaign against their "own" working class or against the government of the soviets.

. . .

100

The Official Soviet Position in Regard to the "Zinoviev Letter" Incident

[Rakovsky's Acknowledgment of Chamberlain's Note of November 21 and Recapitulation of the Preceding Correspondence, November 28, 1924][26]

. . .

In view of the very great attention given by the British public to this document [the Zinoviev letter], my government, to remove all doubts and establish the unbiased truth, offered to submit it to an investigation by an impartial court of arbitration. Several weeks passed, and my government received no reply to its offer. Meanwhile, many members of the British government had publicly questioned the authenticity of the document, and some of them had even expressed their conviction that it was a forgery.

In view of these doubts, the British government found it necessary, after the election campaign, to appoint an authoritative commission of members of the government, including the prime minister and the foreign minister, to examine the nature and origin of the document. This commission established that neither the government nor any of the government departments of Great Britain had seen the original of the document. This fact was made public on November 4. These curious circumstances explain why world public opinion considers the alleged Zinoviev letter a forgery.

This declaration by the authoritative commission removed every ground for the accusation advanced by Mr. Gregory against the Soviet government at the height of the election campaign, and my government was inclined to consider this declaration as an actual withdrawal of the accusation. Indeed the most elementary rules of jurisprudence forbid basing accusations on unverified, uncertified copies of documents that none of the accusers has ever seen. We understand, moreover, that the delegation from the British trade unions, after investigating the authenticity of the "Zinoviev letter" in Moscow, expressed its absolute and unanimous conviction "that the document is a forgery and that no evidence to the contrary can be produced, which alone can explain the refusal of the Russian offer of arbitration."

Consequently, my government expresses its extreme surprise that the present government of Great Britain has seen fit to ignore its predecessor's conclusions, and that after declining to submit the document to the examination of an impartial court, it has made statements unsupported by any evidence concerning the authenticity of the document. My government cannot accept such unproved allegations.

My government believes that it has even more reasons for rejecting the unfounded declaration made by the British government, since in the past accusations have repeatedly been made against the Soviet government, based on documents which on closer examination were found to be forged, and of which the actual origin

---

[26] *Anglo-sovetskie otnosheniia so dnia podpisaniia tozgovogo soglasheniia do razryva (1921–1927 gg.)*, pp. 85–87 (cited hereafter as *Anglo-sovetskie otnosheniia*); also *Daily Herald*, November 29, 1924, p. 3. Complete text in Degras, I, 477–80.

was established. My government considers as established and proved the fact that, in a number of cities in Europe and America, there exist organizations, under the leadership of Russian counterrevolutionary emigrés and other dubious elements, engaged in the fabrication of false documents with a view to undermining the international position of the Soviet Union. Quite recently I presented to the [British] foreign minister documentary evidence proving that in Great Britain itself there exist political organizations engaged in the fabrication and distribution of false documents concerning the U.S.S.R.

In the name of my government I express my deep regret that the British government bases its political actions, which have the greatest bearing upon further relations between the U.S.S.R. and Great Britain, on unchecked documents coming from very doubtful sources, and by so doing makes the relations between the two states precariously dependent on foreign, malicious, and dubious persons and political organizations pursuing their own selfish ends.

My government considers that the declaration made by the British government commission on November 4 as to the absence of the document referred to by Mr. Gregory in his note of October 24 fully disproves the accusation made by him.

My government wishes to believe that the British government will in the future be more circumspect in its accusations and will examine more carefully the facts on which it bases official correspondence. Inasmuch, however, as the present government of Great Britain wishes to ignore the declaration of the government commission on November 4 and to insist again on the accusation based on a forged document, the Soviet government, on its part, is forced to insist on its offer of arbitration as the sole means to an unbiased settlement of this question. This offer was made in its note of October 27, which unfortunately was "lost" during the change of government in Great Britain, but the content of which, according to Mr. Gregory's note, is known to you. The British government must be aware that by rejecting the arbitration court offer, it convinces the public of all countries that it cannot substantiate the accusations put forward during the election campaign.

Further, my government regrets that in its note of November 21 the British government evaded a direct answer to the question of referring the "Zinoviev letter" to arbitration, but found it appropriate to pass on to general unfounded accusations against the Soviet government in connection with the activities of the Communist International.

As regards these accusations, I am instructed by my government to repeat the declarations, which have already been made repeatedly, concerning the absolute political and organizational independence of the Communist International and the government of the U.S.S.R. My government has never undertaken, and can never undertake in the future, to refuse the right of asylum to the Communist International or to other workers' organizations, and still less can it undertake to exercise pressure upon them.

My government considers any further discussion of attacks on the international workers' organizations useless and fruitless, and has requested me to declare that it has loyally carried out, and will carry out in the future, on the principle of reciprocity, the obligations it has undertaken.

Please accept . . .

THE CAPITALISTS' PARTIAL STABILIZATION AND THE COMMUNISTS' TASKS AT HOME AND ABROAD

101

Excerpts from the Theses on Tactics Adopted at the Fifth Congress of the Communist International, June 17–July 8, 1924[27]

•   •   •

XIII. *Two Prospects*

The epoch of international revolution has begun. The tempo of its development as a whole or in part, the rate of development of revolutionary events on any particular continent or in any particular country, cannot be predicted with precision. The whole situation is such that two prospects are open: either (a) a slow and prolonged development of the proletarian revolution, or (b) since the ground under capitalism has been undermined to such an extent and the contradictions of capitalism as a whole have developed so rapidly, a crisis in one country or another in the not too distant future.

The Comintern must allow for either possibility. It must be able to adapt itself rapidly to new developments. But even if things happen slowly, the Comintern must remain an irreconcilable mass communist party of proletarian revolution, a party that attracts the masses and trains them for the revolutionary struggle for power.

XIV. *The Bolshevization of the Party and the Formation of a Single World Communist Party*

The Comintern's most important task now is to bolshevize its sections, and not simply by mechanically applying the experience of the Bolshevik Party in Russia to all other parties. The special features of a Bolshevik party are the following:

(a) The party must be really a mass party: that is, while being a legal party, or if obliged to become illegal, it must maintain unseverable ties with the working masses and serve as the expression of their needs and aspirations.

(b) It must have the ability to maneuver: that is, its tactics must not be dogmatic or sectarian; it must be able to resort to every strategic maneuver against the enemy that will enable it to remain true to itself. It is one of the chief errors of our parties that they frequently fail to understand this.

(c) It must be essentially a revolutionary and Marxist party, undeviatingly and in spite of all circumstances proceeding toward the goal and making every effort to bring nearer the hour of the victory of the proletariat over the bourgeoisie.

(d) It must be a centralized party, prohibiting factions, tendencies, and groups. It must be a monolithic party, hewn of one piece.

(e) It must carry on regular definite propaganda and organizational work in the bourgeois armies.

To bolshevize the party means to apply to our sections those principles of Russian bolshevism which have been and are international in character and applicable in general.

Only to the degree that the sections of the Comintern become really converted into Bolshevik parties will the Comintern become truly an international Bolshevik party imbued with the ideas of Leninism.

[27] *Piatyi Vsemirnyi Kongress K.I.*, II, 47–48; also *International Press Correspondence*, No. 62, August 29, 1924, pp. 652–53.

102

The Workers' United Front

[Joint Declaration of International Unity by the Anglo-Russian Conference of Trade Unions in London, Which Met on April 6, 7, and 8, 1925][28]

1. The joint conference confirms that the national and international unity of the workers of all countries is the first condition for making the trade union movement capable of (*a*) defending its present position against the advance of capital, and (*b*) getting its social and political demands (as stated in various workers' declarations) accepted.

2. The political situation is characterized in all so-called civilized countries by the triumph of reaction, and in many countries by a definite increase in the power of the united capitalist forces. . . .

. . .

7. It has become clear that a new war, more horrible and more devastating than any before experienced, is being prepared . . .

8. Only one force can save humanity from another world catastrophe. Only one force can defend the workers . . . This force is the working class itself, if it is well organized, well disciplined, and true to its interests, if it is resolved to struggle against all those who wish to prevent or hinder its full liberation.

Once the working class is united nationally and internationally, it will become an irresistible force against capitalist oppression, and will serve as an unbreakable pledge of peace and economic security. The workers can conquer all those reactionaries who wish to keep them from uniting. . . .

Therefore, the representatives of the trade union movement in the U.S.S.R. and in Great Britain confirm the agreement made in Moscow between the representatives of organized labor in Great Britain and the U.S.S.R. for the purpose of strengthening the international solidarity of the workers in the interests of international peace.

As a result of the discussions and agreements at the present London Conference, mutual steps have been outlined, upon the recommendation of the British delegation, to persuade the Amsterdam International to agree to the convocation of a conference, free of any preliminary conditions, with representatives of the trade unions of the U.S.S.R.

. . .

Proletariat of the world, unite! Long live the World Federation of Trade Unions!

103

Chicherin's Report to the Third Congress of Soviets on the Relation of Propaganda to Relations with Capitalist Governments in General and Soviet-British Relations in Particular, May 14, 1925[29]

. . .

For the past few months the official attitude of the British government toward us has been vacillating and changeable. At the beginning of the year, in the period when Britain failed to arrive at an understanding with the continental states con-

[28] *Izvestiia*, No. 87, April 15, 1925, p. 3.
[29] *Izvestiia*, No. 110, May 16, 1925, p. 5; also *International Press Correspondence*, No. 45, May 28, 1925, p. 582; also Degras, II, 33–34.

cerning a whole series of questions such as Morocco and Tunis, the official position of the British government was as follows: The Soviet government may propose negotiations; we are prepared to negotiate; the Soviet government may make proposals; we will examine these proposals. At that time we declared: We are ready at any moment, and with the greatest pleasure, to commence and to conduct these negotiations; we only want to know in what respect the treaty signed by MacDonald is unacceptable to the new British government. We cannot make proposals if we do not know what points in our former proposals proved to be unacceptable. "Submit proposals," we are told, but we say "There is the treaty, show us wherein it is unacceptable, and then we will know what proposals are possible." However, this was not done.

The present position of the British foreign minister is somewhat different. He says that normal relations cannot be established with the Soviet Union until the Soviet Union abandons propaganda. This is another question. It is a literal repetition of the words of Lord Curzon when we met in Lausanne.

When I asked Lord Curzon what possibilities he saw for improving our relations, he replied that no better relations were possible so long as we continued our propaganda. I then asked him: "What is propaganda? We have a government and official government machinery. The government and its employees pledge themselves not to carry on any propaganda, but the government cannot accept responsibility for what any private citizen may say. If a private citizen infringes the laws or the treaties, then he will be held responsible. We cannot, however, compel the Communist Party to cease to be a communist party; we cannot compel the members of the Communist Party to cease to act as Communists."

And Curzon replied: "If this is to be a question of a fifty per cent reduction in propaganda and not a hundred per cent cessation, His Majesty's Government will not negotiate."

The same idea can be seen in Chamberlain's declaration: "Cease conducting propaganda."

But what is propaganda? We face the main question of our foreign political relations. Our government is prepared to accept, and does accept, all the obligations inherent in international relations. If the British government proves that we are misusing our diplomatic connections, our diplomatic rights, or our diplomatic machinery, or that an official Soviet representative is violating international obligations, then we are prepared to assume the responsibility for what is demanded of us in this respect.

If, however, we are told that all propaganda in general must cease in the Soviet Union, it is tantamount to demanding that the Communist Party cease to be a communist party. This is then a question of whether we shall remain a party, or not. [Of course] we shall remain a party. The experience of our first years has demonstrated that we cannot be overthrown, that we are here, and that we shall stay here: *"J'y suis, j'y reste."*

The basic question concerns our relations with the capitalist world by which we are surrounded. . . .

They [the British] must understand that between Britain and ourselves, between the capitalist states and our state, a *modus vivendi* must be created. But in order to create a *modus vivendi*, the British government must adopt its former position—that is to say, regulate the relations of government with government. The British government must abandon its present position, which demands that the Communist Party cease to be a communist party. Everything that is possible by way of government policy or official government agreements and obligations, our government is prepared to undertake and will undertake.

On this basis, concrete demands should be advanced and definite agreements arrived at. We may mention that when we concluded the provisional treaty with

Britain in 1921, which still remains in force, we proposed that Britain should not limit herself to this short and all too general agreement. We proposed that all questions of mutual interest be examined and a compromise reached, an acceptable *modus vivendi* between ourselves and Britain. This proposal was rejected at that time. The government of Lloyd George did not desire such a conference. Even MacDonald did not undertake an exhaustive, concrete examination of all the problems in dispute.

So long as this is not done, there will exist between Britain and ourselves, and thus throughout international politics, that element of uncertainty which the capitalist states find so painful today. And if Chamberlain says that the cause of this uncertainty is the existence of the Soviet Union, then Chamberlain is guilty of not attempting to arrive at a compromise with us . . .

The working masses in all countries understand this. They see that it is our government that favors the peaceful settlement of [international] problems, and that the actions which lead to further uncertainty in international relations do not come from us.

104
The International Situation and the Military Tasks of the Soviet Union

[Speech by M. V. Frunze at a Meeting of Cadets, Commanding Officers, and Political Workers of the Moscow Garrison, February 16, 1925][30]

One of the greatest and most gifted military scholars, the German general Clausewitz, said as early as the beginning of the last century that "war is but the extension of foreign policy by other means."

By this he meant that a state's war aims are absolutely determined by its policy. This is clearly true, and applies not only to war but to peace. In times of peace, military affairs, military activity, and the development of armed forces are also determined by the general political situation. This applies particularly and fully to us, to our workers' and peasants' Red Army. . . .

Our enemies' hopes for our economic bankruptcy have been wrecked before their eyes. In all spheres we are well on the way to recovery. Our finances have become sound; our industry is reviving; our agriculture is developing at a rapid pace.

On the basis of this economic improvement, the existence of which cannot now be disputed, the political consolidation of our Soviet Union is advancing rapidly. . . .

It would be natural to expect that, as a consequence, our international position would be considerably strengthened and the danger of war diminished. This, indeed, is partly true. Our economic growth and internal consolidation have been supplemented by a series of great diplomatic successes. During the past two years we have been formally recognized by all the great bourgeois countries, except the United States of America.

But, comrades, we should not make the mistake of assuming that these facts have lessened the danger of war for our republic. The danger has not diminished. On the contrary, as a result of our economic consolidation, it has increased.

Why? Because the news of our economic, cultural, and political growth sounds to the bourgeois capitalist world like a death knell; because our enemies have lost the bets they placed on the inevitability of our economic collapse; because the consolidation of the workers' and peasants' state has, independently of our will, become the strongest means of agitation and propaganda, the strongest weapon for undermining the bourgeois capitalist world. . . .

[30] *Pravda*, No. 41, February 19, 1925, p. 5; also *International Press Correspondence*, No. 19, March 12, 1925, pp. 279–82.

The Communist parties of all countries are speedily ridding themselves of the last remnants of the old opportunist inheritance and transforming themselves into a real revolutionary force. Bolshevism has already been deeply rooted in the workers' class movement in Europe, so much so that the ruling bourgeois circles tremble once again before the Communist danger. We see how, as a result of these facts, attempts are being made in all countries not only to create a united front against the Comintern, but to combine the forces of the bourgeois countries in a united front against the Soviet Union. . . .

However, the antagonisms in our enemies' camp remain for the present unchanged. They are so great, so serious, that even the fear of the insurrection of the colonial peoples and of the consolidation of the Soviet Union cannot induce the bourgeois groups, which are hostile to us, to drop their dissensions and to create a united front against us. In this respect the most recent attempt to organize an anti-Soviet bloc is especially instructive.

It is quite clear to us that England has taken the initiative in the organization of this bloc. We have, it is true, recently heard the leader of British foreign policy, Chamberlain, assert that England has no aggressive intentions against the Soviet Union and is not working for the creation of an anti-Soviet bloc. These are very fine words, but difficult to believe.

We know, of course, that the ruling groups in England today have no complete unity of opinion; we know that there are not only advocates of Curzon's old policy of attack and ultimatum, but also representatives of sounder and more moderate views.

And knowing this, comrades, even though the present British government's policy is hostile to our interests, we will not give up our attempt to reach a peaceful agreement. First, however, British policy must definitely renounce every attempt to intimidate us. We are fully convinced that the British Conservative government cannot carry on an armed campaign against us in opposition to the will of the British working class. And no government can force the British worker into a war against the Soviet Union.

We have always been ready to negotiate in a matter-of-fact way for the peaceful solution of the points of dissension that divide us. From our point of view, the life and blood of one hundred workers and peasants is more valuable than any other advantage we might gain. For that reason, we have maintained, do maintain, and shall maintain, to Britain and other bourgeois countries, the position that peace must be protected and ensured.

Nevertheless, we know that the objective course of international relations will induce the groups hostile to us to interfere in our affairs and to pursue a policy opposed to our interests. Therefore, while in every respect we put our peace policy into practice and are ready to agree to any tolerably acceptable proposal, we must not neglect the consolidation of our military power. More than that, nothing but the development of our military power will prevent our enemies from attacking us.

The other important country of Western Europe on which war or peace depends is France.

We shall soon be sitting round the conference table with France.[31] What are the prospects for these negotiations?

[31] This conference, which dealt mainly with the problem of Russia's prewar debts to France, opened a year later, February 25, 1926, after some preliminary negotiations. Kh. G. Rakovsky, the Soviet ambassador to France, represented the Soviet government. Negotiations were suspended in July 1926, were resumed in March 1927, and finally bogged down in mid-1927, probably because of the effect on the French government and public of the break in Soviet-British relations in May 1927. (For particulars see A. J. Toynbee, *Survey of International Affairs, 1927*, pp. 278–81, and Louis Fischer, *The Soviets in World Affairs*, II, 617–22.)

The workers and peasants of the Union and the Red Army must know that the Soviet delegation will be faced at this conference by tasks of enormous difficulty. The reason for these difficulties is that the old tsarist government was deeply in debt to French capital. . . .

If French capital insists that we acknowledge these debts, no serious negotiations can, of course, take place. We are of the opinion that the October Revolution definitely and irrevocably solved this question. We can discuss no changes in this course, and only a few corrections. These corrections may lead to an understanding by which the Soviet Union satisfies a certain number of the holders of old tsarist promissory notes, on the condition that it involves no burden of taxation for our working classes and peasantry.

Is such an arrangement in any way thinkable? Certainly. We could agree to it if a loan were made to us that would enable us to satisfy the French holders of tsarist bonds on the basis of the difference between the rate of interest and the investment on the loan. . . .

A positive factor for the approaching negotiations with France is this: There are no irreconcilable opposing interests between us and France. Whereas British capital is afraid of our revolutionary ideas, unhappy about the consolidation of the Soviet state, and anxious about its position on the Asiatic continent, France's outlook is decidedly more favorable. . . .

We are firmly convinced that every year of our peaceful existence, every year of our peaceful economic and cultural and political success, will represent an enormous gain in our struggle against world imperialism, and in the consolidation of our foreign political position. Our peace policy is no empty phrase intended to deceive our opponents. No, this policy is in harmony with our own interests, and with our own domestic conditions and international position as we interpret them. For this very reason, however, we cannot ignore the danger that international capital may, at a suitable moment, decide to attack the Soviet Union and try to destroy the threat we pose to the security and [even] the existence of the whole capitalist world.

In the East we have recently had a great success: the peace treaty with Japan.[32] This treaty returned to us the last bit of Soviet land in the East that was still under the yoke of foreign imperialism—the northern half of Sakhalin.

Our treaty with Japan has definitely improved our political situation in the East by enabling us to consolidate our position in China, which in the immediate future will be the center of interest of all the countries of the world. An enormous revolutionary movement is developing there, and the prestige of the Soviet state is steadily increasing in the eyes of China's hundreds of millions of people. . . .

This, indeed, describes the essentials of our relations with the greatest bourgeois countries. There remains only the United States of America. Is American recognition of the Soviet Union to be hoped for in the immediate future? According to our diplomats, many signs indicate that this recognition may not be far off. . . .

In our foreign political situation, a new period is now beginning, a period of formal relations with all the bourgeois countries. Representatives of all foreign states will be present in our Red capital. This leads to a new, a far more complicated situation. Thousands of unfriendly eyes will be fixed on our successes and our failures; new plots will be hatched which aim at throttling us one way or another.

We must remark that the prospect of an anti-Soviet bloc is without doubt bound up with the hopes for our internal disintegration. I have in mind, in particular, that discussion which was started in the columns of our party press and which caused the change in the leadership of the Red Army.[33]

[32] The Soviet-Japanese Treaty was signed at Peking on January 20, 1925. Text in Shapiro, I, 283-85.

[33] This is a reference to the Stalin-Trotsky conflict and Trotsky's removal as Commissar of War.

Every one of you grasps the meaning of these events. Our enemies have tried to make political capital out of them, have seen in them the beginning of the disintegration of the Red Army and the approaching collapse of Soviet power. The foreign White Guardist press, the Polish, Estonian, and Finnish press, and the press of the great bourgeois countries have been crammed with all sorts of insinuations about the international situation in the Soviet Union.

.   .   .

Our task . . . under the circumstances is to greatly increase the armed strength of the Soviet Union. We must eliminate the possibility of another Curzon ultimatum. We must advance so far that no one will dare to speak to us in Curzon's language . . .

A few words as to the details of the task.

I said that the state must give more attention to defense, and use more of its resources for defense. . . .

I can assure you that even today the Red Army is a strong armed force; if today we found ourselves obliged to test the force of our weapons in the field of battle, I do not doubt for a moment that the Red Army and the Red Navy would be equal to their tasks.

Nevertheless, all is not as it should be. The greatest shortcoming is the unsatisfactory condition of our war industry, our war technique. . . . More attention should be given to war industry. The Red Army must have at its disposal all those means of war that our potential enemies will have.

The second task is to bring our territorial formations up to a fit level. . . .

The third task is to improve the military education of our soldiers and commanders. . . .

Our fourth task is to build iron revolutionary discipline.

Our fifth task is to educate the army in the spirit of the commands of our great teacher, Comrade Lenin. Under the leadership of the Communist Party, the army and the navy of the republic must become the most powerful support for communism and for the cause of revolution. . . .

105

The Extension of the Breathing Space for Soviet Russian Foreign Policy

[Directives to the Central Committee by the Fourteenth Congress of the Russian Communist Party, December 18–31, 1925][34]

The Fourteenth Congress of the VKP (B) fully endorses the political and organizational policy of the Central Committee. This policy has ensured for the party, the working class, and the entire country the general improvement of the national economy, and has at the same time consolidated the socialist position, both within and outside the country.

As an international consequence of this policy, the Soviet Union has been recognized by several capitalist countries and has signed trade and concession agreements with them. It has increased its foreign trade and has consolidated its international position in general.

.   .   .

In the field of international relations, we are witnessing the extension of the breathing space into a long period of so-called peaceful coexistence between the U.S.S.R. and the capitalist countries, even though the antagonisms between these

[34] *V.K.P. v rezoliutsiiakh*, II, 47–49.

two camps have not diminished but increased. Thus the Soviet Union is given a chance for internal reconstruction. Economic relations with other countries will definitely help speed up our economic reconstruction; on the other hand, the increasing contact between our economy and world capitalism increases our dependence on the latter, which creates new dangers. The party, in its work of socialist reconstruction, must take these dangers into account.

The following facts in the capitalist countries must be taken into account: the partial stabilization of capitalism and the relative consolidation of the political power of the bourgeoisie in Europe; the vast expansion of the role of the United States of America (which is close to dominating world finances); the gradual decline of the role of the British Empire as a world power; the conflicts of interest between the victors and the vanquished of the last imperialist war; the conflicts in the camp of the victors themselves; the conflicts between the United States of America and Europe; the uprooting of the entire imperialist system by the colonial and semicolonial peoples of China, India, Syria, and Morocco, who are now being politically awakened (movements within these countries have in some places taken the form of national wars of liberation, and have reached tremendous and unprecedented development); and finally, the growth—in new forms—of the workers' movement in Europe and its close connection with the proletariat of the U.S.S.R. (the struggle for unity in the trade union movement, workers' delegations to the U.S.S.R., and so forth).

The relative stabilization, and so-called "pacification," of Europe under the hegemony of Anglo-American capital has led to a whole system of economic and political blocs. The latest of these are the conference in Locarno and the so-called "guarantee pacts," directed against the U.S.S.R. These blocs and agreements, under cover of the allegedly pacifist League of Nations and the false and noisy manifestations of the Second International concerning disarmament, actually constitute the alignment of forces for a new war. To offset these blocs . . . there is an increasing drawing together of the proletariat of the advanced countries and the proletariat of the U.S.S.R., primarily under the slogan of the struggle for peace and the struggle against new imperialist wars or armed attacks on the U.S.S.R.

Taking these facts into consideration, the Congress instructs the Central Committee to base its policy upon the following principles:

(*a*) To strengthen as much as possible the alliance between the proletariat of the U.S.S.R. and the Western European proletariat and the oppressed peoples, aiming at the development and victory of the international proletarian revolution;

(*b*) To carry on the policy of peace, which must be the core of the government's entire foreign policy and which must guide the government's basic actions and statements;

(*c*) To carry on economic reconstruction with a view to transforming the U.S.S.R. from an importer of machinery and equipment into a producer of machinery and equipment; so that, though encircled by capitalists, the U.S.S.R. will not become an economic appendage of the capitalist world economy, but will represent an independent economic unit constructed in accordance with socialist methods, and a powerful force for revolutionizing the workers of all countries and the oppressed colonial and semicolonial peoples;

(*d*) So far as possible, to prepare economic reserves that will insure the country against all eventualities in both domestic and foreign markets;

(*e*) To take every possible measure to consolidate the defense of the country and to increase the power of the Red Army, the Red Navy, and the air fleet.

In the realm of *economic reconstruction*, the Congress starts with the fact that our country, the country of the dictatorship of the proletariat, possesses "all that is necessary to build a fully socialist society" (Lenin). The Congress believes that our party's primary task is socialist reconstruction in the U.S.S.R. The year under consideration has fully proved the correctness of this principle. The working class, in alliance with the masses of the peasantry, has already achieved its first serious successes in socialist reconstruction without the so-called "help" of foreign capital, while continually struggling against private capital in its own country. The [Russian] working class was able to achieve these successes even though the proletariat of other countries, for all their support [to the Russian workers], have not themselves seized power.

The past year has seen the rapid development of the whole national economy and an approach to prewar levels. . . .

And so we are witnessing the economic development of the proletariat on the basis of the New Economic Policy, and the progress of the economy of the U.S.S.R. toward socialism. More and more, socialist state industry becomes the vanguard of the national economy, and leads the national economy as a whole. . . .

LOCARNO

106
Karl Radek on Locarno[35]

The guarantee pact between Germany and France, Great Britain, and Belgium marks a further liquidation of the Versailles peace, which had been regarded as an expression of the victory of France and Britain. The guarantee pact presents a new coalition of forces, led by the United States and Britain. [Analyzes the struggle for European leadership from Versailles to Locarno.] . . .

In 1924 France tried to take advantage of the brief existence of a pacifist-inclined Labour government (which, despite its desires, could not carry out the foreign policy of British imperialism) to get French security guaranteed by the Geneva Protocol,[36] which, by improving the clauses of the Covenant of the League of Nations, would have placed Britain's fleet and all her military resources at the disposal of France against Germany. The ensuing Conservative government refused to ratify the Geneva Protocol and began new negotiations for a guarantee pact with France and Germany. These negotiations ended with the Locarno Conference.

What are the results of that conference?

(1) Germany is to enter the League of Nations. What is the meaning of this decision? The League of Nations was created by the Treaty of Versailles, and the Covenant of the League of Nations is included in that treaty, but in spite of this, Germany, which is now ordered to enter the League, was not permitted to enter it in the year 1919. The League was created as an organ of the victors and their satellites. By including Germany now, these powers symbolically acknowledge that they no longer regard Germany as an enemy. Great Britain goes even further, and sees in Germany a future instrument of her policy. France hopes to see Germany's coming expansion fettered by the network of obligations that her membership in the League would entail.

(2) Such obligations as Germany has contracted toward states that do not belong to the League of Nations and that might come in collision with it are to be covered by elastic diplomatic formulas. This is simply intended to facilitate Germany's entry into the League.

[35] K. Radek, "Garantiinyi pakt," *Izvestiia*, No. 242, October 22, 1925, p. 2; also *International Press Correspondence*, No. 79, November 5, 1925, pp. 1195–96.

[36] See our pp. 270–71.

The most important political fact is not the political form, but the fact that Germany accepts these obligations.

(3) Great Britain undertakes to guarantee the inviolability of the . . . frontier between France and Germany, and between Belgium and Germany. But contrary to France's former intentions, Britain comes forward as a guarantor not only as regards France and Belgium, but also as regards Germany. . . .

(4) Germany is to sign arbitration treaties with her eastern neighbors, Poland and Czechoslovakia. Thus Britain, by refusing to guarantee the frontiers of Poland and Czechoslovakia, indicates to Germany that they may be altered.

(5) France, in the event of a German attempt to alter the Polish-German frontier, cannot act independently of the League of Nations in order to protect her allies. The Franco-Polish and Franco-Czech alliances, by being placed under the control of the League of Nations, in which England plays a very important role, lose much of their strength. In this way French hegemony on the Continent is considerably weakened.

But what is the ultimate meaning of Locarno? Does it mean a liquidation of the Treaty of Versailles?

The Western frontiers decided upon at Versailles are confirmed, and yet they are altered; they are in a certain sense internationalized and made dependent upon special British guarantees. The Versailles decisions that were favorable to the program of French imperialism, the program of Marshal Foch, lose all their validity. Not that France abandons the decisions permitting the occupation of the Rhine province and the Saar district; on the contrary, she will try to retain these rights and use them in fighting against the complete subordination of Germany to Britain. Britain, seeing in them a means for driving a future bargain with Germany as well as for embittering relations between France and Germany, has not insisted upon their abolition. But France's goal in getting these decisions embodied in the Treaty of Versailles—that is, her plan to use them as a springboard for a further advance into Germany—now becomes unattainable.

The eastern decisions of the Locarno Conference indicate that Poland is to be the new tool by means of which changes in the international political situation will be effected. [On the other hand] the subordination of Germany to the League of Nations is a step toward creating a European concert of powers directed against the U.S.S.R. and against the East [in general].

From this brief survey we can see that the Locarno decisions signalize important political regroupings. Although they do not abolish the Treaty of Versailles, they reveal a new balance of power, in which Germany will play a new role, even if it is not the role of equal partner of which the German bourgeois politicians are dreaming.[37]

107

The Meaning of Locarno for the U.S.S.R.

[Statement by Rakovsky][38]

. . .

Why has our working class, guided by its instinct, adopted a negative attitude toward the Locarno agreements from the first, even though these agreements have been camouflaged by pacifist phraseology? Because everyone has drawn a very

---

[37] In two further articles on the guarantee pact (*Izvestiia*, No. 244, October 24, 1925, p. 2, and No. 245, October 25, 1925, pp. 2–3) Radek dealt with the economic condition of the British Empire, with victorious American imperialism, and with the awakening East.

[38] Kh. G. Rakovsky, *Liga natsii i SSSR*, pp. 45, 47–54.

simple and obvious conclusion: If the capitalist states unite, if they try to iron out their conflicts, their strength will increase. And since we know they disapprove of our Soviet government, our socialist economy, our monopoly of foreign trade, our nationalized industries, and our nationalization of the land, we naturally conclude that if one of these states—Britain, for example—finds it necessary to advance against us, it will try to make use of this newly acquired strength.

What is the purpose of the groupings, duets, and quartets that are now so numerous? . . . Every state that has undertaken certain obligations and has made certain sacrifices, whether real or fictitious, will, of course, try to use these groupings to its own advantage against us. This is simple logic, though it naturally differs from that formal logic with which they [the capitalists] try to lull us when they tell us that these agreements are not directed against us.

[Refers to warnings to Russia not to start a preventive war.] . . .

We do not intend to resort to any preventive war for two simple reasons: the weakness of our technology, and our geographic situation. Our geography, our resources, and our technology make the Soviet Union invincible in a defensive war . . .

There are also other reasons why we cannot conduct a preventive war. Our best ally—and in this respect we can say that we are the least isolated country of all—is the sympathy, the solidarity, of the working masses of all countries. But we can count on this solidarity and this sympathy only while we pursue a peaceful defensive policy, a policy without even a hint of an attempt to conquer or to seize new territories. . . . And so the suspicion that we desire to wage a preventive war falls to pieces.

But there is a grain of truth in what is said to us. When the so-called balance of power is reached, then the strongest country may be tempted to obtain its goal by means of threats, intimidation, and ultimatums. . . .

Despite their limited character, the Locarno agreements have created a new balance of power in Europe. It is here that we find a threat to peace, and a direct threat to us. This threat derives from the fact that the Locarno agreements, like the League of Nations, have attached themselves by one thick root to the interests of the imperialist states while another thin root has fastened itself to the pacifist mood of the working masses.

We cannot be indifferent to this fact. Does not the Second International try to blame us for undermining the cause of peace, while claiming that all others are striving for it? A partly class-conscious worker, or one lacking class-consciousness, can easily be deceived by the splendid pacifist phraseology found in abundance in the Locarno agreements, such terms as peace, disarmament, arbitration, the restoration of Europe, etc., etc.—terms similar to the term "justice" often mentioned in the Covenant of the League of Nations. Our task must be to disclose the pseudo-pacifist nature of the Locarno agreements with the entire force of our criticism. I believe we can do this without much difficulty.

One result of the Locarno agreements already confronts us: a direct or indirect conflict over the Mosul question.[39] The states that signed the Locarno agreements, having purposely ignored Turkish interests, formed a bloc in regard to Mosul. Thus Locarno's first actual consequence was to intensify the [West's] policy of undermining the interests of the nationalities and states of the East.

Our interests are contrary to those of the imperialists; we are in favor of the independence, restoration, and unification of all the nationalities of the East. In a question such as Mosul, the difference between our policy and that of the imperialist states, the unification of which was greatly assisted by the contacts made at Locarno, becomes especially clear. From this I do not conclude that the bloc on colonial or Eastern problems is maintained absolutely consistently or, in particular, that com-

[39] See our p. 278.

plete agreement on colonial policy has been reached between England and France. . . .

We view with great anxiety the fact that despite our many offers during the year to renew negotiations with the British government, we have received no response from Britain. Reasoning from the absolutely false premise that it is not Britain who needs us, but we who need her, and that Britain can therefore wait patiently for a suitable moment, the British government has systematically declined all our attempts to reopen negotiations. Since this situation prevailed even before Locarno, now, after this conference, which made Britain the heroine of the day, she will maintain her former position with still greater obstinacy. . . . The fact that our offers to negotiate have been declined gives us every reason to suppose that Britain is waiting for an advantageous moment when she can gather all her forces against us and bring special pressure to bear upon us with the greatest chance for success. . . .

How, then, can we prove to the broad masses in the West that all the widely proclaimed pacifist intentions are simply deceit; that certain governments' intentions toward us are absolutely contrary to their declarations about peace, about abolishing the use of force, and about settling disputes by arbitration, declarations that are so prevalent in the text of the Locarno agreements? The best thing for us is to make these states show their cards to their people. This is exactly what we are now doing. As they declare that the Locarno agreements mean the consolidation of peace, we say: "If, in reality, you signed peaceful agreements in Locarno, if your intentions are to consolidate peace, if you are not going to use Locarno against us, prove it to us—settle the questions in dispute and the misunderstandings that have accumulated between the Soviet and capitalist governments." In Paris we formulated our policy as follows: "Take the anti-Soviet sting out of the Locarno treaties." This would be possible only if all the states that signed the Locarno agreements were also to sign an agreement or a treaty with us containing a mutual guarantee to abstain from attack, blockade, or intervention. It is easier for us to talk about such an agreement because we have already signed one: our treaty with Turkey.[40] The Turkish treaty was our reply to Locarno, and by it we demonstrated in practice the kind of treaty that should be concluded, and that can be called truly peaceful.

What chance have we to develop this policy? Can we look forward to signing treaties, if not like the Soviet-Turkish treaty, at least formulated in the same spirit? In general, what chance have we for a rapprochement with the capitalist states, and especially with the signatories of the Locarno agreements? In trying to answer these questions we must follow this everyday practical rule: There is no agreement that might not be changed with changing circumstances and interests, for irreconcilable differences arise anew every day in the life of states.

[Speaks of the statements that appeared in French newspapers directly after Locarno, concerning the need for a rapprochement between France and the U.S.S.R. in order to provide better guarantees for France against Germany.] . . .

Locarno proved, among other things, that the alleged secret military agreement between us and Germany was simply a legend. Had it existed, Germany would not have joined the League of Nations and would not have ventured to accept the obligations ensuing from Article 16[41] of the League Covenant. It is clear, therefore, that our hands are clean; that we had, and I hope shall have in the future, friendly relations with Germany based on mutual interests but unconnected with armed military forces. Previously, when France, under her former government, occupied the

[40] The Soviet-Turkish treaty of friendship and neutrality signed December 17, 1925, at Paris. Text in Shapiro, I, 313.

[41] According to this article, if one League member attacks another, the rest are to support the attacked member against the aggressor. Further, members will "support one another in resisting any special measures aimed at one of their number by a covenant-breaking State," and allow Covenant-enforcing states to send troops through their territory.

Rhine provinces, our relations with Germany worried her considerably. Now they can no longer worry her because she has signed the Locarno treaty with Germany. Thus, the Locarno agreements have given us a certain freedom of action.

I shall not enumerate here all the trends in European politics. However, in international politics the conflicts between Britain's industrial interests and those of America are already evident. In addition there is now a chance for German industry to stand on its own feet once more, for the sake of which Germany consented to concessions at Locarno. But when German industry is again consolidated, it will be confronted with the rivalry of British industry; in short, we shall face the same economic conflict between Germany and Britain that led to the World War. I do not say that this will happen today or tomorrow, but the possibility of such a conflict is already becoming clear.

There is also another point worth noting. More than once we have heard Germany say something like this: "When did we depend on Britain most of all? When our relations with France were strained during the occupation of the Ruhr in 1923. At that time our only support and hope was Britain; we looked to her for advice and help, and so forth. But the rapprochement with France will give us a certain freedom of action in so far as Britain is concerned." I refrain from drawing any conclusion from this. I only note that the Locarno agreements bear the germ of a development in international relations that would paralyze the aggressive efforts of separate states against us.

It is very characteristic that at first the Locarno agreements were given considerable approval in America . . . Now a certain amount of disappointment in them is manifest. Why? Because there has been talk of the creation of a United States of Europe. Against whom? Against America. . . .

Here again we see the conflict of interest between America and Europe, between American and European capital. If the policy of American and British capitalists in Europe agrees on some points, it disagrees on others. If America is interested in creating a durable and stable political regime in Europe, and in making peace between France and Germany, Britain, so some people say, is not interested in that at all. The antagonism between France and Germany will make it possible for Britain to play the role of arbiter, and to maintain her predominant influence in Europe. If the continental states were to unite, if French policy were to permit a rapprochement (I do not speak of alliance) between France, Germany, and Poland, it would mean the emancipation of Europe from England.

All this confirms my earlier remarks that the Locarno agreements present a grave danger to us, and we do not conceal this fact. On the other hand, while remaining active, we can now insist calmly and patiently on an agreement with every state individually, in order to render harmless, if only partially so, [those sections of] the Locarno agreements which are directed against us.

108
Rykov on the League of Nations

[Excerpt from the Report to the Fourteenth Moscow Province Party
Conference, December 5, 1925][42]

The League of Nations an Instrument of War and Not of Peace

Judging by what the responsible statesmen of the bourgeois world say, a whole series of economic and political conferences will be held in the immediate future. The bourgeoisie is trying to bridge over its present and potential conflicts of interest in order, as it is customary to say, "to pacify Europe."

[42] *Izvestiia*, No. 280, Dec. 8, 1925, p. 5; also *International Press Correspondence*, No. 89, Dec. 24, 1925, pp. 1345–47.

This enormous number of conferences, treaties, and agreements between the separate states can neither eliminate the conflicts that are fatal to capitalism nor prevent wars.

Symptomatically, the bourgeois and Menshevik press and statesmen of considerable repute have recently begun to invite the Soviet Union to join the "League of Nations." It has been especially pleasing to read invitations of this kind in British newspapers, which have hitherto regarded the government of our Union as a gang of robbers. Only a year ago, the Conservative Party won the election by displaying the forged Zinoviev letter and calling for a struggle against the republic of soviets. Are we to believe in the sincerity of such an abrupt change? Obviously not.

. . . In the present political circumstances the newspaper campaign to draw the Soviet Union into the League of Nations aims at discrediting us in the eyes of that part of the working class which still cherishes pacifist illusions.

The world's "MacDonalds" are persistently telling the working class that the League of Nations will ensure the peaceful development of mankind. So long as there are sections of the working class who, in their hatred of war, place any kind of hope in the League of Nations, it is to our enemies' political advantage to take just this tack, in order to represent the U.S.S.R. as an enemy of peace. This is Chamberlain's line in his struggle against the Soviet Union, and the Second International's line in its struggle against our party . . .

As a matter of principle, we support the view that the League of Nations is an instrument not of peace but of war, not of liberation but of oppression; we consider the propaganda that capitalist society might furnish a remedy for war to be a crime, and not an error, on the part of the Second International. In our opinion, war was, is, and will be, inevitable under capitalism; war is insolubly bound up with capitalism and is part of its very nature.

· · ·

Why Do We Not Join the League of Nations?

What does the bourgeoisie expect from our joining the League of Nations? I have read in a bourgeois paper a very exact answer to this question. It is expected that the entrance of the Soviet Union into the League of Nations will bring about a "political capitulation in the East and an economic capitulation in the West." This is expressed very clearly and exactly.

The League of Nations is a little business undertaking that deals in peoples; it passes them over as it sees fit, in the form of mandates, to the so-called states of high culture, which defend their mandate rights by force of arms and mercilessly enslave the peoples under their tutelage. For this reason, the East would naturally regard us as traitors if we were to stand behind the counter of this shop. We shall not do so. We shall continue to rejoice in the development of the movement for national liberation among the oppressed colonial peoples.

Joining the League of Nations would mean for us economic capitulation in the West, because as a member we should be bound by the resolutions of the bourgeois majority in economic questions also.

In my opinion, the governments and newspapers that propose our joining the League of Nations are dishonest. I believe they know we shall not join, and propose that we join solely to enable MacDonald and the rest to tell the workers . . . that "the Soviet Union, by refusing to join the League of Nations, is responsible for its own isolation," as was stated in the resolution of the Second International. . . .

New Wars Are Being Prepared Under the Mask of Pacifism

The present period has seen a new attempt to consolidate imperialism under the mask of pacifism. This attempt is dictated (1) by the extremely straitened financial situation of the most important imperialist countries of Europe; (2) by America's attempts to have her debts in Europe paid more or less punctually; (3) by the fear of new wars that prevails among the peoples; and (4) by the failure of recent efforts to bolster imperialism by direct military action (occupation of the Ruhr, Morocco, Syria, events in China, anti-Soviet bloc, etc.).

I believe that the task of the day for the Communist International and the revolutionary trade unions is to explain the danger inherent in just this pacifism, for under the mask of pacifism new wars have been and are being prepared.

Another reference to the threat of Red imperialism has recently appeared in the papers. This theme, invented by Kautsky, crops up from time to time in foreign newspapers. We must combat this malicious calumny with all the means at our disposal. It must be pointed out that as early as at Genoa, the republic of soviets was the first country to propose the only possible plan for the radical disarmament of all states. We did the same in 1922 in the negotiations with our Baltic neighbors. Every worker within and without the Soviet Union should thoroughly understand that our party will fully support universal and absolute disarmament, that the Soviet government will be the first to declare itself prepared to dissolve the armed forces of our country and to destroy our whole war industry, on the one and only condition that other countries do the same. . . .

It would be stupid beyond words to believe that economic stabilization and so-called "political pacification" of the bourgeois countries can overcome the fatal conflicts of capitalism. True, capitalism is stronger today than it was in 1920–21, a period of great crisis in many countries, but the stabilization is in itself transitory. Throughout the period of stabilization there will be crises of varying intensity, crises that the workers' movement in the West must make use of in order to organize its revolutionary forces, to prepare itself for the period when further attempts to stabilize capital will prove impossible.

THE MOSCOW NONAGGRESSION AND NEUTRALITY PACTS

109

On the Impossibility of Solving Disputes by Arbitration[43]

The principle of settling disputes by arbitration, which has often been mentioned in international law, . . . presupposes complete and absolute trust in the party called upon to resolve the conflict, and also that party's absolute and irreproachable impartiality.

No one will deny the validity of the suspicion with which the U.S.S.R. views the possibility of the settlement by a state authority in the hands of the bourgeoisie of disputes in which the Union's interests are threatened.

No one will deny that the capitalist states themselves, hostile as they are to the U.S.S.R. because of the nature of their political organization, will never agree to the solution by the U.S.S.R. of a conflict resulting from their imperialist policy (say, in China!). . . .

These alone are decisive reasons for the Union's negative attitude toward the principle of arbitration. But there is still another reason, which, although subordinate to the first, is nevertheless very important.

Even if we were to assume, in theory, that an impartial decision could be reached through arbitration, we would observe that such arbitration would not actually fulfill

[43] I. M. Bogolepov, "Arbitrazh i imperialisticheskaia deistvitelnost," *Mezhdunarodnaia Zhizn*, No. 4, 1927, pp. 50–55.

its purpose, i.e., would not lead to a peaceful, nonmilitary settlement of international disputes. Arbitration as practiced by the bourgeois states fully confirms this thesis. In order to see its absolute worthlessness it is sufficient to examine briefly the role of arbitration in international relations during the fifteen years preceding the World War. The principle of arbitration is not new; a number of international treaties declare the desirability and, in some cases, the obligation of submitting international conflicts and complications to arbitration. History, however, knows not a single case in which two parties threatened by war as a result of a dispute resorted in practice to arbitration (and this in spite of previous treaties making arbitration obligatory). Such conflicts as have been settled by arbitration have concerned secondary problems or technical matters exclusively. . . . During the first fifteen years of the present century alone we have had a sufficient number of sanguinary wars—the Boer War of 1899–1901, the Chinese war in 1900, the Russo-Japanese War in 1904–5, the Italo-Turkish war in 1911, the Balkan Wars in 1912–13, and finally, the World War of 1914–18. What better way than arbitration could have been used to prevent these wars! Yet "the most efficient and acceptable way to settle disputes which cannot be resolved through diplomacy" (decisions of the First and Second Peace Conferences at The Hague in 1899 and 1907) was forgotten, as were the numerous treaties on "permanent" peace and friendship.

[Shows that the same thing happened after World War I.] . . .

Even the famous Mosul dispute was settled, actually, by "direct action" . . . ; only the appearance of a decision by the League of Nations as arbitrator was created. It is no secret that the League of Nations, which is an obedient tool in the hands of "great" powers, was a mere mouthpiece for Britain's wishes, and that Britain actually dictated its own decision to the League. [Attempts to confirm this point of view by references to similar views of bourgeois scholars.]

. . .

Our conclusion, therefore, is clear: the principle of arbitration cannot be accepted by those who are truly interested in a permanent guarantee of peaceful relations.

110
First Soviet Nonaggression Treaty
[Litvinov on the Soviet-Turkish Treaty of Friendship and Neutrality, December 17, 1925][44]

. . .

The treaty strengthens the existing relations between the two countries. The nature of these relations excludes any aggressive or hostile act by one country against the other.

I shall not conceal the fact that the official consolidation of these relations and the hastening of the signing of the treaty was due in part to persistent false reports by the Anglo-American press of an alleged agreement between the U.S.S.R. and Italy directed against Turkey.

The Soviet government, on the other hand, was aware of the efforts of certain governments to draw Turkey into combinations hostile to the U.S.S.R.

The signing of the treaty now ends these alarming rumors and any other doubts about the strength of Soviet-Turkish friendship. . . .

I find it necessary to state in the most categorical manner that there are no additional secret clauses or protocols attached to the treaty. The best proof of the peaceful

[44] *Pravda,* No. 294, December 24, 1925, p. 6; also Degras, II, 79–80. Text of this treaty appears in Shapiro, I, 313.

nature of the treaty can be found in the readiness of the Soviet government to conclude similar agreements with all other countries with whom it maintains normal
relations.

Only a system of agreements among all states similar to the Soviet-Turkish treaty,
and not the machinations of the League of Nations or Locarno, can eliminate the
possibility of hostile groups and alliances and really lead to the prevention of wars.[45]

111

Litvinov on the Signing of the Soviet-German Treaty and Russia's Desire for Peace

[Excerpt from a Speech to the All-Russian Central Executive Committee, April 24, 1926][46]

In line with [our] peace policy, we have for a long time been offering all countries
the chance to sign agreements with us for mutual neutrality in the event of armed
conflict with a third party. A few months ago we signed such a treaty with Turkey.

I am able to tell you now, with the deepest satisfaction, that a similar treaty has
been signed today in Berlin with Germany.

[Reads the text of the treaty.]

In signing the treaty the plenipotentiaries of both countries exchanged notes or
declarations. Germany's note declared that the treaty will help the maintenance of
general peace, and that both governments will be guided in their negotiations, as
stated in Article I of the treaty, by the principle of general peace.

Germany further elaborated her view of the League of Nations. She believes
that the League's basic purpose is to regulate international disputes by peaceful and
just means, and that from this point of view the treaty does not contradict the League's
regulations. The German government outlined the probable nature of its conduct
in the event the League of Nations should reveal intentions that were either against
the basic concept of peace or one-sided and directed against the U.S.S.R.

The German government also outlined its views on Articles 16 and 17 of the
Covenant of the League of Nations. As you know, these articles provide for international sanctions and international reprisals against countries named as aggressors
by the League. The German government stated that the League can decide whether
the U.S.S.R. is an aggressor (in an armed conflict with a third power) only with
German consent, as was stipulated in the well-known German declaration at Locarno.

Further, it was proposed that the two countries sign a special convention on the
settlement of conflicts by peaceful means, that is, by means of arbitration and conciliation boards. To this note we replied that . . . we too consider the purpose of
this treaty to be the maintenance of peace, and that we are ready to sign a convention
on arbitration and conciliation boards.

It will not be amiss to state here that all that was signed today in Berlin will be
published in full, and that there are no secret agreements, no secret protocols or
amendments attached to this treaty.

The treaty is a supplement or rather an elaboration of the Rapallo treaty, and

---

[45] Similar treaties were signed with other Near Eastern countries: the Treaty of Paghman (Afghanistan), August 31, 1926, and the Treaty of Moscow (Persia), October 1, 1927.
Texts of these treaties appear in Shapiro, I, 322–23 and 340–41, respectively.

[46] *Izvestiia,* No. 95, April 25, 1926, p. 2. Complete text of this speech appears in Degras,
II, 104–7. This treaty was preceded by a commercial treaty, dated October 12, 1925, which
included seven separate agreements (an economic agreement, a railway agreement, a fiscal
agreement, etc.) ; and two separate agreements of the same date, one for reciprocal legal
assistance in civil matters, the other a consular agreement. Complete texts of all these documents appear in Shapiro, I, 288–308.

it fully corresponds to the friendly relations that have been established between the Union and Germany, and to the mutual desire to maintain these relations in the future.

The Rapallo treaty was inspired in its time by both countries' desire for friendship, by their community of interests, and by the dangerous international situation in which they found themselves, surrounded as they were by an ocean of hostility. Since then great changes have taken place in international relations. I do not know whether Germany can count many friends among the European states, whether she considers that after Locarno and Geneva her relations with other European countries are sufficiently pacified and consolidated, and whether she considers herself free from all danger. That is Germany's own affair. For our part, although we have improved our relations with a number of states and gained their *de jure* recognition, our Union's position is still dangerous, and the Western and non-Soviet world's general animosity toward it persists. Since attacks on the Union cannot, therefore, be regarded as impossible, the purpose of Soviet diplomacy is to reduce this danger of the formation of anti-Soviet blocs and of joint attacks. The reduction of this danger naturally raises the chances of general peace.

The policy of other countries, in so far as we have recently seen it expressed in military alliances and military assistance treaties—for example, the Polish-Rumanian treaty[47]—this policy of forming military groupings similar to those which led to the great slaughter of 1914, our Union meets by the policy of nonaggression treaties, treaties for the maintenance of peace and noninterference in the armed conflicts of third parties. If our policy were consistently pursued by other states, more would be done toward ensuring general peace and eliminating at least large-scale and international wars than has been achieved by all the well-known measures taken by the League of Nations in the past, and all those it is capable of taking in the future.

European diplomacy and its press have been shaking their heads in the last few days over whether the Soviet-German treaty contradicts the so-called spirit of Locarno. The question and the reproaches, of course, are not addressed to us, because we have retained complete freedom of action, and are not tied down by any Locarno or other treaties.

But speaking objectively, the answer to this question depends on the purposes of Locarno itself. If Locarno, as its initiators try to convince us, aims at bringing peace to Europe and consolidating the relations between European countries, then the supporters of Locarno, it would seem, should warmly welcome the Soviet-German treaty as a new step toward the consolidation of friendship between two great peoples. But if Locarno, as we have always suspected, has as one of its aims the formation of a single anti-Soviet front, the isolation of our Union, then one must admit that the treaty signed today does contradict the spirit of Locarno, and we can only rejoice that we have succeeded to a certain extent in removing the anti-Soviet sting from Locarno. I say "to a certain extent" because judging by the fury and malice of the attacks on Germany for signing this treaty, we must admit that Locarno continues to exist as a threat to our Union.

Another indication of friendly relations between the Union and Germany is provided by the recent agreement of the German government to partially guarantee [to Russia] credit to the amount of 300 million marks. The German government has correctly evaluated the importance of the moment for the consolidation of economic relations between Germany and Russia during the coming years. A guarantee of 60 per cent [credit] has already been provided, partly by the central German government and partly by the local German governments (Saxony, Prussia, etc.). The realization of credits, unfortunately, has been delayed, because the German banks greedily insist on too high a rate of interest, to which we cannot agree. . . .

The friendship with Germany in no way precludes our desire to re-establish

[47] A military alliance was concluded between Poland and Rumania on March 3, 1921, and renewed in 1926.

friendly relations with other countries. We must remember, however, that our general and separate agreements with Germany have been made easier by the fact that since Rapallo the German government has placed national interests above the private interests of separate groups or persons, and that it agreed to a mutual annulment of material claims. This national point of view, unfortunately, has not been accepted by other countries, and material claims act like a millstone in our relations with a number of states with whom we would like to and could establish very friendly relations.

112

The Fourth Nonaggression Treaty

[The Treaty of Neutrality and Nonaggression Between Lithuania and Soviet Russia, Known as the Treaty of Moscow, September 28, 1926][48]

Seven years ago the victors in the imperialist war began to disarm the vanquished nations completely, allegedly "for the purpose of preparing the limitation of armament for all nations." . . . However, during the last seven years the Allies have only accomplished the disarmament and annihilation of the military might of the vanquished. As to their own disarmament, these "defenders of peace" have forgotten about it. On the contrary, the growth of armament in Europe proceeds at full speed. . . .

But the Soviet Union stands in the way [of armament].

The truly peaceful policy of the workers' and peasants' state prevents the imperialists of various colors from proceeding calmly with their Cain's [i.e., treacherous] task. . . . Therefore, the League of Nations has done everything it can to prevent a delegation of the U.S.S.R. from attending [any conference] at which plans were being made for new wars instead of disarmament.

The U.S.S.R. is true to its slogan of struggle against the threats of war. Because its numerous offers of disarmament have not found response, it has chosen the road of nonaggression and neutrality. The fourth of these treaties was signed yesterday in Moscow. After the treaties with Turkey, Germany, and only a few days ago Afghanistan, the Soviet Union has now signed a treaty of nonaggression with Lithuania. . . .

113

The Nonaggression Treaties and the System of Coexistence

[An Editorial in *Izvestiia*][49]

· · ·

One of the fundamental questions of our existence as a type of state previously unknown in history, and in radical contradiction to the bourgeois world, has been from the start as follows: On what basis can true coexistence between this state and the [capitalist] world be attained, without either an endless struggle or the assimilation [of the new state] by the bourgeois states? Our terms provide a clear answer, and probably a complete answer to this question for the present.

Outwardly these terms are only negative; that is, we and our cosignatories must not attack each other, we must not participate in any combinations against each other, and neither party may take advantage of the other's difficulties in the event of war

[48] *Izvestiia*, No. 224, September 29, 1926, p. 1. Text of this treaty appears in Shapiro, I, 323.

[49] *Izvestiia*, No. 96, April 27, 1926, p. 1.

[with a third party]. But although all these terms contain "do not," they neverthe-less solve the coexistence problem so satisfactorily that we might be led to ask why they have not been thought of before.

Unfortunately, these [apparently] simple principles actually have been very dif-ficult to apply, since there have been no proper conditions for them. So far the diplomatic efforts of the bourgeois statesmen have been along quite a different plane. They have been concerned not with peace, but with war, with how to increase one state's territorial power at another's expense, and [once this is] done, how to protect it from other imperialist designs—that is, from acts of vengeance by the enemy whose territories and wealth have been seized.

These efforts, which correspond to the nature of [these] bourgeois states, result in political and military alliances of an offensive or defensive nature.

[It appears that] before our own diplomacy could find the new terms it sought [for coexistence], it was necessary for some states—states that were once powerful and proud, and that still have much vitality—to be forced by circumstances to direct all their efforts, just as we do, to healing the wounds dealt them by war and inter-vention (the Ruhr was also intervention!) and restoring their economy. In order to do this, these states must work hard, and have no time to fight a war . . . We are truly proud to have created these new terms, as yet unprecedented in history, which our cosignatories, to their great honor, have fully accepted.

The Soviet-German treaty is important not only because it links two peoples who are very seriously interested in friendship, but also because it signifies a new political system in international relations in general. We do not conceal the fact . . . that we are ready to conclude treaties with other powers on the same basis. Least of all would we wish to have our present treaty with Germany interpreted as a diplomatic move against some third party, and in particular against our nearest neighbors . . .

If all other countries would demonstrate their willingness to sign such an agree-ment as Germany and we have signed, Europe would present quite a different political picture. Instead of leagues that serve as curtains to conceal intrigue and violence, and instead of Geneva conferences that lead only to new armament and new devasta-tion—if instead of all this deceit for which the peoples pay so dearly we were to have true and (so far as possible) full co-operation among the peoples, we could then truly cut down armament without any abstract calculation of "potential" and actual rifles, and so turn at least some of our swords into ploughshares. Will any other governments adopt this course? Both treaties, the Soviet-Turkish and the Soviet-German, now call for a reply from other peoples.

THE MEANING OF "SOCIALISM" IN ONE COUNTRY"

114

Zinoviev on the Theory of Socialism in One Country

[Excerpt from a Speech at the Fourteenth Party Conference, April 29, 1925][50]

. . .

We must speak not merely of one stabilization, but of two stabilizations. The connection between the victory of the proletarian revolution in one country and this country's obligations toward other countries has now become especially urgent. This

[50] *Izvestiia*, No. 100, May 5, 1925, p. 4; also *International Press Correspondence*, No. 46, May 30, 1925, pp. 602–3, 605.

question was solved theoretically by Lenin. To obviate every possible objection, to avoid any misunderstanding, and to throw every possible light on this question from every standpoint, we have considered this question in our theses mainly from Comrade Lenin's viewpoint.

. . . In 1915 Comrade Lenin stated the problem in its most general form for the first time, saying that the revolution would consist of long years of battle, and of periods of advance intermingled with counterrevolutionary convulsions.

In his article, published in the collection "Against the Stream" . . . and directed against Kautsky and in part against Comrade Trotsky, Comrade Lenin formulated his law of capitalism, which demonstrates the unevenness of capitalist development. Comrade Lenin's book on imperialism is based on this law. In 1917, after the February Revolution, Comrade Lenin formulated the program of the Russian revolution in his well-known letter to the Swiss workers, and declared that "the Russian proletariat cannot carry the socialist revolution through to a victorious conclusion alone; it can only begin it." . . .

In his admirable article "Left-Wing Communism: An Infantile Disorder," Comrade Lenin mentioned the famous "chicken." He wrote:

"Socialism is unthinkable without the rule of the proletariat in the state. This is another platitude. History . . . develops in such a peculiar manner that in the year 1918 two separate halves of socialism were born, lying side by side like two future chickens in one eggshell of world imperialism. In 1918 Germany and Russia represented the most graphic object lessons of the material realization of the economic, productive, and socioeconomic prerequisites of socialism on one hand, and of its political prerequisites on the other."

Then followed *Kautsky the Renegade,* in which a whole chapter was devoted to this subject. Then came Lenin's declaration of March 13, 1919, that we are living in the midst of a system of states, and that two different systems cannot both continue to exist permanently. In the end, one or the other will be victorious. In other places Comrade Lenin stressed that "in the end" does not mean "at the beginning of the beginning." A number of other important statements followed: the highly important speech in Moscow on November 27, 1920, on concessions; the speech at the Third Congress of the Comintern; the remarks in 1921 on the original plan for taxes in kind; and finally the last statements, to which we must accord special attention—his political legacy and the notes from his diary of 1922–23, in which the ideas on co-operatives and on the East are of unusual importance. We have given them in full in our theses.[51] The extracts show us clearly that Vladimir Ilich believed that a country such as ours could attain complete socialism, even by way of co-operatives alone, if we were safe from international intervention. But at the same time, as an international proletarian revolutionist, he emphasized that final victory was possible only on an international scale, and that without the international revolution our victory would be neither permanent nor final. I shall also mention his statement on the East, which is well known to all of you.[52] . . .

Lenin was an international revolutionist; he knew that final victory was possible only on an international scale, that victory on an international scale is the single sure

[51] These were the "Theses on the Tasks of the Comintern and the VKP (B)" adopted at the Fourteenth Party Conference, April 27–29, 1925. The text appears in *V.K.P. v rezoliutsiiakh,* II, 25–31.

[52] Lenin wrote in 1923: "In the last analysis, the outcome of the struggle will be determined by the fact that Russia, India, China, etc., have the overwhelming majority of the population of the globe. And it is precisely this majority of population that, during the past few years, has been drawn into the struggle for its emancipation with extraordinary rapidity, so that in this respect there cannot be the slightest shadow of doubt what the final outcome of the world struggle will be. In this sense, the final victory of socialism is fully and absolutely assured." (Lenin, *Sochineniia,* XXVII, 416–17.)

guarantee against the restoration of bourgeois conditions. But at the same time, his articles defended and promulgated the idea that our country, with its patriarchal, semisavage customs and its *Oblomovshchina*,[53] can be changed into a socialist country. In his last speech in the Moscow soviet he bequeathed us a great legacy: to convert the Russia of the N.E.P. into a socialist Russia.

This legacy is now of the utmost importance to us all. The partial stabilization of capitalism in Europe is wrongly interpreted by some party members, especially our young students, who are thus led on to the wrong track. We as a party must promulgate the Leninist principle that socialism can be established even in our poor country—even though we are inside the capitalist encirclement. We have all acknowledged the partial stabilization of capitalism in Europe. We have all acknowledged that the world revolution is developing less rapidly. But does this mean that a petty bourgeois degeneration is inevitable in Russia? Does it signify a stagnation or even a retrogression in our revolutionary development? It may be safely asserted that no such definite point of view actually exists. However, there is a feeling of it in the air, and this feeling is perfectly comprehensible in the present stage of the revolutionary movement.

There are two dangerous trends of thought inherent in the present situation. They are these:

(1) If final victory is really possible only in the event of world revolution, and if we recognize that world revolution is moving forward slowly, if we have no adequate outside aid, shall we be able to develop socialism in Russia? . . . Does the present situation perhaps signify that we, the Russian Communist Party, are unable to fulfill our historical mission as a Bolshevik party, as a party of international proletarian revolutionists? . . .

(2) What do we care about the international revolution? We can arrange our own affairs very comfortably; we possess unlimited territory, we are in power, we are in a position to consolidate our victory and concern ourselves but little with the events taking place in the international arena. . . .

Although these trends of thought have not yet taken any definite form, still we must face the danger of their doing so. Otherwise we should not be the party created by Lenin, capable of looking forward and of coping with possible dangers. We must prevent the genesis of such ideas. We must continually remind all our comrades that we are proletarian revolutionists, international proletarian revolutionists; that we can only imagine our victory on an international scale; that we do not and cannot forget this even for a moment; and that, after having won victory in one country, we shall do our utmost to promote the revolutionary movement in other countries.

We are now confronted with the necessity of safeguarding ourselves against these two possible dangers in our own ranks. Our next task, then, will be to associate very closely with the Comintern, to afford it maximum support, to help it draw upon the treasury of our practical and political experience—especially the fund of experience gained between 1907 and 1914—so as to enable it to lead the international proletariat through all the difficulties of the present situation.

. . .

We want to look upon the world with open eyes; we want to comprehend what is going on around us. In 1921 Lenin wrote: "Ten to twenty years of good relations with the peasantry and international victory is guaranteed, even though the pace of international revolution slows down." This length of time of course is not obligatory. We hope that victory will be won earlier, that the revolution will be victorious

[53] *Oblomovshchina* is a word derived from the fictional figure Oblomov, the central character of Goncharov's novel of that name. The novel and its protagonist have become celebrated because they present a type of Russian intellectual who, although given to dreams of an active and useful life, is absolutely incapable of arousing himself to action.

in other countries much sooner than this. But if this does not take place as quickly as we hope, then we shall work on, systematically, for ten or twenty years or longer if necessary, under the conditions of the slower development of the revolution. Our party always has been, and remains, in the front rank of the Comintern. It is the party of the working masses, the party of the international proletariat, the party of the international proletarian revolution.

115

The Temporary Nature of Capitalist Stabilization and the Tasks of the Comintern

[Resolution on the Immediate Problems of the International Communist Movement, Adopted at the Sixth Enlarged Plenum of the ECCI, February 17–March 15, 1926][54]

"Stabilization" of Capitalism and Tactics of the World Revolution

The previous Enlarged Plenum of the ECCI (March 1925) recorded a certain partial stabilization of capitalism, and at the same time indicated the entirely relative and uncertain nature of this stabilization. The past year has fully confirmed the Communist International's analysis. . . .

The period of the decline of capitalism continues, but within this period temporary and partial recoveries are possible. The Communist International recorded such a recovery, such a "stabilization" of capitalism, in 1925. This "stabilization" is a fact. It should be understood, however, not as a permanent consolidation of capitalism—a consolidation denoting a new epoch of ascendancy of the capitalist order in general—but merely as a certain relative stability compared with the earlier postwar years. From this viewpoint, the relative and uncertain character of this "stabilization" becomes especially apparent.

At the beginning of 1926, capitalist Europe is experiencing a whole series of new and serious crises. In Britain, a predominantly industrial crisis; in France, a predominantly inflationary crisis; in Germany, an acute economic crisis, the beginning of the Dawes Plan crisis; in Poland, almost an economic catastrophe; in Austria, also, a crisis, etc. The past year confirmed with remarkable clarity the instability of "stabilization" in a number of important European countries.

· · ·

The East

The past year has also absolutely confirmed the last Enlarged Plenum's Leninist appraisal of the development of events in the East. The national-revolutionary liberation movement in the East has made a great stride forward, and in some countries has developed more rapidly than was expected. Because of the gradual industrialization of the East, events there are particularly important.

· · ·

The U.S.S.R.

Simultaneously, at the other end of the globe, in the U.S.S.R., in the union of countries wrested by the proletariat from the bourgeoisie, we witness a remarkable economic development and a consolidation of the economic and political power of the proletariat. In spite of the continuous attempts of bourgeois states to isolate and encircle the U.S.S.R., in spite of the terrible inheritance of the civil war, the U.S.S.R.

[54] *Kommunisticheskii Internatsional v dokumentakh*, pp. 529–30, 536–39, 546–48, 554–56; also *International Press Correspondence*, No. 40, May 13, 1926, pp. 613–24.

has been able to raise its economy to the prewar level and to achieve considerable success in socialist construction, which is bound to extend and continue to grow. . . . Even Social Democratic leaders, who for years carried on a fierce struggle against the Russian revolution and the Soviet power, are now compelled by the workers to admit that the U.S.S.R. is growing strong and overcoming the greatest obstacles . . . The U.S.S.R. is becoming the center of attraction for the proletarians of all countries, the pivot of the international proletarian revolution.

In the present world situation there are everywhere fundamental differences between two systems, two worlds, between which a more or less unstable equilibrium is as yet maintained: on one side, the world of capitalism headed by America; on the other, the world of proletarian revolution headed by the U.S.S.R. American imperialism continues to run the capitalist world. In the domain of international politics, America, whenever it so desires, draws to its side Britain as an ally (the Anglo-American bloc). But this does not mean that there are no conflicts within this bloc over such cardinal questions as China, Mosul, and Mexico. Neither does it mean that the other sectors of the bourgeois world, which to a certain extent are under pressure from the Anglo-American bloc, are free from internal conflicts of their own.

.   .   .

The situation may be summed up as follows:

1. There is a consolidation of capitalism in America and in some other trans-oceanic countries.

2. In the second half of 1925, economic crises became more acute in all the most important capitalist countries of Europe.

3. The concentration of the means of production in the hands of trusts and cartels backed by bank capital has increased enormously, notably in America, Britain, France, and Germany.

4. The economic antagonism between America and Britain is becoming increasingly acute. Like the antagonism between Britain and Germany before the first imperialist world war, the present antagonism between America and Britain is developing rapidly. (In this connection, the significance of other important antagonisms—between America and Japan, Britain and France, etc.—should not be underestimated.)

5. The Dawes Plan has begun to fail.

6. There are five million unemployed (the figure is much higher if families are included).

7. The middle classes are becoming impoverished in almost all the countries of Europe.

And at the same time:

1. On territory embracing one-sixth of the globe [the U.S.S.R.], socialism is in the course of construction—although with great difficulty.

2. On territory embracing nearly one-quarter of the population of the world (China), the national-liberation movement is growing, and the revolutionary movement of the workers is growing along with it, and at its head.

3. In Morocco and Syria the national-liberation movement has developed into actual war; in India and Egypt it is ripening slowly but surely.

4. Throughout the capitalist world, communist parties are becoming more and more efficient, and the labor movement—although subject to fluctuations in the industrial situation—is growing.

The Communist International rejects hasty conclusions, conclusions made as if there were no "stabilization" of capital. But it rejects as emphatically as before the "conclusion" of the Social Democratic leaders that capitalism has become consolidated for another historical epoch.

The past year has shown over and over again the steadfastness of the fundamental Leninist policy of the Communist International—the policy of world proletarian revolution. The absence of a directly revolutionary situation during the epoch of partial and untenable stabilization of capitalism can and must impel the Communist International to make corresponding changes in the methods of its work, but the aim and the basis of the Comintern's activity remain as of old.

· · ·

IV

Tasks of the Comintern

1. With the objective conditions for the victory of socialism in Europe becoming increasingly mature, the subjective factor has become increasingly significant: To what extent will the working class become consolidated? How strong will the communist parties become? To what degree will they become really Bolshevik parties? Will they prove equal to the historical situation? Although the proletarian revolution may well develop slowly, owing to the partial stabilization of capitalism, the communist parties should nonetheless do their utmost to prepare themselves for a more rapid development of the revolution. The most important task of the Communist International during the coming years is to pay more attention to the political training of communist parties, to their tempering, organizational consolidation, ideological firmness, revolutionary determination, and knowledge of how to approach the masses.

2. At the present time, when many of the most important European capitalist states, despite the partial "stabilization" of capitalism, are facing an economic impasse, when the productive forces of capitalist Europe are declining or marking time [etc.] . . . the task of the communist party is this: to put before the masses more extensively, more decisively, and more persistently than ever before, its program for saving Europe by means of the proletarian revolution, the dictatorship of the proletariat, and the formation of the United States of Socialist Europe (a plan approved by the Communist International in 1923), and for realizing the slogan "Proletarians of all countries and oppressed peoples of the world, unite!"

In propagating the idea of forming a United States of Europe to liberate the proletariat and the peoples of Europe from twofold oppression—by national and North American capital—the following circumstances should be considered. First, the United States of Europe should be understood as a political organization uniting and controlling the relations between the soviet socialist republics of Europe, which will come into being as a result of a victorious proletarian revolution in the European countries. Second, the victorious proletarian revolution in Europe should not necessarily be understood as a simultaneous victory of the proletariat throughout the whole of Europe. Rather, it should be interpreted as a whole period of revolutionary upheavals, during which the proletarian revolution may be victorious first in separate countries, or in one European country, and only later extend to all the countries of Europe. Third, the establishment of a federated United States of Europe by the liberated nationalities of Europe will proceed on an entirely voluntary basis, with complete recognition of the rights of nations to self-determination. Fourth, while the plan of the United States of Europe means the establishment of the proletarian dictatorship [in Europe], it carries with it at the same time the liberation of the colonial and semicolonial countries and the establishment of collaboration between them [and the United States of Europe] on a completely voluntary basis. . . .

At the same time in many European countries (France, Italy, the Balkans, Poland, Czechoslovakia, Germany) the slogan for a workers' and peasants' government should be emphatically advanced.

The United States of Socialist Europe in alliance with the Union of Soviet Socialist Republics, in alliance with the oppressed peoples of the world, in alliance with the socialist nucleus of the American proletariat, would represent a tremendous force against which imperialist America would be helpless. . . .

5. The desire for Unity is the main desire of the workers throughout the world. . . . The popularity of the slogan for unity among the working class masses, and in particular the slogan for trade union unity, are the main features of the present-day workers' movement.

6. On this basis the united front tactic should now be developed particularly extensively. . . . It is the tactic of the proletarian vanguard for a whole period, right up to when we win the majority of the working class to our side; hence the united front tactic should adapt to the changing situation . . .

7. The present key element in the united front is the trade union movement . . . The Left elements of the trade unions must be assisted; their efforts to rally the forces of the working class must be supported; every effort must be made to establish trade union unity in each individual country and to form a single international organization of [proletarian] trade unions . . .

24. Efforts to extend the mass influence of the communist parties have already been made in practically all the capitalist countries, but they have been unsystematic and largely ineffective. They must henceforth be systematic and thorough. . . .

The illegal communist parties, no less than the legal parties, must direct their efforts toward organizing revolutionary work among the masses. . . .

25. Consumers' co-operatives are also a form of mass organization. The communist parties must work systematically and practically to win over the broad masses of the co-operatives' members, and to enroll the co-operatives in the united proletarian fighting front against capital. Many sections have badly neglected this work.

27. . . . The attention of the workers of the whole world should be fixed more and more on the economic development and construction of socialism in the U.S.S.R. Widespread aid from the international proletariat in the work of industrializing the U.S.S.R.!

More attention to the East! Teach the workers to understand that the national-liberation movement in the East has the closest and most intrinsic connection with the revolutionary struggle of the proletariat.

More attention to the new continents—to the workers' movement in Latin America, Africa, and Australia!

Struggle for the peasantry! Struggle for the middle strata of the population! Struggle for the most important elements of the urban and [rural] petty bourgeoisie . . .

116

"Socialism in One Country" and the World Policies of Soviet Russia and the Communist Party

[Excerpts from Stalin's Speech at the Fifteenth Party Conference, November 1, 1926][55]

We are faced by three questions:

(1) Is the victory of socialism possible in our country, considering that so far our country is the only country of the dictatorship of the proletariat, that the pro-

[55] Stalin, *Sochineniia*, VIII, 246–52, 262–66; also *Izvestiia*, No. 256, November 5, 1926, pp. 3–4.

letarian revolution has not yet been victorious in other countries, and that the tempo of the world revolution has slowed down?

(2) If victory is possible, can we call it a complete victory, a final victory?

(3) If this victory cannot be called final, what is necessary to render it a final victory?

These three questions are involved in the general question of whether socialism can be victorious in one country, that is, in our country.

.   .   .

Lenin was a great continuator of Marx and Engels precisely because he was never a slave to the letter of Marxism. In his studies he always followed Marx's direction when he said (more than once) that Marxism was not a dogma but a guide for action. . . . Lenin's greatness lay precisely in his capacity to cast about openly, honestly, and without any vacillation for a new formula for the victory of the proletarian revolution in separate countries. Lenin did this knowing full well that the opportunists of all countries would cling to the old formula, trying to conceal their opportunist teaching behind the names of Marx and Engels.

.   .   .

Lenin was the first Marxist to submit imperialism to a really Marxian analysis as the new and last phase of capitalism, to raise the question of the victory of socialism in separate capitalist countries, and to provide a positive solution to this problem. I have in mind Lenin's leaflet *Imperialism, the Highest Stage of Capitalism*, and his article "O lozunge Soedinennykh Shtatov Evropy" ["On the Slogan of the United States of Europe"], which appeared in 1915. I have also in mind the polemics between Lenin and Trotsky concerning the slogan of the United States of Europe or of the World, at the time when Lenin first formulated his thesis on the possibility of socialism in a single country. In this article Lenin wrote as follows:

The United States of the World would scarcely make a correct independent slogan because on one hand it merges with socialism, and on the other it might erroneously suggest the impossibility of the victory of socialism in one country and of relations between such a country and other countries.

Uneven economic and political development is an absolute law of capitalism; consequently, the victory of socialism in a few capitalist countries, or even a single one at first, is possible. The victorious proletariat of this country, after having expropriated the capitalists and organized socialist production, would rise against the remaining capitalist world, draw to their side the oppressed classes of other countries, inciting them to insurrection against the capitalists, and proceeding, if necessary, with military force against the exploiting classes and their states. . . . [For] a free association of the nations under socialism is impossible without a more or less prolonged and tenacious struggle between the socialist republics and the other states. (See [Lenin, *Sochineniia*] XVIII, 232–33.)

.   .   .

We can and must defeat the capitalist elements in our [national] economy; we can and must work at building up a socialist society. But can this victory be called a final victory? No, it cannot. We can defeat our capitalists, we can build up socialism, but this does not mean that we can secure the country of the proletarian dictatorship from external dangers, from the dangers of intervention and the restoration of the old order. We are not living on an island, but in the midst of capitalist encirclement. The fact that we are building socialism, and thus revolutionizing the workers of the capitalist countries, is bound to arouse the hatred and enmity of the capitalist world. . . . Therefore, we cannot regard our victory as final so long as we are within the capitalist encirclement; we cannot regard it as final until the proletariat is victorious in at least several countries. However great our success in [socialist] construction at home, we cannot regard the country of the proletarian dictatorship as secure from outside dangers. Therefore, in order to win full victory we must see to it that our present capitalist encirclement is supplanted by a socialist environment; we must see to it that the proletariat is victorious in at least a few other countries. Only then can we consider our victory complete and final. That is why we consider the victory of our country not as a goal in itself, not as something that has a significance of its own, but as a step, as a means, as the way toward the victory of the proletarian revolution in other countries. . . .

Hence it follows that the danger of military intervention still exists, and will long continue to exist. Whether the capitalists can undertake a serious intervention against us now is another question. Much depends upon the attitude of the workers in the capitalist countries, on how sympathetic they are toward our country and toward socialism. For the time being, they cannot support our revolution by a revolution against their own capitalists. It is equally true, however, that the capitalists are not in a position to arouse "their own" workers to a war against our republic, or to carry on such a war without exposing capitalism to deadly danger. This is clear from the innumerable workers' delegations that visit our country to see how we are building socialism, and also from the far-reaching sympathy felt for the Soviet republic by the working class all over the world. The international position of our republic is based on this sympathy. Without it we should be confronted today by a new series of attempts at intervention; we should be exposed to interruptions in our constructive work and deprived of our breathing space.

But if the capitalist world is not now able to launch a military intervention against us, it may well be able to do so at some future date. . . .

Lenin was therefore right when he said: "So long as our Soviet republic remains the sole boundary of the whole capitalist world, it would be . . . a ridiculous flight of imagination, a Utopia, to think of the disappearance of this or that danger. So long as the fundamental antagonisms exist, these dangers continue to exist as well, and there is no escape from them." (See [Lenin, *Sochineniia*] XXVI, 29.)

And this again was Lenin's reason for saying: "The final victory is possible only on an international scale and through the combined efforts of the workers of all countries." (See [Lenin, *Sochineniia*] XXIII, 9.)

What, then, is the meaning of the victory of socialism in our country?

It means the establishment of the dictatorship of the proletariat and the realization of socialism, the overcoming of the capitalist elements of our economy by the inner forces of our revolution.

And what is the meaning of the final victory of socialism in our country?

It means the creation of a complete guarantee against all attempts at intervention or restoration, a guarantee based on the victory of the socialist revolution in at least several countries.

If to achieve socialism in one country means to solve the internal contradictions that can be fully solved in one country (we are naturally thinking of our own country), then to achieve the final victory of socialism means to solve the contradictions between the country of socialism and the countries of capitalism, contradictions that can be overcome only by the forces of the proletarian revolution in several countries.

Those who confuse these two groups of contradictions are either hopeless muddleheads or incorrigible opportunists.

That is the basic line of our party.

117

The Main Tendencies of Capitalism and the Aims and Effects of Socialist Policies

[Excerpts from Bukharin's Report Prepared for the Seventh Enlarged
Plenum of the ECCI, November 22–December 16, 1926][56]

. . .

Beyond any doubt the acute crisis that has affected the entire capitalist world and that reached its highest point in 1920–21 is now somewhat less acute . . . During the last few years, capitalism has been able to mend its fences. Consequently, there is no direct revolutionary situation in the principal centers of capitalist economy . . . [and so] it becomes necessary to determine to what extent capitalism has succeeded in extricating itself from the mire of the profound postwar crisis. It is also necessary to point out the present main tendencies of capitalism and consequently the fate of capitalism in general.

. . .

The development of socialist industrial relations within the U.S.S.R. represents an important factor for the repression of capitalism. Economically, politically, culturally—from every angle the U.S.S.R. is, in the final analysis, an instrument for the disintegration of the capitalist order in other countries. In terms of the international situation, the capitalist world and the U.S.S.R. cannot be regarded as two absolutely independent entities. The present importance of the U.S.S.R. is quite exceptional, and the so-called "Russian question," which is in fact the most important contributor to the international revolutionary situation, is [at the same time] the most troublesome problem that confronts the world bourgeoisie and its political leaders. Consequently, the problem must be examined from several angles:
1. The exclusion of the Soviet territories from normal trade relations has caused a very considerable breach in the development of world economy. . . .
2. To the bourgeois world, however, the restoration of commercial relations between capitalist countries and Russia—now the U.S.S.R.—present a constant menace by accelerating the development of state industries and the national economy in the land of the proletarian dictatorship. True, these relations (along the lines of commerce, credits, and possible concessions) represent also a certain outlet for the capitalist world, now so much in need of markets for its goods and capital, and thus contribute to a certain degree to the stabilization of capitalism. However, only the dullest ultra-Left renegades and Social Democratic charlatans would claim that the country of the proletarian dictatorship abandons its revolutionary mission when it establishes economic contacts with the capitalist states. Obviously such contacts do more for the revolutionary forces than for the capitalist forces. While economic relations with Soviet Russia provide a certain (though extremely small) outlet to a number of capitalist countries, they . . . greatly facilitate the economic development of the Soviet Union. Russia's [planned economy] makes for far greater efficiency and productive effect than can be attained in the laissez-faire countries, our superior results being due to the socialist organization of the "commanding heights" of our economy. Consequently, [economic] relations between the capitalist world and the Soviet Union serve to strengthen and consolidate the basic stronghold of the international proletarian movement.

[56] *Puti mirovoi revoliutsii,* I, 30–31, 40–45, 48; also N. I. Bukharin, *Capitalist Stabilization and Proletarian Revolution,* pp. 3, 14–16, 20, 23. For Bukharin's oral report, an abridgment of his written report, see *Puti mirovoi revoliutsii,* I, 19–30, or *Pravda,* No. 273, November 25, 1926, pp. 1–2.

3. What our economic development is like and how it compares in tempo with that of the capitalist countries is, of course, of paramount importance. . . .

Clearly our rate of development is much more rapid than the rate of stabilization of capitalism. No other country anywhere suffered so much destruction (as a result of the imperialist war, civil war and intervention, etc.) as the U.S.S.R. . . . Nonetheless, the U.S.S.R. has approached prewar [economic] levels almost as quickly as the capitalist world. It is not difficult, therefore, to note the great rapidity of the U.S.S.R.'s development. Precise statistical data will confirm it also.

· · ·

The rapid growth of socialism in the U.S.S.R., the most important and fundamental factor of all, is a mighty lever of the international proletarian revolution, and consequently the most important contributor to the disintegration of the forces of international capital. The powerful influence of the U.S.S.R., and its importance as a rallying center for all the forces directed against the capitalist order, must be considered the most powerful obstacle to the consolidation of the world capitalist system.

A final important factor in the disintegration of the capitalist order in Western Europe is the profound decline of the British Empire, at one time the almost indisputable ruler of the waves. The great British Empire—this former stronghold of world capitalism, "workshop of the world," etc.—is slipping from its former position and turning from a classic example of omnipotent capitalism into a classic example of capitalism's decline. A large number of causes have contributed to this decline.

· · ·

In view of the systematic decline of British capitalism and the increasing acuteness of the class struggle, the working class of Great Britain will infallibly be led by history to the problem of seizing power. In Great Britain more than in any other country in Europe a "direct revolutionary situation" is developing, although such a situation will not necessarily be brought about by the present [miners'] strike. At the same time the decline of British capitalism and its consequences are causing a tremendous breach even in the relative stability of modern capitalism.

· · ·

PART V

Renewal of Suspicion and Hostility
1926–1927

PART V

By 1926 Joseph Stalin was well entrenched as the leading figure within the U.S.S.R. and the international communist movement. He had outmaneuvered and defeated his principal rivals but had not finally disposed of them. He took a greater interest in and exerted greater influence on Soviet foreign affairs. His policy of "socialism in one country," which had become the party line, was based on his belief that the U.S.S.R. could not count on social revolution in the West for at least ten to twenty years. He made this estimate in 1925.[1]

As the years 1926 and 1927 progressed, events seemed to challenge the soundness of the theory of a twenty-year breathing space. Soviet leaders began to emphasize again the danger of capitalist intervention, and some were saying that the period they had previously described as a "pacifist-reformist" era in the West was about to end.

The British General Strike and the Arcos Raid

Soviet relations with Great Britain, in particular, deteriorated rapidly during this period, and were finally broken off altogether. As noted in Part IV, Anglo-Soviet relations had run into troubled waters as early as November 1924, when the then newly elected British Conservative government refused to recognize the treaty negotiated with the Soviets by the preceding Labour government. Certain powerful British interests had demanded complete termination of relations at that time, but a compromise was effected: The treaty was not ratified, but diplomatic and commercial relations continued. Then in July 1925, troubled by disturbances in Shanghai that were attributed to Russian influence, certain British circles once more demanded the end of all relations. Again the British government successfully opposed the step.

In May 1926, a miners' strike in Great Britain was followed by a general strike. These strikes, and the Soviet reaction to them, precipitated another major crisis in Anglo-Soviet relations. Some Soviet leaders greeted the news of the strikes jubilantly, seeing in them the harbingers of revolution, and Soviet trade unions immediately sent large sums of money to aid the cause. The British government held that the striking miners might accept the Soviet funds, on the ground that the miners' strike was a legal industrial dispute. The British Trades Union Congress itself, however, refused the proffered aid.

When Soviet unions also sent funds to promote the general strike, the British government intervened. It declared the strike illegal, and the Russian offer a hostile act and a breach of the Soviet guarantee of June 4, 1923.[2] On June 12, 1926, a British note pointed out to the Soviet government that the action of the Soviet Commissariat of Finance in forwarding money to aid the general strike "does not conduce to the friendly settlement the Soviet Government profess to desire."[3]

Within a few days the Soviet government replied that it could not legally

---

[1] Stalin, *Sochineniia*, VII, 166.
[2] See our p. 188.
[3] *The Times* (London), June 17, 1926, p. 14.

prohibit Soviet trade unions from sending money to help trade unions of other countries, that the funds in question had been sent to the General Council of the British Trades Union Congress by the All-Russian Central Council of Trade Unions, and that the Soviet government itself had had no part in the affair.[4]

Soviet leaders attached great significance to the British strikes. Stalin, who spoke at length on the strikes and their failure, saw them as bearing out Lenin's theory of imperialism as the last stage of capitalism—i.e., as workers' unrest caused by Great Britain's loss of her monopoly of world trade, and the subsequent drop in the British workers' living standards. The workers' interests had been sacrificed, Stalin argued, to the necessity of winning new markets by producing cheaper goods. The Conservative Party had wanted the strikes, had been preparing for them, and could not continue to exist without conflicts both in Britain and elsewhere.

The strikes failed, said Stalin, because the British capitalists were well organized, the General Council of the Trades Union Congress was disunited, the capitalist leaders were stronger than the union leaders, and the Conservative Party was willing (as the unions were not) to resort to political methods of struggle.

The British labor leaders either did not or would not understand that such a strike could be won only by international proletarian solidarity—a reference, apparently, to the refusal of the British trade unions to accept assistance from the Soviet unions.

According to Stalin, the failure of the strike, and the fact that the British bourgeois government had used the powers of the government against the workers, would point up the need for an intensified struggle and for new, more revolutionary working class leaders.

Moreover, said Stalin, the failure of the strike demonstrated that the capitalist stabilization, however temporary and provisional, had not ended. He called upon Communists everywhere to organize a united front of workers in order to turn the predicted future attacks into counterattacks and revolutionary offensives.[5]

The Soviet support of the British strikes, the open help the Soviets gave the antiforeign, anti-imperialist movements in China in 1926,[6] and the continuance of Soviet-inspired and anti-British propaganda throughout the world, all combined to undermine the relations between the two countries. Early in 1927 the British government sent a note to the Soviet representative in London, A. P. Rosengolts, which foreshadowed the break to come. This note, dated February 23, 1927, referred to the Soviet government's official guarantee of June 4, 1923, not to support efforts to spread discontent or foment rebellion in any part of the British Empire. It also recalled previous British representations regarding this guarantee, and denied all Soviet allegations of British designs against the Soviet republic:

> So long as the present rulers of the Union of Soviet Socialist Republics, be they technically members of the Government or members of the Politbureau, which is the real dominating authority in the Union, or its ambassadors abroad, persist in making public utterances in defamation of Great Britain, or in advocacy of a world

---

[4] Kliuchnikov and Sabanin, III, 345–46.

[5] Stalin, *Sochineniia*, VIII, 155–68; see Document 121.

[6] See the companion volume, *Soviet Russia and the East, 1920–1927*.

revolution, no improvement [in the relations of the two countries] is possible. . . .

His Majesty's Government are indeed well aware of the delusion under which M. Chicherin and many of his colleagues are suffering that Great Britain is continually occupied in plotting against the Union of Soviet Socialist Republics and for this purpose has never ceased to guide the policy of such countries as Poland and the Baltic states and Persia into an orientation directed against Soviet Russia . . . Its continuance . . . can only be based on a rooted, even perhaps temperamental, hostility in the minds of the Soviet authorities themselves and a corresponding credulity in regard to false reports from interested informants.

After some further references to defamatory statements by Soviet leaders about Great Britain and her colonies, the note concluded: "His Majesty's Government trust that this protest and warning will be received by the Union of Soviet Socialist Republics with the attention they require, and that no further cause of complaint may be given."[7]

Litvinov, then Assistant Commissar of Foreign Affairs, replied to the British note on February 26, 1927:

The note of the British government merely enumerates a number of public utterances of Soviet public men within the U.S.S.R., and of newspaper articles in the Soviet press. I must, therefore, give the reminder that there is no agreement between the U.S.S.R. and Great Britain limiting the freedom of speech and of the press within the confines of the two countries. . . . To consider the agreement of 1923 or the agreement of 1921 as affecting printed or oral utterances within the confines of the U.S.S.R. is arbitrarily to extend the scope of these agreements.

After noting that similar anti-Soviet statements had been made by British Conservatives, Litvinov ended by pointing to the benefits that Great Britain as well as Russia derived from the trade and diplomatic relations between the two countries.[8]

Rykov interpreted the British note as ideological preparation for creating an anti-Soviet bloc, a new *cordon sanitaire*. Behind the anti-Soviet agitation, he told the Fourth Congress of Soviets of the U.S.S.R., were three things: a new attempt to force the Soviet Union to recognize tsarist debts, British displeasure at the demonstration of solidarity between the working masses of Britain and the Soviet Union, and the sympathy of the Soviet workers for the British strike and for the Chinese people.

Rykov, like other Soviet spokesmen, declared that the Soviet government would not allow anyone to prevent Soviet workers from sending assistance to workers in other countries. He also added that a rupture of diplomatic relations with Great Britain at that time would make the maintenance of peace more difficult.[9]

But the Conservative cabinet took a different view. On May 12, 1927, the British Home Secretary, after consulting the Foreign Secretary, Sir Austen Chamberlain, authorized a police search of the premises of Arcos Ltd., a branch of the Soviet trade delegation in London. Arcos and the Soviet trade delegation occupied offices in the same building, known as Soviet House. Under

[7] *A Selection of Papers Dealing with the Relations between His Majesty's Government and the Soviet Government, 1921–1927* (Cmd. 2895), pp. 45–50.

[8] Kliuchnikov and Sabanin, III, 366–69.

[9] *Izvestiia*, No. 90, April 20, 1927, pp. 1–2; see Document 123.

the commercial treaty of 1921 between Great Britain and the U.S.S.R., the chief of the Soviet trade delegation enjoyed diplomatic immunity and the right to use code. Arcos, however, had no such immunity. The British justified the search of May 12 on the ground that a confidential document relating to the armed forces of Great Britain[10] had been taken into the Arcos building and there photostated for transmission to the Soviet government.

On May 16 the British government announced that although the police had not found the missing document, they had found abundant proof of the existence of a vast Soviet espionage organization, enough to justify severing relations with the Soviet Union.

The Soviet government protested the raid and demanded to know whether Great Britain desired to continue diplomatic and trade relations, on the basis of strict observance of the trade agreement and noninterference with Soviet economic organs in Britain.[11]

On May 24, 1927, the British prime minister informally answered the Soviet question in a speech in the House of Commons. Evidence in British hands, he said, revealed that Soviet agents, under orders from the Russian trade delegation, were trying to get confidential documents relating to Great Britain's armed forces. Documents found during the Arcos raid proved the existence of a regular system for conveying subversive documents secretly from various organizations in Russia to communist agents in Great Britain and elsewhere, and showed conclusively that military espionage and subversive activities throughout the British Empire and North and South America were directed and carried out from Soviet House. He added that no distinction could be discovered between members of the trade delegation and employees of Arcos, that both organizations appeared to be involved in anti-British espionage and propaganda, and that the Soviet trade delegation was thus breaking the agreements under which it had been received in Great Britain. His government, therefore, would terminate the trade agreement and require the withdrawal of the trade delegation and the Soviet mission. However, rather than end trade relations and recall the British mission from Moscow, the prime minister was prepared to make arrangements for continuing ordinary trade between the two countries.[12]

In the debate that followed Mr. Baldwin's speech, Liberal and Labour spokesmen naïvely took the line that the Arcos raid had revealed more smoke than fire, and that the subversive and espionage activities attributed to the Soviet officials were similar to activities carried on by other governments, including that of Great Britain.

On May 26 a formal note from the British government to the Soviet government terminated the trade agreement of March 1921, suspended diplomatic relations between the two governments, and asked Soviet diplomatic and trade representatives to leave the country.[13] They complied, after being given a lunch-

---

[10] For communist approval of propaganda among the armed forces of foreign countries, see Document 101.

[11] *Anglo-sovetskie otnosheniia*, pp. 116–20; see Document 124.

[12] The British prime minister's statement on the termination of trade agreements with Soviet Russia, May 24, 1927. *Debates 1927* (Great Britain, House of Commons, Fifth Series, Vol. 206), pp. 1842–49.

[13] *A Selection of Papers Dealing with the Relations between His Majesty's Government and the Soviet Government, 1921–1927* (Cmd. 2895), pp. 69–70.

eon in the House of Commons by members of the Labour Party. The break was not as complete as it appeared to be: Arcos Ltd. and "a reasonable number" of its personnel were permitted to remain in England to carry out "legitimate commercial operations." The British government, however, reserved the right to choose which employees might remain.[14]

The Soviet leaders explained to the peoples of Russia that the British action was no surprise, and that it must be regarded, as Litvinov put it, "as an energetic preparation for war."[15] The Moscow soviet said that the British government had been inspired by "class hatred for the first proletarian state," and a desire to form a "united counterrevolutionary front of capitalist powers against the Soviet Union."[16] In the face of this alleged war threat, the Moscow soviet called on all Russian people to work harder, consolidate relations with the workers and oppressed peoples of all countries, support every measure of the Soviet government, and buy more state bonds. Protest meetings were organized and the Russian people were treated to a mild war scare. The Soviets took the opportunity to denounce the Social Democrats and the nearly defunct Second International and to send warm greetings to the toilers of China. The government seized the occasion to arrest and liquidate a number of persons suspected of espionage.

France: Tsarist Debts and the Rakovsky Affair

Although the French government had recognized the U.S.S.R. *de jure* in October 1924, the two governments' differences remained. The French continued to press for Soviet recognition of tsarist debts, and the Communists continued to refuse to consider such recognition except in conjunction with new loans.

Informal discussions of the debt and loan question went on intermittently through 1925. Chicherin reached an understanding with Briand concerning political relations in general, a possible commercial treaty, and a conference to discuss debts and credits in February 1926.

As February approached, it became apparent that French financial opinion was divided. One group was willing to agree to the Soviet demands for long-term credits if, in return, the Soviet government would grant large-scale petroleum concessions in the Caucasus. A second group, which included the National Association of Russian Bondholders, objected that the Soviet plan to repay debts out of surplus profits from nationalized industry, after using French credits to help restore that industry, was entirely unworkable. This group insisted that the nationalized property be restored to its former owners.

The Franco-Soviet conference opened February 25, 1926, and dragged on until July, but little was accomplished. In mid-July it was announced that no basis for agreement had been found and that further discussion would be postponed until autumn. By the following March, when negotiations were at last reopened, tension in Franco-Soviet relations had so greatly increased that the talks were soon suspended. The Anglo-Soviet break seems to have contributed

[14] *Ibid.*, p. 70.

[15] *Pravda*, No. 117, May 26, 1927, p. 1; see Document 125.

[16] A. I. Rykov, *Angliia s SSSR; doklad na plenume moskovskogo soveta l iiunia 1927 g.*, p. 44; see Document 126.

something to the failure of the talks; the activities of French Communists and the ensuing reaction of the French government contributed even more. Most damaging of all was the action of the Soviet ambassador to France, Rakovsky, who signed on August 9, 1927, a declaration of the Trotsky opposition calling for the "defeat of all the bourgeois states that carry on war against the Soviet Union."[17]

The French government protested, and after an exchange of notes between the two governments, Rakovsky was replaced in October 1927 by V. S. Dovgalevsky, the former Soviet ambassador to Japan.

Poland: the Pilsudski Coup

Soviet relations with Poland, never cordial, were worse than usual in 1926. In May of that year, Josef Pilsudski took control of the Polish government by a *coup d'état*. The Polish Communists indirectly supported him by helping the armed forces of the insurgents rather than attempting to assume leadership of the masses themselves. In commenting upon the fact that the revolutionary-minded workers and peasants of Poland rallied to Pilsudski rather than to the Polish Communist Party, Stalin remarked on June 10: "The Polish Communist Party has been weak, very weak, and it became still weaker in this struggle by its incorrect support of Pilsudski's troops. [By taking an] unrevolutionary position . . . our Polish comrades have actually made a very grave mistake."[18]

Soviet-Polish relations were also aggravated by the Soviet-Lithuanian non-aggression treaty of September 28, 1926, in which, by inference, the Soviet government recognized the city of Vilna as part of Lithuania, although it was at that time not only claimed but occupied by Poland.

While Poland and the U.S.S.R. were discussing a neutrality and nonaggression treaty, the Soviet ambassador to Poland, P. L. Voikov, was assassinated by a young Russian emigré, Boris Kowerda. In the ensuing exchange of notes, the Soviets blamed the Polish government for not breaking up a terrorist organization to which the assassin was alleged to have belonged,[19] but on the whole the incident was discussed with remarkable restraint on both sides. The treaty talks went on, and on September 27, 1927, the Polish foreign ministry stated officially that agreement had been reached on certain points.[20] Some years were to pass, however, and substantial changes were to take place in the international scene before Poland and Soviet Russia finally completed a nonaggression treaty in 1932.

Soviet efforts to conclude neutrality and nonaggression pacts with the Baltic countries have been mentioned elsewhere.[21] After Russia's rejection of the principle of a multipartite pact, advanced jointly by Latvia, Estonia, and Finland on May 5, 1926, these countries agreed reluctantly in August of the same year to conduct separate negotiations. Negotiations with Finland, however, broke down on November 24, 1926, and Russo-Estonian negotiations were also soon suspended. A Russo-Latvian neutrality treaty was initialed in 1927, but not

---

[17] Text in *L'Europe nouvelle*, No. 504, October 8, 1927, p. 1353.

[18] Stalin, *Sochineniia*, VIII, 171–72.

[19] Text of correspondence between the two governments appears in *Kliuchnikov and Sabanin*, III, 385–89.

[20] *Le Temps*, September 29, 1927.

[21] See Part IV, pp. 280–82.

formally signed. Instead, the Latvian government sent a delegation to Moscow to negotiate a commercial treaty, which was duly signed on June 2, 1927.[22]

World Economic Conference

In spite of the generally increased tension in Soviet diplomatic relations with the Western powers and the accompanying Soviet fear of renewed intervention, the U.S.S.R. continued to participate in international gatherings. In 1927 Soviet delegates attended two important international conferences called by the League of Nations: the World Economic Conference and the Preparatory Commission for the Disarmament Conference.

The World Economic Conference—a renewed attempt to find some solution of the general economic problems growing out of World War I—was proposed by France at the sixth assembly of the League, September 26, 1925:

The Assembly, Firmly resolved to seek all possible means of establishing peace throughout the world; Convinced that economic peace will largely contribute to security among the nations; Persuaded of the necessity of investigating the economic difficulties which stand in the way of the revival of general prosperity, and ascertaining the best means of overcoming these difficulties and of preventing disputes; Invites the Council to consider at the earliest possible moment the expediency of constituting on a wide basis a Preparatory Committee which, with the assistance of the Technical Organizations of the League and the International Labour Office, will prepare the work of an International Economic Conference.[23]

The conference, which convened at Geneva on May 4, 1927, was attended by 194 delegates and 226 experts from member and nonmember states. The Soviet delegates expected little; *Izvestiia* stated flatly that "the world economy cannot be cured by such means." Moreover, said *Izvestiia*, Soviet participation in the conference did not indicate Russia's willingness to back down on economic matters; no such concessions would be made and the Soviet monopoly of foreign trade would be maintained.[24]

During the conference sessions, Soviet spokesmen stressed that the contradictions inherent in world capitalism made for a constant world crisis, with acute phases taking the form of revolutions and armed conflicts and less acute phases marked by a gradual growth of trusts and monopolies. This being so, said the Soviet delegates, the only hope lay in change to a socialist system.

By way of further political propaganda the Soviet delegation introduced a number of proposals, most of which, had they been adopted, would have been as unacceptable to the Soviet Union as to the rest of the assembled powers. They suggested that the powers cancel war debts, raise industrial wages, introduce a six-hour day in mines and an eight-hour day in general, recognize the right of free association and the right to strike, introduce a system of real and effective assistance for the unemployed, prohibit price raising by cartels, remove barriers to the migration of surplus populations, abolish protectorates and mandates and introduce self-determination in political and economic life, end

[22] Text of this treaty appears in Shapiro, I, 333–36.

[23] *Report and Proceedings of the World Economic Conference Held at Geneva, May 4th to 23rd, 1927*, I, 3. (Cited hereafter as *World Economic Conference, Geneva, 1927*.)

[24] *Izvestiia*, No. 97, April 30, 1927, p. 1.

military intervention in China, end the economic and political boycott of the Soviet Union, and undertake total disarmament.[25]

Although the Soviet delegation abstained from voting on the proposals adopted by the conference, it nevertheless characterized the conference as a step toward the "practical realization" of the Soviet formula on "the *de facto* co-existence of the two systems and the structural links which exist in the world economic system."[26]

The Preparatory Commission on Disarmament

From 1927 on, the Soviet government also participated in the Preparatory Commission for the Disarmament Conference. Since its inception the League had been concerned with the problems of disarmament and security. As previously noted,[27] a draft of a guarantee pact, known as the "Geneva Protocol for the Pacific Settlement of International Disputes," had been prepared in September 1924 by the fourth and confirmed by the fifth assembly of the League on October 2, 1924, but owing to the opposition of the British government, it had never been put into effect.

On September 25, 1925, at the League's sixth assembly, methods of disarmament were again discussed. Again it was a question of priorities—should disarmament come before security or security before disarmament? This time the Assembly tried to deal with the two problems simultaneously. It directed the League Council "to make a preparatory study with a view to a Conference for the Reduction and Limitation of Armaments, in order that, as soon as satisfactory conditions have been assured from the point of view of general security . . . the said Conference may be convened and a general reduction and limitation of armaments may be realised."[28]

Accordingly, on December 12, 1925, the League Council set up the machinery for establishing an organization to study the problem—the Preparatory Commission for the Disarmament Conference. Delegates were invited to participate in the commission's deliberations from the ten states represented on the Council; from the then non-League states of Germany, the United States, and the U.S.S.R.; and from certain other states whose geographical position or other special circumstances warranted their inclusion, namely, Bulgaria, Finland, Yugoslavia, the Netherlands, Poland, and Rumania.

Although scheduled to meet on February 15, 1926, the Preparatory Commission did not actually convene until May 18, 1927. By the end of January, 1927, all invited governments except the U.S.S.R. had indicated their willingness to send delegates. The U.S.S.R., although willing in principle to participate, said it would send a delegation only if the meetings were held outside of Switzerland. The stipulation was the result of Swiss-Soviet differences follow-

25 *World Economic Conference, Geneva, 1927*, I, 129; see Document 128.

26 *Ibid.*, p. 165; see Document 129.

27 See Part IV, pp. 270–71.

28 *Documents of the Preparatory Commission for the Disarmament Conference Entrusted With the Preparation of the Conference for the Reduction and Limitation of Armaments*, Series I, p. 5. (Cited hereafter as *Preparatory Commission for the Disarmament Conference*.)

ing the assassination of V. V. Vorovsky, the Soviet representative at the Lausanne Conference.[29]

The commission's first session was held in Geneva (May 18–26, 1927). Soviet delegates did not participate, nor, in fact, did they join the deliberations until November, by which time the difficulty with Switzerland had been settled.

In the meantime, Rykov repeated the Russian Communists' view of the League of Nations to the Fourth Congress of Soviets of the U.S.S.R. in April 1927. He characterized the League as merely "an instrument in the hands of a small group of some of the biggest imperialist states for supremacy over the other states," and the disarmament conference as a conference "on how to preserve, with the least possible expenditure, the military supremacy of those countries that now dominate the world."[30] He reaffirmed the Soviet position, with which no other government agreed, that only total disarmament could accomplish the desired objectives.

Karl Radek added other Soviet explanations of the origin of the League's disarmament commission:

. . . the serious financial situation of all the European states, the impossibility of satisfying the minimum social demands of the working masses, is compelling the governments to flirt with the idea of the reduction of armaments. Pacifist hypocrisy is the political weapon of all bourgeois governments. In addition to this, none of them would be sorry to see a reduction of the armaments of others.

The League had convoked the commission, said Radek, because England and France wanted to frustrate an American scheme to increase American strength by using the pressure of indebtedness to force the European powers to disarm. Furthermore, the commission's sessions were held on Swiss soil with the specific intent of keeping the Soviets from attending, because the Great Powers wanted to conceal "the role of the Soviet Union as the only fighter for the emancipation of humanity from the burden of armaments."[31]

The Soviet-Swiss incident was resolved in time for the Soviet government to send a delegation to the commission's fourth session. On November 30, 1927, shortly after the Soviet delegation arrived, Litvinov, its head, introduced a proposal for total disarmament, reiterating the Soviet view that "under the capitalist system no grounds exist for counting upon the removal of the causes giving rise to armed conflicts. Militarism and navalism are essentially natural consequences of the capitalist system." He justified Soviet participation in the commission's sessions on the ground that "the people in all countries, however enfeebled and impoverished by the imperialist world-war of 1914–18, are imbued with the determination to struggle against imperialist wars and for the guaranteeing of peace between nations." He went on to say that by participating the Soviet government "demonstrates in the face of the whole world its will to peace between the nations and desires to make clear to all the real inspirations and true desires of the other States with regard to disarmament."

Condemning as "Utopianism" the commission's attempt to link disarmament

[29] See our p. 223. The invitation to the U.S.S.R. was sent by the Secretary General of the League of Nations on December 12, 1925. The Russian reply of January 16, 1926, is given in *The Soviet Union and Peace* . . . , pp. 128–30.

[30] *Izvestiia*, No. 90, April 20, 1927, p. 2; see Document 131.

[31] Karl Radek, "The Disarmament Conference," *International Press Correspondence*, No. 10, January 28, 1926, pp. 133–34.

and security guarantees, Litvinov declared that such an approach, by evoking endless and fruitless arguments on so-called military potential, would indefinitely postpone the fundamental discussion of the actual dimensions of disarmament. He proposed "the complete abolition of all land, naval and air forces" within a year after the disarmament conference. He further proposed destroying all military supplies, discontinuing military training, destroying fortresses and naval and air bases, scrapping all war industry, discontinuing all military appropriations, breaking up all military staffs, prohibiting all military propaganda and education, prohibiting the right to patent military weapons, and withdrawing or altering any legislative acts, either national or international, that might infringe any of these stipulations.

Litvinov added that in the event the proposal for immediate abolition of all armed forces was rejected, the Soviet government "is prepared to make a proposal for complete disarmament to be carried out simultaneously by all contracting States, by gradual stages, during a period of four years, the first stage to be accomplished in the course of the coming year."[32]

Answering for the majority of the commission, Paul-Boncour of France said in effect that this Soviet proposal was too simple to be sound. Total disarmament without any other provisions

would always leave the small nations at the mercy of the great ones. Supposing you had total disarmament, if there were no international organization taking charge of security, if you had no international force to ensure the maintenance of this security, if you had no international law such as we are endeavouring to lay down here, a powerful and populous nation with great resources would always have the means of imposing its will, when it wished to do so, on a small nation—equally disarmed, but less populous and less well-equipped to resist an attack which might be made upon it. . . . Accordingly, the last Assembly decided to link more closely . . . the work of security with the work of disarmament. . . . The day when you admit . . . that we cannot effect an international reduction of armaments without an international organisation for security, the co-operation of the great country which you represent in this positive work of the international organisation of security will give an impetus to our labours which will put them above all criticism.[33]

Beneš of Czechoslovakia pointed out that Litvinov's proposals actually contained nothing new, that the League had discussed the question of total disarmament at length in 1921 and 1922. He suggested, therefore, that the conference "should proceed to the execution of the task which has been entrusted to us by the Assembly and constitute the Committee on Arbitration and Security."[34] Soviet delegates did not join this committee, but agreed to attend as observers.

At the fourth meeting of the fifth session of the commission, March 20, 1928, Lord Cushendun replied in detail to Litvinov's proposal for total disarmament:

Complete and general disarmament has been an ideal of mankind since the dawn of history, and, I say, as a general proposition I certainly am in favour of it. But if it comes to the question: Is it practicable? Can it be done now, in the existing condition of the world and having a view of realities—then I am bound to express very profound doubt, and I say that that is a question which deserves and must have examination in detail.

[32] *Preparatory Commission for the Disarmament Conference*, Series V, pp. 9–12; see Document 132.
[33] *Ibid.*, p. 14.
[34] *Ibid.*, p. 15.

He questioned the spirit in which the Soviet government sent delegates to the conference, and referred to the Soviets' scornful attitude toward the League of Nations during its seven years of existence. Without absolutely rejecting the proposals, he made it clear that they required "the most careful, laborious and detailed examination."[35] The other speakers also emphasized that the claims of security should be considered simultaneously with the requirements of disarmament. The Soviet representatives, despite the rejection of their plan for total disarmament, continued to participate in the work of the commission.

When the commission planned to create a security committee to consider disarmament in relation to security, Litvinov repeated that this would merely postpone the real work of disarmament.[36] Back home late in 1927, Litvinov reported in detail to the Fifteenth Party Congress on the commission's work, concluding with the familiar communist dogma that "complete disarmament and the end of wars can come only from the soviet state, and can be accepted and carried out only when the soviet system has spread to other states of the world, because then the principles that now guide the U.S.S.R. will form the basis of the policy of these states as well."[37]

Stalin was even more emphatic. Reporting to the Fifteenth Party Congress in the name of the Central Committee of the party, he declared that the League-sponsored discussions of peace and disarmament had accomplished nothing except to deceive the masses, promote the growth of new armaments, and speed up and accentuate conflicts. In this speech he also gave a new official communist interpretation of the world situation. The era of "peace policy" and "disarmament policy" in the West had come to an end, and the temporary stabilization of capitalism was giving way to a period in which new imperialist wars and new revolutionary upheavals were inevitable.[38]

Behind Soviet hostility toward the work of the Preparatory Commission, with its emphasis on relating national security to disarmament, was, of course, the Soviet desire to overthrow rather than to preserve the post-Versailles status quo in Europe. An editorial in *Izvestiia* put it this way:

The essence of the French theory concerning the necessity of creating security guarantees *before* disarming expresses the tendency to obtain by every available means a guarantee of the post-Versailles status quo in Europe, a state of affairs established by the peace treaties and by the entire network of conventions worked out by French diplomacy. Therefore, any additional "guarantee of security" means the consolidation of French hegemony on the European continent.[39]

Soviet leaders, while advocating disarmament without security guarantees, continued their efforts to provide for their own security through bilateral guarantees of neutrality and nonaggression. Further, they continued to press for the settlement of international disputes through courts of conciliation without recourse to arbitration, a principle they thoroughly distrusted.

Later Soviet efforts in the direction of disarmament and peace lie beyond the scope of this book. It should be added, however, that the Preparatory Commission rejected not only Litvinov's plan of total disarmament, but also his al-

---

[35] *Preparatory Commission for the Disarmament Conference*, Series VI, pp. 245–46.
[36] Text of Litvinov's speech appears in *ibid.*, pp. 268–76.
[37] *XV sezd Vsesoiuznoi Kommunnisticheskoi Partii (B). Stenograficheskii otchet*, p. 954 (cited hereafter as *XV sezd V.K.P.*). See Document 133.
[38] *XV sezd V.K.P.*, pp. 42–43, 46; see Document 134.
[39] *Izvestiia*, No. 17, January 20, 1928, p. 1.

ternative proposal of a four-year gradual disarmament, the latter on the ground that it failed to provide security. Nevertheless, when the disarmament conference itself was finally held in Geneva in 1932, the Soviet government actively participated in it.

The Kellogg-Briand Pact

A few words must also be said about the Soviet attitude toward the Kellogg-Briand Pact to outlaw war, though the pact itself is beyond our chronological limits. On June 20, 1927, Aristide Briand, then French foreign minister, proposed to the United States the conclusion of a bilateral treaty, with Article I reading as follows: "The high contracting powers solemnly declare, in the name of the French people and the people of the United States of America, that they condemn recourse to war and renounce it respectively as an instrument of their national policy towards each other."[40] In reply, on December 28, 1927, Secretary of State Kellogg suggested that this pact be multilateral. After some negotiations the pact was signed on August 27, 1928, by Germany, the United States, Belgium, France, Great Britain and the Dominions, Italy, Japan, Poland, and Czechoslovakia.[41] Moscow naturally did not overlook the omission of Russia's name from the list of states invited to participate in later general negotiations. On August 5, 1928, Chicherin offered this explanation:

The exclusion of the Soviet government from these negotiations leads us, in the first place, to the assumption that among the real objectives of the initiators of this pact there obviously was and is an endeavor to make of this pact a weapon for isolating and fighting the Soviet Union. The negotiations regarding the conclusion of the Kellogg Pact are obviously an integral part of the policy of encircling the Soviet Union, which at the present moment occupies the central point of the international relations of the whole world.[42]

The Soviet leaders also criticized the wording of the pact for not going far enough in the renunciation of war and for failing to cover all methods of aggression. Nevertheless, Russia expressed its desire to join the pact and later did so.

Disarmament and the Territorial Militia Program

During these years in which communist leaders had been urging total disarmament abroad, at home they had been engaged in working out a long-range program—military, industrial, and agricultural—for almost total armament. Radical changes were to be introduced into every phase of Soviet life. All available and reliable workers and peasants were to be trained and organized into a territorial militia army; industrial production was to be brought under over-all five-year plans, and agricultural production was to be collectivized. At the Third Congress of Soviets of the U.S.S.R., on May 19, 1925, M. V. Frunze, People's Commissar for Military and Naval Affairs, said of this broad scheme:

We must have an army such as can protect the frontiers of Soviet territory on all sectors and from all directions in the event of a serious encounter. In practice this means that a system of defense is necessary such as would enable the entire mass of toilers capable of bearing arms to take the field. . . . We must construct the eco-

40 *The General Pact for the Renunciation of War. Text of the Pact as Signed. Notes and Other Papers,* p. 4.
41 For the text see *ibid.,* pp. 1–3.
42 *Izvestiia,* No. 181, August 5, 1928, p. 1.

nomic system of our country and direct our economics in both the industrial and the agricultural field in such a way as will meet the needs of defense. Every one of our enterprises, or groups of enterprises in the form of trusts, should calculate the necessities of defense when organizing its peacetime production, and should build up its economic system so that it will be easier to change over to supplying the needs of a future army of many millions in wartime.[43]

Dedicated as they were to promoting revolution abroad and building up defensive strength at home, the Communists were disposed rather to increase than to reduce the armed strength of the Soviet state. But disarmament, like peace, was a popular cause among the war-weary. For this reason, and because they would have been glad to see their enemies disarm, the Communists committed themselves to advocating total disarmament. The Western powers, moreover, had some difficulty explaining why they did not at once accept so simple and appealing a proposal.

The Soviet leaders next had to reconcile their advocacy of disarmament with their obvious intention of increasing their military potential—hence the expedient of a territorial militia. In this way they could cry up decreases in the strength of the Red Army, while training every reliable element in the population to take part in the national preparedness program. Frunze frankly discussed the political aspects of this policy on February 27, 1925:

The expansion of our armed forces is possible only by increasing the cadres of our regular army or by developing the militia system. For both financial and political reasons the first method is closed to us. . . . One reason for our strength and our moral influence in the eyes of millions of workers and peasants abroad is their absolute faith in the peaceful nature of our military policy. . . . If we were to increase the permanent numerical strength of our regular army, we would give our enemies a strong weapon, the "threat of Soviet imperialism," with which to intimidate their own petty bourgeoisie and perhaps even some proletarian elements. . . . I consider it politically inexpedient to provide food for such agitation . . . Therefore the numerical increase of our regular forces is, in my estimation, absolutely out of the question. There remains another way—expanding the militia. We are doing this, and shall go on doing it. Every year our militia organization will become more and more the basis of [our] revolutionary forces.[44]

That the Soviet government hoped, by expanding the territorial militia, ultimately to militarize the entire nation was clearly stated by another Red Army leader, I. S. Unschlicht, in an address delivered on February 23, 1927, the ninth anniversary of the founding of the Red Army:

Our military slogan of the day is as follows:

Mass propaganda and diffusion of military knowledge and habits among the entire population of the country, the effecting of close contact between the Red Army and the population, the militarization of the entire population of the country.

The territorial system is the basis for implementing this slogan. . . .

The broad participation of the toilers of the Union in defense work and socialist reconstruction under the leadership of the Leninist party will guarantee the victory of the Red Army over the capitalist armies, and the victory of socialism.

The Red Army now faces its last task, which is to serve as a bulwark for the coming socialist revolution in Europe.[45]

[43] M. V. Frunze, *Sobranie sochinenii*, III, 219.

[44] *Ibid.*, p. 136; see Document 136.

[45] *Izvestiia*, No. 44, February 23, 1927, p. 1; see Document 137.

The idea of training a whole population as a territorial militia was not new to communist ideology, as Frunze pointed out in 1925:

As for the interpretation of the principles of militia organization, we have the opinions of our outstanding Marxists. In particular, the late member of the German Social Democratic Party, Mehring, and Friedrich Engels were interested in this question. Their writings supply sufficiently exhaustive interpretation of the principles of militia organization.[46]

The Second Congress of the Russian Social Democratic Labor Party in 1903 had also advocated the substitution of a people's militia for a standing army.[47] So-called Red Guard units were formed in certain factories after the Bolshevik revolution in 1917, and for a short time a militia system was contemplated. But for military and political reasons during the civil war a standing Red Army was organized under Trotsky's direction, and no changes in this system were proposed until 1924, when Trotsky was replaced as People's Commissar for Military and Naval Affairs by Frunze, an Old Bolshevik and a civil war commander. As early as March 1919, the Eighth Party Congress had passed a resolution advocating the creation of a territorial militia and linking this with planned economic developments:

Theoretically it may be regarded as indisputable that the best army is one formed on the basis of the obligatory training of workers and toiling peasants under conditions close to their daily work. The general improvement of industry, the improvement of industrial production, and the increase of collective methods and production in agriculture would provide the sanest basis for the organization of the army: companies, battalions, regiments, brigades, divisions would coincide with workshops, factories, villages, cantons, counties, provinces, etc. An army of that nature, the organization of which would proceed side by side with the economic development of the country and the parallel training of the commanding personnel, would become the most invincible army in the world. It is for such an army that we are striving, and it is such an army that sooner or later we shall have.[48]

Frunze himself was a proponent of the militia system, but he was also enough of a realist to advocate a slow transition to that system.

By 1925, however, he felt the time for large-scale transition to a territorial militia organization had come. On February 27, 1925, he said:

I believe that the psychological moment has arrived for us to be completely reconstructed on a new basis. Our Red Army should no longer be considered a regular Red army, but an armed nation of workers and peasants, who are duty-bound and ready to bear arms and fight the enemy at any moment. This should be our psychological mood and the mood that we should bring about among our workers' and peasants' masses.[49]

He also believed that Russia had "a number of the prerequisites for a militia army" of which Engels and Mehring had spoken: "Power is now in the hands of the working class. The most important means of production are in the hands of the state. The state, in control of the apparatus of persuasion, both political

[46] M. V. Frunze, *Sobranie sochinenii*, III, 135.
[47] Point 12 of the program of the Russian Social Democratic Labor Party, adopted at the party's Second Congress, July–August, 1903. *V.K.P. v rezoliutsiiakh*, I, 22.
[48] *Vosmoi sezd R.K.P.*, pp. 403–4.
[49] M. K. Frunze, *Sobranie sochinenii*, III, 137–38; see Document 136.

and cultural, can mold public opinion and influence the psychology of the toiling masses." In elaborating his views, Frunze made a significant reference to the relation of collectivized agriculture to military preparedness: "Our agriculture has produced only the embryo of collective forms of economic management. In the main, the individual farm still predominates in our country. This state of our agriculture does not provide the collective spirit and discipline that we need."[50]

Tukhachevsky, the hero of the Polish war and chief of staff of the Red Army and Red Navy, mentioned other advantages of the territorial militia system to the Soviets:

It enables the State to provide the large number of toilers with military training with the expenditure of minimum funds. . . . The territorial system in the hands of the Soviet state is a powerful lever for reinforcing Lenin's chief watchword of an alliance of workers and peasants and for getting Party and Soviet influence to reach the wide masses of toilers.[51]

The industrial and agricultural phases of the long-contemplated domestic reorganization, aimed at building up the economic power and industrial potential of the Soviet Union, were officially presented at the Fifteenth Party Congress in December 1927. By this time the territorial militia system was well established. It was at this Fifteenth Party Congress that the first over-all Five-Year Plan for industrial development was introduced and the plan for the future collectivization of agriculture detailed.

The First Five-Year Plan

The Five-Year Plan for industrialization had been worked out over a period of years by the Gosplan, the State Planning Commission, and was introduced to the congress by its director, G. M. Krzhizhanovsky. After reviewing Soviet economic reconstruction and describing the N.E.P. as correct for the period it covered, he stated that the Five-Year Plan would increase Soviet industrial production by 82 to 100 percent by 1931. Of the drafting of the plan he said: "Here we find not merely the work of State Planning Commission people working out state plans, but the embodiment of the efforts of thousands of industrial administrators in all our republics throughout the country." Of the plan's objectives and its operation, he declared: ". . . the plan must not become bureaucratic; it must give the necessary chances for economic maneuvers, particularly for the republics and economic districts. . . . The plan will decisively and finally overcome anarchy in all spheres of the economy."[52]

The Five-Year Plan also dealt with the defense of the country. "I believe," said K. E. Voroshilov, who succeeded Frunze in 1925 as People's Commissar for Military and Naval Affairs, in his report to the congress, "that it has now become a well-known truth that mankind is facing an inevitable new world slaughter. Therefore, in outlining our five-year plan, we are duty-bound to accept the necessity of building our defense." Having discussed at some length

[50] *Ibid.*, pp. 135–36.
[51] M. N. Tukhatchevsky (Tukhachevsky), "The Territorial System in the Red Army," *International Press Correspondence*, No. 66, October 14, 1926, p. 1126.
[52] *XV sezd V.K.P.*, pp. 794, 807.

the measures taken and the preparedness for war achieved by other countries, he added:

In view of these facts . . . we must on no account treat lightly the question of defending our country and preparing our entire economy for defense. We shall continue, of course, our firm policy of peace. The Soviet Union does not need war; our interests require peaceful work for the development of our national economy. Nevertheless, the Soviet Union should be always ready to parry the imperialist attack . . . In comparison with capitalist countries, we have one very considerable advantage, a planned economy. . . . But our disadvantage lies in the fact that we are extremely poor.

Having analyzed the need of developing various branches of Soviet industries, Voroshilov summed up as follows:

In addition to the five-year plan for economic construction, we have a five-year plan for building up our armed forces. This plan stresses a great increase in the technical resources of the Red Army. The number of men in the armed forces remains the same. The increase in the budget for the army is used exclusively for technical resources and supplies . . . Our chief aim and the basic purpose of the five-year plan is to raise the technical power of the Red Army to the level of the first-class modern armies.[53]

The Fifteenth Party Congress

The Fifteenth Party Congress met in an atmosphere of increasing tension in Soviet foreign relations. Soviet leaders appeared to believe that the breathing space was drawing to an end, although the danger of attack was doubtless played up to prepare the country for the strain of the Five-Year Plan or to justify the expulsions from the party. Trotsky and Zinoviev were expelled; Rakovsky, Radek, Kamenev, and other Old Bolsheviks were slated for expulsion but recanted their heresies. Stalin was not yet ready to deal with the so-called "Right Deviationists"—Bukharin, Tomsky, and Rykov.

In his political report to the congress, Stalin declared that the "crisis of capitalism, resulting from the victorious October Revolution . . . , is not only not overcome but becoming more intense." Europe was "definitely entering a phase of new revolutionary upheaval," there was a "revival of interventionist tendencies among the imperialists," and "the policy of isolating and encircling the U.S.S.R." was everywhere in evidence. He explained that because the British bourgeoisie were the most threatened by revolution, Britain had taken the initiative in encouraging intervention. Happily, Great Britain's aggressive intentions conflicted wth a more conciliatory point of view represented by several other countries, and this conflict had prevented Great Britain from organizing a united front against the Soviets, if only temporarily.

In the light of the war menace Stalin urged the Communists to make the most of the contradictions among the capitalists, to postpone war by paying them off, and to "take all measures to preserve peaceful relations." He referred to Lenin's statement that in building socialism "much depends on how well we succeed in delaying war with the capitalist world. Such a war is inevitable, but it can be delayed either until the proletarian revolution in Europe has matured, or until the colonial revolutions have fully ripened, or, finally, until the capitalists

[53]*Ibid.*, pp. 868, 874, 876, 885; see also Document 138.

have plunged into war among themselves for the repartition of the colonies."
While urging the temporary preservation of peaceful relations with the capitalist
world, Stalin reiterated his theory of the possibility of the coexistence of capitalism and communism. "The basis of our relations with the capitalist countries
is the admission of the coexistence of two fundamentally different systems."[54]

In the same report Stalin also outlined the "party line" on the international
revolutionary movement and on foreign policy.

Hence, the tasks of the party are:

1. Along the lines of the international revolutionary movement—
(*a*) A struggle for the development of the communist parties throughout the
world;
(*b*) A struggle for the consolidation of the revolutionary trade unions and the
united front of the workers against the capitalist offensive;
(*c*) A struggle for strengthening the friendship between the working class of
the U.S.S.R. and the working class of the capitalist countries;
(*d*) A struggle for a stronger alliance between the working class of the U.S.S.R.
and the liberation movement of the colonial countries.
2. Along the lines of U.S.S.R. foreign policy—
(*a*) A struggle against the preparation of new imperialist wars;
(*b*) A struggle against the interventionist tendencies of Britain and a strengthening of the defensive capacity of the U.S.S.R.
(*c*) A peace policy and the preservation of peaceful relations with the capitalist
countries;
(*d*) An extension of our trade relations with the outside world on the basis of
the consolidation of the foreign trade monopoly;
(*e*) Rapprochement with the so-called weak and unequal countries, which are
suffering from the oppression and exploitation of the dominating imperialist powers.[55]

Somewhat earlier, on the occasion of the tenth anniversary of the October
Revolution (November 1927), Stalin had spoken of that revolution's "world
significance," declaring that it not only had ushered in a new era of colonial
revolutions, but also had created

a powerful and open center for the world revolutionary movement, a center such as
it never possessed before and around which it can now rally and organize a united
revolutionary front of the proletarians and the oppressed peoples of all countries
against imperialism.
This means . . . that the October Revolution has inflicted a mortal wound on
world capitalism, a wound from which the latter will never recover. . . . Capitalism
may become partially stabilized; it may rationalize production, turn over the administration of the country to fascism, temporarily hold down the working class;
but it will never recover the "tranquillity," the "assurance," the "equilibrium," and
the "stability" that it flaunted before; for in the crisis now reached by world capitalism the flames of revolution must inevitably break out—now in the centers of imperialism, now on the periphery—reducing to naught the capitalist patchwork and
daily bringing nearer the fall of capitalism.[56]

[54] *Ibid.*, pp. 45–47; see Document 143.
[55] *Ibid.*, pp. 48–49.
[56] Stalin, *Sochineniia*, X, 239–46; see Document 140.

DOCUMENTS

THE DISINTEGRATION OF CAPITALISM AND THE
TASKS OF SOVIET DIPLOMACY

118

Stalin on the International Significance of Building
Socialism in One Country

[Report to the Seventh Enlarged Plenum of the ECCI, December 7, 1926][1]

. . .

2. *The Factors of the* Peredyshka [*Breathing Space*]

The second question concerns the present international position of the U.S.S.R., the conditions of the *peredyshka* during which the work of establishing socialism has begun in our country. We can and must establish socialism, but in order to do so we must exist, and to exist we need a *peredyshka*. . . . We require certain minimum international conditions in order to exist and build socialism.

What, then, is the basis of the present international position of the republic of soviets? What determines the present "peaceful" period of development of our country in its relations with capitalist countries? What is this *peredyshka* based upon? If the danger of intervention exists and will continue to exist, if it can be removed only by the victory of the proletarian revolution in a number of countries, then what sustains the *peredyshka*—what deters the capitalist world from serious intervention and creates the necessary conditions for building socialism in our country?

The present *peredyshka* is based on at least four fundamental facts.

First, the antagonisms in the camp of the imperialists, which continue to remain acute and make it difficult for them to come to an understanding directed against the republic of soviets.

Second, the antagonisms between imperialism and the colonial countries; the growth of the movement for liberation in the colonial and dependent countries.

Third, the growth of the revolutionary movement in the capitalist countries and the growing sympathy of the proletarians of all countries for the republic of soviets. The proletariat in capitalist countries is as yet unable to support the proletariat in the U.S.S.R. by direct revolution against the capitalists, but the capitalists of imperialist states are already unable to move their workers against the proletariat of the U.S.S.R., because the sympathy of the proletarians of all countries toward the republic of soviets is increasing and is inevitably bound to increase from day to day. Yet it is impossible to conduct war without the working class now.

Fourth, the strength and power of the proletariat of the U.S.S.R.; the success of its socialist construction; the power and organization of the Red Army.

The combination of these and similar conditions creates the *peredyshka* . . .

---

[1] Stalin, *Sochineniia*, IX, 25–28; *Izvestiia*, No. 285, December 9, 1926, p. 2; *International Press Correspondence*, No. 1, January 5, 1927, pp. 5–6.

3. The Unity and Inseparability of the National and International Tasks of the Revolution

The third question is that of the national and international tasks of the proletarian revolution in various countries. The party holds that the national and international tasks of the proletariat of the U.S.S.R. merge into the one general task of emancipating the proletariat of all countries from capitalism, that the interests of building socialism in our country wholly and completely merge with the interests of the revolutionary movement in all countries into one common interest in the victory of the revolution in all countries.

What would happen if the proletariat of all countries did not sympathize with and support the republic of soviets? There would be intervention, and the Soviet republic would be destroyed.

What would happen if the capitalists were to succeed in destroying the republic of soviets? A period of the blackest reaction would set in in all capitalist and colonial countries. The working class and the oppressed peoples would be crushed. The strongholds of international communism would be destroyed.

What will happen if the support and sympathy of the proletariat of all countries for the republic of soviets increase and grow? This will considerably facilitate socialist construction in the U.S.S.R.

What will happen if the achievements of socialist construction increase in the U.S.S.R.? This will immeasurably improve the revolutionary position of the proletariat of all countries in the struggle against capital; it will undermine the strongholds of international capital and enormously increase the international proletariat's chances of victory.

Clearly, then, the interests and tasks of the proletariat of the U.S.S.R. are interwoven and inseparably connected with the interests and tasks of the revolutionary movement in all countries. It is therefore a profound error to contrast the national tasks of the proletariat of any country with its international tasks. To describe the zeal and passion displayed by the proletariat of the U.S.S.R. in socialist construction as a symptom of "national insularity" and "national self-sufficiency," as the opposition sometimes does, is nothing but madness or childishness. To consider the interests and tasks of the proletariat of one country one and indivisible with the interests and tasks of the proletariat of all countries—this is the surest guide to the victory of the revolutionary movement of the proletariat of all countries.

It is precisely for this reason that the victory of the proletarian revolution in a single country is not an end in itself, but a means, a lever, for the development and the victory of the revolution in all countries.

Therefore, to establish socialism in the U.S.S.R. means to serve the common cause of the proletariat of all countries. It means to forge victory over capitalism not only in the U.S.S.R., but in all capitalist countries as well, because the revolution in the U.S.S.R. is part of the world revolution—it is its beginning and the base for its expansion.   .   .   .

119

Bukharin on the International Revolution

[Excerpt from His Report on the International and Domestic Situation at the Fifteenth Moscow Province Party Conference, January 1927][2]

1. The Problem of Markets and Profits. The "Russian Problem"

It has long been recognized that the relations of the capitalist states to the Soviet Union are determined by two main factors: first, by their need, if only a relative

[2] *Izvestiia*, No. 10, January 13, 1927, p. 2; also *International Press Correspondence*, No. 10, January 28, 1927, pp. 189–94.

need, to maintain commercial relations with us; and second, by their fear that our Soviet Union may become too mighty and powerful a factor, that it will awaken, support, and organize international proletarian revolutionary sentiment everywhere, including among the oppressed colonial peoples.

.   .   .

We may understand the so-called "Russian problem," that is, what the capitalist bourgeoisie is thinking and planning in regard to us, in the light of this increased aggravation of the problem of finding markets. . . .

2. *The Soviet Union—Seat of the World Revolution*

.   .   .

It is impossible to ignore the tremendous influence exercised by the U.S.S.R. over the Chinese revolution and other liberation movements in the East. Nor can it be concealed that the working class of our country—precisely because our country is the country of the proletarian dictatorship—sent aid to the British miners as no other working class did. Finally, the main elements of the Western European working class, which send their delegations to us, conclude that we are the center of socialist construction.

All these facts, taken together, have a definite effect upon the bourgeoisie. The bourgeoisie has formed a two-sided and peculiarly inconsistent opinion about us. On one hand it sees in us a great market, and the prospect of flooding this market with capitalist goods is more attractive now than ever before; on the other hand it notes the powerful movement in China, the ever-growing sympathy of the international working class for the U.S.S.R., the help to the British miners, and Soviet Russia as the seat of the great international ferment among the oppressed masses. This inconsistency has existed from the beginning and will continue to exist so long as the Soviet Union is surrounded by a capitalist world. The vacillation between these two standpoints—that is, between trade interests and revolution—has always existed and will continue to exist.

3. *German Vacillation and the Belligerent British Policy*

.   .   .

During the great imperialist war Comrade Lenin spoke of the possibility that the war might end in the complete defeat of one of the flourishing state organizations of imperialism, and that this nation, even though maintaining a bourgeois regime, might fall into a position radically and fundamentally different from its wartime position. In such a case Comrade Lenin held a national war of liberation against the rule of imperialism to be possible. In my opinion, this was Germany's position after the war, and therefore the Soviet state was right to express its sympathy with oppressed Germany and all communist parties were perfectly right to support Germany against the imperialist states, despite her bourgeois regime. This could be done and had to be done, for Germany was at that time completely isolated, and her struggle was not based on any imperialist tendencies whatsoever.

Bourgeois politicians in Germany, their Social Democratic mouthpieces, and ultra-Left renegades from communism are now doing their best to represent our position on this question as a fall from virtue, an iniquity. To these we declare once more from this tribune that the Communist Party of our country, and the Soviet state led by the Communist Party, will always be found on the side of all oppressed and enslaved states, even nationalist bourgeois states, if they are attacked on all sides by imperialist robbers. We have laid down this line and followed it, and we shall continue to follow it when similar emergencies arise in the future.

Matters now are very different. Germany has successfully raised herself from the pit into which she fell a few years ago. . . . Germany has turned fairly decisively toward the West, owing to the revival of the German economy, promoted to a great extent by American capital. Germany now enters the concert of imperialist states possessing "full and equal rights," and she turns away from the East, steering a course toward the West.

This does not by any means signify that she breaks off every connection with us. Although Germany is again an imperialist state, her position differs from that of the other imperialist states, since she faces more acutely than the others the necessity of finding markets. . . .

And since Germany is suffering with extraordinary severity from the unsound economic conditions of the present epoch, and is still held in the clutches of the Versailles treaty, for the immediate future she is condemned to a policy of vacillation, and the conciliatory attitude of many of her bourgeoisie toward the U.S.S.R. is inevitable.

Thus Germany remains, though far less than before, among the bourgeois states that pursue a comparatively conciliatory policy toward us.

The direct opposite of Germany's attitude to the U.S.S.R. is Britain's. Britain has received and continues to receive severe blows of late from two different quarters: from the mighty Chinese revolution and from her own working class.[3] They undermine more and more daringly the traditionally conservative regime of the great British Empire.

This circumstance, combined with the mighty influence of our Union, has forced Britain to become the bourgeoisie's champion against the Soviet Union. Of late, since the revolutionary tendencies in the East have grown much more acute, since the Chinese revolution has begun to exercise a gigantic and unparalleled influence all over the East, and since the victorious advance of the armies of national revolution has been clearly resounding throughout the world, and not merely in its capital cities—since all this, Britain has begun to reveal still more clearly her hostile attitude toward us.

We have seen of late that attempts are being made to encircle us on all sides: by diplomacy, by military tactics, and by a system of every imaginable conspiracy inspired by the British government. With the help of the British government, under its leadership, and with its instruction, a large number of diplomatic and military conventions have been agreed upon: the Rumanian-Italian treaty, the Franco-Rumanian agreement, the Polish-Rumanian convention, the Polish-Czech convention, the Polish-Yugoslav treaty, and the conference of the diplomats and General Staff officers of the Baltic border states. Britain's activity against us in Persia is part of these tactics, her action in Afghanistan is directed against us, and so is her government's aggressively bloody work in China, which the British press does not trouble to conceal. All this shows that the attempt to encircle the Soviet Union is being carried on with greatly increased energy. The instigator, initiator, and financial supporter of this policy of encirclement is the English bourgeoisie, the government headed by the King of England. It is under Britain's leadership that military operations are being prepared against us; in Poland, especially, these preparations are being made with feverish energy. Only recently Rumania obtained a loan of several million lire in Italy (Italy is one of Britain's closest allies), securing ammunition orders and the construction of a naval base in Constanta with the aid of British experts. It is Britain who is financing Wrangel's men,[4] who continue to maintain their military organization and hold themselves in readiness.

This is the aggressive and actively hostile policy Britain now pursues against us.

---

[3] A reference to the miners' strike.

[4] After the defeat of General Wrangel's army in the civil war in November 1920, a number of his men succeeded in escaping from the Crimea and eventually settled in different European countries, mainly in the Balkans and in France. Bukharin's statement that they were financed by Great Britain in 1927 is incorrect.

The policy of our government, of the government of the proletarian dictatorship, has been and always will be a policy of peace. Last year we concluded a large number of nonaggression treaties, treaties of a demonstrably peaceful character. One was with Turkey, another with Lithuania; and we have proposed still others to the border states. The latest reply to our policy of peace has been the fascist *coup d'état* in Lithuania,[5] which destroys or will destroy every one of the model treaties concluded between our government and the so-called *Randstaaten*, that is, the states bordering us. Of course the Lithuanian *coup d'état* is not simply a matter of the executions that have aroused so much proletarian protest against, indignation toward, and abhorrence of the Lithuanian butchers; its import lies much deeper than this. Behind the scenes of this supported nationalist *coup d'état* we may see the Poland of Marshal Pilsudski, ready at any moment to devour this new fascist Lithuania. Poland has been waiting for this morsel long enough, and Poland's participation in the *coup d'état* became obvious when we learned that its most prominent leaders were naturalized Poles, men who have been most zealous of late in altering their names to the Lithuanian form, so that they might play the part of resident Lithuanian patriots and combine the roles of "Lithuanian" landlords and bearers of Polish influence into Lithuania.

Behind Poland we find Britain, to whom belongs the doubtful honor of being the leading wire-puller in the events in Lithuania. But what is particularly astonishing is this (and I believe this has not yet been published in our newspapers): Some reports show that the Germans, too, have taken active part in the Lithuanian *coup d'état*. "Democratic" Germany, obviously fearing an increase in Polish influence, has acted both to offset this increase and to gain a concrete strategic position of influence in Lithuania. Germany thus shares with the Polish and British governments the responsibility for all the fascist misdeeds committed by the new Lithuanian government. . . .

We have reports showing that a similar coup is being prepared in Latvia; we hear the same from Finland. On all sides our enemies are working feverishly to draw a cordon of despicable fascist scoundrels around the U.S.S.R., in order to do as much damage as possible to socialist construction in our country. It is especially noteworthy that Pilsudski does not even deem it necessary to conceal from the world the smallest part of his notorious program of expansion "Eastward," to be accomplished mainly at our expense.

4. *From Social Democrats to Monarchists*

All over Europe open and semilegal "ideological and moral" preparations for war against the Soviet Union are being made. The entire gigantic machinery of ideological influence upon the masses is now being set in action essentially against us.

This "moral" mobilization of the masses against the U.S.S.R. has found perhaps its most patent and despicable expression in the tale of the so-called "Soviet shells,"[6] first mentioned in the columns of the British liberal paper, the *Manchester Guardian*. The information originated in German circles and is based on an agreement that we had, and still have, with the Junkers firm. This firm, as *Pravda* correctly observed a few days ago, does not manufacture sausages; it makes airplanes. We do not conceal, and have never tried to conceal, our agreement with Junkers, nor have we denied that airplanes have been constructed and are being constructed. We can declare quite openly that we shall not fail to profit by the advantage offered us by any capitalist state that will send us instructors, and for a due sum of money will construct on our territory planes and other armaments required for the defense of

---

[5] The *coup d'état* took place on December 18, 1926, in Kaunas, the capital of Lithuania. The old government was deposed by the military, and a new one headed by Augustinas Voldemaras (a nationalist) came to power.

[6] See our pp. 173-75.

our country. Although we have fewer armaments proportionately than any of the Great Powers, we are not such fools as to let ourselves be disarmed at a time when all other countries are arming, or to let other people lead us by the nose in our efforts to establish socialism . . . We know that our enemies are sharpening their teeth against us, and we are prepared to utilize every available possibility—of this we give notice to all concerned—for the most efficient defense of the U.S.S.R.

The bourgeois states are preparing for a new imperialist war; they are doing their best to "encircle" us, and getting ready to open an actual campaign against us. They must know, however, that it is no longer 1914, and that the broad masses of workers and peasants are crying out for peace. Therefore, the whole strategy of the capitalist class is directed toward maintaining the assertion that it is we, the Union of the Soviet Socialist Republics, who are the great disturbers of peace. . . .

This is the cry of the Second International, the Social Democrats and the leaders of the Amsterdam International, the renegades from the communist movement expelled from the Comintern, etc. All these are lending their fullest support, both to the bourgeois slanders and to the bourgeoisie's preparations against the Soviet Union. . . .

Thus we see alarming symptoms arising on all sides in the international situation: from Rumania, from Poland, from the Russian emigrés financed by various foreign states, and especially by Britain. . . . To be sure, we need not be particularly alarmed by all this, for our enemies well know that war against us is a very risky business. But nonetheless we must look the growing danger of war clearly in the face. Our enemies shrink from nothing. Only today we received a telegram informing us that a number of foreign papers have published provocative reports of a concentration of Soviet troops on our Western frontier. Our bourgeois adversaries grasp at every means, and resort first of all to lies and provocation.

5. For the Peace Policy, For Proletarian Defense

We must continue to pursue, openly and demonstrably our policy of peace. We have amply proved our peaceful attitude in our nonaggression treaties with various countries, and during the conflict with Chang Tso-lin over the Chinese Eastern Railway. . . . Here again our attitude has furnished renewed and ample proof that we pursue and shall continue to pursue a policy of peace.

It goes without saying that our policy of peace does not exclude, but presupposes, our sympathies for every liberation movement. We must repeat again and again that we have sided and shall always side with the oppressed in every part of the world. We believe in the mighty revolutionary powers of the toiling masses, of the working class, of the tremendous movement now taking place in China. . . .

We shall pursue a demonstrable peace policy; but should anyone attempt to attack us, he must remember that it is no longer 1905 or 1914. . . . Our whole policy, every single diplomatic step we take and every single diplomatic note we dispatch abroad, must be permeated with this striving for peace. We cannot repeat often enough that we not only lose nothing by maintaining peace, but gain a great deal by it. Nevertheless, we can assure all our enemies that the long breathing spell we have enjoyed while working at our economic development has by no means reduced us to simple-minded harmlessness, nor has it caused us to cease to be the fighting party of the communist proletariat. At the slightest threat of danger to the proletarian dictatorship, the working class of our country and its Communist Party will reply by closing ranks with unexampled determination, and will present such a front that each and every foe and adversary will break his teeth on the steel of our bayonets!

Comrades, we are often told that we made a miscalculation in our hopes for international revolution—that we have been preaching international revolution all the time, but that our hopes were disappointed at the decisive moment; that international revolution has "not come about," and that we must resign ourselves to the bitter necessity of ceasing to be what we have hitherto been. In my opinion our first reply to this must be: The international revolution not only will come, but is already an accomplished fact. It is wrong, naïve, and nonsensical to imagine the international revolution as one single event in which all countries begin, at a certain concerted signal, to take part at one and the same moment in a "world conflagration." It is absurd to suppose there is one certain "hour," mystically determined beforehand, in which "His Majesty" the proletariat comes into power.

The international revolution is a gigantic process involving decades. This process began in many countries during the imperialist war, leading in our country to a more and more firmly established dictatorship of the working class, and in Central Europe rolling various kingly crowns in the dust. It has suffered various reverses, and has been brought to a standstill, but it is already kindling again at another point. If we look to the East and properly evaluate the great events in China, we cannot but realize that the Chinese revolution is a constituent part of the international revolution, the international revolution that does not need to "come about" somehow and somewhere but has already arrived.

The world revolution will complete its course when it triumphs in all countries. But we must not talk as if it had not even begun, and as if we should pray to some communist God and the communist Holy Virgin to take pity on us and send down international revolution upon the sinful earth. Our building up of socialism is a constituent part of the international revolution; so is the defeat of the English imperialists in China by the national-revolutionary armies; so is the position of the [British] miners, who came close to [understanding] the problem of seizing power.

The international revolution takes many forms, is expressed in many ways, sometimes suffers reverses and defeats; but nonetheless we are in the midst of international revolutionary events, and surely only born idiots or blind men can turn around with uncertainty in this vortex of events and ask, "But where is this intangible international revolution?" In view of the tremendous struggles going on around us, we cannot but become more and more firmly convinced that the strengthening of capitalism in some countries—and capitalism has been strengthened to some extent—can never erase the fact that at the other end of the capitalist organism, the source of international revolution is sending forth mighty currents. Knowing this, we can maintain an ever greater discipline and self-control in the face of open or concealed preparations for war.

We repeat once more that we feel no fear of coming events, whatever they may be, for we are intensely conscious of having right on our side from the standpoint of the history of the world, nor do we ever doubt even for a minute that our cause will triumph in the end. . . .

120

The Fundamental Principles of the Foreign Policy of the U.S.S.R.

[Outlined by A. I. Rykov, Chairman of the Council of People's Commissars, at the Fourth Congress of Soviets of the U.S.S.R., April 19, 1927][7]

.   .   .

What then are the principles underlying our policy, which we have carried out during the whole of the past period and which, in the view of the government, we must continue to carry out?

[7] *Izvestiia,* No. 90, April 20, 1927, p. 2; also *Russia's Foreign Policy Outlined by Mr. A. I. Rykov,* pp. 17–24.

Analyzing the attitude of foreign powers toward us, we must bear in mind two fundamental factors in the so-called "Russian question":

(1) The growth of economic interest in the U.S.S.R. caused by her consolidation, the development of her economic might, and the extension of her markets.

(2) The growth of antagonism toward the U.S.S.R. (on the part of the dominant political groups) as her international significance and political influence increases. . . .

As for the political treaties that we have concluded with various countries during the period under review, and the relations those treaties have established, I must indicate the fundamental difference between our political treaty relations and those of the Western European states among themselves. They have a system of so-called groupings, by which they endeavor to guarantee their influence and supremacy in peacetime and their united action in time of war. In certain cases there are already agreements and even military alliances, as for instance between Poland and Rumania. This system serves the purpose of organizing the proper distribution of forces in case of war.

We have not participated and do not participate now in any of these groupings.

Our treaties bear, so to speak, a two-sided character; that is, they are concluded by two states only. Their aim, so far as we are concerned, is to guarantee real peace, and to assure the neutrality of the two contracting parties in case of military actions. Thus our system, unlike the grouping system, not only makes no preparations for new wars, but, on the contrary, localizes possible military conflicts by its provisions for maintaining neutrality.

Permit me, in conclusion, to discuss very briefly our relations with the various countries of Europe and Asia, with the exception of Britain and China. . . .

Germany

. . . I must say that during the five years since Rapallo we have been given no cause for complaint by the relations between the U.S.S.R. and Germany. . . .

In connection with the Locarno Conference and the entry of Germany into the League of Nations, the press of a number of countries began to affirm that Germany was now obliged to permit the armed forces of other countries to cross her territory in the event of war between those countries and the U.S.S.R. The German government, however, has declared that it has taken no such obligations upon itself. This declaration was made officially by the German foreign minister, Herr Stresemann, both in the German Reichstag and specially to the government of the U.S.S.R. Since the government of the U.S.S.R. cannot but believe the official declarations of the German government, we must assume that in no conceivable intrigues against the U.S.S.R. will Germany be induced to let herself be used for armed attacks against us.

Moreover, our economic and cultural relations with Germany, which are more extensive than with any other country, are becoming stronger year by year. During the last few years the German government has guaranteed special credits for our industrial orders in Germany. . . . We have used these credits entirely to purchase machinery and equipment that we need for our industrialization. Hence, the policy laid down at the time of the Rapallo agreement has been fully justified.

France

After a certain interval the work of the Franco-Soviet conference has resumed.

Clearly an agreement between the U.S.S.R. and France would exert a considerable influence, not only on the development of economic relations between these two countries, but on the peace of Europe. There are no direct political and economic conflicts between the Soviet Union and France. The absence, however, of an agreement on controversial problems is hindering the extension of commercial relations between the two states, and is thus depriving both sides of economic advantages.

The principles on which we base our economic and commercial negotiations with the French government (on claims, debts, etc.) are the same principles on which we based our negotiations with MacDonald's government.

Poland

During the period under review our relations with the Baltic states and Poland have been of considerable importance. Our whole policy—against war and for peace —makes it highly desirable for us to conclude a nonaggression and neutrality pact with the border states generally, and with Poland in particular.

One obstacle to concluding such pacts has been Poland, who desires to be a sort of guardian or guarantor of the other Baltic states, and who would like to see a solid chain of states from Rumania to Finland come to an agreement with us through Poland and with Polish help.

The government of the U.S.S.R. has rejected this point of view, since it considers that the creation of such a united front of countries from the Baltic to the Black Sea (united with respect to their relations with the U.S.S.R.) would in no way serve the interests of the consolidation of peace. This has been one of the chief sources of disagreement between us. In recent times a number of Polish statesmen have declared that a treaty should be speedily concluded. Unfortunately, although we agree with such declarations, so far they have not been followed by acts on the other side.

The Baltic States

A short time ago we concluded a nonaggression and neutrality agreement with Lithuania. This treaty remains in force despite the changed situation in Lithuania.

As is well known, we have initialed an agreement with Latvia. Negotiations to determine the final form of certain documents to be appended to the main agreement are now in progress.

It is to be hoped that our negotiations with Finland and Estonia will proceed satisfactorily.

In its negotiations with the border states, the government of the U.S.S.R. is continuing the policy of peace which in 1922 led to the calling of the Moscow Conference for the Limitation of Armaments.

We are trying not only to establish and consolidate friendly political relations with the Baltic countries, but also to extend our economic relations with them.

The economic development of most of the Baltic countries depends to a considerable extent on their economic co-operation with the U.S.S.R., since their economic organization, their industry, and their railways were an integral part of tsarist Russia before the October Revolution. . . .

The principle upon which the negotiations for a trade agreement with Latvia are being conducted, our readiness to extend export-import operations with Latvia and to place a number of orders there, provides the best possible proof of the desire of the U.S.S.R. not only to proclaim in words, but also to show by deeds, the need for developing economic relations with the Baltic states.

Turkey

Relations with Turkey, the most important country of the Near East, have been adequate ever since the conclusion of the 1921 treaty, which was followed up by the neutrality treaty of December 17, 1925, and the trade agreement of 1927.[8] It is necessary to develop still further economic relations between the two states. . . .

[8] Text appears in Shapiro, I, 326–29.

Persia

The development of friendly relations between the U.S.S.R. and Persia continues to be a cardinal aim of Soviet policy. . . .

The presence in Moscow just now of the Persian foreign minister, Mr. Ansari, who is here to negotiate with us for a new settlement of Soviet-Persian relations, gives us reason to hope that these negotiations will end quickly and successfully and that an agreement will at length be signed.

Afghanistan

A short time ago we signed a neutrality pact with Afghanistan, which has now been ratified by both governments. . . . Measures must now be taken to use this agreement to extend economic relations between the two countries.

Japan

The preservation of peace in the Far East depends to a considerable extent upon Japan, and hence upon the relations between the three chief Eastern countries: Japan, the U.S.S.R., and China. The government of the U.S.S.R. is therefore endeavoring in every way possible to develop peaceful relations with Japan, and to arrive at a settlement of all those questions upon which negotiations are still proceeding between the two governments. . . .

We must remember that there are no serious points of difference between ourselves and the government of Japan, and consequently no great obstacles to a further rapprochement.

The interests of both countries in Manchuria are also no obstacle to the conclusion of an agreement between them.

Japanese public opinion, which at first feared that the republic of soviets would continue the tsarist government's policy of aggression in the East, has begun to understand the fundamental difference between this policy and the peace-loving policy of the republic of soviets. One obstacle to the development of trade relations with Japan is the fact that the [current] economic negotiations, particularly on a fishing convention, are not yet concluded. The government of the U.S.S.R. is endeavoring to accelerate these negotiations and to start as soon as possible on a commercial agreement. Unfortunately, for reasons independent of us, these negotiations have dragged on longer than is really necessary in the interests of the two states; we can only hope that they will end in agreement in the very near future.

The Austrian government has adopted a measure for guaranteeing credits to us. Elsewhere, nothing requiring mention at this congress has occurred. The government of the Soviet Union, basing itself upon the principles of international policy described above, is ready to apply them in its relations with any and every country.

We Desire Peace—But We Are Ready for Defense

. . . [However] it must be stated that despite the improvement and development of our relations with such countries as Germany and Turkey, and the possibility of reaching an agreement with such countries as Japan and France, our general international position is far more disturbing than it was at the time of the last congress of soviets.

Remember that as the difficulties of the capitalist system become more acute, as the so-called stabilization of capitalism becomes more and more uncertain, an endeavor will undoubtedly be made to blame these shortcomings and failures in both foreign and domestic affairs—the struggle at home with the working classes—very largely upon the republic of soviets. In so far as the movement in China develops under the slogan of friendship and sympathy toward our state, in so far as the revolutionary movement—any working class movement [in other countries]—proceeds under similar slogans, the attacks upon the U.S.S.R. will also increase.

It is no accident that now, when the fate of imperialism is to some extent in the balance, aggression against our Union is increasing from day to day. Will this aggressive movement lead to military ventures against us? No one can say. The existence side by side of the two systems, socialism and capitalism, over a long historical period may of course very well lead to armed conflicts between them.

The government of the Union will take every possible measure to keep from being taken unawares.

We shall insist in the future as in the past on a determined, firm policy of peace against all hostile combinations.

But however firmly we may endeavor to carry through this policy, neither the government nor those here present can guarantee that our socialist territory will not be attacked. Consequently we must also be prepared for the very worst that may come.

THE MINERS' STRIKE AND THE GENERAL STRIKE IN GREAT BRITAIN

121

Lessons of the British Strike

[Excerpt from Stalin's Speech Delivered at a Meeting of the Railway Shop Workers in Tiflis, June 8, 1926][9]

. . .

What are the lessons of the general strike in Britain, at least the most important ones? They are as follows:

First: The crisis in the coal industry of England and the general strike connected with it raised point-blank the question of socializing the means of production in the coal industry and establishing workers' control, [in other words] the question of introducing socialist practices. Obviously, the only way to settle the crisis in the coal industry is the way offered by the British Communist Party. The crisis in the coal industry and the general strike place the British workers face to face with the task of bringing about socialist order in their country.

Second: The British working class must see from its own experience that the main obstacle in its way is the political authority of the capitalists, in this case the authority of the Conservative Party and its government. Although the General Council of the Trades Union Congress was terribly afraid to recognize the indissoluble connection between the economic struggle and the political one, the British workers are now bound to see that in their hard struggle against organized capital the question of power is basic, that to solve the crisis as a whole they must first settle the question of power.

Third: The history of the general strike will convince the working class in England that Parliament, the constitution, the King, and the other authorities of the bourgeois government are nothing but a weapon of the capitalist class directed against the proletariat. The strike has destroyed the myth of the untouchable sanctity

[9] Stalin, *Sochineniia*, VIII, 164–68; also *Izvestiia*, No. 136, June 16, 1926, p. 2.

of Parliament, and has shown the present constitution to be an instrument of the bourgeoisie directed against the workers. The workers are bound to see that they need their own workers' constitution to use against the bourgeoisie. I believe that the acceptance of this truth will represent a tremendous achievement for the working class of England.

Fourth: The strike is bound to convince the British working classes that their old leaders, men schooled in the old British policy of compromise, are unfit and must be replaced by new ones, by revolutionary leaders.

Fifth: The British workers will see now that the British miners form the vanguard of England's working class, and that supporting the coal strike and ensuring its victory are, therefore, a task for that entire class. The whole story of the strike points to the absolute truth of this lesson.

Sixth: The British workers were unquestionably convinced during the difficult period of general strike, when the platforms and programs of the different parties were applied in practice, that the only party capable of defending their interests to the end, boldly and decisively, was the Communist Party.

Such are the general basic lessons of the general strike in England.

Now I pass to some practical conclusions. First, consider the stabilization of capital. The strike in England has shown the Comintern's warning—that the stabilization in question was temporary and unreliable[10]—to be absolutely correct. The attack by British capital upon the British miners was an attempt to transform the provisional and unreliable stabilization into a durable and permanent one. This attempt did not succeed and could not succeed. The British workers, who replied to it with a great strike, showed the entire capitalist world that no durable capitalist stabilization was possible in this postwar period, and that attempts to establish one were pregnant with the threat of the defeat of capitalism. The opposite thesis, however, is equally incorrect, namely, that the stabilization is over, that it has been ended, and that we have now entered a period of great revolutionary upheaval. The stabilization of capitalism is temporary and provisional, but this stabilization exists.

Further, it is exactly because of the provisional and temporary nature of the present stabilization that the capitalists will try in the future to attack the working class. Of course, the lessons of the English strike are bound to show the capitalist world how much it risks by making experiments like the one made by the British Conservative Party. That this experiment will have its repercussions both within the Conservative Party and among the capitalists of all countries can no longer be doubted. Nevertheless, capital will again try to attack the working class, for it no longer feels safe, and it craves security. The working class and the Communist Party must muster their forces to repulse the coming attacks. They must also continue organizing a united front of workers, with a view to changing the capitalists' attack into their own counterattack, into a revolutionary offensive by the workers, into a struggle to establish the dictatorship of the proletariat and to liquidate capitalism.

Finally, in order to carry out these tasks of the day, the working class of Britain must first of all free itself of its present leaders. One cannot wage war on capitalists with such leaders as Thomas and MacDonald. One cannot expect victory when there are in the rear such traitors as Henderson and Clynes. The working class of England must learn to replace such leaders by better ones because it has a choice to make: Either the British working class will learn to drive away Messrs. Thomas, MacDonald & Co., or it will never see victory.

Such, comrades, are some conclusions that appear evident.

[10] The theses on "The Problems of the Day in the International Communist Movement," adopted by the Sixth Enlarged Plenum of the ECCI, February 17–March 15, 1926. (*Kommunisticheskii Internatsional v dokumentakh*, pp. 529–31.)

122
Analysis of the Soviet Reply to the British Warning Concerning Diplomatic Relations, February 1927[11]

In recent times there has appeared, in close connection with the bitter campaign waged against the U.S.S.R. by the "die-hard" wing of the Conservative Party, a certain tension in Anglo-Soviet relations. It was up to those who actually direct the foreign policy of Britain, up to the responsible leaders of the British government, to convert the bad relations between the two countries into normal business relations. Instead, Mr. Chamberlain's note to the Soviet government, published in today's *Pravda*, . . . which contains a large number of impermissibly sharp expressions and even threats against our government, shows that the British government prefers to complicate rather than improve Anglo-Soviet relations.

Let us try to determine the nature and political meaning of the British note. . . .

This note, unlike the equally remarkable, ill-famed "Zinoviev letter" [note], is not based upon deliberately false documents. . . . To this extent it directly reflects the bankruptcy of the former "method of procedure" toward us. It does not, however, have that "firm substance" which is obligatory for important documents passing between the great states of the world.

The British note contains not a single concrete accusation, not a single concrete revelation, not a single concrete fact to prove that we have violated the treaties existing between the two countries. It contains absolutely none of these things.

On the other hand, the British note, which bears the character of a "discussion," contains carefully selected extracts from speeches of VKP leaders, from articles in our press, from reports at party conferences and sessions of the Communist International. . . .

As usual, the note identifies the Political Bureau of the Central Committee of the VKP with the Soviet government. We do not wish to refute for the thousandth time this petty bourgeois wisdom. One might as well say that the British cabinet is identical with the British Conservative Party, and that all the latter's actions are to be treated as acts of the former.

No matter how one may turn the extracts from the speeches quoted in the note, one cannot conclude from them that the Soviet government is "making" the world revolution, "creating" the Chinese revolution, "making" the British strike, and so forth. In declaring, say, that a powerful anti-imperialist revolutionary movement is developing in China, our leaders are only recording the existence of an objective historical process, not creating this process.

[11] Editorial, *Pravda*, No. 46, February 25, 1927, p. 1; also *International Press Correspondence*, No. 17, March 3, 1927, pp. 339–40.

A note from the British Foreign Secretary, Sir Austen Chamberlain, warned the Soviet government on February 23, 1927, that the toleration shown Soviet agents by the British government did not imply either ignorance of their designs or acquiescence in the unprecedented relationship between the two countries. After summarizing certain Soviet anti-British acts, Chamberlain stated that continuation of such acts "must sooner or later render inevitable the abrogation of the Trade Agreement, the stipulations of which have been so flagrantly violated, and even the severance of ordinary diplomatic relations." (*A Selection of Papers, 1921–1927*, p. 50.)

On February 26 Litvinov replied in part: ". . . it is impossible really to regard as anti-British propaganda [either (1)] an analysis and estimate of the foreign policy of the British government and of its relation to the Soviet Union, or [(2)] party workers' reasonings, based on general principles, pointing to the inevitability of a world revolution or the significance of the national-revolutionary movement in the East." He repeated once again that the Communist Party and its international institutions were not to be confused with the Soviet government. (Kliuchnikov and Sabanin, III, 367.)

When, however, the British note charges us with the "crime" of sympathizing with the oppressed peoples, then we venture to assure the honorable members of the British government that this has nothing to do with our actual business, trade, and diplomatic obligations, just as the British Conservative Party's undeniable sympathy, let us say, for Italian fascism [has nothing to do with its business, trade, and diplomatic obligations]. In different states there are different parties in power, and hence there are different "sympathies" that cannot be removed even by diplomatic notes.

The British note seems to "accuse" our government of the fact that the VKP members, in appraising world political events, proceed on the basic principles of revolutionary Marxism and Leninism. Even from the standpoint of the Conservative politicians themselves, this "accusation" is exceedingly ill-advised. What would they say if we were to demand that they abandon their Conservative program, with its sacred principles of "the family, property, and religion"? They would describe this, at the very least, as interference in the internal affairs of Great Britain. Similarly, their ridiculous demand that members of the VKP be "compelled" to abandon the program of the Communist Party is interference in the internal affairs of the U.S.S.R.

When Mr. Chamberlain accuses the Soviet government of base and offensive attacks on members of the British government, he again adopts a very disadvantageous standpoint for the British cabinet.

First, Mr. Chamberlain's quotations do not prove his thesis.

Second—not to speak of the thousands of impertinent articles against the U.S.S.R. appearing in the British Conservative press—we could remind the forgetful preachers of "good manners" of dozens and hundreds of "beautiful expressions" used by influential members of the British government, expressions that would be difficult to find not only in a book of diplomatic terms but even in an ordinary simple lexicon. . . .

One cannot help being surprised at the astounding shortsightedness with which Mr. Chamberlain decides to give us lessons in politeness and good behavior!

The British note's charges are unfounded. We would not trouble to deal with them in detail were it not that the note clearly threatens to break off diplomatic relations between Britain and the U.S.S.R. Obviously such a threat is in general, and particularly now, a foreign political adventure of the very worst sort. Even MacDonald describes the sending of this note as "an extremely stupid and damaging procedure." The entire labor movement of Great Britain, including even its moderate elements, opposes such a policy. We assume for our part that the present British government can only be the loser in pursuing a policy that will have immediate repercussions upon its political position both at home and abroad.

123
Rykov on Relations with Britain
[Speech at the Fourth Congress of Soviets of the U.S.S.R.,
April 19, 1927][12]

. . .

Anglo-Soviet Relations

We can see the real reason for the Conservative government's note[13] only after examining the anti-Soviet agitation that is being conducted by a considerable section, if not the whole, of the Conservative Party.

The chief issues of this propaganda are: (1) tsarist debts; (2) the solidarity

[12] *Izvestiia*, No. 90, April 20, 1927, pp. 1–2; also *Russia's Foreign Policy Outlined by Mr. A. I. Rykov*, pp. 4–14.

[13] Chamberlain's note, described in footnote 11.

of the Soviet working class with the British working masses and, more particularly, with the miners' strike; (3) the imperialists' displeasure at the Chinese people's sympathy for our Union. This the imperialists call "participation" by the Soviet Union in the Chinese liberation movement. Their dissatisfaction is directed against us because the U.S.S.R. is the first country of the "October Revolution," the first country to lay the foundation for a new socialist epoch. It is quite natural that other oppressed peoples use our experience when fighting for their freedom. The first point concerns the material claims against the October Revolution; the other two deal with so-called propaganda, but actually concern the sympathetic attitude of the working masses and oppressed peoples of the whole world toward our Soviet Union. I consider that these three "claims" form the real reasons for the British note and for the mobilization of conservative public opinion in Britain against us.

I believe it essential to emphasize that none of these questions was ever discussed between official representatives of the Soviet and British governments. Despite our repeated efforts to enter into business negotiations, the present Conservative government has consistently refused to subject these so-called controversial problems to official negotiations. Nevertheless, the British Conservatives, basing themselves on these three points, are conducting an agitation in England which not only blocks the development of our economic and commercial relations, but might, under certain circumstances, lead to a rupture of relations. A rupture in diplomatic relations between two such great states as the U.S.S.R. and Britain cannot but affect the whole political situation in Europe. It cannot but make more difficult the maintenance of peace. What the Conservatives are doing—namely, worsening and possibly rupturing relations [with us] by exploiting issues on which they have not even permitted official negotiations—must consequently be considered criminal.

In view of the great importance of these questions in international politics, I consider it necessary to treat them in some detail.

Disputes on the Workers' Question

As to the position of the working class in our Union and their rights and relations with the world working class movement, everyone, even the Conservatives, must remember that our republic is a working class state. Consequently not only the toiling masses and the workers' organizations, but our government itself, may declare quite openly its fraternal and class solidarity with the working class and the laboring masses of other countries.

Every attempt to force the working class of the U.S.S.R. to renounce this, their natural right, or to force our government to keep our working class from cementing relations with and aiding the working classes of other countries, is due to a desire to alter the very nature of the Soviet state. Our state is based on the dictatorship of the proletariat; this historic fact and its natural results cannot be annihilated.

Consequently, it is politically unrealistic to consider the events of October 1917 a crime of the Soviet government. We surely cannot consider it a crime of Sir Austen Chamberlain that there exists in Britain a capitalist system, that the Conservative Party is in power there, and that consequently he now sympathizes, let us say, not with the Chinese coolie, but with the Chinese mandarin, the Chinese militarist. . . .

Similarly, our sympathies with the British miners cannot be considered interference by the Soviet government (as a contracting party to established treaty relations) in the internal affairs of Britain. A workers' dictatorship obviously cannot deprive the workers of the right to organize trade unions and to help the workers of other countries in any way they choose. The chief difference between our state and the British is this: It is unthinkable that our Congress should consider a law limiting the rights of trade unions. But in Britain this is not only thinkable—it is actually happening. Herein lies the difference in structure between the two states.

In a workers' state, the trade unions are at liberty to do what they wish. If we were to forbid them this freedom, we should cease to be a government of workers and peasants.

During the British miners' strike, the working masses of the U.S.S.R. collected money through their trade unions. The government of the Soviet Union itself, however, sent no money to the miners.

To support the assertion that the Soviet government helped organize the miners' strike and similar conflicts between labor and capital, the Conservatives attribute to the Soviet government responsibility for the appeals, speeches, and acts of workers' organizations both in the U.S.S.R. and elsewhere—and, indeed, not only of communist organizations, but often of simply democratic ones, even those that actively oppose the communist movement. We were blamed for the rising in the Hawaiian Islands and in Nicaragua, and certain British papers and statesmen even attributed the British strike to "instigation from Moscow."

The British strike is only one part of the world conflict between capital and labor, a conflict that even bourgeois economists and politicians have long considered inevitable and for which both sides have long been preparing. Consequently, it is absolutely ridiculous to attribute the strike to the "pernicious agitation of Soviet agents." . . . Nevertheless, the Conservatives endeavored to blame the Soviet government for both the inception of the strike and the heroic endurance of the British miners. An interesting comment on the impartiality of the British Conservatives is the fact that, whereas the British government declared its neutrality during the miners' strike, it did its best to block assistance to the starving strikers and their families by working-class organizations, and at the same time gratefully accepted the strikebreaking efforts of Russian White Guards. Of course, this is a matter for the British government, and we understand quite well that the British government did precisely what its class interests dictated. No sane politician could expect anything else. The workers of our Union, on their side, also fulfilled their class duties, and may be expected to do the same again under similar circumstances. The question of our relations with the working class movement, of our prohibiting our workers from assisting the working classes of other countries, must be altogether removed from the order of the day. The Soviet government will permit no change in its policy on this matter.

The Debts

On the second question, that of the debts, the Soviet government has repeatedly stated its views, which were to a certain extent reflected in the treaty with the former British government. This treaty was signed by the then British premier, MacDonald, and by the chairman of our delegation, Comrade Rakovsky.

This treaty took into account all the circumstances and the interests of both sides. It pointed out the way to settle outstanding questions, and was at that time considered advantageous both to the English and to ourselves. With the coming to power of the Conservative government, however, the treaty was not ratified. Presumably, if the new Conservative government of Britain had sincerely desired to come to terms with us, it would have pointed out exactly what it disagreed with in the treaty that had already been signed; it would have indicated what, in its opinion, should be changed, and in what way: and it would have drafted a new treaty. No such concrete proposals have been received by our government. Although our representatives in Britain, Rakovsky, the late Krasin, and Rosengolts, have repeatedly requested notice of such modifications of the treaty as the British side might desire, I must state that the British government has evaded these requests and has made no new proposals.

We cannot regard the Conservative stand on this matter as indicating that the British government is waiting for a favorable moment to force the U.S.S.R. to a one-sided recognition of the debts. If the British government, which sees itself as a European legal adviser in the matter of the tsarist debts, desires to wait and see, this is its affair, but I cannot see how such an attitude benefits either the economic relations between the two countries or the creditors themselves.

Our Position

The British government's note threatened a rupture of relations. Our reply sufficiently controverted the [British] position and the accusations officially made against us by the British government. At the same time, it clarified the Soviet government's position regarding the possible rupture and the responsibility for it. To judge by what certain British ministers have said, no rupture occurred only because they considered the time unsuitable owing to Britain's international and internal difficulties. These difficulties forced the Conservative government to renounce the idea of a rupture for the moment.

The anti-Soviet campaign of the Right-wing Conservatives is continuing; in their opinion, the wisest thing their party could do would be to break off relations with the Soviet Union. Therefore, it is hard to predict what line the Conservatives will follow in Anglo-Soviet relations.

The government of the U.S.S.R., in pursuance of its general policy of peace, has never refused to enter into negotiations, and considers it both desirable and possible to remove the present strained relations.

The government of the Soviet Union is convinced that the friendly relations between the peoples of the U.S.S.R. and the British people will continue to develop and that the attempts of the British Conservatives to further evade the development of economic and political relations with the U.S.S.R. are doomed to failure. . . .

[Goes on to discuss the Chinese revolution.]

The British Note. The Bessarabian Protocol

Comrades! It seems to me that the British note had not only the aims of which I have spoken, but another aim: the ideological preparation, so to speak, of an anti-Soviet bloc. Why would businesslike Englishmen have sunk to the level of using a diplomatic note as a propaganda proclamation, unless to convince the bourgeoisie everywhere of the necessity of encircling our Union? And, indeed, many Conservative papers have been speaking recently of this necessity, of "annihilating the Bolshevik danger," of "forming a *cordon sanitaire*," and so on. Such agitation forms in essence a preparation for encirclement, a psychological preparation for intervention. There has now begun almost an open bidding for an anti-Soviet orientation.

In the light of this anti-Soviet campaign and this public bidding, the Italian government's ratification of the protocol legalizing Rumania's seizure of a part of Soviet territory—Bessarabia—is distinctly significant. For a long time the Italian government considered it unnecessary and untimely to ratify this protocol, but just now, during the anti-Soviet campaign, it renounces this point of view. With regard to the Bessarabian protocol and the annexation of Bessarabia by Rumania, we must say once and for all that no papers, notes, ratifications, or affirmations have any significance whatever, nor can they have, unless the Soviet government participates in them.

·   ·   ·

THE END OF SOVIET-BRITISH RELATIONS AND THE DETERIORATION OF RELATIONS WITH FRANCE

124

The Soviet Government Protests the Raid on Arcos

[Litvinov to William Peters, British Representative in Moscow, May 17, 1927][14]

.   .   .

Immediately after the end of the intervention and after the lifting of the blockade against the U.S.S.R., the Soviet government proceeded to establish economic relations with Great Britain and other Western states. The Soviet government firmly believed that its [trade] organs, which were to conduct business with other states on the principle of state monopoly of foreign trade, must insist on an explicit guarantee of the complete immunity of state documents, instructions, circulars, orders, etc., sent by them abroad—just as private firms insist on the preservation of their commercial secrets. This was especially important since these organs concentrated in their hands the Soviet state's entire import and export activity, and carried out their operations in accordance with previously formulated state plans and intentions. For this reason, in its negotiations with Great Britain and other Western states for the establishment of diplomatic relations and for commercial treaties, the Soviet government put forward with special emphasis the demand that its commercial agencies abroad be assured complete immunity and inviolability. At the same time the Soviet government took into consideration the hostile atmosphere in which the commercial agents of the first Soviet state would have to work in capitalist countries, and the extraordinary attention that might be paid them by reactionary police circles in those countries.

The principle of the immunity of trade delegations and representatives of the Soviet Union has now been recognized by nearly all the countries with which the Soviet government has treaty relations. No objections to this principle were raised by the British government, in the person of Sir Robert Horne, then Minister of Trade, during the negotiations with the late Krasin in 1921.

This principle, which was embodied in Article Five of the Soviet-British trade agreement of 1921, has now been violated by British authorities in the most gross and insulting manner.

According to our information, the search warrant for "Soviet House" on Moorgate Street, which was not presented until an hour after the arrival of the police, named both Arcos Ltd. and the Soviet trade delegation. Although Arcos is officially a trading corporation registered in accordance with the British laws, the British authorities were bound to know that it was engaged mainly, if not exclusively, in carrying out the commercial instructions of Soviet economic organs. A police raid on a large British trading company, with good references in British business circles, with an annual turnover of tens of millions of pounds sterling, and accurately fulfilling its obligations, is altogether unprecedented in the history of the city of London. The raid could only have been designed to damage Soviet interests connected with Arcos' activities, by compromising Arcos and creating around it an atmosphere of

[14] *Anglo-sovetskie otnosheniia*, pp. 116–20; also *International Press Correspondence*, No. 31, May 26, 1927, pp. 630–31.

lack of confidence and hostility. From this point of view the Soviet government feels that it has a right to protest the raid on Arcos.

However, if the British authorities, ignoring the most elementary demands of correctness, commercial usage, and even expediency, can refer to their formal right in regard to Arcos, there is no doubt whatever that the violent invasion by the police of the trade delegation's premises and what they did there are a gross violation of the agreement of 1921. If, according to Article Five of this agreement, the official agent of the U.S.S.R. is granted the right to use cipher correspondence, it clearly follows that this correspondence and the ciphers themselves can in no circumstances be examined by the agents of another state or by any other persons from outside without the sanction of the head of the Soviet delegation. If, according to the same article, the official agent of the Soviet Union is granted the right, on the grounds of his diplomatic immunity, to receive sealed packets by special couriers, then the immunity of the contents of these packets is obvious to everybody.

Nevertheless, police agents, having forced their way into the trade delegation's premises and into the personal desk of Mr. Khinchuk, an official agent enjoying diplomatic immunity, examined and took away without discrimination all papers found there including ciphered correspondence, codes, and papers received by diplomatic mail. At the same time, officials of the cipher department of the trade delegation, Miller and Khudiakov, who were fulfilling their duty and who protested against the illegal demands of the police, were subjected to acts of violence and were even beaten, while the wife of the acting chargé d'affaires of the U.S.S.R., Mrs. Maisky, who was on the premises and has a diplomatic passport, was forcibly detained and searched.

No less significant is the political aspect of the British government's act. The absolutely uncalled-for police raid on a government institution of another state, apart from the question of treaty rights involved, is in itself a most hostile act, and undoubtedly threatens an end to relations between the interested states, with all the consequences ensuing therefrom. The trade delegation's behavior gave no justification for such a raid; the British government never once complained about its activities. The police authorities themselves who undertook the raid apparently did not expect to find any documents incriminating the delegation, or they would have taken good care to guarantee themselves against the abuses possible in such searches and thus ensure confidence in the results of the search. By having refused to let the trade delegation's representatives remain during the search to certify the authenticity of the documents that were removed by drawing up a proper list and protocol, the police authorities deprived the search of any formal significance.

The British government undoubtedly knows of the Soviet government's note protesting the police raid recently made in the same way and in similar circumstances in China. To provide the search with even the most elementary legal guarantees was under the circumstances most necessary, in view of the ominous role already played by a forged document in the relations between the Soviet Union and Great Britain.

It is impossible not to recall today the note of February 23, in which Sir Austen Chamberlain sought reasons for the tension between the Soviet Union and Great Britain in the conduct of the Soviet press and of certain Soviet statesmen and public leaders. The present raid and the motives underlying it clearly show where the true reasons should be sought. As against the unfounded, absolutely unconfirmed, although often repeated accusation that the Soviet government has not lived up to its obligations and has violated the rules of international relations, the Soviet government can irrefutably prove that the British government has violated the Soviet-British agreement of 1921 and visited the most offensive treatment upon persons enjoying the right of diplomatic immunity, while totally ignoring the requirements of international law and recognized international usage.

The actions of the British government prove that it is not only undisturbed by the Anglo-Soviet tensions it complains of in its note of February 23, but apparently intent upon bringing these tensions to a climax as soon as possible. Its actions refute its frequent references to its efforts to maintain peace and to improve European economic conditions. They show the whole world where the really destructive forces working to increase the economic chaos and anarchy of Europe are to be found, and this at the very time of the World Economic Conference called by the League of Nations (of which Great Britain is the leading member) to strengthen international economic relations and remove obstacles to economic co-operation.

Putting the interests of peace above all, and desiring to ensure peaceful conditions for internal construction within the U.S.S.R., the Soviet government has for a long time patiently suffered a series of gross attacks and provocative acts from individual members of the British government and from the government itself. The Soviet government has repeatedly declared its willingness to do everything in its power, within the limits of normal relations and negotiations on equal terms, to help settle the misunderstandings and disputes between the two governments. With this object in view, it has not discontinued trade relations with Great Britain, but has tried to enlarge them wherever British business circles would go halfway to meet the Soviet government and so long as the British government did not interfere with such efforts. It has noted with satisfaction the city of London's growing interest in the Soviet market and the London banks' growing confidence in Soviet economic organizations, as testified to by the agreement regarding a credit of 10,000,000 pounds sterling concluded with one of these banks just before the raid.

However, the absolutely unprecedented and unrestrained campaign of hate that culminated in the raid on the premises of the trade delegation, a campaign recently encouraged by members of the British government, compels the Soviet government to ask, with all the earnestness and frankness the alarming situation demands, whether the British government desires to preserve and develop Anglo-Soviet relations or intends in the future to hamper them.

For its part the Soviet government categorically declares that the continuation of trade relations is possible only if the British government strictly observes the trade agreement, and guarantees Soviet economic organs the right to uninterrupted, quiet, and normal work.

The Soviet government declares just as resolutely that while realizing its self-appointed tasks of internal development according to a definite economic plan, and while co-ordinating its operations in foreign trade with this plan, it cannot permit these operations to be made dependent upon casual party combinations in England, electioneering maneuvers, or the fantastic ideas of this or that minister.

The Soviet government feels that it has the right to demand from the British government both a clear and unequivocal reply, and satisfaction for the British government's violation of its treaty obligations, for insults suffered, and for material losses caused by the action of the police.

Requesting you, Sir, to bring the above to the attention of the British government, I beg you to accept the assurance of my sincere regard.

125
Litvinov's Statement on Soviet-British Relations
[An Interview with Representatives of the Soviet Press, May 1927][15]

The decision of the British government to break off diplomatic and economic relations with the U.S.S.R. is no casual and unexpected event connected with the

[15] *Pravda*, No. 117, May 26, 1927, p. 1.

raid on Arcos or the alleged duplicity of the Soviet trade organization. The decision must be considered a logical conclusion of the anti-Soviet policy that the present Conservative government has pursued from the very day when, having deceived its electorate by a forged document, it came into power.

While basing its policy on ruthless struggle against the working class in England and upon the enslavement of China, India, Egypt, and other countries, the Conservative government could not be reconciled to the existence of a workers' and peasants' government, a government that did not conceal its sympathy for the class struggle of the proletariat and the national movement of oppressed peoples.

Therefore, the desire to overthrow the Soviet government has been the core of the activity of the British Conservative government. All through its existence this government has carried on anti-Soviet intrigues, with the object of isolating and weakening the Soviet Union so as to destroy it the more successfully. The only reason the British government delayed the rupture until now was that it expected to find allies in a joint attack on our Union. When this hope was disappointed, the British government decided to attack the U.S.S.R. alone, and did so openly and independently, hoping again to rally other states by its example.

The rupture of diplomatic relations with the U.S.S.R. and the threat of war are also in perfect harmony with the general policy of the British government, which consists of inciting and arming one country against another with a view to preventing the stabilization of peace and calm, both in Europe and elsewhere. This government's role in Egypt, in China, and lastly in wrecking Anglo-Soviet political and economic relations is so evident to all that I need not dwell on it.

Sir Austen Chamberlain himself repeatedly declared that the breaking off of Anglo-Soviet relations would menace world peace. These relations having nonetheless been broken off, the Nobel peace laureate must admit that the danger of war not only does not trouble him, but is desirable to him and forms part of the political plans of his government.

The rupture of diplomatic relations must be interpreted as an energetic preparation for war; otherwise it would be absurd from the point of view of England's own interests. Indeed, the rupture could hardly aim merely at depriving English industry of Soviet orders worth many millions of pounds and English consumers of cheap raw material, or at increasing unemployment and releasing the Soviet government from all obligations to Britain.

Clearly all that has occurred makes further trade relations with Britain impossible. The Soviet government now has no guarantees against raids, against the seizure of commercial correspondence, even against the confiscation of goods belonging to our state organizations. Neither can Arcos continue its operations, inasmuch as its commercial activity was based on the sale of Soviet state commodities and the purchase of English goods.

This [the rupture] is what the British government has been aiming at for a long time; [now,] having rendered further commercial relations practically impossible and having assumed the entire responsibility for breaking them off, [it] has achieved its object. Characteristically, Arcos and the trade delegation were raided the day after the Midland Bank had agreed to finance Soviet orders to English factories to the extent of 10,000,000 pounds sterling, thus opening up further prospects for the rapid development of economic relations between the two countries.

In the light of these facts, Mr. Baldwin's attempts yesterday in the House of Commons to justify the rupture by displaying a kind of movie—with all the elements of American hit movies—are ludicrous and unconvincing. After his speech, who will doubt that the rupture is the result of the raid, and that the raid itself was undertaken with the object of preparing a rupture? Indeed, Mr. Baldwin failed to justify the raid even from the purely police point of view. He was compelled to admit that the mythical lost document, in search of which the London police undertook their blustering and formidable expedition, was not found on the premises of the trade delegation.

Consequently Mr. Baldwin himself recognized that Mr. Hicks[16] had sytematically deceived British public opinion when he referred to this document as the reason for the raid. Having dismally failed on this central point, entailing catastrophic consequences to the cause of peace, Mr. Baldwin pitifully and unworthily clings to other "documents" allegedly discovered. Again, however, he could produce no documents compromising the trade delegation's activities. Indeed, we cannot take seriously the private letters allegedly taken from the pockets of members of the staff, even granting that the police report is true, which, naturally, remembering the "Zinoviev letter," may well be doubted.

Even if it were proved that some member of the staff of Arcos or the trade delegation engaged in "criminal" correspondence with trade unions or other labor organizations, can the institution where such collaborators were employed be held responsible? Indeed, except for the chief of the trade delegation no member of the staff of the delegation, still less of Arcos, enjoys immunity. All bear full personal responsibility for personal actions. The police could have searched their pockets outside the delegation's premises and, if they had discovered "criminal" documents, could have acted in accordance with the law.

The Foreign Office is well aware that our plenipotentiary representatives and trade delegation in London, as well as elsewhere, engage all members of their staffs by a written document warning them of dismissal and legal prosecution if they should violate the laws of the country in which they reside, interfere with its internal affairs, or engage in any propaganda [in that country]. If any employee breaks this obligation either intentionally or unintentionally, the trade delegation obviously cannot be held responsible.

We must reject as a wicked insinuation the charge of espionage advanced against the trade delegation. The raid did not substantiate this accusation. If, as Mr. Baldwin asserts, the English police knew of members of the trade delegation staff who engaged in espionage, why were they not prosecuted? Obviously because there is no such evidence, and the charge advanced is absolutely groundless. . . .

126

The British Break Interpreted as New Evidence of Class Hatred

[Resolution of the Plenum of the Moscow Soviet on the Report of A. I. Rykov, June 1, 1927][17]

"Having listened to the report of the chairman of the Council of People's Commissars, Comrade Rykov, on the international position of the U.S.S.R., the plenum of the Moscow soviet fully endorses the government's steps to maintain peace and defend the interests of the toilers of the Soviet Union. In spite of all the provocatory adventures of Messrs. Chang Tso-lin, Hicks, and Chamberlain, the government of the U.S.S.R. did not yield [to provocation] and was able to check [these attempts] worthily.

"The plenum of the Moscow soviet, jointly with all the toiling masses of the U.S.S.R., with all class-conscious workers of the world, and with all the oppressed masses of the toilers of all countries, brands the British government's breaking off

---

[16] Sir William Joynson-Hicks, Home Secretary in Baldwin's government, 1924–29.

[17] A. I. Rykov, *Angliia i S.S.S.R.; doklad na plenume moskovskogo soveta 1 iiunia 1927 g.*, pp. 43–47.

of the commercial agreement and of diplomatic relations with the U.S.S.R. as a new attempt dictated by class hatred for the first proletarian state.

"Having come to the helm by means of the fabricated 'Zinoviev letter,' the British Conservative government has consistently carried out a defiant and provocatory policy toward the U.S.S.R., and has not ceased even for a moment its attempts to create a united counterrevolutionary front of capitalist powers against the Soviet Union, which by the very fact of its existence and the successes of its socialist construction has become the basis of the world proletarian revolution.

"The entire period during which the consequences of the world imperialist slaughter have been liquidated is also a period of international preparation for new imperialist wars, and first of all for war against the U.S.S.R. by the capitalist governments and their lackeys, the Second International.

"The U.S.S.R. is so greatly hated precisely because it is one of the most serious hindrances to the robbers' intentions of the imperialists, headed by the Conservative government of Britain.

"The working class and the toiling masses of the world are facing the danger of a new and even more formidable war, and still more infamous treachery by the Social Democrats and the Amsterdam International.

"The plenum of the Moscow soviet considers that the threat of war must be met by intensifying the proletarian and peasant forces on the economic front, and by special vigilance and firmness in preparing for the defense of the country. In the face of this threat there can be no place for lack of discipline, wastefulness, or slovenliness.

"The plenum of the Moscow soviet calls upon the toiling masses of the city and province of Moscow to reply to the insolent impertinence of the British diehards by redoubling their efforts along the lines of economic and cultural construction and the establishment of socialism; by further consolidating the ties of international solidarity with the proletariat and the oppressed peoples of all countries; and finally by supporting the Red Army to the utmost and preparing themselves to decisively repel the impudent imperialist attack on the U.S.S.R.

"The plenum of the Moscow soviet declares on the part of the toilers of Moscow its readiness to support every measure of the Soviet government directed toward the decisive defense of the first country of the dictatorship of the proletariat.

"The plenum of the Moscow soviet fully approves the decisions of the Council of People's Commissars to transfer all the country's export and import operations to those countries with which normal relations are maintained and in which our economic organs have been given a sufficient guarantee of uninterrupted and systematic work.

"In answer to the threat of an economic blockade of our Soviet Union, the plenum of the Moscow soviet calls upon the proletariat and peasantry of the city and province of Moscow, and of the Union as a whole, to contribute to their own defense by unanimously supporting state loans for the restoration of the economy.

"The plenum of the Moscow soviet sends its warm proletarian greetings to the toilers of China, who are fighting heroically for their own liberation, and calls upon the proletariat of all countries to guard peace vigilantly before the new threat of imperialist slaughter, as well as to strike a shattering blow at the new attempt on the U.S.S.R., the bulwark of the world proletarian revolution."

In addition to the above resolution, the plenum unanimously approved the following proposition:

"The plenum of the Moscow soviet considers that the Soviet government must not accept any offer to discuss regulating the material claims of British subjects until full diplomatic relations are re-established between the U.S.S.R. and Great

Britain, and until the British government gives sufficient satisfaction for all the injuries and material losses its actions have cost the U.S.S.R."

127
Soviet-French Relations

[Declaration of the Assistant Commissar of Foreign Affairs, Litvinov, to Representatives of the Press, Moscow, September 16, 1927][18]

1. When I returned from abroad recently, I was inclined to think that the war scare at home was somewhat exaggerated and untimely. But the anti-Soviet campaign that has now been opened in France, a campaign similar in scope and method to the one conducted in Britain prior to the break in Soviet-British relations, forces me to think that the apprehension is perhaps rather underestimated than overestimated, and that the preparation for war has a solid foundation which is not limited to Britain alone.

2. Only the most naïve people or international political deceivers can say that the anti-Soviet campaign in France is directed against our present plenipotentiary representative there, Comrade Rakovsky, personally, for having signed the well-known declaration of the opposition.[19] . . .

Clearly this incident serves only as a pretext. Reactionary French circles have another aim in the campaign they have started, namely, to end Soviet-French relations and negotiations concerning debts.

3. We have pointed out more than once, and so have the serious political leaders of France, that there is no real reason for the misunderstanding between the U.S.S.R. and France. We were assured at one time by the French side that only the debt question blocked further rapprochement between the two states. But we recently succeeded in settling this problem to the satisfaction of both the French and the Soviet delegations by outlining a plan for annual payments by the U.S.S.R. of sixty million gold francs. This plan would profit millions of holders of Russian bonds which are now absolutely valueless, and, by providing for credits in order to finance Soviet orders to be placed with the French firms, would enlarge the export markets of French industries. It opened new possibilities for the economic and political rapprochement of the two states.

Therefore, we cannot consider it incidental that the anti-Soviet campaign [in France] started the day after this agreement was reached, because this campaign aims first of all at scrapping the outlined agreement, after which a policy similar to Great Britain's is to be pursued. It is not in vain that the French press, without naming names, stated that the anti-Soviet campaign was inspired and started by the same circles that a few months ago brought about the Anglo-Soviet rupture. In France, of course, as in England, a major role is being played by the internal party struggle. However, if we try to speak of it, we might be accused of interfering in internal affairs.

4. But let them not tell us that they are concerned only with getting a "guilty" plenipotentiary representative replaced. Actually, at present the fate of the Soviet-French conference is being settled, the fate of the agreement that has already been reached, the fate of the whole complex of Soviet-French relations. I do not know whether the circles hostile to us and their obedient press realize, as Anglo-Soviet relations have already proved, that there can be no agreement, claims, or payments

---

[18] Kliuchnikov and Sabanin, III, pp. 398–99.

[19] This so-called Platform of Eighty-Three was circulated in the summer of 1927 among party members. It urged the Central Committee to reopen discussion on controversial matters.

if relations deteriorate, still less if normal diplomatic relations are ended. Because of this, the above-mentioned circles take upon themselves a heavy responsibility before their own countrymen, the numerous holders of Russian bonds. Even if we do not regard the campaign as the result of conscious effort by these circles, we must admit that events have their own logic. It is now clear to everyone in Western Europe that the Anglo-Soviet rupture has created a definite threat to general peace, that it has further strained the international situation by creating new dangers of war. The Franco-Soviet rupture will increase these dangers still more. That is why we can flatly characterize the zealots of the anti-Soviet campaign in France as war-mongers and as the incendiaries of the world conflagration. We do not lose hope, however, that the French government and the peace-loving section of French public opinion will see this danger and will be able to avoid its consequences.[20]

THE WORLD ECONOMIC CONFERENCE

128

Soviet Estimate of the World Economic Situation

[Speech by the Soviet Delegate, Obolenski-Ossinski, at the World
Economic Conference, Geneva, May 7, 1927][21]

. . . The present world economic system is a veritable maze of contradictions. We find them everywhere. Though interlinked, they are infinite in number and variety. It would be impossible to enumerate them all, but no adequate review of the present situation can be given without a brief reference to the most important of them. That is not only possible but is very necessary if we are to obtain a clear idea of the true situation.

Suppose for a moment that we proceed to classify, in order of economic prosperity, the countries represented at this Conference, and also those not represented here.

We should give first place to the United States, the economic victor of the world war. We should place next the neutral States and the British Dominions; next would come England and France, the military victors, conquered Germany and the new States in Eastern Europe; and, finally, we should have the agricultural countries of the East and the semi-colonial and colonial territories.

If the experts who prepared the documentation for the Conference had drawn up a comparative table showing the conditions obtaining in all these countries—their national wealth, the national income per head of the population, the consumption of certain commodities, the average wages paid, the average length of the working day and so on—we should find a pitiful state of affairs attended by startling inequalities.

These inequalities existed before the war, it is true, but they have since been accentuated. It must be remembered that the whole population of the world—about 2,000 million—were caught in the backwash of the war. Even the most backward countries were aroused from their age-long slumber. All are now aspiring to economic and social equality, and no one who fails to grasp that truth can ever find the key to the social psychology of the age.

[Gives examples.] . . .

[20] A note of September 21, 1927, from the chairman of the Soviet delegation of the Franco-Soviet conference, Rakovsky, to the chairman of the French delegation, de Monsie, in connection with the Soviet-French negotiations on debts and credits, appears in Kliuchnikov and Sabanin, III, pp. 399–403.

[21] *World Economic Conference, Geneva, 1927*, I, 125–29.

To return, however, to the contradictions in the economic system of the world. The most general and the most obvious is the enormous disparity that exists between the productive capacity of industry and the purchasing-power of markets. It is revealed by the incomplete use that is being made of the instruments of production. Even in the United States, one of the most prosperous countries in the world, 25 per cent of the ironfounding plant and 25 per cent of the mechanical engineering plant is standing idle.

In England, 41 per cent of the metallurgical and 45 per cent of the textile plant is unused. In Poland, the figures are higher still. This phenomenon is so well known that I need not trouble you with fuller details. The root-causes of the situation are the reduction of the purchasing-power of the working and peasant classes in the majority of countries, the ruin of whole States, and the policy of boycotting and violence applied to large countries such as the U.S.S.R. and China. As the result of the late war, certain States are burdened with payments which oblige them to sell commodities, to throw them on the market—a senseless procedure from the economic point of view—or, conversely, to refuse to buy commodities that they actually require.

The reduction in the purchasing-power of the working-classes is one particular feature of another contradiction which has been greatly accentuated. I refer to the contradiction between the economic position of the working classes and that of the business capitalists. This contradiction is particularly striking in the United States. [Cites statistics.] . . .

Despite the upward trend of wages, the gulf between capital and labour has widened. During that period the class-consciousness of the workers, their economic claims and their demands for social equality greatly increased. There are in the world to-day not only what are known in Russia and Germany as "the scissors" between the curves of industrial and agricultural prices, but also social-economic "scissors" which are no less important and no less sharp.

In Europe, real wages are, at best, on the same level as before the war. East of the Elbe they are—except in the U.S.S.R.—below the pre-war level. . . .

At first sight, it may seem strange that, with so much unemployment in the world, the working day should be lengthened for those actually employed; yet this process —one of the lesser contradictions in the economic field—is very much on the increase. The Washington Resolutions of 1919 concerning the eight-hour day have never been ratified. The U.S.S.R. is the only country where the working day does not exceed eight hours, and is indeed only six hours in the mines. The working day in England, Germany and other countries is tending to become longer. . . .

All these facts are illustrative of the general offensive conducted by industrial capitalists against the working classes. This offensive is already taking the form of an attack against the trade-union right of association and the right to strike. From the economic point of view it is a sure sign of the sharpening of the contradictions that exist between labour and capital. For, I repeat, class-consciousness and the just claims of the working classes have grown apace.

An equally sharp contradiction is that which exists between capitalist industry and agricultural production. . . .

. . . In the capitalist world itself we find a whole series of contradictions—of conflicts. Let us pass over the less important of these—between capitalists in various branches of industry and between industrial, business and banking capital. The principal contradictions are between the powerful national capitalist groups in control of the big Powers to-day. A fierce struggle is raging in this domain, the struggle for sea and rail routes, for export markets, for sources of raw materials, for openings for capital investment. . . . The struggle for raw materials is the most plainly visible, but it is not the most important. It is astonishing to think that none of these problems are suggested as subjects for discussion at a Conference which is asked to study the economic difficulties that threaten the peace of the world.

While the great contradictions between the imperialist systems themselves were assuming vast proportions, some of these countries transformed into a contradiction of the sharpest kind the innate contrast that exists as between the capitalist system of the European-American world and the Socialist system of the Soviet Union.

The existence of this contrast does not imply that these two parties must necessarily come into actual conflict. The Soviet Union at any rate sees no inherent necessity for that. Socialism is not merely a system of economic and national equality; it stands primarily for peace. A peaceful foreign policy is a permanent feature and forms an organic part of the policy of the Soviet State. The fact that dissimilarity exists between two economic systems, which are forced for a given period to exist side by side, by no means precludes the possibility of a practical understanding between them. On the contrary, such an understanding is perfectly feasible. For that reason, the economic and financial boycotting of the U.S.S.R. which has been attempted with partial success in recent years has formed an unnecessary addition to the confusion already existing in the world. The share taken in world trade by the territory now comprised in the U.S.S.R. amounted before the war to 4 per cent. By 1925 it had fallen to a little over 1½ per cent, chiefly through the lack of requisite credits. Nevertheless, the part played by the Soviet Union in world trade and in the world money market is capable of increasing to dimensions even larger than before the war. The absence of the U.S.S.R. from these markets and its partial exclusion from world trade have aggravated the effect of the disturbances resulting from the reduced purchasing-power of the world as a whole.

The contradiction between the great empires of the world is closely connected with the other great contradictions in economic life to-day. The powerful groups which control the contemporary world States are causing violent conflicts between the interests and rights of the mother-countries and their colonies. The struggle for export markets, sources of raw materials and openings for capital investment is also a struggle for economic exploitation with the maximum yield. . . .

This contradiction, which already existed before the war, became sharply accentuated after the close of hostilities. The whole world having been divided up, the next step was to intensify the exploitation of the colonies. But the national consciousness of the colonial peoples and the class-consciousness of colonial workers have also grown. The ineradicable sympathy which the first Socialist republic of the world feels for colonial peoples, and more particularly for the people of China, in their struggle for their rights, is consonant with the inexorable laws of history.

The contradictions of the world capitalist regime may be described as constituting one long and constant world crisis, independent of the periodic economic crises and the periodic alternations of activity and depression.

In their more acute phases these contradictions take the form of a series of revolutions and armed conflicts which for the time being are only in the nature of guerilla warfare. But the large-scale armaments which are still being maintained together with the acute economic struggle now being waged render the menace of a new war, a fresh world cataclysm, a very real one.

What are the reasons for all these contradictions, and what has made them so intensely acute? The primary cause undoubtedly lies in the actual character of the economic system under which they have arisen. [Goes on to interpret the capitalist system as a growth of trusts and monopolies eventually resulting in armed competition among capitalist monopolies.] . . .

There is no real way out of the newly formed complex of these contradictions in world economy, or, rather, there is only one way out—to transform the whole economic system, or, in other words, to change over from the capitalist system, based on private ownership, to the socialist system. The contradictions that exist in the world economy of to-day will not disappear, nor will the menace of war be permanently removed, until the producers themselves take over the management of producers' trusts, which to-day have assumed nation-wide proportions, and until production, instead of being carried on in private interests, is designed to satisfy the requirements of the producers themselves. All other solutions are vain, and will only aggravate these contradictions, or at best temporarily mitigate their harmful effects, only, perhaps, to give rise to still more serious troubles in the future. [Analyzes and condemns proposals put forth by Loucheur and Jouhaux.][22] . . .

. . . I shall be told, the schemes for the reorganisation of Europe on socialistic lines have no bearing upon conditions at the present day or even in the present year. If the co-existence of the bourgeois and the Socialist systems for a limited period is regarded as feasible, it is *ipso facto* implied that the bourgeois system still has a further lease of life before it.

The world economic system is passing through a period of acute crisis. The consequences of that crisis will have a far-reaching effect on the situation of the masses. What are the measures that should be taken or that can be taken to remedy the worst of these contradictions, to improve the situation of the workers and to facilitate the transition to a new era in world economy? The following concrete proposals may furnish the answer to this question.

It is essential that:

1. All war debts and all payments relating to the war should be cancelled, this being the sole means of liquidating the contradictions which are the direct heritage of the war of 1914–18. The cancellation of such debts would be a great step towards the restoration of world trade.

2. The wages of industrial workers should be raised.

3. The eight-hour day should be restored and a six-hour day should be introduced in mines and in occupations that are especially arduous or unhealthy.

4. The working classes should be given full and genuine freedom of association and an absolute right to strike.

5. A system of real and effective assistance should be introduced for the unemployed, particularly for those thrown out of work through what is known as the rationalisation of production. For this purpose, heavier taxes should be levied on the incomes of the wealthy classes, and all unproductive forms of consumption (expenditure on army and navy, civil service, luxury articles, etc.) should be cut down.

6. Strong measures should be taken to combat the raising of the prices of industrial commodities, particularly by cartels.

7. All barriers to the migration of the surplus population of one State to another should be removed.

8. Protectorates and mandatory systems should be abolished, troops should be withdrawn from the colonies and all nations should be allowed self-determination in both the political and the economic field.

9. All military intervention in China should cease. China should be granted full political and economic self-determination with a view to the re-establishment of normal economic relations between herself and the rest of the world.

10. The economic and political boycott, in whatever form, of the Soviet Union should cease, and the relations established should be based on acceptance of the fact that two different systems must exist side by side. The Soviet Union should be granted credits to strengthen its purchasing-power; concessions should be given in the Soviet Union to foreign capital; technical co-operation and a system of exchange of information in the sphere of industrial technology should be established; no further attacks should be made upon institutions which form an indissoluble and organic part of the Socialist system—in particular, the State monopoly of foreign trade.

11. There should be complete and effective disarmament, and all permanent land

[22] Loucheur and Jouhaux represented France at the conference.

and sea forces should be abolished. All plant and equipment intended for military purposes should be dismantled under the supervision of the workers' and peasants' organisations.

Public opinion in the Soviet Union unanimously holds that not only is peace as dear to the heart of all peoples as life is to man but that it is the fundamental condition essential for all work in the economic sphere. Public opinion in the Soviet Union repudiates the capitalist and imperialist system for the very reason that it leads to war. The Soviet Union will do its utmost to support all practical measures to reduce the dangers of war and to save the lives of the workers in every country. It is itself prepared to take all measures that may be necessary to this end.

129

Obolenski-Ossinski Sums up the Results of the Conference at the Session of May 23, 1927[23]

Mr. President, ladies and gentlemen—The work of the World Economic Conference is nearing its conclusion, and the present moment appears to me to offer a suitable opportunity to draw certain conclusions from the point of view of the Soviet delegation.

Members of the Conference, Press representatives, the public, and all who have been following the proceedings of the Conference have been asking one another the same question during these last few days: Has the Conference been a success, or have its activities resulted in failure?

I shall endeavour first to reply to this question.

In the view of the Soviet delegation, the Conference might have proved a great success, and a very real success, if the decisions passed and the practical measures derived therefrom—to quote my first speech—had been such as to "remedy the worst of these contradictions, to improve the situation of the workers and to facilitate the transition to a new era in world economy."

Such a success would have involved the acceptance of the Soviet delegation's proposals, which were set forth in the eleven points[24] mentioned at the end of the speech I have just quoted. As you know, these proposals were not accepted, and most of the questions with which they deal were not even examined by the Conference.

The representatives of the capitalist States present here had assigned another task to this Conference, and tried to find other means of promoting what they called "the alleviation of world economic difficulties."

These means they sought to find by making minor changes in the economic and social policy of the capitalist States. They were thus helping to consolidate and stabilise the capitalist system, wherever it exists. Are such achievements of any value? Does this Conference, in the opinion and judgment of those assembled here, represent—for the moment, of course, only psychologically—any real progress in the stabilisation of the capitalist economic system? For such stabilisation is a fact, as we have repeatedly noted. Its existence is not assured forever, or even perhaps for very long, but at present it is a fact.

If this Conference really marks a further step in this direction, it must be confessed that it is only a very timid one, considering the acute differences of opinion and the divergency of interests and the enormous difficulties presented by the arrangement and the abstract form of the decisions taken, which are themselves due to those differences and that divergency.

One very far-reaching question was submitted to this Conference. I refer to

23 *World Economic Conference, Geneva, 1927*, I, 165–66.
24 See our pp. 385–86.

the question of establishing measures for the peaceful co-existence of two economic systems—the socialist system in the Soviet Union and the capitalist system in other countries.

The Soviet delegation suggested this practical formula, a formula which is inevitable in view of the *de facto* co-existence of the two systems and the structural links which exist in the world economic system. In proposing this formula we did not renounce a single one of the principles upon which our socialist system is based. We spoke advisedly of the co-existence of two different, two opposed economic systems.

Does this Conference mark a step forward towards the practical realisation of our proposal? It does. That is an actual fact, and it is one of the successes achieved by the Conference. This fact, like many others, is not yet fully established, but in the relevant resolution the principle has been enunciated sufficiently clearly.

As regards this point I should like to refer to a statement made by M. Jouhaux to the French Press. M. Jouhaux thinks we are inconsistent in condemning his very enthusiastic attempt to arrive at a compromise with the capitalist class while at the same time ourselves concluding compromises with the capitalist States.

Surely M. Jouhaux must see the fundamental difference. To begin with, what he calls our "compromises" do not mean a renunciation of the principles of the socialist system existing in the Soviet Union. Our compromise consists in a desire to promote exchanges of commodities between two entirely different economic systems. Such exchanges would in no way prejudice the interests of the working classes or compromise the principles upon which the socialist system in the Soviet Union is based.

M. Jouhaux's compromises are quite different in character. They simply amount to economic and political concessions to the capitalist class in the name of the workers.

Again, does M. Jouhaux not realise that, when the political and economic power of the whole State is in the hands of the workers, the relations between that State and capitalist States are not the same as relations between the different classes in any single State? Collisions between States mean war. Hence those who are opposed to war must seek for some scheme of peaceful co-existence. We deem it our duty to endeavour to find some such solution in our relations with States whose economic system is different from our own.

The position of the workers within a capitalist State is obviously quite different.

To return to questions which directly concern the Conference. I beg to inform you that the Soviet delegation will abstain when a vote is taken on the resolutions of the Conference as a whole. This we shall do because, although opposed to many of the principles, statements and concrete decisions formulated in this report, we find in it and in the resolutions as a whole various concrete decisions which we think right. There is, for instance, the formula—to us a vital formula—concerning economic co-operation between all countries irrespective of differences in their economic systems.

We do not wish to raise any formal obstacle which would prevent the realisation of those of the decisions which we approve. Therefore we shall abstain from voting on the report as a whole.

As regards the separate parts of the report, we expressed our opinion when voting on the individual motions.

I should mention that we have not been able to approve the proposals entrusting the execution of certain measures to different organs of the League of Nations. We are not Members of the League, and we have no intention of applying for admission. We cannot regard the League as an instrument of peace, for in our opinion it constitutes, in its present form, an instrument which serves the interests of the ruling Powers of the world and is often employed as a cloak to cover acts of violence committed at the expense of weaker States.

We propose, therefore, in conjunction with these States, to seek other means whereby the measures we take to carry out the resolutions that we approve may be co-ordinated with the measures taken by other States. We shall do our utmost to carry out these resolutions by rapid and energetic means, and we earnestly hope that the other States and nations will adopt, without delay and to the fullest possible extent, such parts of the Conference's work as may lead to positive results.

THE PREPARATORY COMMISSION ON DISARMAMENT

130

Zinoviev on How to Prevent War[25]

How can we prevent a new war?

The most important means for achieving this is the revolutionary enlightenment of the masses, the organization of the masses under the leadership of the Communist Party.

The best issue for the whole of humanity would be if the European revolution were to come to pass before a new imperialist war broke out. Our whole policy should be directed toward this end. This would be the most economical, the "most peaceful" issue (not from the pacifist, but from the revolutionary point of view).

In any case, it is our greatest revolutionary concern to postpone war as long as possible, to try with every means in our power to prevent it. After the imperialist war which so seriously hit the industrial life of our country, peace is the most necessary condition both for our socialist growth and for the preparation and consolidation of the Communist Parties in other countries. The later imperialism sets war against us in motion, the stronger we will be, we, the Soviet Union and the world proletariat with us.

Our task is:

1. The building up of Socialist economy; we must build up without a moment's respite, build in the teeth of all difficulties by which we are faced. 2. We must civilize ourselves, we must work at carrying through successfully the "cultural revolution," we must work at our own development and 3. we must with all our might, promote the cause of the international revolution—such is Lenin's command and this command will be fulfilled. . . .

131

The U.S.S.R., the League of Nations, and Disarmament

[Excerpt from Rykov's Report to the Fourth Congress of Soviets of the U.S.S.R., April 19, 1927][26]

At the present time the bourgeoisie is endeavoring to use our attitude toward the League of Nations in its campaign against us; it is accusing the government of the U.S.S.R. of refusing to join the League and to take part in the general work of "peace." Our relations with the League of Nations may now again become a key

25 *International Press Correspondence*, No. 14, February 17, 1927, pp. 293–94.
26 *Izvestiia*, No. 90, April 20, 1927, p. 2; also *Russia's Foreign Policy Outlined by Mr. A. I. Rykov*, pp. 14–16.

question, both because of the general international situation and because the "geographical" obstacle to our participation in the work of special business commissions of the League of Nations has now been removed. A few days ago our plenipotentiary representative in Germany, Comrade Krestinsky, and the Swiss ambassador in Berlin, with the consent of both governments, signed a protocol ending the conflict between the U.S.S.R. and Switzerland caused by the murder of Vorovsky during the Lausanne Conference. . . .

Is the League of Nations really struggling for peace? As is well known, both China and Britain are members of the League of Nations. May it not be asked in what way this membership has affected the relations between these two countries? British armed forces in China are as active as they were before the League was organized, if not more so, and the League has not even placed the discussion of the war in China on its agenda. During recent times there have been a number of armed conflicts, a number of wars, a number of violations of the peace, a whole series of very acute conflicts. . . . The League of Nations is only an instrument in the hands of a small group of some of the biggest imperialist states for supremacy over the other states.

The League of Nations never has played and does not now play any other role, unless we take into account certain harmful illusions about its nature, illusions that persist even though they are at variance with all actual occurrences. The League is said to be an organization to prevent war; our refusal to join it is interpreted as unwillingness "to struggle for peace." We have supported and shall continue to support by every means in our power every real movement in the struggle for peace, and we are ready to give every possible measure of support to any really pacifist organization, but we do not desire to enter into an organization of the character of the League of Nations.

Conference on Disarmament

The League of Nations is endeavoring to prove its love of peace by calling a conference on disarmament. Voices have been heard to say that if this conference fails, its failure will arise mainly from the nonparticipation of the U.S.S.R. Actually the unlikelihood of its success has already become apparent during the preparatory work, which shows the conference to be not really on disarmament, but on how to preserve, with the least possible expenditure, the military supremacy of those countries that now dominate the world. The draft plans, the contents of which have now filtered through to the press, show that the dominant powers are endeavoring to establish an "armaments regime" to prevent other states from becoming strong enough to defend themselves against the strongest imperialist states.

Our Proposals

We have more than once expressed our attitude toward disarmament in principle, but I think it would be well to reaffirm our position. We are prepared to agree, and we call upon all other countries to agree, to the most radical measures for preventing war and armed struggle. We propose the complete destruction of war industries, and the establishment of a real control by representatives of the people, the workers, trade union organizations, and peasants.

We propose also the control of financial resources that might be used for war preparations. The people's representatives should be responsible for seeing that not a single farthing is spent on war matériel. We sincerely call upon all states to co-operate in this work. Recently in the British Parliament our state was basely accused of surpassing other states in its preparations for chemical warfare. . . . I here declare that there is no branch of war industry in which any of the big Western European states does not excel us in both resources and means. Moreover, of all the European countries and America, only the U.S.S.R. has been spending on its army since the imperialist war less than half of what was formerly spent.

This slander is evident: Consider only the backwardness of our technical development, particularly in the chemical industry, compared with that of the chief imperialist states. Demagogical speeches of this character are due to the [Allies'] wish to justify their own preparations for chemical warfare. . . .

132

Total Disarmament Proposed by Litvinov at the Preparatory Commission on Disarmament, November 30, 1927[27]

M. Litvinoff (Union of Socialist Soviet Republics).—The Government of the Union of Socialist Soviet Republics, having been unable to participate in the three sessions which have already been held by the Preparatory Commission of the Disarmament Conference, has entrusted its delegation to the fourth session of the Preparatory Commission to make a declaration covering all questions connected with the problem of disarmament.

I. The Government of the Union of Socialist Soviet Republics adheres to the opinion it has always held that under the capitalist system no grounds exist for counting upon the removal of the causes giving rise to armed conflicts. Militarism and navalism are essentially natural consequences of the capitalist system. By the very fact of their existence, they intensify existing differences, giving a vast impetus to all potential quarrels and inevitably converting these into armed conflicts.

The people in all countries, however enfeebled and impoverished by the imperialist world-war of 1914–18, are imbued with the determination to struggle against imperialist wars and for the guaranteeing of peace between the nations.

This is precisely what has made it possible for the Soviet Government to accept the invitation of the League of Nations, the latter having expressed itself in favour of disarmament. In so doing, the Soviet Government demonstrates in the face of the whole world its will to peace between the nations and wishes to make clear to all the real inspirations and true desires of the other States with regard to disarmament.

. . .

In now sending its delegation to the fourth session of the Preparatory Commission on Disarmament, the Government of the Union of Socialist Soviet Republics has authorised it to present a scheme for general and complete disarmament.

II. The delegation of the Union of Socialist Soviet Republics is authorised by its Government to propose the complete abolition of all land, naval and air forces.

The Government of the Union suggests the following measures for the realisation of this proposal:

(a) The dissolution of all land, sea and air forces and the non-admittance of their existence in any concealed form whatsoever.

(b) The destruction of all weapons, military supplies, means for chemical warfare and all other forms of armament and means of destruction in the possession of troops or in military or general stores.

(c) The scrapping of all warships and military air vessels.

(d) The discontinuance of calling up citizens for military training either in armies or public bodies.

(e) Legislation for the abolition of military service, either compulsory, voluntary, or recruited.

27 *Preparatory Commission for the Disarmament Conference*, Series V, pp. 9–12.

(f) Legislation prohibiting the calling-up of trained reserves.

(g) The destruction of fortresses and naval and air bases.

(h) The scrapping of military plants and factories and of war industry equipment in general industrial works.

(i) The discontinuance of assigning funds for military purposes both on State budgets and those of public bodies.

(k) The abolition of military, naval and air ministries, and the dissolution of general staffs and military administrations, departments and institutions of every kind.

(l) The legislative prohibition of military propaganda and military training of the population and of military education both in State and public bodies.

(m) The legislative prohibition of the patenting of all kinds of armaments and means of destruction with a view to the removal of incentives to the invention of the same.

(n) Legislation making the infringement of any of the above stipulations a grave crime against the State.

(o) The withdrawal or corresponding alteration of all legislative acts, both of national or international scope, infringing the above stipulations.

III. The delegation of the Union is empowered to propose the execution of the above programme of complete disarmament as soon as the Convention in question comes into force, in order that all the necessary measures for the destruction of military stores be completed in a year's time.

The Soviet Government considers that the above scheme for the execution of complete disarmament is the simplest and the most conducive to peace.

In the case, however, of capitalist States rejecting immediate actual abolition of standing armies, the Soviet Government, in its desire to facilitate the achievement of a practical agreement on complete disarmament, is prepared to make a proposal for complete disarmament to be carried out simultaneously by all contracting States, by gradual stages, during a period of four years, the first stage to be accomplished in the course of the coming year.

National funds, freed from war expenditure, to be employed by each State at its own discretion, but exclusively for productive and cultural purposes.

IV. Whilst insisting upon the views just stated, the delegation of the Union of Socialist Soviet Republics is nevertheless ready to participate in any and every discussion of the question of the limitation of armaments whenever practical measures really leading to disarmament are proposed.

V. The delegation declares that the Government of the Union fully subscribes to the Convention on the prohibition of the application to military purposes of chemical and bacteriological substances and processes, expresses its readiness to sign the Convention immediately while insisting on an early date being fixed for its ratification by all States, and considers that, in order to ensure the practicability of the Convention, it would be necessary to raise the question of the establishment of workers' control over those chemical industries susceptible of being rapidly converted to war purposes in States having a highly developed chemical industry.

We have laid before you our programme of disarmament, but realise that its radical and exhaustive nature may make it appear at the first glance complex, difficult of realisation and perhaps even Utopian. This, however, is merely because the problem of complete disarmament has always been treated as a forbidden subject and never yet thoroughly dealt with. We understand perfectly that the realisation of this programme may not be compatible with certain political interests, chiefly those of the great Powers, the interests of war industries or those of the numerous groups of speculators, but I contend that in itself the problem of complete disarmament presents no difficulties and is capable of rapid and easy solution.

It is in any case a great deal simpler, and would require far less time to work out in detail, than the schemes which have so far been used as a basis for the work of the Preparatory Commission. I confess that, on acquainting myself with the findings of this Commission, I was aghast at the complexity, confusion and multiplicity of the questions with which that of disarmament had become involved. The Commission has, in effect, devoted several sessions to the discussion of the enumeration and headings of the clauses to make up an international Convention for limitation of armaments. Unanimity has only been achieved with regard to certain trivial and common points. The overwhelming majority of the clauses—or rather their head-ings—evoked dissensions which have so far failed to be reconciled either by the Commission itself or by private negotiations between the Governments concerned. If and when, however, these dissensions have been reconciled, the Commission will still only be at the threshold of its real difficulties. The Commission will have to agree to the satisfaction of all as to what constitutes security for each country and, indi-vidually, the extent and importance of its international obligations, its geographical peculiarities and other special features, before the level of its effectives, technical armaments, military and air vessels, etc., can be established.

The mere enumeration of these questions will suffice to bring before us the utter hopelessness—more, the Utopianism—of expecting this question to be solved within any imaginable period.

The latest manifestations of international life, various international treaties recently concluded, lead not to the unification but rather to the still further division of the European and non-European countries into political groupings, and to the intensification of their mutual antagonisms, and do not afford the slightest grounds for optimism as to the outcome of the questions before the Preparatory Commission.

To crown all, attempts are still being made to delay for a long time to come the work of the Preparatory Commission pending the solution of a series of political questions not less confused and complex than those I have already mentioned.

One thing is certain: if the present basis of the Preparatory Commission's work is not changed, it is—even if not exploded by the abundance and weight of its own internal differences—condemned to years, if not decades, of work either completely sterile or productive of quite intangible results.

We live in a time in which the outbreak of fresh wars is no mere theoretical danger. This is not merely our opinion; many responsible statesmen in capitalist countries have expressed the same fears quite recently. The imminence of war is making itself felt everywhere. If it is to be averted, something will have to be done. In our opinion, the best guarantee of security for all peoples and all countries is immediate complete disarmament. This problem should be faced immediately and solved in the shortest possible time. Those countries postponing the solution of this problem are taking upon themselves an enormous responsibility. I therefore beg to move on behalf of the Soviet delegation the following resolution:

> Whereas the existence of armaments and the tendency they show to growth by their very nature inevitably lead to armed conflicts between nations, diverting the workers and peasants from peaceful productive labour and bringing in its train countless disasters;
>
> Whereas armed force is a weapon in the hands of great Powers for the oppression of peoples in small and colonial countries; and
>
> Whereas the complete abolition of armaments is at present the only real means of guaranteeing security and affording a guarantee against the outbreak of war.
>
> The fourth Session of the Preparatory Commission for the Disarmament Conference resolves:
>
> (1) To proceed immediately to the working out in detail of a draft Con-vention for complete and general disarmament on the principle proposed by the Delegation of the Union of Socialist Soviet Republics;

(2) To propose the convocation, not later than March 1928, of a Disarmament Conference for the discussion and confirmation of the proposals provided for in paragraph (1).

We are fully aware that certain circles will endeavour to stigmatise our programme and resolution as propaganda. We are quite ready to accept this challenge and declare that we are making propaganda for peace and shall continue to do so. If the Preparatory Commission for the Disarmament Conference is not a suitable place in which to make peace propaganda, then apparently we are here under a misunderstanding. The Soviet Government pursues, and has always pursued, a resolute peace policy which it has always shown, and is still showing, in deeds as well as in words. . . .

133

Litvinov's Comments on the Preparatory Commission for the Disarmament Conference

[Report to the Fifteenth Party Congress, December 14, 1927][28]

. . . In its correspondence with the League of Nations concerning the invitation to the conference on disarmament, the Soviet government emphasized sufficiently strongly its distrust of the League's efforts in this field. . . . What we saw and heard at Geneva did not in the least alleviate our distrust. . . .

As the result of the labors [of the Preparatory Commission] we have a document entitled the Draft International Convention on Disarmament.[29] This is a very curious document. No eloquent description can convey the League's methods as clearly as a thorough examination of this document. It consists of several sections with about fifty articles, subarticles, subclauses, notes, and so forth. But even the first introductory article is given in three parallel versions, French, English, and German. Then follow several articles enumerating the kinds of armament and army formations that should be reduced. In vain you will look to this document for a single figure, for a single coefficient dealing with disarmament. Figures are absolutely absent. The kinds of arms and ammunition to be reduced are named, but how this reduction is to be effected, within what limit, by what criterion—the commission has simply not dealt with these questions yet. This is so because even the drafting of the above-described articles aroused a great many disagreements and arguments among the bourgeois countries. There is hardly any important article in the document regarding which several proposals, several plans—French, English, Japanese, German, and so forth—were not made. Since the Preparatory Commission itself could not settle these differences, its work is to be supplemented by private diplomatic negotiations among the interested powers. Only after these negotiations bear fruit will the commission meet again to discuss what figures are to be substituted for the x's and y's scattered throughout the draft; that is, the present algebraic formulae will be changed into a concrete project. These figures, it is expected, will indicate the maximum possible reduction in various kinds of armament, personnel, command, ships, and airplanes, but all this, mind you, for each country separately. No general criteria for limiting armaments were given, and it is proposed to discuss the armament levels for each country separately . . . in accordance with its degree of security, its international obligations, its geographical position, and, so the proposals read, "its other

[28] *XV sezd V.K.P.*, pp. 946–54.

[29] For the text of the Draft Convention see *Preparatory Commission for the Disarmament Conference*, Series X, pp. 425–61.

peculiarities." These matters in turn must obviously be discussed, because agreement and unanimity on them must be reached among the powers. . . . But please, comrades, do not think that even after unanimity is reached . . . the convention will present any categorical and definite statements, or will provide any guarantee against the horrors of a war such as we witnessed ten years ago. Nothing of the kind! The draft includes the [following] article, which I will read to you in full: "The provisions of the present Convention shall not prevent any of the High Contracting Parties from increasing its land, naval or air armaments beyond the agreed figures: (1) If a war in which it is a belligerent has broken out," (that is, the convention provides no security whatever, and every country is free to increase its armaments to a maximum) "or (2) If it is threatened with a rebellion, or" (they did not forget this either!) "(3) If this increase is effected with the consent of the Council of the League of Nations."[30]

Here we come to the question of so-called potential, that is, of granting each country, in case of war, the right to raise its armament upon its own initiative. Consequently, the countries that are well-developed industrially and capable of mobilizing their war industries will immediately acquire a very great superiority over the countries with lesser industrial development—that is, over the small nations in general.

Another, equally curious article reads: "If, during the term of the present Convention, a High Contracting Party considers that the requirements of its national security are materially affected by any change of circumstances, it may be authorised to exceed the limits for armaments fixed under the present Convention by a unanimous decision of the following High Contracting Parties: . . ."[31] The space that follows is to be filled later with the names of the judges who will be given the right to decide which country can increase its armament despite the convention. This, comrades, is called a "sober realistic approach to the matter," in contrast to the "Utopian, idealistic" proposals made by the Soviet delegation.

It would seem, comrades, that the plan outlined by the Preparatory Commission would make for endless sessions and conferences over a great many years, so that the adversaries of disarmament have nothing to fear on this score. But actually even this snail-like pace appears to make some apprehensive. Thus, at the last session of the League of Nations, additional measures were taken to prevent not only any untimely disarmament, but even the discussion of the problem of disarmament. (Laughter, shouts: "That is how they disarm!") For this purpose there was invented and created the so-called Security Committee, charged with discussing additional guarantees of security for the League's members—in other words, guarantees of a secure digestion of war spoils and of the forceful territorial robberies that have been carried on in violation of the Versailles, Saint-Germain, and other treaties. This committee must also examine, with the same purpose, the relevant articles of the League's Covenant and seek means to strengthen them. Only after this committee has finished its work will the Draft Convention on which I am reporting to you be discussed.

Here, comrades, is the balance of the work of the League of Nations on disarmament which our delegation found in Geneva.

The fourth session of the Preparatory Commission, in which we participated, had an insignificant agenda consisting of two points: (1) settling the date for the next session, and (2) creating the Security Committee.

If we ignore the creation of the committee, whose connection with the Preparatory Commission was disputed by others besides ourselves, it follows that the representatives of twenty-six powers from all over the world went to Geneva simply to

[30] *Ibid.*, Article XA, p. 452.
[31] *Ibid.*, Article ZE, p. 454.

settle the date for the next session. It is not surprising, therefore, that when the Soviet delegation raised in the Preparatory Commission the question of actual disarmament, its action was taken to be a sacrilege, an attack on the principles of the commission of the League of Nations, a violation of every rule of proper behavior.

．　．　．

The commission's leaders, however, did everything possible, on various pretexts, to ignore our proposal and proceed with the agenda. This they needed to do . . . mainly because actually they had nothing to say against our suggestion, as was soon proved during the short discussion to which the commission was obliged to agree.

Indeed, what objections did we hear to our program? They said it was too simple. True enough. It is so simple that it calls for a simple answer: It does not permit the discussion, argument, and delay to which the League is accustomed. From this point of view, the simplicity of our program presents inconveniences to some people.

They said that our program was too good not to have been thought of before, and that if our ancestors had never thought of it, we too should not consider it. Moreover, they said, the commission already had its own plan for a convention, upon which it had spent much time and effort, and which therefore must not simply be shelved (laughter); we must engage ourselves in this plan, and not in our own. At the same time they openly acknowledged that discussions of their plan have led to a hopeless impasse. . . . It was also said that some countries, despite the convention on full disarmament, might continue to arm—this argument can be applied to any agreement. It seems to me much easier to police a [disarmed] state that violated a promise not to arm, than to control an armed state that promised only partial disarmament and then secretly broke its promise. All such arguments are absolutely nonsensical.

．　．　．

Some bourgeois newspapers, even some of a liberal trend, rejected our program on philosophical grounds: the militant nature of man in general, his love of fighting, and the inevitability of struggle. If complete disarmament takes place, they said, people will have to fight with their fists, and this is a withdrawal from civilization and a return to barbarism. The companions of civilization [so it seems] are gunpowder, lead, tanks, dumdum bullets, submarines, bomb-carrying planes, the destruction of cities, poison gas, and other paraphernalia of modern warfare. Without them, it appears, civilization is impossible.

Our plans have produced quite a literature abroad. Every paper, every periodical had something to say about them. Although I followed closely what they said, I found no arguments other than those enumerated above.

The position of the representatives of the capitalist states on the commission was indeed tragic. They could not say that they declined the plan for total disarmament. Did not the disarmament conference, and the Preparatory Commission, stem from the fact that the capitalist governments, even the most reactionary of them, are obliged to pay some heed to public opinion, which demands guarantees against future wars and which wants relief from the military burden? They could not therefore come out against complete disarmament, but neither could they disclose their reasons for opposing it, reasons that we, comrades, know very well. Meanwhile, they were naturally unable to argue seriously against our program, or to prove it inapplicable, granted a desire to disarm. And that is why, having first tried to circumvent any discussion, they later thwarted such discussion.

．　．　．

We were also obliged to disagree with the other members of the Preparatory Commission over the date for the following session. The Soviet delegation proposed the nearest possible date; it was prepared to continue the work without returning home, and to work on holidays. In view of the recess (already decided upon) during the sessions of the League of Nations, however, and the other delegations' evident unwillingness to work during holidays, the Soviet delegation suggested that the commission's fifth session meet on January 10. But, of course, the commission has its own tempo of work. . . .

We then introduced a final resolution maintaining that there was no connection between the Preparatory Commission's work and that of the Security Committee. The German delegation, having introduced some minor amendments, supported our resolution as a whole. It also insisted on the earliest possible convocation of the next session of the Preparatory Commission. However, it soon began to vacillate, gave up its positions, and agreed to a suggested compromise, namely, that the next session be held on March 15.

In this and other cases, the German delegation went with us for a certain time, although its motives were different from ours. The German delegation is also interested in settling the disarmament question as soon as possible. Disarmed by the Versailles treaty, Germany bases her demand for other countries' disarmament on one of the articles of the Covenant of the League of Nations. If this article is violated, Germany may have the right to insist on her own armament.

Germany, jointly with us, believed that keeping the Preparatory Commission's work separate from the Security Committee's would speed up the commission's work. But being bound by the decisions of the League of Nations, of which she is now a member, she could not defend her demands as persistently as the Soviet delegation did.

As a result, in all the questions discussed by the commission a clear dividing line has been drawn between us and the rest of the members. This is understandable. We cannot complain about it. You, comrades, must understand that under the circumstances we could not always speak when we wished, or say what we wanted to say.

Now a few words about the Security Committee. We refused to join this committee as a full-fledged member. We saw the committee as a device to postpone disarmament, and we could not assume responsibility for such tactics. Besides, not being a member of the League of Nations, not recognizing its Covenant, we naturally could not examine, explain, and amend separate articles of the Covenant, or in general take part in any decision of the League Council or of the League itself. However, in view of the technical connection, established against our will, between the Preparatory Commission and the Security Committee, we agreed to join the committee as observers, for information purposes. The rights of so-called observers in the League of Nations are not regulated and are provided for in each case separately and by agreement.

I was present as an observer at the first session of the Security Committee, and if I had wished to take the floor on any question, I presume I would not have been prevented from doing so. But I did not make use of this opportunity, chiefly because the questions the committee discussed had no relation to us whatsoever.

The committee simply outlined the program of its [future] work. Two tendencies immediately became manifest. First, an attempt was made to resurrect the so-called Geneva Protocol dealing with obligatory arbitration and mutual guarantees, the same protocol that was accepted in principle, but not officially, by the MacDonald government, only to be repudiated by the present Conservative government of Great Britain. The British delegate, spotting this attempt, stated definitely that the protocol should be considered as dead and buried. If the committee wished to consider this protocol, it could of course do so, but he wished to warn the committee that no one present would live until the discussion was over. (Laughter.)

．　．　．

Second, the first exchange of views in the Security Committee gives a clear picture of the battles that will take place there in the future, and also serves as a splendid confirmation of the view expressed by us: i.e., that to establish mutual dependence between the Preparatory Commission and the Security Committee is the best way to doom the work on disarmament to complete sterility, or at best to endless delay.

The sum total of our participation in the work at Geneva is this: For the first time the problem of actual disarmament has been seriously and concretely advanced. Let our adversaries say, as Beneš says, that our program lacks novelty. Nevertheless, for the first time in history there has been advanced a plan for total disarmament, and thus for an end to wars—not resolutions or pious wishes by some pacifist society, but a carefully worked out and concrete program proposed by a state that occupies one-sixth of the globe. It is impossible to ignore this proposal, nor shall we allow it to be ignored. Although we found no co-operation in Geneva, we have many supporters and co-thinkers all over the world, to judge from the large number of telegrams, letters, and resolutions that we received in Geneva and are continuing to receive at home. Resolutions have been adopted not only by pacifist societies, but even by some parties of the Second International, conceding the greatness of our program and seeking to join it, at least verbally. That the bourgeoisie is very much disturbed by our plans is clear from its efforts to discredit our proposals. The bourgeoisie even resorts to the most "heroic" measures, that is, it fabricates [new] "Zinoviev letters" . . . [cites examples].

Some "socialist" from the Second International announced a few days ago: "Let Soviet Russia set an example for others, let her disarm, and we may then follow this example." (Laughter, exclamation: "We are not such fools!") This suggestion, of course, is not naïve, but it is stupid, and deserves no answer. We know very well that there are those who strongly wish not total disarmament, but the disarmament of the Soviet state alone, so that they can seize it with bare hands. But they will not succeed in this attempt. We have declared before and we declare now that we are fully ready to apply our program if other countries agree to do likewise. If the capitalist states doubt our sincerity, they can test us by joining our program. Let them take this risk. If they do not, if they cannot, if they do not wish to, then they reveal, against their own wishes and before the whole world, that the proposal for complete disarmament and the end of wars can come only from the soviet state, and can be accepted and carried out only when the soviet system has spread to other states of the world, because then the principles that now guide the U.S.S.R. will form the basis of the policy of these states as well.

134

Stalin on Capitalist Disarmament

[Excerpt from the Political Report of the Central Committee of the VKP to the Fifteenth Congress of the Party, 1927, Delivered by Stalin, December 3, 1927][32]

. . .

(b) During the period under review were there any attempts made at a "peaceful settlement" of the developing military conflicts? Yes, there were. More attempts were made than might have been expected, but they resulted in nothing, absolutely

---

[32] *XV sezd V.K.P.*, pp. 42–44; also *Report of the Fifteenth Congress of the Communist Party of the Soviet Union*, pp. 27–29.

nothing. Moreover, these attempts merely proved to be screens to cover the preparatory work of the "powers" for new wars, screens designed to deceive the workers and peasants.

Let us take the League of Nations, which, according to the deceitful bourgeois press, and the equally mendacious Social Democratic press, is an instrument of peace. What good results has the League's chatter had in bringing about peace, disarmament, and the curtailment of armaments? None, except the deception of the masses, new attempts at armament, a new aggravation of the ripening conflicts. Can it be regarded as a mere accident that, although the League of Nations, supported by the so-called Second International, has for three years been giving out lying twaddle about peace and disarmament, the "nations" keep on arming and arming, increasing the old conflicts between the "powers" and piling up new ones, thus undermining the cause of peace? What does the failure of the Three-Power Conference on the Reduction of Naval Armaments (England, America, and France) indicate if not that the Pacific problem is the source of new imperialist wars, that the "powers" do not want to disarm or reduce their armaments? What has the League of Nations done to avert this danger? Or consider the recent proposal of the Soviet delegation in Geneva for real (and not decorative) disarmament. How can we explain the fact that the straight and honest declaration of Comrade Litvinov on complete disarmament stunned the League of Nations and proved to be "absolutely unexpected"? Does this not show that the League is an instrument not of peace and disarmament, but for concealing new armaments and preparations for new wars? The corrupt bourgeois press of all countries, from Japan to Britain, from France to America, clamors about the "insincerity" of the Soviet disarmament proposals. Then why not test our sincerity and proceed now with practical disarmament, or at least with a serious reduction of armaments? What prevents this? Consider, for example, the present system of "treaties of amity" of capitalist states, the agreement between France and Yugoslavia, the agreement between Italy and Albania, the "treaty of amity" between Poland and Lithuania now being prepared by Pilsudski, the "Locarno system," the "spirit of Locarno," etc.—what is all this if not a system of preparing new wars and allocating forces for them? Or take, for instance, the following facts: The numerical strength of the armies of France, Britain, Italy, the United States of America, and Japan increased between 1913 and 1927 from 1,888,000 to 2,262,000 men; during the same period the war budgets of the same countries increased from 2,345,000,000 gold rubles to 3,948,000,000 rubles; the number of airplanes in active service in these five countries increased between 1923 and 1927 from 2,655 to 4,340; the tonnage of cruisers of these five powers increased from 724,000 tons in 1922 to 864,000 tons in 1926. As for war chemicals, the chief of the Chemical War Service of the United States, General Fries, has stated that "one air-chemical bomb of 450 kg. charged with Lewisite can make ten districts of New York uninhabitable, and 100 tons of Lewisite dropped from 50 airplanes can make all New York uninhabitable at least for a week." What do these facts show if not that new wars are being prepared at top speed in all countries?

Such are the results of the "peace policy" and "disarmament policy" of the bourgois states in general, the League of Nations especially, and the Social Democratic capitalist lackeys in particular.

. . . Is it not clear that the growth of these armaments is dictated by the inevitability of new imperialist wars among the "powers," that the "war spirit" is the fundamental substance of the "spirit of Locarno"?

. . . It would suffice to shake up the present "peaceful relations" somewhere in Albania or Lithuania, China or North America, to cause the whole "structure of peaceful relations" to fall to the ground. . . .

From stabilization arises the inevitability of new imperialist wars.

. . .

SOVIET MILITARY PREPAREDNESS

135

M. V. Frunze on Soviet Military Organization, 1922

[Excerpts from an Article Entitled "Regular Army and Militia,"
March 1922][33]

Can we expect our militia, which will inevitably be nine-tenths peasant, to acquire in short periods of training the teamwork and discipline that provide the basis for military preparedness?

I think we can. . . . If we organize our political education correctly, we shall still have units that will be fully unified and disciplined for mass action.

We must also take into account the existence among the peasant masses, and particularly among the Great Russians, of traditions and habits that are survivals of former patriarchal relations. This considerably simplifies our work of putting across the spirit of solidarity. In the process of collectivizing the peasant economy, these habits will be stressed, and the situation will be further improved.

It is interesting to note that in the old Russian army the feeling of contact between individuals [sviaz], a reflection of the existing peasant psychology, was an important morale factor. This has been noted many times by military experts, not only in Russia but abroad. . . .

Engels speaks of it as follows: "The Russian soldier is indisputably courageous. So long as the tactical outcome of the battle depends upon attack by closed ranks of infantry masses, he is in his element. The entire past experience of the Russian soldier has taught him to co-operate closely with his comrades. The semicommunist *obshchina* [village commune] in the countryside, artels in towns, produce joint responsibility [krugovaia poruka] everywhere. The Russian soldier has seen around him an organization of society that continually demands co-operation and that always emphasizes the helplessness of separate individuals left to their own devices. This psychology guides the Russians in battle. The soldiers are placed in tightly knit columns. The greater the danger, the stronger the soldiers' inclination to close ranks." (Engels on the Prussian military problem, 1865.)

This opinion shows that military discipline in the Russian army was the discipline not of a regular army, but of militia, that is, the discipline that followed from the soldier's conditions of labor and life.

136

Soviet Armed Strength Based on the Principle of the Territorial Militia System

[Frunze's Report to the Secretaries of Party Cells, February 27,
1925][34]

The army is an instrument of war. The defense system of any state is necessarily determined by the [nature of the expected] armed conflicts and by its war potential.

When we ask what form our army organization should take, we must also ask what sort of war our Red Army may be expected to wage.

[33] M. V. Frunze, *Sobranie sochinenii*, I, 433-34. Frunze was made People's Commissar for Military and Naval Affairs in 1924 after the removal of Trotsky. He held this post until his death in 1925, when he was succeeded by K. E. Voroshilov.

[34] *Ibid.*, III, 131-34, 136-38.

The nature of such a war will be fully and absolutely determined by the nature and character of our state, by the development of its productive forces, and by its position in relation to other states. What do we find in this last regard? Our state definitely, absolutely, and irreconcilably opposes the capitalist world that encircles us. This opposition forces us, militarily speaking, to plan on being confronted in future military encounters by the united forces of all imperialist camps. If we remember that the clash between these two mutually exclusive worlds can only end with the victory of one or the other, we will see clearly that our task, as military workers, is to prepare ourselves for that clash.

When the great and serious war breaks out between the Union of Soviet [Socialist] Republics and the union of the largest bourgeois states, no limited aims will be pursued. The task will not be to drive the enemy from this or that area, this or that sector. If such a war actually breaks out, it will be a gigantic life-and-death struggle. The nature of this struggle determines our entire military work.

We must organize our future armed forces for just this life-and-death struggle. Therefore, it becomes imperative for us to have in readiness all the forces of both the Red Army and the Soviet state.

The numerical strength of the forces we will have to send into the battle against imperialism becomes evident. We shall clearly have to deal with huge armies, millions of men strong. Hence we need a peacetime organization that will allow us at the time of mobilization, at the moment when the struggle begins, to call millions of our own fighters to the colors and send them to the battlefield. Here, then, is our first deduction from the nature of future wars, namely that we will need enormous numbers of trained men.

The second deduction is that all efforts of the workers and peasants throughout the country must be strained to the utmost. There is, of course, nothing new in this conclusion, a lesson of the past imperialist war. . . .

[But] we expand its scope. When we speak of "mobilization" . . . we apply it to the workers and peasants behind the lines, to our entire national economy, as well as to our educational efforts, and so forth.

· · ·

Our third deduction is that very broad military propaganda will be necessary throughout the length and breadth of our workers' and peasants' country. . . . The present rapid development of aviation and of chemical and other means of warfare indicates that a long and stationary line at the front cannot long be maintained. There will always be an opportunity to reach the enemy's rear, to deal a blow to the enemy's bases and even to places without direct military significance.

This technical character of future wars calls for the timely preparation and training not only of those who are liable to military service, but of the masses in general, particularly those who live close to the front line, since there is no longer a distinction between the "rear" and the "front" . . .

I want to dwell on two aspects of our work: the organization of the armed forces and the psychological propaganda and technical preparedness of the rear for the conditions of future wars.

You can see from what I have said that we must find some new way to organize the armed forces. This search for new ways is inevitable; we cannot produce the huge armies we shall need from the numerically insignificant cadres in the present regular army. These new ways we have seen and we now see in the development of the system of militia and territorial units.

· · ·

The expansion of our armed forces is possible only by increasing the cadres of our regular army or by developing the militia system. For both financial and political reasons the first method is closed to us. . . .

One reason for our strength and our moral influence in the eyes of millions of workers and peasants abroad is their absolute faith in the peaceful nature of our military policy. True enough, that is what our policy has always been. Not only in words, but also in actions, we have applied and are now applying the policy of peace. By doing so we in no way repudiate or betray our revolutionary class position, which works in the interests not only of the working class of the Soviet Union but of the international proletariat. . . . If we could only secure for ourselves by peaceful means the chance for cultural, economic, and political development, by this fact alone we could overthrow the bourgeois world, because by devoting our utmost effort to the consolidation of our economy we would rapidly reach the [economic] level of modern bourgeois countries. There could be no better revolutionary propaganda than this, no more powerful spur to the class proletarian movement in all countries. We are not, however, given this opportunity, and we must therefore undertake to consolidate our military power.

If we were to increase the permanent numerical strength of our regular army, we would give our enemies a strong weapon, the "threat of Soviet imperialism," with which to intimidate their own petty bourgeoisie and perhaps even some pro-letarian elements. . . . I consider it politically inexpedient to provide food for such agitation . . . Therefore the numerical increase of our regular forces is, in my estimation, absolutely out of the question. There remains another way—expanding the militia. We are doing this, and shall go on doing it. Every year our militia organization will become more and more the basis of [our] revolutionary forces. I believe that the psychological moment has arrived for us to be completely recon-structed on a new basis. Our Red Army should no longer be considered a regular Red Army, but an armed nation of workers and peasants who are duty-bound and ready to bear arms and fight the enemy at any moment. This should be our psycho-logical mood and the mood that we should bring about among our workers' and peasants' masses. This task belongs chiefly to us. Our military propaganda . . . must be devoted chiefly to indoctrinating the broad masses of workers and peasants with this concept of the Red Army. . . .

137

The Militarization of the Entire Population

[I. S. Unschlicht, Acting People's Commissar for Military and Naval Affairs, on the Ninth Anniversary of the Red Army][35]

.   .   .

In its present form [our] Red Army represents only the nucleus of the armed forces of the Union.

The future war will impose heavy obligations upon all the forces and resources of the country, and will require the active participation of all toilers in the defense of the country. It is imperative for the entire population to become aware of the existing danger, and of the necessity of defending the October achievements with guns in our hands.

With the least possible expenditure by the state, and not through enlistment in the [regular] Red Army, it is imperative to provide at least preliminary military training to the largest possible number of people capable and worthy of bearing arms.

The activities and self-expression of the large masses of the population are on

[35] *Izvestiia*, No. 44, February 23, 1927, p. 1.

the increase. It is imperative to direct these activities, among other things, into the general current of preparing the country for defense. Military training . . . must interfere as little as possible with their daily peacetime work. It must be closely connected with general training in athletics, with work at schools and factories, and with the entire economic activity of the country.

Our military slogan of the day is as follows:

Mass propaganda and diffusion of military knowledge and habits among the entire population of the country, the effecting of close contact between the Red Army and the population, the militarization of the entire population of the country.

The territorial system [of military training] is the basis for implementing this slogan. . . . This system will be bolstered by pre-enlistment training, by the sharp-shooters' circles, by the militarization of the *Vuzy* [higher institutions of learning], etc.

.   .   .

The broad participation of the toilers of the Union in defense work and socialist reconstruction under the leadership of the Leninist party will guarantee the victory of the Red Army over the capitalist armies, and the victory of socialism.

The Red Army now faces its last task, which is to serve as a rampart for the coming socialist revolution in Europe.

138

K. E. Voroshilov, People's Commissar for Military and Naval Affairs, on the Five-Year Plan for the Army

[Speech at the Fifteenth Party Congress, December 1927][36]

.   .   .

In addition to the five-year plan for economic construction, we have a five-year plan for building up our armed forces. This plan stresses a great increase in the technical resources of the Red Army. The number of men in the armed forces remains the same. The increase in the budget for the army is used exclusively for technical resources and supplies. . . .

Now that absolutely satisfactory conditions in the organization, training, education, and battle preparedness of the Red soldiers and the commanding personnel have been achieved, our chief aim and the basic purpose of the five-year plan is to raise the technical power of the Red Army to the level of the first-class modern armies.

.   .   .

1. The five-year plan for the national economy must proceed from the inevitability of an armed attack upon the U.S.S.R. and the consequent necessity of organizing, in accordance with our material resources, a defense of the Soviet Union that would ensure victory over the united forces of our possible adversaries.

2. Our country's capacity is determined by its industrial potential. Therefore military considerations must affect the planning of industrial construction. In particular, (a) the location of industrial enterprises must correspond to the requirements of strategic safety; (b) our ferrous and especially nonferrous metallurgy must be built up within the next few years to where it can supply the minimum requirements for defense; (c) sufficient funds must be allocated to the weakest branches of our economy and our defense (automobile and tractor construction, chemistry, and so forth).

[36] *XV sezd V.K.P.*, pp. 885–87.

3. The rural economy must be developed with a view to making the U.S.S.R. self-sufficient agriculturally as quickly as possible.

4. The stockpiling of reserves (both natural and monetary) must be based on the all-round consideration of defense needs.

5. The development of the armed forces (the workers' and peasants' Red Army, Navy, and Air Force) must be based on the necessity of raising their technical and fighting capacities to the level of a first-class European army.

6. It is imperative to start immediately to supplement the five-year plan with a detailed plan for our entire national economy in case of war.

I would like to close with the following statement from our theses: "In connection with the outlining of the five-year plan, it is imperative that defense matters be given the attention not only of our economic planning organs but of the whole party."

139

Stalin on the Need for a Strong Red Army

[Excerpt from a Speech at a Plenary Session of the Central Committee of the Party, January 19, 1925][37]

. . . In view of the growing complications within the countries that surround us, the question of our army, of its strength and its preparedness, is bound to confront us in all its seriousness. This does not mean that we are pledged to intervene against anybody anywhere. We are not, and if anyone thinks we are, he is wrong. As before, our banner is that of peace. But if war begins, we shall not be able to sit with folded arms. We shall have to come out, but we shall be the last ones to come out. And we shall come out in order to throw the decisive weight on the scales.

It follows that we must be prepared for anything; we must prepare our army; we must equip and train it; we must improve its technique, our chemical warfare, our aviation; in general, we must raise our Red Army to its full height. This is required of us by the existing international situation.

COMMUNIST ESTIMATE OF THE WORLD SITUATION AT THE END OF 1927

140

Stalin on the World Significance of the October Revolution

[On the Occasion of the Tenth Anniversary of the October Revolution][38]

The October Revolution is not only a revolution "within national limits." It is, primarily, a revolution of an international, world significance, for it marks the departure from the old, capitalist world to the new, socialist world. . . .

It is precisely for this reason that the victory of the October Revolution marks a radical change in the history of mankind, a radical change in the historical destiny of world capitalism, a radical change in the liberation movement of the world proletariat, a radical change in the methods of struggle and the forms of organization,

[37] Stalin, *Sochineniia*, VII, 14.
[38] *Ibid.*, X, 239–50.

in the life and the traditions, in the culture and the ideology of the exploited masses throughout the world.

This is the basic reason why the October Revolution is a revolution of an international, a world order. . . .

1. The October Revolution is remarkable primarily for having broken the front of world imperialism, for having overthrown the imperialist bourgeoisie in one of the biggest capitalist countries, and for having put the socialist proletariat in power. . . .

This means that the October Revolution has ushered in a new era, the era of proletarian revolutions in the imperialist countries. . . .

But the October Revolution did not, and could not, stop there. Having destroyed what was old and bourgeois, it began to build what was new and socialist. . . . The indisputable successes of socialism in the U.S.S.R. on the construction front have demonstrated that the proletariat can successfully govern the country without the bourgeoisie and against the bourgeoisie; that it can successfully build industry without the bourgeoisie and against the bourgeoisie; that it can successfully direct the whole of the national economy without the bourgeoisie and against the bourgeoisie; that it can successfully build socialism in spite of the capitalist encirclement. . . .

2. The October Revolution has shaken imperialism not merely in the centers of its domination, not merely in the "mother countries." By undermining the rule of imperialism in the colonial and dependent countries, it has also struck blows at the rear of imperialism, at its periphery. . . . The October Revolution accomplished these national-colonial revolutions in the U.S.S.R. not under the banner of national enmity and international conflict, but under the banner of mutual confidence and fraternal rapprochement among the workers and peasants of the various nationalities of the U.S.S.R.; not in the name of nationalism, but in the name of internationalism, . . . thereby setting a contagious example for the oppressed nations of the whole world.

This means that the October Revolution has ushered in a new era, the era of colonial revolutions, revolutions that are being conducted in the oppressed countries of the world in alliance with the proletariat and under the leadership of the proletariat.

3. Having sown the seeds of revolution in both the centers of imperialism and its rear, having weakened the might of imperialism in the "mother countries" and having shaken its domination in the colonies, the October Revolution has thereby jeopardized the very existence of world capitalism as a whole. . . .

More than that, while shaking imperialism, the October Revolution has at the same time created—in the first proletarian dictatorship—a powerful and open center for the world revolutionary movement, a center such as it never possessed before and around which it can now rally and organize a united revolutionary front of the proletarians and the oppressed peoples of all countries against imperialism.

This means, first of all, that the October Revolution has inflicted a mortal wound on world capitalism, a wound from which the latter will never recover. Capitalism will never recover the "equilibrium" and "stability" it possessed before October. Capitalism may become partially stabilized; it may rationalize production, turn over the administration of the country to fascism, temporarily hold down the working class; but it will never recover the "tranquility," the "assurance," the "equilibrium," and the "stability" that it flaunted before; for in the crisis now reached by world capitalism the flames of revolution must inevitably break out—now in the centers of imperialism, now on the periphery—reducing to naught the capitalist patchwork and daily bringing nearer the fall of capitalism. . . .

4. The October Revolution is not only a revolution in the domain of economic and sociopolitical relations, but a revolution in the minds, in the ideology of the working class. The October Revolution was born and gained strength under the banner of Marxism, under the banner of the idea of the dictatorship of the proletariat,

under the banner of Leninism, which is Marxism in the epoch of imperialism and of proletarian revolutions. That is why it marks the victory of Marxism over reformism, the victory of Leninism over Social Democracy, the victory of the Third International over the Second International. . . .

The era of the domination of the Second International and of Social Democracy in the workers' movement has come to an end.

The era of the domination of Leninism and of the Third International has begun.

141

The Future Is on the Side of the Comintern

[Bukharin's Final Remarks in His Speech at the Fifteenth Party Congress, December 10, 1927][39]

. . .

We must first note that we are entering a new phase of international development, a phase favorable for the Comintern. In Western Europe we witness the development of contradictions in the capitalist stabilization, producing a decided veering to the Left among the broad masses of the working class. We see how the internal differences in the stabilization, especially economic differences, have intensified class conflict. We see how the working class, having recovered somewhat from its defeats of the last few years, is beginning to close its ranks and to hold up its banner; we see it moving toward the Left, growing more revolutionary, emphasizing once more the problems of the class struggle and thus paving the way for increased communist work among the masses. We are entering a phase not of pacification, but of increasing struggle in the colonial countries; the great Chinese revolution is not dead but lives and develops, inspiring by its powerful influence the revolution in India. India, now in a state of deep ferment, is bound to step out into the great historical arena of struggle against imperialism.

We see how European capitalism is endeavoring to corrupt the working class by new methods, to which end it has allied itself with the Social Democrats; but at the same time we see that European capitalism has no good foundation for such methods, and that, despite a temporary increase in prosperity, it faces the prospect of renewed and tremendous differences, accompanied by an ever-increasing class struggle. We can see, comrades, how, despite pacifist illusions and idylls and the deception of the Social Democrats, tremendous conflicts are growing within the womb of capitalist society.

Let the Social Democratic Philistines and the vulgar elements console themselves with their illusory hopes of a new age of peace under the capitalist regime, a regime that is allegedly to free mankind from wars. Sober Marxist analysis ruthlessly reveals the fundamental reality of our times. The capitalist regime is inevitably leading humanity toward gigantic disasters, disasters that will dwarf the war of 1914. At the same time this Marxist analysis shows how within capitalist society itself, forces prepared to resist the catastrophes of the imperialist period have ripened. The future promises us no rest; it promises a fierce struggle. But the communist workers are no longer entering this struggle as isolated champions, as Liebknecht and others once did. They are entering the struggle in full consciousness as an organized force that has formed its first communist detachment. And though we cannot guarantee that the entire mass of workers will rise at once at the very first shot fired against the Soviet Union, we may rest assured that the first shot will arouse and mobilize all the best forces in the workers' movement, and that eventually, perhaps after many

[39] *XV sezd V.K.P.*, pp. 625–26; also *International Press Correspondence*, No. 1, January 5, 1928, p. 19.

painful [inner] struggles, and after various stages of doubt and vacillation, we will form an oceanic revolutionary wave that will sweep away all capitalist barbarity!

(Stormy and prolonged applause. Bukharin receives an ovation. All rise and sing the Internationale.)

142

Establishing Socialism in the U.S.S.R. Essential to the World Communist Movement

[Stalin at the Plenum of the Central Committee and Central Control Commission of the Party, October 23, 1927][40]

. . .

History shows that not a single young state in the world has developed its industry, particularly heavy industry, without foreign help and foreign loans, or without plundering foreign countries, colonies, etc. That is the usual way of capitalist industrialization. England developed her industry in the past by plundering other countries and colonies for centuries, and investing the proceeds of her robbery in her industry. In recent years Germany has been able to develop only with the aid of American loans, amounting in value to several billions [of rubles]. We, however, cannot follow either of these two ways. Our whole policy excludes colonial robbery. We do not get any loans. There remains to us only one way, that indicated by Lenin : developing our industry and re-equipping it by domestic means. The opposition constantly croaks that we cannot do this. As early as April 1926, the opposition, in their polemic against Comrade Rykov delivered at the plenum of the Central Committee, maintained that our domestic means were not sufficient to re-equip our industry. At that time the opposition prophesied one defeat after another. As it turned out, however, we have made headway in the past two years in re-equipping our industry.

. . .

. . . The aim of our foreign policy, in so far as diplomatic relations with the bourgeois states are concerned, is to secure peace. What have we achieved in this sphere? We have achieved peace, despite the capitalist encirclement, despite the hostile work of the capitalist governments, despite the provocative raids in Peking, London, and Paris—in spite of everything we have not responded to any provocation and have been able to defend the cause of peace. Despite the manifold prophecies of Zinoviev and others, we have no war; against this basic truth the opposition's cries are impotent. And peace is important to us, since only under peaceful conditions can we build up socialism as quickly as we desire. And how often we have heard war prophesied. Comrade Zinoviev prophesied that we would have a war last spring; then he prophesied war for autumn. It is already winter, and still we have no war.

These are the results of our policy of peace.

. . .

. . . Only a blind man can deny that the communist parties of the world, from China to America, from England to Germany, are growing. Only a blind man can deny that the crisis of capitalism is growing and not declining. Only a blind man can deny that the growth of socialist construction in our country, the successes of

[40] Stalin, *Ob oppozitsii*, pp. 739–41 ; also *International Press Correspondence*, No. 64, November 17, 1927, pp. 1433–34.

our policy within our country, constitute one of the main causes of the growth of the communist movement in the whole world. Only a blind man can deny the continual growth of the influence and authority of the Communist International in all countries.

. . .

143
Stalin on the Capitalist World and the U.S.S.R.
[Excerpt from His Report to the Fifteenth Party Congress,
December 3, 1927][41]

. . .

We have all the symptoms of an intense crisis and growing instability in world capitalism. If the temporary postwar crisis of 1920–21, with all its chaos within capitalist countries and the break-up of their foreign relations, has given way to a period of partial stabilization, nonetheless the general and main crisis of capitalism, resulting from the victorious October Revolution and the separation of the U.S.S.R. from the world capitalist system, is not only not overcome but is becoming more intense, shattering the very foundations of world capitalism. Stabilization, far from ameliorating this main crisis, has abetted it. The growing struggle for markets, the need of new spheres of influence and [therefore] of a new partition of the world, the failure of bourgeois pacifism and the League of Nations, the feverish work to form new coalitions for a possible new war, the frantic growth of armaments, the brutal oppression of the working class and the colonial countries, the growth of the revolutionary movement in the colonies and throughout Europe, the growing authority of the Comintern throughout the world, and finally, the consolidation of the Soviet Union's power and its authority among the workers of Europe and the toiling masses of the colonial countries—these are the facts that shatter the very foundations of world capitalism.

The stabilization of capitalism is becoming more and more rotten and unstable.

If two years ago we had to speak about an ebb of the revolutionary wave in Europe, we now have every ground for claiming that Europe is definitely entering a phase of new revolutionary upheaval. I do not speak here of the colonial and dependent countries, where the situation of the imperialists is becoming more and more catastrophic.

Events have shattered the capitalists' hope that the U.S.S.R. would be tamed and its authority decline among the workers of Europe and the toiling masses of the colonial countries. The U.S.S.R. is growing, and growing toward socialism. Its influence among the workers and peasants throughout the world spreads and strengthens. The very existence of the U.S.S.R. as a country engaged in establishing socialism helps demoralize world imperialism and undermine its stability in both Europe and the colonial countries. The U.S.S.R. is definitely becoming a symbol for the working class of Europe and the oppressed colonial peoples.

Therefore, in order to clear the ground for future imperialist wars, to choke its "own" working class more thoroughly and muzzle its "own" colonies to strengthen its rear, capitalism must first of all (so the bourgeois policy makers believe) muzzle the U.S.S.R., the heart and nursery of revolution and at the same time one of the greatest markets for capitalist countries. Hence the revival of interventionist tendencies among the imperialists, and of the policy of isolating and encircling the U.S.S.R., the policy of preparing for war against the U.S.S.R.

[41] *XV sezd V.K.P.*, pp. 45–49; also Stalin, *Sochineniia*, X, 285–91.

The strengthening of interventionist tendencies in the imperialist camp and the menace of war against the U.S.S.R. is one of the main characteristics of the present situation.

The most "threatened" and "affected" party in the developing crisis of capitalism is the British bourgeoisie. It has therefore taken the initiative in intensifying interventionist tendencies. . . .

Thus the struggle between two tendencies of the capitalist world toward the U.S.S.R., an aggressive military tendency (primarily Britain) and a tendency to continue peaceful relations (several other capitalist countries), is now the principal fact in our foreign relations.

Here are facts showing a tendency toward peaceful relations during the period covered by the report: the nonaggression treaty with Turkey; the neutrality pact with Germany; the customs agreement with Greece; the agreement with Germany on credits; the neutrality pact with Afghanistan; the nonaggression pact with Lithuania; the initialing of a similar pact with Latvia; the trade agreement with Turkey; the settlement of the conflict with Switzerland; the neutrality pact with Persia; the improved relations with Japan; and the growing business relations with America and Italy.

Here are facts showing an aggressive military tendency during the same period: the British note about the money sent to the striking miners; the raids on Soviet diplomatic premises in Peking, Tientsin, and Shanghai; the raid on Arcos; the rupture between Great Britain and the U.S.S.R.; Voikov's assassination; the terrorist acts of British agents in the U.S.S.R.; and the deterioration of relations with France over the question of recalling Rakovsky.

If about two years ago it was possible and necessary to speak of a period of relative equilibrium and "peaceful coexistence" between the U.S.S.R. and the capitalist countries, we have now every reason to say that this period has given way to a period of imperialist attacks on the U.S.S.R. and [accompanying] preparations for intervention.

British attempts to set up a united front against the U.S.S.R. have so far been unsuccessful, owing to the conflicting interests within the imperialist camp, the interest displayed by some countries in having business relations with the U.S.S.R., the peaceful policy of the U.S.S.R., the opposition of the European working class, and the imperialist fear that war with the U.S.S.R. would bring revolution at home. This, however, does not mean that Britain will stop trying to organize a united anti-Soviet front, or that it will not succeed in doing so. The war menace still exists despite Britain's temporary failure.

We must accordingly observe the contradictions in the imperialist camp, postpone war by "paying off" the capitalists, and take all measures to preserve peaceful relations. We cannot forget Lenin's words that in building [socialism] much depends on how well we succeed in delaying war with the capitalist world. Such a war is inevitable, but it can be delayed either until the proletarian revolution in Europe has matured, or until the colonial revolutions have fully ripened, or, finally, until the capitalists have plunged into war among themselves for the repartition of the colonies. The preservation of peaceful relations with the capitalist countries is, therefore, a necessary task for us.

The basis of our relations with the capitalist countries is the acceptance of the coexistence of two fundamentally different systems. Experience has fully justified this arrangement. The question of debts and credits is sometimes a stumbling block. Our policy on this question is clear. It is based on the formula "give and take." Give us credit to develop our industry and you will receive a certain part of the prewar debts, which we will regard as additional percentage on credit. If you will not give, you will not receive. Facts show that we have done quite well in securing industrial credits. I refer here not only to Germany, but also to America and Britain. What is the secret? It is this: Our country is the greatest market for imported equipment, and the capitalist countries need precisely such a market.

[Sums up points made above.]

Hence, the tasks of the party are:

1. Along the lines of the international revolutionary movement—

(*a*) A struggle for the development of the communist parties throughout the world;

(*b*) A struggle for the consolidation of the revolutionary trade unions and the united front of the workers against the capitalist offensive;

(*c*) A struggle for strengthening the friendship between the working class of the U.S.S.R. and the working class of the capitalist countries;

(*d*) A struggle for a stronger alliance between the working class of the U.S.S.R. and the liberation movement of the colonial countries.

2. Along the lines of U.S.S.R. foreign policy—

(*a*) A struggle against the preparation of new imperialist wars;

(*b*) A struggle against the interventionist tendencies of Britain and a strengthening of the defensive capacity of the U.S.S.R.;

(*c*) A peace policy and the preservation of peaceful relations with the capitalist countries;

(*d*) An extension of our trade relations with the outside world on the basis of the consolidation of the foreign trade monopoly;

(*e*) Rapprochement with the so-called weak and unequal countries, which are suffering from the oppression and exploitation of the dominating imperialist powers.

CHRONOLOGY

1920

January 10	League of Nations comes legally into existence.
January 16	Allied Supreme Council lifts the blockade of Soviet Russia.
February 2	Treaty of peace between the R.S.F.S.R. and Estonia.
February 12	Agreement between Great Britain and Soviet Russia on the exchange of prisoners of war.
February 24	Allied Supreme Council recommends to the states bordering on Soviet Russia that they come to an agreement with the Soviet government. Soviet peace offer to the United States, Japan, and Rumania.
February 27	Soviet peace offer to Czechoslovakia.
March 13–19	Military putsch in Germany headed by Dr. Kapp.
March 29–April 5	Ninth Party Congress recommends transforming some Red Army units into "labor armies" until such time as the men might be needed again as soldiers.
April 6	Formation of the Far Eastern Republic.
April 20	Agreement between France and the R.S.F.S.R. and Ukrainian S.S.R. for mutual repatriation of nationals; similar agreement between the R.S.F.S.R. and Belgium.
April 23	Soviet-German agreement for repatriation of prisoners of war.
April 25–October 12	Soviet-Polish open warfare.
April 27	Soviet-Italian agreement on prisoners of war and interned civilians.
May 5–June 12	Polish troops and Petliura's Ukrainian forces occupy Kiev.
May 7	Peace treaty between Soviet Russia and Menshevik Georgia.
May 12	British trade delegation arrives in Moscow.
May 21	Agreement between Hungary and the R.S.F.S.R. and Ukrainian S.S.R. for repatriation of prisoners of war and civilians.
June 7	Karelian Labor Commune founded.
July 5	Treaty between Austria and the R.S.F.S.R. and Ukrainian S.S.R. for the repatriation of prisoners of war.
July 8	The United States passes a trade embargo against Russia.
July 12	Soviet-Lithuanian peace treaty.
July 14	Soviet-Lithuanian agreement regarding the passage of troops through Lithuanian territory.

July 15	International Revolutionary Council of Trade Unions (Profintern) founded.
July 19–August 7	Second Congress of the Communist International adopts the Twenty-one Conditions for admission to the Comintern, passes resolutions on the party's role in the proletarian revolution, formulates theses on the agrarian, nationalities, and colonial questions.
July 30	Opening of the First International Conference of Communist Women in Moscow.
July 31	"Council of Action" formed in Great Britain to oppose intervention in Soviet Russia.
August 8	Belorussian S.S.R. proclaimed.
August 11	Soviet-Latvian peace treaty.
August 14	Treaty between Czechoslovakia and Yugoslavia, initiating the "Little Entente." Soviet troops reach the outskirts of Warsaw.
August 1920–April 1921	Tambov peasant insurrection, known as "Antonovshchina" after the leader Antonov.
September 1–8	First Congress of the Peoples of the East, in Baku.
September 3–15	Armed clashes between workers and police in Italy; workers attempt to organize collective management of industrial enterprises, and to proclaim soviet republics in Trieste and Trento.
October 4	Soviet-Finnish peace treaty.
October 12	Soviet-Polish armistice signed.
October 15	Miners' strike in Great Britain.
October 28	Bessarabia Protocol, recognizing Rumania's sovereignty over Bessarabia, signed by Britain, France, Italy, Japan, and Rumania.
November 23	Decree of Council of People's Commissars granting concessions to foreign capitalists.
December 28	Treaty of alliance between the R.S.F.S.R. and the Ukrainian S.S.R.

1921

January 16	Treaty of alliance between the R.S.F.S.R. and the Belorussian S.S.R.
January 21	The Soviet representative in the United States, Ludwig Martens, leaves the country after an unsuccessful attempt to establish official diplomatic relations between his country and the United States.
February 22	Workers' unrest and strikes in Petrograd.
February 26	Soviet-Persian treaty of friendship.
February 27	Martial law proclaimed in Petrograd.
February 28	Soviet-Afghan treaty of friendship.
February 28–March 8	Kronstadt revolt: rebelling sailors demand re-election of soviets with secret ballot, freedom of assembly, union, and peasant organizations; release of political prisoners, annulment of political departments, etc.

March 3	Secret military convention allegedly signed between Poland and Rumania.
March 8–16	Tenth Party Congress adopts the New Economic Policy and passes a resolution prohibiting party factions.
March 12	Agreement allegedly signed by France and Japan for transferring Wrangel's remaining forces from Constantinople to Vladivostok.
March 16	Soviet British trade agreement. Soviet-Turkish treaty of friendship. Stalin elected to the Politburo and Orgburo of the party's Central Committee.
March 18	Treaty of Riga between Poland and the R.S.F.S.R. and Ukrainian S.S.R.
March 21	Litvinov's offer to the United States to re-establish diplomatic relations.
March 22–31	Workers' uprising in Germany; clashes with police; seizure of factories.
March 25	Secretary of State Hughes rejects the Soviet offer.
March 31	Beginning of miners' strike in Great Britain.
May 6	Soviet-German provisional agreement on exchanging prisoners of war.
May 21	Treaty of alliance between the R.S.F.S.R. and Soviet Georgia.
May 26–28	Tenth Party Conference convened to work out N.E.P.
Summer and Fall	Famine in the R.S.F.S.R.
June 22–July 12	Third Congress of the Communist International. Emphasis on capitalist stabilization; search for new tactics. Lenin says the Comintern's immediate and main strategic task is to capture the majority of the working class.
June 26	*Pravda* admits that twenty-five million Russians are starving.
July 3–19	First Congress of the Red Trade Union International (Profintern).
July 13	Maxim Gorky appeals to the peoples of the world to help the starving Russians.
August	Formation of Mezhrabpom (International Workers' Aid).
August 20	Agreement signed between Russia and the American Relief Administration.
November 12– February 6, 1922	Washington Conference on Naval Disarmament and Far Eastern Affairs.
December 19–22	Eleventh Party Conference defines the limits of the N.E.P.; nationalized land, large-scale industry, and transportation and the monopoly of foreign trade are to be retained at all costs.
December 26	Soviet-Italian preliminary economic and political agreement.
December 29	Stalin becomes People's Commissar of Workers' and Peasants' Inspection.

1922

| January 10 | Allied Supreme Council decides to invite Soviet Russia to participate in the Genoa Conference to discuss the world economic and financial problems. |

February 6	The Treaty of Washington between Great Britain, France, Italy, Japan, and the United States on limitation of naval armaments.
March 12	Formation of the Transcaucasian S.F.S.R.
March 13–17	Conference held in Warsaw between the Baltic States and Poland providing for arbitration and a defensive league in the event of attack by another power.
March 20–28	Soviet representatives attend for the first time a conference convened by the League of Nations (Pan-European Health Conference).
March 29–30	The Russian delegation on the way to the Genoa Conference confers in Riga with the representatives of Estonia, Latvia, and Poland on trade between their respective countries and the consolidation of peace in Eastern Europe. Riga Protocol signed.
April 2–6	Conference of the representatives of the three Internationals meets in Berlin.
April 3	Stalin elected General Secretary of the party upon Lenin's recommendation.
April 10–May 19	The Genoa Conference for the Economic and Financial Reconstruction of Europe.
April 16	Treaty of Rapallo signed by the Russian and German delegations at the Genoa Conference.
June 1	New Soviet-Finnish agreement designed to assure safety of the two countries' frontiers.
June 5	Soviet-Czech provisional treaty of friendship.
June 6	Ukrainian-Czech provisional treaty of friendship.
June 26–July 20	The Hague Conference on Russia.
July 3	Soviet-British trade agreement extended to include Canada.
August 4–7	Twelfth Party Conference: abolition of the foreign trade monopoly proposed and rejected along with the British industrialist Urquhart's request for a concession to operate his former Russian enterprises.
October 20	Central Committee appoints Stalin a delegate to the Fourth Congress of the Communist International.
November 5– December 5	Fourth Congress of the Communist International; Lenin's last speech to communist representatives of foreign countries; conclusions and resolutions of the Third Congress reaffirmed.
November 14	Far Eastern Republic decides to join the R.S.F.S.R.
November 20	Lenin's last speech delivered at the plenum of the Moscow soviet, on transforming the Russia of the N.E.P. into a socialist Russia. Opening of the Lausanne Conference on Near Eastern Affairs.
December 3–13	Moscow Conference on Disarmament convened upon Russian initiative and attended by representatives of the R.S.F.S.R., Poland, Estonia, Latvia, and Finland.
December 10–15	World Congress on War Against War convened by the Amsterdam International at The Hague, Soviet representatives participating.

| December 24–27 | Tenth Congress of Soviets of the R.S.F.S.R. ratifies the Treaty of Union between the R.S.F.S.R., the Ukrainian S.S.R., the Belorussian S.S.R., and the Transcaucasian Federation. |
| December 30 | First Congress of Soviets of the U.S.S.R. issues a declaration concerning the formation of the Union. |

1923

January 11	French and Belgian troops begin occupation of the Ruhr following the Reparation Commission's declaration that Germany is in default.
March 3	All-Russian Central Council of Trade Unions resolves to send food to the starving Ruhr workers; offer declined by the German government.
March 14	Conference of Allied Ambassadors delimits new frontier between Poland and Lithuania, giving Vilna to Poland.
April 17–25	Twelfth Party Congress.
April 26	Stalin reappointed General Secretary of the party.
May 9	Soviet government receives the "Curzon Ultimatum" and replies on the next day.
July 6	Assassination of V. V. Vorovsky, Soviet delegate to the Lausanne Conference in Switzerland. Central Executive Committee ratifies the constitution of the U.S.S.R.
July 13	Central Executive Committee announces to the world the establishment of the U.S.S.R.
July 24	Lausanne agreement signed by Turkey and the governments of the principal Allied powers.
October 8	Trotsky tells the Politburo that the Central Committee is heading the country for ruin.
October 10–16	First International Peasant Conference held in Moscow; International Peasant Council (Krestintern) founded.
October	Communists and Left Social Democrats form a government in Saxony and Thuringia.
October 18	Saxon government overthrown by government troops sent from Berlin.
October 23–28	Communist uprising in Hamburg.
December 8	Trotsky publishes "The New Course," an attack upon the government of the U.S.S.R.
December 16	Chicherin proposes resumption of diplomatic relations to the United States.
December 18	Secretary of State Hughes declines Chicherin's offer.

1924

| January 21 | Lenin's death. Stalin, Zinoviev, and Kamenev emerge as the leading figures of the party and the government. |
| January 26–
February 2 | Second Congress of Soviets of the U.S.S.R.; adoption of the constitution (January 31) formally establishing the Union. |

February 1   *De jure* recognition of Soviet Russia by Great Britain.
February 7   *De jure* recognition by Italy.
February 15   *De jure* recognition by Norway.
February 25   *De jure* recognition by Austria.
March 8   *De jure* recognition by Greece.
March 15   *De jure* recognition by Sweden.
March 24   *De jure* recognition by Canada.
April 9   The Dawes Plan for Germany's financial reconstruction submitted to the Reparations Commission by the Committee of Experts under the chairmanship of Charles G. Dawes.
April 16   Germany accepts the Dawes Plan.
May 23–31   Thirteenth Party Congress adopts a plan to reorganize the Red Army on a territorial militia basis, and condemns certain deviations of Comintern members.
May 31   Resumption of official relations between the Peking and Soviet governments.
June 17–July 8   Fifth Congress of the Communist International; Stalin assumes open leadership in the Congress and its chief commissions; theses on tactics and a resolution on the bolshevization of communist parties adopted.
August   Insurrection in Georgia, suppressed within a few days.
October 2   Geneva Protocol for the pacific settlement of international disputes brought forward by British prime minister Ramsay MacDonald.
October 25   "Zinoviev Letter" of September 15, 1924, addressed to the British Communists, published in *The Times* (London).
October 28   *De jure* recognition from France.
November 18   French and Belgian troops of occupation finally withdrawn from the Ruhr district.

1925

January 15   Central Executive Committee dismisses Trotsky as People's Commissar of War.
January 17   Central Committee decides to warn Trotsky and replace him as Chairman of the Revolutionary War Council.
January 20   Convention between Soviet Russia and Japan.
April 6–8   Anglo-Russian Conference of Trade Unions held in London.
April 10   Tsaritsyn renamed Stalingrad.
April 27–29   Fourteenth Party Conference notes the failure of the revolutionary movement in Central Europe; its progress in the colonies and dependent countries; the possibility of revolutionary advances in Britain, the Balkans, and the Far East; and the party's obligation to support the Comintern.
October 12   Soviet-German commercial agreement.
October 16   The Pact of Locarno between Germany, France, Belgium, and Italy.
December 17   Treaty of neutrality and friendship between Soviet Russia and Turkey.

| December 18–31 | Fourteenth Party Congress; Stalin urges peaceful socialist construction and calls for struggle against Left and Right deviations. |

1926

January 15	Soviet Russia agrees to participate in the work of the Preparatory Commission for the Disarmament Conference.
March 5	Soviet government proposes nonaggression pacts to the governments of Lithuania, Latvia, Estonia, Finland, and Poland.
April 24	Soviet-German neutrality and nonaggression agreement.
May 3–12	General strike in Great Britain, with miners' union continuing the strike until November 19.
May 12–13	Pilsudski *coup d'état*. Pilsudski becomes premier and minister of war and assumes dictatorial power.
August 31	Treaty of neutrality and nonaggression between Soviet Russia and Afghanistan.
September 8	Germany admitted to the League of Nations.
September 28	Soviet-Lithuanian treaty of neutrality and nonaggression.
October 20	Vilna question raised by Poland at the Ambassadors' Conference.
October 23	Trotsky, Kamenev, and Zinoviev expelled from the Politburo of the Communist Party.
October 26–November 3	Fifteenth Party Conference instructs its Comintern delegation to pursue "the policy of further bolshevization of the communist parties."

1927

February 23	British government accuses the Soviet government of violating the 1921 trade agreement and of propaganda.
March 11	Treaty of commerce and navigation with Turkey.
May 4	Opening of the World Economic Conference at Geneva, with fifty nations (including the U.S.S.R.) represented.
May 12	British police raid Arcos.
May 26	Great Britain severs diplomatic relations with the U.S.S.R and terminates the 1921 trade agreement.
July 29–August 9	Joint plenum of the Central Committee and Central Control Commission admits the economic and political consolidation of capitalism in Europe, Japan, and the United States.
August	Opposition leaders accuse the Politburo and the Central Committee of intending to dissolve the Comintern, betray the Chinese revolution, recognize tsarist debts, abolish the foreign trade monopoly, and adopt a policy favoring the kulaks.
October 1	Treaty of nonaggression and neutrality between Soviet Russia and Persia.
October 21–23	Joint plenum of the Central Committee and Central Control Commission orders the drafting of the Five-Year Plan. The

	plenum also resolves to expel Trotsky and Zinoviev from the Central Committee.
November 7	The opposition organizes antiparty demonstrations in Leningrad.
November 12	Congress of the Friends of the U.S.S.R. held in Moscow.
November 30	Litvinov proposes immediate and complete disarmament to the Preparatory Commission for the Disarmament Conference in Geneva.
December 2–19	Fifteenth Congress of the Russian Communist Party.

BIBLIOGRAPHY

BOOKS AND ARTICLES

Aikhenvald, A. Iu. *Sovetskaia ekonomika. Ekonomika i ekonomicheskaia politika SSSR* (Soviet economics. Economics and economic policy of the U.S.S.R.). Moscow, 1929.

Aleksandrov, B. "Vilenskii vopros" (The Vilna question). *Mezhdunarodnaia Zhizn*, No. 11, 1926, pp. 3–16.

Bajanov, Boris G. *Avec Staline dans le Kremlin*. Paris, 1930.

Bakh, M. G. [Gertsbakh, M. I.]. *Politiko-ekonomicheskie vzaimootnosheniia mezhdu SSSR i Pribaltikoi za desiat let (1917–1927)*. (Ten years of politico-economic relations between the U.S.S.R. and the Baltic states, 1917–1927). Moscow, 1928.

Bakshiev, D. *Tsentralizm i demokratizm bolshevistskoi partii* (Centralistic and democratic principles of the Bolshevik party). Moscow, 1948.

Bantke, S. (ed.). *Borba bolshevikov za sozdanie Kommunisticheskogo Internatsionala. Materialy i dokumenty, 1914–1919 gg.* (The Bolshevik struggle for the formation of the Communist International. Materials and documents, 1914–19). Moscow, 1934.

Barbusse, Henri (comp.). *The Soviet Union and Peace; the Most Important of the Documents Issued by the Government of the U.S.S.R. concerning Peace and Disarmament from 1917 to 1929*. London, 1929.

Batsell, W. R. *Soviet Rule in Russia*. New York, 1929.

Beloff, M. *The Foreign Policy of Soviet Russia, 1929–1941*. 2 vols. London, 1947–48.

Berdyaev, Nicolas. *The Russian Idea*. New York, 1948.

Bilmanis, Alfred. *Baltic States in Post-War Europe*. Washington, D.C., 1943. Includes historical background and the story of the unsuccessful communist putsch in Estonia in 1924.

Blücher, Wipert von. *Deutschlands Weg nach Rapallo; Erinnerungen eines Mannes aus dem zweiten Gliede*. Wiesbaden, 1951.

Bogolepov, I. B. "Arbitrazh i imperialisticheskaia deistvitelnost" (Arbitration and imperialist reality). *Mezhdunarodnaia Zhizn*, No. 4, 1927, pp. 5–55.

Bolshaia Sovetskaia Entsiklopediia (Large Soviet encyclopedia). 65 vols. Moscow, 1926–31.

Boretskii, B. *Liga natsii-orudie voiny* (The League of Nations—an instrument of war). Moscow, 1927.

Borilin, B. S. "Lenin i problema imperializma" (Lenin and the problem of imperialism). *Pod Znamenem Marksizma*, No. 5–6, 1925, pp. 110–39.

Borkenau, F. *The Communist International*, London, 1938.

Brandler, G. "Polozhenie v Germanii nakanune Genui" (The situation in Germany on the eve of Genoa). *Vestnik N.K.I.D.*, No. 4–5, 1922, pp. 67–72.

British Labour Delegation to Russia, 1920. *Report*. London, 1920.

Budecki, Zdislaw. *Stosunki polsko-litewskie po wojnie swiatowei 1918–1928. Z przedmova d-ra Juljana Makowskiego* (Polish-Lithuanian relations after the World War, 1918–1928. With a foreword by Dr. Julian Makowski). Warsaw, 1928.

Bukharin, N. I. *The A B C of Communism.* London, Communist Party of Great Britain, 1922.

———. *Building up Socialism.* London, Communist Party of Great Britain, 1926.

———. *Capitalist Stabilization and Proletarian Revolution; Report to the VII Enlarged Plenum of the E. C. of the Comintern on Point I on the Agenda. "The World Situation and the Tasks of the Comintern."* Moscow, 1926.

———. *Lenin as a Marxist.* London, Communist Party of Great Britain, London, 1925.

———. "O kharaktere nashei revoliutsii i o vozmozhnosti pobedonosnogo sotsialisticheskogo stroitelstva v SSSR" (On the nature of our revolution and the possibility of victorious socialist construction in the U.S.S.R.). *Bolshevik,* No. 19–20, October 31, 1926, pp. 28–59.

———. *Put k sotsializmu i raboche-krestianskii soiuz* (The road to socialism and the workers' and peasants' union). Moscow, 1925.

Bunyan, James, and H. H. Fisher. *The Bolshevik Revolution 1917–1918. Documents and Materials.* Stanford, Calif., 1934.

Burckhardt, Julius. *Der deutsch-russische Rechts- und Wirtschaftsvertrag vom 12 Oktober 1925 nebst Wirtschaftsprotokoll vom 21 Dezember 1928.* Würzburg, 1930.

Cardwell, Ann Su (Super, Margaret Low [Stump]). *Poland and Russia: The Last Quarter Century.* New York, 1944.

Carr, E. H. *The Bolshevik Revolution, 1917–1923.* 3 vols. London and New York, 1951–53.

———. *The Interregnum, 1923–1924.* London and New York, 1954.

———. *International Relations since the Peace Treaties.* London, 1938.

———. *Soviet-German Relations between the two World Wars, 1919–1939.* Baltimore, 1951.

Celtus (pseud.). *La France à Gênes; un programme français de reconstruction économique de l'Europe.* Paris, 1922.

Chaikin, V. A. *K istorii rossiiskoi revoliutsii (Kazn 26 bakinskikh komissarov)* (On the Russian revolution. The execution of the twenty-six Baku commissars), Vol. I, Moscow, 1922.

Chakste, Mintauts. "Soviet Concepts of the State, International Law and Sovereignty." *The American Journal of International Law,* Vol. 43 (1949), pp. 21–36.

Chastenet, Jacques. *Vingt ans d'histoire diplomatique 1919–1939.* Genève, 1945.

Chicherin, G. V. *The Foreign Policy of Soviet Russia; Report Submitted by the People's Commissariat for Foreign Affairs to the Seventh All-Russian Congress of Soviets (Nov. 1918 to Dec. 1919).* London, B[ritish] S[ocialist] P[arty], 1920.

———. "Lozanskaia konferentsiia i mirovoe polozhenie" (The Lausanne conference and the world situation). *Mezhdunarodnaia Zhizn,* No. 2, 1923, pp. 3–6.

———. *Two Years of Foreign Policy; the Relations of the Russian Socialist Federal Soviet Republic with Foreign Nations from November 7, 1917 to November 7, 1919.* New York, The Russian Soviet Government Bureau, 1920.

———. *Vneshniaia politika Sovetskoi Rossii za dva goda. Ocherk sostavlennyi k dvukhletnei godovshchine raboche-krestianskoi revoliutsii* (Two years of Soviet Russia's foreign policy. An outline prepared for the second anniversary of the workers' and peasants' revolution). Moscow, 1920.

Child, Richard Washburn. *A Diplomat Looks at Europe.* New York, 1925.

Chuvikov, P. "Uchenie Lenina-Stalina o voinakh spravedlivykh i nespravedlivykh" (Lenin's and Stalin's teaching on just and unjust wars). *Bolshevik,* No. 7–8, 1945, pp. 14–26.

Ciliga, Anton. *The Russian Enigma.* London, 1940. Deals with opposition groups.

Craig, Gordon A., and Felix Gilbert (eds). *The Diplomats 1919–1939.* Princeton, 1953.

Cressey, George B. *Asia's Lands and Peoples. A Geography of One-Third of the Earth and Two-Thirds of Its People.* New York and London, 1945.

———. *The Basis of Soviet Strength.* New York, 1945.

Cumming, C. K., and Walter W. Pettit (comps. and eds.). *Russo-American Relations. March 1917–March 1920. Documents and Papers.* New York, 1920.

D'Abernon, Viscount, Edgar Vincent. *An Ambassador of Peace; Pages from the Diary of Viscount D'Abernon (Berlin, 1920–1926).* 3 vols. London, 1929–30.

Dąbski, Jan. *Pokój Ryski; wspomnienia, pertraktacje, tajne układy z Joffem, listy* (The Riga peace; reminiscences, deliberations, secret negotiations with Ioffe, letters). Warsaw, 1931.

Dallin, David J. *Russia and Postwar Europe.* New Haven, 1943.

Danilevsky, N. Ia. *Rossiia i Evropa. Vzgliad na kulturnyia i politicheskiia otnosheniia slavianskogo mira k germano-romanskomu,* St. Petersburg, 1871. Also in German: *Russland und Europa* . . . Stuttgart and Berlin, 1920.

Davis, Kathryn (Wasserman). *The Soviets at Geneva; the U.S.S.R. and the League of Nations, 1919–1933.* Geneva, 1934.

Dawes, Charles G. *A Journey of Reparations.* London, 1939.

Dawes, Rufus C. *The Dawes Plan in the Making.* New York, 1925.

Deborin, G. A. *Pervye mezhdunarodnye akty sovetskogo gosudarstva i ego vneshniaia politika v gody inostrannoi interventsii i grazhdanskoi voiny (1917–1922 gg.)* (The first international acts of the Soviet state and its foreign policy during the years of intervention and civil war, 1917–1922). Moscow, 1947. Lecture delivered on June 1, 1947.

Degras, Jane (Tabritsky) (comp.). *Calendar of Soviet Documents on Foreign Policy, 1917–1941.* London, 1948.

———. *The Communist International, 1919–1943; documents* . . . , London, 1956–.

———. *Soviet Documents on Foreign Policy.* 2 vols. London and New York, 1951–52.

Denisov, A. I. *Teoriia gosudarstva i prava* (The theory of state and law). Moscow, 1948.

Dennis, A. L. P. *The Foreign Policies of Soviet Russia.* New York, 1924.

Deutscher, Isaac. *The Prophet Armed: Trotsky, 1879–1921.* New York and London, 1954.

———. *Stalin, A Political Biography.* London, 1949.

Domsky, L. "Pilsudchina i fashizm" (The Pilsudski regime and fascism). *Mirovoe Khoziaistvo i Mirovaia Politika,* No. 5–6, 1926, pp. 34–38.

Dostoevsky, F. M. *The Diary of a Writer;* translated and annotated by Boris Brasol. 2 vols. London, 1929.

Dranov, B. A. *Chernomorskie prolivy; mezhdunarodno-pravovoi rezhim* (The Black Sea Straits under the rule of international law). Moscow, 1948.

Dukes, Paul. *Red Dusk and the Morrow: Adventures and Investigations in Red Russia.* Garden City and New York, 1922.

Durdenevsky, V. "Soiuz sovetskikh sotsialisticheskikh respublik" (The Union of Soviet Socialist Republics). *Sovetskoe Pravo,* No. 1 (4), 1923, pp. 3–35.

Engels, F. "Die auswärtige Politik des russischen Zarenthums." *Die Neue Zeit,* Jhrg. 8, Stuttgart, 1890, pp. 193–203.

Erusalimsky, A. S. *Germaniia, Antanta i SSSR* (Germany, the Entente, and the U.S.S.R.). Moscow, 1928.

Eudin, Xenia J. "Moscow's Views of American Imperialism." *The Russian Review,* October 1954, pp. 276–84.

——, and Robert C. North, *Soviet Russia and the East, 1920–1927; a Documentary Survey,* Stanford, Calif., 1957.

Evropa posle Lokarno (Europe after Locarno). Moscow and Leningrad, 1926.

Fainsod, Merle. *International Socialism and the World War.* Cambridge, Mass., 1935.

Farbman, M. *After Lenin; the New Phase in Russia.* London, 1924.

Fedoseev, P. "Marksizm-Leninizm ob istokakh i kharaktere voin" (Marxism-Leninism on the origin and nature of wars). *Bolshevik,* No. 16, 1945, pp. 31–59.

Filippov, N. *Ukrainskaia kontr-revoliutsiia na sluzhbe u Anglii, Frantsii i Polshi* (The Ukrainian counterrevolution in the service of England, France, and Poland). Moscow, 1927. Includes texts of two conventions between Poland and the Ukraine: (1) political convention, April 21, 1920, and (2) military convention, April 24, 1920.

Fischer, Louis. *Oil Imperialism; the International Struggle for Petroleum.* New York, 1926.

——. *The Soviets in World Affairs. A History of the Relations Between the Soviet Union and the Rest of the World, 1917–1929.* 2d ed., 2 vols. Princeton, 1951.

Fischer, Ruth. *Stalin and German Communism; a Study in the Origins of the State Party.* Harvard, 1948.

Fisher, H. H. *The Communist Revolution; an Outline of Strategy and Tactics.* Stanford, Calif., 1955.

——. *The Famine in Soviet Russia, 1919–1923; the Operations of the American Relief Administration.* New York, 1927.

Florinsky, Michael T. *World Revolution and the U.S.S.R.* New York, 1933.

Freund, Heinrich, *et al.* (comps.). *Russlands Friedens- und Handelsverträge 1918/1923, auf Grund amtlichen Materials aus dem russischen übertragen von Dr. Heinrich Freund . . .* Berlin and Leipzig, 1924.

Frunze, M. V. *Sobranie sochinenii* (Collected works). 3 vols. Moscow, 1926–29.

G-bach, M. "K fashistskomu perevorotu v Litve" (On the fascist *coup d'état in* Lithuania). *Mirovoe Khoziaistvo i Mirovaia Politika,* No. 12, 1926, pp. 9–13.

G-vich, M. "Borba vokrug ugolnogo voprosa v Anglii" (The struggle over the coal problem in Britain). *Mirovoe Khoziaistvo i Mirovaia Politika,* No. 5–6, 1926, pp. 17–33.

Ganetsky, Ia. S. *Angliiskii imperializm i S.S.S.R.* (British imperialism and the U.S.S.R.). Moscow, 1927.

Gankin, O. Hess, and H. H. Fisher. *The Bolsheviks and the World War: The Origin of the Third International.* Stanford, Calif., 1940.

Genkina, E. B. "Gosudarstvennaia deiatelnost V. I. Lenina v period perekhoda k mirnomu stroitelstvu (Ianvar–fevral 1921 g.)" (V. I. Lenin's government work in the period of transition to peaceful reconstruction, January–February, 1921). *Voprosy Istorii,* No. 1, January 1, 1948, pp. 3–21.

——. "Iz istorii borby bolshevistskoi partii za ukreplenie ideologicheskogo fronta (1921–1922)" (A sketch on the struggle of the Bolshevik Party for the consolidation of the ideological front, 1921–1922). *Voprosy Istorii,* No. 1, 1949, pp. 16–38.

——. *Obrazovanie S.S.S.R.* (The formation of the U.S.S.R.). 2d enlarged ed. Moscow, 1947.

——. "Sovetskaia strana v period perekhoda k novoi ekonomicheskoi politike" (Soviet state in the period of transition to the New Economic Policy). *Istorik-Marksist,* No. 5–6 (75–76), 1939, pp. 38–66.

Gershuni, G. *Die Konzessionspolitik Sowjetrusslands.* Berlin, 1927.

Gessen, S. Ia. *Okrainnye gosudarstva; Polsha, Finliandiia, Estoniia, Latviia i Litva* (The border states; Poland, Finland, Estonia, Latvia, and Lithuania). Leningrad, 1926.

Glasgow, George. *From Dawes to Locarno: Being a Critical Record of an Important Achievement in European Diplomacy, 1924–1925.* London, 1925.

Gogol, N. V. *Polnoe sobranie khudozhestvennykh proizvedenii.* Moscow, 1916.

Goikhbarg, A. "Lenin o gosudarstve" (Lenin on the state). *Sovetskoe Pravo,* No. 6 (12), 1924, pp. 3–23.

———. "V. I. Lenin i sovetskoe pravo" (Lenin and Soviet law). *Sovetskoe Pravo,* No. 2 (8), 1924, pp. 3–6.

Gordon, Leland. *American Relations with Turkey, 1830–1930.* Philadelphia, 1932.

Graham, Malbone W. *New Governments of Eastern Europe.* New York, 1927.

———. "Russian-American Relations, 1917–1933." *American Political Science Review,* Vol. XXVIII, No. 3, June 1934.

———. *The Soviet Security System.* New York, 1928.

———. "The Soviet Security Treaties." *American Journal of International Law,* Vol. XXIII, No. 2, April 1929.

Greg. "Krizis Maloi Antanty" (The crisis of the Little Entente). *Mezhdunarodnaia Zhizn,* No. 9, 1926, pp. 38–50.

Gregory, J. D. *On the Edge of Diplomacy; Rambles and Reflections, 1902–1928.*

Gregory, J. E. *The Land of the Soviets.* New York, 1946. Maps by J. F. Horrabin.

Gurian, Waldemar. *Bolshevism; Theory and Practice.* New York, 1932.

[Gurko-]Kriazhin, V. "Razdel Turtsii vo vremia mirovoi voiny" (The partition of Turkey during the World War). *Novyi Vostok,* No. 4, 1923, pp. 49–57.

Gurvich, G. S. "Printsipy avtonomizma i federalizma v sovetskom systeme" (The principles of autonomy and federalism in the Soviet system). *Sovetskoe Pravo,* No. 3 (9), 1924, pp. 3–39.

Gurvich, I. "Pritiazaniia Antanty k Rossii v svete mezhdunarodnogo prava" (The Entente's claims to Russia in the light of international law). *Sovetskoe Pravo,* No. 2 (5), 1923, pp. 33–42.

Halecki, O. *A History of Poland.* New York, 1943.

Hallgarten, George W. F. "General Hans von Seeckt and Russia, 1920–1922." *Journal of Modern History,* Vol. XXI, No. 1, March 1949, pp. 29–34.

Hanisch, Erdmann. *Geschichte Sowjetrusslands, 1917–1941.* Freiburg, 1951.

Hazard, John H. *Law and Social Change in the U.S.S.R.* London, 1953. Published under the auspices of the London Institute of World Affairs.

———. "The Soviet Concept of International Law." *Proceedings of the American Society of International Law at its Thirty-third Annual Meeting Held at Washington, D.C., April 27–29, 1939,* pp. 33–51.

Historicus (George Morgan). *Stalin on Revolution,* New York, 1949. Reprinted from *Foreign Affairs,* January 1949.

Hoffmann, Karl. *Öl Politik und angelsächsischer Imperialismus.* Berlin, 1927.

Howard, Harry N. *The Partition of Turkey. A Diplomatic History, 1913–1923.* Norman, Oklahoma, 1931.

Iakubovskaia, S. I. *Obedinitelnoe dvizhenie za obrazovanie S.S.S.R. (1917–1922)* (The movement for unification and the formation of the S.S.S.R., 1917–1922). Moscow, 1947.

Ioffe, A. A. "Germanskaia revoliutsiia i rossiiskoe posolstvo" (The German revolution and the Russian embassy). *Vestnik Zhizni,* Moscow, No. 5, 1919, pp. 35–46.

———. *Mirnoe nastuplenie* (A peaceful offensive). Petersburg, 1921.

————. *Organizatsiia interventsii i blokady sovetskoi respubliki, 1918–1920; ocherk* (The organization of intervention and the blockade of the Soviet republic, 1918–1920; an outline). Moscow, 1930.

————. "Pered Genuei" (Before Genoa). *Vestnik N.K.I.D.*, No. 4–5, April-May, 1922, pp. 3–6.

Ipatieff, V. N. *The Life of a Chemist*. Stanford, Calif., 1946.

Iur. "Okkupatsiia Reina i Rura" (The occupation of the Rhine and the Ruhr). *Mezhdunarodnaia Zhizn*, No. 1, 1924, pp. 3–16.

Ivanov, L. N. "Anglo-amerikanskie otnosheniia" (Anglo-American relations). *Mirovoe Khoziaistvo i Mirovaia Politika*, No. 3, 1926, pp. 55–72, and No. 4, 1926, pp. 33–49.

————. *Anglo-frantsuzskoe sopernichestvo, 1919–1927 gg.* (Anglo-French rivalry, 1919–1927). Moscow, 1928.

————. "Lokarno v svete anglo-frantsuzskikh protivorechii" (Locarno in the light of Anglo-French differences). *Mezhdunarodnaia Zhizn*, No. 3, 1926, pp. 27–48.

————. *Morskoe sopernichestvo imperialisticheskikh derzhav* (The naval rivalry of the imperialist powers). Moscow, 1936.

————. *SSSR v imperialisticheskom okruzhenii* (The U.S.S.R. in the imperialist encirclement). Moscow, 1928.

————, and P. Smirnov. *Anglo-amerikanskoe morskoe sopernichestvo* (The Anglo-American naval rivalry). Moscow, 1933.

Ivanovich, V. *Pochemu Angliia boretsia s Sovetskim Soiuzom* (Why Britain struggles against the Soviet Union). Moscow and Leningrad, 1927.

James, C. L. R. *World Revolution, 1917–1936; the Rise and Fall of the Communist International*. London, 1937.

Jordan, W. M. *Great Britain, France and the German Problem, 1918–1939*. London and New York, 1943. Also in Russian: W. M. Dzhordan. *Velikobritaniia, Frantsiia i germanskaia problema v 1918–1939 gg.* Moscow, 1945.

Kakurin, N. E., and V. A. Melikov. *Voina s belopoliakami 1920 g.* (War with White Poles in 1920). Moscow, 1925.

Kantorovich, A. Ia. "Amerika i Genuia" (America and Genoa). *Vestnik N.K.I.D.*, No. 4–5, April-May, 1922, pp. 33–47.

————. *Borba za Tikhii Okean . . .* (The struggle for the Pacific . . .). Moscow, 1932.

————. "Frantsuzskaia burzhuaziia i Sovetskaia Rossiia" (The French bourgeoisie and Soviet Russia). *Vestnik N.K.I.D.*, No. 1–3, January–March, 1922, pp. 95–113.

Karelsky, Iu. "Pribaltiiskie strany i peregovory o garantiinom dogovore" (The Baltic states and negotiations on the guarantee pact). *Mirovoe Khoziaistvo i Mirovaia Politika*, Nos. 7–8, 1926, pp 3–12.

Keeton, G. W., and Dr. R. Schlesinger. *Russia and Her Western Neighbors*. London, 1942.

Kennan, George F. *American Diplomacy, 1900–1950*. Chicago, 1951.

————. "The Sisson Documents." *The Journal of Modern History*, Vol. XXVIII, No. 2, June 1956, pp. 130–54.

Khinchuk, L. M. *K istorii anglo-sovetskikh otnoshenii* (An outline of Anglo-Soviet relations). Moscow, 1928.

Kitaigorodsky, P. "Na volnakh nefti" (On petroleum waves). *Kommunisticheskaia Revoliutsiia*, No. 1 (40), January 1923, pp. 71–75.

————. "Vopros o kapituliatsiiakh na Lozanskoi konferentsii" (The problem of capitulations at the Lausanne Conference). *Novyi Vostok*, No. 5, 1924, pp. 114–24.

Kliuchnikov, Iu. V. (ed.) "Dokumentatsiia po voprosam mezhdunarodnoi politiki" (Documentation of the problems of international politics). *Mirovoe Khoziaistvo i Mirovaia Politika,* No. 4, 1926, pp. 126–40.

――――. "Liga Natsii i razoruzhenie" (The League of Nations and disarmament). *Mezhdunarodnaia Zhizn,* No. 1, 1925, pp. 85–106.

――――. "Liga Natsii kak 'orudie ekonomicheskogo mira' " (The League of Nations as an "instrument of economic peace"). *Mezhdunarodnaia Zhizn,* No. 7, 1927, pp. 31–46.

――――. "Politicheskaia i pravovaia metodika razoruzheniia" (Political and legal methodology of disarmament). *Mezhdunarodnaia Zhizn,* No. 5, 1926, pp. 16–35.

Knight-Patterson, W. M. (Wladyslaw Kulski). *Germany from Defeat to Conquest, 1913–1933.* London, 1945.

Kohn, Hans. "The Permanent Mission: An Essay on Russia." *Review of Politics,* Vol. X, No. 3, July 1948, pp. 267–89.

Kolarz, Walter, *Russia and Her Colonies.* London, 1952.

Kon, F. "Panskaia Polsha, Antanta i Sovetskaia Rossiia" (The gentry's Poland, the Entente, and Soviet Russia). *Kommunisticheskaia Revoliutsiia,* No. 10 (49), June 1, 1923, pp. 27–35.

Konovalov, Serge (ed.). *Russo-Polish Relations; an Historical Survey.* Princeton, 1945.

Korovin, E. A. "Liga Natsii i ee evoliutsiia" (The League of Nations and its evolution). *Sovetskoe Pravo,* No. 1 (4), 1923, pp. 36–43.

――――. *Mezhdunarodnoe pravo perekhodnogo vremenni* (International law of the transition period). Moscow, 1923.

――――. "Mezhdunarodnoe priznanie SSSR. . . i iuridicheskie ego posledstviia" (International recognition of the U.S.S.R. . . . and its legal consequences). *Sovetskoe Pravo,* No. 3 (9), 1924, pp. 76–86.

――――. "*Ogovorka rebus sic stantibus* v mezhdunarodnoi praktike RSFSR" (*Rebus sic stantibus* in the international practice of the R.S.F.S.R.). *Sovetskoe Pravo,* No. 3 (6), 1923, pp. 53–57.

――――. *Osnovnye printsipy sovetskoi vneshnei politiki. Stenogramma publichnoi lektsii prochitannoi 25 maia, 1947 goda v Lektsionnom zale v Moskve* (The basic principles of Soviet foreign policy. Stenographic report of a lecture delivered on May 25, 1947, in the Lecture Hall in Moscow). Moscow, 1947.

――――. "La République des Soviets et le droit international." *Revue Générale de Droit International Public,* Tome XXXII, 1925, pp. 292–312.

――――. *Sovremennoe mezhdunarodnoe publichnoe pravo* (Contemporary public international law). Moscow, 1926.

――――. "Voprosy mezhdunarodnogo prava perekhodnogo vremeni" (The problems of international law in the transition period). *Mezhdunarodnoe Pravo,* No. 1, 1928, pp. 39–56. With a summary in French.

――――,*et al. Zahraniční politika SSSR od říjnové revoluce až po naše dny* (Foreign policies of the U.S.S.R. from the October Revolution to the present day). Praha, 1949.

Kotliarevsky, S. "Pravovoe polozheniie avtonomnykh respublik" (The legal status of the autonomous republics). *Sovetskoe Pravo,* No. 6 (18), 1925, pp. 37–45.

Krasin, L. B. *Vneshtorg i vneshniaia ekonomicheskaia politika sovetskogo pravitelstva* (The Commissariat of Foreign Trade and the foreign economic policy of the Soviet government). Petersburg, 1921.

――――. *Voprosy vneshnei torgovli* (Problems of foreign trade). Moscow, 1928.

"Krasnye granaty" (The red grenades). *Znamia Borby,* No. 20–21, March 1927, pp. 19–22. Deals with the Soviet-German secret military deal.

Krichevsky, M. "Rossiia No. 2 i Genuia" (Russia No. 2 [i.e., anti-Soviet groupings] and Genoa). *Vestnik N.K.I.D.*, No. 4-5, April-May, 1922, pp. 60–67.

Krivitsky, W. G. *In Stalin's Secret Service; an Exposé of Russia's Secret Policies by the Former Chief of the Soviet Intelligence in Western Europe.* New York and London, 1939.

Krotkov, V. T. "Angliia i Genuia" (England and Genoa). *Vestnik N.K.I.D.*, No. 4-5, 1922, pp. 18–33.

Krylov, S. B. "Istoricheskii protsess razvitiia sovetskogo federalizma" (The historical process of the development of soviet federalism). *Sovetskoe Pravo*, No. 5 (11), 1924, pp. 36–66.

———. "Sovetskoe konsulskoe pravo" (Soviet consular law). *Sovetskoe Pravo*, No. 1 (7), 1924, pp. 111–24.

Kunina, A. "Iz istorii imperialisticheskoi ekspansii S. SH. A. v Evrope posle pervoi mirovoi voiny (Deiatelnost ARA v 1918–1919 gg.)" (An account of American imperialist expansion in Europe after World War I. The activity of the A.R.A. in 1918–1919). *Voprosy Istorii*, No. 3, March 1948, pp. 80–92.

Kutrzeba, Stanislaw. "La question de Wilno." *Revue Générale de Droit International Public*, Tome XXXV, 1928, pp. 624–44.

Ladyzhensky, A. "Instruktsiia konsulam RSFSR" (Instructions to the consuls of the R.S.F.S.R.). *Mezhdunarodnaia Zhizn*, No. 16 (134), November 30, 1922, pp. 22–27.

Lagarde, Ernest. *Priznanie sovetskogo pravitelstva* (Recognition of the Soviet government). Moscow, 1925. Translated from the French.

———. *La reconnaissance du gouvernement des soviets.* Paris, 1924.

Lamont, Corliss. *The Peoples of the Soviet Union . . .* New York, 1946. With maps, plates, diagrams.

Lan, V. *S. SH. A. ot pervoi do vtoroi mirovoi voiny* (The United States from World War I to World War II). Moscow, 1947.

Lapradelle, A. G. de. *Le marxisme tentaculaire; la formation, la tactique et l'action de la diplomatie soviétique, 1920–1940.* Issoudun, 1942.

Laserson, Max M. *Russia and the Western World; the Place of the Soviet Union in the Comity of Nations.* New York, 1945.

———. "The Development of Soviet Foreign Policy in Europe, 1917–1942. A Selection of Documents . . ." *International Conciliation*, No. 386, January 1943, pp. 3–95.

See also Shotwell

Leites, N. C. *The Operational Code of the Politburo.* New York, 1951.

Lemin, I. M. "Tridtsat let borby SSSR za mir i bezopasnost" (Thirty years of the U.S.S.R.'s struggle for peace and security). *Mirovoe Khoziaistvo i Mirovaia Politika*, No. 10, 1947, pp. 25–55.

———. *Vneshniaia politika Velikobritanii ot Versalia do Lokarno, 1919–1925* (The foreign policy of Great Britain from Versailles to Locarno, 1919–1925). Moscow, Akademiia Nauk S.S.S.R. (Academy of Sciences of the U.S.S.R.), 1947.

Lenin, V. I. *Sochineniia* (Works), 1st ed., Vol. XVII. Moscow, 1923.

———. *Sochineniia* (Works). 2d ed., 30 vols. Moscow and Leningrad, 1926–32.

———. *Leninskii sbornik* (Lenin's miscellaneous notes). 35 vols. Moscow, 1924–45.

———. *Selected Works.* 12 vols. New York, 1935–38.

Leontiev, A. "Leninsko-stalinskoe uchenie o postroenii sotsializma v nashei strane" (Leninist-Stalinist teaching on the building of socialism in our country). *Proletarskaia Revoliutsiia*, No. 3, 1939, pp. 29–76.

Levidov, M. *K istorii soiuznoi interventsii v Rossii. Tom I: Diplomaticheskaia pod-*

gotovka (An account of Allied intervention in Russia. Vol. I: Diplomatic preparation). Leningrad, 1925.

Litvinov, M. M. *Mirnaia politika sovetov; doklad i preniia na IV sessii TSIK S.S.S.R. 4-go sozyva* (The peace policy of the Soviets; report and discussions at the fourth session of the Central Executive Committee of the Fourth Congress of the U.S.S.R.) Moscow and Leningrad, 1929.

———. *Protiv voin. Za vseobshchee razoruzhenie. Sovetskie predlozheniia o polnom i chastichnom razoruzhenii* (Against wars. For universal disarmament. Soviet plans for total or partial disarmament). Moscow and Leningrad, 1928.

Liubimov, N. N. *SSSR i Frantsiia; franko-russkaia finansovaia problema v sviazi s mezhdunarodnoi zadolzhenostiu* (The U.S.S.R. and France; the Franco-Russian financial problem in connection with international debts). Leningrad, 1926.

Londonskaia konferentsiia (16 iiulia–16 avgusta 1924 g.) (The London Conference, July 16–August 16, 1924). Moscow, Communist Academy, 1925. Introduction by Karl Radek.

Lozovsky, A. (S. A. Dridzo). "Lozanna i Rur" (Lausanne and the Ruhr). *Pravda,* No. 35, February 16, 1923.

Lukashova, O. M. *Sovetskaia strana v period perekhoda na mirnuiu rabotu po vosstanovleniiu narodnogo khoziaistva. Obrazovanie SSSR (1921–1925 gg.)* (The Soviet country in the period of transition to peaceful work for the reconstruction of the national economy. Formation of the U.S.S.R., 1921–1925). Moscow, 1952.

Mahaney, Wilbur Lee, Jr. *The Soviet Union, the League of Nations and Disarmament: 1917–1935.* Philadelphia, 1940.

Maisky, I. *Vneshniaia politika RSFSR, 1917–1922* (The foreign policy of the R.S.F.S.R., 1917–1922). Moscow, 1922.

Makowski, J. "La question lithuanienne," *Revue Générale de Droit International Public,* Tome XXXVII, January–April, 1930, pp. 43–61.

Malaia Sovetskaia Entsiklopediia (Small Soviet encyclopedia). 10 vols. Moscow, 1930–31.

Manuilsky, D. "Bolshevization of the Parties," *Communist International,* No. 10, 1925, pp. 46–68.

Marchlewski, Julian. "Mir s Polshei" (Peace with Poland). *Kommunisticheskii Internatsional,* No. 14, 1920, pp. 2751–54.

———. *Polsha i mirovaia revoliutsiia* (Poland and the world revolution). Moscow, 1920.

———. *Voina i mir mezhdu burzhuaznoi Polshei i proletarskoi Rossiei* (War and peace between bourgeois Poland and proletarian Russia). Moscow, 1921. Translated from the Polish.

Marriott, Sir John A. R. *Anglo-Russian Relations 1689–1943.* London, 1944.

Medvedev, A. R., and Ia. L. Berman. *Uchenie o proletarskoi diktature i sovetskom prave* (The theory of proletarian dictatorship and Soviet law). Moscow and Leningrad, 1928.

Melville, Cecil F. *The Russian Face of Germany, an Account of the Secret Military Relations between the German and Soviet-Russian Governments.* London, 1932.

Menkes, M. "Raspad Maloi Antanty" (The disintegration of the Little Entente). *Mezhdunarodnaia Zhizn,* No. 2-3, 1924, pp. 79–93.

Mersmann-Soest, O., and Paul Wohl (comps. and eds.). *Die deutsch-russischen Verträge vom 12 Oktober 1925 nebst Schlussprotokollen, Notenwechsel, Denkschrift sowie Zusammenstellungen wichtiger Sowjet Dekrete über den Aussenhandel, usw. . . .* Berlin, 1926.

Mikhailov, Nicholas. *Land of the Soviets. A Handbook of the U.S.S.R.* New York, 1939. Translated from the Russian.

Miliukov, P. N. " 'Neitralizatsiia' Dardanell i Bosfora" (The "Neutralization" of the Dardanelles and the Bosporus), in *Voprosy mirovoi voiny. Sbornik* . . . (The problems of world war. A collection of articles . . .). Petrograd, 1915, pp. 532–48.

——. *La politique extérieure des Soviets.* Paris, 1934.

Mills, J. Saxon. *The Genoa Conference.* New York, 1922.

Mirkine-Guetzévitch, B. [Mirkin-Getsevich]. *La doctrine soviétique du droit international.* Paris, 1926.

Mirov, N. T. *Geography of Russia.* London, 1951.

Mitskevich-Kapsukas, V. "Oktiabrskaia revoliutsiia i rabochee dvizhenie Pribaltiiskikh stran" (The October Revolution and the workers' movement in the Baltic countries). *Krasnyi Internatsional Profsoiuzov,* No. 10 (81), October 1927, pp. 399–406.

Moore, Barrington. *Soviet Politics: the Dilemma of Power; the Role of Ideas in Social Change.* Cambridge, Mass., 1950.

Morrison, John A. "Russia and Warm Water: A Fallacious Generalization and Its Consequences." *United States Naval Institute, Proceedings,* Vol. 78, No. 11, Whole No. 597, November 1952, pp. 1169–79.

Mousset, Albert. *La Petite Entente; ses origines, son histoire, ses connexions, son avenir.* 2d ed. Paris, 1923.

Münzenberg, Willi. "Five Years of Workers International Relief." *International Press Correspondence,* No. 61, September 9, 1926.

Nansen, Fridtjof. *Russia and Peace.* London, 1923.

Neiman, G. *Puti razvitiia sovetskoi torgovli* (The ways of development of Soviet trade). Moscow, 1934. Edited by E. I. Kviring.

Nemanoff, Leon. *La Russie et les problèmes de la paix.* Paris, 1945.

Nicolsky, N. *Le Peuple russe; sa carrière historique, 862–1945.* Neuchâtel, 1945.

Nicolson, H. *Curzon: The Last Phase, 1919–1925. A Study in Post-War Diplomacy.* Boston and New York, 1934.

Nikiforov, P. M. *Istoricheskie dokumenty o deistviiakh i zamyslakh mezhdunarodnykh khishchnikov na Dalnem Vostoke* (Historical documents on the activities and plans of the international vultures in the Far East). Moscow, 1923.

Norton, H. K. *The Far Eastern Republic of Siberia.* London, 1923.

Odi. "Lokarnskaia konferentsiia" (The Locarno Conference). *Mezhdunarodnaia Zhizn,* No. 4-5, 1925, pp. 3–22.

Osinsky, I. "K voprosu o vseobshchei stachke v Anglii" (On the general strike in England). *Mirovoe Khoziaistvo i Mirovaia Politika,* No. 5–6, 1926, pp. 3–6.

Oudendijk, Willem J. *Ways and By-Ways in Diplomacy.* London, 1939.

Ouraloff, A. (A. Avtorkhanov). *Staline au pouvoir.* Paris, 1951.

Pankratova, A. M. *Sovetskaia diplomatiia v borbe protiv popytok kapitalisticheskikh stran obrazovat edinyi front (1925–1932 gody)* (Soviet diplomacy in the struggle against attempts by the capitalist countries to erect a united front, 1925–1932). Moscow, 1947. Stenographic report of a lecture delivered on June 15, 1947.

Papukchieva, Maria. *La politique de la Russie à l'égard des Détroits.* Lausanne, 1944.

——. *Partiia i Komintern o "staroi" i "novoi" oppozitsii. Sbornik rezoliutsii i postanovlenii* (The party and the Comintern on "old" and "new" opposition. A collection of resolutions and decisions). Moscow, 1926.

Pashukanis, E. B. *"Dolgi" i kredity (K peregovoram SSSR s Frantsiei)* ("Debts" and credits. On Soviet negotiations with France). Moscow, 1927.

——. "K voprosu o zadachakh sovetskoi nauki mezhdunarodnogo prava" (On the question of the tasks of Soviet scholarship in international law). *Mezhdunarodnaia Zhizn,* No. 1, 1928, pp. 7–18. Summary in French.

Pavlovich, *see* Veltman

"Pered opasnostiu nepopravimogo shaga" (The danger of an irreparable decision). *Izvestiia,* No. 218, September 24, 1925. Deals with Germany and the Locarno agreement.

"Piat let mezhdunarodnykh otnoshenii Sovetskoi Rossii, 1917–1922" (Five years of Soviet Russia's international relations, 1917–1922). *Mezhdunarodnaia Zhizn,* No. 15 (133), November 7, 1922. The entire issue is dedicated to the above subject.

Pilsudski, Jósef. *L'Année 1920. Edition complète avec le texte de l'ouvrage de M. Toukhatchevski "La Marche au-delà de la Vistule."* . . . Translated from the Polish.

———. *Rok 1920; z powodu książki M. Tuchaczewskiego "Pochód za Wisle"* (The year 1920; concerning M. Tukhachevsky's book "The March Across the Vistula River"). 2d ed. Warsaw, 1927.

Pipes, Richard. *The Formation of the Soviet Union: Communism and Nationalism, 1917–1923.* Cambridge, Mass., 1954.

Popov, K. "Ob istoricheskikh usloviiakh pererastaniia burzhuazno-demokraticheskoi revoliutsii v proletarskuiu" (On the historical conditions for the transformation of the bourgeois-democratic revolution into a proletarian one). *Bolshevik,* No. 21–22, 1928, pp. 35–42; No. 23–24, 1928, pp. 70–86; No. 1, 1929, pp. 70–85.

Popov, N. "Turtsiia i Lozanskaia konferentsiia" (Turkey and the Lausanne Conference). *Kommunisticheskaia Revoliutsiia,* No. 15 (39). December 15, 1922, pp. 57–67.

Post-skript. "Polsko-litovskii konflikt" (The Polish-Lithuanian conflict). *Mezhdunarodnaia Zhizn,* No. 12, 1927, pp. 61–67.

Potemkin, V. P. (ed.). *Istoriia diplomatii* (History of diplomacy). 3 vols. Moscow, 1941–45.

Preobrazhensky, E. *Itogi gennezskoi konferentsii i khoziaistvennye perspektivy Evropy* (The results of the Genoa Conference and the economic outlook of Europe). Moscow, 1922.

Przybylski, Adam. *Wojna Polska, 1918–1921* (The Polish war, 1918–1921). Warsaw, 1930.

Purlitz, F. M. (ed.). *Deutscher Geschichtskalender: sachlich geordnete Zusammenstellung der wichtigsten Vorgänge im Inland und Ausland.* I. Band, Januar-Juni, 1924.

—r. "Sovetsko-germanskii dogovor" (The Soviet-German treaty). *Mirovoe Khoziaistvo i Mirovaia Politika,* No. 3, 1926, pp. 3–9.

Rabenau, Friedrich von (ed.). *H. von Seeckt, aus seinem Leben, 1918–1936* . . . Leipzig, 1941.

Radek, K. *Die auswärtige Politik des deutschen Kommunismus und der hamburger nationale Bolschewismus.* N. d., n. p.

———. *Die auswärtige Politik Sowjet-Russlands.* Hamburg, 1921.

———. "The Disarmament Conference." *International Press Correspondence,* No. 10, June 28, 1926, p. 133.

———. *Das dritte Jahr des Kampfes der Sowjet Republik gegen das Weltkapital.* Leipzig, 1921.

———. "Garantiinyi pakt" (The guarantee pact). *Izvestiia,* No. 242, October 22, 1925, p. 1. Deals with the Locarno agreement.

———. *Gegen den Nationalbolschewismus! Zwei Aufsätze von Karl Radek und August Thalheimer.* N. p., 1920.

———. "Golod v Rossii i kapitalisticheskii mir" (The famine in Soviet Russia and the capitalist world). *Vestnik Agitatsii i Propagandy,* No. 22–23, November 1921, pp. 1–3.

————. *The International Outlook. Report of Comrade Radek to the Enlarged Executive Committee at the Sixth Session on June 15, 1923.* London, Communist Party of Great Britain, 1923.

————. "Itogi 'ery demokratii i patsifizma' " (The results of the "era of democracy and pacifism"). *Kommunisticheskii Internatsional,* No. 2 (39), February 1925, pp. 77–93.

————. *Leo Schlageter, der Wanderer ins Nichts.* Berlin, 1923.

————. *Likvidatsiia versalskogo mira; doklad IV kongressu Kommunisticheskogo Internatsionala.* Petrograd, 1922. Also in English: *The Winding-up of the Versailles Treaty. Report to the IV Congress of the Communist International.* Hamburg, 1922.

————. *Mezhdunarodnaia Politika. Obozrenie za 1924 god. Plan Daussa. Rabochee pravitelstvo v Anglii. Levyi blok vo Frantsii. Kitaiskaia revoliutsiia. Sushchestvo i itogi tak nasyvaemoi ery demokratii i patsifizma* (International policies. Review of the year 1924. The Dawes Plan. Workers' government in Britain. The Left bloc in France. The Chinese revolution. The nature and results of the so-called era of democracy and pacifism). Moscow and Leningrad, 1925.

————. *Na sluzhbe germanskoi revoliutsii* (In the service of the German revolution). Moscow, 1921. Translated from the German.

————. *Piat let Kominterna* (Five years of the Comintern). 2 vols. in one. Moscow,

————. *Portraits and Pamphlets.* London, 1935. Translated from the Russian.

————. "Posle Anglii—Italiia" (After England—Italy). *Pravda,* No. 32, February 9, 1924, p. 1.

————. "Stabilizatsiia kapitalizma (Doklad v Institute Mirovogo Khoziaistva i Mirovoi Politiki 13 noiabria 1926 g." (The stabilization of capitalism. Report delivered at the Institute of World Economy and World Politics, November 13, 1926). *Mirovoe Khoziaistvo i Mirovaia Politika,* No. 10–11, 1926, pp. 11–20.

————. *Vneshniaia politika sovetskoi Rossii* (Foreign policy of Soviet Russia). Moscow, 1923.

Rakovsky, Kh. G. *Liga natsii i SSSR. Prilozhenie: G. V. Chicherin, Liga natsii i SSSR* (The League of Nations and the U.S.S.R. Supplement: G. V. Chicherin, "The League of Nations and the U.S.S.R."). Moscow, 1926.

————. "Mezhdunarodnoe polozhenie" (The international situation). *Mirovoe Khoziaistvo i Mirovaia Politika,* No. 2, 1926, pp. 3–15. Lecture delivered at the Mendeleev Institute, Moscow, January 30, 1926.

————. *Nakanune Genui.* (On the eve of Genoa). Moscow, 1922.

————. *Rumyniia i Bessarabiia; k semiletiiu anneksii Bessarabii* (Rumania and Bessarabia; on the seventh anniversary of the annexation of Bessarabia). Moscow, 1925. Also in English, *Roumania and Bessarabia* (London, 1925), and French, *Roumanie et Bessarabie* (Paris, 1925).

Rezanov, A. S. *Le travail secret des agents bolchévistes; exposé d'après des documents authentiques émanant des bolchéviks.* Paris, 1926.

Romani, S. "Politicheskie itogi shestoi sessii Ligi Natsii" (Political results of the Sixth Session of the League of Nations). *Mezhdunarodnaia Zhizn,* No. 4–5, 1925, pp. 23–43.

Rosenberg, A. *A History of Bolshevism from Marx to the First 5 Years' Plan.* London, 1934.

————. *A History of the German Republic.* London, 1936.

Rosinski, Herbert. *The German Army.* London, 1939.

Rotshtein, F. A. (ed.). *Mirovaia politika v 1924 godu; sbornik statei* (World politics in 1924; a collection of articles). Moscow, 1925.

————. "Kakaia polza ot priznaniia" (What advantage from recognition?). *Pravda,* No. 59, March 12, 1924, p. 1.

Rubinshtein, M. " 'Kolonizatsiia' Evropy amerikanskim kapitalom. Itogi Londonskoi konferentsii" (The "Colonization" of Europe by American capital. Results of the London Conference). *Bolshevik,* No. 12-13, 1924, pp. 28–37.

Rubinshtein, N. L. *Sovetskaia diplomatiia v borbe protiv izoliatsii SSSR i ustanovlenie diplomaticheskikh otnoshenii s kapitalisticheskimi stranami; stenogramma publichnoi lektsii prochitannoi 8 iiunia 1947 goda v Lektsionnom zale v Moskve.* (Soviet diplomacy in the struggle against isolation of the U.S.S.R. and the establishment of diplomatic relations with capitalist countries. Lecture delivered June 8, 1947, at the Lecture Hall in Moscow). Moscow, 1947.

————. *Sovetskaia Rossiia i kapitalisticheskie gosudarstva v gody perekhoda ot voiny k miru, 1921–1922 gg.* (Soviet Russia and the capitalist states in the years of transition from war to peace). Moscow, 1948.

————. "Sovetskaia Rossiia na genuezskoi konferentsii" (Soviet Russia at the Genoa Conference). *Voprosy Istorii,* No. 2-3, 1946, pp. 3–32.

————. *Tridsat let sovetskoi vneshnei politiki; stenogramma publichnoi lektsii . . .* (Thirty years of Soviet foreign policy; stenographic notes of a public lecture . . .). Moscow, 1948.

Rubinshtein, P. "Zapadnaia Ukraina i Zapadnaia Belorussiia. Kratkaia istoricheskaia spravka" (The Western Ukraine and Western Belorussia. A short historical account). *Istoricheskii Zhurnal,* No. 10, 1939, pp. 10–15.

Rudolf, N. *Osnovy mezhdunarodnoi politiki sovetskoi vlasti* (The bases of the foreign policy of Soviet Russia). Moscow, 1933.

Rykov, A. I. *Angliia i SSSR; doklad na plenume moskovskogo soveta 1 iiunia 1927 g.* (England and the U.S.S.R.; report at the plenary session of the Moscow soviet, June 1, 1927). Moscow and Leningrad, 1927.

————. *Russia's Foreign Policy Outlined by Mr. A. I. Rykov (Chairman of the Council of People's Commissaries) at the Soviet Congress of the Union of Socialist Soviet Republics on April 19th, 1927.* London, 1927.

————. *Sotsialisticheskoe stroitelstvo i mezhdunarodnaia politika SSSR. Doklad na IV sezde sovetov SSSR* (Socialist construction and the international policy of the U.S.S.R. Report to the Fourth Congress of Soviets of the U.S.S.R.). Moscow and Leningrad, 1927.

Sabanin, A. V. *Khronologicheskii perechen mezhdunarodnykh mnogostoronnikh dogovorov, zakliuchennykh s 1919 po 1933 g. s kratkim izlozheniem ikh soderzhaniia* (A chronological enumeration of the international multilateral treaties signed from 1919 to 1933 with their brief summaries). Moscow, 1933.

————. "Mezhdunarodnoe pravo v sovetskom prave" (International law in Soviet law). *Mezhdunarodnoe Pravo,* No. 1, 1927, pp. 19–38. Summary is given in French.

————. "Pervyi sovetskii kurs mezhdunarodnogo prava" (The first Soviet textbook on international law). *Mezhdunarodnaia Zhizn,* No. 2, 1925, pp. 116–26.

————. "Sovetskaia vlast i mezhdunarodnoe pravo" (Soviet government and international law). *Mezhdunarodnaia Zhizn,* No. 15 (133), November 7, 1922, pp. 10–16.

St. Graur, Stefan. *Les relations entre la Roumanie et l'U.R.S.S. depuis la traité de Versailles.* Paris, 1936.

Sandomirsky, G. "Venskaia konferentsiia i sudby 'Romania Mare' (Velikoi Rumynii)" (The Vienna Conference and the fate of "Romania Mare" (Great Rumania)). *Mezhdunarodnaia Zhizn,* No. 2-3, 1924, pp. 36–56.

Schapiro, L. B. "The Soviet Concept of International Law," in *The Year Book of World Affairs, 1948* (London, 1948), pp. 272–310.

Scheffer, Paul. *Seven Years in Soviet Russia. With a Retrospect.* New York, 1932. Translated from the German.

Seeckt, Hans von. *Gedanken eines Soldaten.* Berlin, 1929.
Semashko, N. "Pochemu oni vzbesilis" (Why they got mad). *Izvestiia*, No. 93, April 28, 1922, p. 1. On the Allies' attitude toward the Rapallo treaty.
Seraphim, Ernst. *Deutsch-russische Beziehungen 1918–1925.* Berlin, 1925.
Serge, Victor. *From Lenin to Stalin.* New York, 1937. Translated from the French.
Shapiro, B. "Ocherednaia problema sovetskogo konsulskogo prava" (The immediate problem of Soviet consular law). *Sovetskoe Pravo*, No. 2 (14), 1925, pp. 144–51.
Shotwell, James T. *Turkey and the Straits. A Short History.* New York, 1940.
———, and Max M. Laserson. *Poland and Russia, 1919–1945.* New York, 1945.
Shtein, B. E. "Anglo-frantsuzskie protivorechiia" (Anglo-French contradictions). *Mezhdunarodnaia Zhizn*, No. 2, 1923, pp. 7–24.
———. "Balans 'idei razoruzheniia'" (The balance of the "ideas on disarmament"). *Mezhdunarodnaia Zhizn*, No. 3, 1926, pp. 3–12.
———. *Gaagskaia konferentsiia* (The Hague Conference). Moscow, 1922.
———. *Genuezskaia konferentsiia* (The Genoa Conference.) Moscow, 1922.
———. *"Russkii vopros" na Parizhskoi mirnoi konferentsii (1919–1920 gg.)* ("The Russian problem" at the Paris Peace Conference, 1919–1920). Moscow, 1949.
———. *Sovetskaia Rossiia v kapitalisticheskom okruzhenii. Torgovaia politika RSFSR* (Soviet Russia in the capitalist encirclement. Trade policy of the R.S.F.S.R.). Moscow, 1921.
———. *Torgovaia politika i torgovye dogovory sovetskoi Rossii 1917–1922 gg.* (Trade policy and commercial treaties of Soviet Russia in 1917–1922). Moscow, 1923.
Shubin, I. (Samarin). "Novye puti polskoi politiki" (The new course of Polish policy). *Mezhdunarodnaia Zhizn*, No. 2, 1923, pp. 35–59.
Shverma (Ia.) [member of the Central Committee of the Communist Party of Czechoslovakia]. "Istoricheskii put Kommunisticheskogo Internatsionala (K dvadtsatiletiiu osnovaniia Kominterna)" (The historical path of the Communist International. On the twentieth anniversary of the foundation of the Comintern). *Proletarskaia Revoliutsiia*, No. 2, 1939, pp. 67–100.
Shtiurmer, B. "Zhenevskaia konferentsiia Ligi Natsii. Dogovor o 'garantiiakh' i vopros o 'razoruzhenii'" (The Geneva Conference of the League of Nations. The "guarantee" treaty and the problem of "disarmament"). *Mezhdunarodnaia Zhizn*, No. 4-5, 1924, pp. 25–46.
Shtiurmer, Kh. "Turtsiia posle Lozanny" (Turkey after Lausanne). *Mezhdunarodnaia Zhizn*, No. 2-3, 1924, pp. 57–58.
Slovès, Ch. H. *La France et l'Union soviétique.* Paris, 1935.
Sobolev, M. N. (ed.). *Ekonomika i politika vneshnei torgovli. Sbornik* (The economics and politics of foreign trade. A collection of articles). Moscow, 1928.
Sobolevicius, Elias (Sobolevitz). *Les Etats baltes et la Russie soviétique (relations internationales jusqu'en 1928).* Paris, 1930.
Sorin, V. G. *Partiia i oppozitsiia; iz istorii oppozitsionnykh techenii . . . I: Fraktsiia levykh kommunistov* (The party and the opposition; a sketch of opposition tendencies . . . Vol. I: Communist Left faction). Moscow, 1925. Preface by N. I. Bukharin.
Speeches and Addresses of Warren G. Harding, President of the United States. Delivered During the Course of His Tour from Washington, D.C., to Alaska and Return to San Francisco, June 20 to August 2, 1923. N.p., n.d. Reported and compiled by James W. Murphy.
Spektator, M. "Promyshlennyi krizis v Anglii" (The industrial crisis in Britain). *Mirovoe Khoziaistvo i Mirovaia Politika*, No. 5-6, 1926, pp. 7–16.
Stalin, I. V. *Interview with Foreign Workers' Delegation.* New York, 1927.

————. "K mezhdunarodnomu polozheniiu" (On the international situation). *Bolshevik*, No. 11, 1924, pp. 8–20.

————. *Ob oppozitsii; stati i rechi, 1921–1927 g.g.* (On the opposition; articles and speeches, 1921–1927). Moscow and Leningrad, 1928.

————. *Sochineniia* (Works), Vols. I–. Moscow, 1946–.

————. *The Theory and Practice of Leninism.* London, Communist Party of Great Britain, 1925.

————. *Voprosy leninizma.* 11th ed. Moscow, 1947. Also in English: *Problems of Leninism.* Moscow, 1943.

————. *Works*, Vols. I–. Moscow, 1954–.

Stern-Rubarth, Edgar. *Three Men Tried. Austen Chamberlain, Stresemann, Briand and Their Fight for a New Europe.* London, 1939.

Stuchka, P. I. *Revoliutsionnaia rol prava i gosudarstva. Obshchee uchenie a prave i gosudarstve* (The revolutionary role of law and state. General principles of law and state). Moscow, 1921.

Sumner, B. H. *A Short History of Russia.* New York, 1942.

Surface, Frank M., and Raymond L. Bland. *American Food in the World War and Reconstruction Period; Operations of the Organizations Under the Direction of Herbert Hoover, 1914 to 1924.* Stanford, Calif., 1931.

Suslov, P. V. *Politicheskoe obespechenie sovetsko-polskoi kampanii 1920 goda* (Political guarantee of the Soviet-Polish campaign, 1920). Moscow and Leningrad, 1930.

Sworakowski, Witold. "An Error Regarding Eastern Galicia in Curzon's Note to the Soviet Government of July 11, 1920," *Journal of Central European Affairs,* Vol. 4, No. 1, April 1944.

Tanin, M. *Amerika na mirovoi arene* (America in the world arena). Moscow and Leningrad, 1927.

————. "Anglo-sovetskii razryv i problema edinogo imperialisticheskogo fronta" (The Anglo-Soviet break and the problem of the united imperialist front). *Bolshevik*, No. 11–12, June 15, 1927, pp. 59–68; No. 13, July 1, 1927, pp. 70–80; No. 14, July 31, 1927, pp. 55–66.

————. *Mezhdunarodnaia politika SSSR (1917–1924)* (The international policy of the U.S.S.R., 1917–1924). Moscow, 1925.

————. *10 let vneshnei politiki SSSR (1917–1927)* (Ten years of U.S.S.R. foreign policy, 1917–1927). Moscow and Leningrad, 1927.

Taracouzio, T. A. *The Soviet Union and International Law, a Study based on the Legislation, Treaties, and Foreign Relations of the Union of Socialist Soviet Republics.* New York, 1935.

————. *War and Peace in Soviet Diplomacy.* New York, 1940.

Towster, Julian. *Political Power in the U.S.S.R., 1917–1947; the Theory and Structure of Government in the Soviet State.* New York, 1948.

Toynbee, Arnold J. (ed.). *Survey of International Affairs, 1920–1927.* 7 vols. London, 1925–28.

Trainin, I. P. "Questions of Guerrilla Warfare in the Law of War." *The American Journal of International Law.* Vol. 40 (1946), pp. 534–62.

Treviranus, G. R. *Revolutions in Russia; Their Lessons for the Western World.* New York, 1944. Deals with Soviet-German military collaboration.

Trotsky, L. D. *The First Five Years of the Communist International.* 2 vols. New York, 1945.

————. "K voprosu o perspektivakh mirovogo razvitiia" (On the prospects of world progress). *Izvestiia*, No. 177, August 5, 1924.

————. *The Lessons of October, 1917.* London, 1925. Translated from the Russian.

——. *My Life: An Attempt at an Autobiography.* New York, 1930.

——. *The New Course.* New York, 1943. Translated from the Russian.

——. *The Real Situation in Russia.* New York, 1928. Translated from the Russian.

——. *Sochineniia, tom XII: Osnovnye voprosy proletarskoi revoliutsii* (Works, Vol. XII: The basic problems of the proletarian revolution). Moscow and Leningrad, 1925.

——. *Sochineniia, tom XIII: Kommunisticheskii Internatsional* (Works, Vol. XIII: The Communist International). Moscow and Leningrad, 1926.

——. *Sochineniia, tom XVII: Sovetskaia respublika i kapitalisticheskii mir* (Works, Vol. XVII: The Soviet republic and the capitalist world). 2 parts. Moscow, 1926.

——. *Stalin, an Appraisal of the Man and His Influence.* New York and London, 1941. Edited and translated from the Russian by Charles Malamuth.

——. *The Stalin School of Falsification.* New York, 1937.

——. *The Strategy of the World Revolution.* New York, 1930. Translated with an introduction by Max Shachtman.

——. *The Suppressed Testament of Lenin . . .* New York, 1935.

——. *The Third International After Lenin.* New York, 1936. Translated by John G. Wright.

——. *Zapad i vostok; voprosy mirovoi politiki i mirovoi revoliutsii* (West and East; the problems of world politics and world revolution). Moscow, 1924.

Trutko-Gul [F. I.]. "O sovetskom konsule i konsulskom kodekse" (On the Soviet consul and the consular code). *Sovetskoe Pravo,* No. 1 (13), 1925, pp. 79–84.

Tukhachevsky, M. N. "The Territorial System in the Red Army." *International Press Correspondence,* No. 66, October 14, 1926, p. 1126.

Turubiner, A. "Konstitutsiia RSFSR 1925 goda" (The R.S.F.S.R. constitution of 1925). *Sovetskoe Pravo,* No. 6 (18), 1925, pp. 14–24.

Turok, V. M. *Lokarno* (Locarno). Moscow, Akademiia Nauk, 1949.

——. "Ot plana Dausa k garantiinomu paktu" (From the Dawes Plan to the guarantee pact). *Voprosy Istorii,* No. 6, June, 1928, pp. 22–41.

Umiastowski, Roman. *Russia and the Polish Republic, 1918–1941.* London, 1945.

L'U.R.S.S. et la paix; recueil de documents, propositions de paix et de désarmement du gouvernement des Soviets aux gouvernements d'Europe, Amérique, etc., 1917–1929 . . . Paris, 1930. Issued by Les Amis de l'Union Soviétique.

Varga, E. *The Decline of Capitalism; the Economics of a Period of the Decline of Capitalism after Stabilization.* London, Communist Party of Britain, 1928. Translated from the Russian.

——. *The Process of Capitalist Decline. Report to the IV Congress of the Communist International.* Hamburg, 1922.

Vaucher, Georges. "Le Comité international de secours à la Russie et son haut commissariat." *Revue Internationale de la Croix Rouge,* No. 37, January 15, 1922.

Veltman, M. L. (M. Pavlovich). *The Foundations of Imperialist Policy; a Course of Lectures Read to the Academy of the General Staff in 1918–1919.* London, 1922. Translation from the Russian.

——. *Iaponskii imperializm na Dalnem Vostoke* (Japanese imperialism in the Far East). Moscow, 1923. Vol. IV in the series *RSFSR v imperialisticheskom okruzhenii* (The R.S.F.S.R. in the imperialist encirclement).

——. "Lozanskaia konferentsiia" (The Lausanne Conference). *Novyi Vostok,* No. 3, 1923, pp. 3–34.

——. *Pered ugrozoi budushchikh voin* (Under the threat of future wars). Moscow, 1924.

———. *"Russkii vopros" v angliiskoi vneshnei politike (1922–1924)* ("The Russian question" in British foreign policy, 1922–1924). Moscow, 1924.

———. *Sovetskaia Rossiia i kapitalisticheskaia Amerika* (Soviet Russia and capitalist America). Moscow, 1922. Vol. III of *RSFSR v imperialisticheskom okruzhenii* (The R.S.F.S.R. in the imperialist encirclement).

———. *Sovetskaia Rossiia i kapitalisticheskaia Angliia (ot epokhi tsarizma do pravitelstva Chemberlena-Bolduina 1925 g.)* (Soviet Russia and capitalist Britain; from the tsarist period to the Chamberlain-Baldwin government, 1925). Moscow, 1925. Vol. II of *RSFSR v imperialisticheskom okruzhenii*.

———. *Sovetskaia Rossiia i kapitalisticheskaia Frantsiia* (Soviet Russia and capitalist France). Moscow, 1922. Vol. I of *RSFSR v imperialisticheskom okruzhenii*.

———. "Vashingtonskaia konferentsiia" (The Washington Conference). *Vestnik N.K.I.D.*, No. 9-10, 1921, pp. 3–12.

Ves SSSR. Spravochnaia i adresnaia kniga na 1926 god (The U.S.S.R.: Reference and address book for 1926). Moscow and Leningrad, 1926.

Vilensky, V. D. (Sibiriakov). "Dva soglasheniia" (Two agreements). *Izvestiia*, No. 192, May 24, 1924, p. 1. Concerns Turkey.

———. "Politika mira" (The policy of peace). *Izvestiia*, No. 240, October 20, 1923, p. 1.

Voitkevich, M. "Oktiabrskaia revoliutsiia i proletariat Polshi" (The October Revolution and the proletariat of Poland). *Krasnyi Internatsional Profsoiuzov*, No. 10 (81), October 1927, pp. 380–85.

von Laue, Theodore H. "Soviet Diplomacy: G. V. Chicherin, People's Commissar for Foreign Affairs, 1918–1930," in Gordon A. Craig and Felix Gilbert (eds.), *The Diplomats 1919–1939*, Princeton, 1953, pp. 234–81.

Vyshinsky, A. Ia. *Voprosy mezhdunarodnogo prava i mezhdunarodnoi politiki* (The problems of international law and international politics.) Moscow, 1949.

———. *Voprosy teorii gosudarstva i prava* (The theory of state and law). 2d ed. Moscow, 1949. Also published in English.

Vysnepolsky, S. "Svoboda morei v epokhu imperializma" (Freedom of the seas in the epoch of imperialism). *Sovetskoe Gosudarstvo i Pravo*, No. 1, 1949, pp. 13–25.

Wheeler-Bennett, J. W. *Disarmament and Security Since Locarno, 1925–1931; Being the Political and Technical Background of the General Disarmament Conference, 1932*. New York, 1932.

Wolfe, Bertram D. *Three Who Made a Revolution, a Biographical History*. New York, 1948.

Wollenberg, Erich. *The Red Army*. London, 1938. Translated from the German. Deals with Soviet-German military collaboration.

Zernov, Nicolas. *Three Russian Prophets: Khomiakov, Dostoevsky, Soloviev*. London, 1944.

Zinoviev, G. E. "K godovshchine gamburgskogo vosstaniia" (The anniversary of the Hamburg rising). *Pravda*, No. 242, October 23, 1924, p. 1.

———. *Les problèmes de la révolution allemande*. Paris, 1923.

———. *Rurskie sobytiia i zadachi Kominterna* (The Ruhr events and the tasks of the Comintern). Moscow, 1923.

———. *Speech in Reply to Discussion of Report on the Work of the E.C.C.I. Delivered by G. Zinoviev, June 26, 1924. Resolution on the Report of E.C.C.I* Moscow, 1924.

———. *The "Zinoviev" Letter. Report of Investigation by British Delegation to Russia for the Trades Union General Council, November–December, 1924*. London, 1925.

OFFICIAL PUBLICATIONS, TREATIES, AND CONFERENCES
OFFICIAL PUBLICATIONS

Finland. Ministry of Foreign Affairs. *Livre vert. Actes et documents concernant la question carélienne (1922).* Helsinki, 1922.

――――. *La question de la Carélie orientale. Documents publiés par le Ministère des affaires étrangères.* 2 vols. Helsinki, 1922–24.

Germany. *Verhandlungen des Reichstags. III. Stenographische Berichte. Wahlperiode 1924. Band 391 (von der 225 Sitzung am 3 November 1927 bis zur Sitzung am 5 Februar 1928).* Berlin, 1927.

Great Britain

Parliamentary Debates. Commons. Fifth Series: *1920*, Vol. 125; *1924*, Vol. 176; *1927*, Vol. 206.

Anglo-Russian Parliamentary Committee. *U.S.S.R. and Disarmament. Discussion of Russia's Disarmament Proposals at Geneva. March 16–24, 1928. Convention for Partial Disarmament, etc.* Compiled by W. P. Coates.

Foreign Office. *Correspondence between His Majesty's Government and the Soviet Government respecting the Relations between the two Governments.* Cmd. 1869. Accounts and Papers, 1923, Vol. XXV. London, 1923.

――――. *Correspondence with M. Krassin respecting Russia's Foreign Indebtedness.* Cmd. 1546. Accounts and Papers, 1921, Vol. XLIII. London, 1921.

――――. *Documents Illustrating the Hostile Activities of the Soviet Government and Third International against Great Britain.* Cmd. 2874. Accounts and Papers, 1927, Vol. XXVI. London, 1927.

――――. *Further Correspondence between His Majesty's Government and the Soviet Government respecting the Relations between the two Governments.* Cmd. 1890. Accounts and Papers, 1923, Vol. XXV. London, 1923.

――――. *Notes from His Majesty's Government to the Government of the Union of Soviet Socialist Republics respecting the Relations existing between the two Governments and Note in Reply, February 23/26, 1927* . . . Cmd. 2822. Accounts and Papers, 1927, Vol. XXII. London, 1927.

――――. *Reply of the Soviet Government to His Majesty's Government respecting the Relations between the Two Governments.* Cmd. 1874. Accounts and Papers, 1923, Vol. XXV. London, 1923.

――――. *A Selection of Papers Dealing with the Relations between His Majesty's Government and the Soviet Government, 1921–1927.* Cmd. 2895. Accounts and Papers, 1927. Vol. XXV. London, 1927.

Latvia. Latvian Legation, Washington, D.C. *Latvian-Russian Relations, Documents.* Washington, D.C., n.d. Compiled by A. Bilmanis.

Lithuania. Ministry of Foreign Affairs. *Documents diplomatiques. Conflit Polono-lituanien. Question de Vilna, 1918–1924.* Kaunas, 1924.

――――. Lithuanian Information Bureau, London. *The Lithuanian-Polish Dispute.* 3 vols. London, 1921–23.

Poland. Ministry of Foreign Affairs. *Documents diplomatiques concernant les relations polono-lituaniennes* . . . 2 vols. Warsaw, 1920–21.

――――. Polish Embassy, U.S. *Polish-Soviet Relations. 1918–1943. Official Documents Issued by the Polish Embassy in Washington by the Authority of the Government of Poland.* Washington, D.C., 1944.

Russia

Academy of Sciences of the U.S.S.R. Institute of History. *Obrazovanie S.S.S.R.; sbornik dokumentov, 1917–1924* (The formation of the U.S.S.R.; a collection of documents, 1917–1924). Moscow, 1949. Edited by E. B. Genkina.

All-Russian Communist Party (B). *Desiatyi sezd R.K.P. (B). Mart 1921 g.* (Tenth Congress of the Russian Communist Party (Bolshevik). March 1921). Moscow, 1933.

——. *Dvenadtsatyi sezd Rossiiskoi Kommunisticheskoi Partii (Bolshevikov). Stenograficheskii otchet, 17–25 aprelia 1923 g.* (Twelfth Congress of the Russian Communist Party (Bolshevik). Stenographic report, April 17–25, 1923). Moscow, 1923.

——. *History of the Communist Party of the Soviet Union (B). .Short Course.* . . . New York, 1939. Translated from the Russian (see next entry).

——. *Istoriia Vsesoiuznoi Kommunisticheskoi Partii (Bolshevikov). Kratkii kurs. Pod redaktsiei Komissii TsK VKP (B), odobren TsK VKP (B), 1938 g.* (History of the All-Union Communist Party (B). Short course. Edited by a commission of the Central Committee of the party and authorized by the Central Committee, 1938). Moscow, 1938.

——. *XV sezd Vsesoiuznoi Kommunisticheskoi Partii (B). Stenograficheskii otchet* (Fifteenth Congress of the All-Union Communist Party (B). Stenographic report). 2d ed. Moscow and Leningrad, 1928.

——. *Report of the Fifteenth Congress of the Communist Party of the Soviet Union.* London, Communist Party of Great Britain, 1928.

——. *Trinadtsatyi sezd Rossiiskoi Kommunisticheskoi Partii (Bolshevikov). Stenograficheskii otchet, 23–31 maia 1924 g.* (Thirteenth Congress of the All-Russian Communist Party (B). Stenographic report, May 23–31, 1924). Moscow, 1924.

——. *Vosmoi sezd RKP (B). 18–23 marta 1919 g.* (Eighth Congress of the Russian Communist Party (B), March 18–23, 1919). Moscow, 1933.

——. *Vsesoiuznaia Kommunisticheskaia Partiia (B) v rezoliutssiakh i resheniiakh sezdov, konferentsii i plenumov Ts. K. (1898–1935)* (The All-Union Communist Party (B) in resolutions and decisions of its congresses, its conferences, and the plenums of its Central Committee, 1898–1935). 5th ed., 2 vols. Moscow, 1936.

[Laws, etc.] *The Fundamental Law (Constitution) of the U.S.S.R. together with the Constitution (Fundamental Law) of the R.S.F.S.R.* Moscow, 1932.

[——.] *Sobranie Uzakonenii i Rasporiazhenii Rabochego i Krestianskogo Pravitelstva, 1917–* (Collected laws and regulations of the workers' and peasants' government, 1917–). Moscow, 1919–. Title varies.

People's Commissariat of Foreign Affairs. [Adam, E. A. (ed.)] *Konstantinopol i prolivy. Po sekretnym dokumentam b. Ministerstva Inostrannykh Del* (Constantinople and the Straits. According to secret documents of the former Ministry of Foreign Affairs). 2 vols. Moscow, 1925–26.

——. *"Akty mirnoi politiki Sovetskogo pravitelstva. 1917–1921"* (Acts of peace policy of the Soviet government, 1917–1921). *Vestnik N.K.I.D.*, No. 5–6, July 1, 1921, pp. 3–12. Chronological data.

——. *Anglo-sovetskie otnosheniia so dnia podpisaniia torgovogo dogovora do razryva (1921–1927 gg.)* (Anglo-Soviet relations from the day of signing the trade agreement to the break of relations, 1921–1927). Moscow, 1927.

——. *Desiat let sovetskoi diplomatii. Akty i dokumenty* (Ten years of Soviet diplomacy. Acts and documents). Moscow, 1927.

——. *Ezhegodnik Narodnogo Komissariata po Inostrannym Delam na 1925 god* (Yearbook of the People's Commissariat of Foreign Affairs for 1925). Moscow, 1925.

——. *Ezhegodnik Narodnogo Komissariata po Inostrannym Delam na 1926 god* (Yearbook of the People's Commissariat of Foreign Affairs for 1926). Moscow, 1926.

——. *Godovoi otchet za 1923 g. Narodnogo Komissariata po Inostrannym Delam k II sezdu sovetov S.S.S.R.* (Annual report for 1923 of the People's Commissariat of Foreign Affairs to the Second Congress of Soviets of the U.S.S.R.). Moscow, 1924.

———. *Godovoi otchet Narodnogo Komissariata po Inostrannym Delam za 1924 g. k III sezdu sovetov S.S.S.R.* (Annual report for 1924 of the People's Commissariat of Foreign Affairs to the Third Congress of Soviets of the U.S.S.R.). Moscow, 1925.

———. *"Krasnaia Kniga." Sbornik diplomaticheskikh dokumentov o russko-polskikh otnosheniiakh. 1918–1920 gg.* ("The Red Book." A collection of diplomatic documents dealing with Russo-Polish relations, 1918–1920). Moscow, 1920.

———. *"Livre Rouge." Documents et correspondence diplomatique russo-finlandaise concernant la Carélie orientale.* Moscow, 1922.

———. *Mezhdunarodnaia politika R.S.F.S.R. v 1922 g. Otchet Narodnogo Komissariata po Inostrannym Delam* (The international policy of the R.S.F.S.R. in 1922. Report of the People's Commissariat of Foreign Affairs). Moscow, 1923.

———. *Sovetskaia Rossiia i Polsha* (Soviet Russia and Poland). Moscow, 1921. Also in Polish, *Rosja Sowiecka a Polska* (Moscow, 1921), and French, *La Russie des Soviets et la Pologne* (Moscow, 1921).

Vtoroi Sezd Sovetov Soiuza Sovetskikh Sotsialisticheskikh Respublik. Stenograficheskii otchet (Second Congress of Soviets of the *U.S.S.R.* Stenographic report). Moscow, 1924.

United States

Annual Message of the President of the United States [Coolidge] to a Joint Session of the Senate and the House of Representatives, December 6, 1923. Washington, D.C., 1923.

Committee on Public Information. *The German-Bolshevik Conspiracy.* Washington, D.C., 1918. Documents collected and reported on by Edgar Grant Sisson.

Congress. Senate, Committee on Foreign Relations. *Russian Propaganda.* Hearing before a Sub-Committee of the Committee on Foreign Relations . . . 66th Cong., 2d sess. Washington, D.C., 1920.

Department of State. *Papers Relating to the Foreign Relations of the United States, 1918[–1919]. Russia* . . . (4 vols., Washington, D.C., 1931–37). ———, *1919. The Paris Peace Conference* (13 vols., 1942–47). ———, *1920* (3 vols., 1936). ———, *1921* (2 vols., 1936). ———, *1923* (2 vols., 1938).

TREATIES

Adamov, E. A. (ed.). *Sbornik dogovorov Rossii a drugimi gosudarstvami, 1856–1917* (A collection of treaties between Russia and other states, 1856–1917). Moscow, 1952.

"Dogovor ob ekonomicheskom soiuze mezhdu Rossiiskoi Sotsialisticheskoi Sovetskoi Respublikoi i Dalne-Vostochnoi Respublikoi" (Treaty of economic alliance between the R.S.F.S.R. and the Far Eastern Republic). *Vestnik N.K.I.D.*, No. 6, 1922, pp. 174–78.

Dogovory o neitralitete, nenapadenii i o soglasitelnoi protsedure zakliuchennye mezhdu Soiuzom S.S.R. i inostrannymi gosudarstvami (Treaties of neutrality, nonagression, and procedure for reaching agreement between the U.S.S.R. and foreign states). Moscow, 1934.

The General [Kellogg-Briand] Pact for the Renunciation of War. Text of the Pact as Signed. Notes and Other Papers. Washington, D.C., 1928.

Kliuchnikov, Iu. V., and A. V. Sabanin (eds.). *Mezhdunarodnaia politika noveishego vremeni v dogovorakh, notakh i deklaratsiiakh* . . . (International policies in recent times as expressed in treaties, notes, and declarations . . .). Moscow, 1925–28. In three parts.

Shapiro, Leonard (comp. and ed.). *Soviet Treaty Series: A Collection of Bilateral Treaties, Agreements and Conventions, etc., Concluded between the Soviet Union and Foreign Powers,* Vol. I: *1917–1928.* Washington, D.C., 1950.

Trade Agreement between His Britannic Majesty's Government and the Government of the Russian Socialist Federal Soviet Republic. Cmd. 1207. Accounts and Papers, 1921, Vol. XLIII. London, 1921.

Treaty between the Principal Allied Powers and Roumania respecting Bessarabia signed at Paris, October 28, 1920. Cmd. 1747. London, 1922.

The Treaty of Peace between Finland and the Russian Soviet Republic. Helsingfors, 1921.

CONFERENCES

Baku Congress. *I-yi sezd narodov Vostoka, Baku, 1–8 sentiabria 1920 g. Stenograficheskie otchety* (The First Congress of the Peoples of the East, Baku, September 1–8, 1920. Stenographic reports). Moscow, 1920.

Conference at the Hague. 1. Non-Russian Commission. 2. Russian Commission, June 26–July 20, 1922. Minutes and Documents. The Hague, 1922.

Conférence de Moscou pour la limitation des armements, 1922. Moscow, 1922.

Genoa Conference

Les Documents de la Conférence de Gênes. Rome, 1922.

The Genoa Conference for the Economic and Financial Reconstruction of Europe. April 10 to May 19, 1922. Joint Report of the Canadian Delegates . . . Ottawa, 1922.

Materialy genuezskoi konferentsii. Podgotovka, otchety, raboty komissii, diplomaticheskaia perepiska i pr. (Materials on the Genoa Conference. Preparation, stenographic report of the sessions, work commissions, diplomatic correspondence, etc.). Moscow, 1922.

Inter-Allied Conference on Reparations and Inter-Allied Debts. Held in London and Paris, December 1922 and January 1923. Reports and Secretaries' Notes of Conversations. London, 1923.

Lausanne Conference on Near Eastern Affairs, 1922–1923. Record of Proceedings and Draft Terms of Peace. Cmd. 1814. Accounts and Papers, 1923, Vol. XXVI. London, 1923.

The Locarno Agreements and the League of Nations, Supplement to the monthly summary of the League of Nations, December 1925. Nancy, 1925.

Londonskaia konferentsiia 16 iiulia–16 avgusta 1924 (The London Conference [on Reparations and Inter-Allied Debts] of July 16–August 16, 1924). Moscow, 1925.

Report and Proceedings of the World Economic Conference Held at Geneva, May 4th to 23rd, 1927 . . . Geneva, 1927.

Report of the International Peace Congress Held at The Hague under the auspices of the International Federation of Trade Unions, December 10–15, 1922. Amsterdam, 1923.

INTERNATIONAL ORGANIZATIONS

Communist International

Kommunisticheskii International v dokumentakh: resheniia, tezisy i vozvaniia kongressov Kominterna i plenumov IKKI, 1919–1932 (The Communist International in documents: resolutions, theses, and appeals of the congresses of the Communist International and the plenums of its Executive Committee, 1919–1932). Moscow, 1933.

Rapports sur le mouvement communiste internationale presentés au deuxième congrès de l'Internationale Communiste, Moscou, 1920. Petrograd, 1921.

The Second Congress of the Communist International. Proceedings of Petrograd

Session of July 17th and of Moscow Sessions of July 19th–August 7th, 1920. Moscow, 1920.

Vtoroi Kongress Kominterna, iiul-avgust 1920 g. (Second Congress of the Communist International, July-August, 1920). Moscow, 1934.

Der zweite Kongress der Kommunistischen Internationale; Protokoll der Verhandlungen vom 19. Juli in Petrograd und vom 23. Juli bis 7. August 1920 in Moskau. Hamburg, 1921.

IV Vsemirnyi Kongress Kommunisticheskogo Internatsionala, 5 noiabria–3 dekabria 1922 g.; Izbrannye doklady, rechi i rezoliutsii, Moscow, 1923.

Piatyi Vsemirnyi Kongress Kommunisticheskogo Internatsionala 17 iiunia– 8 iiulia, 1924 g. Stenograficheskii otchet (Fifth World Congress of the Communist International, June 17–July 8, 1924. Stenographic report). Moscow, 1925. 2 vols. in one.

Communist International between the Fifth and the Sixth World Congresses, 1924–1928. London, Communist Party of Great Britain, 1928.

Kommunisticheskii Internatsional pered Shestym Vsemirnym Kongressom; obzor deiatelnosti IKKI i sektsii Kominterna mezhdu V i VI kongressami (The Communist International before the Sixth World Congress; a survey of the activities of the ECCI and the Comintern's sections between the Fifth Congress and the Sixth). Moscow, 1928.

ECCI

Deiatelnost Ispolnitelnogo Komiteta i Prezidiuma IK Kommunisticheskogo Internatsionala ot 13-go iiulia 1921 g. do 1-go fevralia 1922 g. (Activities of the ECCI from July 13, 1921, to February 1, 1922). Petrograd, 1922.

Otchet ispolkoma Kominterna, Aprel 1925 g.–Ianvar 1926 g. (Report of the ECCI, April 1925–January 1926). Moscow, 1926.

Preparations Committee. *Thesis on the Propaganda Activity of the Communist International and Its Sections . . .* Moscow, 1921.

Rasshirennyi plenum Ispolnitelnogo Komiteta Kommunisticheskogo Internatsionala 12–23 iiunia 1923 g. Otchet ([Third] Enlarged Plenum of the Executive Committee of the Communist International, June 12–23, 1923. Report). Moscow, 1923.

Rasshirennyi plenum Ispolkoma Kommunisticheskogo Internatsionala 21 marta–6 aprelia 1925 g. Stenograficheskii otchet ([Fifth] Enlarged Plenum of the ECCI, March 21–April 6, 1925. Stenographic report). Moscow, 1925.

Shestoi rasshirennyi plenum Ispolkoma Kominterna 17 fevralia–15 marta 1926 g. Stenograficheskii otchet. (Sixth Enlarged Plenum of the ECCI, February 17–March 15, 1926. Stenographic report). Moscow, 1927.

Sixth Session of the Enlarged Executive Committee of the Communist International, February–March, 1926. An offprint from *International Press Correspondence,* March 4–May 13, 1926.

Puti mirovoi revoliutsii; sedmoi rasshirennyi plenum Ispolnitelnogo Komiteta Kommunisticheskogo Internatsionala 22 noiabria–16 dekabria 1926 g. Stenograficheskii otchet (The paths of world revolution. Seventh Enlarged Plenum of the ECCI, November 22–December 16, 1926. Stenographic report). 2 vols. Moscow, 1927.

VIII Plenum Ispolnitelnogo Komiteta Kommunisticheskogo Internatsionala 18–30 maia 1927 goda. Tezisy, rezoliutsii i vozvaniia (Eighth Plenum of the ECCI, May 18–30, 1927. Theses, resolutions, and appeals). Moscow, 1927.

League of Nations

Assembly. *Records of the Second Assembly. Plenary Meetings. Text of the Debates.* Geneva, 1921.

Council. *Procès verbal . . . Minutes of the Ninth Session of the League of Nations held in Paris from 16th to 20th September, 1920.* Geneva, 1921.

Preparatory Commission for the Disarmament Conference. *Documents of the Preparatory Commission for the Disarmament Conference Entrusted with the Preparation of the Conference for the Reduction and Limitation of Armaments.* Series I–XI. Geneva, 1926–31.

―――. *S.S.S.R. v borbe za razoruzhenie. Sovetskaia delegatsiia na IV sessii podgotovitelnoi komissii po razoruzheniiu. Fakty i dokumenty* (The U.S.S.R. in the struggle for disarmament. The Soviet delegation at the fourth session of the Preparatory Commission on disarmament. Facts and documents). Moscow, 1928.

Secretariat. *Report on Economic Conditions in Russia with Special Reference to the Famine of 1921–1922 and the State of Agriculture,* Annex IV.

Commission Internationale de Secours à la Russie. *Procès verbaux . . . Séances tenues à Bruxelles les 6, 7 et 8 octobre 1921.* Typewritten manuscript in the Hoover Archives, Hoover Library, Stanford University. The Commission was set up by the Supreme Council of the Allied and Associated Powers.

Resolutions and Decisions. Third World Congress of the Red International of Labor Unions Held in Moscow, July 1924. Chicago, 1924.

NEWSPAPERS AND PERIODICALS

Newspapers

Berliner Tageblatt. Berlin. Daily.

Daily Herald. London. Daily.

L'Humanité. Paris. Daily.

Izvestiia (News). Petrograd, Moscow. Organ of the Central Executive Committee of Soviets. Daily. Subtitle varies.

Krasnaia Gazeta (Red Gazette). Petrograd. Daily.

Manchester Guardian. Weekly.

The Observer. London. Weekly.

Petrogradskaia Pravda (Petrograd Truth). Petrograd. Daily. Continued as *Leningradskaia Pravda* (Leningrad Truth).

Pravda (Truth). Moscow. Organ of the All-Russian Communist Party (B). Daily.

Die Rote Fahne. Berlin. Daily.

Le Temps. Paris. Daily.

The Times. London. Daily.

Periodicals

American Relief Administration Bulletin. March 17, 1919–April 1926. Paris and New York.

Biulleten Oppozitsii (Bolshevikov-Lenintsev) (Bulletin of the Bolshevik-Leninist Opposition). Paris, Berlin, New York. Trotskyite organ.

Bolshevik. Moscow. Organ of the Central Committee of the All-Russian Communist Party (B).

L'Europe Nouvelle. Paris. Weekly.

International Press Correspondence. Vienna, Berlin, London. Superseded by *World News and Views,* January 1, 1954. Appears also in French, German, and Spanish.

Istoricheskii Zhurnal (History Journal). Moscow. Organ of the Institute of History of the Soviet Academy of Sciences. Preceded by *Borba Klassov.* Absorbed *Istorik-Marksist* in 1941. Superseded by *Voprosy Istorii,* July 1945.

Istorik-Marksist (Marxist Historian). Moscow. Organ of the Institute of History of the Soviet Academy of Sciences. Absorbed in 1941 by *Istoricheskii Zhurnal.*

Journal of Central European Affairs. Boulder, Colo.

Kommunisticheskaia Revoliutsiia (Communist Revolution). Moscow. Organ of the Central Committee of the All-Russian Communist Party (B).

Kommunisticheskii Internatsional (Communist International), 1919–1943. Moscow. Organ of the ECCI. Also appeared in English, French, and German.

Krasnaia Nov (Red Virgin Soil). Moscow. Organ of the Union of Soviet Writers.

Krasnyi Arkhiv (Red Archives). Moscow. Organ of the Chief Office of Soviet Archives.

Krasnyi Internatsional Profsoiuznov (Red Trade Union International). Moscow.

Krestianskii Internatsional (Peasant International). Moscow. Organ of the International Peasant Council.

Mezhdunarodnaia Zhizn (International Life). Moscow. Organ of the People's Commissariat of Foreign Affairs.

Mirovoe Khoziaistvo i Mirovaia Politika (World Economy and World Politics). Moscow. Organ of the Institute of World Economy and Politics of the Soviet Academy of Sciences. Changed to *Voprosy Ekonomiki* in 1948.

Der Monat; Eine International Zeitschrift für Politik und Geistiges Leben. Berlin. Office of Military Government, Information Service Division, 1948.

Novyi Vostok (The New East). Moscow. Organ of the All-Russian Association for Eastern Studies.

Pod Znamenem Marksizma (Under the Marxist Banner). Moscow. Philosophical and socioeconomic journal.

Problemy Marksizma (Problems of Marxism). Leningrad. Organ of the Leningrad Section of the Communist Academy.

Proletarskaia Revoliutsiia (Proletarian Revolution). Moscow. Organ of Marx-Engels-Lenin Institute. Publication suspended in 1932 and 1937.

Revue Générale de Droit International Public. Paris.

Russian Information and Review. London. Organ of the Russian trade delegation in London. Superseded by *Soviet Union Review* in 1925.

Sotsialisticheskii Vestnik (Socialist Messenger). Berlin, Paris, New York. Organ of the Russian Social-Democratic Labor Party (Mensheviks), 1921.

Sovetskoe Gosudarstvo, see Sovetskoe Gosudarstvo i Pravo.

Sovetskoe Gosudarstvo i Pravo (Soviet State and Law). Moscow. Organ of the Institute of Law of the Soviet Academy of Sciences. Title varies: 1930, *Sovetskoe Gosudarstvo i Revoliutsiia* (Soviet State and Revolution); 1931–38, *Sovetskoe Gosudarstvo* (Soviet State). Publication suspended May 1941–December 1945.

Soviet Russia. New York. Chicago. Official organ of the Friends of Soviet Russia. After being renamed *Soviet Russia Pictorial,* it was combined in 1924 with *Labor Herald* and *Liberator* to form *Workers' Monthly.*

Vestnik Agitatsii i Propagandy (Agitation and Propaganda Messenger). Moscow. Organ of the Central Committee of the All-Russian Communist Party (B).

Vestnik Narodnogo Komissariata po Inostrannym Delam (Messenger of the People's Commissariat of Foreign Affairs). Moscow. Referred to as *Vestnik N.K.I.D.*

Vestnik 2-go Kongressa Kommunisticheskogo Internatsionala (Messenger of the Second Congress of the Communist International). Petrograd and Moscow, 1920.

Vestnik Zhizni (Messenger of Life). Moscow, 1918–19. Organ of the Central Executive Committee of the R.S.F.S.R.

Vlast Sovetov (Soviet Power). Moscow. Organ of the All-Russian Central Executive Committee of Soviets.

Voprosy Istorii (Problems of History). Moscow. (Organ of the Institute of History of the Soviet Academy of Sciences). Superseded *Istoricheskii Vestnik.*

INDEX

Abramovitch, Rafail Abramovitch, 120
American Relief Administration, 28–30, 66, 74–75, 165, 193, 276
Amsterdam International, *see* International Federation of Trade Unions
Anglo-Russian Trade Union Committee, 270; conferences preceding formation of, 269–70, 309
Anglo-Soviet trade agreement (1921), 20–23, 64–66, 93, 157, 185, 186, 187, 223–28 *passim*, 265, 344, 375–76
Arbitration, Soviet views on, 277, 280, 282, 322–23, 351
Arcos (Russian Trading Corporation in London), 267, 343–45, 375–79, 408

Babushkin, Soviet embassy employee, 226
Baku Congress of the Peoples of the East (1920), 22, 41 n.
Baldwin, Stanley, 179, 190, 344, 378–79
Balfour, Arthur James Balfour, 1st earl of, 175
Baltic States, *see* Estonia; Finland; Latvia; Lithuania
Barthou, Jean Louis, 103, 169, 202
Bauer, Colonel, 204
Beneš, Eduard, 76 n., 231, 243, 350, 397
Berens, Evgenii Andreevich, 119
Berzin, Jan Antonovich, 11
Bessarabia, 33 n., 192, 239, 292, 294, 374
Bittker, Soviet official, 207
Bogdanov, Petr Alekseevich, 207
Bolsheviks, *see* Russian Communist Party
Bozengardt, Soviet trade delegation employee, 277
Brandler, Heinrich, 178, 179, 183, 184, 212, 221–22
Brest-Litovsk, Treaty of (1918), 14, 38, 45, 46, 50, 63, 67, 72, 83, 110, 123, 203, 275, 289
Briand, Aristide, 100, 103, 125, 209 n., 271, 345, 352
British Communist Party, 265, 269, 302, 303–4, 368, 369
British Trades Union Congress, 19, 52, 81 n., 265, 269, 305, 341, 342, 368
Brown, Walter Lyman, 29, 30
Budenny, Semen Mikhailovich, 39, 40, 291
Bukharin, Nikolai Ivanovich, 178, 188, 270, 356: on Anglo-Soviet crisis of 1923, 187; on the coming revolutionary upsurge (1927), 405–6; on communist expansion (1922), 122, 159; on communist policy in England (1924), 266; on failure of German revolution, 183–84; on growth of socialism and crisis of capitalism (1926), 285, 336–37; on the international revolution (1927), 359–64; on military alliances with bourgeois states, 174–75, 209–10; on

the Ruhr occupation, 177, 211; supports Stalin against Trotsky (1926), 258
Bulakh-Balakhovich, Major, 33
Bullitt, William Christian, 45
Butkiewicz (Budkiewicz), Monsignor Konstanty, 185, 187, 188, 227 n.

Campbell, John Rich, 264
Cannes Resolution (1922), 98, 99, 102, 103, 107, 124–25, 127, 130, 132; *see also* Genoa Conference
Chamberlain, Sir Austen, 271, 306, 310, 311, 312, 321, 343, 370, 371, 372, 376, 378, 379
Chang Tso-lin, 363, 379
Chester, Admiral C. M., 147 n.
Chiang Kai-shek, 257
Chicherin, Georgii Vasilievich, 17, 21, 53, 57, 168, 236, 343: accepts French *de jure* recognition, 237; on Anglo-Soviet treaties of 1924, 261, 296; on British demand that U.S.S.R. cease anti-British propaganda (1925), 270, 310; calls for an international conference (1921), 79–80; on co-operation with U.S., 165; on the Estonian Treaty (1920), 7–8; at Genoa Conference, 101, 102–3, 131–33, 277; on imperialist threat to U.S.S.R. (1924), 194–95, 242; on the international situation (1923), 165–66, 197–99; interviews with Seeckt, 206; on the Kellogg-Briand Pact (1928), 352; at Lausanne Conference, 114–16; on the League of Nations (1926), 280; negotiations with Germany and Poland (1925), 277; note to President Coolidge (1923), 240; pre-Genoa Conference report, 99, 126–28; protests Polish conduct at Genoa Conference, 170; replies to Allied proposals re Lausanne Conference, 143–44; replies to the Colby note, 70–73; on the Ruhr occupation, 198–99; seeks famine relief, 28; on Soviet-British relations (1925), 309–11; sums up Lausanne Conference, 117, 145–48; on the Treaty of Rapallo, 169, 202; on U.S. refusal to recognize U.S.S.R. (1924), 241–42
Churchill, Winston, 37 n., 39
Cieplak, Archbishop Janusz, 227
Clynes, John Robert, 369
Colby, Bainbridge, 27, 66–69, 70–73 *passim*; text of Colby note, 66–69
Communist International (Comintern): AF-FILIATED INTERNATIONALS: Communist Youth International, 267, 268; Peasants' International (Krestintern), 267, 268–69; Red Sport International (Sportintern), 267, 268; Red Trade Union International (Profintern), 81, 149, 265, 267, 268, 269 ;— and Anglo-Soviet crisis of 1923, 186, 188,

443

226; CONGRESSES: Second (1920), 16, 22, 41–44, 88, 150–51, 301; Third (1921), 35, 77, 80–90, 156, 166, 201, 245, 267, 328; Fourth (1922), 31, 32, 122, 156–60, 166–67, 174, 186, 201–2, 209–10, 267; Fifth (1924), 32, 184, 221, 222, 262, 264, 265–66, 267, 269, 298–99, 301–2, 308;—Co-operatives' Section, 267; criticized in Colby note (1920), 69; distinguished from Soviet government by Soviet spokesmen, 226, 241, 307; FIFTH CONGRESS: manifesto to world proletariat, 298–99; outlines tasks of British Communists, 302; theses on tactics, 308;—Fourth Congress, "Theses on the Tactics of the Communist International," 166–67, 201–2; and German revolution of 1923, 178–84, 212–22; International Women's Secretariat, 267; party line in 1926, 283–85, 330–37; position in 1921 summarized, 35; proclamations on Poland (1920), 16–17; Third Congress, theses on the world situation and communist tasks, 84–90; the united front, 167, 201–2, 219–20, 222, 266–70, 285, 333; and Zinoviev letter, 265–66, 301–7; see also Executive Committee of the Communist International; Russian Communist Party

Communist Party of the Soviet Union, see Russian Communist Party

Communist Youth International, 267, 268

Congress on War Against War (The Hague, 1922), 119–21, 148–50

Conradi, M., 223 n.

Coolidge, Calvin, 194, 239–40

Co-operatives' Section (of the Communist International), 267

Cuno, Wilhelm, 178, 206

Curzon, George Nathaniel (Lord Curzon), 21, 34, 56, 114, 115, 116, 152, 176, 230, 243, 303, 306, 310, 312; Curzon ultimatum (1923), 184–88, 222–28, 230, 232, 233, 243, 314

Cushendun, Ronald John McNeill, 1st Baron, 350

Czechoslovakia: Little Entente, 33, 76–77, 110, 133, 134, 200; relations with R.S.F.S.R. (1920–22), 25; Zinoviev appraises, as threat to German revolution (1923), 216

D'Abernon, Edgar Vincent, 1st Viscount, 168

Dąbski, Jan, 18, 59–60

Daniszewski, Karol, 54–57

Dariac, French Deputy, 198

Davison, British engineer, 226, 227

Dawes, Charles Gates, 221, 247, 262, 296–98; Dawes Plan, 180, 246, 247, 262–64, 296–300, 302, 330, 331

Debts and claims: Anglo-Soviet negotiations and treaty (1924), 259–62, 292–96, 373; concession on tsarist debts offered by R.S.F.S.R. (1921), 34, 79, 80; Franco-Soviet conference on, 312–13, 345–46, 365–66, 382 n.; Genoa Conference, 98–109, 125, 127, 129–31, 132, 157–58; Hague Conference, 109–11, 134; Litvinov on (1927), 381–82; Rykov on (1927), 373–74

Denikin, Anton Ivanovich, 3, 15, 37, 39, 40, 48, 54, 61, 129

Deutsch, Felix, 205

Disarmament: Congress on War Against War, 119–21, 148–50; Kellogg-Briand Pact, 352; League of Nations draft treaty (1923) and Geneva Protocol (1924), 270–71; Preparatory Commission for the Disarmament Conference, 348–52, 388–98; proposed by Soviet delegation at World Economic Conference, 348, 385–86; Rome Conference, 117–19; and Soviet militia program, 352–55, 399–402; Soviet proposals for (1922), 102–3, 111–13, 132–33, 135–37, 138–41, 322; Stalin on (1927), 351, 397–98

Dmowski, Roman, 15

Dovgalevsky, Valerian Savelievich, 346

Draft International Convention on Disarmament, 393–94

Dukes, Paul, 226

Dzierzynski, Felix, 16

Eastman, Max, 255

Ebert, Friedrich, 174, 206, 221

ECCI, see Executive Committee of the Communist International

Enckell, Carl J. A., 136

England: Anglo-Soviet crisis of 1923, 184–89, 222–28; Arcos raid (1927), 343–45, 375–79, 408; Bukharin on anti-Soviet activity of (1927), 361, 362; Chicherin's appraisal of (1922), 126–27; de jure recognition of U.S.S.R., 190, 233, 259, 265; general settlement treaties with U.S.S.R. (1924), 259–62, 264, 265, 274, 292–96, 305, 373; labor delegation visits R.S.F.S.R. (1920), 19, 53–54; Lausanne Conference, 113–17, 141–48; Lenin's appraisal of (1920), 46–47, 152; Locarno Conference, 270–73, 316–20; miners' strike and general strike (1926), 270, 337, 341–42, 343, 360, 361, 364, 368–69, 370, 372, 373; political situation analyzed by Kamenev (1924), 229–30; relations with U.S.S.R. (1926–27), 341–45, 370–81, 382; relations with U.S.S.R. analyzed by Chicherin (1925), 309–11; trade agreement with R.S.F.S.R. (1921), 20–23, 64–66, 93, 157, 185, 186, 187, 223–28 passim, 265, 344, 375–76; Zinoviev letter, 264–66, 301–7

Estonia: communist coup of 1924, 281; Moscow Conference, 112–13, 135–41; negotiations with Poland, Finland, Latvia, and U.S.S.R. (1925–26), 280–82, 346; peace treaty with R.S.F.S.R. (1920), 7–9, 48, 49–51, 204; Riga Protocol, 111–12, 170

Executive Committee of the Communist International (ECCI): on communist tactics (1926), 284–85; expounds the united front, 266, 285; and the failure of the German revolution, 218, 220; PLENUMS: Second (1922), 266; Third (1923), 171–72, 188–89; Fifth (1925), 184, 221–22, 330; Sixth

(1926), 284–85, 330–33, 369 n.; Seventh (1926), 258, 268, 285, 336–37; — recommends preparedness to Red Army (1924), 265; resolution on the immediate problems of international communism (1926), 330–33; Stalin-Trotsky showdown, 258–59; and Zinoviev letter, 303–6 *passim*; *see also* Communist International
Experts' plan, *see* Dawes Plan

Facta, Luigi, 102
Famine of 1921–23, 28–33, 73–76
Far Eastern Republic, 45, 80, 83 n., 127, 153, 164
Finland: Moscow Conference, 112–13, 135–41; negotiations with Poland, Baltic states, and U.S.S.R. (1925–26), 280–82, 346; peace treaty with R.S.F.S.R. (1920), 11–14; troubles with R.S.F.S.R. (1920–22), 12–14
First International, 42, 43
Five-Year Plan, First, 355–56, 402–3
Foch, Ferdinand, 223, 317
Fotieva, Lidiia Aleksandrovna, 75
France: accused of inciting Poland and Rumania, 77–78; adamant at Genoa and Hague conferences, 103, 108, 110; conference on debts with U.S.S.R. (1926–27), 312–13, 345–46, 365–66, 382 n.; *de jure* recognition of U.S.S.R., 192, 236–39; designs on Germany assessed by Stalin (1924), 299–300; Litvinov on anti-Soviet campaign in (1927), 381–82; Locarno Conference, 270–73, 316–20; policies criticized by Chicherin, 127, 147; the Rakovsky affair (1927), 346, 381, 408; and the Ruhr, 176–78, 179, 198–99, 210–12, 245, 262; situation appraised by Zinoviev (1923), 216; support of anti-Bolsheviks objected to by R.S.F.S.R., 20, 26, 33, 77–78
Franklin-Bouillon, Henri, 147
Fries, General, 398
Frunze, Mikhail Vasilievich, 113 n.: on collectivization and army requirements, 352–53, 355; on expanding the militia, 353, 354–55, 400–401; on the international situation and Soviet military tasks (1925), 311–14, 399–401; on Soviet military organization (1922), 399

Galperin, Dr., Soviet official, 207
Geneva Protocol (1924), 271, 316, 348, 396
Genoa Conference (1922), 98–109, 110, 111, 123–33, 153, 157, 158, 168, 169, 170: analysis and aftermath, 108–9; Chicherin's speech at, 102–3, 131–33, 277; preliminaries, 98–101, 123–31; Rakovsky on, 100–101, 128–31; Report on the Reconstruction of Russia, 104–5, 107; Soviet appraisals of international situation before, 123–28; Soviet replies to Western proposals, 105–6, 107, 108; *see also* Treaty of Rapallo
German Communist Party, 25, 171, 172, 179, 182–84, 204, 212–22 *passim*, 245
German Social Democratic Party, 25, 171,

172, 177, 179, 182, 184, 208–22 *passim*, 245, 247
Germany: Berlin raid and commercial treaty with U.S.S.R. (1925), 277–78; Bukharin on situation in (1927), 360–61, 362; and the Dawes Plan, 262–64, 296–300; and the League of Nations, 271–75, 279, 280, 283, 316–17, 319–20, 324–25, 365; neutrality and nonaggression treaty with U.S.S.R. (1926), 279–80, 324–26, 327, 408; occupation of the Ruhr, 176–78, 179, 198–99, 210–12, 245, 262; resumption of relations with R.S.F.S.R. (1920), 25, 204; revolution of 1923, 178–84, 212–22, 245; Rykov on Soviet relations with (1927), 365; Soviet rapprochement with (1920–23), 167–78, 202–10; Spartakusbund and Zimmerwald movement, 5, 24, 38, 40, 221; Treaty of Rapallo, 106–7, 168–70, 202–3, 206
Gessler, Otto, 174
Gompers, Samuel, 194, 248
Gorbunov, Nikolai Petrovich, 75
Gorky, Maxim, 28–29, 73–74
Great Britain, *see* England
Gregory, John Duncan, 306, 307
Guarantee pact, *see* Locarno Conference
Guest, Leslie Haden, 53

Haber, Fritz, 207
Hague Conference (1922), 109–11, 133–35, 153, 158
Harden, Maximilian, 70
Harding, Stan, 226, 227
Harding, Warren Gamaliel, 27, 125, 194
Harrison, Marguerite E., 226
Harvey, George Brinton McCellan, 124, 127
Haskell, Colonel William N., 75
Hasse, General von, 205, 206
Heilman, Ernst, 204
Henderson, Arthur, 369
Herriot, Edouard, 192, 236, 237, 238, 239, 242, 264, 299, 300
Hintze, Paul von, 205
Hodgson, British official, 185, 223, 227
Hoover, Herbert, 28–29, 30, 66, 74–75
Horne, Sir Robert, 65, 375
Hughes, Charles Evans, 28, 193–94, 240–42, 264, 300, 305, 306

Inter-Allied Conference on Reparations and Inter-Allied Debts (London Conference), 242, 262, 264, 299–300
International Commission for Russian Relief, 32–33
International Committee for Russian Relief, 30
International Federation of Trade Unions (I.F.T.U.), 44, 81, 85, 119, 149, 202, 269, 270, 363, 380
International law, Soviet theory of, 275–77; *see also Historical Introduction*
International Organization to Aid the Revolutionary Fighters (M.O.P.R.), 31–32
International Peace Congress, *see* Congress on War Against War

International Women's Secretariat (of the Communist International), 267

International Workers' Aid, 31

Ioffe, Adolf Abramovich: expelled from Germany (1918), 24; on his subversive work in Berlin in 1918–19, 72 n.; in negotiations with Poland (1920–21), 17, 18–19, 60–61; on peace with the Baltic states, 48–51; on peace treaty with Poland (1921), 63–64

Ipatieff, Vladimir Nikolaevich, 174, 207–8

Ismet Pasha, 114, 115

Italy: de jure recognition of U.S.S.R., 190, 230, 234; Soviet trade agreements with (1920–21), 23–24, 190; workers' uprising in 1920, 63; see also Mussolini

Joffe, Adolf, see Ioffe

Jouhaux, Léon, 385, 387

Joynson-Hicks, Sir William, 379

Kalinin, Mikhail Ivanovich, 17, 57, 233, 237

Kamenev (Rosenfeld), Lev Borisovich, 75, 97, 152, 255, 356: analysis of the international situation (1924), 228–33, 291–92; on de jure recognition, 189, 230–32, 291–92; on Soviet foreign policy (1921), 36, 91–94

Karakhan, Lev Mikhailovich, 141, 186, 193

Karakhanian, Soviet embassy official, 226

Karelian Labor Commune, 12

Kautsky, Karl Johann, 322, 328

Kellogg, Frank Billings, 352

Kellogg-Briand Pact (1928), 352

Kemal Atatürk (formerly Mustafa Kemal Pasha), 40, 107 n., 114 n., 146

Kerensky, Aleksandr Fedorovich, 37

Khinchuk, Lev Mikhailovich, 267, 376

Khudiakov, Arcos employee, 376

Kirov, Sergei Mikhailovich, 14

Kolchak, Aleksandr Vasilievich, 3, 15, 38, 40, 45, 48, 54, 61, 129

Kolomiitsev, I. I., 226

Kopp, Viktor Leontievich, 25, 168, 182, 204, 231

Korovin, E. A., 276, 277

Kowerda, Boris, 346

Krasin, Leonid Borisovich, 53, 143, 373: on Anglo-Soviet trade agreement (1921), 65–66; negotiations with German industrialists, 168, 205; in trade negotiations with England (1920–21), 20, 21–22, 375

Krasnov, Petr Nikolaevich, 15

Krestinsky, Nikolai Nikolaevich, 168, 209, 277, 389

Krestintern, see Peasants' International

Krivitsky, Walter, 179

Kronstadt revolt, 3, 65, 93

Kropp, Archbishop, 204

Krzhizhanovsky, Gleb Maksimilianovich, 355

Kun, Bela, 5

Kuusinen, Otto Vilhelm, 304

La Follette, Robert Marion, 269

Latvia: Moscow Conference, 112–13, 135–41; negotiations with Poland, Finland, Estonia, and U.S.S.R. (1925–27), 280–82, 366; neutrality and commercial treaties with U.S.S.R. (1927), 282, 346–47, 366, 408; peace treaty with R.S.F.S.R. (1920), 10–11, 48–49; Riga Protocol, 111–12, 170

Lausanne Conference (1922–23), 113–17, 141–48, 153, 199, 349

Law, Bonar, 54

League of Nations: appealed to in Karelian dispute, 13; attitude toward disarmament criticized by Soviet leaders (1927), 388–89, 393–98; commission of inquiry rejected by R.S.F.S.R., 19, 52–53; criticized by Soviet spokesmen (1925), 273–75, 320–22; decides Mosul dispute, 278, 318, 323; draft treaty on mutual assistance (1923) and Geneva Protocol (1924), 270–71, 316, 348, 396; effects armistice in Vilna dispute (1920), 9; Germany enters, 271–75, 279, 280, 283, 316–17, 319–20, 324–25, 365; Lenin on ineffectiveness of, 145, 151–52; Locarno Conference, 270–75, 316–20; Preparatory Commission for the Disarmament Conference, 347, 348–52, 388–98; recognizes Finnish claim to Aaland Islands, 13; refuses to take lead in relieving Russian famine, 31; Soviet attitude toward (1920–23), 117–19, 121–22, 145, 155–56, 195; Soviet participation in health conference of (1922), 195; World Economic Conference (1927), 347–48, 377, 382–88

Lenin (Ulianov), Vladimir Ilich: absent from Genoa Conference, 101; on the Black Sea Straits, 144–45; on emancipation of Asia, 328 n.; on England (1920), 46–47, 152; estimate of the international situation (1921), 82–84, 97, 123–24; on exploiting capitalist differences, 90, 169, 203; on foreign trade and concessions, 6, 44–48, 99, 100; on forthcoming Genoa Conference, 99, 100; illness and death, 165, 178, 254–55; on ineffectiveness of League of Nations, 145, 151–52; instructions to Soviet delegates to Congress on War Against War, 119, 148–49; on interdependence of R.S.F.S.R. and Germany, 24, 47; letter to British workers (1920), 53–54; on the New Economic Policy, 4; on objectives of Russian foreign policy (1921), 90, 123–24; on peace with Estonia, 48; proposes warning to Poland, Finland, and Rumania (1921), 78–79; seeks help against famine, 28, 31, 75–76; on socialism in one country, cited by Zinoviev, 328–29, by Stalin, 334–35; testament recommends replacing Stalin, 255; theory of revolution cited by Stalin, 256–57, 286–91 passim, 334–35; on the war with Poland, 61–62

Liebknecht, Karl, 5, 38, 40, 405

Lithuania: dispute over Vilna, 9–10, 111, 280, 282, 346; fascist coup of 1926, 362; Moscow Conference, 112–13, 135–41; neutrality and nonaggression treaty with U.S.S.R. (1926), 282–83, 326, 346, 362, 366, 408; peace treaty with R.S.F.S.R. (1920), 9–10, 55

Little Entente (Czechoslovakia, Rumania, Yugoslavia, Poland), 33, 76–77, 110, 133, 134, 200

Litvinov, Maksim Maksimovich (Maxim Litvinov) : on arbitration, 277 ; on Arcos raid, 345, 375–79 ; in Copenhagen (1920), 19–20, 21, 53 ; in famine relief negotiations, 29, 30 ; at Hague Conference, 109, 110 ; on the League of Nations (1925), 274–75 ; on Locarno Conference, 279, 325 ; at Moscow Conference, 112, 135–37 ; and the Preparatory Commission for the Disarmament Conference, 349–52, 390–97, 398 ; proposes trade relations with U.S. (1921), 27 ; replies to British protest (1927), 343, 370 n. ; replies to Curzon ultimatum, 223–28 ; on severance of Soviet-British relations (1927), 377–79 ; on Soviet-French relations (1927), 381–82 ; on Soviet-German treaty of 1926, 279, 280, 324–26

Lloyd George, David, 7, 21, 97, 98, 100, 102, 109, 125, 126, 129, 157, 158, 176, 229, 230, 261, 311

Locarno Conference (1925), 270–75, 279, 283, 315, 316–20, 325, 365, 398

London Conference, see Inter-Allied Conference on Reparations . . .

London Memorandum of Experts (1922), 100, 104–5, 107

Loriot, Fernand, 39, 40

Loucheur, Louis, 385

Lozovsky, A. (Solomon Abramovich Dridzo), 119, 120 : on importance of trade unions, 269 ; on the Ruhr occupation, 176

Ludendorff, Erich Friedrich Wilhelm, 203, 204

Luxemburg, Rosa, 5

McCully, Newton A., 67

MacDonald, Ramsay, 229, 230, 234, 238, 241, 242, 247, 260, 264, 266, 292, 299–305 passim, 310, 311, 321, 366, 369, 371, 373, 396

McLean, Neil, 40

McManus, Arthur, 304

Maisky, Mrs., 276

Malinovsky, A. A., 119

Maltzan, Baron Adolf von, 168

Manuilsky, Dmitrii Zakharievich, 63, 258–59

Marchlewski, Julian, 62

Martens, Ludwig C. A. K., 26–27

Mehring, Franz, 5 n., 354

Militia, Soviet plans for, 352–55, 399–402

Miller, Evgenii Karlovich, 15, 21

Miller, Arcos employee, 376

Molotov (Skriabin), Viacheslav Mikhailovich, 19

Monsie, Pierre de, 382 n.

Moscow, Treaty of (R.S.F.S.R. and Lithuania, 1920), 9–10, 55

Moscow, Treaty of (U.S.S.R. and Lithuania, 1926), 282–83, 326, 346, 362, 366, 408

Moscow, Treaty of (U.S.S.R. and Persia, 1927), 279, 324 n., 408

Moscow Conference on the Limitation of Armaments (1922), 112–13, 135–41, 201, 366

Münzenberg, Willi, 31

Mur, Austrian socialist, 203

Mussolini, Benito, 190, 230, 234, 244, 292, 296, 300

Nansen, Fridtjof, 30, 31

New Economic Policy, 3–4, 6, 23, 125, 157, 253, 316, 355

Nitti, Francesco Saverio, 24

Noske, Gustav, 208, 221

Noulens, Joseph, 32, 33, 77

Obolenski-Ossinski, Valerian Valerianovich, 382–88

O'Grady, James, 20

Paghman, Treaty of (1926), 278–79, 324 n., 326, 367, 408

Paris, Treaty of (1925), 278, 319, 323–24, 326, 327, 362, 366, 408

Pašić, Nikola, 76 n.

Paul-Boncour, Joseph, 350

Pavlovich (Veltman), Mikhail Lazarevich, 22 n.

Peasants' International (Krestintern), 267, 268–69

People's Commissariat of Foreign Affairs, see Chicherin

Peters, William, 375

Petliura, Semen Vasilievich, 15, 33

Pilsudski, Józef, 15, 54, 204, 346, 362, 398

Podvoisky, Nikolai Ilich, 268

Poincaré, Raymond, 100, 108, 109, 129, 146, 175, 176, 177, 192, 198, 211, 234, 242, 243, 271, 299

Poland : communist activity in, 16, 42–43, 62–63, 77, 346 ; likelihood of intervention in Germany, Zinoviev on (1923), 216 ; Moscow Conference, 112–13, 135–41, 201 ; negotiations with Baltic states for defense agreement (1925), 280–81 ; negotiations with U.S.S.R. (1927), 346, 366 ; peace treaty with R.S.F.S.R. (1921), 17–19, 54–64, 282 ; the Pilsudski coup, 346 ; Provisional Revolutionary Committee of (1920), 16 ; reaction to Treaty of Rapallo, 170 ; Riga Protocol, 111–12, 170 ; Soviet concern over (1923), 177–78, 181–82, 217–18, 223 ; Soviet suspicions of (1921), 33–34, 76–79 ; and Vilna, 9–10, 282, 346 ; war with R.S.F.S.R., 14–18, 22, 54–64, 151–52

Ponsonby, Arthur, 261

Preparatory Commission for the Disarmament Conference, 347, 348–52, 388–98

Profintern, see Red Trade Union International

Purcell, Arthur A., 269

Radek, Karl, 22 n., 119, 120, 356 : on Anglo-Soviet crisis of 1923, 188–89 ; on Cannes Resolution, 99, 124–26 ; on collaboration with fascists, 172 ; contacts with German nationalists in 1919–20, 168, 203–5 ; and German revolution of 1923, 171–72, 179, 183, 184, 213, 221–22 ; heads revolutionary activities in Germany (1919–20), 25, 171–73, 203–5 ; on the international situation (1922), 122, 156–59 ; interviews with Seeckt, 205, 206 ; on Italy's de jure recognition of U.S.S.R., 190, 234 ; on Locarno Conference, 316–17 ; on the Preparatory Commission for the Disarmament Conference, 349; on problems confronting Comintern's Third Congress, 80–82; on revolutionary possibilities in Germany (1923), 171–72, 179, 213

Radziwill, Prince Janusz, 137–38

Rakovsky, Khristian Georgievich, 168, 356, 373: and Franco-Soviet debt conference (1926–27), 312 n., 382 n.; on Genoa Conference and economic matters, 100–101, 128–31; on Locarno Conference, 274, 317–20; in negotiations with England (1924–25), 260, 274, 292–96; the Rakovsky affair (1927), 346, 381, 408; on Zinoviev letter, 306–7

Rapallo, Treaty of (1922), 106–7, 163, 168–70, 202–3, 206, 279, 324–25, 326, 365

Raskolnikov, Fedor Fedorovich, 186, 225

Rathenau, Walter, 168, 203, 205

Red Sport International (Sportintern), 267, 268

Red Trade Union International (Profintern), 81, 149, 265, 267, 268, 269

Reibnitz, Baron, 203–4

Renaudel, Pierre, 299

Reparations, see Dawes Plan; Debts and claims

Report on the Reconstruction of Russia (1922), 104–5, 107

Riga, Treaty of (1921), 17–19, 54–64, 282

Riga Protocol (1922), 111–12, 170

Rome Conference on the Limitation of Naval Armament (1923), 117–19, 155–56

Rosengolts, Arkadii Pavlovich, 207, 342, 373

Rotshtein, Fedor Aronovich, 119, 149–50, 193 n., 235

Rubinshtein, Nikolai Leonidovich, 111

Ruhr, occupation of, 176–78, 179, 198–99, 210–12, 245, 262

Rumania, see Bessarabia; Little Entente

Russia, see Russian Socialist Federated Soviet Republic (to 1924) or Soviet Union (1924 on)

Russian Communist Party: agrees on necessity of united front (1922), 266; and Baku Congress, 22 n.; CONFERENCES: Fourteenth (1925), 327–30; Fifteenth (1926), 283, 333–35; — CONGRESSES: Eighth (1919), 254, 354; Tenth (1921), 3, 91–94, 164; Eleventh (1922), 4, 100, 266; Twelfth (1923), 154 n.; Thirteenth (1924), 183, 222, 243, 255; Fourteenth (1925), 257, 314–16; Fifteenth (1927), 351, 355, 356–57, 393–98, 402–3, 405–6, 407–9; — directives on domestic and foreign policy (1926), 314–16; numerical strength of, 1917 and 1920, 40; position in 1921 summarized, 35–36; and socialism in one country, 283–84, 327–30, 333–35; struggle for power within, 254–59, 341, 356, 406; see also Communist International

Russian Socialist Federated Soviet Republic: Anglo-Soviet crisis of 1923, 184–89, 222–28; attitude toward the League of Nations, 117–19, 121–22, 145, 155–56, 195; and Baltic states (1920), 7–14, 48–51; beginning of "peaceful coexistence" (1922–23), 97–160; Bessarabian dispute with Ru-

mania, 33 n., 192, 239, 292, 294, 374; CONGRESSES OF SOVIETS: Eighth (1920), 24, 44–48; Ninth (1921), 34, 78–79, 97, 123–24; Tenth (1922), 152 n., 164, 201;—diplomatic triumphs and revolutionary failures (1922–24), 163–249; the famine of 1921–23, 28–33, 73–76; first diplomatic contacts with Allied powers and Germany, 19–28, 64–73; general situation in 1920–21, 3–6, 37–48; IN INTERNATIONAL CONFERENCES: Congress on War Against War, 119–21, 148–50; Genoa, 98–109, 124–33; The Hague, 109–11, 133–35; Lausanne, 113–17, 141–48; Moscow, 112–13, 135–41; Rome, 117–19, 155–56;—objectives of foreign policy (1921), 90–94; objects to French support of anti-Bolshevik forces, 20, 26, 33, 77–78; offers concession on tsarist debts (1921), 34, 79, 80; PEACE TREATIES: with Estonia (1920), 7–9, 48, 49–51, 204; with Finland (1920), 11–14; with Georgia (1920), 14; with Latvia (1920), 10–11, 48–49; with Lithuania (1920), 9–10, 55; with Poland (1921), 17–19, 54–64, 282;—position on Black Sea Straits (1922–23), 113–17, 119, 141–48, 199; proposals for disarmament (1922), 102–3, 111–13, 132–33, 135–37, 138–41, 322; rapprochement with Germany (1920–23), 167–78, 202–10; reactions to occupation of the Ruhr, 176–78, 179, 198–99, 210–12; relations with United States, 26–28, 66–73, 193–95, 239–42; reopening window to West (1920–21), 3–94; resumption of relations with Germany (1920), 25, 204; suspicion of Little Entente (1921), 33–34, 76–79; TRADE AGREEMENTS: with England (1921), 20–23, 64–66, 93, 157, 185, 186, 187, 223–28 passim, 265, 344, 375–76; with Italy, 23–24, 190; with Scandinavian and Central European countries, 25–26;—treaties of friendship with Near Eastern countries, 26; Treaty of Rapallo, 106–7, 163, 168–70, 202–3, 206, 279, 324–25, 326, 365; troubles with Finland (1920–22), 12–14; war with Poland (1918–20), 14–18, 22, 54–64, 151–52; see also Soviet Union

Russian Trading Corporation, see Arcos

Rykov, Aleksei Ivanovich, 236, 237, 270, 356, 379, 406: on British protest of 1927, 343, 371–74; on international position of the U.S.S.R. (1926), 283; on the League of Nations, 273–74, 320–22, 349, 388–89; on proposed disarmament conference (1927), 349, 389; on Soviet foreign policy (1927), 283, 364–68

Saunus, Lithuanian diplomat, 137

Savinkov, Boris Viktorovich, 33, 34, 79

Schein, S., 207

Schlageter, German nationalist, 171, 184

Schleicher, Kurt von, 205, 206

Schmidt, Gustav, 204–5

Second (Socialist) International, 40, 44, 81 n., 84, 86, 149, 159, 234, 241, 247, 248, 264, 274, 318, 321, 345, 363, 380, 397, 398, 405

Second-and-a-Half International (Vienna), 84, 159
Seeckt, Hans von, 172–73, 205–6
Seljamaa, Julius, 136
Sforza, Count Carlo, 23
Shaw, Tom, 53, 229
Shtein, Boris Efimovich, 108
Shumiatsky, Boris Zakharievich, 186
Sisson, Edgar Grant, 72 n.
Smirnov, A. P., 269
Snowden, Philip, 229
Sokolnikov, Grigorii Iakovlevich, 186, 226
Souvarine, Boris, 174
Soviet diplomacy, see R.S.F.S.R.; Soviet Union; Chicherin; Litvinov; Rakovsky
Soviet Union: commercial treaty with Germany (1925), 277–78; conference on debts with France (1926–27), 312–13, 345–46, 365–66, 382 n.; CONGRESSES OF SOVIETS: First (1922), 152 n., 155, 164; Second (1924), 152 n., 164, 189, 195, 228–33; Third (1925), 270, 309–11, 352; Fourth (1927), 283, 343, 349, 364–68, 371–74;— DE JURE RECOGNITION: from England (1924), 190, 233, 259, 265; from France (1924), 192, 236–39; from Germany (1922), 168; from Italy (1924), 190, 230, 234; from lesser countries (1924), 190–92;—formation of, 152 n., 155, 163–65; general settlement treaties with England (1924), 259–62, 264, 265, 274, 292–96, 305, 373; international position in 1926 assessed by Rykov, 283; and Kellogg-Briand Pact, 352; military reorganization, 314, 352–55, 356, 399–403; and Mongolia, 253 n.; negotiations with Poland (1927), 346, 366; negotiations with Poland, Finland, and Baltic states (1925–27), 277, 280–82, 346, 366; NEUTRALITY AND NONAGGRESSION TREATIES: with Germany (1926), 279–80, 324–26, 327, 408; with Latvia (1927), unratified), 282, 346–47, 366, 408; with Lithuania (1926), 282–83, 326, 346, 362, 366, 408; with Turkey (1925), Afghanistan (1926), and Persia (1927), 277–79, 319, 323–24, 326, 327, 362, 366–67, 408;—official position on the Zinoviev letter, 306–7; and Preparatory Commission for the Disarmament Conference, 347, 348–52, 388–98; reactions to Arcos raid, 345, 375–79; reactions to Dawes Plan, 262–64, 298–300; reactions to de jure recognition, 189–93, 228–39, 253; reactions to Locarno Conference, 273–75, 279, 316–20, 325; relations with England (1926–27), 341–45, 370–81, 382; relations with France (1927), 381–82; renewal of suspicion and hostility (1926–27), 341–409; "socialism in one country" and the pacificist-reformist interlude (1924–26), 253–337; Stalin on reasons for forming, 152–54; the Stalin-Trotsky struggle (1924–27), 254–59; theory of international law, 275–77 (see also Historical Introduction); trade delegations in foreign countries, 276–78, 343–45, 375–79; views on arbitration, 277, 280, 282, 322–23, 351; views on the League

of Nations (1925), 273–75, 320–22; and World Economic Conference (1927), 347–48, 382–88; see also Russian Socialist Federated Soviet Republic
Spartakusbund, 5, 24, 38, 40, 221
Sportintern, see Red Sport International
Stalin, Iosif Vissarionovich (Dzhugashvili), 121, 163, 183, 270: advocates caution in Germany (1923), 178–79, 212; on the British general strike, 342, 368–69; China policy under attack, 257; on the Dawes Plan, 264, 299–300; on disarmament, 351, 397–98; on growing popularity of U.S.S.R., 300–301; on history of the proletarian dictatorship (1920), 37–41; on international situation (1924), 195, 243–44; on international situation and party tasks (1927), 356–57, 407–9; justifies his policies (1927), 406–7; on need for confederation of soviet republics, 150–51, 164; on need for a strong Red Army (1925), 403; on reasons for forming U.S.S.R. (1922), 152–54; rebukes Polish Communist Party, 346; rise to prominence (1919–24), 254–55; on socialism in one country, 256–57, 258, 283–84, 289–91, 333–35, 341, 358–59, 406–7; on socialist and capitalist camps (1922), 154; struggle for power (1924–27), 254–59, 341, 356, 406; on theory of proletarian revolution, 256–57, 286–89; on world significance of the revolution (1927), 357, 403–5
Stamboliisky, Aleksandr, 195 n.
Stampfer, editor of Vorwärts, 204
Steklov, Iurii Mikhailovich, 170: on approaching doom of capitalism, 176; on failure of Hague Conference, 133–35; on French de jure recognition of U.S.S.R., 192, 237–39; on League of Nations, 117–19; on the Little Entente, 76–77, 200; on Soviet economic position (1922), 110–11, 134–35; on threat of war (1923), 166, 200–201; on trade agreement with England, 64–65
Stinnes, Hugo, 176
Stolzenberg, Dr., German official, 207
Straits, Black Sea, see Lausanne Conference; see also Historical Introduction
Stresemann, Gustav, 178, 179, 209 n., 231, 245, 271, 365
Stuchka, Petr Ivanovich, 275

Tartu, Treaty of, between R.S.F.S.R. and Estonia (1920), 7, 8–9, 48, 49–51, 204
Tartu, Treaty of, between R.S.F.S.R. and Finland (1920), 11–14
Tchitcherin, see Chicherin
Thalheimer, August, 184, 221–22
Third International, see Communist International
Thomas, James Henry, 369
Tomsky, Mikhail Pavlovich, 270, 356
Trade Union International, see International Federation of Trade Unions or Red Trade Union International
Trotsky (Bronshtein), Lev Davidovich, 193, 254, 328, 334, 346, 356: at Brest-Litovsk, 14, 275; on Curzon memorandum, 187,

188; denies that Lenin's testament was concealed (1925), 255; on failure of German revolution, 183, 245; on the Far Eastern situation (1924), 247–48; on the international situation (1924), 196, 244–49; on the pacifist-reformist era in Europe, 244–49; on postwar imperialism (1920), 41–44; on the price of peace (1923), 166; on prospects of revolution in Germany (1923), 180, 217; struggle with Stalin, 255–59; on the war with Poland, 42–43, 62; warns Poland against intervening in Germany, 181–82, 217–18

Trumbić, Ante, 76 n.

Tsarist debts, see Debts and claims

Tukhachevsky, Mikhail Nikolaevich, 355

Turkey: Lausanne Conference, 113–17, 141–48, 199; neutrality and nonagression treaty with U.S.S.R. (1925), 277–78, 319, 323–24, 326, 327, 362, 366, 408; treaty of friendship with R.S.F.S.R. (1921), 26, 142

Ukraine: Anticommunist activity in, 15–16, 33; becomes part of U.S.S.R., 152 n., 164; provisional and preliminary treaties with the West (1920–22), 24 n., 25; right to participate in Lausanne Conference, 114, 142, 144; in Russo-Polish negotiations (1920–21), 15–16, 17, 18, 19, 55–61

Unions, see British Trades Union Congress; International Federation of Trade Unions; Red Trade Union International

United States: American Relief Administration, 28–30, 66, 74–75, 165, 193, 276; Chicherin's views on (1922), 127; the Colby note, 27, 66–69; the Dawes Plan, 180, 246, 247, 262–64, 296–300, 302, 330, 331; relations with R.S.F.S.R. (1919–21), 26–28, 66–73; resists Soviet efforts at rapprochement (1922–24), 193–95, 239–42; Trotsky on imperialistic designs of, 246–49

Unschlicht, I. S., 353, 401–2

Urquhart, John Leslie, 147, 153, 223

U.S.S.R., see Soviet Union

Vandervelde, Emile, 120–21

Vasilev, A. N., 253 n.

Veltman (Pavlovich), Mikhail Lazarevlch, 22 n.

Vienna Conference (1924), 292, 294

Vilna, 9–10, 55 n., 111, 280, 282, 346

VKP, see Russian Communist Party

Voikov, Petr Lazarevich, 346, 408

Voldemaras, Augustinas, 10 n., 362 n.

Voroshilov, Kliment Efremovich, 355–56, 399 n., 402–3

Vorovsky, V. V., 24, 223, 349, 389

Washington Conference (1921–22), 117, 119, 126, 156, 234

Webb, Sidney James, 229

Weinstein, Soviet official, 227

Wesmanis, Latvian diplomat, 136

Wilson, Woodrow, 41–42, 163

Wirth, Karl Joseph, 206

Women's Committee for the Recognition of Russia, 193

World Economic Conference (Geneva, 1927), 347–48, 377, 382–88

Wrangel, Baron Petr Nikolaevich von, 21, 26, 39, 40, 53, 54, 62, 152, 361

Yudenich, Nikolai Nikolaevich, 3, 7, 8, 15, 38, 48, 54, 61

Zeligowski, General Lucjan, 9

Zetkin, Klara, 5 n., 267

Zimmerwald movement, 5 n.

Zinoviev, Grigorii Evseevich (Hirsch Apfelbaum), 22 n., 178, 184, 193, 223, 356, 406: on British Labour government, 262, 301–2; calls Zinoviev letter a forgery, 305–6; on failure of German revolution, 183, 218–20; on how to prevent war (1927), 388; on importance of trade unions, 269; on prospects of revolution in Germany (1923), 181, 213–17; retains hope for German revolution (1924), 220–21; on socialism in one country, 327–30; on Soviet foreign policy (1924), 195; in the struggle for power (1924–27), 255, 258, 406; on united-front tactics, 167, 219–20; Zinoviev letter, 192 n., 238 n., 264–66, 301–7, 321, 370, 380, 397